THE BIBLE is full of stories featuring forms of magic and possession – from Moses battling with Pharaoh's wizards to the supernatural actions of Jesus and his disciples. As, over the following centuries, the Christian church attempted to stamp out 'deviant' practices, a persistent interest in magic drew strength from this Biblical validation. A strange blend of mumbo-jumbo, fear, fraud and deeply serious study, magic was at the heart of the European Renaissance, fascinating many of its greatest figures.

This is a book filled with incantations, charms, curses, summonings, cures and descriptions of extraordinary, shadowy, only half-understood happenings from long ago. It features writers as various as Thomas Aquinas, John Milton, John Dee, Ptolemy and Paracelsus, along with anonymous ancient and medieval works which were, in some cases, viewed as simply too dangerous even to open.

Brian Copenhaver's wonderful anthology will be welcomed by everyone from those with the most casual interest in the magical tradition to anyone drawn to the Renaissance and the tangled, arcane roots of the scientific tradition.

THE BOOK OF MAGIC

THE BOOK OF

Magic

FROM ANTIQUITY
to the ENLIGHTENMENT

Selected and Translated with an
Introduction and Notes by
BRIAN COPENHAVER

PENGUIN BOOKS

PENGUIN CLASSICS

UK | USA | Canada | Ireland | Australia
India | New Zealand | South Africa

Penguin Classics is part of the Penguin Random House group of companies
whose addresses can be found at global.penguinrandomhouse.com.

Penguin
Random House
UK

First published in Penguin Classics 2015
001

Set in 10.5/14 pt Adobe Caslon Pro
Typeset by Jouve (UK), Milton Keynes
Printed in Great Britain by Clays Ltd, St Ives plc

ISBN: 978–0–241–19856–8

www.greenpenguin.co.uk

Penguin Random House is committed to a
sustainable future for our business, our readers
and our planet. This book is made from Forest
Stewardship Council® certified paper.

Contents

Introduction   xv

THE BOOK OF MAGIC

I

Study No Abomination:
The Hebrew Bible and Apocrypha

1   A Wonder-working Contest: Exod. 7:1–8:15   9

2   Who Parts the Red Sea? Exod. 14:5–31   12

3   A Snake on a Pole: Num. 21:4–9   15

4   Messengers from Heaven: Gen. 28:10–19   16

5   Thou Shalt Not Suffer a Witch to Live: Exod. 22:17–19 17

6   Urim and Thummim: Exod. 28:3–30   18

7   Sun, Moon and Stars: Deut. 4:15–20   19

8   A Goat for Azazel: Lev. 16:1–10   20

9   Prophets and Diviners: Deut. 18:9–21   21

10 The Witch of Endor: 1 Sam. 28   23

11 Sinning with Omen-takers and Ghost-talkers: 2 Kings 21:1–15 25

12 Angels at the Throne: Isa. 6:1–3   27

13 A Vision of the Enticer: 1 Kings 22:1–38   28

14 Dry Bones and the Spirit: Ezek. 37:1–10   31

15 Lilith and the Goat-demons: Isa. 34:8–16   32

16 The Adversary in the Court of Heaven: Job 1:6–12   34
17 Satan Incites David: 1 Chron. 21:1–5   35
18 The Angel Raphael: Tobit 4–6   36

2

Power in the Name of Jesus: The Greek New Testament

1   God Sent the Angel Gabriel: Luke 1:5–38   43
2   Astrology Guides the Magi: Matt. 2:1–12   45
3   Get Away from Me, Satan! Matt. 4:1–11   47
4   A Battle of Angels: Rev. 12:1–9   48
5   The Sheep and the Goats: Matt. 25:31–41   50
6   Principalities, Powers and Dominations: Ephes. 1:15–23   51
7   My Name is Legion: Mark 5:1–42   52
8   Expelling Demons in the Name of Jesus: Mark 9:38–40   55
9   Signs and Wonders, True or False? Mark 13:1–23   56
10 Jesus and Beelzebub: Matt. 12:22–8   57
11 Can a Man Who Sins Produce Such Signs? John 9:1–17   58
12 Jesus Frenzied in the Spirit: John 11:1–48   60
13 To Touch Even the Fringe of His Robe: Mark 6:45–56   62
14 The Fig Tree that You Cursed: Mark 11:12–24   64
15 Apostles Make the Lame Walk: Acts 14:8–20   65
16 In the Name of Jesus Christ, Come Out of Her: Acts 16:16–32 67
17 She Opened Her Eyes and Sat Up: Acts 9:32–43   68
18 He Astonished Them with Acts of Magic: Acts 8:4–25   69

3

Fire Priests, *Magoi* and *Mageia*

1   The Will of Ohrmazd and Ahriman: *The Greater
    Bundahishn*, 1.1–32   77

2 Sacred Fire Slays the Demons: *Vendidad*, 8.73–81   80

3 Night-roamers and Magi: Heraclitus, frg. 14   82

4 The Wisdom of the Magi: Plato, I *Alcibiades*, 121A–22A   83

5 Rites in Fire Temples: Strabo, 15.3.15   85

6 Skills of the Magi: Pausanias, 5.27.1–6   86

7 Magic From the Orient: Diogenes Laërtius, 1.1–9   88

4

Drugs, Charms and Fair Words: Greco-Roman Antiquity

1 Deadly Drugs or Lucky: Homer, *Odyssey*, 10.275–306   99

2 Magi, Purifiers, Gypsies and Con-men: Hippocrates, *The Sacred Disease*, 1–6, 21   101

3 A Charm to Go with the Medicine: Plato, *Charmides*, 155B–58C   104

4 A Science of Erotics: Plato, *Symposium*, 185E–88D   107

5 Love, Divination and Incantations: Plato, *Symposium*, 201D–3A   110

6 All Trickery and Magicking: Plato, *Laws*, 908C–10D   113

7 A Law on Poisoning: Plato, *Laws*, 932E–33E   115

8 A Haunted House: Plautus, *Mostellaria*, 447–531   117

9 Foreseeing the Future: Cicero, *On Divination*, 1.1–5, 30–35   121

10 Drawing Down the Moon: Virgil, *Eclogue*, 8.64–75   124

11 This Dark Technology of Magic: Virgil, *Aeneid*, 4.474–515   126

12 Down to Hell the Trip is Smooth: Virgil, *Aeneid*, 6.33–314   128

13 Who Invented Such Things? Pliny, *Natural History*, 28.4–32   133

14 This Most Fraudulent of the Arts: Pliny, *Natural History*, 30.1–18   136

15 Configurations of Sun, Moon and Stars: Ptolemy, *Treatise in Four Books*, 1.1–2   140

16 Dangerous and Forbidden Sorceries: Apuleius, *The Defence*   143

17 Brokers, Greeters and Carriers: Apuleius,
     On the God of Socrates, 4–11   150

18 Testing an Amulet: Galen, *On Simple Medicines*, 6.3.10   152

5

The Primal Mage and Sorcerer: Late Antiquity

1   A Philosopher and an Honest Man: Philostratus,
     Life of Apollonius, 1.1–2   163

2   A Thunderbolt Struck the Table: Philostratus, *Life of Apollonius*,
     4.42–5   165

3   Totally Unsolvable Problems: Alexander of Aphrodisias,
     Problems, prologue   168

4   An Indwelling Spirit of the More Divine Degree: Porphyry,
     Life of Plotinus   170

5   The Reigning Sympathy: Plotinus, *Enneads*, 4.4.40–44   174

6   Artful, Shape-shifting Hell-dweller: Greek Magical Papyri,
     4.2708–84   178

7   The Holy Books of Hermes: Zosimos, *On the Letter* Ω   180

8   Formed in the Likeness of the Cosmos: Firmicus Maternus,
     Instruction, 2.1–2   185

9   Compelled by Fatal Necessity: Firmicus Maternus,
     Instruction, 1.7.13–22   188

10 Demons and Heroes: Iamblichus, *On the Mysteries
     of Egypt*, 2.2–10   190

11 Statues Ensouled and Conscious: *Asclepius*, 23–4, 37–8   194

12 Natural Powers, Sympathies and Antipathies: *Kyranides*,
     prologue and 1.13   197

13 That Art is Not Theurgy: Iamblichus, *On the Mysteries*, 3.28–31   200

14 Undescribable Properties: Pseudo-Galen, *On Kidney Diseases*,
     5.676–9   203

15 Jynxes: Synesius, *On Dreams*, 1.1–3.2   205

16 Attracting by Likeness: Proclus, *On the Priestly Art*   207

6

Armies of Sorcery and Flights of Angels:
Early Christian Europe

1 The Fall of Simon Magus: *Acts of Peter*, 30–33   219

2 Belly-talkers: Origen, *On the First Book of Kings*   222

3 Lies of a Demon-ridden Hag: Eustathius of Antioch, *Against Origen's Thesis*, 27–30   224

4 Unclean and Inconstant Spirits: Lactantius, *Divine Institutes*, 2.15–17   226

5 The Rites Are No Good: Lactantius, *Divine Institutes*, 4.27   228

6 The Great Pan is Dead: Eusebius, *Preparation for the Gospel*, 5.16–17   231

7 The Coals of the Devil's Deceit: Athanasius of Alexandria, *Life of Anthony*, 3–9   233

8 Magic and Sorcery Fail: Athanasius of Alexandria, *Life of Anthony*, 73–79   235

9 This Noxious and Criminal Science: Augustine, *City of God*, 8.19   237

10 Chronic Superstition: Augustine, *City of God*, 8.22   239

11 Deluded by Lying Angels: Augustine, *On Christian Teaching*, 4.30–45   241

12 Angelic and Demonic Sex: Augustine, *The City of God*, 15.23   244

13 Nine Revelatory Names: Dionysius, *The Celestial Hierarchy*, 2.1–3, 6.1–2   246

14 The Wicked and the Unquiet Dead: Martin of Braga, *Correcting the Ways of Peasants*   248

15 A Deal with the Devil: Paul the Deacon, *A Miracle of Holy Mary*   251

16 Jesus Defiled by Judas: *The Generations of Jesus*   255

7
Arts of Magic That Astonish Us:
The Middle Ages

1 The Three Parts of the World's Philosophy: *The Emerald Tablet*   271

2 Have You Believed? Burchard of Worms, *Corrector*,
   5.60–70, 151–3, 170–80   272

3 Illusions and Phantoms: Gratian, *Decretum*, 2.26.5.12   275

4 An Excellent Astrologer: Pseudo-Ptolemy, *The Book of a
   Hundred Sayings*, 1–10   277

5 Making a Golem: Eleazar of Worms, *Commentary
   on the Book of Formation*   279

6 The Name of This Science is Necromancy: *Picatrix* 1.2, 4   281

7 Make No Mistakes with the Names: *Picatrix* 1.5   284

8 Images, Forms and Figures: *Picatrix* 2.11   287

9 Talismans at the Apex of Astronomy: Albert the Great,
   The Mirror of Astronomy   289

10 Forms and Powers in Stones: Albertus Magnus,
   On Minerals, 1.1.6   296

11 Magic in Nature: Albert the Great, *On Minerals*, 2.3.5–6   298

12 Magic Philosophized: Thomas Aquinas, *Summa
   Against the Heathens*, 3.104–7   300

13 Witchcraft, Impotence and Frigidity: Aquinas,
   Commentary on the Sentences, 4.34.3   305

14 Incubus and Succubus: Aquinas, *Summa of Theology*, 1.51.2–3   307

15 Sulphur, Arsenic and Mercury: Geber, *Summa on
   Completing*, 1.24–30   309

16 Preparing the Stone: Geber, *Summa on Completing*, 3.24–30   313

17 An Art to Answer All Questions: Ramon Lull, *The Brief Art*   317

18 Hell's Doorkeeper: Dante, *Inferno*, 5.1–45   322

19 No Need for Demons: Nicole Oresme, *On the Causes
   of Wonders*   325

20 Spirits Inside the Circle: A Magic Manual   328

21 Repairing the Book of Consecrations: A Magic Manual 331

22 Invoking Satan as Mirage: A Magic Manual 333

8

Ancient Wisdom and Folly: The Earlier Renaissance

1 Why Witches Must Be Killed: Kramer and Sprenger, *The Hammer of Witches*, 1.1 341

2 Sex with Demons: Kramer and Sprenger, *The Hammer of Witches*, 2.1.4 343

3 Why Most Witches Are Women: Kramer and Sprenger, *The Hammer of Witches*, 1.6 345

4 The Metaphysics of Magic: Marsilio Ficino, *On Life*, 3.1 347

5 A Mean Between Body and Soul: Ficino, *On Life*, 3.3–4 349

6 To Capture the Power of a Star: Ficino, *On Life*, 3.8 351

7 From Each and Every Star Hangs a Series: Ficino, *On Life*, 3.13–14 353

8 Testing Talismans: Ficino, *On Life*, 3.15 356

9 Images They Used to Make: Ficino, *On Life*, 3.18 359

10 Astral Spirits Kept Inside Them: Ficino, *On Life*, 3.20 362

11 Singing to a Star: Ficino, *On Life*, 3.21 364

12 A Demon in Charge of Each Person: Ficino, *On Life*, 3.23 366

13 How Impure the Superstition: Ficino, *On Life*, 3.26 368

14 This Natural Magic: Pico, *Oration*, 214–33 372

15 The Ancient Mysteries of the Hebrews: Pico, *Oration*, 234–57 375

16 Magic, Kabbalah and the Divinity of Christ: Pico, *Conclusions* 379

17 Kabbalah, Angels and Demons: Pico, *Conclusions* 382

18 Whatever Other Kabbalists May Say: Pico, *Conclusions* 384

19 The Demon Makes Fools of Them All: Champier, *Dialogue Against the Destructive Arts of Magic*, 2.3 387

9

Ancient Wisdom Modernized:
The Later Renaissance

1 These Effects Are Real: Pomponazzi, *On Spells*, chap. 13   399

2 A Higher and Holier Philosophy: Agrippa, *The Occult Philosophy*, 1.1–2   402

3 Naming the Demons and Angels: Agrippa, *The Occult Philosophy*, 3.18, 20, 24–5   404

4 An Anatomy of Magic: Paracelsus, *The Labyrinth*, 9   410

5 The Philosopher's Stone: *A Rose Garden of Philosophers*   415

6 A Practical Part of Natural Philosophy: Porta, *Natural Magick*, 1.3   418

7 An Excellent Art Discredited: Porta, *Natural Magick*, 5 pr.–2   420

8 Desiring the Company of Iron: Porta, *Natural Magick*, 7 pr.–2   422

9 So May a Man Secretly See: Porta, *Natural Magick*, 17 pr.–2, 5   425

10 The Monad's Progeny: John Dee, *The Hieroglyphic Monad*   427

11 Instructions from Angels: John Dee's Diaries   431

12 Love is the Great Demon: Bruno, *A General Theory of Bonds*, 3.12–15   434

13 The Bonds of Magic: Bruno, *On Natural Magic*, 49–83   436

14 Abominable and Devilish Inventions: Scot, *Discoverie*, 1.7–9   441

10

Magic Seen, Heard and Mocked

1 Merlin's Enchanted Sword: Spenser, *The Faerie Queene*, 2.8.17–22   453

2 Within This Circle: Marlowe, *Doctor Faustus* (A–Text), 1.3   456

3 Fairies and Hobgoblins: Shakespeare, *A Midsummer Night's Dream*, 2.1   459

4 A Spirit Too Delicate: Shakespeare, *The Tempest*, 1.2   464

5 The Simple Idiot Should Not Learn It: Jonson, *The Alchemist*, 2.2   468

6   Fake Magic Goes to College: Mewe, *False Magic*, 3.6–7   473

7   A Summons to Pandaemonium: Milton, *Paradise Lost*, 1.253–798   476

8   Peccant Humours: Molière, *The Doctor In Spite of Himself*, 2.4   482

9   A Virtue Dormitive: Molière, *The Imaginary Invalid*, finale   485

10 A Cunning Man, Hight Sidrophel: Butler, *Hudibras*, 2.3   488

II

Magic in an Age of Science

1   Noble Ends: Bacon, *The Advancement of Learning*, 1.4.1–11   513

2   News of the Invisible Brethren: *A Rosicrucian Manifesto*   516

3   Heresy No Magic: Naudé, *Apology*   523

4   Crazies and Contagion: Naudé, *Apology*   526

5   Cold Slain by Heat: Campanella, *On Sense and Magic*, 2.26   529

6   Consensus: Campanella, *On Sense and Magic*, 3.13–14   532

7   Science is Magic: Campanella, *On Sense and Magic*, 4.5–6   534

8   A Little World in Action: Fludd, *Mosaicall Philosophy*   535

9   Proof Positive: Hopkins, *Discovery of Witches*   542

10 The Ancient Real Theosophy: Vaughan, *Anthroposophia
    theomagica*   548

11 The True Philosophick Cabbala: More, *Conjectura
    cabbalistica*, 2.3   551

12 Magnetisms: Athanasius Kircher, *Nature's Magnetic Kingdom*, 1   556

13 A Demon Witnessed by Multitudes: Joseph Glanvill to
    Lord Brereton   558

14 Angel Midwives: Leibniz, Letter to Thomasius   565

15 Intercourse with Good Spirits: Boyle, *Dialogue on the
    Converse with Angels*   567

16 The Kingdom of Darkness: Leibniz, Correspondence
    with Clarke, 1 and 5   570

    Bibliography   573
    Notes   585

Figure 1: The Eucharist, *c.* 1475

Introduction

Disenchantment and the Evil Eye

Some enchanted evening,
You may see a stranger,
You may see a stranger
Across a crowded room.
And somehow you know,
You know even then,
That somewhere you'll see her
again and again . . .

Who can explain it?
Who can tell you why?
Fools give you reasons;
Wise men never try.

Some enchanted evening: you see a stranger across a crowded room, and the evil eye may be the least of your worries. As you look across, chances are you won't fear bewitchment – in the strong sense of that word – if someone on the other side looks back at you. That's because your world is 'disenchanted', no longer full of magic – if Max Weber was right. This antiseptic feature of your world is a modern one, only a few centuries old. This book is about an older world that was full of magic – until the magic, or some kinds of magic, went way.

In those bygone days, the author of a scientific encyclopedia wrote that the skin of a hyena's head will ward off the evil eye. From the same Roman author – Pliny the Elder – Marsilio Ficino learned about people from faraway places (the Balkans) who had two pupils in each eye and whose angry looks could kill. Pliny's word for this was *fascinatio*: 'spell-casting' or perhaps 'enchantment'. Writing in the Renaissance, more than a millennium after Pliny, Ficino cited the Roman sage's *Natural History*. Ficino was a physician, a philosopher and also a priest. What Pliny wrote was authoritative for him.

But the words of Jesus were more than that: they were sacred. And Jesus says in the Sermon on the Mount that 'the light of thy body is the eye: if therefore thine eye be *single*, thy whole body shall be full of light. But if thine eye be *evil*, thy whole body shall be full of darkness.'[1]

Is the message metaphorical and ethical? Light and darkness often signify good and evil. Maybe an eye is evil if it can't see through the darkness to the 'treasures in heaven' promised by Jesus just moments before. But why is the eye belonging to an enlightened body 'single' – in the King James translation of the Gospels? Why does the Evangelist see 'single' and 'evil' as opposites? *Haplous*, Greek for 'single', might mean 'single-hearted' or 'wholehearted' but also 'simple', 'pure', 'healthy' or even 'generous'. The eye that is not single is 'evil' – *ponêros*, which also has many meanings. The Devil is *ponêros* and so are his demons. Ficino, the first to translate all of Plato's dialogues from Greek, knew those words well. He also knew about the Balkan killers with eyes whose pupils were not single but double. Maybe Matthew had something more concrete in mind, more physical than ethical – the evil eye as a transmitter of magical power.

The difficulty of the passage, which has stumped students of the Gospels, opens it to interpretation. 'Who can explain it?' When the song asks that question about enchantment in the evening, the answer is that 'wise men never try'. Maybe so. This book will try, however, taking heart from Max Weber's sociology of religion – which is also a sociology of magic – to tell a story about magic through a selection of texts. There are many sociologies, anthropologies, histories and other such studies of magic. I single Weber's work out from them for two reasons: first, his writing about magic is brilliant and illuminating; second, it helps describe my very different approach, which is textual, historical and philosophical, not social-scientific.

Nonetheless, the social science of the last two centuries is a matrix for this book, one of whose polestars is an anthropologist, E. E. Evans-Pritchard. After criticizing Weber's views on religion as 'too vague, too general, a bit too easy', he summarizes his own position and says that 'religion is what religion does'.[2] Taking that to be a nominalist restriction on the study of religion, I apply it to magic as well.

Evans-Pritchard did the same in his famous book on *Witchcraft, Oracles and Magic Among the Azande*, aiming 'to describe what Azande understand by *mangu*, *soroka* and *ngua*'. For those Zande words and several others, he supplies 'the English words that I use' – 'witchcraft' for *mangu*, 'oracles' for *soroka*, 'magic' for *ngua* – adding that if anyone prefers 'terms other than those I have used, I should raise no objection'.[3] *Ngua* is what the local expert on *ngua* says it is – whatever we choose to call it in a different language, with different preoccupations. If we choose 'magic', the choice confers no essence on anything. *Ngua* has no essence, neither does magic, and the same goes for religion.

Two key words in this book – the Greek *mageia* and *magia* in Latin – are ancestors of 'magic', the English term that Evans-Pritchard chooses for *ngua*. Most of the texts translated here were written in Greek or Latin – fewer in Hebrew, English, Persian or other languages. My story is not about the words *mageia*, *magia* and 'magic', but it is about concepts signified by them – in the past – at particular times and places. In my opinion, there is no essence to be distilled from all those concepts and labelled 'magic', such that the label will be informative and accurate for all times and places.

'Magic' (like 'religion') as the name of an essence will be uninformative because eliminating contradictions to keep the word accurate will also make it very abstract too abstract for the relevant domains, which are moral, social and cultural. Keeping the word accurate will be hard because the concepts tagged by 'magic' and its cousins, with all the freight that they carry, have emerged in Western and Christian environments in response to Western and Christian problems. Applying the word 'magic' – free and clear – to something non-Christian and non-Western (like *ngua*) will be difficult, maybe impossible. Since that conclusion is controversial and cannot be defended here, let me refer to another book by me that engages the issue extensively.[4]

Meanwhile, a quick look at Weber's writings will show how he theorizes about magic – however vaguely, according to Evans-Pritchard.

Magic is ritual where religion is ethical, according to Weber. Magic coerces, but religion supplicates. Magic goes to particulars, religion generalizes. Magic is emotional, religion rational. Deeply learned, writing with patience and finesse, Weber knows that these facile dichotomies cannot stand. By his lights, Moses, Elijah and Jesus were magicians. If those heroes of the Abrahamic faiths were all magicians, how can magic be distinct from religion on axes like ethics v. ritual, reason v. emotion, and so on? No such distinctions can hold, as Weber concedes again and again. But then – on the trail of 'typical pure magicians' and something 'essentially magical' – he applies the distinctions again, seduced by 'always' and 'all', words meant to distinguish *all* magic *always* from religion – or the reverse – in order to isolate an essence.[5]

Thinking like a philosopher, Weber wants to generalize, but he keeps finding facts that stymie generalization. Then he responds with 'ideal types'. In the book that made him famous, he explains that such items, constructed to present religious ideas in a logically consistent form . . . have rarely existed in historical reality . . . Precisely because of the impossibility of drawing clear boundaries in historical reality, we can only hope to arrive at the specific effects of those ideas by examining their most logically consistent form.

By Weber's standard of logical consistency, the following argument looks good. Ritualism is magic; sacraments are rituals; the Eucharist is a sacrament; the sacramental heart of Roman Catholicism is the Eucharist; hence, the Catholic religion is magical at its core. Writing as a Protestant mainly for Protestants, Weber opposes ethics to ritual, just as he links ritual with magic, concluding at the end of his *Sociology of Religion* that 'only ascetic Protestantism completely eliminated magic'.[6]

Weber, formally a Protestant, had evolutionism in his soul. He saw a certain kind of Protestant faith as progressive. Emulating the followers of Yahweh in ancient Israel, ascetic Calvinists won 'the struggle against magic'. Such a struggle needs a stable target, so magic needs an essence. Mere enchantment – something strange and cloudy across a crowded room – won't be enough. Disenchantment, by Weber's reckoning, is a moment of rationalization and modernity. It is also a term of art that needs defining:

Making progress by intellectualizing and rationalizing does not mean general progress in the conditions of our lives. It means something else – knowing or believing that we can figure this out at any time, whenever we want. The upshot (in principle) is that no mysterious forces are in play, eluding calculation, and that our calculations can (in theory) master everything. The disenchantment of the world: that is the point. We need no longer rely on magic as a device for mastering spirits or pleading with them – unlike the savages for whom such mysterious forces used to exist. Calculation and technical equipment do the job.

Weber captures the spirit of modernity: fair enough. What his analysis says about the pre-modern past is a different question.[7]

Weber respects history's irreducible complexity. As others had said, philosophy generalizes, but history – whatever else it does – tells stories by assembling particulars. If history's engagement with particulars is solid, a historically informed sociology that attends to the facts, as apart from the data, will be stuck between generalizing and getting it right. That was Weber's dilemma in his sociology of magic. In his scheme of history, progress requires breakthroughs *away* from something distinct (like magic) and *towards* something distinct (like ethical and ascetic religion). He needs ideal patterns of evolution as tracks for ideal types – types and patterns too artificial to qualify as essences, essences too remote from the past to make a good fit with history.[8]

Like many intellectuals of his day, Weber treats evolution as a scientific principle, whereas his wobbly essentialism is just a philosophical reflex. He struggles with essentialism, but he can't fix it and can't do without it. But Evans-Pritchard eliminates it with his austere nominalism. My choice of Evans-Pritchard's way – a choice that has no grounding at all in social-scientific theory or practice – is just my response to the texts selected for this book, texts that were not selected because I see them that way. Others would make different choices: I hope that students of magic will see mine as reasonable.

Weber's moment of disenchantment comes at the end of my story, with the early Enlightenment (of the young Benjamin Franklin) as a chapter in his tale of rationalization.[9] By that time, the concepts represented by 'magic', 'religion' and 'science' were available to people who tried to understand one of them (magic) by contrasting it with the others. In biblical antiquity, where my story starts, there were no such concepts, nor the words to name them. My task is to show – by selecting texts and supplying brief comments – how such ideas developed over a very long time, more than two millennia.

Part of that development was the construction of theories to explain magical effects and evaluate them – not to verify them, however, since the effects were usually just accepted as real. The explanations were often philosophical. The evaluations sometimes applied moral categories to magical actions.

In his book *On the Occult Philosophy*, completed for publication in 1532, Cornelius Agrippa von Nettesheim did both, writing philosophy as a moral critic. Like Ficino, he knew from Pliny and others about the Balkan people (*fascinatores*, he says, and women) who killed people by looking at them. He brings this up in a discussion of 'natural powers', where the evil eye might be seen as dangerous but not malevolent – no more than venom from a snake. Later, however, he mentions that a 'lust for killing' drives witches (*malefici* not *maleficae*, so presumably male) whose eyes cast spells (*fascinare*).[10]

Is the enchantment called *fascinatio* a blind force of nature or a conscious will to evil? Agrippa wavers on that question while constructing a framework to answer it, along with many other such enquiries. His 'occult philosophy' is a theory of magic, explicit and well articulated, that sums up centuries of debate about *mageia*, *magia*, *magie* and 'magic'. The English noun ('arts of *magic*') and adjective ('*magic* arts') – born of Greek and Latin words by way of French – were both used in the fourteenth century. Today in North America, where 'the Magic' is a basketball team from a Disney city in Florida, the word is looser than it used to be. Stage conjuring can be magic, also anything seen as faked, unexplained, mysterious, supernatural or just very, very impressive (like Earvin Johnson, a wizard with the ball).

The magic in this book – ruined by disenchantment – used to be more serious and was, in fact, better understood. Accusations of magic caused people – many people – to be executed by civil and religious authorities. Experts like Agrippa offered explanations of magic that relied on the deepest understandings and best practices of other experts in theology, philosophy and especially natural philosophy – the pre-modern ancestor of modern science. This book uses 'magic' in the way that Agrippa, Ficino and Pliny often used *magia* – very broadly.

In the relevant sense, 'magic' is not just some person's theory (like the *mageia* of Proclus; see section 5.16) or someone's practice (like the magick that ravished Faustus; see 10.2). It is a general term that includes not only such practices and theories – magic in the narrower sense – but also alchemy, astrology, demonology, divination, Kabbalah, witchcraft and many other items, some as petty as the evil eye, some as grand as Satan, included by Agrippa in his occult philosophy.

Texts that describe and debate those things fill most of this book. The texts are arranged historically in eleven sections, starting with the wizardry of Moses in the Hebrew Bible and ending with a letter from Leibniz, that icon of Enlightenment and failed hero of disenchantment: Voltaire mocked him as Dr Pangloss in a book where 'crude doggerel attacking old women and witches' had finally become unacceptable.[11] Each of the eleven sections is introduced by a few pages of comment on the texts selected: these remarks are thematic, however, not chronological. Within each section, the texts themselves are in chronological order, more or less, if the chronology is known. A cursory headnote precedes each text. Cross-references in the headnotes point to other parts of the book.

Translations from Greek, Hebrew, Latin and the modern vernaculars are by me, unless otherwise noted. Other English translations (not always available) are cited in the bibliography solely for the reader's convenience – not because they are my versions or because I recommend them: some are excellent translations, some less so. For the Hebrew Bible, I went from the original text to standard versions like the King James, the Jewish Study Bible, and so on. In a few cases – Jowett's Plato and McKenna's inimitable Plotinus – I have used translations by others because they cannot be surpassed – by me, anyhow – only adapted and lightly modernized. For older texts in English, like Shakespeare's plays and John Dee's diaries, I have not modernized the original language, and my notes address some of its obscurities. Texts longer than a paragraph or two have often been shortened by subtraction and elision, indicated by an ellipsis (three dots). Since the compression is sometimes great, a look at the original may be helpful. Suggestions for further reading in the bibliography are just that, and my lists are far from complete. Especially for texts that may be hard to find, internet addresses have been added if online versions are available.

I am grateful to Michael Allen, John Coldewey, Greg Copenhaver, Kathleen Copenhaver, Rebecca Copenhaver, Tony Grafton, Fabrizio Lelli, Larry Principe, Teo Ruiz and Simon Winder.

NOTES

1. Matt. 6:22–3; Plin. *NH* 7.16, 28.101; Ficino, *On Life*, p. 324 (3.16).
2. Evans-Pritchard, *Primitive Religion*, pp. 118–20.
3. Evans-Pritchard, *Witchcraft*, pp. 8–12.
4. Copenhaver, *Magic in Western Culture*.
5. Weber, *Judaism*, pp. 97, 110, 220; *Sociology of Religion*, pp. 6–7, 25–30, 37, 47, 78, 89, 100, 102, 108, 150–51, 163, 186, 191, 227, 270.
6. Weber, *Sociology of Religion*, pp. 74–5, 89, 152–3, 269; Weber, *The Protestant Ethic*, p. 69.
7. Weber, *Judaism*, p. 167.
8. Weber, *Sociology of Religion*, pp. 67–8; 'Wissenschaft als Beruf,' *Schriften: 1894–1922*, ed. D. Kaesler (Stuttgart: Kröner, 2002), p. 488.
9. Weber, *The Protestant Ethic*, pp. 8–15.
10. Cornelius Agrippa, *Opera* (Lyon: Bering, 1600), I, pp. 39–40, 233–4.
11. Voltaire, *Romans et contes*, ed. F. Deloffre and J. van Den Heuvel (Paris: Gallimard, 1979), p. 217.

THE BOOK OF MAGIC

I

Study No Abomination:
The Hebrew Bible and Apocrypha

Figure 2: God, Angels and Devils

The Bible is full of familiar stories. The people and things in them are sometimes ordinary but sometimes not. When Moses parts the Red Sea, for example, something extraordinary happens. Through Moses, God gives power to the Israelites fleeing from Egypt, power that is not at all normal. A reader today might say that the Bible puts the parting of the waters outside the limits of nature – though there is no word like 'nature' in biblical Hebrew.

Thinking of the story in religious terms, the same modern reader might say that a miracle happened, one of those 'prodigious signs and marvels' that 'the Lord has not given you a mind to understand'. Conspicuously, however, Moses relies on a device – a rod or a wand – already used by his brother Aaron against Pharaoh in a contest involving magic. The contestants on Pharaoh's side, whose wands are also in working order, are commonly called 'sorcerers' and 'magicians'. Do those English words render the Bible's terminology correctly? Nothing like the generic 'magic' or 'religion' occurs in the Hebrew Bible. As for the terms that are used in the relevant passages, the Bible says little about what they meant in ancient Israel.

Yet what those words describe is authenticated by what the Bible says so sparingly – starting with 'portents and wonders', named as such and promoted by God himself. Because God authorizes them, extraordinary events that we might call 'magical' are not only real – meaning that they are factual, not illusory – but also legitimate. Without God's authorization they would be illegitimate, though still perhaps real: when Pharaoh's wizards turn their wands into snakes, the Egyptian sorcery is evil, unsuccessful but not ineffective.

Moses waves his wand and parts the sea: what he does is effective and not only legitimate but also remarkable enough to sustain the faith of the Israelites in the God for whom Moses speaks. When Moses holds his wand out over the water, is his gesture magical or religious or both or neither? The Bible is harsh in condemning such actions if the agents are not on God's side. But the holy book gives no help with analytical distinctions that might respond to our questions about the marvels that it takes for granted.

Prophecy and idolatry are prominent in the Bible, which distinguishes prophecy from the divination practised by foreigners while also setting idolatry apart from the worship that God demands for himself alone. Idolatry is a deceit: the gods honoured by idols are not the true God. But those 'false gods' are not false in the way that tricks, mirages or hallucinations are false. The gods worshipped by idolaters are less powerful than God but not unreal: stars and planets, depicted by idols, are plainly real, and they are also *persons* of high standing – lesser divinities but gods nonetheless, in some sense. Perhaps 'gods' is not the best name for them: 'angels' or 'demons' might be better. Pagan diviners who worship demons do not usually speak for the true God, who speaks officially only through true prophets, like Moses. And yet the Creator uses pagan divination to manipulate human creatures, making those procedures effective, authenticated and condoned – if not authorized.

Divinatory magic, even done by gentiles, will be good if God wants it done. Not all magic is bad, then, and no magic is absolutely bad since none of it escapes God's plan even when it violates his law. Such illicit magic is malevolent, harmful and permitted without being approved. To make these distinctions, 'good' and 'bad' are helpful words, like 'licit' and 'illicit' and 'effective' and 'ineffective'. A clear account deploying such terms is not to be found in the Bible, however, which asserts the reality of a magic – or better, some ancient correlate of what 'magic' now sometimes refers to – that is sometimes good, sometimes bad; sometimes licit, sometimes illicit; sometimes effective, sometimes ineffective.

Some agents of magic are humans, identified by pejoratives like 'sorcerer' or 'witch' but also by approving terms like 'priest' or 'prophet'. Other agents of magic are not human but are persons – angels and demons. In earlier parts of the Bible, their standing as persons is not obvious and their personalities are indistinct. Even hazier is the 'spirit', which sometimes is God's prophetic voice, and at other times an autonomous person, a conscious agent of good or evil. Satan – the best-known demonic person, and eventually the personification of Evil – acquires the name 'Satan' only late in the Bible story. Only two good angels are named in the Hebrew Bible, Gabriel and Michael, and only in a few places. Raphael's much richer story – linked with the demon Asmodeus – is non-canonical.

In summary: the book that Christians call the 'Old Testament' authenticates the reality of magic and its human and non-human agents, generally but not always to condemn it because magic is usually not approved by God, even though God himself makes it possible and makes use of it, not only through heroes like Moses but also through dubious characters like 'the Witch of Endor'.

I.1

A Wonder-working Contest:
Exod. 7:1–8:15

Before this episode begins, Moses has pleaded his unfitness to speak in God's name before Pharaoh. To assure him and his brother Aaron that they are worthy, God instructs them to challenge Pharaoh's experts to a magic duel, using a *mattah* – a wand, or perhaps a staff or rod (see 1.2; 4.1, 9, 12). Opposing the two Israelite heroes are Egyptian *mekashfim* (sorcerers, but see 1.5, 9) and *hartumim* (magicians) who use *latim* (mysteries) to make their wands work. When Moses and Aaron defeat the Egyptian wizards, they win not because Egyptian magic is powerless but because the true God makes Israelite magic more powerful – directed by 'the finger of God', in the words of the humbled Egyptians. The God of Israel wants to increase his own 'portents and wonders', like the signs produced by Moses and Aaron to prove whose God is mightiest: after Aaron turns the Nile into blood, God says, 'By this shall you know that I am YHVH.'

*

Then YHVH said to Moses, 'See, I have made you a god to Pharaoh, and your brother Aaron will be your prophet. You shall say everything I command you, and your brother Aaron shall tell Pharaoh to let the children of Israel go out of his land. I will harden Pharaoh's heart, however, so that I may multiply my portents and wonders in Egypt, and when Pharaoh does not listen to you, I will lay my hand upon Egypt and bring my troops – my people, the children of Israel – out of Egypt with mighty judgements. And the Egyptians shall know that I am YHVH when I stretch out my hand over Egypt and bring the children of Israel away from them.' Moses and Aaron did this, exactly as YHVH commanded them. Moses was eighty years old and Aaron eighty-three when they made their speech to Pharaoh.

YHVH said to Moses and Aaron, 'When Pharaoh says to you, "produce a sign for yourselves," say to Aaron, "Take your wand and throw it down in front of Pharaoh," and it will become a snake.' So Moses and Aaron went before Pharaoh and did just as YHVH commanded. Aaron threw his wand down in front of Pharaoh and his court, and it became a snake. Pharaoh then summoned experts and sorcerers, and the Egyptian magicians did the same with their mysteries: each threw down his wand and it became a snake. But Aaron's wand swallowed their wands. Yet Pharaoh's heart stiffened, and he would not listen to them, just as YHVH had said.

Then YHVH said to Moses, 'Pharaoh's heart is unfeeling; he refuses to let the people go. Go to Pharaoh in the morning as he comes out to the water. Stand in front of him on the bank of the Nile, holding in your hand the wand that turned into a snake, and say to him, "YHVH, God of the Hebrews, has sent me to say to you: 'Let my people go, so that they may worship me in the wilderness.' But up to now you have not listened. This is what YHVH says: 'By this shall you know that I am YHVH.' Look, with the wand that is in my hand I will strike the water of the Nile, and it will be turned into blood. The fish in the Nile will die, and the Nile will stink so that the Egyptians will be unable to drink the Nile's water."' YHVH said to Moses, 'Tell Aaron, "Take your wand and stretch your hand out over the waters of Egypt – the streams and canals, the ponds and all the pools of water – so that they will turn to blood. There will be blood all throughout the land of Egypt, even in things of wood and stone."'

Moses and Aaron did just as YHVH commanded. He raised his wand and struck the Nile water in the sight of Pharaoh and his court, and all the Nile water turned into blood. The fish in the Nile died, the river smelled so bad that the Egyptians could not drink the Nile water, and there was blood all throughout the land of Egypt. When the Egyptian magicians did the same with their mysteries, Pharaoh's heart stiffened, and he would not listen to Moses and Aaron, just as YHVH had said. He turned and went into his house, but not even this touched his heart. Because they could not drink the Nile water, all the Egyptians dug beside the Nile for water to drink.

Seven days passed after YHVH had struck the Nile, and YHVH said to Moses, 'Go to Pharaoh and say to him, "So says YHVH, 'Let my people go so that they may worship me. But if you refuse to let them go, I will plague all your borders with frogs.' The Nile will swarm with frogs: they will come up and get into your house, into your bedroom, on your bed and into the houses of your court and your people, into your ovens and kneading troughs. The frogs will come up on you, your people and your whole court."'

YHVH said to Moses, 'Say to Aaron, "Hold your hand with your wand out over the streams, canals and ponds, and bring the frogs up on the land of Egypt."' And Aaron held his hand out over the waters of Egypt, and the frogs came up and covered the land of Egypt. And the magicians did the same with their mysteries, bringing frogs up on the land of Egypt.

Then Pharaoh summoned Moses and Aaron, saying, 'Beg YHVH to take the frogs away from me and from my people, and I will let your people go to sacrifice to YHVH.' And Moses said to Pharaoh, 'Take this victory over me: on your behalf and your court's and your people's, when shall I beg to have the frogs removed from you and your houses and remain only in the Nile?' 'Tomorrow,' he answered. And Moses said, 'As you say: so that you may know that there is none like YHVH, our God, the frogs will leave you, your houses, your court and your people, remaining only in the Nile.' Then Moses and Aaron left Pharaoh, and Moses cried out to YHVH about the frogs that he had brought upon Pharaoh. And YHVH did what Moses asked: the frogs died away in the houses, courtyards and fields. They heaped them up in piles, making the land stink. When Pharaoh saw that there was relief, he hardened his heart, and he did not listen to them, as YHVH had said.

YHVH said to Moses, 'Say to Aaron, "Hold your wand out and strike the dust of the earth, and it shall become lice all throughout the land of Egypt."' This they did. And Aaron held his hand out with his wand and struck the dust of the earth, and there were lice upon man and beast; all the dust of the earth turned to lice all throughout the land of Egypt. The magicians did the same with their mysteries to get the lice out, but they could not, and there were lice upon man and beast. So the magicians said to Pharaoh, 'It is the finger of God.' Pharaoh's heart was unfeeling, however, and he would not listen to them, as YHVH had said.

Who Parts the Red Sea?
Exod. 14:5–31

Instructed and empowered by God, Moses performs the stunning miracle that finally releases the Israelites from bondage in Egypt. As they march into the sea, the waters withdraw on their right and left to clear a safe path, recalling the miracle of creation when God first divided water from land. To defeat Pharaoh's army, God orders Moses to 'raise your wand' and use the power that had already defeated the King's wizards (see 1.1; 4.1, 9, 12). The messenger (or angel) who moves to the rear of the army comes from God, and the cloud that moves to the front carries a curse (see 1.4). But some of what follows – like the 'pillar of fire and cloud' – might be natural, if unusual: soldiers could be stranded by strong winds and a changing tide, as mud immobilizes their chariots. Water standing 'like a wall' to expose a sea bottom is nothing natural, however: this marvel makes even the Egyptians see God's glory, and the 'immense might' of true divinity is Israel's basis for faith and fear of God – a supernatural basis, one might say. Yet the story itself makes no explicit distinction between *natural* and *supernatural* events or powers: the Hebrew word *teva*, 'nature', is not biblical (see 4.1–2, 7). Even so, some *normal* or *ordinary* course of events is implicit: this is the background against which God and Moses work their wonders.

*

When it was reported to the King of Egypt that the people had fled, Pharaoh and his court had a change of heart towards the people and said, 'What have we done, freeing Israel from serving us?' So he hitched up his chariot and took his people with him. He picked six hundred of his best chariots along with the remaining chariots of Egypt, with officers for them all. YHVH hardened Pharaoh's heart – the King of Egypt – and he chased after the children of Israel.

The children of Israel marched out with fists raised, and the Egyptians chased after them, overtaking them encamped by the sea – all Pharaoh's chariot horses, his horsemen and his troops, near Pi-hahiroth, facing Ba'al

Zephon. Pharaoh approached, and the children of Israel looked up to see the Egyptians coming at them. They were very frightened, and the children of Israel cried out to YHVH. They said to Moses, 'Are there no graves in Egypt, and this is why you have led us into the wilderness to die? What have you done by taking us out of Egypt? Is this not exactly what we told you in Egypt when we said, "Leave us alone, and we will serve the Egyptians, because we would rather serve the Egyptians than die in the wilderness."' Moses said to the people, 'Have no fear! Stand and see what YHVH will do for you today – what his salvation is: you shall never again see the Egyptians as you have seen them today. YHVH will fight for you. Say no more!'

YHVH said to Moses, 'Why do you cry out to me? Tell the children of Israel to move on. Raise your wand, hold your hand out over the sea and split it, and then the children of Israel can go on dry ground into the sea. Look: I will harden the hearts of the Egyptians so that they come after you, and I will win glory through Pharaoh and all his troops, his chariots and his horsemen. The Egyptians shall know that I am YHVH when I win glory through Pharaoh and his chariots and through his horsemen.'

Then God's messenger, who had been going in front of Israel's army, moved and went behind them, and the pillar of cloud went from in front of them and stood behind them, coming between the Egyptian army and the army of Israel. The cloud was there with darkness, then, and this put a curse on the night, and one army did not come near the other all night long. Moses held his hand out over the sea, and YHVH led the sea all night with a strong east wind, turning the sea into dry ground and splitting the waters, so that the children of Israel went on dry ground into the sea, whose waters were like a wall for them on their right and their left. The Egyptians came chasing after them into the sea – all Pharaoh's horses and chariots and his horsemen.

Then, during the morning watch, YHVH looked down on the Egyptian army from a pillar of fire and cloud, throwing the Egyptian army into panic. He locked the wheels of their chariots, making them hard to move. And the Egyptians said, 'Let us run away from Israel: YHVH is fighting for them against Egypt.'

Then YHVH said to Moses, 'Hold your hand out over the sea, and let the water come back on the Egyptians and on their chariots and horsemen. So Moses held his hand out over the sea, and in the morning, as the Egyptians fled from the sea, it held steady again. YHVH threw the Egyptians into the sea, and the waters came back and covered the chariots and horsemen, with Pharaoh's whole army following them into the sea: not one survived. But the children of Israel had gone through the sea on dry ground, and for them the water was like a wall on their right and their left. On that day YHVH saved Israel from the might of the Egyptians, and Israel saw Egypt dead on the shore of the sea. Israel saw the immense might that YHVH used on the Egyptians: the people feared YHVH, and they believed in YHVH and in Moses, his servant.

1.3
A Snake on a Pole:
Num. 21:4–9

Weary of wandering in the desert after the escape from Egypt, the Israelites question God's purpose and doubt the leadership of Moses. God sends snakes to punish their insolence, but then he gives them a cure for snakebite, directing Moses to put a metal snake on a pole. The 'fiery snakes' that deliver the venom are seraphim, a word that Isaiah uses for angels who blaze around God's throne (see 1.12). Since the copper snake resembles the golden calf of Exodus 32, a notorious case of idolatry, readers of this passage were troubled. In other circumstances, a graven image would be not only an idol but also a tool of illicit magic. Here it is a vessel of God's mercy.

*

Journeying from Mount Hor along the way to the Red Sea to go around Edom, the people became annoyed as they travelled and spoke against God and against Moses. 'Why did you bring us out of Egypt,' they asked, 'to die in the wilderness? There is no bread or water, and we hate this awful food!' Then the Lord sent fiery snakes against the people to bite them, and many Israelites died. The people came to Moses and said, 'We sinned by speaking against the Lord and against you. Ask the Lord to take the snakes away from us.' So Moses prayed for the people, and the Lord said to him, 'Make an image of a fiery snake and put it on a pole so that anyone who is bitten can look at it and will live.' So Moses made a snake out of copper and put it on a pole, and when anyone was bitten by a snake and looked at the copper snake, that person lived.

I.4
Messengers from Heaven:
Gen. 28:10–19

Rebekah, Jacob's mother, has warned him away from his brother, Esau, who is in a rage: Jacob tricked their father, Isaac, into giving him the blessing due to Esau as the older son. Jacob runs away to Haran, where his uncle lives. As God addresses him directly for the first time, restating the covenant made with Abraham, the patriarch dreams of a grand stairway reaching to the sky, where *mal'akim* go up and down: in the Septuagint, the official Greek version of the Bible, the *mal'akim* in this passage are *angeloi*. The Greek and Hebrew words, *mal'ak* and *angelos*, can both mean simply 'messenger', including the human couriers who in Latin would be *nuntii*. But the Jacob story in the official Latin Bible has *angeli* – unknown in classical Latin. The older Greek translation influenced the Latin version: by the time that text was produced in late antiquity, biblical and extra-biblical Hebrew writings were using *mal'akim* for 'angels', like the current English word: for intermediate and later developments, see 1.7, 12, 15, 18; 2.1, 4, 6; 5.10–11, 15; 6.4, 11.

*

Jacob left Beersheba to go towards Haran. Reaching a certain point, he stopped for the night because the sun had set. When he lay down to sleep, he took one of the stones there to put under his head. He dreamed of a stairway set on the ground with its top reaching to the sky, and God's messengers were going up and down on it. Beside him stood the Lord and said, 'I am the Lord, the God of your father Abraham and the God of Isaac. I will give you and your descendants the ground on which you lie. Your descendants will be like the dust of the earth . . . I will not leave you until I have done what I have promised you.' Waking from his sleep, Jacob said, 'Surely the Lord is in this place, and I did not know!' He was shaken and said, 'How fearsome this place is! This is none other than the house of God, which is heaven's gate.' Early in the morning, Jacob took the stone he had put under his head, set it up as a pillar and poured oil on top of it. That place he called Bethel, though its name had been Luz.

1.5
Thou Shalt Not Suffer a Witch to Live:
Exod. 22:17–19

After Moses came down from Sinai to deliver God's Ten Commandments, he also provided civil and criminal laws in more detail, followed by moral and religious regulations. One rule forbids deeds so heinous that the person who does them may not live: she is a *mekashefah*, a woman who does *keshef* – Hebrew for 'magic' or 'sorcery' (see 1.1). But when Jews translated the Hebrew into Greek, they used *pharmakous*, a masculine plural, for 'poison-makers', not the feminine singular that would correspond to *mekashefah*. The Latin translation made by Christians has *maleficos* (see 4.16), also masculine plural – literally 'evildoers'. Later, when the King James Bible declared 'thou shalt not suffer a witch to live', the condemned were not always female, though the notorious *Hammer of Witches* had explained at some length why most of them should be (see 8.3). The next offences listed in Exodus are bestiality and idolatry, establishing the context for the *mekashefah*'s crime, seen as repugnant and antisocial as well as irreligious.

*

You shall not allow a potion-maker to live. Whoever lies with an animal shall be put to death. One who sacrifices to gods other than YHVH shall be cast out.

1.6

Urim and Thummim:
Exod. 28:3–30

Exodus gives detailed instructions for making vestments for the High Priest, Aaron, and his sons, specifying colours and types of fabric, metal and gems, all in intricate patterns. One vestment is the 'ephod', which supports a breastplate carrying sacred objects called Urim and Thummim, used by the priest to discover God's will in an authorized rite of divination (see 1.9). The Book of Numbers, describing Joshua's selection to succeed Moses, says that 'Eleazar the priest shall seek the decision of the Urim', and the first Book of Samuel indicates that the procedure involved 'casting lots' – meaning stones, bones, dice and so on.

*

Say to all who are wise at heart, those I have filled with the spirit of wisdom, that they are to make Aaron's garments to consecrate him as priest in my service. These are the garments for them to make: a breastpiece, an ephod, a robe, a chequerered tunic, a cap and a sash . . . Let them make the ephod of gold, blue, purple and crimson wool and of fine linen twisted and worked into designs . . . You shall make a breastplate of decision, worked into a design, and make it like the work of the ephod, of gold, blue, purple and crimson wool, and fine linen twisted . . . When Aaron enters the sanctuary, let him carry over his heart the names of the sons of Israel in the breastplate of decision, as a reminder before YHVH at all times. You shall put the Urim and the Thummim into the breastplate of decision so that they will be over Aaron's heart when he comes before YHVH, and Aaron will carry the judgement of the children of Israel over his heart before YHVH at all times.

1.7
Sun, Moon and Stars:
Deut. 4:15–20

Unlike the gods of other nations, the God of Israel described here is bodiless and invisible, sharing no form with any creature – although 'God created man in his image' in the Genesis story. This formless and ubiquitous God is all-powerful, having no body to confine him in space and time: Israel is to serve no other deity nor make any idol in human, animal or even celestial form. Although an army of stellar and luminary powers fills the heavens with light, those lesser forces too are God's creatures, whom Israel may not worship by making idols (see 1.11–13, 16).

*

Watch yourselves and be careful, for on the day YHVH spoke to you at Horeb out of the fire, you saw no shape of any kind. Do not become corrupt, then, and make yourselves an idol, a likeness in some shape, in the form of a man or woman, or like some animal on earth or a bird that flies on wings in the air, or like something that crawls on the ground or some fish in the waters beneath the earth. And when you look up at the sky and see the sun, moon and stars – the whole army of heaven – do not be lured into bowing down to them in worship. These YHVH, your God, has assigned to all nations under heaven. But you YHVH took and brought out of Egypt, that furnace of iron, to be his own people, as you now are.

1.8

A Goat for Azazel:
Lev. 16:1–10

After destroying Nadab and Abihu, Aaron's sons, for going their own way with ritual, God directs Moses to make sure that his brother follows instructions exactly – above all in rites of purification and atonement, which the tiniest lapse can ruin. Azazel, a demon of the wilderness, gets one of two goats sacrificed for Israel's sins: for demonic animals, see 1.15.

*

The Lord spoke to Moses after the death of the two sons of Aaron who died when they came too close to the Lord. The Lord said to Moses: 'Tell your brother Aaron that he is not to come as he likes into the holiest place behind the curtain, in front of the cover on the ark, or else he will die, for I appear in the cloud over the cover. This is how Aaron is to enter the holiest place – bringing a bull from the herd for a sin offering and a ram for a burnt offering . . . He is to take two male goats from the community of Israel for a sin offering and a ram for a burnt offering. Aaron is to offer the bull for his own sin offering . . . and then take the two goats and make them stand before the Lord at the entrance to the meeting tent. He is to put lots on the two goats, marking one for the Lord and the other for Azazel. Aaron shall bring the goat marked by lot for the Lord and offer it as a sin offering, but the goat marked by lot as the scapegoat is to be left alive, standing before the Lord to be used for making atonement and sending into the wilderness for Azazel.'

1.9
Prophets and Diviners:
Deut. 18:9–21

Divination includes many techniques for knowing what is unknown or normally cannot be known because it is remote in time or space – often but not always in the future. Moses is a *navi*, or prophet, authorized by God to speak for him, unlike the diviners employed by Israel's Canaanite enemies. Although the genuine prophet's main role is to mediate between God and Israel, prophecies often involve predictions, whose truth or falsity tests the prophet's standing. Besides *navi* and *mekashef*, however, this passage uses eight other words and phrases for Canaanite specialists, prohibiting them in Israel because God has not licensed them – not because they are ineffective (see 1.5). Since Moses bans the *study* of the Canaanite practices, he assumes that they can be studied: these crimes are techniques or arts – like the 'mysteries' of Pharaoh's wizards – not just innate abilities or knacks (see 1.1). A *hover haver* is an expert at binding with spells, a *sho'el hammetim* has a method for questioning the dead. However, not all the Hebrew words in this list reveal so much about the techniques that they name, and some of the corresponding English terms, like 'soothsayer' and 'augur', are place-holders more than translations: exactly what the Hebrew words signified at the time is hard to say. One puzzle for later readers was the *sho'el 'ov* – 'ghost-questioner', perhaps – also present in the much-debated tale of the Witch of Endor, who was certainly no 'witch' in the later sense (see 1.10; 6.2–3). That the proscribed deeds were repulsive, however, is clear: they are the atrocious crimes of hostile aliens.

*

When you have come to the land that YHVH, your God, gives you, you shall not study the abominations of those nations and copy them. Let there be no one found among you who passes his son or daughter through fire, no diviner or augur, omen-taker or sorcerer; no spell-caster, ghost-questioner, consuler of familiars or necromancer. For whoever does these things is an abomination to YHVH, and because of these abominations, YHVH, your God, drives them out from before you. Be whole before YHVH, your God. Those nations that you shall conquer listen to augurs and diviners, but to you YHVH, your God, has not given such things. YHVH, your God, will raise up a prophet, like me, from among you and your brothers, and him shall you heed . . . And YHVH said to me . . . 'The prophet who presumes to speak a speech in my name that I did not command him to speak or who speaks in the name of other gods, that prophet shall die.' But suppose you ask yourselves 'how will we know which word YHVH did not speak': if a prophet speaks in YHVH's name and what he says does not happen and the saying does not come about, this is the saying that YHVH did not speak; the prophet has spoken it in insolence, and you shall have no fear of him.

I.10
The Witch of Endor:
1 Sam. 28

Saul, Israel's first king, learns in this story that he is doomed: he has not heeded warnings sent by God through Samuel, the first great prophet after Moses. On the eve of Saul's final battle with the Philistines, Samuel has died, having banished the unauthorized diviners condemned by earlier laws. Lacking an authorized source of advice after Samuel's death, Saul sins again by consulting an unauthorized ghost-talker – a necromancer (see 1.6–7, 9, 11; 4.12; 6.2–3). But this necromancer is a clever, cooperative, generous, persuasive woman whose behaviour belies her traditional label: the Witch of Endor. No malicious hag, she shares her best food with the King and his men, after talking her royal guest out of his hysterical terror. Although prophecy, dreams (like Joseph's in Egypt) and the Urim have failed the King, her illicit divining gives him what he wants: Samuel appears when she calls (though Saul cannot see him), and what the prophet says through her to Saul is God's own truth. Magic can be illicit and still effective, just as licit magic – like the uninformative Urim – can be ineffective.

*

In those days, the Philistines mustered their troops for war, to attack Israel . . . Samuel had died, and all Israel mourned him, burying him in his own town of Ramah. Saul had expelled the ghost-talkers from the land with those who consult familiars.

The Philistines mustered and went to Shunem to make camp, while Saul gathered all Israel and made camp at Gilboa. When Saul saw the Philistine camp, he was afraid, shaken to his core. He asked YHVH what to do, but YHVH did not answer – through dreams or Urim or prophets. Saul then said to his servants, 'Find me a woman who deals with ghosts, so I can go and ask her.' And his servants said, 'In Endor there is a woman who deals with ghosts.' Saul changed his clothes, disguised himself and went to the woman at night with two men.

'Please use a ghost to divine for me,' he said, 'and raise up for me the one that I shall tell you.' But the woman said to him, 'Look, you know what Saul has done. He has expelled ghost-talkers from the land with those who consult familiars. Why would you entrap me and get me killed?' Saul swore to her by YHVH, 'As YHVH lives, no punishment will come to you for this.' Then the woman asked, 'Whom shall I raise up for you?' 'Raise Samuel up,' he said.

When the woman saw Samuel, she cried out in a loud voice and said to Saul, 'Why have you deceived me? You are Saul!' The king said to her, 'Have no fear. What do you see?' 'I see a godly spirit rising out of the earth,' said the woman. 'What shape is it?' he asked. 'An old man comes up, wrapped in a robe,' she said. Then Saul knew it was Samuel, and he bowed down with his face to the ground, prostrating himself.

Samuel said to Saul, 'Why have you disturbed me to bring me up?' 'I am greatly troubled,' said Saul. 'The Philistines attack me, and God has turned away, no longer answering me, neither through prophets nor through dreams. So I have called you to tell me what to do.' 'Why ask me,' said Samuel, 'now that YHVH has turned away from you and become your enemy? As he foretold through me, so YHVH has done to you. YHVH has ripped the kingdom from your hand and has given it to your partner – to David. Because you did not obey YHVH and make the Amalekites feel his fierce anger, YHVH has done this to you today. YHVH will deliver you and Israel both into the hands of the Philistines: tomorrow you and your sons will be with me. YHVH will also deliver the army of Israel into the hands of the Philistines.' Filled with fear by Samuel's words, Saul threw himself flat on the ground right away. And he had no strength, having eaten no food all day and all night.

When the woman came to Saul and saw that he was terrified, she said, 'Your handmaid has heard you: I took my life in my hands and did as you asked me. Now hear me: let me give you a little food to eat, and you will have strength to go on your way.' He refused and said, 'I cannot eat.' But his men joined the woman in pressing him, and he listened to what they said. He rose from the ground and sat on the couch. The woman had a stall-fed calf in the house. She quickly slaughtered it, took some flour, kneaded it and baked loaves without yeast. This she set before Saul and his men, and they ate. On the same night they rose and left.

I.II

Sinning with Omen-takers and
Ghost-talkers:
2 Kings 21:1–15

Manasseh ruled the southern realm of Judah after Assyria had destroyed Israel, the northern kingdom, near the end of the eighth century. He reversed the religious policies of his father, Hezekiah, who had purged Judah of pagan worship. This story, by a later author hostile to Manasseh, accuses him of restoring the cults of Baal, Asherah and other Canaanite gods – even desecrating the Temple in Jerusalem with their images. This attack, in the language of biblical prophecy, focuses on idolatry (see 1.7) as a violation of the first commandment in the Book of Exodus: 'I am YHVH, your God . . . you shall have no other gods before me.' But Manasseh also sinned with omen-takers, ghost-talkers and others denounced by Deuteronomy (see 1.9). There is no general label here – like 'magic' – for Manasseh's crimes: they are breaches of the covenant committed or inspired by foreigners and therefore 'evil in YHVH's eyes'. Christians would come to see the Deuteronomy crimes not just as irreligious but as a special type of sin against religion distinct from other such offences, like idolatry: the list in the King James version of Deuteronomy includes one who 'useth divination or an observer of times or an enchanter or a witch or a charmer or a consulter with familiar spirits or a wizard or a necromancer'.

*

Manasseh was twelve years old when he became king, reigning fifty-five years in Jerusalem. His mother's name was Hephzibah. He did what was evil in YHVH's eyes, following the abominable practices of the nations that the Lord had driven out before the Israelites. He rebuilt the high shrines that his father Hezekiah had destroyed; he set up altars to Baal; and he made an Asherah – as Ahab, King of Israel, had done. He bowed down to the whole host of the heavens and worshipped them, building altars in YHVH's house, of which YHVH had said 'on Jerusalem will I put my name'. In the two courts of YHVH's temple he built altars to the whole army of the heavens. He passed his own son through the fire, practised divination, took omens and used ghost-talkers and those who consult familiars. He did much that was evil in YHVH's eyes and provoked him.

He took the Asherah idol he had made and put it in the Temple – of which YHVH had said to David and his son Solomon 'on this house and on Jerusalem, which I have chosen out of all the tribes of Israel, will I set my name for ever. I will not again make Israel's feet wander from the land that I gave their fathers, if only they take care to do all I have commanded them, keeping the whole law that my servant Moses gave them.' But the people did not listen. Manasseh led them astray, and they did more evil than the nations that YHVH had destroyed when they faced the Israelites.

Through his servants, the prophets, YHVH said: 'Manasseh, King of Judah, has done these abominable things, doing more evil than the Amorites who came before him and leading Judah into sin with his idols. So says YHVH, God of Israel: I will bring such calamity on Jerusalem and Judah that the ears of everyone who hears of it will sting. On Jerusalem I will use Samaria's measuring line and the plumb line of Ahab's house. As if wiping a plate and turning it over, I will wipe Jerusalem out. I will abandon the remnant of my heirs and deliver them into the hands of enemies, making them prey and plunder for all their enemies because they have done evil in my eyes and have provoked me from the day their fathers left Egypt until this day.'

I.12

Angels at the Throne:
Isa. 6:1–3

One of Manasseh's crimes was to desecrate the Temple by setting up 'altars to the whole army of the heavens' (see 1.7, 11). Those heavenly battalions, for whom Manasseh deprives God of his due worship, are the Lord's winged soldiers in Isaiah's vision. Writing even later than Manasseh's attacker, the author of Isaiah 6 turns the astral powers of the previous 2 Kings passage into God's angelic attendants – though the Bible uses neither the positive 'angel' nor the pejorative 'demon' in these places, where power and splendour are the main features of the celestial troops. The name 'seraph' tells us that Isaiah's angels 'burn' in their brilliance (see 1.3).

*

In the year when King Uzziah died, I saw my Lord sitting exalted on a high throne, and the bottom of his robe filled the Temple. Seraphs stood attending Him, each with six wings: with two he covered his face, with two he covered his feet and with two he would take flight. One called to the other, saying, 'Holy, holy, holy is YHVH of the Armies; the whole earth is full of His glory.'

1.13

A Vision of the Enticer:
1 Kings 22:1–38

As the first Book of Kings closes, the ruler of Israel goes to his death in battle, an end described here as infamous by a critic who can bring himself only once to mention the King's name – Ahab. A large band of prophets wants to please Ahab by encouraging his war on Aram. But one prophet – Micaiah – refuses to be manipulated, and Ahab's ally, Jehoshaphat, King of Judah, behaves cautiously. God, in order to deceive Ahab and destroy him, asks for a volunteer from the celestial army, and one 'spirit' (*ruah*) steps forward to serve as an 'enticer' (see 1.7, 11–12). This tempter is a distinct spiritual person, though the 'spirit' in this story is also God's voice speaking through his prophets, a power that migrates from one person to another. The spirit who steps out of the heavenly brigades as the enticer distinguishes himself by this act from the rank and file of God's army. Micaiah, like Isaiah, sees the heavenly troops in a prophetic vision.

*

Three years passed with no war between Aram and Israel. But in the third year, Jehoshaphat, King of Judah, went down to see the King of Israel. The King of Israel said to his officials, 'You realize that Ramoth-gilead belongs to us, and yet we do nothing to get it back from the King of Aram's control.' And he asked Jehoshaphat, 'Will you go with me to attack Ramoth-gilead?' Jehoshaphat's reply to the King of Israel was this: 'I will do as you do, my troops are your troops, my horses are your horses.' But to the King of Israel Jehoshaphat also said, 'First see what YHVH says.'

So the King of Israel assembled the prophets – about four hundred of them – and asked them, 'Shall I go and attack Ramoth-gilead, or shall I hold back?' 'Go,' they said, 'and the Lord will put it in the King's control.' Then Jehoshaphat asked, 'Is there not another prophet of YHVH here for us to question?' The King of Israel answered Jehoshaphat: 'There is one prophet yet whom we can ask what YHVH says, but I despise him because his prophecy is never helpful, only trouble – Micaiah, son of Imlah.' 'The King should not say that,' Jehoshaphat replied. Then the King of Israel called one of the eunuchs and said, 'Bring Micaiah, son of Imlah, at once.'

On the threshing floor by the entrance of the Samaria gate, the King of Israel and Jehoshaphat, King of Judah, sat on their thrones dressed in their royal robes, and all the prophets prophesied before them. Zedekiah son of Chenaanah had made iron horns for himself and declared, 'So says YHVH: "With these shall you gore the Arameans until you finish them."' All the other prophets gave the same prophecy: 'Attack Ramoth-gilead and win; YHVH will put it under the King's control.'

The messenger who had gone to summon Micaiah said to him, 'Look, the statements of the prophets are all helpful to the King. Let your statement be like theirs, please, and say something helpful.' But Micaiah answered, 'As YHVH lives, I will say only what YHVH tells me.' When he came before the King, the King asked him, 'Shall we attack Ramoth-gilead or not, Micaiah?' 'Go and win,' he answered: 'YHVH will put it in the King's control.' The King said to him, 'How many times must I make you swear to tell me nothing but the truth in YHVH's name?' Micaiah then answered, 'I saw all Israel scattered over the hills like sheep without a shepherd, and YHVH said, "They have no master. Let each go back to his home safely."' The King of Israel said to Jehoshaphat, 'Did I not say that his prophecies are never helpful to me, only trouble?'

'Then hear what YHVH says,' Micaiah answered: 'I saw YHVH sitting on his throne with the whole army of heaven standing around him on his right and left. And YHVH said, "Who will entice Ahab so that he attacks Ramoth-gilead and falls there?" One said this, another that. Then a spirit came forward, stood before the Lord and said, "I will entice him." "How?" asked YHVH. "I will go and be a lying spirit in the mouths of all his prophets," he said. "You shall succeed in enticing him," he replied, "go do it." So you see, YHVH has put a lying spirit in the mouths of all these prophets of yours. YHVH has decreed trouble for you.'

Then Zedekiah, son of Chenaanah, went up to Micaiah, slapped his face and demanded, 'Which way did YHVH's spirit go from me to speak to you?' 'On the day when you go to an inner room to hide, you will find out,' Micaiah answered. Then the King of Israel said, 'Take Micaiah and turn him over to Amon, governor of the city, and to Prince Joash and tell him, "This is what the King says: Put this person in prison and give him a bit of bread and water until I come back safely."' 'If you ever return safely,' Micaiah replied, 'YHVH has not spoken through me,' adding, 'hear, all you peoples!'

Then the King of Israel and Jehoshaphat, King of Judah, marched on Ramoth-gilead. The King of Israel said to Jehoshaphat, 'I will go into battle disguised, while you wear your royal garb.' So the King of Israel went into battle disguised. Meanwhile, the King of Aram had given orders to his thirty-two chariot officers: 'Attack no one, great or small, but the King of Israel.' When the chariot officers saw Jehoshaphat, thinking that he must be the King of Israel, they turned to attack him. But when Jehoshaphat cried out, the chariot commanders saw that he was not the King of Israel and stopped chasing him. Then someone happened to draw his bow and hit the King of Israel between parts of his armour, and the King told his chariot driver, 'Rein about and get me out of the fight; I am wounded.'

The fighting raged all day, with the King propped up in his chariot facing Aram. His wound bled into the chariot, and he died at dusk. As the sun set, a shout went through the army: 'Every man to his town, every man to his land!' So the King died and was brought to Samaria, and in Samaria they buried the King. They washed the chariot at the pool of Samaria, dogs licked the blood and whores bathed in it – as YHVH's word had said.

1.14
Dry Bones and the Spirit:
Ezek. 37:1–10

In Ezekiel's haunting vision of the valley of dry bones, the spirit is the enlivening power of God and also the breath of life itself, akin to the four winds that make the earth move. But this organic, physical and metaphysical force is also a person who can hear, understand and act on God's orders (see 1.13). Like any human person, the spirit gets the word of God from a prophet.

*

YHVH's hand was upon me, and he brought me out by YHVH's spirit and set me in the centre of the valley: it was full of bones. He led me all around them, and I saw many, many bones – very dry bones – on the valley floor. He asked me, 'Can these bones come alive, son of man?' 'Lord YHVH,' I answered, 'you alone know.' Then he said to me, 'Prophesy to these bones and say to them, "Hear the word of YHVH, you dry bones."' This is what the Lord YHVH said to those bones: 'I will make the spirit enter you, and you shall come alive. I will put sinews on you, make flesh grow on you and cover you with skin. I will put the spirit into you, and you shall come alive. Then you shall know that I am YHVH.'

I prophesied as I was ordered. And as I prophesied there was a rattling noise, and the bones came together, bone to bone. I watched as sinews and flesh grew on them and skin covered them, but there was no spirit in them. Then he said to me, 'Prophesy to the spirit; prophesy, son of man, and tell the spirit, "This is what the Lord YHVH says: Come from the four winds, spirit, and breathe into these slain so that they may live."' I prophesied as he ordered me, and the spirit entered them. They came to life and stood up on their feet – a vast multitude.

1.15
Lilith and the Goat-demons:
Isa. 34:8–16

The prophet Isaiah threatens ruin for the alien land of Edom with a list of geological and biological horrors – streambeds clotted with smoking pitch, monuments overgrown with desert weeds and beasts of prey roaming the landscape. These afflictions are assembled by God's spirit, who also sends down unnatural powers, including Lilith, a female demon associated with winds and illicit sexuality. Since several words in this passage are unusual, whether the prophet describes ordinary animals or demons is unclear: in context, however, the *se'erim* seem to be satyrs, not just hairy goats; the arrow-snake (*qippon*) may also be a demon. All come at the command of God's spirit (see 1.8, 13–14).

*

For YHVH there is a day of vengeance,
a year of retribution for Zion's cause.
Edom's streams shall be turned to pitch,
her dirt to burning sulphur;
her land shall be flaming pitch
and not go out, night or day,
its smoke rising for ever.
Through the ages shall Edom lie wasted;
for eternity no one shall pass through it.

Nightjar and screech owl shall take it,
night owl and raven nesting there.
He will take the measure of Edom
with the line of chaos
and the weight of ruin.
'No Kingdom There' shall be its name;
its nobles and princes shall vanish.

Thorns shall grow in the palaces,
nettles and briers in the strongholds.
It shall be a den of jackals,
a house for the ostrich.
Desert cats shall greet hyenas,
and goat-demons bleat to one another;
there the lilith shall lie
and find herself a place to roost.
The arrow-snake shall nest there and lay eggs
to brood and hatch in its shade;
and there shall the buzzards gather,
each with its mate.
Look in YHVH's book and read:
not one shall be missing,
not one shall lack a mate,
for the order has come from his mouth,
and his spirit gathers them together.

1.16

The Adversary in the Court of Heaven:
Job 1:6–12

As the Book of Job opens in heaven, God is attended not by an army but by a court of lesser divinities, including one who has the job of adversary – *ha-satan*, not yet used as a proper name – in mediating between God and his creatures. Although the adversary's task recalls the role of the enticer in the story of Micaiah, his character is stronger and better defined: he debates with God and offers a challenge, yet he remains subordinate and follows orders (see 1.7, 11–13).

*

One day the sons of the gods came to present themselves to YHVH, and the adversary also came with them. YHVH asked the adversary, 'Where have you come from?' To YHVH the adversary said, 'From walking around and prowling over the earth.' Then YHVH asked the adversary: 'Have you thought about my servant Job? There is no one like him on earth. He is a blameless man and upright, fearing God and shunning evil.' 'Is it for nothing that Job fears God?' said the adversary to YHVH. 'Have you not put a hedge all around him and his household and all that he has? You have blessed the work of his hands, and his herds have spread through the land. But now take your hand and touch everything he has, and surely he will curse you to your face.' YHVH said to the adversary: 'All that he has is in your power, then, but do not lay a hand on him.' Then the adversary left YHVH's presence.

1.17
Satan Incites David:
1 Chron. 21:1–5

The word *satan* in this sentence lacks a definite article, so it may be that the adversary who provokes David into taking a census had acquired a proper name – Satan – by the time this passage was written (see 1.16). Although the real instigator of David's statistical sin may have been just a human 'adversary', it was 'Satan' who 'stood up against Israel', according to the King James version. In either case, since the chronicler does not describe David's provoker as an agent of God, Satan (or a lesser adversary) may be acting independently.

*

Satan went up against Israel and incited David to number Israel.

1.18

The Angel Raphael:
Tobit 4–6

The Book of Tobit, translated here from the work called 'Tobias' in the Latin Vulgate, is not part of the canonical Hebrew Bible. The older of the story's two heroes lives in Nineveh in the eighth century BCE, after the Assyrians have deported the Jews of Israel, the northern kingdom. Although Tobit is steadfast in righteousness, he goes blind, causing him to wish for death, but not before sending his son, Tobias, on adventures with an angel, who shows him how to use natural objects – the guts of a fish – to drive demons away (see 2.7, 10–11). The angel and the demon both have names – Raphael (also called Azaria) and Asmodeus – making them more like persons than the nameless angelic and demonic powers in older biblical texts (see 1.7, 11–13, 16).

*

Of the city and tribe of Napthali, Tobias . . . when he was taken captive in the time of Salmanassar, King of Assyria, did not abandon the path of truth even in captivity . . . When everyone went to the golden calves that King Jeroboam of Israel had made, he alone avoided keeping company with them, going to Jerusalem to worship his Lord, the God of Israel . . . When he came of age, he took a wife of his own tribe, Anna, and had a son by her, giving him his own name . . . He fed the hungry, clothed the naked and took care to bury the dead and slain . . .

One day, when the burying had worn him out, he went home, lay near a wall and slept, and warm droppings fell from a sparrow's nest on his eyes and blinded him when he was sleeping . . . But he remained steadfast in the fear of God, giving thanks to God all the days of his life . . .

But on the same day in Rages, a city of the Medes, it happened that Sarah, Raguel's daughter, heard one of her father's maidservants rebuking her because she had been betrothed to seven husbands and a demon named Asmodeus killed them . . . She kept praying, however, begging God in tears to free her from this rebuke . . . And at that moment, the prayers of them both were heard in the glorious sight of God Almighty. Raphael, the Lord's holy angel, was sent to heal them both . . .

Then, since Tobit thought that his prayer for death had been heard, he called his son, Tobias, to him, and said . . . 'When God takes my soul, bury my body and honour your mother all the days of her life . . . I also inform you, my son, that when you were still an infant, I gave ten talents of silver to Gabelus of Rages, a city of the Medes, and here I have the document in his writing. Now find out how to go to him and get that amount of silver from him, giving him back his document . . .'

When Tobias started out, he found a handsome young man standing there, dressed as if for travel. Not knowing that this was God's angel, he greeted him and said, 'Where do you come from, my friend?' 'I am a son of Israel,' he answered, and Tobias said to him, 'Do you know the road that goes to the land of the Medes?' 'I know it,' he answered. 'I have taken many trips and gone there often, staying with our brother Gabelus, who lives in Rages . . . '

Tobias set out on his journey with a dog following, and the first stop was beside the river Tigris. When he went to wash his feet, he saw a huge fish come up and try to eat him. Terrified by the fish, Tobias cried out and said, 'It's coming after me, sir!' And the angel said to him, 'Grab it by the gills and pull it towards you.' When he did this and dragged it on to the dry land, the fish began to gasp near his feet. Then the angel said to him, 'Gut the fish and save its heart, gall and liver, which are needed for medicines that we can use.' After doing so, he cooked its flesh, and they took it with them on the road. The rest they salted – enough until they came to Rages, the city of the Medes.

Then Tobias questioned the angel, saying, 'Please, Azaria my brother, the parts of the fish that you told me to keep, what will they cure?' The angel answered: 'If you put a bit of the heart on the coals, its smoke will get rid of every kind of demon – for a man or a woman – so that it will not return to them again. The gall is good as a salve for eyes that have white spots, and they will be healed.'

'Where do you think we should stay?' asked Tobias. The angel answered, saying, 'There is a man here named Raguel, a relative from your tribe, who has a daughter named Sarah, but he has no child, male or female, except her. All his property is owed you, and you must take her as your wife. Ask her father, then, and he will give her to you in marriage.'

Then Tobias replied, saying, 'I have heard that she was betrothed to seven husbands, who have died, and I have also heard that a demon killed them. I am afraid that the same might happen to me, and since I am the only child of my parents, I will send them below with grief in their old age.'

Then the angel Raphael said to him: 'Listen to me, and I will show you who it is that the demon can overpower. For they that go into marriage by shutting God out from themselves and their minds and giving themselves to lust, like a horse or a donkey that has no intelligence – it is them that the demon has in his power. When you marry her, however, and have entered the bedchamber, do not touch her for three days and do nothing with her but pray. On your wedding night, by burning the fish's liver, the demon will be driven out. On the second night you will be admitted to the embrace of the blessed patriarchs. And on the third night you will get a blessing to beget healthy children. When the third night has passed, take the girl in the fear of the Lord, moved more by love of children than by lust, that you may be blessed with children in the seed of Abraham.'

2

Power in the Name of Jesus:
The Greek New Testament

Figure 3: Jesus Harrows Hell and Satan Presides

What truth could be firmer for Christians than Gospel truth? Although the evangelists say that some magic is fake – tricks done by 'false messiahs and false prophets' – most of the signs and wonders they record are described as real. Magic really works in the New Testament, where magicians draw crowds, angels talk with humans, demons roam the earth and Satan commands an army of devils to deceive the weak and manipulate illicit wizardry. By telling stories about these strange persons and bizarre events, the Greek (Christian) part of the Bible confirms and extends ancient Israel's experience of the magic reported in the Hebrew books.

The evangelists show us, again and again, that Jesus has enormous power: he does many things out of the ordinary, things not at all normal. This happens, they claim, because Jesus is God's agent or even God himself. The signs and wonders done by Jesus are many and astounding. They convince people that his message is true, and the same message attributes otherwise inexplicable happenings to God. But the same marvels provoke the enemies of Jesus. And other people besides Jesus also do such things, some to finish the work that he started, others for reasons of their own. The apostles chosen by him make real wonders happen, but so do their competitors and other neutral parties.

The evangelists locate these events in two frameworks: the social world and the world of nature. As society's saviour, Jesus feeds hungry crowds with a few scraps; he heals the incurably ill, curing ailments acquired or present from birth; he drives out demons who possess and torment their victims; and he brings people back from the dead. As ruler or viceregent of the universe, Jesus can quell storms, walk on water and make a healthy tree wither overnight. When he does something astonishing, the effect sometimes follows a command – a word or phrase of power – that he utters; in some cases, a physical action on his part precedes the effect; in another case, power flows from him by contact; and sometimes the strange phenomenon simply happens, with no prior statement or action. Jesus, who once asks a demon for his name, has a name so charged with power that others use it to work wonders, even without accepting the message that he preaches.

Where else in the world's classics, except in the Gospels, is a story told four times in succession but in two different patterns (synoptic and Johannine) while making the protagonist a compelling character? Where else do we meet angels – both good and evil – as fully or thinly formed as other persons in the story, capable of sustained conversation and psychological interaction with humans? Opposing the good spirits and messengers of God are evil angels under Satan's command.

Both bad angels and good angels are real persons. In a confrontation with Jesus early in the Gospel story – the temptation in the desert – Satan has a concrete personality and his own psychology (cunning, arrogant, malicious). Distinctive physical traits (immense size, reptilian anatomy, a blazing red complexion) come later, in the Book of Revelation at the end of the New Testament. Whether Satan is the Devil or Beelzeboul or has another name, he is the same malevolent figure who commands the bad angels. They are lesser devils or demons, and they are innumerable, plaguing humans with mental and physical ailments that can be cured ritually – by exorcism. Like Satan, they converse and react, but sometimes they act impersonally, as the 'unclean spirits' of mental and bodily disease. Demons are punished for the evil that they do, burning in hell for all eternity with Satan, the supreme fallen angel, once a peer of Gabriel and Michael but now a disgraced prince of a dark realm.

Opposing the forces of evil, the apostles do astonishing things – as Jesus did – and usually in the same ways: healing the sick, expelling demons, even raising the dead. Although their professed aim is to prove the true God's power, the dazzled crowds attracted by Christ's disciples take them for gods. Their own contrary belief is that they can work wonders only because Jesus has told them to do so – unlike others who misuse the name of Jesus as a tool of magic. Their main competitor in Samaria, the unscrupulous Simon, is a magus in his own right, though not a very clever one. More appealing are the Magi of the Christmas story, benevolent sages and astrologers from far away who were masters of magic before Jesus was born.

God Sent the Angel Gabriel:
Luke 1:5–38

The angel Gabriel – one of two angels named in the Hebrew Bible – brings good news along with punishment for weak faith: he announces that Zacharia's aged wife will bear a child, but until the birth the old man will be mute because he doubted the angel's message (see 1.2, 4). Mary is also puzzled by Gabriel's astounding declaration that she is to give birth to 'a Son of God', though when she questions Gabriel, no punishment follows. A scene reproduced in countless images, the angel's announcement to Mary – the Annunciation of Christian liturgy and art – still shows us how to picture an angel.

*

In the days of Herod, King of Judah, there was a priest named Zacharia in the watch of Abia; his wife, named Elizabeth, was also a descendant of Aaron. Both were righteous in God's eyes, keeping without fault all the Lord's commandments and decrees. They had no child, however, because Elizabeth was barren and both were advanced in years. Once, when it was the turn of Zacharia's watch and he was serving as priest before God, it happened – by priestly custom – that he was chosen by lot to enter the Lord's Temple and burn incense. And when it came time to burn the incense, the whole crowd of people outside was praying.

An angel of the Lord then appeared to him, standing to the right of the altar where the incense was burned. Zacharia was startled to see him, and fear took hold of him. But the angel said to him, 'Have no fear, Zacharia: your plea has been heard. Your wife Elizabeth will bear you a son, and you shall give him the name John . . .' Zacharia asked the angel, 'How can I know this? I am old, and my wife is well on in her years.' The angel replied: 'I am Gabriel; I stand in God's presence; I have been sent to speak to you and give you this good news. Now – since you have not believed what I said, which will be done at the appointed time – you will be silenced and unable to speak until the day it happens.' . . . When the days of his service were done, he went back to his house. After this time, his wife Elizabeth conceived and stayed secluded for five months . . .

In the sixth month, God sent the angel Gabriel to a town in Galilee named Nazareth – to a young woman betrothed to a man named Joseph, of the house of David, and the young woman's name was Mary. The angel went to her and said, 'Greetings, favoured woman, the Lord is with you.' At these words she was perplexed, asking herself what sort of greeting this might be. And the angel said to her 'do not be afraid, Mary: you have found favour with God. You shall conceive in your womb and bear a son, and you shall give him the name Jesus. He will be great and will be called Son of the Most High, and to him the Lord God will give the throne of David, his father. He will rule the house of Jacob for ever, and his kingdom will have no end.'

'How can this be,' Mary asked the angel, 'since I know no man?' The angel answered, saying, 'The Holy Spirit will come upon you, the power of the Most High will cover you over, and thus the holy one to come will be called a Son of God. Look at your cousin Elizabeth, who has also conceived a child in her old age: she, who has been called barren, is in her sixth month. For the word of God nothing shall be impossible.' 'You see the Lord's servant,' said Mary, 'let it happen to me as you said.' And the angel left her.

2.2

Astrology Guides the Magi: Matt. 2:1–12

The notorious wizard who challenges the Apostles in Samaria is never called 'Simon Magus' by the Book of Acts, even though he is known for 'doing magic' – *mageuôn* (see 2.18). When Paul, still named Saul, encounters a different *magos* in Cyprus, the culprit – like Simon – is a Jew and also a 'false prophet' and a 'son of the devil', according to the same book (see 2.9). But the Magi of Matthew's Christmas story are benevolent sages of the Orient. As astronomers, they can tell Herod 'the time when the star had appeared', as astrologers, they know what the star portends – the royal birth that terrifies Herod – and as interpreters of dreams, they see through the King's deception (see 4.9, 15; 5.8–9).

*

In the days of Herod the King, when Jesus was born in Bethlehem of Judea, Magi from the East came to Jerusalem, asking, 'Where is the one born King of the Jews? For we saw his star in the East and have come to worship him.' But when King Herod heard this, it troubled him, and all Jerusalem with him. He called together all the high priests and scribes of the people, asking them where the Anointed would be born. 'In Bethlehem of Judea,' they answered, 'for thus was it written by the prophet:

> And you, Bethlehem, a land of Judah,
> are not least among Judah's princes:
> from you will come a ruler
> to shepherd Israel, my people.'

Then Herod called the Magi in secret and learned from them the time when the star had appeared. He sent them to Bethlehem, saying, 'Go and enquire carefully about the child, and if you find him, send me word so that I too may go and worship him.' Having heard the King, they left, and the star they had seen in the East stayed ahead of them until it stood over the place where the child was. When they saw the star, they were overjoyed – with joy abounding. Coming into the house, they saw the child with Mary, his mother, and bowed down to worship him, opening their treasures then and giving him gifts of gold, incense and myrrh. Because a dream warned them not to go back to Herod, they took a different road to return to their country.

2.3
Get Away from Me, Satan!
Matt. 4:1–11

When Shakespeare wrote that 'the Devil can cite Scripture for his purpose', he may have been thinking of this confrontation between Jesus and the Slanderer – *diabolos*, a common noun in Greek – but also the Tempter and Satan, which could be a proper name or might mean 'adversary' (see 1.16–17). Known by many names, the Devil is vicious, devious and powerful, both physically and intellectually. He transports Jesus instantly from the desert to the centre of Jerusalem and then to the top of a mountain, while displaying his mastery of Bible texts in debate with his opponent. When the enticer or adversary of the Hebrew Bible ensnares humans, even one as mighty as David, he acts as God's agent. But if Matthew implies that Jesus is 'the Lord your God' whom 'angels came to attend', it is God himself that Satan tries to test and tempt.

*

Then Jesus was led into the desert by the Spirit to be tempted by the Devil. After fasting forty days and forty nights, he was hungry. The Tempter came and said to him, 'If you are the Son of God, then tell these stones to turn to bread.' Answering, he said, '"Not by bread alone shall man live" is it written, "but by every word that comes from God's mouth."' Then the Devil took him away to the holy city, stood him on top of the Temple and said to him, 'If you are the Son of God, throw yourself down, for this is written: "He will order his angels to take care of you, and with their hands they will lift you up lest you strike your foot against a stone."' Jesus answered him. 'This too is written: "Do not tempt the Lord your God."' The Devil took him away again to a very high mountain and showed him all the kingdoms of the world and their glory. 'All this will I give you if you will bow down and worship me,' he said. Then Jesus said to him, 'Get away from me, Satan! For it is written, "You shall worship the Lord your God, and him only shall you serve."' Then the Devil left him, and angels came to attend him.

2.4

A Battle of Angels:
Rev. 12:1–9

The Book of Revelation is an apocalypse – a vision of the end of time. But this passage also mirrors the creation of the universe, before the 'old serpent' tempted Eve and Adam. The Satan or Accuser of Revelation has evolved from the Adversary or Satan of the Hebrew Bible (see 1.13, 16 –17). He and the dark angels he commands once shone in heaven's armies, before they fell in a battle recorded by non-biblical texts. 'Michael and his angels', who defeated the Devil's legions in the beginning, now stop them from spoiling the birth of the Anointed – Jesus, the Messiah. God shelters the Messiah's mother in the desert – a refuge for the Israelites fleeing Egypt but also the site of Satan's encounter with Jesus (see 1.2–3; 2.3). Although the Devil is doomed to lose, his power is enormous, enough to sweep 'a third of the stars from the sky' with one stroke of a huge saurian tail. Like the flood of Noah's day, the water that the dragon vomits is a torrent of destruction. Some details of this vision became elements of Satan's image: an immense monster, many-headed, horned, reptilian and fiery red.

*

A great sign was seen in heaven: a woman wearing the sun, the moon under her feet and upon her head a crown of twelve stars. With her belly full, she cried out in the travail and torment of birth. Then another sign was seen in heaven, a great dragon, flaming red with seven heads and ten horns and seven crowns on its heads. Its tail swept a third of the stars from the sky, hurling them to the earth. The dragon stood facing the woman as she was about to deliver – to eat her child as soon as she had birthed it. She gave birth to a son, a male, who will 'herd the whole flock of nations with an iron wand'. And her child was snatched up to God and his throne. The woman fled to the desert, where God had prepared a place to feed her for 1,260 days.

Then there was a fight in heaven. Michael and his angels fought against the dragon; the dragon and his angels fought back. But he was not strong enough,

and they could find no place in heaven. The great dragon was hurled down –
the old serpent called the Devil and Satan, the one who deceives the whole
world, was hurled to earth, and his angels were hurled with him. And I heard
a great voice in heaven say

> Now salvation and power have come
> with the kingdom of our God
> and the authority of his Anointed
> to hurl down the Accuser of our brothers
> who accuses them to our God day and night.
> They overcame him
> by the blood of the Lamb,
> by the word of their witness,
> by facing death and not loving their lives.
> Rejoice, then, you heavens
> and you who dwell in them,
> but woe to the earth and the sea:
> the Devil has gone down to you, raging mightily,
> seeing that his time is short.

When the dragon saw that he had been hurled to earth, he went after the
woman who had given birth to the male child. And the two wings of the
great eagle were given to the woman so that she could fly to the place prepared for her in the desert to feed her for an age, for ages and for half an age,
out of the serpent's sight. Coming after the woman, the serpent vomited a
torrent of water from his mouth to sweep her away in the flood. But the
dragon helped the woman, opening the mouth of the earth and swallowing
the river that the serpent had ejected from his mouth. Enraged at the woman,
the serpent went off to do battle with the rest of her seed – those that keep
God's commandments and have the witness of Jesus.

2.5
The Sheep and the Goats:
Matt. 25:31–41

The eternal prison of the Devil and his angels is a fiery hell, ready to receive the damned at the Last Judgement (see 3.1; 4.12; 6.2, 6, 12; 7.18; 10.2, 7).

*

When the Son of Man comes in his glory and all the angels with him, he will sit upon his throne of glory. Gathered before him will be all the nations, and he will separate them from one another as a shepherd separates sheep from goats. He will station the sheep to his right and the goats to his left. Then the King will say to those on his right, 'Come, you blessed of my Father, and claim your inheritance, the Kingdom prepared for you since the foundation of the world . . .' Then to those on his left he will say, 'Get away from me, you accursed, into the eternal fire prepared for the Devil and his angels.'

2.6

Principalities, Powers and Dominations: Ephes. 1:15–23

Paul chants this prayer for a growing Christian community in Western Asia, dominated by the city of Ephesus and its god Artemis, but also home to lesser gods, the principalities, authorities, powers and dominations feared by Christians as evil demons (see 5.10; Fig. 6). The Magical Papyri invoke Artemis as mistress of such spirits, whose names were tokens of power for users of those spells (see 5.6). Thinking of the Psalms, where 'the Lord said unto my Lord, sit thou at my right hand, until I make thine enemies thy footstool', Paul assures the Ephesians that Christ's 'exceedingly great power' will prevail over the magicians and their demons, whose domain is cosmic but lower than God's throne. From 'every name that is named' the threat is real yet transitory: Jesus, having vanquished death, will defeat the ministers of death. Later generations of Christians, confident that the old gods had been beaten, would use the same terminology – principalities, powers, thrones and dominations – to classify angels (see 6.13).

*

Once I heard about the faith that you have in the Lord Jesus and your love for all the saints, I have not stopped giving thanks for you or remembering you in my prayers, asking the God of our Lord Jesus Christ, the Father of Glory, to give you the spirit of wisdom and revelation, so that you might come to know him, so that your heart's eyes might be enlightened to know the hope of his call, the wealth of his glorious inheritance in his saints and – for us believers – his exceedingly great power when his mighty rule is working, which was worked in Christ by raising him from the dead and seating him at his right hand in the heavens, far above every principality and authority, power and domination, and every name that is named, not only in this age but also in that to come: God put them all under his feet and gave him headship over them all.

2.7

My Name is Legion:
Mark 5:1–42

Across the Jordan in a region where gentiles live, Jesus brings his power down to earth, showing that his authority over hostile forces operates not just on heaven's distant heights but also in the here and now (see 2.4–6). He meets a man tormented by unclean spirits – enough demons to fill a legion – and subdues them with just a few words, even before asking the primary demon to reveal his (or their) name (see 9.3). A spectacular exorcism follows, astonishing the onlookers and those who hear the story later. But collateral damage – drowning a huge herd of livestock – alienates the local people, who ask Jesus to leave. When he moves on to heal a woman's chronic illness and bring a young girl back from the dead, some still laugh at him. But his power is stupendous: Jesus heals the woman by physical contact alone, without conscious action on his part (see 2.13). After the woman touches his clothing, he senses 'in his own body that power had gone out of him', discharging the healing force as if it were electricity. Perhaps the crowds had already seen such displays from travelling magicians (see 5.1–2). All or most of what Jesus says to them will have been Aramaic, turned into Greek for the Gospels. But when Jesus touches the daughter of Jairus to bring her back to life, the evangelist transliterates and translates the words – *taleitha kum* – treating them as exotic and incantatory.

*

They went to the other side of the lake to the district of the Gerasenes. When Jesus got out of the boat, a man with an unclean spirit came straight up from the tombs to meet him. He had a place to live in the tombs, and even with a chain no one could bind him any longer. Often, in fact, he had been bound with shackles and chains, but he tore the chains off and broke the shackles apart. No one was strong enough to overpower him. All night and day in the tombs and in the hills he kept shrieking and cutting himself with stones.

Seeing Jesus from far away, he ran and bowed down to him. In a loud voice he shrieked, 'What do you want with me, Jesus, Son of the Most High God?

Swear to God not to torture me!' For he had said to him, 'Come out of this man, unclean spirit!' Then he asked him, 'What is your name?' 'Legion is my name,' he answered, 'because there are many of us.' And he kept begging Jesus not to send them out of the district.

A huge herd of pigs was there, feeding near the hillside. They begged him: 'Send us to the pigs and let us go into them.' He let them do it, and the unclean spirits came out and went into the pigs. The herd rushed over the bank towards the lake – about two thousand of them – and they drowned in the lake. Hurrying off to town and the countryside, those feeding the pigs reported this, and people went out to see what it was. When they came to Jesus and saw the man possessed by demons sitting and wearing clothes, quite sane – the one who had a legion of them – they were afraid. Those who had seen what had happened to the demon-ridden man told them about it – and also about the pigs. Then they started asking Jesus to leave their territory.

As he was getting into the boat, the man with the demon asked to go with him. He did not let him, instead saying to him 'go to your home and your people and tell them how much the Lord has done for you and how kind he has been to you'. So he went away and in the Ten Cities started to tell how much Jesus had done for him, and they were all amazed.

When Jesus had crossed again to the other side by boat, a big crowd gathered around him and he stayed near the lake. One of the masters of the synagogue – Jairus by name – came up, and when he saw him, he fell at his feet and begged for help, saying 'my daughter is near the end: please come and put your hands on her so that she might be saved and live'. And Jesus went off with him, but a big crowd followed, pushing towards him – including a woman whose blood had kept flowing for twelve years.

After many physicians treated her for many illnesses, she had spent all her money, yet nothing helped and she got worse instead. Having heard things about Jesus, she went into the crowd behind him to touch his robe. 'If I even touch his robe,' she said, 'I shall be saved,' and when the stream of blood dried up right away, it felt like her body had recovered from a beating.

Jesus, surrounded by the crowd and sensing in his own body that power had gone out of him, turned and asked, 'Who touched my robe?' 'You see the crowd pushing towards you,' said his students, 'and you ask, "Who touched me?"' As Jesus looked around to see who had done it, the woman, realizing what had happened to her, came in fear and trembling to kneel before him and tell the whole truth. 'Daughter,' he said to her, 'your confidence has saved you. Leave in peace and be healed from your pain.'

Jesus was still speaking when people came from where the master of the synagogue lived to tell him, 'Your daughter has died: why keep bothering the teacher?' Jesus overheard what they said and told the master, 'Don't be afraid; just be confident.' And he let no one follow him but Peter, James and John – James's brother. When they reached the master's house, he saw a crowd in an uproar, with much wailing and shouting. Going in, he asked, 'What's all the uproar and wailing? The child hasn't died. She's just sleeping.' And they laughed at him.

After making them all leave, and taking with him the child's father and mother and his students, he went in to where the child was, took hold of her hand and said to her '*taleitha kum*', which translated is 'I'm telling you to get up, little girl.' She stood up right away and walked around: she was twelve years old. At once they were totally astonished, and he gave them full and strict instructions to let no one know about it, also telling them to give her something to eat.

2.8
Expelling Demons in the Name of Jesus:
Mark 9:38–40

The name of Jesus itself is a word of power: others use it to work wonders against demons, just like Jesus himself, but without accepting the message that Jesus proclaims. Perhaps all publicity is good publicity.

*

John said to him: 'Teacher, we have seen someone driving out demonic spirits in your name, and we stopped him because he is not one of our followers.' 'Do not stop him,' said Jesus, 'for no one who does something powerful in my name can then abuse me, since anyone not against us is for us.'

2.9

Signs and Wonders, True or False? Mark 13:1–23

True 'signs and wonders' done by Jesus and his followers cause the amazement that stimulates faith and sustains it (see 1.1–2; 2.7). Real wonders are also done by people who do not follow Jesus (see 2.8). But other dazzling sights are deceptions, illusions devised by the 'false messiahs and false prophets' who will worsen the chaos of the last days, signalled by the 'ruinous horror' – a heathen desecration of the Temple described by the Book of Daniel.

*

As he left the Temple, one of his students said to him, 'Look, teacher: what magnificent stones and amazing buildings!' 'Do you admire all these immense structures?' Jesus asked. 'Not one stone here will be left on another and not thrown down.'

As he was sitting on the Mount of Olives facing the Temple, Peter, James, John and Andrew talked among themselves and questioned him: 'Tell us when these things will happen. What will be the sign that they are all about to be done?' Jesus started to explain: 'Watch that no one fools you. Many will come in my name, saying, "I am he," and many will be fooled by them . . . When you see the "ruinous horror" standing where it must not stand (let the reader note), those in Judah should then flee to the mountains . . . No creature would survive had the Lord not cut those days short. But he has shortened the days for the sake of the chosen – those of his own choosing. At that time, if anyone says to you, "Look, here is the Messiah," or, "Look, there he is," do not believe. For false messiahs and false prophets will be seen, giving out signs and wonders to mislead even the chosen, if they can. Watch out, then: I have told you everything in advance.'

2.10

Jesus and Beelzebub:
Matt. 12:22–8

Another astonishing cure by Jesus annoys his critics, who resent competition in healing the possessed (see 2.7, 11). They accuse Jesus of complicity with Beelzeboul – probably 'Prince Baal', not 'Lord of the Flies' – who is Satan going by a different name and heading a hierarchy of demons: they can be commanded not just 'by God's spirit' but also for unrighteous purposes (see 1.13–15).

*

Then a man, blind and mute, was brought to him with a demon, and he healed him, so that someone mute could both speak and see. This amazed everyone, and they asked, 'Could this be the Son of David?' But when the Pharisees heard this, they said, 'This person drives out demonic spirits only by Beelzeboul, the demon prince.' He knew what they were thinking and said to them, 'Every kingdom divided against itself will be laid waste, and no city or house divided against itself will stand. If Satan drives Satan out, he divides himself. How will his kingdom stand, then? And if I drive demons out by Beelzeboul, by whom do your followers drive them out? On that account, they will be your accusers. But if it is by God's spirit that I drive the demons out, then for you the kingdom of God has come.'

2.11

Can a Man Who Sins Produce Such Signs? John 9:1–17

Just as Jesus drives out demons, he also rids the sick of bodily afflictions (see 2.10). When he heals a man blind from birth, he uses natural objects, dirt and saliva, to make the paste that he applies (see 1.18). Is the dirt itself a natural cure? Or is it an ingredient in a recipe for imitative magic, reinforced by – and contrasting with – an official ritual: washing in Jerusalem's Pool of Shiloah? If Jesus is divine, why use any such devices? Why not just command the healing (see 2.7, 12, 14)? Perhaps physical circumstances are relevant. At night, Jesus notes, 'No one has the power to work.' Will darkness inhibit the magic that brings light, or is night a metaphor for the darkness of sin? John's story goes on for twice the length of this passage, as the befuddled Pharisees grind away at the credibility of the healed man, who insists that his cure is 'a marvel'.

*

Moving on, he saw a man blind from birth, and his students questioned him, asking, 'Who sinned, Rabbi, this person or his parents, for him to be born blind?' 'Neither he sinned nor his parents,' Jesus replied: 'it was for the works of God to be shown in him. While it is still day, we must do the works of him who sent me. Night is coming, when no one has the power to work. While I am in the world, I am the world's light.' After saying this, he spat on the ground, made mud with the spit and smeared it on the man's eyes, telling him, 'Go and wash in the Pool of Siloam' – the word means 'sent'. Then the man went and washed and left with his sight.

The man's neighbours – and those who saw him before as a beggar – asked, 'Is this not the same one who used to sit and beg?' Some said, 'That's him,' while others said, 'No, but he looks like him,' and he said, 'It's me!' Then they asked him, 'So how were your eyes opened?' 'The man called Jesus made mud and smeared it on my eyes,' he replied, 'and then he told me to go to Siloam and wash. So I went and washed, and then I saw again.' 'Where is this man?' they asked him, and he said, 'I don't know.'

They brought him to the Pharisees – the one who had been blind. But it was the Sabbath on the day when Jesus made the mud and opened his eyes. So the Pharisees asked him again how he came to see anew. 'He put mud on my eyes,' the man answered, 'I washed, and I see.' Some of the Pharisees said, 'This man is not from God since he does not observe the Sabbath.' But others asked, 'How can a man who sins produce such signs?' And there was disagreement among them. Then they spoke to the blind man again: 'What do you say about him, now that he has opened your eyes?' 'He is a prophet,' he said.

2.12

Jesus Frenzied in the Spirit: John 11:1–48

Because Jesus cured the blind, some thought that he could also raise the dead, a greater marvel (see 1.10; 2.7, 11). Details in John's story – time passes, we smell the decay, see the grave uncovered and watch the shroud unwrap – show that the death in question is real and presumably irreversible. By delaying his trip to Bethany, however, Jesus sets the stage for an astonishing reversal, choosing *not* to heal his friend Lazarus before he dies so that God – and God's Son – will be glorified when death is defeated. When he finally arrives, the mourners greet him, wondering why he came too late. At that moment, when 'Jesus wept', his response to the family's grief was normal. But what put him in a frenzy – literally, 'snorting' or 'roaring'? Does the agitation suggest ecstasy, preparing for a deed of power? After Jesus prays to thank the Father, his next step is the short command that calls Lazarus back to life – and worries the authorities who see so many turning to Jesus because of his signs.

*

A certain man was ill, Lazarus of Bethany, from the village of Mary and her sister Martha . . . The sisters sent word to Jesus: 'Lord, one that you love is sick.' When he heard this, Jesus said, 'This illness does not lead to death. It is for the glory of God, to glorify God's Son through it.' Jesus loved Martha and her sister and Lazarus. Yet when he heard that he was ill, he stayed for two days where he was.

After that, he said to his students, 'Let us go back to Judah.' To this the students said, 'Just now the Jews tried to stone you, and you are still going back there?' Jesus answered: . . . 'Our friend Lazarus has fallen asleep, and I am going to wake him up.' 'If he is sleeping, Lord, he will get better,' answered the students. Jesus had been talking about his death, but they thought he meant falling asleep. Then he told them plainly, 'Lazarus is dead, and I am glad – for your sake, to make you believe – that I was not there. But let us go to him.' . . .

When he got there, Jesus found that Lazarus had been four days in the tomb . . . When Martha heard that Jesus was coming, she went to meet him, but Mary stayed at home . . . Later she went back and took her sister Mary aside, saying, 'The Teacher is here, asking for you.' Hearing this, she got up quickly and went to him . . . Then, when Mary got to where Jesus was and saw him, she fell at his feet and said, 'Had you been here, Lord, my brother would not have died.'

When Jesus saw her crying, and the Jews who had come with her also crying, he was frenzied in the spirit, disturbed within himself. 'Where have you put him?' he asked. 'Come and see, Lord,' they said. Jesus wept. Then the Jews said, 'See how he loved him!' But some of them said, 'This person who opened the blind man's eyes – could he not do something so that this person would not die?'

Jesus, frenzied again within himself, came to the tomb. It was a cave with a stone covering. 'Lift up the stone,' he said. But Martha, the sister of the deceased, said, 'By this time it stinks: it has been four days.' Then Jesus told her, 'Have I not said that if you believe, you would see the glory of God?' So they lifted the stone. Then Jesus lifted his eyes and said, 'Father, I thank you for hearing me. You always hear me – that I know. But for the crowd standing here I have said this, for them to believe that you have sent me.' Having said this, Jesus called in a loud voice, 'Lazarus, come out!' The man who had been dead came out, his hands and feet wrapped in the shroud, and a cloth around his face. Jesus said, 'Loosen them and let him go.'

And then many of the Jews who came to Mary believed in him, having seen what he did. But some of them went to the Pharisees and told them what Jesus had done. Then the chief priests and the Pharisees assembled the Sanhedrin and asked, 'What are we doing, while this man does so many signs? If we let him go like this, everyone will believe in him.'

2.13

To Touch Even the Fringe of His Robe:
Mark 6:45–56

After feeding a crowd of five thousand with a few loaves and fishes, Jesus sends his
students across the lake. Although he sees them rowing hard against bad winds, his
aim is not to rescue them when he walks across the water. On the contrary, the sight
of Jesus moving over the waves terrifies his followers, who have missed the point of
the loaves and fishes: in both cases – like Moses dividing the waters – Jesus has the
power to alter, in astounding ways, the ordinary course of events (see 1.2). Crossing
the lake, he does not command the water to support him; he simply walks over it, as
if it were dry land. When he gets to the other side, sick people are cured just by
touching him (see 2.7). No words of power are required, and the cures are many – a
mass phenomenon.

*

As he released the crowd, Jesus made his students get into the boat right away
and go on ahead of him to the Bethsaida side. After he said farewell to them,
he went up the hill to pray. The boat was in the middle of the lake when evening came, and he was on land by himself. He saw that the rowing was torture
because the wind was against them.

At night, around the fourth watch, he went out to them, walking on the
lake and meaning to go past them. But when they saw him walking on the
lake, they thought it was an illusion. They all saw him and were terrified, and
they screamed. Right away he spoke to them, saying, 'Have courage! It's me.
Don't be afraid.' Then he got up into the boat with them, and the wind died
down. They were completely beside themselves, not having understood about
the loaves: the heart within them was hardened.

When they had crossed over to the land, they came to Gennesaret and
anchored there. Once they got out of the boat, people recognized Jesus
right away: they rushed about through that whole district, carrying those

who were not well on mats to wherever they heard he was. And wherever he went – villages, towns or countryside – they put the sick in the marketplaces. They begged him to let them touch even the fringe of his robe, and all who touched it were healed.

2.14
The Fig Tree that You Cursed: Mark 11:12–24

Mark breaks this strange little story in two, to frame his account of Jesus throwing the merchants out of the Temple. The intended lesson is that prayer strengthens faith: every heartfelt plea will be answered, even asking for something as outlandish as moving a mountain, though one must first pray in a spirit of forgiveness. The words that Jesus had spoken just a day before were a curse, however, not a prayer – as Peter notes – a curse aimed unforgivingly at a tree doing what trees ought to do: not bearing fruit out of season. Jesus had blasted the tree, inspiring awe and fear more than faith with this anomalous and destructive intervention in the non-human world – so unlike the kindnesses to humans that feed a crowd, heal the sick, expel a demon or raise the dead (see 2.7–13).

*

The next day when they left Bethany, he was hungry. Seeing a fig tree in leaf at some distance, he went to see if there was anything on it. When he got to it, he found nothing but leaves since figs were not in season. Then he spoke to the tree, saying, 'May no one ever eat fruit from you again,' and his students heard him. Going into Jerusalem, they went to the Temple, where he began throwing the sellers and buyers out . . . When evening came, they left the city.

As they went on their way in the morning, they saw the fig tree dried up from the roots. Peter remembered and said to him, 'Look, Rabbi! The fig tree that you cursed has dried up.' And Jesus answered, telling them to 'have confidence in God: truly, I tell you that if anyone says to this mountain, "Get up and throw yourself into the sea" – with no doubt in his heart but believing that what he says will happen – it shall be so for him. So I say to you, all things that you ask for in prayer, believe that you have received them, and it shall be so for you. And as you stand praying, if you hold anything against anyone, let it go so that your Father in heaven may let your sins go for you.'

2.15
Apostles Make the Lame Walk:
Acts 14:8–20

Travelling through Asia Minor, Paul and Barnabas spread the faith by preaching and working wonders. Paul is a remarkable person. In this story, he sees into the heart of a stranger – a lame man – and then survives a stoning meant to kill him. When he makes the lame man walk with a few words of power – like Jesus in John 5 and Luke 13 – the crowd takes him and his partner for gods. Paul's emphatic response is that he and Barnabas are fellow sufferers, mere mortals. Their marvels work only by the power of 'the living God who made heaven and earth', as Paul explains. But the crowd – having heard stories about wizards – cannot distinguish true divinity from the 'powerless things' that Paul scorns (see 5.1–2).

*

Sitting in Lystra was a man who could not use his feet, being lame from his mother's womb and unable to walk. He heard Paul speaking, and Paul looked straight at him. Seeing that the man believed he would be healed, Paul said in a loud voice, 'Stand straight on your feet,' and he jumped up and walked around. Seeing what Paul had done, the crowd raised a shout in the Lycaonian tongue, saying, 'Gods looking like humans have come down to us!' They called Barnabas 'Zeus' and Paul – since he took the lead in speaking – 'Hermes'. The priest of Zeus, being near the city, brought bulls and wreaths to the gates, wishing like the crowd to offer a sacrifice.

But when the apostles – Barnabas and Paul – heard about this, they tore their robes and raced out into the crowd, shouting, 'Brothers, what are you doing? We too are human, suffering like you but bringing you good news, telling you to turn away from these powerless things to the living God who made heaven and earth and the sea and everything in them. In generations past, he let all nations go their own way. Yet he has not left himself without a witness, showing kindness by giving you rain from heaven and seasons that bear crops, filling you with food and making your hearts glad.'

Even after saying this, they had a hard time keeping the crowd from sacrificing to them. Then Jews came from Antioch and Iconium and won the crowd over. They stoned Paul and dragged him outside the city, supposing that he had died. But after the students banded around him, he got up and went into the city.

2.16

In the Name of Jesus Christ, Come Out of Her: Acts 16:16–32

The author of Acts, having travelled in Asia Minor with Paul and others, tells a tale about expelling a demon after Jesus left the apostles: the demon does some good, however, by telling the future and making a living for the owners of a slave girl possessed by the demon (see 1.6, 9–11; 2.7–10). The fortune-teller's unwelcome enthusiasm – awkward for preachers of a true gospel – provokes Paul to drive the mantic spirit out of her. But the exorcism does not please the girl's owners, who have Paul and his companions jailed – until an earthquake releases them.

*

On our way to the synagogue, we happened to meet a slave girl who had a python spirit and did a great deal of business for her masters by telling fortunes. She followed Paul and us, shouting, 'These men are servants of the most high God who are telling you about the path of salvation.' She did this for many days, irritating Paul so much that he turned on the spirit and said, 'I order you in the name of Jesus Christ to come out of her' – and at that moment out of her it came.

When her masters saw that their hope of business was gone, they attacked Paul and Silas and hauled them into the marketplace to face the authorities. They brought them before the magistrates and said, 'These men – these Jews – are throwing our city into turmoil by preaching behaviour that is unacceptable to us and unfit for Romans.' The crowd fell upon them, and the magistrates ordered their robes removed for a caning. After giving them many blows, they threw them in jail, ordering the jailer to guard them carefully. Taking these orders, he threw them into the inner jail and locked their feet in stocks.

About midnight, Paul and Silas were praying and singing hymns to God, and the other prisoners were listening to them. Suddenly there was an earthquake so great that the jail's foundations shook. At once all the doors flew open, and the chains fell from everyone.

2.17
She Opened Her Eyes and Sat Up:
Acts 9:32–43

Another healing by Peter's words of power attracts little notice from the author of Acts, who has more to say when the chief apostle brings a girl back from the dead (see 1.10; 2.7, 12). As when Jesus went to Lazarus, time has passed since Tabitha's death, and rites of burial have begun. Like Jesus, Peter prays before commanding the girl to stand up – in a two-stage resurrection. Lydda is now Lod near Tel Aviv in Israel.

*

Going from place to place, he went on to visit the saints living in Lydda. There he found a man named Aeneas, who for eight years had been lying in bed because he was paralysed. And Peter said to him, 'Jesus Christ heals you, Aeneas. Get up and make your bed,' and he got up right away. All those living in Lydda and Sharon saw him and turned to the Lord.

In Joppa there was a female student named Tabitha (Dorcas, the gazelle); she was full of good works and gave to the poor. In those days she became ill and died, so they washed her and took her upstairs. Since Lydda is close to Joppa, when the students heard that Peter was in Lydda, they sent two men to him and urged him, 'Please don't delay in coming to us!' Peter got up and went with them, and when he arrived they took him upstairs. All the widows standing around him wept and showed him the robes and dresses that Dorcas had made while she was still with them.

Sending all the widows outside, Peter went to his knees, prayed and turned towards the body, saying, 'Tabitha, get up.' She opened her eyes and sat up when she saw Peter. He gave her his hand and stood her up. Then he called for the saints, including the widows, and presented her to them alive. This became known all over Joppa, and many believed in the Lord.

2.18

He Astonished Them with Acts of Magic: Acts 8:4–25

Despite persecution by Saul (before his conversion) in Judah and Samaria, Peter, Philip and John remained active, competing with others who also attracted crowds with their deeds of power (see 5.1–2). Two questions motivate this story. What works? And is it authorized? Simon – explicitly said to be doing magic – is an effective rival. But he is a boaster, soon overwhelmed by the might of the apostles, though even then he thinks that their success can be bought. This is a natural mistake, since magic in Simon's day was commercial: recipes, charms, curses, amulets, talismans and love potions were bought and sold (see 5.6). Simon may have been a third-rate wizard, but this unfriendly account never calls him a fake. When Philip's 'signs and great acts of power' amazed Simon, were the apostles doing counter-magic in the villages of Samaria?

*

Those who had been scattered went around preaching the word. Philip went down to a city in Samaria to proclaim the Messiah to them. When the crowds heard what Philip said and saw the signs he produced, they came together and listened closely. Unclean spirits – howling loud – left many who had them, and many were healed who had been lame or paralysed: so there was great joy in that city.

A certain man named Simon had been in the city doing magic and astonishing the people of Samaria, boasting that he was an important person. And all the people, both small and great, listened to him, saying, 'This person is the Power of God called the Great One.' They listened to him for a long time because he astonished them with acts of magic. But since they believed Philip when he brought good news of God's kingdom and the name of Jesus Christ, men as well as women were baptized. Even Simon himself believed, and he was baptized, sticking close to Philip, astonished to see the signs and great acts of power.

When the apostles in Jerusalem heard that Samaria had accepted the word of God, they sent Peter and John to them. When they arrived, they prayed for the Samaritans to receive the Holy Spirit, who had not yet come upon any of them since they were only baptized in the name of the Lord Jesus. Then Peter and John laid their hands on them, and they received the Holy Spirit.

Because Simon saw that the Spirit was given when the apostles laid their hands, he offered them money, saying, 'give me this authority too so that anyone on whom I lay hands receives the Holy Spirit'. But Peter said, 'May your silver go with you to destruction because you imagined you could buy God's gift with money! You have no part or share in this discussion because your heart is not right before God. Repent of this wickedness and beg the Lord that perhaps he might forgive your having such a notion in your heart. The bile of bitterness and being captured sin is what I see in you.' Then Simon replied: 'Plead with the Lord for me so that nothing you have said may come upon me.' After giving more witness and speaking the Lord's word, Peter and John returned to Jerusalem, bringing the good news to many Samaritan villages.

3

Fire Priests, Magoi *and* Mageia

Figure 4: Regal Magi Guided By a Star

What is magic? Is it religion gone bad? Is it failed science? Can we trace magic to ignorance – theoretical or practical or both – of a primitive kind? Is magic characteristically primitive, a defective way of thinking left behind on the way to modernity? Answering 'yes' has been common since the late nineteenth century, when James Frazer wrote the book that still defines magic for many people: *The Golden Bough*. Hailing the science of his day as enlightened progress, while seeing religion – with Protestant Christianity at its apex – as the evolutionary prelude to science, Frazer puts magic in the earliest phase of human culture, locating it in the primitive way of life recently put on display for him and other Europeans by anthropology. Just as sociology, another new social science, responded to economic, industrial and demographic changes sparked by Europe's revolutions, so anthropology was an academic reflex of European imperialism and colonialism.

Magic became a special object of study for anthropologists. Why did they use the word 'magic' for what they studied and called 'primitive'?

Evidence to answer that question had been gathered by professors like Frazer, who – unlike Frazer himself – seldom thought of themselves as anthropologists. Frazer's teachers at Cambridge and their teachers were classicists and philologists. They studied ancient languages – Greek, Latin, Hebrew, Sanskrit – and texts written in those languages, the classical and biblical works at the heart of elite education in Europe. Mastery of those books – or just knowing their titles – gave prestige to admirers of the classics, who commanded the armies, organized the commerce and supported the missionary work through which Europe controlled its colonial subjects. In 1912 Lucien Lévy-Bruhl described what he took to be the social psychology of the colonized in his *Fonctions mentales dans les sociétés inférieures*, known to its large Anglophone audience as *How Natives Think*. The natives, because their thinking was pre-logical and thus magical, simply could not reason like the colonizers: hence their assumed inferiority.

Europeans had been using the word 'magic' for well over two millennia by the time of Lévy-Bruhl and Frazer. When Heraclitus wrote about 'night-roamers, *magoi*, bacchants, revellers and initiates' around 500 BCE, he used *magoi* as a pejorative, grouping it with words for people whose religious behaviour he found repellent. The *mageia* of the *magoi* was offensive to Heraclitus and alien, nothing like proper Greek rituals, but there was nothing primitive about it. *Mageia* was the Greek word for what *magoi* did, and they were Persians, priests of an enemy whose organizational skill and military might would nearly destroy Greek civilization. When Greeks called the Persian invaders 'barbarians', mocking their speech as gibberish and their religion as weird, they were raging against equals whom they feared, not dismissing a lesser people whom they scorned.

The sophistication of Persian culture is evident in documents of the Zoroastrian religion, whose dualist theology impressed few Greeks enough to motivate serious study of its metaphysics or morality. Greeks focused such efforts on the home-grown enterprise that they called 'philosophy', organizing their 'love of wisdom' in durable institutions shortly after the Persian Wars. Centuries later, however, when Diogenes Laërtius cobbled together a sloppy digest of philosophical opinions, he opened his book with accounts that traced philosophy to regions east of the Hellenic heartland, to alien cultures that the Greeks regarded as far older than their own – but not primitive. 'Some say that doing philosophy began with the barbarians,' wrote Diogenes, 'claiming that these were the Magi in Persia', among other favourites of this Greek orientalism.

The Greeks and the Romans knew as much as they ever would about ancient Persian culture by the time Strabo wrote his *Geography* in the era of Augustus. He says only a little about the fire temples that Pausanias also describes in his guidebook to Greek monuments, compiled when the Antonine emperors ruled Roman Europe. 'A magus carries dry wood to the altar,' says Pausanias, 'first putting a tiara on his head and then – in barbarous words utterly incomprehensible to Greeks – chanting an invocation.'

Some people seem strange to us, and sometimes we find their ways primitive: this was a common reaction of early anthropologists to what they called 'magic'. Some people we hate, though their threats to us are not at all primitive: as clever and strong as we are, such aliens have what it takes to do us in. At first, Greeks reacted that way to the Persians, also describing them as users of *mageia*. Other people from faraway places, whose culture is also not our own, entertain us as exotic just because of their strangeness, which gives us a way to account for what had to have been new – and hence unfamiliar – in the earliest chapters of our own story. Greeks eventually saw the *magoi* in that way, as outlandish voices of a primal (but not primitive) alien wisdom: this is the 'wisdom from the Magi' that Plato identifies with 'the worship of the gods'.

The Will of Ohrmazd and Ahriman:
The Greater Bundahishn, 1.1–32

Although the *Greater Bundahishn* or *Creation* was written in Middle Persian in the ninth century BCE, this work preserves older traditions about the teachings of Zarathustra or Zoroaster, a religious reformer on the steppes of southern Russia late in the second millennium. Challenging the prevailing polytheism, his creed entered eastern Iran by about 1200 and moved west to the Iranian tribes of Media by about 600. The passage that follows puts two divinities, Ohrmazd and Ahriman, at the centre of a cosmic struggle between good and evil, light and darkness. The Evil Spirit has *devs* or demons to help him, but Ohrmazd and his forces are mightier.

*

So it is revealed in the Good Religion that Ohrmazd was on high in omniscience and goodness. For boundless time He was always in the light, the light that is the space and place of Ohrmazd. Some call it Endless Light . . . Ahriman was abased in slowness of knowledge and the lust to smite. The lust to smite was his sheath and darkness his place. Some call it Endless Darkness. And between them was emptiness.

They both were limited and limitless: for what is on high, which is called Endless Light . . . and what is abased, which is Endless Darkness – those were limitless. But at the border both were limited since emptiness was between them, and there was no connection between the two so that the two Spirits were both limited in themselves. But because of the omniscience of Ohrmazd, all things, the limited and the limitless, were within Ohrmazd's knowledge. For He knew the measure of what is within the two Spirits – then the entire kingship of the creation of Ohrmazd, in the body to come for ever and ever – which is limitless. The creation of Ahriman, at the time when the body to come will be, shall be destroyed: that truly is limited.

Ohrmazd by His omniscience knew that the Evil Spirit existed – what he plotted to do in his envy, what he would commingle, what the beginning would be and what the end, what and how many the tools with which He would make an end. And He created in the spirit state the creatures He would need as those tools. For three thousand years creation stayed in the spirit state. The Evil Spirit, because of his slowness to know, was not aware of Ohrmazd's existence. Then he arose from the deep and came to the boundary and beheld the light, rushing forward when he saw the intangible light of Ohrmazd and attacking to destroy it because of his lust to smite and his envious nature.

Then he saw valour and supremacy greater than his own. He crawled back to darkness and shaped many *devs*, the creation that destroys. And he rose for battle. When Ohrmazd saw the Evil Spirit's creatures, they appeared to Him frightful and putrid and evil, and He did not desire them. But when the Evil Spirit saw Ohrmazd's creatures, they appeared to him most profound and fully informed. And he desired the creatures and creation of Ohrmazd. Then Ohrmazd, in spite of His knowledge of creation and how things would end, approached the Evil Spirit to offer peace, saying, 'Evil Spirit! Help my creatures and give praise, so that in return you may be immortal.' . . .

Snarling, the Evil Spirit said, 'I will not help your creatures and will not give praise, but I will destroy you and your creatures for ever and ever. And I will persuade all your creatures to hate you and love me.' And Ohrmazd said, 'You are not all-powerful, Evil Spirit, so you cannot destroy me, and you cannot influence my creatures to not return to being mine.' Then in His omniscience Ohrmazd knew this: 'If I do not set a time for that battle of his, then . . . for eternity he can mix things up and make strife for my creatures. He will be able to lead my creatures astray in the Mixture and make them his own.' Then Ohrmazd said to the Evil Spirit: 'Set a time, so that by this truce we may postpone battle for nine thousand years.' For He knew that by setting a time He would destroy the Evil Spirit.

The Evil Spirit, unable to foresee the end, then agreed to the pact. This too Ohrmazd knew in His omniscience, that within those nine thousand years, three thousand years would go according to the will of Ohrmazd; the three thousand in the Mixture would go according to the will of Ohrmazd and Ahriman both; and at the last battle Ahriman could be made powerless, and the assault from His creatures could be warded off.

Then Ohrmazd recited the Great Prayer aloud. And He showed the Evil Spirit His own final victory, the Evil Spirit's powerlessness, the destruction of the *devs*, also the resurrection and the body to come as well as the freedom of creation from Assault for ever and ever. When the Evil Spirit saw his own powerlessness, along with the destruction of the *devs*, he fell prostrate and unconscious. He fell back again into hell, even as He says in the Scriptures that when He had spoken one third, the Evil Spirit crouched in fear; when He had spoken two thirds, the Evil Spirit sank to his knees; when He had spoken it all, the Evil Spirit became powerless to do evil to Ohrmazd's creatures. And for three thousand years he lay prostrate.

3.2
Sacred Fire Slays the Demons:
Vendidad, 8.73–81

Recorded in a late form of the Gathic or Avestan language around 200 CE, this passage describes fire rituals that preceded the fire temples of the fourth century BCE and later. Fire, the divine son of Ahura Mazda (Ohrmazd), helps his father overcome the evil demons and the human wizards who assist them (see 3.1).

*

'Creator of the world of bodies, Most Holy Spirit and just! If worshippers of Mazda, walking or running, riding or driving, come upon a fire on which carrion is being cooked . . . what should they do, as worshippers of Mazda?'

Then Ahura Mazda said: ' . . . they should slay the cooker of carrion, they should remove the pot, they should remove the container of bones. From that fire you should kindle new blazing tinder or twigs that nourish fire, and by picking up the fire-sustaining tinder, one may carry it away and separate it so that the polluted fire goes out as quickly as possible. The first time, one should take as much blazing tinder as a man can hold and lay it down on the ground, a good arm's length away from the fire on which carrion was cooked. From this he should take blazing tinder away again and separate it to put the second fire out as quickly as possible. The third time, as much blazing tinder as a man can hold . . . The ninth time, one should lay down on the ground as much blazing tinder as a man can hold . . . to put the eighth fire out as quickly as possible.

'Then Spitama Zarathustra, if one duly brings fuel of sandalwood or gum or aloe or pomegranate or any other sweet-smelling plants to the ninth fire, from whichever and to whichever side the wind shall carry the fragrance of the fire, from that side and to that side the son of Ahura Mazda, the Fire, will turn, slaying thousands of invisible demons born of the wicked darkness, slaying twice as many sorcerers and witches.

'Creator of the corporeal world, Most Holy Spirit and just! If a man brings a carrion-burning fire – thus purified – to an appointed place, how great will that man's reward be after the separation of body from consciousness?' Then said Ahura Mazda: 'As great as if he had brought ten thousand pure embers to an appointed place in this material life.'

3.3
Night-roamers and Magi:
Heraclitus, frg. 14

Heraclitus lived on the west coast of Asia Minor, where Greeks met Persians and Medes more often than they were seen by their cousins across the Aegean. His experiences were remembered seven centuries later by Clement of Alexandria, a Christian critic of the ancient Greeks who saw their religion as infected by magic. The serpent that Clement mentions may have been used in the Eleusinian mysteries – rites that Heraclitus regards as sacred but defiled by improprieties of some sort. The text preserved in part by Clement but written around 500 BCE is the earliest statement in Greek to mention *magoi* – priests of the Zoroastrian religion of Achaemenid Persia, the great empire that fought Greece for half a century until 449 BCE. Clement starts by mocking a Hellenic ritual – the Eleusinian mysteries – revered by Greeks who despised the Persians.

*

And this is the pledge in the Eleusinian mysteries: *I have fasted, I have drunk the drink, and what I have taken from the basket, I have put it into the hamper after that part of the rite and then out of the hamper back into the basket* – fine things to see befitting a goddess, mysteries worthy of the night, of the fire! Also worthy of the exuberant or rather loose-talking people of the Erechtheids along with the other Greeks who are 'awaited by what they hope the end will not bring them'. And it is just for those people that Heraclitus of Ephesus utters his vatic words – 'night-roamers, *magoi*, bacchants, revellers, initiates', threatening them with what comes after death and predicting fire for them because 'they make a sacrilege out of what people treat as mysteries'. Law and public opinion are irrelevant, then, and the serpent's mysteries are a fraud.

3.4

The Wisdom of the Magi:
Plato, I *Alcibiades*, 121A–22A

Plato or a follower wrote the first of two dialogues called *Alcibiades* around 350 BCE. Making fun of the cocky young Alcibiades, Socrates praises the Persians to provoke him, associating them with piety, royalty and wisdom as a cardinal virtue, along with justice, moderation and courage – even though Greeks criticized the Persians as fabulously wealthy and therefore decadent. In Plato's account, where Socrates – as often – is joking, the wisdom of the Magi that came from Zoroaster and Oromazdos (Ohrmazd) keeps good company with the classical Greek virtues (see 3.1). Alcibiades enters bragging about his ancestors.

*

'My family goes back to Eurysaces, and he goes back to Zeus!'

'Mine too, noble Alcibiades, to Daedalus, and then Daedalus to Hephaestus, the son of Zeus. But such kings come from kings going back to Zeus – those of Argos, of Lacedaemon or of Persia for ever – and at various times of Asia, as the Persians are now, whereas we and our fathers have been just ordinary people . . . The Persian king is so exalted that no one ever suspects that a prince might be born from any man other than him. That's why fear alone guards the king's wife. When the eldest son and heir is born, everyone in the kingdom celebrates . . .'

'After this the child is tended not by some worthless little nanny but by the best of the royal eunuchs . . . At twice seven years the boy is handed over to people called 'the royal schoolmasters'. These are four grown men, selected because they are seen as the best among the Persians: the wisest one, the most just, the most temperate and the bravest. From Zoroaster, the son of Oromazdos, the first teaches him wisdom from the Magi – this being the worship of the gods – and also teaches him a king's duties. The second, who is the most just, teaches him always to tell the truth as long as he lives. Then, so that he gets used to being a free man and a real king, the most temperate teacher forbids him to allow any pleasure to rule him, requiring that he govern himself first and never be his own slave. The bravest prepares him to be unafraid and undaunted since fear is slavery.'

'On the other hand, Alcibiades, the tutor that Pericles put in charge of you was Zopyrus the Thracian, a slave of his so old that he was useless.'

3.5
Rites in Fire Temples:
Strabo, 15.3.15

The geographer Strabo was still alive when Cappadocia, in south-eastern Asia Minor, became a Roman province in 17 CE. Acknowledging his reliance on Herodotus and other sources, Strabo also travelled widely and claims to have seen the Persian rites and temples that he describes – a continuation of customs that had lasted for four centuries.

*

In Cappadocia, where the tribe of Magi, also called Fire People, is large, are many temples of the Persian gods. These people too use no swords in their sacrifices, taking a branch from some tree for a cudgel to club the victims. They also have Fire Temples – shrines worth noticing. In the middle is an altar with embers all over it where the Magi keep the fire always lit. Coming there every day, they chant for nearly an hour, holding a bunch of sticks in front of the fire while wearing felt tiaras with cheekpieces hanging down on both sides to cover their lips. The same customs hold in the temples of Anaïtis and Omanus, which also have shrines where they march in with a wooden statue of Omanus. These things I have seen myself, but the rest and what comes after is what the histories say.

3.6
Skills of the Magi:
Pausanias, 5.27.1–6

Pausanias, active in the middle of the second century CE, wrote centuries after the first events described in this passage, which reports that Phormis – probably a playwright from Arcadia who moved to Syracuse before 478 BCE – had dedicated statues of horses and drivers at the great shrine of Olympia. One of the horses, though especially ugly, carried the notorious 'horse-madness' that drove stallions into sexual frenzy, causing them to 'burst into the Altis', a sacred space. Although a Persian *magos* could have been present at this time and place, when Pausanias mentions 'someone who is a magus', he may just mean 'a wizard of the Orient'. But then he (or his source) underlines the Persian theme by leaping from the Olympian *hippomanes* to temples with eternal fires in Lydia – once a Persian province in Western Asia Minor, though it was Roman when Pausanias wrote. A 'man who is a magus' performs a fire-ritual, and spontaneous flames are the work of 'magi and their skill'.

*

Across from the offerings I have listed are others in a row turned towards the south and close to the area devoted to Pelops, among which are those dedicated by Phormis of Maenalia . . . His offerings at Olympia are two horses and two drivers, with the man who was driving placed next to each horse . . . The first of the horses and men are by Dionysius of Argos . . . and this horse – so the Eleans say – is also the one in which the horse-madness lies.

It is clear, furthermore, that what happens to this horse comes from the skill of someone who is a magus. In size and shape it falls far short of the other horses standing there inside the Altis, and to make it uglier still its tail has been cut off. And yet every day, not just in spring, male horses are hot to go for it. They actually burst into the Altis, breaking their fetters, running away from their grooms and jumping up on it much more frantically than on a living horse, even the most beautiful . . .

I know another marvel, unlike the horse of Phormis but not free of magi

and their skill, for I have seen it in Lydia. Lydians called Persians have temples both in the city named Hierocaesarea and in Hypaipa: in each of these
temples is a chapel, and in the temple on an altar are ashes, though the ashes
are not ashen in colour. Entering the chapel, a man who is a magus carries dry
wood to the altar, first putting a tiara on his head and then – in barbarous
words utterly incomprehensible to Greeks – chanting an invocation to one of
the gods and reading the chant from a book. The wood must start burning
without any fire, then, and produce visible flames.

3·7
Magic From the Orient: Diogenes Laërtius, 1.1–9

To establish philosophy's cultural credentials at the start of his sketchy history of that subject, Diogenes repeats (and rejects) stories about its foundation by Egyptian gods, Indian sages, Druid priests and other wise men from Thrace, Libya, Phoenicia, Judaea, Syria, Chaldaea and points east. He has much to say about the Indian 'gymnosophists', while noting that these naked sages and the Jews may both have descended from ascetic Persian Magi, devotees of prayer, theology and divination who knew nothing of 'the sorcerer's magic'. By the time Diogenes wrote after 200 CE, the antics of figures like Apollonius of Tyana required him and other admirers of the Magi to distance them from their own *mageia* (see 4.2; 5.1–2). Meanwhile, authorities like Aristotle had calculated that these followers of Zoroaster were 'even older than the Egyptians' – primordial as well as exotic.

*

Some say that doing philosophy began with the barbarians, claiming that these were the Magi in Persia, the Chaldaeans in Babylonia and Assyria, the Naked Sages in India and people called Druids or the Devout among the Celts and Gauls: their sources are Aristotle in his *Magic* and Sotion in book 23 of his *Succession*. They also say that Mochos was a Phoenician, Zamolxis a Thracian and Atlas a Libyan. According to the Egyptians, however, a son of the Nile – Hephaistos – started philosophy, with priests and prophets taking the lead: 48,863 years passed between this Hephaistos and Alexander of Macedon, marked by 373 eclipses of the sun and 832 of the moon.

But in his book *On Mathematics*, Hermodorus the Platonist says that 5,000 years passed between the Magi, starting with the Persian Zoroaster, and the fall of Troy. And yet Xanthus of Lydia says that Xerxes invaded 6,000 years after Zoroaster, who was followed by many Magi in succession – Ostanes, Astrampsychos, Gorbryas, Pazates – until Alexander conquered the Persians. These people forget that the feats they attribute to barbarians belong to the Greeks, not just philosophy but the origin of the human race itself . . .

But those who claim that philosophy began with the barbarians also discuss the way it was done by each group. They say that the Naked Sages and Druids spoke tersely in riddles and philosophized about revering the gods, doing no wrong and practising courage. Clitarchus in his twelfth book says that the Naked Sages think little even of death, adding that the Chaldaeans work at astronomy and predictions and that the Magi spend their time on worshipping the gods, sacrifices and prayers – as if only their prayers were heard.

They also discuss the substance of the gods and their origin, and how they are fire, earth and water. But they condemn statues, especially the opinion that the gods are male and female. They hold discussions about justice and think it irreligious to burn the dead in fire. They believe intercourse with a mother or daughter to be religious, however, as Sotion says in book 23. They also practise divination and predicting, stating that the gods become visible to them. But they add that the air is full of vaporous shapes that flow and penetrate the eyes of the sharp-sighted. Fancy clothes and jewellery they forbid. They dress in white and sleep on straw, eating greens, cheese and cheap bread. For a staff they use a reed, sticking it into the cheese – they say – to pick it up and gnaw on it.

Of the sorcerer's magic they know nothing, however, according to Aristotle in his *Magic* and Dinon in the fifth book of his *Histories*. Dinon also says that the translation of 'Zoroaster' is 'sacrifices to stars', which Hermodorus claims as well. In his first book *On Philosophy*, Aristotle writes that they are even older than the Egyptians, noting that their first principles are two, a good spirit and an evil spirit, the one named Zeus and Horomasdes, the other Hades and Areimanios. In his first book *On the Magi*, Hermippus says this too, along with Eudoxus in his *Voyage* and Theopompus in his eighth *Philippic*, adding that humans will come back to life, according to the Magi, and become immortal – also that existence will endure because of their invocations, as Eudemus of Rhodes also notes. But Hecataeus claims that they treat the gods as being born.

Writing *On Education*, Clearchus of Soli says that the Naked Sages are also descended from the Magi, and some say that the Jews come from them as well. Moreover, those who have written about the Magi attack Herodotus, claiming that Xerxes would never have thrown spears at the sun nor let chains down into the sea since sun and sea are gods in the traditions of the Magi – though it was natural enough for him to pull statues down.

4

Drugs, Charms and Fair Words: Greco-Roman Antiquity

Figure 5: Ancient Sages

S hortly after 156 CE, a provincial essayist and novelist named Apuleius
went to court in North Africa to defend himself against a charge of
magic. His strategy turned on two distinctions: first, between magic
and other activities, like cooking, healing and worship; second, between good
magic and bad magic. Perhaps Apuleius could convince his judges that when
he chose a special fish for dinner or cared for a statuette of a god, none of this
was magical. If that defence failed, he could still argue that his magic was all
and only the good kind – something that no upstanding intellectual would
find shameful.

To make his case, Apuleius had to prove that he had done no *maleficium*,
no 'harmful sorcery', and that none of his *magia* – had there been any – would
have been criminal. Three centuries earlier, when Plautus was also writing in
Latin, the word *maleficium* was available to the playwright, but only to talk
generally about some 'offence' or 'injury', with no suggestion of *magical*
wrongdoing or sorcery. Also, if pressed to be more specific, Plautus could not
say that some *maleficium* is *magia* because that second word had not yet
entered the Latin language. *Magia* first showed up more than a century later
when Cicero and other educated Romans needed Latin terminology for what
Greek authors had said about their *mageia*, with its exotic Persian background. The word in Greek was not native or archaic. Homer had never heard
of *mageia*: without uttering that word, Circe turns people into pigs and Odysseus calls ghosts up from the underworld.

When Apuleius insists that '*magia* is an art approved by immortal gods', he
means 'the magic that Plato describes as the royal education given by the
Persians to their young princes', citing a line from Plato's first *Alcibiades*, written around 350 BCE. More than five centuries later, Plato's dialogues had
become part of a classical heritage invented by Greeks and adopted by their
Roman admirers – like Apuleius and many, many others. These heirs of the
classical tradition – students of Aeschylus, Aristotle, Epicurus, Euripides,

Herodotus, Hesiod, Hippocrates, Homer, Isocrates, Pindar, Plato, Sopho-cles, Thucydides and other eminent authorities – inherited magic when they inherited the Greek classics, and this inheritance had the philosophical cre-dentials to make magic respectable, or so Apuleius assumed.

Writing about the *daimôn* who steered Socrates through life's rapids, Apuleius had to discuss the Latin word *demon*: an important source was Pla-to's *Symposium*. In that dialogue and elsewhere, Plato's role in giving magic a philosophical basis was original, enduring but not straightforward: he shows how magic works, but in his *Laws* he also argues for penalizing it severely.

When he recalls a talk about charms and amulets that Socrates had with his students, how those remedies function is not the issue, and conversation about such magical devices was evidently nothing unusual for educated Athe-nians. Socrates suggests that dialectic heals the intemperate just as a headache charm cures pain: he assumes that people use such charms but not that they understand them. On other occasions, however – notably the dinner party described in his *Symposium* – Plato wants to show what makes magic effect-ive, finding analogies for action at a distance in emotional signalling, musical resonance and the physiology of complex organisms. Familiar psychological or physical phenomena – often organic – are models for the less familiar magical effects that need explaining.

The best models come from ordinary experience: one person responding emotionally to another, one organ in a body affecting another, one lute reso-nating with another. Local phenomena, since they are familiar, help explain (assuming that the analogies hold up) global phenomena, like a planet's influ-ence on a disease, that are unfamiliar and poorly understood. Thinking on a global, cosmic scale, Plato appeals to love as the divine harmonizer of all the world's antipathies and sympathies. This cosmic love might be an abstract force, like Newton's gravity. But Plato is talking about Love as a god – a per-sonal agent who makes some actions work at a distance, apparently without contact.

A magnet here attracts iron from over there. This lute resonates with that lute. With a wicked look – the evil eye – a person on one side of a room harms a person on the other side. Contact seems absent in all these cases, and that is the problem of action at a distance. Impersonally and abstractly, what solves the problem is mediation: if the celestial Jupiter is to heal what ails me, some-thing must bridge the distance between me and the far-off planet. But in Plato's world the planet is also a god – an ensouled person with a mind. And persons mediate in a special way, communicating with signs (explaining, complaining, threatening, pleading, praying, and so on) that link minds with one another. Some interpersonal mediation is the job of lesser gods (*daimones*) who cross the immense distances between mortals and the great gods on high. Among all these gods, Love is a very great *daimôn*, according to Plato.

Plato's *daimones* are not the demons of Christian belief: they are not agents of evil. Greater worries for the philosopher are humans 'full of cunning and deceit . . . all trickery and magicking'. Because those malicious cheats use 'chants and sorcery to attack and utterly destroy individuals and whole houses and states', Plato rules severely against them and their secret devices in his ponderous *Laws*. Seeing customary religion as part of the civic order and a bulwark for it, he condemns diviners and sorcerers as threats to the city. Some of Plato's language in these legal passages is precise and transfers well into modern terminology: his legislation against diviners is aimed, more or less, at people who might still be called 'diviners'. And yet, while the philosopher plainly wants to protect conventional religion, he never shows just where religion stops when magic starts. In our time, there is still no agreement about that boundary – or even whether there is a boundary – after millennia have passed and many philosophers have continued what Plato started.

Late in the first century CE, when the elder Pliny wrote summarily about magic, he knew he could draw on philosophy's august authority. Speaking of magic, he reports that 'Pythagoras, Empedocles, Democritus and Plato went abroad to learn it . . . and when they came back they told people about it'. In this context and others, Pliny – assembling an encyclopedia in thirty-seven books – realized that he was the recipient of a learned tradition: the one we call 'classical'. In part, that tradition was native and Roman, in part imported and Greek.

The first complete Latin documents on the native side are the comedies written by Plautus, starting in the later third century BCE. The language of the plays is demotic, the characters often dissolute and clownish. By Pliny's time, however, all of this was what we now call 'literature': Varro made a list of the plays; Horace read them; and they were studied still later, accumulating the dignity that comes with survival and sustained recognition. Such dignity is authoritative – having the *auctoritas* or esteem reserved for *auctores* – the authorities. So when Plautus makes crude jokes about a ghost in a haunted house, the style and content of his comedy take nothing away from its cultural weight. On the contrary, we take Plautus seriously when he shows us, in concrete and convincing detail, the same trivial superstitions that appalled Pliny, who belittled his fellow Romans because they felt 'obligated to stay silent while cutting their nails'.

'No one is unafraid of being bound by threatening curses,' a fear that Pliny finds shameful: 'when people remove and crack the shells of their eggs or snails or use spoons to break through them – also the describing of love charms by Theocritus in Greece, our own Catullus and recently Virgil'. In Virgil's lyric poems, Pliny could spot the magic that came from the Greek classics, starting with Homer, whose main Latin vehicle was Virgil's *Aeneid*: Greek *mageia* (a word unknown to Homer) becomes Roman *magia* when Aeneas wields his golden wand to clear a path to hell and when Dido, Queen of Carthage, hides her suicide behind the 'dark technology of magic'. Telling Dido's sad story, Virgil shows us the

> black venom milked from juicy plants
> searched out by moonlight and then reaped
> with brazen sickles.

The *Aeneid* is not an ethnography, but this depiction of a ritual could convince no one if the poet were not in touch with the particulars. In context, the details are more than the decor of a good story. In their setting, Virgil's descriptions became official, gaining status when Romans encountered them in their city's patriotic epic. These were the same Romans who saw divination as a state function, carefully classified by Cicero in his study *On Divination*.

'What ancient author does not mention such things,' asks a speaker in Cicero's dialogue: 'let's deny them all, let's burn the records and say that these stories are false.' No such purge was in the cards, however. Pliny, bragging that he had 'often refuted the foolishness of the Magi', collected, compiled and preserved their recipes in order to expose them. But he also concluded that the *magia* named after them had to be studied in a serious way. Part of his enquiry is genetic – the history of magic that opens Book 30 of the *Natural History*. Having gathered a great many facts, Pliny makes a narrative out of them in order to explain his findings and support a moral verdict: that magic is the greatest fraud of all, getting its power from three sources: medicine, astronomy and religion.

'Still very much in the dark' about religion, Pliny does not make it a distinct topic in his encyclopedia of (mainly) natural science, where astronomy gets plenty of attention and medicine even more. The 'astronomy' in his magic is the predictive kind that we now call 'astrology': an amalgam of the two was the best science of the day – as summarized by Ptolemy in his *Four Books*. In later theories of magic, astrology would be fundamental, for reasons that Ptolemy lays out.

Some of the earliest theorizing about magic was motivated by medical debates, reported early on in the Hippocratic treatise *On the Sacred Disease*. The author of this polemic was a contemporary of Socrates. He rails against the 'magi, purifiers, gypsies and con-men' who use 'purifications and chants' to treat a troubling disease – epilepsy. Because of its striking symptoms, people consider this illness not to be natural, even though its causes (says the physician) are like those of any other natural effects. Rightly admired for its vigour and clarity, *The Sacred Disease* could hardly settle all the questions about epilepsy. Galen, just as resolute as the Hippocratic author in his naturalism, was still puzzled by the disease centuries later, still looking for physical causes to explain it. An epileptic boy's erratic behaviour gave Galen evidence that amulets work in that natural way, as he enquired about the same magical cures that had interested Socrates and his students.

4.1

Deadly Drugs or Lucky:
Homer, *Odyssey*, 10.275–306

Told that Circe has turned his shipmates into pigs, Odysseus sets off to rescue them until Hermes, carrying his golden wand, warns him off and describes the dangers that lurk in Circe's house. To neutralize her potent drugs, Hermes gives Odysseus one of his own, called 'lucky' or 'noble': this drug is a plant, *môlu*, named not in Greek but in the language of the gods. Hermes shows Odysseus the plant's 'nature' (*phusis*), using that word – which would be linked with 'magic' until the eighteenth century – for the first time in the records of a Western language (see 1.2; 4.2). In addition to *phusis*, *rhabdos* ('wand') and *pharmakon* ('drug'), Homer uses other words in the Circe story that registered as magical with later readers: *agamai* ('be amazed'), *alexô* ('ward off'), *dênea* ('wiles'), *dolos* ('trick'), *katathelgô* ('enchant') and others. But there is no *mageia* in the *Iliad* or *Odyssey*, whose texts had stabilized by the late seventh century BCE (see 3.7; 4.10). The ancients themselves were struck by 'Homer's total silence about the art in the Trojan War', as Pliny would observe, adding that magic 'is surely the only way to account for Circe and for invoking the underworld' (see 4.13–14).

*

As I was on my way along the sacred wood,
up to the big house where Circe keeps her drugs,
Hermes and his golden wand were with me there . . .
to take my hand and ask me straightaway
'where are you off to, poor fool, with no idea
what place you're headed for or that your mates
are penned like pigs in Circe's deepest sty? . . .
But I shall save you, set you free from harm.
Here: go to Circe's house and take this drug – it's good!
Then walk right in, your head protected against evil.
I'll tell you all about her deadly plans.
She'll fix you up some food and drink and drug them.

But my gift to you – that lucky drug – will take away
all power from her charm. I'll fill you in:
just when Circe hits you with her giant wand,
go for your thigh, pull out your sharpened sword
and run at her – hell-bent to kill her dead.
Cowering, she'll call you to her bed, and then,
if you don't disdain seduction by a god,
she'll release your mates and guide you home.
But – by all that's holy – make her swear a mighty oath
that she'll design no other evils for you
and not unman you like a coward when you're naked.'
This the Argos-killer said and, handing me the drug
that he had dug up from the ground, showed me its nature:
black at the root but milk-like in the flower –
môlu the gods call it – and hard it is to dig for mortal men.

4.2

Magi, Purifiers, Gypsies and Con-men: Hippocrates, *The Sacred Disease*, 1–6, 21

In the fifth century BCE, an unknown physician – traditionally called Hippocrates – made this strikingly lucid declaration of naturalism: since anything that a physician can explain is an effect of physical causes of the same general type, everything known to medicine 'comes and goes' in the same natural landscape (see 1.2). Gods also inhabit that world, but this physician's theism is naturalist: divinity is immanent in an eternal cosmos that has no transcendent Creator. Terrified by the sight of epilepsy, the physician's neighbours tried to cure it with rites and spells, calling it the 'sacred disease' because they did not understand what they feared (see 4.16, 18). As he corrects their errors, the physician deploys the vocabulary of magic that Greeks used in the generations before Socrates was executed for impiety, thus leaving a record of beliefs and practices that violate Hippocratic principles (see 4.1, 3).

*

As for the disease called 'sacred', I find it no more sacred or divine than other diseases. Quite the contrary: it has a nature from which it comes like other ailments. But since it bears no resemblance to other diseases, people hold that its nature and supposed cause is something divine because they are ignorant and astonished. This problem of not understanding the disease makes them stick with the divine, while the problem itself is eliminated because the way of curing – just purifications and chants – makes the treatment simple. Also, if they consider the disease divine out of amazement, not one but many illnesses must be sacred, as I will show. Fevers recurring daily or every three days or four days I find no less amazing and marvellous, yet no one thinks them sacred . . .

It appears to me that the first people to hallow this disease were the type who are now magi, purifiers, gypsies and con-men, the same ones who pretend to be exceedingly pious and to know a lot. Using the divine to cloak and screen their own failure to find a procedure that helps, they have treated the affliction as sacred so that their total inability to understand it will not be obvious. They have chosen the right words to establish a treatment without risk to them, prescribing purifications and chants while ordering their patients not to bathe or eat the many foods that are bad for sick people . . .

They have also forbidden them to put black clothes on since black is for death – also wearing goatskin or sleeping on it or putting one foot on top of the other or one hand on top of the other because it will stop the disease if all those rules are followed. They have made all those recommendations because of the disease's divine character, as if they had more information, while stating other pretexts so that if the patient became healthy, they would gain in reputation for skill, but if he died, their excuses would carry no risk, the pretence being to blame the gods – not themselves – since they have not prescribed anything to eat or drink nor assailed their patients with baths, nothing that might seem to be a cause.

People who live in Libya's interior are never healthy, I suppose, because they sleep on goatskins and live on goat's meat. They have nothing, in fact – no blanket, garment or shoe – that does not come from goats since they herd only goats and cattle. But if eating and wearing such things brings on and aggravates the disease, whereas not eating cures it, the cause is nothing divine, and purifications will not help since only the eating does the healing or harming and the god's power is eliminated.

Hence, people who try to cure these diseases in this way seem to me not to treat them as sacred or divine. For if the ailments are removed by purifications and other such remedies, what stops other devices of this sort from producing sickness to attack people, so that the cause is no longer divine but something human? For anyone who can use purgations and magic to drive out such an affliction could also bring it on by applying the same devices – an explanation that rules out the divine. Talking and doing tricks, they pretend to know more than they really know, and they deceive people by prescribing a pure life and purifications while going on about divinities and spirits. For me, however, while they seem to preach piety, what they are really talking about is impiety, as if there were no gods. Their piety and divinity is impious and unholy, as I will now explain.

If they profess to know how to bring down the moon, to hide the sun, to make the weather good or bad with rain or drought, to make the sea and the land barren and all that other nonsense, it looks to me like impiety, whether they get it from rituals or from other such efforts or actions, either thinking that there are no gods or believing that they exist but cannot help us at all or having no reservations about doing the vilest deeds – must these things not make them horrible to the gods? For if a person does magic and offers a sac-rifice to bring down the moon and hide the sun and make the weather good or bad, I would not find anything divine there but something human, where human effort overcomes and enslaves the power of divinity. But maybe those claims are not true: people who need to make a living contrive all sorts of things like this, including this disease, assigning the cause to a god for each form of the ailment . . .

When they use purifications and chants, they make the divine utterly unholy and ungodly, so it seems to me, using blood and other such things to purify those who have the disease as if they had a defilement or hostile spirits or were under a spell cast by a human or had done some unholy act, when the right thing would have been just the reverse – to sacrifice, pray and go to the temples with gifts to supplicate the gods. Now they do none of that, however, only the purifying, and some of the items for purification are hidden in the ground, some thrown into the sea and others taken to the mountains where no one can touch or step on them. But if a god were really responsible, they ought to take those things to the temples to present to a god . . .

This disease seems no more divine to me than others, however, since like the other ailments it has its nature and its source . . . Like other diseases it starts in a family . . . and the brain is the cause . . . This disease that is called sacred has the same origins as the rest – from what comes and goes, from cold, sun and the shifting, restless winds. Since these things too are divine, there is no need to distinguish one disease from the rest and regard it as more divine: all are divine and all human. But each has a nature and a power of its own, and there is nothing impossible or inexplicable about it . . . Anyone who understands how people change, anyone who can use medicine to make them wet, dry, hot and cold, could also cure this disease if he could pick out the right times to give help – without purifying or doing magic or any other quackery.

4.3
A Charm to Go with the Medicine:
Plato, *Charmides*, 155B–58C

Like the author of *The Sacred Disease*, Socrates knows all about charms, amulets and other magical cures, seeing them as exotic imports into Athens but not taking them too seriously (see 4.2, 18). He specifies that ritual speech, not just physical contact, is needed for an amulet to work (see 2.7–8, 12, 14–17; 3.6). But his conversation with Critias and Charmides turns an amulet and the charm that goes with it into metaphors for stages of dialectical education. Socrates only pretends to know a magical headache cure, which does not mean that he or other Athenians thought such cures ineffective – even though the Hippocratic physician would have found the ritual useless. The 'leaf, and a charm to go with it' might have been a piece of gold or silver foil – a *lamella* – with a charm inscribed on it.

*

'Boy,' said Critias, 'call Charmides, and tell him that I want him to come and see a physician about the ailment that's been bothering him, as he told me the day before yesterday.' Critias also mentioned to me that 'lately he's been complaining of a headache when he gets up in the morning', adding, 'why not make him think you know a cure for headaches?'

'No reason,' I said, 'assuming he comes.'

'Of course he'll come,' he replied, and so it happened . . . He came and sat down between Critias and me . . . Once Critias told him that I was the person who knew the cure, he looked at me with those extraordinary eyes and was just about to ask a question when, with everyone in the gym crowding around us – my noble friend – I looked inside his garment and caught on fire, no longer able to contain myself . . . for I felt I had been grabbed by a wild animal. Still, when he asked me if I knew the headache cure, I answered, with some struggle, that I knew it.

'What is it, then?' he asked. I answered that it was a kind of leaf, and a charm to go with the medicine, and by singing the charm while the medicine touched the skin, this would heal the patient completely, but without the charm the leaf would be useless.

'I'll copy the charm down from you,' he said.

'With my consent,' I said, 'or without it?'

'With your consent, Socrates,' he said, laughing.

'Very good,' I said. 'And are you quite sure you know my name?'

'It would be terrible if I didn't,' he replied, 'since my friends talk about you constantly, and I remember your being with Critias here when I was a child.'

'I'm glad you remember me,' I said, 'since now I can speak more freely with you about what the charm is. Until now I was stuck about how to explain its power. For I tell you, Charmides, that it can do more than just cure a headache. You may have heard that good physicians tell anyone who comes to them with sore eyes that they can't try to cure just the eyes but must treat the head along with the vision if the eyes are to get well – also that it's very foolish to imagine treating the head without the whole body. Reasoning in this way, they prescribe a regimen for the whole body that tries to heal the whole and the part together. Have you noticed that this is what they say and do?'

'Yes,' he said.

'So this is correct, and you'd agree with their reasoning?'

'Yes,' he said, 'certainly.' His approving answers reassured me, and gradually I started to feel better as things heated up again.

'That's how it works, Charmides,' I said, 'including the charm that I learned when I was in the army from one of the physicians of King Zalmoxis of Thrace – doctors who even aim at immortality, so they claim. This Thracian told me that the Greek physicians may be right about what I just said. "But our King Zalmoxis," he added, "is a god and says something else: That as you mustn't try to cure the eyes without the head or the head without the body, so you must also not try to cure the body without the soul.

'"And this," he added, "is why many diseases are unknown to physicians in Greece, because they pay no attention to the whole, which also needs to be examined since the part can never be well unless the whole is well. For every good and every evil in the body comes to the whole person from the soul," he said, "flowing from it like eye problems from the head. If the head and the rest of the body are to be well, then, you must start by curing the soul – that's the main thing. The curing must be done by certain charms, my dear friend, and those charms are fair words. From such words temperance arises in the soul, and where temperance is present, it's also easy to bring health not just to the head but to the whole body."'

'The one who taught me about the medicine and the chants to go with it also said this: "Let no one persuade you to treat the head until he has first given you his soul to be treated by the charm. For this is the big mistake now in treating people, when physicians try to produce each effect separately – temperance and health." And he gave me strict orders: "Let no one, however rich, noble or handsome, convince you to do otherwise." Having made this promise that I must keep, I will obey and use the medicine on your head if you will let me first chant the Thracian's charms for your soul, as the stranger directed. But if not, dear Charmides, I can do nothing for you.'

When Critias heard this, he said, 'The headache will be god-sent for the young man if the pain in his head makes him use his head to think better. And I can tell you, Socrates, that Charmides not only beats his friends in good looks but also in what you claim to use the charm for, which – according to you – is temperance, right?'

'That's right,' I said.

'Then let me tell you that people see him as the most temperate of today's generation and second to none in anything suited to his age.'

'Yes,' I said, 'and I think you should outdo the others in all of that, Charmides ... If you already have temperance, as Critias says, and if your self-control is good enough, then you need no charms from Zalmoxis or Abaris of the Far North, and I can simply give you the headache medicine right away. But if you still seem to need these things, you must have the charm before taking the medicine. So please tell me whether you agree with Critias that you already have enough temperance or not.'

Charmides blushed, making him seem more attractive, and the bashfulness suited his age: he then said quite artlessly that it was hard for him to say yes or no.

4·4
A Science of Erotics:
Plato, *Symposium*, 185E–88D

Eryximachus, a speaker at Plato's drinking party and a contemporary of the author of *The Sacred Disease*, practised medicine in Athens and was a friend of Socrates (see 4.3). This speech of his about Eros, Urania and Polyhymnia – or Love, Celeste and the Songstress, to give them English names – is about gods but also about cosmic forces, the sympathy and antipathy that energize the world and pull it together. Since this energy is life, the universe is more like an organism than a machine for Eryximachus: the biological metaphor explains how cosmic forces work together (like organs in a living body) to act across astronomical distances and propagate magical powers. Since the organic metaphor accommodates musical notions of harmony and discord, the musician's art also underwrites the art of magic. Musical resonance, like living cosmic sympathy, accounts for magical action.

*

'Since Pausanias has got the conversation going well but has not ended it effectively, I suppose I must bring the discussion to a conclusion. I think he is right to divide love into two kinds. I've noticed that this is not just for human souls and about beautiful things, however, but about much else and also in other things – in the bodies of everything that lives, in those that grow in the earth and in all that exists, if I may say so, since from practising my art of medicine I've learned how great and wonderful that god is who reaches through the whole universe to things divine as well as human. So let me start with medicine in order to honour my art.

'Bodies in their nature have these two loves that admittedly are different and dissimilar. Being dissimilar, they long for and love dissimilars, and in the healthy body the love is one thing, another thing when the body is diseased. And to indulge good men is honourable, as Pausanias was just saying, though with debauched people it is shameful, and likewise for bodies: we do well to indulge each body in good and healthy things, and so one should – this is what we call being a physician – while the shame of bad and sickly things must be discouraged, by anyone who wants to excel at this art.

'For medicine can be summed up as the science of the body's loves as we fill and empty it, as the best physician separates good love from bad and converts one into the other, knowing how – if he is a skilled practitioner – to introduce the love that's absent and remove what's present. For he must turn the body's most antagonistic forces into friends and make them love one another. These antagonists are entirely opposed, like hot and cold, bitter and sweet, moist and dry and all the rest. Understanding how to put love and concord into them, my ancestor Asclepius established this art of mine – as the poets here tell us, and I believe them.'

'So all of medicine is ruled by this god, just like training the body and farming, and anyone who gives this a moment's thought will clearly see the same thing going on in music – probably what Heraclitus wanted to say too, though his words are not quite right: "like a well-tuned lyre or bow," the One (he says), "clashes agreeably with itself". But claiming that harmony clashes or is still produced from clashing is absurd. What he probably meant to say is that harmony comes from treble and bass notes that once clashed but were then made to agree by the art of music, though if bass and treble kept clashing, there would be no harmony. For harmony is unison, and unison is agreement: you can't get agreement when things are clashing, as long as they keep clashing, and things that clash can't be harmonized unless they come into agreement.

'In rhythm the same thing happens with long and short beats, which clash at first and are then made to agree. The agreement in all these cases – as with medicine – comes from music, which introduces love and concord, since music too is a science of erotics but regarding harmony and rhythm. And it isn't hard to see the erotics in this alliance of harmony and rhythm, when the love hasn't yet been divided. But if you need to produce rhythm and harmony to help people – whether by writing new songs or by teaching songs and measures correctly after they are already made – it then becomes hard, and you need a good artist. Here the same reasoning applies: in well-behaved people and those who might become better-behaved, we must indulge and protect the love of such things.

'And this is the good love – the heavenly one – the Love born of the Celeste who is a Muse. But then from the Songstress comes the common Love of the streets, whom if we are to befriend we must befriend carefully so that enjoying his pleasure doesn't turn into dissipation, just as in my work a great task is to handle the appetites carefully in the art of eating in order to enjoy the pleasure without illness. In music as in medicine and in all other arts human and divine, each Love must be preserved, as much as can be, since both are involved.

'Even the course of the seasons through the year is full of them both. When hot, cold, wet and dry are well-behaved in their love for one another, mixing and harmonizing temperately – as I was just saying – they bring health and plenty to mankind and all other animals and plants, doing them no harm. But when the Love arrives who brings Wantonness along, he is more over-powering for the seasons of the year, ruining everything and causing damage, for plagues also like to be born from those parents, along with many other diseases of animals and plants. Frost, hail and blight come from the excesses and bad behaviour of those forces when they are in love: the science of them – with the movements of the stars and the seasons of the year – is called astronomy.

'Notice also that for all sacrifices and the whole business of divination – dealing with the relations between humans and gods – the only issue is preserving Love and caring for him since impiety likes to appear only when someone fails to indulge the Love who is well-behaved, honouring not that Love but the other god and putting him first in every action when it comes to one's ancestors, both living and dead, and the gods. The job of divination, then, is to watch over the two Loves and take care of them, and the diviner is the craftsman who makes peace between gods and humans – for humans the science of erotics applied to law and piety.

'Such is the great and mighty or rather universal power possessed by Love – in short, by Love as a whole. But the one who has the greatest power cares for the good and is fulfilled along with temperance and justice, whether for gods or men, and this is what provides all our happiness and makes us friends with the gods who are above us and with one another.'

4.5

Love, Divination and Incantations: Plato, *Symposium*, 201D–3A

The physician Eryximachus describes a universal force of nature, calling it a god, naming it Love and putting that god (or gods) in charge of 'all sacrifices and the whole business of divination' (see 4.4). Later at the same dinner party, Socrates develops this theme in response to a third speaker, Agathon, by recalling his own earlier encounter with Diotima, a woman wise enough to protect Athens from a plague. Love is not supremely divine, lower than a high god yet more than human, a *daimôn* – a formidable spirit whose great powers sometimes help but sometimes hurt humans, just like the two Loves discussed by Eryximachus. But Diotima stresses something different about Love, the *daimôn*'s 'power to interpret and convey things', adding that 'such spirits are many'. When spirits mediate between earthly mortals and the heavenly gods on high, the results are both magical and religious.

*

I'll try to tell you the whole story about Love that I once heard from Diotima, a woman from Mantineia, who understood this and many other things. When the Athenians were offering a sacrifice because the plague was getting close, she made the disease halt for ten years, and it was she who taught me about love – so my story is what she told me, starting with what Agathon conceded to me and going through it by myself, as best I can. As you laid it out, Agathon, I must first say who and what Love is and then what he does, but it seems easiest for me to go back and forth like that woman from abroad when she interrogated me. What I told her was almost what Agathon just said to me: Love is a great god, and beautiful things are his. She proved to me, in words just like I used with him, that by my own account Love is neither beautiful nor good.

'What do you mean, Diotima,' I said, 'is Love ugly and evil, then?'

'What a thing to say! Do you suppose,' she answered, 'that what is not beautiful needs to be ugly?'

'Of course.'

'And ignorant if it is not wise? Or don't you realize that something comes between ignorance and wisdom?'

'What?'

'Having the right beliefs, without having a reason to give, isn't knowledge: how could something be knowledge without a reason? Nor is it ignorance: for how could ignorance just happen upon the truth? Right belief, however, clearly comes between ignorance and understanding.'

'What you say is true,' I replied.

'Then what isn't beautiful need not be ugly, and what isn't good need not be evil. Accordingly, your accepting that Love is neither good nor beautiful doesn't mean that he must be evil and ugly,' she said. 'He could be something in between.'

'Well,' I said, 'everyone agrees that Love is a great god.'

'You mean everyone who doesn't know,' she asked, 'or everyone who knows?'

'All of them together.'

And then she laughed and asked, 'How, Socrates, if they say he isn't a god, could they possibly agree that he is a great god?'

'Who are those people?' I enquired.

'You're one of them,' she said, 'and I'm one.'

Then I answered, 'What are you talking about?'

'It's easy enough,' she said. 'Now tell me, don't you say that all the gods are happy and good? Surely you wouldn't dare claim that any god isn't good and happy?'

'God, no!' I replied.

'And the ones you call happy are those who get what's good and beautiful – correct?'

'Definitely.'

'And you've agreed that Love, because he's in need, desires those good and beautiful things that he needs.'

'Yes,' I agreed.

'But how can he be a god if he has no share of the good and beautiful?'

'He can't, I suppose.'

'So you see,' she said, 'that you also think Love not to be a god.'

'What is Love, then? A mortal?' I asked.

'Not at all.'

'What then?'

'Just as before,' she said, 'between mortal and immortal.'

'What's that, Diotima?'

'He's a great spirit, Socrates, for all the spirit world is part way between god and mortal.'

'What power does he have?' I asked.

'The power to interpret and convey things, to gods from humans with prayers and sacrifices, to humans from gods with commands and repayment for sacrifices. In between the two, Love makes both complete by tying everything in the universe together. Through this moves all divination, all the priestly arts of sacrifice and ritual, all incantations and all prophecy and wizardry. Though gods don't mix with humans, through this spiritual connection come all the communion and all the conversation that gods have with humans, whether waking or asleep. The expert at such things is a spiritual person, while the expert at some craft or handiwork is just a tradesman. But such spirits are many and various, Love being one of them.'

4.6
All Trickery and Magicking:
Plato, *Laws*, 908C–10D

Where religion stops and magic starts is sometimes hard to see in ancient texts, but – in this passage from his immense legal treatise – Plato puts unsanctioned rituals 'outside the law'. A discussion of crimes against the gods, his main topic, exposes beliefs and practices similar to religion that deviate from the religious norms – actual or notional – that Plato respects, moving him to frame laws against those 'who are all trickery and magicking'. Their magic corrupts piety and reverence, the proper attitudes towards the gods – attitudes institutionalized in the city's official religion, whose public character comes to the fore in Plato's analysis. The other side of that coin is the habitual secrecy of magicians, whose heinous crimes against society aggravate their offences against the gods, calling for the harshest punishments.

*

A person may not believe in gods and yet may, by nature, behave in a completely decent way, disliking the wicked. And since this person is unable to commit an injustice because he cannot stand it, perhaps he avoids the wrongs that people do and loves what is right. But another person, besides believing that the world is devoid of gods, lacks self-control when in pleasure or pain, while also having a strong memory and a sharp mind. Although the two share the misfortune of not believing in gods, one does more harm and the other less in the disgrace they bring on others. One may be full of chatter about gods and sacrifices and oaths, and perhaps by laughing at others he will make them like himself – if he goes unpunished. But the other person, who has the same beliefs and whom people call clever, is full of cunning and deceit. Of this type are diviners, who are all trickery and magicking, and sometimes they turn into our bosses, the speechmakers and generals, people who contrive rites of their own in secret – and next we have the sophists, so called, with their own ingenious devices . . .

Becoming like animals, some not only believe there are no gods or that they are uncaring or can be placated, they also despise humanity, guiding away many souls of the living, claiming to guide the dead and promising to win the gods over with sacrifices and prayers, while also using chants and sorcery to attack and utterly destroy individuals and whole houses and states for the sake of money. If such a person is found guilty, the court must sentence him to imprisonment . . . and when he dies he must be thrown out unburied beyond the borders . . .

For all these cases there should be a law in common to mitigate the offences of word and deed that many of them commit against the gods – and also make them less mindless, perhaps – because they will not be allowed to perform religious rites outside the law. Let the law be stated simply to deal with all the issues:

No one may have sacred rites in his own house. When he means to sacrifice to a god, let him go out in public to make the offering and hand it over to the priests and priestesses who care for the purity of those things. Then he should join them in prayer, and anyone else who wishes should pray with him.

The reasons behind this law follow here. To establish gods and temples is not easy, and to do it right takes a great deal of thinking. But the custom is – whether with women or especially anyone ill or in danger or difficulty or, just the reverse, with people having good luck – always to consecrate the occasion by vowing sacrifices and promising shrines to gods, spirits and the children of gods. When ghosts wake people up, when dreams terrify them, when they often remember what they saw in those visions, they make remedies for them in the altars and temples that fill every house and village, standing there in the open air or wherever such events may have occurred.

Thinking of all such cases, we should obey the law just stated, which also applies to enemies of religion, the point being that they cannot conceal these things too in their wicked deeds by supposing that the placement of shrines and altars in their own houses secretly propitiates the gods with prayer and sacrifice, when in fact this does infinitely more wrong and calls down the wrath of heaven on themselves and those – better men than they – who trust them, the result being that the whole city reaps the reward of their irreligion: a strange turn of justice.

4.7
A Law on Poisoning:
Plato, *Laws*, 932E–33E

Plato legislates against two types of poisoning: one uses drugs or other physical substances, the other uses magic. When 'one body does harm to another body' in this way, a physician can analyse the damage that he also knows how to produce. Such injuries are effects of natural causes, not of the magic promoted by sorcerers and diviners (see 1.2; 4.2). Although Plato makes such reprobates as responsible as physicians for turning their expertise into crime, he does not really think of them as experts – unlike physicians, who know what they are doing, more or less (see 4.18; 5.14). The damage done by magic is mainly (using modern categories) psychological and social, yet plainly more widespread and perhaps more destructive than the results of physical poisoning. Because 'poison', 'potion', 'drug' and 'medicine' can all be rendered by a single Greek word – *pharmakon* – a *pharmakeus* can be a druggist, a poisoner or a sorcerer (see 1.5).

*

We have already discussed cases of one person injuring another with poisons shown to have been fatal, but nothing has been said about other cases of freely and purposely injuring another with things to drink, eat or apply to the body. What makes a full account difficult is that there are two kinds of poison to use against humans. There is the kind just mentioned, where one body does harm to another body in a natural way. But another kind convinces the audacious sort that they have the power to hurt people with various acts of magic, incantations and 'binding spells', so called, while convincing others that the sorcery actually has the power to hurt them badly.

With all these things it is hard to see how they might happen naturally, nor would it be easy to convince others if anyone were to figure this out. When people's thoughts about each other have been troubled by seeing wax images on a door or where three roads cross or at a family tomb, trying to persuade them not to worry much about any of this, since there can be no clear idea of it, is not worth the effort.

So the law on poisoning must go two ways, depending on how the poisoning is attempted. But what comes first – through our pleading, exhorting and advising – is not to do such things, not to scare people to death like frightened children nor force legislators and judges to soothe those popular fears, primarily by explaining that anyone who tries poisoning has no idea how to do the kind that works on bodies, unless he happens to know this from being a physician, nor the kind that involves magic, unless he happens to be a diviner or a marvel-gazer.

Let the text of the law on poisoning read as follows, then.

If a physician uses drugs to do harm that is not fatal to a man or to his household, or to do any harm, fatal or not, to his cattle or his bees, and if he is convicted of poisoning, he shall be punished by death, or if he is a layperson, the court shall determine what he is to pay or suffer. But if his reputation is for doing harm with binding charms, spells, incantations or any such methods of poisoning, let him die if he is a diviner or marvel-monger, though if he is convicted of poisoning without any divination, do the same as in the previous case, letting the court decide what he must pay or suffer.

4.8

A Haunted House:
Plautus, *Mostellaria*, 447–531

Although Plautus (254–184 BCE) based his *Haunted House* on an older Greek comedy and set the play in Athens, he wrote when Romans had only started to reshape their culture by borrowing from thinkers like Hippocrates and Plato, bringing alien wisdom – magic included – into Italy (see 4.2–6). Meanwhile, his play got laughs with crude jokes about a spook, a superstitious old man (Theopropides: *Th*) and his cunning, nervy slave (Tranio: *Tr*). The audience had seen it all before in human nature and home-grown habit, long before the word *magia*, a foreign import, had entered the Latin language (see 4.10). The great playwright turned common customs – don't enter or even touch a desecrated place, and if you see a ghost, don't look back or forget to cover your head – into comic art. When Theopropides, with two of his retinue propping him up, returns to his house from a trip, he finds the door locked and his slaves out on the street, with no way to know that his son has been carousing inside for months. Tranio has just entered, after locking the door to protect the boy.

*

Tr *[out of breath]* Theopropides! Welcome, master! You're back safe: excellent! Have you been well, as always?

Th *[barely able to walk]* Never better: just have a look.

Tr *[fawning]* Wonderful!

Th How about you? Have you all gone crazy?

Tr Something wrong?

Th Plainly! Here you are strolling around outside without a living soul inside to watch the house. No one opens the door or says hello. I've almost smashed it in two places by kicking at it.

Tr Oh no! You didn't *touch* the house?

Th Not touch it? How? Haven't I been out here pounding on it enough to break it down?

Tr *[horrified]* So you've touched it?

Th Touched it, yes, and banged on it.

Tr *[more horrified]* Aaahhh!

Th What's wrong?

Tr God help us! That was a *bad* thing to do.

Th What's the problem?

Tr I can't say it – the awful, appalling thing you've done!

Th What? *[rushing towards Tranio, who cowers]*

Tr Get out of there, please! Get away from the house, go, leave, this way, over here by me. Was it the door you touched?

Th I had to knock, didn't I?

Tr My God! *[trembling, word by word]* You've gone and killed . . .

Th *[interrupting]* Who?

Tr . . . your whole household.

Th *[beating Tranio]* What a thing to say: may all the gods and goddesses punish you for it!

Tr *[cringing]* That can't help you or them, I'm afraid: it's no atonement.

Th Atonement for what? What strange stuff are you telling me all of a sudden?

Tr *[irritated]* Oh my! *[whispering, pointing to the helpers]* Tell those two to get out of here.

Th Go away.

Tr *[to the helpers, as they exit]* Don't you touch the house! And also . . . touch the ground.

Th Now speak up, by God! What's wrong?

Tr The fact is that seven months have passed since anyone has set foot inside this house, once all of us got out of it for good.

Th Why should that be?

Tr Careful! Look around: can anyone pick up what we're saying?

Th *[looking around]* The coast is clear.

Tr Check again.

Th *[peering about]* No one here. Speak up! Tell me what's going on!

Tr *[whispering]* A fatal crime has been committed.

Th What? I don't understand.

Tr A crime, I'm telling you – from long ago, an old one in ancient times.

Th Ancient times?

Tr We only just discovered that it had been done.

Th What crime is this? Whodunnit? Come on, talk up!

Tr A host – the same person who sold you the house, I bet – grabbed his guest with his hands and murdered him and . . .

Th *[gasping]* Murdered?

Tr . . . took the guest's gold away and buried the guest there *[pointing]* –
right there in the house.

Th Why did he do this? What do you think?

Tr *[rolling his eyes]* Listen up, and I'll clue you in. One night, when your son
had gone out to dinner, we had all gone to bed after he came back and fell
asleep. But I forgot to put my lamp out, when all of a sudden he cried
out . . .

Th *[agitated]* He? Who? My son?

Tr Shhh! Quiet. Just listen. He said that the dead man came to him in his
sleep . . .

Th Sleeping, you say?

Tr Yes. Now just listen. The man spoke to your son, so he says, in this way . . .

Th The boy was sleeping, right?

Tr How astonishing, had he been awake, since the man had been killed sixty
years before! Sometimes, Theopropides, you're an idiot.

Th I'll be quiet.

Tr Look, here's what the man said.

My name is Diapontius, a guest here from abroad. This is where I dwell –
the dwelling I was given when Hades would not admit me to hell because
I had left this life too soon. Because I trusted, I was tricked. My host
murdered me here, and then that criminal buried me on the same spot
in secret, without a funeral, for the sake of gold. Leave here now! This is
a house of crime, a place where wickedness dwells!

The horrors that happen here I could scarcely tell you in a year . . .

Th *[terrified, as noise comes from the house]* Sshhh!

Tr *[startled]* Oh God! What happened?

Th A noise at the door!

Tr Coming from inside.

Th *[faint with fright]* Not a drop of blood in me, and the dead have come to
haul me to hell alive!

Tr *[aside]* I'm done for! Those idiots in there will make a mess of my story
today. I'm so terrified, and if that's obvious, this old fool will be too much
for me.

Th *[approaching the door]* Why are you talking to yourself?

Tr Don't go near the door, please, get away – my God!

Th Get away? To where? You get away yourself!

Tr I'm not afraid. I'm at peace with the dead.

[voices from inside] Hey! Tranio!

Tr [at the door, angry and whispering] If you have any sense, you won't call out to me. *[aloud]* I'm not the guilty one. I didn't knock on the door.

[voices from inside] Oh, come on . . .

Tr [whispering] Watch what you say!

Th What's this private conversation?

Tr Go away!

Th What's got you worked up, Tranio? Who's that you're talking to?

Tr [relieved] Did *you* call me? God help me, I thought it was that dead man complaining because you knocked on the door. Are you still standing there, not doing what I told you?

Th What should I do?

Tr Go; be careful not to look back; and cover your head.

Th Why aren't *you* going too?

Tr [exasperated] I'm at peace with the dead!

Th [thinking hard] Yes, I know. So why were you scared out of your wits just a second ago?

Tr Don't worry about me, I tell you! I'll take care of myself. You need to keep going as fast as you can, and pray to God.

Th [exit, hurrying] I'm praying to God!

Tr [entering the house] Me too, old man, praying that he'll give you a lot of trouble today. *[grinning]* Oh, God almighty, help me, what a fine mess I've cooked up today!

4.9

Foreseeing the Future:
Cicero, *On Divination*, 1.1-5, 30-35

Divination was built into Rome's culture, politics and military prowess – not just its religion. For public purposes, Roman divination was strongly institutionalized: officials took charge of augury (to study birds, lightning and other natural phenomena), haruspicy (to examine the remains of sacrificial victims) and other specialities, while private persons consulted astrologers, interpreters of dreams and fortune-tellers (see 1.5–6, 9–10; 2.2; 4.11–15; 5.8–9, 15). When Marcus Tullius Cicero became an augur in 53 BCE, he prized that high honour as a career move, though he was no true believer in divination. The philosophers he studied had debated the topic for centuries, sometimes to attack the Stoics for supporting divination: determinism and divine providence were related and contested issues. Although Quintus Tullius Cicero, the great man's brother, was an Aristotelian, he makes the Stoic case in Book 1 of this dialogue *On Divination*, setting up a sceptical refutation by Marcus in Book 2. Cicero takes his typology of divination from Greek philosophy, but many of his examples are native. The Romans themselves thought that Etruscans, famed as experts and inventors of the most prestigious divinatory techniques, were the original masters of those arts. Quintus, taking the lead in Book 1, challenges the sceptical Marcus.

*

'There is an old belief, traced back to the age of heroes and confirmed because the Roman people agree with every other nation, that some type of divination works for humans: the Greeks call it *mantikê* – foreseeing and knowing the future. This is a helpful and impressive thing – provided that it exists – enabling our mortal nature to come close to the power of the gods. Accordingly, having done many other things better than the Greeks, we do so again by naming this most extraordinary item for the "divinities" – though the Greeks, as Plato explains, derived it from "madness".

'No people that I know of, in fact, no matter how cultured and learned, no matter how savage and barbarous, doubts that the future can be shown by

signs that some can understand and then make predictions. Note first of all
the Assyrians – if I may go to the most remote authorities for support: because
the places where they lived were so broad and flat, giving them a clear line of
sight to view the sky from every quarter, they made careful observations of
the passages and movements of the stars and, having noted what they saw,
they kept records of what this meant for each person. A part of that nation
was "Chaldaean", so called not from the Chaldaean art but from a tribal
name: people think that by watching the stars every day they produced a science that enabled them to predict what would happen to each person and the
fate that each was born to. People also believe that the Egyptians acquired
the same art over a very long and almost measureless stretch of time . . .

   'The divining done for public and private purposes is not of a single type.
Leaving other nations aside, how many different types has our own people
embraced? At the start they say that Romulus, our city's parent, not only
founded Rome by taking the auspices but was also a renowned augur himself.
The rest of the kings also used augurs later on, and, after the kings were
expelled, no public business was undertaken, either at home or by the military, without auspices. Because important results seemed to come from the
science of inspecting entrails by interpreting omens for advice and then avert-
ing their effects, they used to employ all this Etruscan science so that no type
of divination would seem neglected.

   'Since there are two ways, beyond any understanding or reasoning, to
excite the mind with its own free and uncontrolled activity, one in a frenzy,
the other in a dream, and since they thought that the Sibylline verses are the
best vehicle of divination by frenzy, they decided to choose ten citizens to
interpret the Sibyl. Of this type, they often thought that mad predictions by
prophets and seers should also be heeded . . . Nor, if they seemed to bear on
public affairs, were dreams of a more serious kind to be ignored in the highest
councils . . . My own view is that our ancestors approved of these things more
because they learned from events than because reason instructed them,
though there are collections of various careful arguments proposed by philosophers to show why divination is real . . .

   'That staff of yours, the proudest badge of an augur's office, where did it
come from? Everyone knows that this is the staff used by Romulus to lay out
the neighbourhoods when he founded the city. The actual staff that belonged
to Romulus – a bent wand curving slightly from the top that got its name
from a "staff" for playing music – was found undamaged when it was put in
the Hall of the Leapers on the Palatine and the Hall burned down. What
ancient author does not mention such things? . . . Let's deny them all, let's

burn the records and say that these stories are false – anything rather than admit that the gods care about human affairs. But look: here's something you wrote about Tiberius Gracchus; doesn't this confirm the teachings of augurs and entrail-readers? . . .

'I agree with those who have said that there are two types of divination, one having a technical component, another lacking technique. For there is a technique when some proceed by inference to find new facts, after learning the old ones by observation. But others lack technique and get advance knowledge of the future not by reasoning or making inferences – after observing and recording the signs – but from mental excitement of some sort when the mind moves free and uncontrolled.

'This also happens in many cases when people dream, and on some occasions when they make predictions in a frenzy – like Bacis in Boeotia, Epimenides in Crete and the Sibyl in Erythrae. Also to be included in this type are oracles, not those taken from balanced lots but those that pour from a divine impulse or inspiration. Even this use of lots should not be dismissed if it also has the weight of antiquity, like those we have sanctioned as sprung from the earth: when drawing such lots makes a good fit for events, I believe the lots may be divinely inspired to fall that way.

'As with grammarians studying poetry, those who analyse all these different cases seem to accept divination if they stick closely to what is analysed. What cleverness is it, then, that wants to overturn things – with lies – when antiquity has made them strong? "I do not find a cause," you say. Perhaps the cause lies hidden, wrapped in the dark folds of Nature, since God did not want me to understand such things, only to use them. Use them I shall, then, and I shall not be persuaded that all of Etruria is mad about entrails or that the same people gets lightning wrong or gives a false interpretation of portents since, when the earth rumbles, when it roars and when it shakes, many such events have made true and troublesome predictions for our Rome and for many other states.'

4.10

Drawing Down the Moon:
Virgil, *Eclogue*, 8.64–100

About twenty years before he died in 19 BCE, Virgil composed his *Eclogues*, Latin pastorals inspired by Theocritus, whose Greek lyrics showed him how to turn magic into poetry. Alphesiboeus, a shepherd, sings in the voice of a nameless peasant girl who is helped by Moeris, a wizard from the Black Sea, to prepare the spells that will win back her lover, Daphnis. In the phrase 'magic rites', Virgil was one of the first users of that adjective in Latin literature, and he associates magic with Homer's Circe (see 4.1, 8, 11).

*

Bring water to these altars with soft woollen bands.
Burn fat herbs and grains of frankincense.
With magic rites and wanting only spells,
I'll try to steal my lover's common sense:
bring Daphnis home from town, my secret spells.

Spells can draw the moon down from the skies.
Circe changed Ulysses' crew with spells.
A meadow snake bursts cold when spells are sung:
bring Daphnis home from town, my secret spells.

I'll first tie threads of triple hue around you
to wrap three times your image carried thrice
around these altars in procession since
uneven is the number that God loves:
bring Daphnis home from town, my secret spells . . .

Moeris brought me all these plants from Pontus
where all the growth is poison: using these
I've often seen him turn into a wolf
and hide deep in the woods – that Pontic Moeris –
often pulling souls deep from their tombs
and shifting full-grown crops to neighbour fields:
bring Daphnis home from town, my secret spells.

4.11

This Dark Technology of Magic:
Virgil, *Aeneid*, 4.474–515

Devastated by the certainty that Aeneas will leave her, Queen Dido of Carthage decides to kill herself and persuades her sister Anna to help her prepare a magnificent self-immolation – fit for jilted royalty. Dido hides the real plan from Anna, however, by concocting a story about a sorceress from far away – an expert on love magic (see 4.10). The magician has instructed her, she claims, to make a bonfire of everything owned or touched by Aeneas, thus resorting to a 'technology of magic' with traditional ingredients – though the poet has shaped tradition for his own purposes (see 3.6; 5.11–12). Had Plautus produced a scene like this, he would not have called the art or method 'magical' because – as far as we know – the Greek *mageia* had not yet been Latinized as *magia*, as it was when Virgil wrote the *Aeneid* and the *Eclogues* (see 4.8).

*

Done in by grief and taking on the madness,
Dido decided she would die but kept the means
and moment to herself and hid the plan,
showing a happy face and calm to her sad sister.
'I've found a way, my darling, so be glad,
a way to get him back or free myself
from love, so hear me out: at ocean's bound
and near the setting sun in farthest
Ethiopia, where tallest Atlas
lifts a turning sphere that burns with stars,
from there a priestess shown to be Massylian,
guardian of a temple for the Western Ones,
has come to visit me. She's fed the dragon,
saved the limbs that drip with honey sweet
and kept the soporific poppy plant.
Her promise is to liberate what minds

she likes with holy incantations
or else to send hard cares to ruin others,
to stop the waters flowing in the rivers,
make the stars run backward in their paths
and also call up ghastly midnight wraiths.
Beneath her feet you'll find the earth will groan
and ash trees slide down lofty mountainsides.

Sister dearest, you and all the gods
and your sweet self will surely testify
how much against my will I arm myself
with this dark technology of magic.' . . .

They stacked a pyre tall inside the palace,
under air with pine and logs of oak,
and all around that place the Queen laid wreaths
to make her funeral garland. On a bed
she put the sword and clothing he had left
and next to them a replica of *him* –
fully knowing what was coming next.
Altars there, and there the foreign priestess,
hair unbound and roaring loud like thunder,
called up three hundred gods: black Erebus,
Chaos, Hecate three-roaded and Diana,
the girl who has three faces – them she called –
while she sprinkled fluids taken (so she said)
from the stinking lakeside of Avernus
and black venom milked from juicy plants
searched out by moonlight and then reaped
with brazen sickles, while she sought to tear
love's cure-all from the forehead of a foal
and take it from the hungry birthing mare.

4.12

Down to Hell the Trip is Smooth: Virgil, *Aeneid*, 6.33–314

Virgil transforms Book 11 of Homer's *Odyssey* into a Roman fantasy (or nightmare) with Greek scenery. Since the Sibyl's prophecies figure in legends about Rome's first kings, it was plausible for Virgil to make the Sibyl's skills at divination available to Aeneas when that hero needs to find his father in the underworld, where he also meets other noble Greeks and Romans (see 4.9). Aeneas can see and talk with the dead after the Sibyl shows him the required rituals – which animals to sacrifice to which gods, for example. His best known piece of equipment – the golden bough – is poetry's most famous magic wand (see 1.1–2). What Aeneas does, in effect, is mass necromancy since 'death had undone so many' – Dante's thoughts in Eliot's English – the many who show themselves to Aeneas in a landscape that inspired Dante's hell and its menagerie of monsters (see 1.9–11; 7.18).

*

Achates comes back then
and Sibyl Scarefoe with him, priest of Phoebus
and Diana's of the crossroads, Grey Eye's girl,
declaring 'now's no time to gawk about, my prince.
Now from an uncut herd take seven bulls,
and pick out seven ewes, our custom says.'

This to Aeneas, whose men obey her orders,
the priest's who calls them to her shrines up high
in Euboea where a hundred holes
hollow a cliff's wide face – a hundred mouths
issuing that many voices: answers from the Sibyl.
They've reached the entry, then at once she screams
'now ask your fates, look, there's the god before you!' . . .

This prophet, still unsubmissive to Apollo,
the more she rages through the cave to shake
that spirit off, the more he wears her out
in rabid speech to make her wild heart tame,
pushing and shaping, until the cavern's mouths –
all hundred – yawn wide on their own,
breathing prophetic sayings through the air . . .

So from her sacred lair Cumae's Sibyl
sends the dread enigmas sounding loud
all through her cave – truths wrapped up tight in black –
raging as Apollo jerked the reins,
then stuck a spur into her pulsing breast.
Frenzy ceased, the crazy talk died down,
and next the brave Aeneas started in.

'No troubles, woman, ever touch me new
or startle – foreknown every cut
that hurts my heart. Just this
I ask: since here, they say, the Lord
of Hell has built his shadowed gates
where Acheron's dark swamp leaks out its ooze,
let me walk through and see my father's face.
Show me the road to pass the Doors of Doom . . . '

The Sibyl spoke. 'Earthborn of heaven's blood
in Troy and from Anchises: down to Hell
the trip is smooth; wide gapes the Gate of Dis
by night and day. Ascending then
is rough, recovering the air –
that's a task, that's work to wear you out!
Few in fairness loved by Jove himself
or drawn by courage to the heights beyond
have done it – even sons of God.
Thick forest in the middle, next Cocytus,
winding black and slow amid the murk.
But if you're so impassioned, so desirous
to swim the pool of Styx a second time
and yet again to view the night in Tartarus,

happy to begin that maddened labour,
first hear what you must do.

A tree gives shade
to hide a leafy bough with pliant stems –
all gold and sacred to the Queen of Hell
who's Juno. A whole grove thrives
to hide it, closed in deep ravines and tarns
of darkness dim. Only one who tears
this glory gold-haired from the tree
can then explore the underpaths of earth . . .'

He's quick to carry out the Sibyl's orders.

The cave was deep, its great mouth gaped,
the rugged entry sheltered by a pit
and stands of sombre trees that birds
could never fly above – so vile a cloud
rose from foul black jaws to stain the sky,
that place whose name in Greek is Birdbane.

First the priest brings in four dark-skinned bulls,
sprinkling their yearling heads with wine
and snipping bristles from between the horns,
first portions fit to feed the holy fire,
then calling loud to Hecate who rules
in Hell and Heaven. Drawing knives to kill,
the others come with broad-brimmed bowls to catch
the cooling gore. Aeneas takes his blade
and makes a gift, a black-fleeced ewe,
to Night, who birthed the Furies (bless
their name), but sends to you, Persephone,
her mighty sister, a forlorn barren cow.
Then at night he lights new altars up
for Styx's ruler, and on the flames
he puts the undivided viscera of bulls,
oiling the burning guts with fat.

Then look! Near sunrise and first light
the dark earth groans beneath their feet,

wooded ridges start to shake and dogs
are seen to howl and greet the goddess
coming through the dark. 'Away, away,
unholy ones,' the Sibyl shouts: 'evacuate
the grove! And you, Aeneas, start
your march and draw your sharpest sword:
now you'll need heart and fearless, boldest spirit' –
her words while raging down the open cave,
her lead to follow unafraid with valiant,
equal steps.

All gods! And rulers of the dead,
all voiceless shades with Chaos, Riverflame,
wide silent passages of night, let it be
right for me to tell what I have heard!
Blessed by you, let it be mine to say
what things lie buried deep in earthy darkness!

In lonely night they went like merest shadows
through gloom and all the vacant properties
of Pluto, realms depopulated,
like walking in the woods by shifty light,
a moon off course when Jupiter beclouds
the sky and black night blots all colour.

In the very anteroom, right at the front
of Hell's own maw, the vengeful Cares
have put their couches, where pallid
Sickness lives with sad Old Age
and Fear, and Hunger sits dispensing
bad advice alongside sordid Need –
shapes all horrible to see: then Death
and Toil and then Death's cousin, Sleep,
who dreams of anxious joys. Next across
the sill, deathdealing War attends
the Furies in their rooms of iron, and raging
Discord mad, her hair done up in bands
of bleeding snakes.
Branched in the middle space, an aged dismal elm spreads wide
and huge, holding – so the story goes – false dreams

attached to every leaf. Weird monsters too
fill that place in many shapes: doorways
stabling Centaurs, biformed Scyllas and Briareus
of the hundred arms, the ugly hissing Hydra,
beast of Lerna, the Chimaera clad in flame,
Gorgons, clawing Harpies, then a shade
in form three-bodied – Geryon – and now
Aeneas, shuddering in sudden fear, still shows
them his drawn blade as they come on at him.
But for his ally's lesson, unaware
how disembodied forms flit hollow yet alive,
he would have wasted iron to slash at phantoms.

From there the path in Tartarus leads on
into the boiling muds of Acheron,
a boundless whirlpool spitting all its sand
at Cocytus in rage. To take the toll
and supervise those streams and waters –
that filthy horror Charon, hair uncombed
and hoary, thick sprouting from his chin,
but eyes of flame and staring, set above
a soiled, knotted cloak on aged shoulders,
his raft he poles himself and tends the sails,
transporting corpses in a rust-red craft –
a god, hence fresh and green though old in shape.
Tumbling towards him down the banks, a crowd
complete with men and women rush, and heroes
great-souled too, their bodies void of life,
and boys and girls unwed – great expectations
put on pyres to be viewed by parents:
count them like the leaves that fall from trees
when autumn feels an early killing frost,
or like the birds, when frigid winter blows
across the water, sent rolled up in balls
to fly the whirling deeps towards sheltering sands
in sunny parts of earth. They stand and beg:
let me go first! I need that further shore!

4.13
Who Invented Such Things?
Pliny, *Natural History*, 28.4–32

The elder Pliny, born in 23 CE shortly after Virgil died, knew the Greek literature on magic; he cites Virgil in this passage as a recent Roman user of that imported lore (see 4.10–12). But he looks homeward as well, at hair-trimming, nail-cutting, spindle-twirling and other everyday activities governed by 'attitudes shared by us all'. His investigation also covers stranger practices, like eating baby's brains and drinking blood from living adults. Pliny would like to pin such gruesome behaviour on 'foreigners and barbarians' – not just Rome's Greek neighbours but also exotic people like the Snake-Born from Cyprus and the Persians who sent Osthanes to Greece (see 4.14). Yet venerable Roman documents testify to a native system of divination and even magic words and spell-casting – more threatening than the superstitious reflexes of daily life. Some of the habits that worry Pliny can be justified by theoretical notions like sympathy and antipathy, ideas that bring a little order to the abundant information in his encyclopedic *Natural History* (see 4.4–5; 5.5).

*

We shall start with the human who seeks to use himself to heal himself, though a large problem confronts us right away. Epileptics actually drink blood from gladiators as if they were living chalices . . . Others want the brains of babies and marrow from their legs . . .

Who invented such things, Osthanes? The blame goes to you, the subverter of human law and artisan of horrors who first produced them, I believe, to make yourself unforgettable. Who began to eat the parts of the body one by one? What omen led to that? How could this medicine of yours have started? Who made remedies more toxic than poisons? Foreigners and barbarians had devised those practices. Good. But did the Greeks have techniques of their own? We have books by Democritus in which bones from a felon's head are better for one ailment, but for others take them from a friend or a guest . . .

Of remedies with human origins, the main one raises a large question that never has been answered: are words and chanted formulas effective? If so, the credit rightly goes to human nature. Man for man, the greatest sages put no trust in this, and yet the whole world trusts the unseen, day in and day out. They really think that sacrificing victims without a prayer does not work unless the gods have been duly addressed. In addition, some words are for good omens, others ward off evil and others give praise, and we see our highest officials praying in fixed formulas . . .

When King Tullus Hostilius used Numa's books to make an identical sacrifice for calling Jupiter down from the sky, he was struck by lightning because he failed to do certain things correctly, for many say that words change the signs and outcomes of great events . . . But the effect of signs is really in our own power, and the results depend on how we take them. The augurs clearly agree, teaching that no premonition, destructive or not, affects those who start out by refusing to pay any attention to it, and divine benevolence gives us no greater gift. Really? Do we not find these words – 'whoever has cast a spell on the crops' – in the Twelve Tables? And in another section: 'whoever has cast an evil spell' . . .

No one is unafraid of being bound by threatening curses. This applies when people remove and crack the shells of their eggs or snails or use spoons to break through them – also the describing of love charms by Theocritus in Greece, our own Catullus and recently Virgil. Many believe that pots can be broken in this way, some that snakes are crushed but that the snakes undo the charm, which is all they know how to do, and at night when asleep they are collected together by an incantation of the Marsi. People also write prayers on walls to keep fire away.

Which is a better destroyer of credibility is hard to say: the outlandish words that we cannot pronounce or the remarkable Latin that one can only think ridiculous, always expecting something huge that deserves a god's attention – no, something to command a deity. Homer said that Ulysses used a spell to stop the blood flowing from his wounded thigh. Theophrastus had one to cure sciatica. Cato reported a spell to fix dislocated limbs . . .

Let me settle this point by noting attitudes shared by us all. Why do we start the year like cheerful prophets with good hopes for everyone on the first day? Also, when making a public sacrifice for purification, why do we pick people with lucky names to bring the victims in? Why counteract the evil eye with a special ritual, in which some invoke Nemesis – a Greek divinity whose statue stands on the Capitoline for just this reason – even though her name is not Latin? When we mention the dead, why insist that this is no offence to their memory? Why believe that odd numbers have more power for all purposes, as seen by keeping track of the days in fevers. In the season of first fruits, why say that 'these are old' while hoping for a new and different crop? Why say 'good health' when someone sneezes? . . .

When market day comes in Rome, many feel obligated to stay silent while cutting their nails and to start with the index finger, but cutting the hair on the seventeenth moon or the twenty-ninth keeps it from falling out and prevents headaches. On many farms in Italy a peasant custom forbids women to twirl their spindles or even carry them uncovered while walking on the roads because this dashes everyone's hopes – especially for the crops.

Marcus Servilius Nonianus, an important man in the city, used to be so worried about sore eyes that he had a piece of papyrus inscribed with the Greek letters rho and alpha, then put a string around it and hung it below his neck – doing this before he ever mentioned the disease or anyone else spoke about it. Mucianus, who was consul three times, did the same thing with a living fly in a bit of linen cloth. Both claimed that these remedies eliminated sore eyes. Chants certainly exist against hail, against various diseases, against burns, and some are based on experience, but I am too uneasy to report them because opinions about them vary so much. So each person must judge for himself.

When I discussed the odd practices of different nations, I mentioned people who have strange natures and the evil eye, along with many special properties of animals, so it would be repetitious to describe them here. In some of them the whole body has positive effects, like those who come from families that frighten snakes and heal those who have been bitten by touching them or sucking out the fluid: members of this group are the Psylli, Marsi and Snake-Born – so called – on the island of Cyprus . . . By the antipathy innate in all these peoples – so the experts agree – they can heal someone just by meeting him, just as wounds get worse if someone comes in who has ever been hurt by a snake's tooth or a dog's. Such people also spoil the eggs of sitting hens and cause cattle to abort their young. Once the wound has been inflicted, so much poison remains that those who have been harmed by poison become the poisoners.

4.14

This Most Fraudulent of the Arts: Pliny, *Natural History*, 30.1–18

Persuaded that magic is foolishness, or mostly so, Pliny wants to understand why it is also ubiquitous and indestructible (see 4.13). He concludes that the 'consensus on magic all over the world' has three sources. Two of them, medicine and astrology, produce predictions that corroborate divination (see 4.2, 15, 18; 5.8–9). Religion, a third basis for magic, also relies on ritual, even though the magic used by foreign peoples conflicts – according to Pliny – with their reputed piety. Records of 'outrageous rites' like human sacrifice show, in his opinion, that magic had also polluted the old Roman religion. In his own day, however, magic was proved false when even the depraved Nero gave up on it (see 5.1–2). 'The Magus Tiridates', a Parthian who brought Zoroaster's exotic wisdom to Rome, was Nero's teacher or accomplice (see 3.7). To enrich his orientalism, Pliny reviews the Greek scholarship on Zoroaster's chronology (see 3.1–3). Although the Persian prophet was the patriarch of magic, Homer, Plato and other learned Greeks also helped propagate what Pliny finds 'detestable, ineffective and useless' (see 4.1–5, 16–17).

*

To be sure, I have often refuted the foolishness of the Magi in the earlier part of my book, as the issues and topics demanded it, but I shall expose it here as well. On a few points there is still more to say about the subject, given that this most fraudulent of the arts has had such huge effects throughout the world for so long a time.

Its immense influence should surprise no one since it is the only art that has taken into itself the three others that most control the human mind. That it first came from medicine no one will doubt. Under the guise of something healthy, it crept in as a higher and holier way to heal. To those most enticing and pleasing promises were added the powers of religion, about which the human race is still very much in the dark. And when that was also a success, the techniques of astronomy were mixed in because no one is less than anxious to know his future, believing the truest account to be found in the skies. Thus, with human feelings chained by this triple bond, magic rose so high that even today it prevails over many peoples, ruling Kings of Kings in the Orient.

Without doubt its origin was in Persia with Zoroaster, as the authorities agree. But was this just one person, or was there also another Zoroaster later? This is not clear. Eudoxus, wanting magic to be recognized as the most famous and useful of the schools of wisdom, reported that this Zoroaster lived six thousand years before Plato died – and Aristotle said this too. Hermippus – while covering the whole art with the greatest care, explicating two million verses composed by Zoroaster, putting titles on his books, and citing Agonaces as the teacher by whom he had been instructed – reported that Zoroaster came five thousand years before the Trojan War.

That the art and its tradition have lasted so long is a great surprise since the commentaries have been destroyed and no famous line of interpreters has continued to preserve the memory. Very few indeed have information on those they have heard about, knowing only their names: the Medes Apusorus and Zaratus, the Babylonians Marmarus and Arabantiphocus or Tarmoendas the Assyrian, of whom there is no further record. The greatest surprise, however, is Homer's total silence about the art in the Trojan War, even though so much of his material on the wanderings of Ulysses comes from the same art that the whole work has no other basis – assuming that they take his passages on Proteus and the Sirens to have no other explanation, which is surely the only way to account for Circe and for invoking the underworld.

After all that, no one has explained how magic came to Telmessus, a city entirely devoted to religion, or when it crossed over to the 'mothers of Thessaly', whose name has lasted long in our world, even though the art was alien to that race – at least in the days of Troy, when Chiron's medicines satisfied them and they looked only to Mars for thunderbolts. I am actually astonished that the scandal of magic stuck with the people of Achilles, which is why Menander – born with unmatched precision as a writer – gave the title *Thessala* to a comedy full of women's wiles for drawing down the moon. Had all of Thrace, the land of Orpheus, not been free of magic, I would think it was he who first brought it from nearby territories to his neighbours and that medicine was the source of his superstition.

As far as I can tell, the first to write something about magic that still survives was Osthanes, a companion of Xerxes. When the Persian King brought war to Greece, Osthanes sowed the seeds of this horrific art, infecting the whole world as he travelled back and forth. Before this person the more accurate sources locate another Zoroaster, who came from Proconnesus. The fact is that this Osthanes, more than anyone else, made the Greeks crazy for his science, which was no mere fad. Yet I note that people have sought the summit of fame and glory from this science since ancient times – if not for ever. Pythagoras, Empedocles, Democritus and Plato certainly went abroad to learn it – in exile, not just on a trip – and when they came back they told people about it, while also making it arcane.

Democritus explicated Apollobex the Copt and Dardanus from Phoenicia, searching the tomb of Dardanus for his books and basing his own writings on their teachings. Life shows us nothing more astonishing than the acceptance – by anyone – of these doctrines and the subsequent tradition. So utterly unbelievable are they and so offensive that those who admire other things in Democritus deny that these works are his. But this is useless since the experts agree that he in particular made magic something worth considering. It is also quite stunning that both these arts – I mean medicine and magic – flourished at the same time: Democritus explained one of them in the same period when Hippocrates dealt with the other, around the time of the Peloponnesian War in Greece, which started in the three hundredth year of our city.

There is also another party of magicians who descend from Moses, Jannes, Lotapes and the Jews, but this was several thousand years after Zoroaster. More recent by as much is the Cypriot group. A second Osthanes added considerable influence to this business in Alexander the Great's day. Openly outfitted as one of Alexander's retinue, which no one could question, he travelled the whole world in full view.

As for Italian peoples, traces of magic certainly exist in the Twelve Tables, based on my own findings and other evidence presented in an earlier book. Since it was only in year 657 of the City, when Gnaeus Cornelius Lentulus and Publius Licinius Crassus were consuls, that the Senate resolved against sacrificing any human, we know that outrageous rites were performed until that time.

Magic certainly kept is grip on the provinces of Gaul, even in living memory, since it was the government of Tiberius Caesar that killed off their Druids – a tribe of seers and healers. But why mention this about an art that has also crossed the sea and sailed on to nature's empty spaces? An awe-struck Britain still practises magic today, with rites so magnificent that you might think it was she who gave the art to the Persians – such is the consensus on magic all over the world, even among peoples who disagree or do not even know one another. How much people owe the Romans is incalculable: it was they who wiped out the ghastly rituals where killing a human and then eating him to stay healthy was the most religious act of all.

As Osthanes explained, the art has several forms. In fact, he claims that divination works from water, the spheres, the air, the stars, lamps, bowls, axes and in many other ways, and also by communicating with ghosts and the underworld. In our day the Emperor Nero found that these are all lies and frauds.

Nero was just as mad about magic as about singing and playing the lyre, longing for it in the evil depths of his soul when his worldly fortunes were at their peak; his special desire was to command the gods, and he wished for nothing more noble. No art has had a more energetic patron, with all the necessary resources: wealth, power, the capacity to learn and anything else (or more) that the world allowed. Nero's abandonment of this art is immense and unquestionable proof of its falsity, though he ought to have brought his doubts to the gods of hell, or any other gods, rather than doing research with pimps and whores. Surely there is no rite, however barbarous and savage its performance, that would not have been gentler than his thoughts. He filled us up with ghosts, and no one has been crueller.

The Magi are evasive in various ways: the gods do not indulge people with freckles, for example, and are not seen by them. Could this have been their problem with Nero? There were no marks on his body. He was free to select the ceremonial days, and it was easy for him to get completely black sheep. As for sacrificing humans, it was his greatest pleasure. The Magus Tiridates had come to him bringing an entourage for the Armenian triumph caused by himself, and the expense for the provinces was huge. He refused to go by sea because they think it wrong to spit into the sea or to offend nature in other ways when people do as they must. He brought Magi with him and initiated Nero at banquets of the Magi. Yet even though Nero gave Tiridates a kingdom, he could not get an art of magic from him. This should persuade us that magic is detestable, ineffective and useless, and if it has some shadows of truth, their power comes from the poisoner's art, not from magic.

4.15

Configurations of Sun, Moon and Stars: Ptolemy, *Treatise in Four Books*, 1.1–2

The mathematician Ptolemy, Galen's contemporary and like him a great scientist, wrote the definitive synthesis of ancient astronomy in his *Almagest* (see 4.18). Here in this separate work, he introduces an equally influential account of predictive stargazing, while making no clean distinction between 'astronomy' and 'astrology' (see 2.2; 5.8–9). (Astronomy itself makes predictions – by forecasting eclipses, for example.) Although astrology quickly becomes technical – thick with terms like 'figuration' and 'configuration' – what makes it broadly credible is ordinary human experience, challenged, as far as Ptolemy can see, only by ignorance and cynicism. The sun gives us heat and life. The moon moves the massive oceans. What better evidence that stars and planets also influence us? If the heavens are divine, the argument is all the more compelling (see 1.7; 5.5, 13). Accordingly, Ptolemy will follow Aristotle and use 'regular philosophical procedures' to treat astrology as a key part of the normal science of his day. His universe is finite but immense, a sphere centred on the earth with stars and planets (wandering stars) moving in between and riding on concentric spheres above the moon, the lowest heavenly body. Everything celestial, including the moon, surrounds the earth, and the surrounding motions cause all the surrounded motions and thus all that changes on earth, including the birth, life and death of every human.

*

Of studies aiming at astronomical prediction, my dear Syrus, two are especially important: using the one that comes first in rank and effect, we grasp each figuration of the solar, lunar and stellar motions with one another and with the earth; using the second, we investigate changes produced in the surrounded objects by special physical features of those same figurations. The first study has a theory of its own that is worth investigating, even without the results that come from linking it with the second. It also has its own *Treatise* where, as best I could, I have given you a systematic and demonstrative explanation of the theory. Here, with regular philosophical procedures, I shall give you an account of the second, which in itself is not so complete.

No one who wants the truth should ever compare his grasp of the second study with the first, as if the second were always as reliable, since faint and obscure material qualities are linked with it in many cases. Yet no one should hesitate to investigate – where this is possible – since most larger events clearly exhibit a cause from what surrounds them. In its nature, nonetheless, anything hard to understand is easily misrepresented by most people. And of the two studies mentioned, the first could be slandered only by the blind, while there are plausible grounds for attacking the second. Some parts of it are difficult, encouraging the view that it is totally incomprehensible. Or else people ridicule the effort as useless because its predictions are hard to prevent.

Before giving a part-by-part sketch of such predictions, I shall try to look briefly at two issues – their possibility and their utility – and possibility comes first . . .

Some power from the aether's eternal nature spreads over the whole region around the earth and permeates it, making it everywhere subject to change for the following reason: of the primary elements beneath the moon, fire and air are surrounded and altered by motions in the aether, and those elements in turn surround everything else – earth, water and the animals and plants that are in them.

This needs little discussion and is completely clear to everyone since the sun, along with what surrounds it, is in some way always affecting everything all over the earth. This happens not only through yearly changes of season that cause animals to give birth, plants to bear fruit, waters to flow and bodies to change, but also through daily cycles that make things hot, wet, dry and cold in a pattern following figurations that fit us when the sun is at its zenith. And the moon, being closest to the earth, gives most of her influence to the earth, since most things, soulless and ensouled, change in sympathy with her. As rivers flow, they rise and fall with her changing lights. Seas turn along with her as their own tides ebb and flow. Plants and animals, in part or whole, wax and wane like her. And the courses of the stars, both non-wandering and wandering, produce many signs of heat, wind and snow in the environment, disposing things on land in the same way.

As the dispositions meet and mix, their configurations with one another produce many complicated changes. For although the sun's power dominates the ordering of quality as a whole, the other heavenly powers work with the sun or against it in various ways. This is more visible and frequent when the moon is new, half or full; it is less distinct and more intermittent when stars rise, set and approach one another . . . In fact, the more observant farmers and shepherds guess the quality of their products from winds that coincide with mating and the planting of seed. In general, we see that the broader conditions signalled by configurations of sun, moon and stars are usually predicted, even by people who simply observe them without investigating their natures.

Completely uneducated people – even some animals that lack reason – understand the greater forces of a simpler type, like annual shifts of seasons and winds, because the global cause is the sun. Lesser forces are understood by those who are already used to making observations because they must, like sailors: they have detailed information about cyclical signs of storms and winds coming from configurations of the moon and the wandering stars with the sun. Because they are ignorant, however, and cannot have precise knowledge of the times and places involved – or of the cycles of the wandering stars that greatly complicate them – it turns out that they often make mistakes.

But if someone has more precise knowledge of the motions of all the stars and the sun and moon . . . what precludes the possibility, on any given occasion, of describing special features of environment – like growing warmer or wetter – from the state of the appearances at that moment? And what makes it impossible, for each single person, to see the overall quality of a particular temperament from the surroundings when the person comes into existence, such that the body is like this, the soul is like that, and things happen according to the times, when some state of the surroundings fits some state of the temperament and tends towards good health, while another state does not fit and tends towards illnesses? . . .

As for the study of nativities, however, and for individual temperaments in general, one can see that there is nothing small or accidental about causes working together to produce particular features in those who come into existence . . . Unless each circumstance is examined together with the causes that come from the surroundings, even though the latter has the greatest effect (since the surround causes the circumstances to be as they are, which is not so for the circumstances), this can lead to large problems for people who think that everything can be settled in such cases just by the motion of things on high – even where that procedure would not be enough.

4.16

Dangerous and Forbidden Sorceries:
Apuleius, *The Defence*

To help a friend secure an inheritance, Apuleius married Pudentilla, his friend's mother and a widow older than himself. But relatives of the new wife and her son – the Aemilianus and Rufinus refuted by *The Defence* – objected: they brought Apuleius to court before the proconsul, Claudius Maximus, charging that he had deceived the ageing widow with criminal sorcery (*maleficium*) by using the love magic that was on sale everywhere (see 1.5; 4.10–11; 5.5–6). *The Defence* is a selective record of the proceedings by the defendant, who was well educated in literature, rhetoric, law and philosophy. Writing in North Africa after 158 CE, he treats magic as a classical tradition with roots going back to Zoroaster and patrons as renowned as Plato and Virgil (see 3.4, 7; 4.3–5, 9–12). If magic is the crime of *maleficium*, Apuleius pleads not guilty. But he also maintains that magic can be grounded in philosophy and more than just respectable. Although he asserts his religious probity and parades his expertise as a naturalist, he does not distinguish magic, as such, from religion and science. His task, amid courtroom acrobatics and virtuoso rhetoric, is to track details of theory and practice – religious, medical and scientific as well as magical – that prove him an upright, learned philosopher who has been falsely accused (see 4.2, 18). Knowing what fish are best to eat is no crime, surely: but what about the fish in magic manuals like the *Kyranides* (see 5.12)?

*

Monstrous crimes, dangerous and forbidden sorceries, abominations of the art – can you prove those charges? . . . I come now to the actual accusation of magic. The huge commotion you've made has fanned the flames of prejudice against me. But what a disappointment for everyone – pouring cold water on the whole thing with stories for old ladies! . . . In fact, since there was just one point to everything claimed by Aemilianus – that I'm a magus – I'll put one question to learned counsel: what is a magus?

Now what I've read in many sources is that *magus* in the Persian tongue is 'priest' in ours: what's the crime, then? Being a priest, knowing what to do, having information and experience about ritual procedure, how to perform the rites and follow the rules of religion – isn't this the magic that Plato describes as the royal education given by the Persians to their young princes? I recall the exact words of that godlike man . . . 'The first teaches him wisdom from the Magi – this being the worship of the gods – and also teaches him a king's duties.' . . .

Are you listening, with your mindless complaints about magic? *Magia* is an art approved by immortal gods because of everything she teaches about hon-ouring and worshipping them – exactly that pious sage and arch-priestess of heavenly power who came to us from her sires, Zoroaster and Oromazes. Yes, this art of magic was among the first lessons for their kings, and the Persians were quite thoughtful about allowing someone to become a magus – just as thoughtful as in choosing a king.

Plato – in a different passage about a certain Zalmoxis, Thracian by birth and skilled in the same art – also left the remark that 'those charms are fair words'. If that's correct, why may I not be allowed to know both the 'fair words' of Zalmoxis and Zoroaster's priestly lore? But if these people share the vulgar view that a magus communicates secretly with gods and can really do any unbelievable thing he wants by the power of some spell, I'm completely baffled: aren't they afraid to attack a person who – by their account – can do such things? What could guard against a power, unlike all others, which is secret and divine? . . .

But people who know nothing nearly always make the same mistake by bringing these charges against philosophers, whom some think irreligious for digging into physical causes, pure and simple. They claim that this eliminates the gods – in the way of Anaxagoras, Leucippus, Democritus, Epicurus and other defenders of nature. But some use the name magus in a vulgar way (as if knowing that something is done were also knowing how to do it) for philosophers – like Epimenides, Orpheus, Pythagoras and Ostanes in bygone days – who undertake the quite painstaking enquiries into providence that pay more honour to the gods. The same mistrust, in later times, fell upon Empedocles and his *Purifications*, upon Socrates and his guardian spirit and upon Plato and his Good. So, since I too am counted among such great men, I congratulate myself! . . .

'Why,' my accuser asks, 'have you looked for certain types of fish?' Perhaps a philosopher, in pursuit of knowledge, may not do exactly as a voluptuary does, pursuing food and pleasure? 'Why has a free woman, thirteen years a widow, married you?' Is the greater wonder just her marrying after all those years, perhaps? . . . And there are more such charges. 'Apuleius keeps some-thing in his house that he worships as sacred.' A bigger crime, perhaps, would be nothing at all to worship? 'Apuleius was there when a boy fell down.' So what if a young man – an old man, for that matter – collapsed because a phys-ical illness took hold or just because the ground was slippery, and I was standing there: what of it?

You prove magic with evidence like this: a boy falls down, a woman weds and fish are relished? . . . I will deny none of these accusations, true or false, conceding that exactly those things happened . . . And first I will refute your arguments, showing that none of this has to do with magic. Next, I will prove that there has never been any reason or any occasion – even if I were the world's greatest magician – for these people to put me on trial for harmful sorcery . . .

'You look for fish,' he says, and I will not deny it. But I have a question for him: is anyone who looks for fish a magus? No more, I suppose, than if I had been looking for rabbit or boar or a plump chicken. Or is it just fish, more than other groceries, that have something secret in them – something known to magi, nonetheless? If you know what this is, then truly you are the magi-cian. But if you don't know, you need to confess that you don't understand the charge. How can you possibly be so ignorant – not just of the whole literature but also all the popular stories – that you can't even cook up something plaus-ible? What good is a stiff, cold fish – or anything else that we look for in the sea – for lighting the fire of love? . . . Had you read your Virgil, you would certainly know that we usually hunt for other things to do that job.

Virgil, if I recall, mentions bands of wool, fat herbs, frankincense and threads in different colours, in addition to the fragile laurel, clay that gets hard and wax that melts. Later he wrote about other things in a serious work where a witch searched

> . . . by moonlight and then reaped
> with brazen sickles, while she sought to tear
> love's cure-all from the forehead of a foal
> and take it from the hungry birthing mare.

But you, as a prosecutor of fish, equip magicians with far different tools, not to extract charms from delicate foreheads but to catch them as they fall from scaly backs, not plucking them from a field but hauling them from the deep, to hook them with barbs, not mow them with sickles. In the end, when Virgil talks about harmful sorcery, he names a poison, but you recommend a sauce;

he lists plants and sprouts, and you discuss scales and bones; he crops a
meadow, you explore the tides. I might also have reminded you of similar
lines from Theocritus, others from Homer and many from Orpheus, and for
much material I could have gone back to the Greek comedies, tragedies and
histories, had I not noticed your inability to read Pudentilla's letter in
Greek . . .

Why catch a fish except to cook it for dinner? For magic it looks like fish
are no good at all . . . You're the only person I can find – after searching the
literature – who transports the power of plants, roots, sprouts and stones from
hilltops into the sea and sews it up in fish guts, as if nature were all jumbled
up. At rites of the Magi, it used to be that Mercury was invoked to carry
incantations, Venus to charm the heart, the moon for all nocturnal science
and She of the Triple Crossroads for power over ghosts, but – by your people –
Neptune, salty Salacia, Portunus of the harbour and Phocus with his whole
chorus of seals are all transferred from the surging sea to hot, heaving
passion . . .

Since we've now looked far enough inside the fish, take another concoction
that's just as stupid but much more deceptive and injurious . . . They've made
up a story about a secret place where no one watches – just a small altar, a
lantern and a few accomplices: there a certain boy was put under a spell, and
then he collapsed as soon as the incantation was done, and when they tried to
wake him he stayed unconscious. They dared take this lie no further. But to
finish the tale they should also have added that the same boy made many
predictions in a prophecy, and this we take to be the pay-off for enchantments: predicting and divining.

That boys do this miracle is confirmed not just by popular belief but also by
the authority of learned men. In writings of the philosopher Varro – superbly
educated and very well informed – I recall reading various such accounts,
including the one 'about Tralles, an enquiry by magic into the outcome of the
Mithridatic War by taking advice from a boy as he gazed at an image of Mercury in water and chanted the coming events in a hundred and sixty verses'.
Varro also writes that Fabius, after losing five hundred denarii, went to consult Nigidius. 'He used spells to inspire boys who then showed where to dig
for a bag that held part of the money and where the rest would be spread
around. The philosopher Marcus Cato even had one of the missing coins,
which he admitted getting from a servant to donate to Apollo.'

Granted: I see many authors reporting this and other things about boys
and magic, though I don't know that I should think them possible. Yet I
believe Plato's claim that some divine powers are positioned – by nature and

by place – midway between gods and humans, governing all the divinations and miracles that magicians do. Yes: this is my own view of the human spirit, especially if it is childlike and innocent. When diverting chants or alluring fragrances produce ecstatic oblivion of the here and now, so that physical consciousness fades from memory, then the spirit withdraws to its own nature – returning to the immortal and divine, of course, in a sort of slumber – and has presentiments of the future.

In any case, if we are to put any trust in such things, some prescient boy – as far as I can see – needs to be physically attractive and in good condition, mentally clever and a smooth talker: either he must provide proper lodgings for the divine power to inhabit (assuming that the power stays in the boy's body) or else his own spirit, when awakened, must get right back to its own divining . . .

But Thallus, the boy you've named, needs a magus less than a physician. Epilepsy has so consumed the poor thing that without any spells he often collapses three or four times a day in a struggle that wears out every part of his body – his face full of sores, skull fractured in front and back, eyes glazed over, nose split and feet tripping. The greatest magician of all is the one who's there when Thallus stays standing: usually the boy just drops, felled by illness or sleep. Yet it was my spells that put him on the floor, so you've claimed, simply because I happened to be there once when he fell . . .

You say a spell did this? The boy knows nothing about it, and I can prove it did not happen. Not even you will dare deny that the child is epileptic. Then why attribute his falling to a spell and not the disease? Why, when I happened to be there, could he not have suffered an attack – just the same as he has at other times with many people present? But suppose my heart's desire were to make an epileptic fall. Why would I need a spell when I read in science books that a quick and effective test for this sickness is burning an asphalt stone. Even in slave markets, a whiff of asphalt is a common way to tell whether young slaves are healthy or ailing. And when a potter's wheel turns, the dizziness quite easily takes hold of a person who has this sickness. Because the sight of the spinning weakens the wounded mind, a potter is far better than a magus for making people go down with seizures . . .

'Why do you look for fish?' 'Why did you examine a sick woman?' 'What did you have in your handkerchief?' . . . 'Have you written a vow on the thigh of some statue? Then you are a magus. Why else did you write it? Have you gone to the temple to pray to the gods in silence? Then you are a magus! But what were you wishing for?' Or go the other way. 'You have never prayed in the temple. Then you are a magus. And why have you not called on the gods?'

It will be the same if I've made a donation, offered a sacrifice or eaten some greens . . .

You ask what I had in my handkerchief, Aemilianus . . . It was completely stuffed – I'll stipulate . . . Would you like me to say what sort of thing was wrapped up in it under the protection of household gods? . . . Just as you wish.

I've participated in several Greek rites as an initiate. I'm careful to keep certain symbols and memorials of those rites that were passed on to me by priests. There's nothing unaccustomed or unfamiliar in what I'm describing. Just think of Father Liber. Some of you here are his initiates: you know what you keep stored up and hidden at home for private worship, away from any defilement. But I – just as I said – being eager for the truth and dutiful to the gods, I've studied *numerous* consecrations, *many* rituals and a *wide* variety of ceremonies . . . To anyone having any notion of religion, can it possibly seem strange that someone with knowledge of so many divine mysteries keeps a few ritual implements at home wrapped in linen cloth – the cleanest covering for sacred objects? . . .

I'm done with that! Now here's the root of the accusation – the reason for the harmful sorcery. Aemilianus and Rufinus must answer this: what would I gain, even if I were the world's mightiest magus, by using my spells and potions to entice Pudentilla into marriage? . . . If you could find even a single tiny reason that might make me want to marry Pudentilla for some advantage of my own, if you could prove even a little gain, then I'd be at your service: a Carmendas or a Damigeron or that Moses or John or Apollobex or Dardanus himself or any other celebrated magus from the line of Zoroaster and Hostanes.

See what a fuss they've made, Maximus, because I've counted off a few magi by name! What's to be done with such wild men, such barbarians? Shall I go back and show them where I've read those names and many others in public libraries, while consulting books by the best authors? Or shall I argue that knowing the names is one thing, involvement in the art quite another, since learned documents and instructional materials must not be treated as a criminal confession? . . .

I had no reason to use potions for seducing Pudentilla into marriage . . . What else, in your judgement, have I not disproved, Aemilianus? What purpose have you found for my magic? Then why should I use potions to soften Pudentilla's heart? . . . And what was your next move? 'He's guilty of many harmful sorceries, and they're as plain as day!' If they really are many, give me just one, even a doubtful or unclear case, since they are so plain.

Otherwise, perhaps I can answer your charges with two words each:

'glittering teeth', cleanliness allowed;
'mirror-gazing', philosophers must;
'making verses', also permitted;   `
'examining fish', studying Aristotle;
'worshipping wood', Plato's advice;
'marriage contracted', obeying laws;
'older woman', often happens;
'marrying money' – dowry paid,
gift recorded,
testament read.

If I've beaten back every accusation, word by word, if I've refuted every slander, if I'm safe – not just from every charge but from all your abusive statements – then philosophy is utterly blameless.

4.17
Brokers, Greeters and Carriers:
Apuleius, *On the God of Socrates*, 4–11

Before discussing a topic that fascinated Platonists – the guardian-spirit who restrained Socrates at critical moments – Apuleius introduces this material with a brief, general description of demons as imagined by some Greeks: demons live in the air, mediate between gods and humans and control various kinds of magic. What Apuleius says is compatible with the elaborate account that Iamblichus would give later – and easier to digest (see 5.10). Later still, Augustine objected to Apuleius because Christian dogma gave a monopoly on intercession to angels and saints, especially the Virgin Mary, greatest of all saints. Mainly through Augustine's rebuttal, the simple sketch by Apuleius became very influential (see 6.9 –10).

*

While humans who inhabit the earth have undying souls, while they delight in reason and prosper in speech, their limbs are doomed to perish, their minds are fickle and anxious and their bodies heavy and sickly . . . because as individuals they are mortal though the whole group is still eternal . . . So you have two classes of the ensouled with no direct means of communication, for gods are very much unlike humans in the loftiness of their place, the eternity of their lives and the perfection of their nature . . .

What? Has nature provided no linkage for herself? Has she let herself be lamed, broken up and split into a divine part and a human – since, as Plato says, no god mixes in with men? . . . But my friend (someone will object), to which one shall I bring my prayer? Whom shall I name in my vow? To whom shall I make a sacrifice? . . . If what Plato says is true and a god never communicates with a human, a stone could hear me better than Jupiter! That's not how it goes, however, and Plato can speak for himself . . .

Besides, some divinities – those through whom our wants and favours travel back and forth to the gods – are powers located in that intermediate layer of air between the aether above and the earth down below. The name

given to them by the Greeks is 'demons', and they are like brokers and greeters who carry things – requests from here, assistance from there – between
earth-dwellers and celestials. These same demons, as Plato states in the *Symposium*, control all prophetic warnings, the various wonders done by magicians
and the many different types of predicting . . .

Stooping to such things is no job for the gods on high: this assignment
goes to middle divinities who live in the tracts of air bordering the earth and
also adjoining the sky – just as there are animals belonging to each sector of
nature – to those that fly in the atmosphere and those that walk on the
ground. Since there are four elements, as everyone knows, and four great
divisions of nature, with animals suited to the earthy, watery and fiery
places . . . why should nature permit only this fourth element of air to be
empty of everything and devoid of its own inhabitants? Should living things
of air not grow in it? . . .

The bodies of such demons must have a little weight of their own, so they
will not just fly off, but they need some lightness too, to keep them from
dropping down. So you won't think I'm talking nonsense – like some poet –
I'll give you the leading example of this well-tempered middleness: we see
clouds condensed in a way not too different from a body of such delicacy . . .
But if every cloud that soars above has risen from the earth and will drift back
down to it, what would you think about a demon's body, which is much more
finely condensed?

4.18

Testing an Amulet:
Galen, *On Simple Medicines*, 6.3.10

Galen of Pergamon, a contemporary of Apuleius, was the most renowned physician of Rome's imperial period. As an expert on sickness and healing, he had no confidence in non-natural forces, and cures for epilepsy had long been notorious as exactly that – supernatural treatments for a sacred disease (see 4.2, 16). The drugs that Galen prescribed were normally ingested, allowing their qualities to be absorbed by the body in order to counteract the damage done by illness – in the way prescribed by the great physician's method (see 5.3, 14). Here he describes an anomalous case: peony root cures epilepsy when worn, like an amulet, without being eaten (see 1.6; 4.3; 6.5, 11). But he still insists on a physical explanation.

*

The sweetlet, which they also call 'five-vetch' and 'peony', has a mildly astringent root with some sweetness, though its rather bitter pungency causes much puckering. It gets the monthlies started, they say, having the power of almond drunk with honeyed milk . . . But on the whole it has a very strong drying effect, so I would also have no reason to believe that wearing it would have any prospect of curing epilepsy in children. Yet I actually saw a boy completely free of epilepsy for eight months when he wore some part of the root. But when the amulet slipped off his neck, he had a seizure right away, and when another was hung around his neck again, he had no symptoms: he seemed fine to me, once again relieved of the disease because of the experiment. Then we hung a big, fresh piece of the root around his neck, and from then on the boy was in perfect health with no more seizures. The likelihood, then, is either that some part of the root fell off and then was drawn in when he inhaled, thus healing the affected places, or the air he breathed was also changed and transformed by the root. For this is also how the juice from Cyrene helps an inflamed uvula, and roasted black cumin visibly dries up colds and sniffles.

5

The Primal Mage and Sorcerer: Late Antiquity

Figure 6: The Many-breasted Artemis on a Magical Papyrus

I n a treatise on astrology written around 337 CE, Julius Firmicus Maternus
describes the last days of an eminent philosopher:

> See how all the might of the Fates landed on him . . . First they stiffened his
> limbs by making his blood cold and sluggish, and bit by bit his sharp eyesight
> lost its brightness as the light weakened. Then a bruising infection broke out all
> over his skin so that his decaying body wasted away as its organs failed from the
> death of the diseased blood. Each day and hour the disease snaked through his
> guts, melting their parts away.

Joint pain, poor circulation, festering skin, weak vision, weight loss and organ
failure made life an agony for Plotinus until death ended it all in the year 270.
Porphyry, his student, had such misery in mind when he wrote the words that
introduce the *Life* of his teacher: 'Plotinus the philosopher, our contemporary, seemed ashamed of being in the body.'

Plotinus, Porphyry and Firmicus – two pagan intellectuals and one convert
to the new Christian faith – lived better than most subjects of the later Roman
Empire. Even for them, however, life was insecure and full of pain, given the
state of nutrition, sanitation, medicine and other basic needs. The body's
frailty had been proverbial even before ascetic withdrawal from it became a
philosophical regimen. The old sages called the body (*sôma*) the soul's tomb
(*sêma*), also warning that the flesh is a corpse, shackled to the soul. Porphyry
was proud that his teacher understood these things and 'seemed ashamed of
being in the body'.

Firmicus, before turning Christian, disagreed, charging that Plotinus had
been reckless in urging his disciples to liberate themselves from imprisonment or entombment in the body. Ignoring those venerable metaphors,
Firmicus promotes a different analogy, between the small world (microcosm)
of an individual human and the great world (macrocosm) of the universe.

'Man was formed in the nature and likeness of the cosmos,' he claims, 'on the same principles that rule and bind the cosmos itself.' And those principles are physical and structural, though Firmicus does not generalize his physics or make it explicit.

The astrological analysis that he presents is detailed, however, expressed in the jargon of 'signs', 'cardines' and 'ascendants'. His system also has physical elements like the 'rays' that run from one heavenly body to another and to us far below. By constructing a geometry of celestial influence, astrologers before Firmicus had drawn a birth-chart for the whole cosmos, thus framing the patterns to be plotted by the horoscopes of individuals. Contemplating those patterns and gazing at the skies, an astrologer could see that 'Saturn will produce celebrated magi, esteemed philosophers or temple priests thought to be famous for magic'.

As Saturn's child, the philosophical magus belongs to a greater whole: he is a citizen (*politês*) of a cosmic state (*kosmopolis*). The Stoics who instructed Firmicus found that thought comforting. They regarded their rule-bound universe as not just an intelligible environment but also a reassuring one. On those grounds, should a wise philosopher not welcome the physicalist determinism that Firmicus asserts? Plotinus thinks not, according to Firmicus, conceding 'nothing to the power of the stars, leaving nothing to the laws of the Fates', which is why the astrologer reminds us of the final torment that the sage could not escape. For Plotinus, his students and his critics in late antiquity, the weight of the body and of bodily matter was heavy. Will the sage carry that load or lighten it or put it down or simply ignore it? Firmicus seems to think that Plotinus wanted the last option, never yielding to laws of Fate that were nonetheless unbending – though Porphyry says only that his teacher was ashamed of his body, not that he imagined escaping it (more than momentarily) in this life.

There is even a kind of naturalism – a restrained naturalism – in the physical and metaphysical framework that Plotinus worked out to explain the magical effects whose reality he took for granted, having felt some of them personally. The framework is universal and more organic than mechanical. The cosmos is a system of concentric spheres, vessels of power nested within one another, and the whole apparatus is alive – energized and harmonized by 'the pull of everything towards any other thing in the living system'. This pull is the force of cosmic sympathy that operates on its own when 'the All . . . purveys spontaneously but . . . purveys also under spell'.

Nature herself is 'the primal mage and sorcerer'. Magical effects are simply natural effects of a special kind: to find and use them requires the skills of a magus. The Nature that produces those effects is a great divinity, but by no means the greatest: far above her are Soul, Mind and the ineffable One. The realm of those three Principles is the sage's true home: Nature and all her works – magic included – are detours away from it. And magic is always already there in the natural cosmos, flowing through it, ready to be switched on. But the sage – retreating within so he can ascend – will not take what Nature offers: 'only the self-intent go free of magic . . . and the entire life of the practical man is a bewitchment'.

To escape matter's witchcraft, the sage will detach from it, separating his inner self as much as possible from the body. Complete disengagement is impossible, however, as Firmicus insisted. Accordingly, his advice is not to abandon the material world but to manage it with a technique – astrology. Having it both ways, however, was the aim of Zosimos of Panopolis in Egypt, a younger contemporary of Firmicus. His technique – alchemy rather than astrology – is a different way to manage or manipulate matter. But like Plotinus, the alchemist also wants a release or redemption.

The techniques described by Zosimos are physical operations illustrated by drawings of equipment. His alchemy improves or ennobles the matter it works on, turning lead or copper into silver or gold. Ennobling a cruder substance by releasing something finer from it, the alchemist achieves a kind of redemption. But what is released or redeemed? The matter's inner spirit or the alchemist's soul or both? To frame such questions, Zosimos appeals to different types of speech, calling them 'embodied' and 'disembodied'. His alchemy is esoteric because the ancients have recorded its procedures in their secret, disembodied language. Recalling their words, Zosimos finds instructions for freeing the spiritual from Fate's embodiment.

Firmicus is content with the material world, or perhaps resigned to it, because astrology can mitigate its hardships by predicting them – without ever escaping Fate. Less satisfied with Fate, Zosimos recommends alchemy as a way out. In the Egypt where he lived, others wanted not just to evade the inevitable but to control it with magic – to compel even the mightiest gods. Those are the audacious promises made by the hundreds of spells collected in the Greek Magical Papyri, written without literary pretension by nameless authors for practical and commercial use.

Plotinus, himself an Egyptian, would have known such recipes and despised them: 'the sage,' he warns, 'will not know . . . enchanted love'. The mechanical rituals in the Papyri, designed for rote repetition, are blasphemous: they invoke many gods, like 'Hecate of the many names', yet the names are empty – pronounced but not felt, much less understood. Such mindless talk insults the gods, and its aims are sordid, like the one-size-fits-all love-spell (one of many) that leaves a blank and says 'let _____ come to my door right away, frenzied . . . from love's fierce need'. The fierce need is anonymous, conjured up for the *innominata* whom the spell-caster also needs. Not at all ashamed of being in the body, the writers of these hackneyed recipes made commodities of the bodies that they promised to enchant.

Suppose you lack the material technology to control your own body, much less the world. Perhaps you can master both with an attitude – like renunciation. Our ancient ancestors celebrated that attitude with extravagant praise, more like worship at times, for a large cast of characters: sages like Plotinus, saints like Anthony of Egypt, holy men like Symeon Stylites and 'divine men' like Apollonius of Tyana. These athletes of austerity and charisma were magnets for mass acclaim and poles of energy, empowering local groups to aggregate around their own ideals while helping them connect with their most remote masters – the gods on high. Evidence that saints and sages could make the heavenly connections were their deeds of power and wonder. Christians would certify their own wonders as 'miracles' – like Peter's stunning exposure of Simon Magus in Rome.

No less astounding was Plotinus in his duel with Olympius, an envious competitor who 'ventured sorcery, seeking to crush Plotinus by star-casting'. Inside the philosopher was such power that the attacker's magic recoiled on him, like light reflected by a polished shield. Feeling the energy go out of him – like Jesus healing the bleeding woman – Plotinus told his companions that Olympius had gone into convulsions, 'his body shrivelled like a money-bag pulled tight'. The hostile star-casting, plainly an aggressive sorcery, relied on a natural force 'discovered by men who thenceforth turn those same ensorcellations and magic arts upon one another'. But Plotinus, whose reflexive magic was even stronger, easily deflected the repeated assaults. Although his power impressed his students, their teacher made nothing of it because the sage who resorts to Nature's lower forces is no sage at all, merely a 'victim of magic'.

In his reputation at least, another such victim – according to his louche biographer – was Apollonius, a pagan saint who toured western Asia while the Gospels were being written. After those texts had been canonized, by the end of the second century, this 'divine man' was still a hit at Nerva's imperial court. Lucius Flavius Philostratus, the sophist who fictionalized his deeds and secured his fame, insisted that this 'expert on the spirit world' was no more a magus than Socrates or Plato, and just as much a philosopher. Philostratus maintains that progressive politics, conspicuous exploits and travels to the distant Orient provoked the enemies of Apollonius to slander him with charges of demonic magic. Charismatic like Plotinus, chaste like that philosopher and every inch the ascetic, he was famed for marvels that also made his name a byword for exotic and disreputable wizardry.

Philostratus and Porphyry both saw their heroes as sages, not sorcerers. But one of those wise men – Plotinus – had laid the foundations for a different and durable distinction, not between magic and philosophy but between two types of magic: natural and demonic. When Plotinus warned philosophers away from magic as merely natural, the perverse result was to encourage others – Christians especially – to see that type of magic as sanitized because its spontaneous effects are physical, not caused intentionally by any person. If the agency were personal, it might be the 'demon's work' that enemies of Apollonius blamed him for.

Physical things could be handled as magical objects in several ways. Manuals like the Hermetic *Kyranides* listed them and recommended the most effective combinations. Physicians and philosophers theorized about them. Alexander of Aphrodisias, commenting on Aristotle at the start of the third century, found them resistant to analysis but still wanted explanations. One durable account could be found in Galenic medicine, whose eclectic theories were partly Aristotelian. Faced with diseases – epilepsy, for instance – that 'do not yield to treatment through a natural property', some medics prescribed the 'undescribable remedies of the ancients . . . that work through the whole substance', a conception that linked magical action with Aristotle's physics and metaphysics. As Aristotle came to dominate Muslim and Christian thinking, the 'undescribable properties' of magical objects evolved into the 'occult qualities' of medieval medicine and philosophy.

Such theorizing was of little interest to the author of the Hermetic *Asclepius*, whose motives were mainly moral and religious. He mentions a 'mixture of plants, stones and spices' only because they 'have in them a natural power of divinity' – power to attract the divine into a statue and bring it to life. The Hermetic author praises the mortals who can fashion their gods in this way, though the gods involved are not the highest, only those 'content to be near to humans'. Only lower divinities could be attracted by the material makings of an idol: that much was clear from the *Enneads* of Plotinus by the time the Latin *Asclepius* was composed around 400 CE.

Iamblichus, next in the line of Neoplatonic masters after Plotinus and Porphyry, was harder on the idol-makers, charging that the life in their statues was not demonic at all, merely the stirring of 'depraved spirits'. Idols are bodies and copies of copies, violating the most basic norms of Platonism.

Iamblichus responded by denouncing what the *Asclepius* glorified as 'god-making', developing his polemic in an intricate hierarchy of divinity – a Neoplatonic demonology that shows how 'a demon differs from a hero and a soul', while also classifying other superhuman persons as angels, archangels and archons.

Properly understood and regarded, beneficent spirits bring health to the body, virtue to the soul and purity to the mind, giving distinct gifts that help humans tell the givers apart. These graded divinities descend to our material world in various manifestations, illuminating earth's darkness in varying degree. Higher powers are simpler than lower ones, also more orderly and calmer: tranquillity trumps energy. But the arrival of a demon, inferior to other spirits, 'makes the body heavy, punishes it with diseases, and drags the soul down to nature . . . never freeing people from Fate's chains'.

To be dragged down to nature is what no philosopher wants, and philosophy alone will not help. The sage needs gods too high to be attracted by demonstrative or dialectical reason – the tools of theological god-talk. Only ritual god-work – theurgy – will do the job, so Iamblichus insists. This theurgy is not idol-making, however, not the statue-magic of the *Asclepius*. And yet, to get the divine work started here on earth, the theurgist will use physical objects like the 'plants, stones and spices' of that text. Iamblichus classifies such natural objects, which are also magical objects, as the 'signs', 'symbols' and 'tokens' that connect the theurgist with the gods by starting an ascent to the supercelestials.

And this is the crux of what Iamblichus teaches: the signs themselves are self-efficacious. 'Even when we are not thinking,' he writes, 'the tokens have the same special effect by themselves. And the undescribable power of the gods, to which the tokens are connected, *on its own* – not because *our thinking* rouses it – recognizes the images that belong to it.' Magic is always all around us, requiring no one's attention or intention – neither from us nor from the gods. Just as a heliotrope turns towards the sun, with never a thought, and just as the sun gives life to the plant, without any effort, magic is always already there, energizing the magus and linking his god-work with the gods. But the gods too are always already there, meaning that Nature's spontaneous magic can never be impersonal, never absolutely detached from divinities or their souls or their minds. And this eliminates the possibility of a purely natural magic without personal agency.

Proclus, the last great voice of ancient Neoplatonism, agrees that magic is natural 'from the sympathy that all visible things have for one another and for the invisible powers'. Writing before the end of the fifth century, he distils the theories invented by his school, calling those ideas 'priestly' because they teach about the gods: since 'the invisible powers' are divine persons, the magic that addresses them cannot be entirely natural, even though it starts with natural objects and can be understood by analogy with physical processes.

One such operation shows how 'ancient wise men brought divine powers into the region of mortals, attracting them through likeness, which . . . is sufficient to join beings to one another'. To grasp how likeness links heaven's heights with our world below, we may contemplate a wick, heated and then lit by a flame above it that never touches it, just as the gods never defile themselves by contact with mortals, who ascend beyond the skies in the blaze of their enduring kinship with the heavens. Natural sympathies – spontaneous, never intentional, yet never impersonal – activate and sustain this reverent theurgy.

The crucial sympathies are always at hand in stones, plants and animals seen everywhere, the same physical things used by physicians like Galen and studied by philosophers like Aristotle. 'Flax-leaved daphne is enough for a manifestation,' according to Proclus, meaning a spirit's 'manifestation' as specified by Iamblichus. Then Proclus points out that 'laurel, box-thorn, squill, coral, diamond or jasper will do for a guardian spirit, but for foreknowledge one needs the heart of a mole and for purification sulphur and salt water'. Embodied earthbound things, despite their entombment in matter, are means to higher ends of ritual purity, divination and theurgy. This was what the ancients taught: 'Mixing some things together and setting others apart . . . while leaving nature and natural energies below, they had dealings with the primary and divine powers.'

A Philosopher and an Honest Man:
Philostratus, *Life of Apollonius*, 1.1–2

Apollonius of Tyana, a 'Pythagorean' wise man and wonder-worker from eastern Asia Minor, was active until the end of the first century CE, at least. For two centuries more, he kept attracting devoted followers: pagan critics of Christianity could cite his astonishing deeds as proof that Jesus was nothing special (see 2.9–12). The fictionalized account of his career by the sophist Philostratus, written before 244 CE or a little earlier, assembles the legends and claims to be based on original records. Julia Domna, Caracalla's mother, commissioned this flashy *Life*: since Julia died by suicide in 217, Apollonius had been famous for a long time. Muslims remembered him even later as the sorcerer Balinas. When Philostratus insists that his hero's exotic wisdom and amazing feats had nothing to do with magic, he links him with Democritus and other philosophers who – according to the author – were likewise misunderstood (see 4.13–14, 16). Philostratus also sees Apollonius as a revolutionary whose righteous asceticism annoyed degenerate tyrants like Nero.

*

The companions of Pythagoras treated as law whatever their master revealed, honouring him as having been sent by Zeus, though silence about the divine was their rule for themselves. For they had heard many divine lessons that were not to be spoken . . . There is much else to say about those who philosophized like Pythagoras, but I must not go into this now, while moving on with the account that I mean to give.

Akin to their practices were those of Apollonius, whose approach to wisdom was a victory over tyrants and more divine than the Pythagorean way. Though he lived neither long ago nor only yesterday, people do not know him for the true wisdom that he practised as a philosopher and an honest man. One praises him for this, another for that, while some – because he associated with the Magi of Babylon and the Brahmans of India and the naked sages in

Egypt – consider him a magus and slander him as an abuser of wisdom. But this is a mistake.

Empedocles and Pythagoras himself and Democritus kept company with magi and described many marvels without yielding to the art. Plato went to Egypt too and – like a painter colouring a sketch – mixed much of what he heard there from prophets and priests into his own teachings. And yet, though he more than anyone was resented for his wisdom, Plato was not seen as a magus. Apollonius, who foresaw and foreknew many things, should not be suspected of that type of wisdom, or else Socrates should also be a suspect because of the foreknowledge that he had from his guardian spirit – and Anaxagoras too with his predictions . . .

People who ascribe these feats to the wisdom of Anaxagoras would rob Apollonius of using wisdom to make his predictions, claiming that he produced them by the art of a magus. It seems to me, then, that I should not overlook the ignorance of many but should give an accurate account of the man, noting the times when he said or did something, and also the sort of wisdom for which he won the reputation of someone inspired and divine.

A Thunderbolt Struck the Table:
Philostratus, *Life of Apollonius*, 4.42–5

Philostratus sets this story in 66 CE, when Nero – 'mad about magic', according to Pliny (see 4.14) – had been on the throne for twelve years, and his low-born praetorian prefect from Sicily, Ofonius Tigellinus, had slaughtered his way to high imperial honours. Meanwhile, Demetrius, Telesinus and Menippus, disciples of Apollonius, were posing as Cynic philosophers and provoked the authorities by ostentatiously despising power and wealth – even in the Emperor's presence. Most of the chapter describes conflicts between Tigellinus and Apollonius, as the holy man tries desperately to manage his students. Philostratus also tacks on a miracle narrative whose details parallel the raising of the daughter of Jairus in the Gospel of Mark (see 2.7).

*

In my discussion of Corinth, I mentioned how Demetrius felt about Apollonius. Later, when Demetrius got to Rome, he paid court to Apollonius while attacking Nero, and the result was to bring everything under suspicion as if it were that great man's stratagem – putting Demetrius up to it, apparently – and the doubts multiplied when Nero finished building a gymnasium that was the city's most astonishing sight. Nero himself, with the Senate and the knights of Rome, was celebrating the happy day when Demetrius swept right by them into the gymnasium to deliver a speech against bathers as limp dicks and wankers, pointing out besides that it was all wasteful extravagance.

After what Demetrius said, the only thing saving him from instant death was that Nero was in excellent voice that day and sang well: he put on a show in a tavern next to the gym, naked down to the knickers like the biggest bum in the bar. But Demetrius could not avoid the backwash from his own rash words. Tigellinus, Nero's sword man, threw him out of Rome because what he had said totally destroyed the bathhouse. He also quietly put a tail on Apollonius, on the chance that he too would say something careless and incriminating.

Apollonius showed no sign either of laughing this off or of dwelling on it, like someone on guard against a threat. He just kept talking about the problems put before him, giving them the attention needed while he discussed philosophy with Telesinus and other people. They did not suppose, even though philosophy was a risky business at the time, that they were taking any risk by studying with him. But he was under suspicion, as I said, all the more because of remarks he made about a sign from heaven.

During an eclipse of the sun, a clap of thunder rolled out – rare in an eclipse, it seems. He then looked up at the sky and said, 'Something great will happen and will not happen.' Those present when he said this could not make sense of his words at first, but everyone had put the meaning together by the third day after the eclipse. While Nero was having his dinner, a thunderbolt had struck the table, breaking apart the cup that was in his hands and not far from his mouth. When Nero was almost hit, it was just as Apollonius had said – something done and not done.

Tigellinus heard the story and started to fear Apollonius as an expert on the spirit world. While thinking he must not bring charges against our master in any visible way – wishing not to be hurt by him in some invisible way – he still turned upon him all the eyes that government sees with. Whether Apollonius was talking or keeping quiet, sitting or walking, Tigellinus observed what he ate and with whom and whether he sacrificed or did not sacrifice.

Just then a sickness struck Rome: physicians named it 'runny nose', complicated by a cough, evidently, and hoarseness if you tried to talk. The temples were full of people supplicating the gods because Nero's throat was swollen and his voice was rough. And Apollonius exploded at the crowd's foolishness, though without striking any one person. He even calmed Menippus down and restrained him when all this got him worked up, urging him to forgive the gods if they found clown-acts entertaining. What he said was soon reported to Tigellinus, who had him hauled into court to answer a charge of impiety against Nero.

To his case they assigned a prosecutor who had already destroyed many people in a string of show trials as grand as the Olympics. He held a document in his hands with the charge written on it, waving it at the master like a sword and saying he had sharpened it enough to kill him. But when Tigellinus unrolled the document, there was not a trace of writing on it – this totally blank book – making him think that a demon had removed the words . . .

Making everyone leave, he pressed Apollonius with questions, asking, 'Who are you?' Apollonius named his father and his country and said why he pursued wisdom, declaring that he did this to gain knowledge of the gods and understand human beings since knowing others is harder than knowing oneself. 'And the demons, Apollonius,' he asked, 'and the phantoms that appear: how do you put them to the question?' 'Just as I would question murderers and people guilty of impiety,' he answered, bantering with Tigellinus, who had been Nero's instructor in cruelty and mindless violence of every kind.

'Would you do some divination for me,' asked Tigellinus, 'if I requested it?' 'How could I,' he replied, 'since I'm not a diviner?' But Tigellinus responded: 'Isn't it you they report as saying "something great will happen and will not happen"?' 'What you've heard is true,' he said. 'But don't ascribe this to divination: it's the wisdom that God reveals to men who are wise.' 'Then why are you not afraid of Nero?' he asked, and Apollonius said, 'Because the God who made him look frightful also gave me the gift of fearlessness.' Then the other asked, 'What do you think of Nero?' 'I think better of him than you think,' Apollonius replied, 'since the lot of you think it fitting for him to sing, while I think that silence is suitable.'

This shocked Tigellinus. 'Get out,' he said, 'but station people here to guarantee your physical presence!' And then Apollonius asked, 'Who guarantees a person's presence if no chains can hold him?' The reply struck Tigellinus as a demon's work and far more than human. As if wary of doing battle with divinity, he said, 'Go where you like: you're too much for me to handle!'

And this is a wonder worked by Apollonius.

After a girl had apparently died just at the moment of her wedding, the bridegroom was following the bier – in full mourning for an unconsummated marriage, and Rome mourned with him because the girl's family had risen to the highest rank. Coming upon this suffering, Apollonius said, 'Set the bier down. I will end your tears for the girl,' at the same time asking, 'What's her name?' Most people thought he was going to give a speech as they do at funerals to stir up the weeping. He did nothing like that, however, just touching her and saying something secret to wake the girl up from her apparent death. The child spoke out loud and – like Alcestis revived by Hercules – returned to her father's house. The girl's relatives wanted to give him 150,000, but he said this was his gift to the child as additional dowry.

Now whether he found some spark of life in her that had escaped the notice of those who were caring for her – for although the sky was drizzling, they say, vapour came from her face – or whether her soul was cold and gone and he warmed it up again and brought her back, the explanation of this is beyond telling, not just by me but by those who were there.

5.3

Totally Unsolvable Problems: Alexander of Aphrodisias, *Problems*, prologue

Aristotle's *Problems*, a long, anecdotal miscellany about natural and other phenomena and their causes, lacks the systematic character of most of the philosopher's writing. Since the content also suggests a more credulous author, the *Problems* or parts of them have sometimes been excluded from the genuine works – likewise the studies of the *Problems* attributed to Alexander of Aphrodisias. Writing around 200 CE, Alexander was the most loyal of the commentators to Aristotle's naturalism, a commitment consistent with the 'endless list' at the end of this prologue, where all but one of the possible explanations is physical or arguably so – and that single exception ('confusion about names') is taxonomical (see 5.12). But Alexander also mentions 'undescribable properties' that are harder to fit into conventional Aristotelian natural philosophy or Galenic medicine: some commonly observed phenomena – magnetism, static electricity, electric fish, erratic poisons, odd animal behaviour – seemed to confirm such properties, which had a long afterlife in medicine and philosophy (see 5.14).

*

Some of the problems are obviously credible and well understood, with no trace of ambiguity or doubt. Tell me this: would anyone with good sense make an issue of why nature gave feathers to winged things? Any intelligent person would say that the feathers are mainly a covering to provide warmth and take the place of a cloak, while beauty comes second . . . But other problems are totally unsolvable and understood by God alone – by the one who causes the thing's essence to exist. For the craftsman who has built some clever work also knows all the causes that make it work, while the ordinary person knows nothing at all about those causes.

Such questions are intractable. Why do people laugh when tickled at the armpits, soles or ribs? Why do some people grit their teeth as soon as they hear pieces of marble rubbed together or sawed or iron scraping or being filed? Why is it that when cold fruit has set your teeth on edge, relief comes from purslane, which itself is cold by nature, making this not a case of curing something with its opposite since these are alike? Or why does the lodestone attract only iron, and why is it that iron filings bring the stone to life? Why does the stone called 'amber' attract only chaff and straws and make them stick to it?

Also, the lion fears only the cock, while the domestic hen that lays eggs cleans herself with straw all over her body. Quail feed on the hellebore that poisons humans. Starlings eat hemlock. But why does bindweed draw out yellow bile, while squash, tree fungus, white hellebore, spurge and flax-leaved daphne draw out phlegm, and black hellebore and dodder draw out black bile? Some who are constipated in the belly by purgatives are purged by binders. One person enjoys a full meal more than another and digests it better. Does anyone not know the sea-stunner and how it numbs the body through a fishing line? Yet a red mullet held in the hand counteracts the stunning.

And I might give you an endless list of such items, known only from experience, which the physicians call 'undescribable properties'. For the so-called 'undescribable' that is said to belong to each such thing goes towards explaining the causes. Some do a wretched job when they lay out countless solutions for such problems, all mixed up and unconvincing . . . They say that the ostrich digests iron, for example, and not by some property but rather by heat, which is absurd, because a lion is hotter than this animal and does not digest iron. Not only physicians but also philosophers and grammarians have their own special properties so that they can classify what they call 'effects' by the uses made of them.

Our job, then, is to undertake an enquiry about the intermediate cases, which are still not certainly known but are capable of solution. Some claims are said to be false and are recognized by everyone; all the true claims are already accessible to demonstrative reasoning; but there are others that someone may call a mix of both . . . All the problems that have solutions are resolved by temperament, conformation, activity, by sympathy between similars, colour, deception of the senses, confusion about names, by increase or decrease in the effectiveness of powers, by being more or less dense or loose or larger or smaller, or by time, phase of life and behaviour, by matters of substance or of accident, or by similarity: these you will find discussed in the problems.

An Indwelling Spirit of the More Divine Degree: Porphyry, *Life of Plotinus*

Porphyry, who followed Plotinus in the Platonic succession, was born in Syria. His teacher, who came from Egypt and had travelled as far east as Syria, did his most important philosophical work in Rome, teaching there until he left the city to die in 270, when Hellenic pagans felt threatened by the new Gnostic and Christian cults (see 5.7). Plotinus 'seemed ashamed of being in the body', Porphyry tells us: his master's personal asceticism flowed from his philosophy, whose ingredients were eclectic but whose soul was thoroughly Platonic. Gods, demons and other spirits populate his universe, whose poles are the immaterial above and the material below, with everything between graded according to its greater or lesser reliance on matter (see 5.10). He and his students – thinkers of great sophistication – took magic seriously: some practised and feared it. Their master's attitude towards magic, as towards everything else, depended on how material it was. He saw it as a distraction, at best, and at worst sinful and repulsive.

*

Plotinus the philosopher, our contemporary, seemed ashamed of being in the body. So deeply rooted was this feeling that he could never be induced to tell of his ancestry, his parentage, or his birthplace . . .

He was often distressed by an intestinal complaint but declined enemas, pronouncing the use of such remedies unbecoming in an elderly man. In the same way he refused such medicaments as contain any substance taken from wild beasts or reptiles: all the more, he remarked, since he could not approve of eating the flesh of animals reared for the table. He abstained from the use of the bath, and . . . in a short while he contracted malign diphtheria. During the time I was with him, there was no sign of any such malady, but after . . . my return to Rome he became hoarse, so that his voice quite lost its clear and sonorous note, his sight grew dim and ulcers formed on his hands and feet.

As he still insisted on addressing everyone by word of mouth, his condition prompted his friends to withdraw from his company: he therefore left Rome for Campania . . . Of his last moments Eustochius has given me an account . . . 'I have been a long time waiting for you,' Plotinus said, 'I am striving to give back the Divine in myself to the Divine in the All.' As he spoke a snake crept under the bed on which he lay and slipped away into a hole in the wall: at the same moment Plotinus died . . .

Despite his general reluctance to speak of his own life, he often related some few details to us in the course of conversation . . . At twenty-seven he was caught by the passion for philosophy: he was directed to the most highly reputed professors to be found at Alexandria, and . . . he followed Ammonius continuously, under his guidance making such progress in philosophy that he became eager to investigate the Persian methods and the system adopted among the Indians. It happened that the Emperor Gordian was at that time preparing his campaign against Persia: Plotinus joined the army and went on the expedition. He was then thirty-eight, for he had passed eleven whole years under Ammonius. When Gordian was killed in Mesopotamia, it was only with great difficulty that Plotinus came off safe to Antioch.

At forty, in the reign of Philip, he settled in Rome . . . In the tenth year of Gallienus, when he was about fifty-nine, I first met him when I was thirty . . . He had a large following . . . and I myself, Porphyry of Tyre, was one of his very closest friends: it was to me he entrusted the task of revising his writings . . .

Among those making profession of philosophy at Rome was one Olympius, an Alexandrian, who had been for a little while a pupil of Ammonius. This man's jealous envy showed itself in continual insolence, and finally he grew so bitter that he even ventured sorcery, seeking to crush Plotinus by star-casting. But he found his experiments recoiling upon himself, and he confessed to his associates that Plotinus possessed 'a mighty soul, so powerful as to be able to hurl every assault back upon those that sought his ruin'. Plotinus had sensed the activity and declared that at that moment Olympius was 'convulsed in his limbs and his body shrivelled like a money-bag pulled tight'. Olympius, perceiving on several attempts that he was endangering himself rather than Plotinus, desisted.

In fact, Plotinus possessed by birth something more than is granted to other men. An Egyptian priest who had arrived in Rome and, through some friend, had been presented to the philosopher became desirous of displaying his powers to him, and he offered to evoke a visible manifestation of the spirit that watched over Plotinus. He readily consented, and the evocation was made in the Temple of Isis – the only pure place, they say, that the Egyptian could find in Rome.

At the summons a divinity appeared, not a being of the spirit-ranks, and the Egyptian exclaimed: 'You are singularly graced: the guiding spirit within you is not of the lower degree but a god.' Yet it was not possible to interrogate or even to contemplate this god any further: the priest's assistant, who had been holding the sacrificial birds to prevent them flying away, strangled them, whether through jealousy or in terror. Thus Plotinus had for indwelling spirit a Being of the more divine degree, and he kept his own divine spirit unceasingly intent upon that inner presence. It was this preoccupation that led him to write his treatise on *Our Tutelary Spirit*, an essay in the explanation of the differences among spirit-guides.

Amelius, who was scrupulous in observing the day of the new moon and other holy days, once asked Plotinus to join in some such celebration. But Plotinus refused: 'It is for those Beings to come to me, not for me to go to them.' What was in his mind in so lofty an utterance we could not explain to ourselves and we dared not ask him . . .

He followed his own path rather than tradition, but in his writings both the Stoic and Peripatetic doctrines are sunk: Aristotle's metaphysics, especially, is condensed in them, all but entire . . . Once on Plato's feast I read a poem on *The Sacred Marriage*. My piece abounded in mystic doctrine conveyed in veiled words and couched in terms of enthusiasm. Someone exclaimed: 'Porphyry has gone mad.' But Plotinus said to me so that all might hear: 'You have shown yourself at once poet, philosopher and hierophant.' . . .

He paid some attention to the principles of astronomy, though he did not study the subject very deeply on the mathematical side. He went more searchingly into horoscopy: once he was convinced that its results were not to be trusted, he had no hesitation in attacking the system frequently both at conferences and in his writings.

Many Christians of this period – among them sectaries who had abandoned the old philosophy . . . – had possessed themselves of . . . revelations bearing the names of Zoroaster, Zostrianus, Nicotheus, Allogenes, Mesus and others of that order. Thus they fooled many, having fooled themselves first. Plato, according to them, had failed to penetrate into the depth of Intellectual Being. Plotinus frequently attacked their position at the conferences and finally wrote the treatise that I have headed *Against the Gnostics*. He left to us of his circle the task of examining what he himself passed over. Amelius proceeded . . . with a refutation of the book of Zostrianus, and I myself have shown on many counts that the Zoroastrian volume is spurious and modern, concocted by the sectaries in order to pretend that the doctrines they had embraced were those of the ancient sage . . .

Apollo was consulted by Amelius, who desired to learn where the soul of Plotinus had gone . . . You shall hear what a full and lofty oracle Apollo produced about Plotinus . . .

Good and kindly, singularly gentle and engaging: thus the oracle presents him, and so in fact we found him. Sleeplessly alert – says Apollo – pure of soul, ever striving towards the divine that he loved with all his being, he laboured strenuously to free himself and rise above the bitter waves of this blood-drenched life. And this is why to Plotinus, godlike and lifting himself often – by ways of meditation and by methods that Plato teaches in the *Symposium* – to the first and all-transcendent God, that God appeared, the God who has neither shape nor form but sits enthroned above the Intellectual-Principle and all the Intellectual-Sphere.

'There was shown to Plotinus the Term ever near': for the Term, the one goal, of his life was to become uniate, to approach to the God over all. And four times, during the period I passed with him, he achieved this Term, by no mere latent fitness but by the ineffable act. To this God, I also declare, I Porphyry, that in my sixty-eighth year I too was once admitted and I entered into union.

We are told that often, when he was leaving the way, the gods set him on the true path again, pouring down before him a dense shaft of light: here we are to understand that in his writing he was overseen and guided by divine powers . . . Thus far the Oracle recounts what Plotinus accomplished and to what heights he attained while still in the body. When he was emancipated from the body, we are told how he entered the celestial circle where all is friendship, tender delight, happiness and loving union with God, where . . . the sons of God are enthroned as judges of souls – not, however, to hold him to judgement but as welcoming him to their company to which are bidden spirits pleasing to the gods: Plato, Pythagoras, and all the people of the choir of immortal Love, there where the blessed spirits have their birth-home and live in days filled full of 'joyous festival' and made happy by the gods.

5.5
The Reigning Sympathy:
Plotinus, *Enneads*, 4.4.40–44

Plotinus gives a philosophical account of magic – its metaphysical basis as well as its physical and moral effects and limitations. A fundamental principle is that anything with 'membership in the All may be affected by another member', making magic – like Newton's gravity – a universal force. But magic is also organic, never lifeless or mechanical. Its energies are natural sympathies and antipathies in a living cosmic organism – like the power of Love as Plato described it (see 4.4–5). Belonging to Nature, magic stays within the natural cosmos, never rising above that goddess to the hypercosmic heights. Confined by her to the bottom of the All, magical power works in humans only on the soul's lower, embodied parts, never controlling the reason or the will. Yet magical forces are always already there for humans to find, just as the gods are there, working on lower beings in ways that those divinities never notice nor intend: 'the giver does not know of the gift but simply gives' (see 5.10). Since magical action is divine, it cannot be impersonal though it operates spontaneously, like resonance in music or one organ affecting another in an organism, where nothing is merely local: 'everything that looks to another is under spell to that other'. Plotinus dispels the dread of Nature's sorcery, however, assuring us that 'no man self-gathered falls to a spell'.

*

But magic spells: how can their efficacy be explained? By the reigning sympathy and by the fact in nature that there is an agreement of like forces and an opposition of unlike, and by the diversity of those multitudinous powers that converge in the one living universe. There is much drawing and spell-binding dependent on no interfering machination: the true magic is internal to the All, its attractions and, not less, its repulsions. Here is the primal mage and sorcerer – discovered by men who thenceforth turn those same ensorcellations and magic arts upon one another.

Love is given in Nature: the qualities inducing love induce mutual approach;

hence there has arisen an art of magic love-drawing whose practitioners, by force of contact, implant in others a new temperament, one that favours union as being informed with love. They knit soul to soul as they might train two separate trees towards each other. The magician too draws on these patterns of power and, by ranging himself also into the pattern, is able tranquilly to possess himself of these forces with whose nature and purpose he has become identified. Supposing the magus to stand outside the All, his evocations and invocations would no longer avail to draw up or to call down. But as things are, he operates from no outside standground. He pulls knowing the pull of everything towards any other thing in the living system.

The tune of an incantation, a significant cry, the gesture of the operator: these too have a natural leading power over the soul at which they are directed, drawing it with the force of mournful patterns or tragic sounds. For it is the reasonless soul, not the will or wisdom, that is beguiled by music, a form of sorcery that raises no question, whose enchantment, in fact, is welcomed and exacted from the performers.

Similarly with regard to prayers: there is no question of a will granting something. The powers that answer to incantations do not act by will: a human being entranced by a snake has neither perception nor sensation of what is happening; he knows only after he has been caught, and his highest mind is never caught. From the Being addressed, in other words, some influence falls upon the petitioner – or upon someone else – but that Being itself, sun or star, perceives nothing of it all.

The prayer is answered by the mere fact that one part and another are wrought to one tone like a musical string which, plucked at one end, vibrates at the other also. Often too, the sounding of one string awakens what might pass for a perception in another, the result of their being in harmony and tuned to one musical scale. Now if the vibration in a lyre affects another by virtue of the sympathy existing between them, then certainly in the All – even though it is made of contraries – there must be one melodic system, for it contains its unisons as well, and its entire content, even to those contraries, is a kinship . . .

The stars have no need of memory or of any sense of petitions addressed to them. They give no such voluntary attention to prayers as some have thought. It is enough, simply in the nature of parts and of parts within a whole, that something proceeds from them whether in answer to prayer or without prayer. We have the analogy of many powers – as in some one living organism – which, independently of plan or as the result of applied method, act without any collaboration of the will. One organ or function is helped or hurt by another in the mere play of natural forces. And the art of doctor or magic healer will compel some one centre to purvey something of its own power to another centre. Just so the All: it purveys spontaneously, but it purveys also under spell.

Some entity is concerned for a member situated within itself and summons the All which, then, pours in its gift . . . The giver does not know of the gift but simply gives, though we must remember that all is one woof and the giving is always consonant with the order of the universe . . . We must hold that the All cannot be affected: its leading principle remains for ever immune, whatsoever happens to its members . . . Thus the stars, in so far as they are parts, can be affected and yet are immune on various counts. Their will, like that of the All, is untouched, just as their bodies and their characteristic natures are beyond all reach of harm. If they give by means of their souls, their souls lose nothing. Their bodies remain unchanged or, if there is ebb or inflow, it is of something going unfelt and coming unawares.

And the sage, how does he stand with regard to magic and love-spells?

In the soul he is immune from magic: his reasoning part cannot be touched by it, he cannot be perverted. But there is in him the unreasoning element that comes from the All, and in this he can be affected, or rather this can be affected in him. Enchanted love, however, he will not know, for that would require the consent of the higher soul to the trouble stirred in the lower. And just as the unreasoning element responds to the call of incantation, so the adept himself will dissolve those horrible powers by counter-incantations. Death, disease, any experience within the material sphere, these may result, yes: for anything that has membership in the All may be affected by another member, or by the universe of members. But the essential man is beyond harm . . .

Even the celestials, the demons, are not on their unreasoning side immune. There is nothing against ascribing acts of memory and experiences of sense to them, in supposing them to accept the traction of methods laid up in the natural order, and to give hearing to petitioners. This is especially true of those closest to this sphere, and in the degree of their concern about it.

For everything that looks to another is under spell to that other: what we look to, that draws us magically. Only the self-intent go free of magic. Hence every action has magic as its source, and the entire life of the practical man is a bewitchment. We move to what has wrought a fascination upon us . . . Now what conceivably turns a man to the external? He is drawn, drawn by the arts not of magicians but of the natural order that administers the deceiving drink and links this to that, not in local contact but in the fellowship of the love-spell.

Contemplation alone stands untouched by magic: no man self-gathered falls to a spell, for he is one, and that unity is all he perceives, so that his reason is not beguiled but holds the due course, fashioning its own career and accomplishing its task . . . But when the agent falls in love with what the good is in his actions, and, cheated by the mere track and trace of the Authentic Good, makes them his own, then, in his pursuit of a lower good, he is the victim of magic. For all dalliance with what wears the mask of the Authentic, all attraction towards that mere semblance, tells of a mind misled by the spell of forces pulling towards unreality. The sorcery of nature is at work in this: to pursue the non-good as a good, drawn in unreasoning impulse by its specious appearance, it is to be led unknowing down paths unchosen. And what can we call that but magic?

5.6
Artful, Shape-shifting Hell-dweller: Greek Magical Papyri, 4.2708–84

The Greek Magical Papyri, manufactured in Egypt during the first seven centuries CE, contain nearly six hundred spells for every conceivable purpose. Like the love-spell from the fourth century given here, they were on sale for use as needed, often by inserting someone's name into a recipe that gives two instructions: what to do and what to say (see 5.12). Addressing gods and demons (Selene/Hecate/Artemis in this case; see Fig. 6) with litanies of names, titles and attributes, many spells invoke a divine presence, often with words meant to seem powerful, especially in Egypt's polyglot culture, because they were unintelligible – ancient hocus-pocus. Some of this concocted language, like *maskelli maskellô*, is formulaic, repeated in many spells. The gibberish may have some meaning, however: parted gates, a threshing floor, eruptions and sleepless fire chime with this love-spell, where labile divine virginity anticipates human sexuality. Although Artemis is a 'holy virgin', the maiden huntress familiar from mythology, here she is also the many-breasted Artemis of Ephesus, the fertility goddess sketched crudely in another papyrus (see 2.6).

*

Another love-spell: Take Ethiopian cumin, fat from a spotted goat – unmated – put the offering together and offer it to Selene on days thirteen and fourteen with coals in a burner made of earth, high on a housetop.

The spell: Here, Hecate, come – giantess and guardian of Dione, Persian, Belly-Bird, arrow-shooter, unwedded, Lydian, untamed, nobly fathered, torch-bearer, Queen, bender of stiff necks, Daughter. Hear me, you parter of gates of indestructible steel, Artemis, who used to watch over us, mightiest Mistress, erupter from the earth, dog-leader, all-subduer, she of the crossroads, three-headed, light-bringer, holy virgin, thee I call, fawn-slayer, artful, shape-shifting hell-dweller: come, three-wayed Hecate, with fire-breathing spectres assigned to bad roads and risky spells, thee, Hecate, I call thee with those who died too early and with heroes who died unwifed and childless, hissing fiercely with anger in their hearts . . .

Standing over the head of _____, steal sweet sleep from her, never let one eyelid stick to the other, and let her feel the pain of waking and worrying about me. But if she holds another lying on her breasts, make her push him away, take me into her heart, forsake him immediately and stand at my door, her soul submissive and in the mood to make love to me. But you, Hecate of the many names, virgin Daughter and goddess, come to my call, shelter and protector of the threshing floor, fire-walking, three-headed, cow-eyed Persephone – BOUORPHORBÊ, the all-feeding PHORBARA, AKTIÔPHI, Ereschigal, NEBOUTOSOUALÊTH by the doors, PUPULÊDEDEDZÔ and gate-breaker: come, Hecate, with your will of fire, I call you to my enchantments   –   MASKELLI   MASKELLÔ!   PHNOUKENTABAÔTH, OREOBAZAGRA, earth-breaking earthsteed, OREOPÊGANUX, MORMORON, TOKOUMBAI (and so on).

Let _____ come to my door right away, frenzied, forgetting children and the company of parents and despising the whole human race, all men and women, except me, and let _____ be there to hold me alone, submissive in her heart from love's fierce need.

THENÔB, TITHELÊB, ÊNÔR, TENTHÊNÔR – the many-named – KUZALEOUSA PADZAOUS, so that KALLIDÊCHMA and SAB shall set the soul of _____ ablaze with the fire that cannot sleep. Orion too and the high-seated Michael: you rule the seven waters and the earth, holding back him that they call the Great Dragon, AKROKODÊRE MOUISRÔ CHARCHAR, ADÔNAI – Zeus, in fact – DAMNAMENEUS Doglife EZAGRA (and so on). iô almighty and iô all-guarding, iô all-nurturing, ZÊLACHNA and SAAD SABIÔTHÊ, NOUMILLON NATHOMEINA, ever KEINÊTH, stout Theseus, a talon, thoughtful DAMNAMENEUS, avenging, mighty goddess and ghost-rite, Persia, SEBARA AKRA, hurry, come fast and let her now be at my door.

5·7
The Holy Books of Hermes:
Zosimos, *On the Letter* Ω

Around 300 CE, as some of the Magical Papyri were pasted together, the first records of alchemy to preserve more than recipes were written by an Egyptian, Zosimos of Panopolis. His fragment *On the Letter* Ω has that title because it introduces a series of notes on alchemical technique classified by the author under *omega*, the last letter of the Greek alphabet. The introduction records a dispute about alchemical apparatus for making tinctures – transmuted substances or agents of transmutation – and using the astrology of Times or constellations (see 4.15; 5.8). *The Letter* Ω reflects religious upheavals, as Christians competed with Jews, Gnostics and Hellenized Egyptian pagans (see 5.4). Before the letter to Theosebeia actually opens, a note introduces an antithesis – embodied v. disembodied, another message of the 'two-parted' *omega* – as a principle of alchemy: transmutation works when dematerialized properties are extracted and detached from a thing's body, seen as bare matter or a featureless substrate, which can then accept different properties, the most obvious being colour. By analogy, the human spirit escapes from the body, where Fate has trapped it, in order to be redeemed (see 5.9). Preferring a liberated spirit to the entombing flesh provoked debates about salvation, thus stimulating interest in Zoroaster, Moses, Hermes, Jesus and other saviours (see 3.7; 4.14). Prominent in the excitement were biblical figures from Adam to the Antichrist, who were alchemical as well as personal agents for Zosimos.

*

The round letter Ω is the two-parted one, the one that rises up to the seventh zone of Kronos, according to the embodied way of speaking, for according to the disembodied way it is different and inexplicable, known only to Nikotheos, the hidden one. Spoken in the embodied way, 'Ocean is the origin and seed,' it says, 'of all the gods,' exactly as stated by the principles that rule the embodied way of speaking. But the expression 'great and wondrous letter Ω' covers the account of apparatus for sulphur water, of all the furnaces – both mechanical and simple – and, simply put, of everything.

Zosimos to Theosebeia: be well always! Deep tinctures well timed, my lady, have made a mockery of the book *On Furnaces*. Many who have had success with the timings when a guardian demon helps them have even mocked the book *On Furnaces and Apparatus* as not being correct. And no account has ever proved that this is the truth and persuaded them – unless their guardian demon says so. And yet, to suit the Times as their Fate changes, the spirit possessing these people is hateful. Hence, with craft and good fortune completely closed to them, as their sayings go both ways randomly, they agree only grudgingly – once their Fate has made things plain – that there is something more to this than they had thought!

Neither God nor the philosophical can accept such people, however. Watching every second, once the figured stars have turned favourable in their Times and the demon treats their bodies well, they give in and change back again, having forgotten how plain everything used to be. They always let Fate lead them, first to one account, then to its opposite. Anything not bodily they cannot imagine – only Fate. Hermes calls such people 'mindless' in his book *On Natures*: they just walk along in Fate's parade, never imagining anything that is not embodied nor even realizing that Fate herself drives them on, and rightly so. No, they speak ill of her lessons about bodily things, imagining nothing beyond the happiness that comes from her.

But Hermes and Zoroaster have said that philosophers are in a class higher than Fate: they keep pleasures under control, never delighting in her happiness; since their path is always inward, her evils cannot hurt them; and looking forward to an end of evils, they take none of Fate's glittering prizes. For this reason Hesiod also brings Prometheus in to advise Epimetheus: 'What do humans suppose is the greatest happiness of all?' 'A shapely woman,' he answers, 'and much wealth.' And Prometheus tells him not to take any gift from Zeus on Olympus, but to refuse and leave it alone, learning from his own brother – through philosophy – to refuse the gifts of Zeus: of Fate, in other words.

Zoroaster claims presumptuously that all Fate's evils – particular and universal both – are averted by understanding all the higher things and by the magic of embodied speech. And yet Hermes, writing *On the Inward*, attacks magic as well, claiming that the spiritual person, once he has found himself, has no need to set anything straight with magic – even if this is considered good – nor to use force against Necessity. Instead, in the natural course of events, he should proceed only by searching for himself, and then, having come to know God, he masters the nameless Triad, even if Fate does as she wants with the clay that belongs to her – his body, in other words.

Having thought and lived freely in this way, says Hermes, 'You will see the Son of God become the All for the sake of holy souls so that he can pull the soul out of the region of Fate into the unbodily. Look: he becomes everything – a god, an angel, a suffering human! Capable of all that he wishes, he also submits to the Father by dissolving through every body. Illuminating each soul's mind, he pushes it up to the region of happiness, where it lived even before being born into the body, and there it follows him, reaching out for him, guided into that Light.'

And in the tablet that Bitos too has written – also the thrice-great Plato and Hermes surpassingly great – notice that the interpretation of *Thoth*, in the original priestly speech, is 'original human', interpreter of all things and maker of names for everything bodily. The Chaldaeans, Parthians, Medes and Hebrews call him Adam, translated as 'virgin earth', 'bloodlike earth', 'flame-coloured earth' and 'earth of the flesh'. You can find this in the libraries of the Ptolemies: in each temple – notably the Serapeion – they put a tablet away at the time when Asenas, High Priest of Jerusalem, was called upon to send Hermes, who translated all the Hebrew into Greek and Egyptian.

So the first man is called Thoth by us and Adam by them, and they have called him that from the language of the angels – not just that language, but also in symbols taken from the four elements of the whole sphere they speak of him as of a body: his letter *alpha* signifies the east, the air; his letter *delta* signifies the west, the earth plunging down because of its weight; [gap in the text] . . . the letter *mu* signifies the south, the ripening fire amid those bodies in the fourth and middle zone. Hence, the fleshly Adam, regarding his outer moulding, is called Thoth, but the Man within this – the spiritual person – also has a special and a common name. At present, the special one is unknown. Only Nikotheos, the undiscoverable, knows these things. But the common name is Light, which is why humans are also said to be lights.

When Light was in the Garden, with the breath of Fate blowing through him, they persuaded him – while he was innocent and not yet active – to clothe himself in the Adam that comes from them, the one from Fate, from the four elements. Being innocent, Light did not turn away from them, and they boasted about using him as their slave. The outer person, as Hesiod said, is a bond with which Zeus binds Prometheus. Along with this bond, he then sends another bond, Pandora, whom the Hebrews call Eve. In fact, by an allegorical account, Prometheus-and-Epimetheus is a single person – soul and body. And sometimes Prometheus has the image of a soul, sometimes of a mind, but sometimes of flesh because of the disregard of Epimetheus as he disregards Prometheus, his own mind. For our mind says, 'The Son of God, all-powerful and becoming all, appears to each one when he wishes and as he wishes.'

Jesus Christ came to Adam and carried him up to where those called 'lights' had lived before. Becoming a human who suffered and was beaten, Jesus appeared even to humans who had no power at all. And in secret he carried off his own lights, for he had not suffered at all but showed how to trample death and banish it. From now until the world ends, he comes both secretly and openly to carry off his own, advising them secretly and mentally to get rid of their Adam, to beat and slay him, the one who led them blindly, envious of the spiritual and enlightened person – and they kill their own Adam.

So it goes until the demon comes who impersonates because he envies the lights and wants to deceive as just before, saying that he is the Son of God, even though misshapen in body and soul. But since they are wiser from perceiving the one who really is the Son of God, they give their own Adam up to him to kill, saving their enlightened spirits for their own region, where they were even before the universe. Before the Impersonator, the Envious, becomes rash enough to do these things, he first sends his precursor from Persia to spread fictitious stories and lead people on under Fate. His name has nine letters (keeping the diphthong) in the same pattern as $\varepsilon\,\iota\,\mu\,\alpha\,\rho\,\mu\,\varepsilon\,\nu\,\eta$ or Fate. After seven cycles, more or less, he will come – even as his natural self.

Only the Hebrews and the holy books of Hermes say this about the enlightened person and his leader, the Son of God, and about the earthly Adam and his leader, the Impersonator, who slanderously and deceptively says that he himself is God's Son. But the Greeks call the earthly Adam Epimetheus, who took the advice of his own mind – from his brother, in other words – not to accept gifts from Zeus. After making his mistake, however, changing his mind and seeking the region of happiness, Prometheus explains everything and gives good advice to all those whose minds have ears. But those whose only ears are bodily belong to Fate, admitting and confessing nothing else.

Those who succeed with their well-timed tinctures talk only of their own skill, mocking the great book *On Furnaces* and also not understanding the poet who says 'nor do the gods give people all their gifts at once'. They are not thoughtful at all, nor do they observe what people do: from a single craft people get results in various ways, practising the same craft differently since their behaviour and the figurations of the stars make the one craft variable, because one of them is a tested craftsman, another a simple craftsman, and because one lags behind while another, even worse, can make no progress.

In all crafts, then, we can see practitioners who differ either in the apparatus and methods they use or in their level of understanding and achievement, and in medicine we can observe this especially – more than in all other crafts. If a bone has been broken, for example, and they look for a bone-setting priest, the priest uses his religion to mend the bone, whose pieces can be heard crunching together as they are set against one another. Even if no priest is found, there is no cause to fear death: they bring in priests who have picture books with lines that are solid, shaded and show everything. As they follow the book, the person is bandaged up with a device, and he goes on with life after regaining health.

There is no question of letting a person die because of not finding a priest to set bones. But when those people have failed, they die of hunger because – in order to get rich and conquer poverty, that incurable disease – they will not bother to understand the skeletons of the furnaces and make sketches of them: and there you have it on this topic.

So let me get back to my project, which is about apparatus. When I received from you the letters that you had written, what I found is that you also want me to write out an account of apparatus for you. I am surprised that you would write to get just those things from me that you should not ask for. Have you never heard the Philosopher saying 'I have passed this over in silence deliberately because it is already there extensively in my other writings.' And you want to learn this from me? Yet I have written nothing more worthy of belief than the ancients, nor could I – you may be sure. But in order for us to understand all that they have said, I am going to set out for you what comes from them. Here it is.

5.8

Formed in the Likeness of the Cosmos:
Firmicus Maternus, *Instruction*, 2.1–2

Julius Firmicus Maternus wrote his *Instruction* on astrology around the middle of the fourth century CE, apparently before he became a Christian and produced a different book attacking the paganism that he had abandoned. Experts on astrology find his wordy account of the subject unreliable, especially on the many technical distinctions that make one horoscope – or 'nativity' – unlike another: since astrology is all about detail, this is no small failing. Astrology studies 'human effects of celestial causes', but only after astronomers have observed and calculated the motions of the stars and planets, as Ptolemy had already explained (see 4.15). Only then can astrologers examine and predict the effects of heavenly motions by applying physics to the rays of light and effusions of heat that sustain and shape human life. In the human microcosm and the universal macrocosm, the same laws operate, forming the decrees of Fate. Fate's pattern can be plotted in a diagram, a 'nativity' or horoscope, a snapshot of causality both in the cosmos as a whole and also for a microcosm – a human born at that moment. Like the 'divine spirit descending from a celestial Mind to sustain a mortal body', cosmic causality goes from above to below – from the surround to the surrounded, as Ptolemy had said.

*

By showing what the godlike ancients taught and by revealing this to everyone, I shall translate into statements the whole content of the *Instruction* that has to do with human effects of celestial causes, thus providing the most complete introduction to the subject for people who want to learn this art.

So my first task . . . is to understand that the God who fashioned man used nature as a guide to produce man's shape, stature and whole being in the image and likeness of the cosmos. For he put man's body together, like the cosmos, by mixing the four elements – fire, water, air and earth – blending and balancing them all to equip a living being whose form imitates God. The Craftsman's divine workmanship assembled man in this way to bring all the strength and substance of the elements together in a small body, so that the human frame – fragile, yes, but resembling the cosmos – could provide lodging for the divine spirit descending from a celestial Mind to sustain a mortal body. This is why a fiery and constant motion, from the five planets as well as the sun and moon, sustains man as if he were a lesser cosmos: so that resources like God's might guide an animal made to imitate the cosmos.

Petosiris and Nechepso, those godlike men who deserve all admiration, whose learning came close to the actual divine secrets, also used their divine mastery of science to pass down to us a nativity of the cosmos, which shows and explains that man was formed in the nature and likeness of the cosmos, to be fuelled for ever by its inexhaustible fires, on the same principles that rule and bind the cosmos itself. Following Aesculapius and Hanubius, to whom Mercury's most potent will entrusted the secrets of this science, Petosiris and Nechepso proposed this nativity for the cosmos. They put the Sun in sector 15 of Leo, the Moon in sector 15 of Cancer, Saturn in sector 15 of Capricorn . . .

Hence, following this nativity, following these positions of the stars and following the evidence that they produce for this nativity, they also propose that men's fates are arranged in these same patterns, as described in the book by Aesculapius called *Myriogenesis*, so that no difference at all is seen between this cosmic nativity and individual human nativities . . .

Saturn located by day sector-wise in the Ascendant – that is, in the sector where the Ascending god is – will produce an infant born with much crying. The newborn will also be senior to all his brothers or else, if one of them was born before him, that child is taken from the parents. Throughout the day in all four cardines, in any case, that god will always produce the first-born children or the first to grow up, or he makes the brothers already born puffed-up with a haughty, prideful spirit. But should Mars hold another cardine of the nativity or be in the cardine's antecedent when Saturn is located sector-wise by day in the Ascendant, this signifies many evils to come, resulting in many dangers and a ruined inheritance. Frequently, however, if no star friendly to the subjects is positioned in a helpful part of the nativity, Saturn will connect through rays that shine strongly, and if Mars receives rays from a waxing Moon, this will produce people who die violently.

But if Saturn is located by night in the Ascendant's sector, long periods of lassitude burden the person who has that god, and great fatigue always presses him down. Saturn will give jobs involving water to some, yet these will always grind them down with wearisome tasks. When Saturn holds the second place from the Ascendant, he produces serious illnesses and enormous destruction . . . But if by day he is in the second sign from the Ascendant, he will slowly and gradually grant increases in inheritance . . .

Positioned in the ninth place, Saturn will produce celebrated magi, esteemed philosophers or temple priests always thought to be famous for magic. Depending on the character of the signs, he also produces diviners, prophets and astronomers famed for correct explanations: it is as if their responses were uttered with almost divine authority. But he will make some pay strict attention to temple worship or preside over religious matters. Sometimes he produces inspired interpreters of dreams, though a long-haired philosopher is often what he makes. When situated in this house by night, however, he will produce anger from gods and hatred from emperors, especially if the Moon's waning light moves towards Saturn from any direction. But greater evils are decreed for someone born in this way when Mars, from any sector, is in aspect with Saturn when he is thus situated with the Moon.

5.9

Compelled by Fatal Necessity:
Firmicus Maternus, *Instruction*, 1.7.13–22

Firmicus chastises Plotinus, a 'long-haired philosopher' ruled by Saturn, for not acknowledging the iron rule of Fate. The philosopher was wrong to boast that 'the essential man is beyond harm', and Porphyry was naïve in his sanctimonious account of his teacher's death (see 5.4–5).

*

Do you still disparage Fate, scorning the power of the stars in your inflexible anger even though you see good people ending badly, the wicked doing well and the guilty escaping harm? To what do you attribute this? On whose orders do you suppose such things happen? It is we who go wrong if, though the commands of the Fates decide all those things for us, we are still inflexible and resist with rigid denials. In the end, it is you who must answer, because the examples given here call on us to do so – in that the guilty party did wrong when forced by Fate, and the innocent person was convicted when compelled by fatal Necessity to suffer a harsh sentence and punishment.

Now let's turn to you, Plotinus, for you are a remarkable man, and I want to defend my claims with recent examples. Is there any part of philosophy that he did not work on? Teaching philosophy would bring him a life of distinction, as he demonstrated what he taught by his own exemplary excellence and not another's. Godlike utterances came from his mouth as if it were a sanctuary. Indeed, this was a man made for virtue's every prize, meant to study the whole of God's plans, a strong, prudent, temperate person who thought that reason and foresight would help him rise above the blows of Fortune.

His first step was to choose a quiet place to live, distancing himself from all the clatter of human conversation. Thus freed from Fortune's grudges, he would give his time only to the rewards of teaching divinity, arming himself against every threat from Fortune with the shield of his virtue – intact and unspoiled . . .

Notice that in some part of his teaching he seems reckless and not cautious, attacking the power of fateful Necessity, severely blaming and censuring people who fear Fortune's decrees, conceding nothing to the powers of the stars, leaving nothing to the laws of the Fates and claiming that everything has been put in our power. To list his views on each point would take a long time: to explain his reasons for eliminating bad luck and the premisses of his argument for throwing its power – Fate and the stars, in other words – into confusion. This was the story he told while still healthy and unhurt, never turning his eyes or thoughts to Socrates at the end or to Plato's demise. Surely there was much to credit to their minds – I suppose – and much to their mistakes.

But see how all the might of the Fates landed on him when he was secure in this bold confidence. First they stiffened his limbs by making his blood cold and sluggish, and bit by bit his sharp eyesight lost its brightness as the light weakened. Then a bruising infection broke out all over his skin so that his decaying body wasted away as its organs failed from the death of the diseased blood. Each day and hour the disease snaked through his guts, melting their parts away. The festering sickness in his body disfigured any part of him that had recently looked healthy. With its whole appearance so ruined and destroyed, his body lost its shape, and once the body was dead – if you'll excuse me – only the mind survived. Consumed by the persistence of an awful disease, compelled by his own pain and convinced by the verdict of reason, he would understand Fate's strength and power, having heard Fortune render her verdict when he was broken by a body spent and mutilated.

Now what to say about this man's celebrated death? Why could his virtues – prudence, temperance, fortitude and justice – not free him from Fortune's punishments? Even he understood Fate's strength and accepted the end that the fiery judgements of the stars had decreed for him.

5.10

Demons and Heroes:
Iamblichus, *On the Mysteries of Egypt*,
2.2–11

Replying around 300 CE to criticisms from Porphyry, Iamblichus locates a magical and religious practice in three frameworks: cosmological, metaphysical and theological (see 5.4). He calls the practice 'theurgy' or 'god-work', as distinct from 'theology', which is just 'god-talk'. And yet one kind of theology – angelology and demonology – dominates his account. His cosmology is tacit and traditional, the same system accepted by Ptolemy, Plotinus, Firmicus and other educated people: the physical cosmos is a vast but finite system of geocentric spheres where large-scale causality is directional, running from above to below, from top to bottom (see 4.15; 5.5, 8). The centre, where humans live, is also the basement of the world, the metaphysical and moral cellar of an edifice whose upper storeys are occupied by gods. In between gods and humans, all other beings in the hierarchy – angels, archangels, archons, demons, heroes and disembodied souls – outrank the mortals entombed below in bodies (see 4.17). The very highest gods are absolutely immaterial, but even they are lower than One, Mind and Soul – the topmost divinities from whom everything else flows in the grand metaphysical procession that constitutes the All. Achieving union with this supreme godhead – 'to become uniate', as Porphyry said of Plotinus – is theurgy's ultimate goal: crucial preliminaries are rituals that call a lesser god down to help the theurgist ascend. Mistakes in the rituals may invite hostile demons, with perilous consequences. Such errors are hard to avoid or even notice because the rites can work automatically, requiring no effort from the theurge: 'It purveys spontaneously,' Plotinus had taught, 'but it purveys also under spell.'

*

I must also show you 'how a demon differs from a hero and a soul, whether essentially or in power or in activity'. When I say 'demons', then, I am talking about generative and creative powers of the gods as the remotest results of

procession produced by the last divisions of all, whereas 'heroes' come from reasons that live among the gods, and for souls the primary and perfect measures
are produced by them both and separated from them. Coming from different
causes, demons and heroes also differ in essence. The demon essence is fit to
make and produce natures for the cosmos and to provide oversight for each individual that comes to be, while the hero essence is life-giving, rational and a
master of souls. To demons one should assign powers of fertility that oversee
nature and the binding of souls to bodies, but the powers rightly assigned to
heroes are those that make life and govern humans yet stay free of becoming.

Next, one must distinguish the activities of each, positing that activities of
demons affect the cosmos and reach further in what they achieve, while those
of heroes reach not as far and involve arrangements for souls. And since soul
stops at the lower limit of the divine orders, souls come after demons and
heroes thus distinguished – the two types of divinity that assign to souls their
various and separate portions of power . . .

Now I move on to their manifestations: how do these differ? For you ask
what is 'the mark of a god's presence or an angel's, an archangel's, a demon's,
some archon's or a soul's'. In a word: the manifestations follow distinctions
among them in essence, power and activity. In keeping with that, they
become manifest to those who call on them, displaying their activities and
exhibiting appearances agreeable to themselves along with marks that are
suitable. To distinguish each one: apparitions of *gods* are of just one type;
those of *demons* are diverse; of *angels*, simpler than with demons but much
inferior to those of gods; and of *archangels*, somewhat nearer to the divine
causes. For *archons*, however – if you mean the worldmasters who control
the elements beneath the Moon – they are diverse but well arrayed by order.
But if the archons are the ones that preside over matter, they are more diverse
and less perfect than the former. Apparitions of *souls* have every sort of
appearance . . .

Moreover, order and quiet attach to the gods, but when those features
belong to archangels, the order and quiet are more energetic. When present in
angels, good order and tranquillity are no longer free of movement, while disorder and confusion go with demonic apparitions, and one sees archons in one
of the two ways just described: turbulent, if wrapped in matter and swept
along by it, or stable if they are the masters, standing still in themselves.
Visions of heroes are mobile, rushed and not free of change, and those of souls
somewhat resemble the heroic ones, though they are inferior even to them . . .

The gifts that come from these beings are not all alike nor do they bear the
same fruit. When gods arrive, they give us health for the body, virtue for the

soul, purity for the mind and – to put it simply – elevation to their native principles for everything within us . . . The arrival of archangels has the same results, except that the benefits are not always given nor given for everything nor are they lasting or complete or undiminishing, and the illumination comes in a way that fits the manifestation. The arrival of angels gives particular benefits that are still more separate, and the activity making this manifest is far weaker than the complete light surrounding an angel. But the arrival of demons makes the body heavy, punishes it with diseases, drags the soul down to nature and does not separate it from bodies nor from the sensing born into bodies: those who are hurrying up towards the fire the demon keeps down here, never freeing them from Fate's chains . . .

The order kept by those that we see emerges when the visions are on display. Gods have gods or angels around them. Archangels are seen with angels on parade – angels either of the same order or coming from below – or else there is some other huge bodyguard of angels stationed near them. Angels show actions fit for the order to which they have come. Good demons hold their own products up for inspection, with the benefits that they bestow. Punishing demons show what the punishments look like, and other demons who are evil in some way are surrounded by various dangerous animals – fierce and bloodthirsty . . .

When some mistake occurs in the technique of theurgy, or the images in visions are not as they should be, and one divinity comes instead of another as lesser orders assume the shape of the more revered and pretend to be the characters they play, they act like fakes, boasting of more power than is theirs . . . Granted: 'ignorance and deceit are outrageous and irreverent'. Yet this does not also make a hoax of proper offerings to the gods and godly actions, for it is not good judgement that connects theurgists with the gods: if that were so, what would stop the philosophers with their theories from attaining theurgical union with the gods?

But this is not really how it is: no, what delivers theurgic union is the ritual doing of deeds beyond description and past all understanding, performed in a godly way, and the power of symbols that cannot be spoken – symbols that only the gods understand. It is not by thinking, then, that we do such deeds: if it were, their effects would be mental and given over to us – neither of which is true. For even when we are not thinking, the tokens have the same special effect by themselves. And the undescribable power of the gods, to which the tokens are connected, on its own – not because our thinking rouses it – recognizes the images that belong to it . . .

The divine tokens themselves, strictly speaking, are what stirs the will of the gods, so that the gods themselves wake the gods, never getting any basis for their own activity from beings below them . . . Even if we know the properties that go along with each type of being, we have not just bumped into the truth about the holy deeds. Real unification is never achieved without knowledge, to be sure, but it is not the same thing.

5.11

Statues Ensouled and Conscious:
Asclepius, 23–4, 37–8

Perhaps a contemporary of Iamblichus, who came from Syria, the Egyptian author of the *Asclepius* wrote originally in Greek, though the text survives mainly in other languages, including this Latin version. Like the surviving Greek *Hermetica*, this dialogue between Hermes Trismegistus and his pupil, Asclepius, is a jumble of contradictory doctrines that underwrite a popular spirituality. The setting is Egypt under Roman rule, and Egypt's temples are on the horizon. The two 'god-making' passages of the *Asclepius* became very famous – or notorious – much later, during the Renaissance, as descriptions of statue-magic by its original practitioners, whose idolatry was condemned even by pagans (see 5.13). Here, however, the same practice shows that humans are cousins of the gods and proves 'mankind's power and strength'. A statue actually becomes a living god, with a divinity 'enticed into the idol' by rituals correctly performed. The rites promoted by the *Asclepius* are not prominent in the rest of the *Hermetic Corpus* – the Greek treatises that focus on popular spirituality, not on magic.

*

'Since this discourse proclaims to us the kinship and association between humans and gods, Asclepius, you must recognize mankind's power and strength. Just as the Master and Father – or God, to use his most august name – is the maker of the heavenly gods, so it is mankind who fashions the temple gods who are content to be near to humans. Not only is mankind glorified; he glorifies as well. He not only advances towards God; he also makes the gods strong. Are you surprised, Asclepius? Surely you don't lack confidence, as many people do.'

'I'm confused, Trismegistus, but I gladly agree to what you say, and I find mankind most fortunate to have attained such happiness.'

'Mankind certainly deserves admiration, as the greatest of all beings. All plainly admit that the race of gods sprang from the cleanest part of nature and that their signs are like heads that stand for the whole being. But the figures of gods that humans form have been formed of both natures – from the divine, which is purer and more divine by far, and from the material of which they are built, whose nature falls short of the human – and they represent not only the heads but all the limbs and the whole body. Always mindful of its nature and origin, humanity persists in imitating divinity, representing its gods in semblance of its own features, just as the Father and Master made his gods eternal to resemble him.'

'Are you talking about statues, Trismegistus?'

'Statues, Asclepius, yes. See how little trust you have! I mean statues ensouled and conscious, filled with spirit and doing great deeds; statues that foreknow the future and predict it by lots, by prophecy, by dreams and by many other means; statues that make people ill and cure them, bringing them pain and pleasure as each deserves.' . . .

'Let's turn again to mankind and reason, that divine gift whereby a human is called a rational animal. What we've said of mankind is wondrous, but less wondrous than this: it exceeds the wonderment of all wonders that humans have been able to discover the divine nature and how to make it. Our ancestors once erred gravely on the theory of divinity: they were unbelieving and inattentive to worship and reverence for God. But then they discovered the art of making gods. To their discovery they added a conformable power arising from the nature of matter. Because they could not make souls, they mixed this power in and called up the souls of demons or angels and implanted them in likenesses through holy and divine mysteries, whence the idols could have the power to do good and evil.'

'Take your ancestor, for example: he was the first to discover medicine, Asclepius. They dedicated a temple to him on the Libyan mountain near the shore of the crocodiles. There lies his material person – his body, in other words. The rest, or rather, the whole of him (if the whole person consists in consciousness of life) went back happier to heaven. Even now he still provides help to sick people by his divine power, as he used to offer it through the art of medicine. And Hermes, whose family name I bear, doesn't he dwell in his native city that was named for him, where mortals come from all around for his aid and protection? Isis, wife of Osiris: we know how much good she can do when well disposed, when angered how much harm!

Anger comes easily to earthly and material gods because humans have made and assembled them from both natures. Whence it happens that these are called holy animals by the Egyptians, who throughout their cities worship the souls of those deified while alive, in order that cities might go on living

by their laws and calling themselves by their names. For this reason, Asclepius, because what one group worships and honours another group treats
differently, Egypt's cities constantly assail one another in war.'

'And the quality of these gods who are considered earthly – what sort of
thing is it, Trismegistus?'

'It comes from a mixture of plants, stones and spices, Asclepius, that have
in them a natural power of divinity. And this is why those gods are enter-
tained with constant sacrifices, with hymns, praises and sweet sounds in tune
with heaven's harmony: so that the heavenly ingredient enticed into the idol
by constant communication with heaven may gladly endure its long stay
among humankind. Thus does man fashion his gods.'

5.12
Natural Powers, Sympathies and Antipathies: *Kyranides*, prologue and 1.13

A worshipper looking for the right 'plants, stones and spices' to lure a divinity into a temple statue could get instructions from manuals like the *Kyranides*, a text with Hermetic authority – like the *Asclepius* – and of exotic Persian origin (see 5.10–11). The first part of this collection, perhaps a little earlier than the *Asclepius*, has twenty-four chapters, one for each letter of the Greek alphabet, each describing a plant, a fish, a bird and a stone. The stone, if it bears the image of a god or some other power, will also be a talisman. Directions for its use often include one of the other three ingredients – all four grouped by names that start with the same letter. Under N, the shipmaster or shipholder called *naukratês* had a long career as a magic object, often (but not here) paired with the *narkê*, the electric ray described elsewhere in the *Kyranides*. Since conventional natural science like Galen's could explain neither the ray's (real) ability to stun nor the tiny shipholder's (fictive) ability to stop a huge vessel, both became evidence for anomalies – the 'undescribable' effects of occult qualities – that helped persuade Plotinus, Porphyry, Iamblichus, Proclus and other intellectuals to theorize about magic, whatever their reservations about related advice that seemed dubious, morally or otherwise, like turning basic botany and pharmacy into necromancy (see 4.18; 5.3, 14, 16).

*

This is the book of Kyranos and a Hermetic book called *The Three*, from both of which a book of natural powers, sympathies and antipathies has been collected – from the two books – both from that first book of Kyranides by Kyranos, King of the Persians, and also from the one by Harpocration of Alexandria to his own daughter.

The contents of the first book by Kyranos are just as we have set them down. Receiving a most valuable gift of God from angels, the thrice-greatest Hermes passed this book of secrets on to all humans capable of receiving it. Do not pass it on to men who lack knowledge, then, but keep it to yourself as a most valuable possession, and, if you can, pass it on only as a father to your children in place of priceless gold and as a possession that has great power, making them swear that only your child will keep it in safety since it comes under divine protection.

In Syriac letters cut into an iron slab, this book was buried under rubble on the Syrian border, as proclaimed in the *Old-Time Book* that preceded it and has been translated by me. But in the book called *Kyranides* are descriptions of 24 stones, 24 winged things, 24 plants and 24 fish. You will find each of these powers commingled and mixed with other powers for the purpose of healing the human body, and also for pleasure and sex, from the all-mastering and all-powerful God, through his knowledge of the effects of plants, stones and fish and of the powers of stones and animals and the nature of beasts, as well as their mixtures with one another and also their oppositions and special properties. Any such knowledge and rich experience comes to humans from the gods.

The whole work, then, will be divided into three Kyranides and arranged by letters so that the contents can be remembered . . .

Letter N: the plant is *nekua*, ghost-mullein; the fish is *naukratês*, the ship-master; the winged thing is *nêssa*, the duck; and the stone is nemesite.

Nekua is the ghost-plant called 'mullein'. The forms of this plant are seven. They say of this plant that when its shoots come up above ground, they burn one piece of it in their lamps instead of candlewick. But since they sprinkle this plant over the basins used for divination with ghosts, this is why people who do such things also call these plants 'ghostlings'.

Nêssa is a winged thing that can swim on the waves, and this duck is quite a large bird.

Naukratês, the shipmaster, is a sea fish – the shipholder. If it sticks to a vessel under sail, this completely prevents the ship from moving unless the fish is removed from the ship's keel. This whole fish is cooked in oil until it becomes like wax, then the oil is filtered and enough wax is taken out to make a poultice for treating gout.

A nemesite is a stone taken from an altar of Nemesis. Carved on the stone is a Nemesis standing with her foot on a wheel. Her image is that of a young girl, holding a ruler in her left hand and a wand in her right hand. Under the stone put a duck's quill and a small piece of the plant. If you then present this ring to a person possessed by a demon, the demon will confess and leave immediately. This also cures the moon-struck when worn around the neck, and it keeps demons from appearing in dreams and babies from being startled by nightmares. But the person wearing it must stay away from everything polluted. This ring shows its wearer how many years he has to live and the place and manner of his death. But the person wearing it must stay away from everything bad.

If you stitch a piece from the shipholder's bones into horsehide and keep it inside you and board a ship and hide it, the ship will not be able to sail at all.

To have foreknowledge of life and death – to put it briefly – you need to take a taste of the sacred aster.

5.13
That Art is Not Theurgy:
Iamblichus, *On the Mysteries*, 3.28–31

The 'priestly art' of theurgy has no need of 'piecemeal matter', according to Iamblichus, nor even of heavenly *bodies* seen in the ordinary way. Embodied planets and stars are mere shadows of bodiless celestial divinities invoked by the theurge who seeks still higher gods – supercelestial and hypercosmic – beyond the world of nature (see 5.4–5, 10–11). The statues praised by the *Asclepius* would be repellent to Iamblichus – fake bodies further defiled by the messy, rotting mixture of 'plants, stones and spices' used to activate them. He denounces the 'idol-maker's craft' that produces such shoddy counterfeits for the purpose of 'wonderworking', calling it sacrilege to confuse trashy idols with higher divinities – the real gods and demons without whom divination and other rituals can never be reliable. Demons are lower than gods, but they are far higher and better than idols. When idol-makers conduct their polluted rites, they attract only 'depraved demons' who are 'anti-gods' and enemies of righteous theurgy.

*

I would be astonished if any of the theurges who gaze upon real forms of gods were to accept what you propose in all seriousness: 'some produce idols that are active'. Why would anyone take idols in exchange for what actually exists and let himself be carried away from the very first beings towards the last? Or do we not realize that all of this is obscure, all the same shadow-painting – that these truly are *phantoms* of truth, *appearances* of good that are not good at all? . . .

This is clear from how they are made. For their maker is no god but a human, who brings them in not from the unitary and intellectual essences but from the matter that he has selected. In that case, what good can come of what grows from matter, from the material, from bodily and matter-bound powers incarnate within bodies? Can any good come of something brought into being by human craftsmanship, which must be weaker than the very human who supplies its existence?

What kind of craft shapes this idol? They say that the craft is the Craftsman's, but that craft produces genuine essences, not just a few idols. The idol-maker's craft is therefore far from any creating of real things, and it bears no likeness to divine making. For it is not by physical movements in the skies nor by piecemeal matter nor by powers parcelled out in this way that God does all his craftwork. No, this comes about from his designs and purposes and immaterial forms – this crafting that God does of cosmic being, both hypercosmic and encosmic. But the maker of idols is said to finish them off with the circling stars. Yet this is not as it seems, nor where they really and truly come from. Although various and countless powers surround the gods in heaven, it is just the last type of all that is in the idols – the physical type . . .

True: image-making draws on the celestial processions, but on a very dim part of them. Mindful of the truth, we must also make it plain that idol-makers do not use the circling stars, the powers contained in them or those naturally settled around them, which the idol-makers are wholly incapable of reaching. And if there is some art that brings idol-makers close to powers that come last by nature and flow forth into the visible world from the uttermost region of the All, that art is not theurgy . . .

Why then does the person who makes idols and does such things give up on himself? For he is better than that and born of better beings, yet he seems to put mistaken trust in soulless idols that breathe in only a semblance of life, idols held together from the outside by an artificial and multiform harmony though they are really made just for a day. Is there something authentic and true in them, perhaps? No: since nothing fashioned by human art is unmixed and pure. Does simple and uniform action or the constitution of the whole prevail in them? They fall completely short. For their visible composition shows that they are put together entirely of manifold and contrary properties. Is some untouched and perfect power to be seen in them? By no means . . .

Then why would a man anxious to learn the truth care so much for this weird wonderworking? As for me, I think it totally worthless. And if a person has knowledge of these things, studies them, spends time on them and sticks with these figments of wholly passive matter, the evil may be simple . . . But if his devotion to the idols makes gods of them, no word can describe nor any deed sustain the absurdity. No divine ray will ever shine on such a soul . . .

If you call the idols 'demons', you are sloppy and the name is incorrect. Demons have a different nature, not like the idols, and a great distance separates the two orders. The Marshal of Idols is also different from the Grandmaster of Demons. Even you concede this when you grant that 'no god or demon is drawn down by them'. Then what value could there be in a ritual act or a prediction of the future that does not commune at all with a god or demon? Although something must be known about the nature of this wonderworking, one must not use it or believe in it.

And there is an even worse interpretation of deeds that are ritually correct, claiming that the cause of divination is 'some type of illusory nature, polymorphous and polyvalent, pretending to be gods, demons and souls of the dead'. I will tell you the account of this that I once heard stated by Chaldaean prophets.

They that are gods in truth are the only givers of good things. Only they converse with good people and associate with those cleansed by the priestly art, driving all evil and suffering away from them. When their light shines, the evil and demonic vanishes, completely displaced by mightier powers as darkness is by light, and this evil makes no trouble for a theurge. Theurges get all the virtues, in fact, making their behaviour perfect, kindly and well ordered.

But those who are sinful assault the divine without law or order, and – because their own energy is spent or because the power they have is deficient – they cannot reach the gods. Or else, owing to some defilement, they are also kept back from conjoining with the unpolluted spirits, making them connect with the evil ones, to be filled by them with the worst inspirations, becoming depraved and unholy, full of unbridled pleasures, loaded with vice, zealots for ways strange to the gods, and – in a word – like the depraved demons to whom they have grown close. These people, since they are full of passions and vice, attract depraved spirits to themselves through kinship, and those spirits excite them to every vice . . .

And when, as it seems, those people celebrate one god in place of another, they sometimes introduce depraved demons instead of gods, calling them anti-gods – never to be mentioned in the same breath with priestly divination! . . .

Hence, just as sacrilegious people struggle mainly against worshipping the gods, those who deal with rogue demons – the ones who cause gross intemperance – fight against the theurges, of course. For every depraved spirit retreats from theurgy and is completely overthrown by it . . . This then is the one and only divination, the kind that is undefiled, priestly and truly divine . . .

5.14
Undescribable Properties: Pseudo-Galen, *On Kidney Diseases*, 5.676–9

The Christian author of this treatise worked in the tradition of Galen, calling that physician's method 'rational' because it applies canons of reason and evidence to make medicine consistent and coherent, systematically related to the best science of the day, especially the theory of four elements (fire, air, water, earth) and associated pairs of qualities (hot/cold, wet/dry). Many medical treatments – mainly botanical drugs – were thought to work rationally and to be explained by the method. When the method failed, however, other 'undescribable' remedies were available but could not be accounted for in the usual way by elements and elementary qualities (see 5.3). Theorists traced the 'undescribable properties' (later called 'occult qualities' by medieval physicians and philosophers; see 7.10; 8.10) of such cures – from plants, stones and some animal ingredients – to 'the whole substance' of the item prescribed. Stones, especially whole stones, uncrushed, were special problems for Christian doctors and patients because hard gemstones were often used to make amulets and talismans (see 4.3; 5.12; 6.10).

*

The best physician must have exact knowledge of how things work in nature, for one who has that exact natural knowledge will also quickly understand what is not natural. Now it is not only the causes already described that completely change the treatment but also specific natures to which the drugs most widely approved do not apply. They often fail, in fact. Because of this, one must watch carefully, and if those natures do not yield to treatment through a natural property or the patient's constitution or something else like that, one must allow a change to drugs that do at least some good.

That this applies not just to drugs but to all other remedies, including some that are undescribable, is not the view of those who are mere beginners in the art – even though they may be more highly regarded than others – but of those who are always hard at work, searching for nature's movements. But if drugs that act through some undescribable property of their own also fail in this medical guesswork, one must urgently and speedily give way to the undescribable remedies of the ancients and those that work through the whole substance, discovered just from experience and from practice that is not reasoned – like the burnt skin of a cave-mouse or a sea-slug, the blood of a billy goat and countless others, both simple and compounded. Most of these are also disgusting, found by unsystematic practice in nature or by fortune or improvising or imitating or from dreams (like the cave-mouse) or from oracles or instruction or other such sources collected in the empiric way.

But for us these are all undescribable, so it is best not to put too much faith in them since how they help is unknown . . . Anyone who wants to be a physician must act according to reason, making proud and confident use of what works because of active qualities, powers and operations, as the power of hot, cool, dry and moist is understood by the method, along with the sour, bitter, acid, sweet, salt, sharp, acrid, clear, coarse and fine, as well as things that act to make the parts dilate, contract, cohere and so on. Since for the most part the matter of medicines made from crushed stones is describable, it is better to use them than those that are undescribable, such as the taming stone, parsley stone, hairy stone and others with similar powers. And since the latter are mainly without effect, it befits us as Christians to have recourse to our own mighty doctrines, the true mysteries.

5.15
Jynxes: Synesius, *On Dreams*, 1.1–3.2

Synesius was born around 370 – just before Iamblichus died (see 5.10). By that time, the successors of Plotinus had found a new holy book, the *Chaldaean Oracles*, a recent medley of verses misattributed to Zoroaster and the Magi (see 3.7; 4.13; 5.13). The *Oracles* entranced Synesius. He cites them frequently in the dream-book that he wrote by 411, when he became a Christian bishop, though without deep commitment to the new faith: *On Dreams* shows no interest in that religion. His little book alludes to the *Oracles*, however, when it mentions 'jynxes' as magical objects that work by feeling and breathing together, 'as limbs of a single whole'. The jynx that Synesius found in the *Oracles* was probably a bird (either a wagtail or a wryneck) whose striking behaviour made some ancient bird-watchers think they were observing deep unison between the universe and its inhabitants. 'If birds had any knowledge,' says Synesius, 'they might use humans to put a technique together about the future, just as we use them.' The Bishop knew that birds were a common source of divinatory information, and he saw the interpretation of dreams as a type of divination (see 1.6, 9; 4.5, 9).

*

Perhaps divination is the greatest of goods since . . . much more comes to humans from divination than belongs to their ordinary nature in that most of them know only the present . . . This is also the reason why a sage is like a god – from trying to get close to the divine with knowledge and from involving himself in the thinking where divinity has its being. There you have proofs that divination is among the finest human pursuits.

But grant that everything is a sign of everything, all akin within the same living thing – the cosmos. And note that those signs are letters of every kind, as in a book: some Phoenician, some Egyptian, others Assyrian. Finally, suppose a sage reads them, that sage whom nature teaches . . . Then that is how sages see the future, some by knowing the heavenly bodies, whether they are fixed stars or stars that cross the skies, some by reading signs in entrails, others by the screams of birds or their flights or where they perch. For other sages the so-called 'tokens' are letters written about the future and quite distinct – also languages that link with some other thing since everything can signify everything else.

Hence, if birds had any knowledge, they might use humans to put a technique together about the future, just as we use them. We are to them, in fact, as they are to us: utterly new, but also most ancient and sources of the best omens. In my view, it must be that the parts of this All, which feel and breathe together, are related to one another as limbs of a single whole. Might the jynxes of the Magi not be such parts? As things signal one another, in fact, they also cast spells. And the sage is a person who sees the kinship among parts of the cosmos, using one part to draw another. For he has near him pledges of things very distant – their voices and materials and figures.

When we feel a pain in the stomach, some other part has the same feeling, and the hurt in a finger comes to rest in the groin even though many parts in between feel nothing. For both are parts of one living thing, with something belonging more to the two of them than to others. Even a stone or a plant from down here suits a god – one of those that live within the cosmos – since the god is affected as they are, yielding to nature and letting the enchantment work . . . Just as with one's relatives, there is also some dissension among the parts since the cosmos is one from many – not one absolutely. In it are parts agreeing with parts but also parts to combat them, and their struggle harmonizes with the unity of the All, just as a lyre combines sounds in discord and concord. The unity that comes from opposites is harmony – of a lyre or of the cosmos.

Archimedes of Sicily wanted a spot beyond the earth in order to balance himself against the earth as a whole, saying that he had no power to act on it as long as he was in it. But a sage stationed outside the world, however much he knew about its nature, could make no use of his learning – using the cosmos in order to go against it. Once the connection is broken, to observe it is useless, and the tokens are sealed up – lifeless. Actually, any divinity outside the cosmos is completely invulnerable to witchery,

standing apart, uncaring, without worry,

for mind is by nature unappeased, and only the affected lets itself be charmed. This is why the bulk of divining and rites of magic come from the multitude of things in the cosmos and from their kinship, such that the manifold is in discord even though they all have kinship in the One. As to the rites, let me not speak of them, in obedience to the law of the state. But no harm is done by giving an account of divination.

5.16

Attracting by Likeness:
Proclus, *On the Priestly Art*

The text that follows, a highly condensed summary, is all that remains of a work by Proclus, who died in 485 CE – last in the ancient succession of Platonic philosophers that started with Plotinus and continued with Porphyry, Iamblichus and Synesius (see 5.4–5, 10, 13, 15). Like Plato and the earlier Neoplatonists, Proclus teaches that bonds of likeness, love and sympathy connect heaven and earth in a universe where 'all things are full of gods' (see 4.3–5). To make his theory of magic clearer, he gives concrete examples of magical objects in the lowest part of the cosmos, where humans live: such objects are stones, plants and animals empowered by kinship with the gods (see 5.3, 11–12). Anyone can see their power working, for example, in solar plants like the lotus and heliotrope. On earth such magical objects occupy the lower ends of 'orders' or 'chains' made of related items – including 'angels, demons, souls, animals, plants and stones' and many others – that go far higher, beyond the boundary of the cosmos. The hierarchical dynamics of the solar order shows why the mighty lion (or a lion demon) fears a puny cockerel (in the barnyard or on a talisman) – because cockerels, being aerial, fly higher in their order than lions roaming the earth. Likewise, consider the analogy between (*a*) lighting an oil-soaked wick by holding a flame above it and (*b*) enticing a god to descend and animate a statue: the familiar experience of *a* clarifies the mystery of *b*, which is theurgy (see 5.13). Like the author of the *Kyranides*, Proclus knows that a magician must choose exactly the right ingredients, like goat fat and Ethiopian cumin if he wants to summon Selene in a love-spell (see 5.6). Such knowledge is empirical, coming from 'evidence of the eyes', yet 'the cause of this is not to be grasped from appearances but from intellectual insight', for which the magus needs the philosopher.

*

Just as lovers systematically leave behind what is fair to sensation and attain the one true source of all that is fair and intelligible, in the same way priests – observing how all things are in all from the sympathy that all visible things have for one another and for the invisible powers – have also framed their priestly knowledge. For they were amazed to see the last in the first and the very first in the last; in heaven they saw earthly things acting causally and in a heavenly manner, in the earth heavenly things in an earthly manner.

Why do heliotropes move together with the sun, selenotropes with the moon, moving around to the extent of their ability with the luminaries of the cosmos? All things pray according to their own order and sing hymns, either intellectually or rationally or naturally or sensibly, to heads of entire chains. And since the heliotrope is also moved towards that to which it readily opens, if anyone hears it striking the air as it moves about, he perceives in the sound that it offers to the King the kind of hymn that a plant can sing. In the earth, then, it is possible to see suns and moons terrestrially, but in heaven one can also see celestially all the heavenly plants and stones and animals living intellectually.

So by observing such things and connecting them to the appropriate heavenly beings, the ancient wise men brought divine powers into the region of mortals, attracting them through likeness. For likeness is sufficient to join beings to one another. If, for example, one first heats up a wick and then holds it under the light of a lamp not far from the flame, he will see it lighted though it be untouched by the flame, and the lighting comes up from below. By analogy, then, understand the preparatory heating as like the sympathy of lower things for those above; the bringing-near and the proper placement as like the use made of material things in the priestly art, at the right moment and in the appropriate manner; the communication of the fire as like the coming of the divine light to what is capable of sharing it; and the lighting as like the divinization of mortal entities and the illumination of what is implicated in matter, which things then are moved towards the others above insofar as they share in the divine seed, like the light of the wick when it is lit.

The lotus also shows that there is sympathy. Before the sun's rays appear, it is closed, but as the sun first rises it slowly unfolds, and the higher the light goes, the more it expands, and then it contracts again as the sun goes down. If men open and close mouths and lips to hymn the sun, how does this differ from the drawing-together and loosening of the lotus petals? For the petals of the lotus take the place of a mouth, and its hymn is a natural one.

But why talk of plants, which have some trace of generative life? One can also see that stones inhale the influences of the luminaries, as we see the sunstone with its golden rays imitating the rays of the sun; and the stone called Bel's eye (which should be called sun's eye, they say) resembling the pupil of the eye and emitting a glittering light from the centre of its pupil; and the moonstone changing in figure and motion along with the moon; and the sun-moonstone, a sort of image of the conjunction of these luminaries, imitating their conjunctions and separations in the heavens.

All things are full of gods, then: things on earth are full of heavenly gods; things in heaven are full of supercelestials; and each chain continues abounding up to its final members. For what is in the One-before-all makes its appearance in all, in which are also communications between souls set beneath one god or another.

In this way, consider the multitude of solar animals, such as lions and cocks, that also share in the divine, following their own order. It is amazing how the lesser in strength and size among these animals are regarded with fear by those greater in both respects. For they say the lion shrinks from the cock. The cause of this is not to be grasped from appearances but from intellectual insight and from differences among the causes. In fact, the presence of sun symbols is more effective for the cock: it is clear that he perceives the solar orbits and sings a hymn to the luminary as it rises and moves among the other cardinal points. Accordingly, some solar angels seem to have forms of this same kind, and though they are formless they appear formed to us held fast in form. Now if one of the solar demons becomes manifest in the shape of a lion, as soon as a cock is presented he becomes invisible, so they say, shrinking away from the signs of greater beings, as many refrain from committing abominable acts when they see likenesses of divine men.

In brief, then, such things as the plants mentioned above follow the orbits of the luminary; others imitate the appearance of its rays (the palm, for example) or the empyrean substance (the laurel, for example) or something else. So it seems that properties sown together in the sun are distributed among the angels, demons, souls, animals, plants and stones that share them.

From this evidence of the eyes, the authorities on the priestly art have thus discovered how to gain the favour of powers above, mixing some things together and setting others apart in due order. They used mixing because they saw that each unmixed thing possesses some property of the god but is not enough to call that god forth. Therefore, by mixing many things they unified the aforementioned influences and made a unity generated from all of them similar to the whole that is prior to them all. And they often devised composite statues and fumigations, having blended separate signs together into one and, by unifying many powers, having made by artifice something embraced essentially by the divine, the dividing of which makes each one feeble, while mixing raises it up to the idea of the exemplar.

But there are times when one plant or one stone suffices for the work.

Flax-leaved daphne is enough for a manifestation; laurel, box-thorn, squill, coral, diamond or jasper will do for a guardian spirit; but for foreknowledge one needs the heart of a mole and for purification sulphur and salt water. By means of sympathy, then, they draw them near, but by antipathy they drive them away, using sulphur and bitumen for purification, perhaps, or an aspersion of sea water. For sulphur purifies by the sharpness of its scent, sea water because it shares in the empyrean power.

For consecrations and other divine services they search out appropriate animals as well as other things. Starting with these and others like them, they gained knowledge of the demonic powers, how closely connected they are in substance to natural and corporeal energy, and through these very substances they achieved association with the [demons], from whom they returned forthwith to actual works of the gods, learning some things from the [gods], for other things being moved by themselves towards accurate consideration of the appropriate symbols. And then, leaving nature and natural energies below, they had dealings with the primary and divine powers.

6

Armies of Sorcery and Flights of Angels: Early Christian Europe

Figure 7: Simon Magus Fails to Levitate

We know little about Eutychianus of Adana, who lived in the sixth century. While he served the church in south-east Asia Minor, the bishop who governed Braga in Iberian Gallaecia, at the other end of the Mediterranean, was named Martin. Martin's official language was Latin, Eutychianus used Greek and both were Christian – like the most ambitious Roman ruler of their age, the great Justinian, and like most well-governed Europeans. By their own reports, however, both clerics lived in a world disrupted by devils – large and small – and full of wicked magic.

A legend recorded by Eutychianus gained fame when Paul the Deacon, an Italian monk who worked for Charlemagne, turned it into Latin: the story is about a priest, Theophilus, who would be promoted to professor when Christopher Marlowe used the same character much later for his Doctor Faustus. Theophilus risks his soul in the earlier telling, and a Jew has helped the Devil snare him. But the boss is really the Devil – 'the cunning Enemy and hostile Adversary'. Satan was also on the prowl in Martin's town of Braga, where he and 'his servants, the demons, were showing themselves to humans in various forms, talking to people and trying to get them to offer sacrifices to them'.

By this time there were no institutions of any size – state, army, schools, temples – loyal to the old gods and capable of returning them to power. The great Pan was dead and gone, and some Christians – in a triumphalist mood – boasted that his passing had been settled once Christ came to save the world. If that were so, if the old ways were long gone, why was Martin having so much trouble with his flock in Braga, those 'ignorant peasants who honoured the demons'? The Bishop – a capable manager, no doubt – surely knew the answer: leadership. Despite their loss of divine status, the little devils who pestered Braga were doing well by doing evil because they had a big Devil to lead them. To set the stage for his Satanic Majesty, Martin tells how Lucifer was ejected from heaven, done in by his own angelic arrogance.

Raging for lost glory, the Devil who offered Jesus the whole world could tempt Martin's peasants with less. Their Bishop begrudged them the tiniest gratifications: a few words muttered to regain control after a sneeze are 'Devil's signs', petty tributes to the Prince of Darkness. Augustine, an acute student of the psychology of superstition, also called out 'the silliest practices . . . like stepping on the threshold when crossing the street in front of your house'. He saw such impulses as contractual, as the fine print in an implicit pact dictated by Satan over a lifetime – a pact to take treachery in exchange for nothing but deception. The deceived sinner, having kept the Devil's small change in circulation, incurs a liability on hell's ledgers and breaks his baptismal bond to renounce Satan, for which he gets no real relief from life's small, relentless shocks.

The explicit contract that Theophilus signs is plainly more serious: that 'despicable pledge of denial' is a formal instrument, written out in a document, sealed in wax with a signet, displayed to horrified witnesses and burned by a bishop. The legalities – those of the priest's ruin and repentance – are crucial, as Augustine would have understood, having studied the Roman law: perhaps legal expertise was what alerted him to 'pacts and marks agreed and contracted with demons'. The really diabolical thing about these superstitions, he suggests, is their indeterminacy. If I tie a stone on a string and hang it around my neck to cure a cold, what am I really doing? Therapy or theurgy? Am I just attaching a bit of healing matter to myself? Or is the stone also a sign, signalling my readiness to take help from a demon?

The stone stops my sneezing, yet I can't explain why and neither can my physician. Is this natural medication also magical? 'All the marvels of magicians,' Augustine insists, 'happen on the instructions of demons,' which also shows why the law goes so hard on magic – and not just laws enacted by Christians. From Apuleius, Cicero, Pliny and other pagan authorities, Augustine knew that the very oldest laws of Rome, the Twelve Tables, penalized 'this noxious and criminal science'. Citing Virgil on the 'dark technology of magic' to underline his point, Augustine assumes that 'the injurious sorceries' are effective. His concern is to show that the magic is nonetheless sinful and disreputable.

Until a few centuries ago, many educated Europeans – like Augustine – loathed magic as evil but also feared it as harmful, both physically and morally. Plotinus had spurned it as a distraction, but that attitude was hard to sustain once Christians had enlisted the Devil's troops as the brigades of sorcery. As a result, the faithful who hated magic seldom scorned it – a distinction that shapes what Augustine says about the 'Witch of Endor' story from the first Book of Samuel. Discussing Samuel's warning to Saul, he concludes that the ritual that raised the prophet must have been effective – though 'no less detestable on that account' – since Samuel's words from the grave were authentic. Also, where Augustine calls the rite at Endor a sacrilege, he says nothing about *necromantia*, a word he uses elsewhere, before it evolved into the medieval *nigromantia* or 'black magic'.

Origen, another immensely learned man, also avoids 'necromancy' when he explicates the story. He comments instead on 'belly-talking' or 'ventriloquism' – though without the vaudeville. His point is that Samuel's appearance was the real thing, not an illusion staged by a shape-shifting Satan. 'We must scrutinize this passage and read it historically,' the great exegete rules. This did not prevent later critics – including Eustathius, the powerful Bishop of Antioch – from accusing him of diluting history with allegory. The woman at Endor, according to the Bishop, was 'a demon-ridden hag: . . . from her belly she utters the nonsense and weird words that the demon puts together there'. She was a 'ventriloquist' in something like our sense of that word, and the necromancy was just a stunt. This reading started with the Greek text of 1 Samuel and probably stopped there, since Eustathius lacked Origen's mastery of the Hebrew behind the Greek.

The Hebrew introduces the mistress of the séance as a *b'alath-'ov* – a woman skilled at whatever *'ov* meant at the time. By the time Rashi struggled with *'ov* in the eleventh century, even experts on biblical Hebrew had lost the trail. A respected modern version makes do with 'a woman who consults ghosts': this tells us *what* she does but not *how* she does it. For Origen and Eustathius, however, the method was the main message of the sacred page, whose Greek version stretches *'ov* into *engastrimuthos*. 'Belly-talker' is probably correct, with *muthos* for 'talk' or 'speech', though the word alone, uninterpreted in the biblical text, will not explain how belly-talking works as divination.

Eustathius gave it a try. Seizing on the exact (by his lights) letter of scripture, he takes *muthos* to be not 'talk' in general but 'myth' in particular. He has already complained that 'the poetry of Homer and Hesiod shows us a false mythology whose main effect is to delude those who hear it at school'. The woman from Endor is – in the crudest physical sense – a mouthpiece for a demon, expert at mythology, who feeds pagan lies to her while gnawing on her innards. The Bishop manages to bait the lions of the old pagan curriculum while manoeuvring with their lessons – laboriously – to attack a better scholar. Carrying the freight of two traditions, classical and biblical, while taking early steps towards a new Christian culture, both Origen and his opponent were handling a bulky part of the load when they confronted the 'witch' of Endor.

Human credulity is a carnival for the Devil and his demons: by the time Eustathius went after Origen, around 330, that view was habitual for learned Christians like them and Lactantius, who wrote in Latin a generation or two before the feisty Bishop. Listing 'astrology, haruspicy, augury, the things called "oracles", necromancy and the art of magic' – while seeing them all in the fabric of the classical tradition – Lactantius repudiates the whole lot as lies invented by demons to fool humans and thwart their salvation. He is so good a classicist, however, that he goes to the classics for evidence against defenders of the old religion, which puts 'almighty Jupiter in the same herd with the demons'.

His strength is in the cross. 'What power this sign has,' he exclaims, and how it panics the unclean spirits! The cross, a novel Christian talisman, 'checks their power and forces them to submit', which is enough to show that the new religion is the real one. The old gods, because they are demons, cannot drive demons away as the cross can, whereas the old rites are useless in the presence of the new sign. Case closed: why say more?

Anthony, a hermit saint and another servant of the cross, had no more to say – at least in the learned speech of Lactantius, Origen and Eustathius. Such a wonder was Anthony, however, that another Christian intellectual, Athanasius of Alexandria, wrote a *Life* to promote the saint, who was illiterate. When philosophers tracked him down in the wilderness to harass him, trying to trick him and 'make syllogisms about preaching the holy cross', Anthony replied that 'we Christians find mystery not in . . . Greek speeches but in the power of faith'. Because the name of Jesus and the sign of his cross 'have chased all the demons away, the ones that you fear as gods . . . magic grows weak and sorcery fails to work. So tell me,' he taunts his inquisitors, 'where are the illusions of the Magi?'

Meanwhile, when Anthony was living in a walled tomb, the old Enemy had already turned to different illusions 'since shape-shifting is easy for the Devil'. To terrify the hermit and test his faith, Satan had his soldiers fill the stinking hole 'full of phantoms – lions, bears, leopards, bulls, snakes, asps, scorpions and wolves – each moving in its own shape'. The Devil himself 'even dared take shape as a woman, behaving like a female in every way, but the young man extinguished the coals of the Devil's deceit'. It is the blaze of God's grace, however, not cold reason, that douses the fire. Having renounced Greek wisdom, Christians like Anthony discarded its philosophical equipment, making a risky trade by exchanging illusions of the Magi for Satan's own phantasmagoria.

But few Christians were like Anthony, for better or worse, nor like

Dionysius the Areopagite. Nothing like Anthony's peasant faith was the delicate glass-bead-game of belief assembled (just after the time of Proclus) by Dionysius. We know that name and little else but what he wrote – except that he was not 'the Areopagite' converted by Paul's preaching in Athens and mentioned in the Acts of the Apostles.

A negative biography suits this impresario of negative theology, often promoted by the Abrahamic religions in their world-fleeing mode. If the Creator is utterly unlike his creatures, not to be contained by vessels as weak as human thought and language, then no positive theology – nothing *asserted* about God – will do: one can only *deny* that God is anything *not* divine. The moral shadow of this self-abrogating syntax is one script for the problem of evil. Since our world, the one we can see, is such a mess, the God who made it must – despite having made it – be inconceivably unlike it and unimaginably far away. To bridge the gap, Dionysius devised an apparatus of go-betweens, the nine orders of angels, by adapting the hierarchies of Iamblichus to biblical tales of divine messengers and manifestations.

The result – still the core of Christian angelology – has been immensely influential, but only by way of other thinkers, less fragile than Dionysius himself, sturdier minds able to implement his moral metaphysics as liturgy and practical religion. Otherwise, when Christians said in prayer that 'the angel of the Lord' – meaning Gabriel – 'declared unto Mary', or if they went to a church named after St Michael, what could the words and labels have meant? Why call a prayer to the Virgin the 'Angelus', and why was that a time to ring church bells? Dionysius, whose whole life was a liturgy, cared about such questions. But it took hardier Christians to answer them with ordinary words and appealing pictures.

Dionysius is wary of the Bible, whose 'intricate hieratic figures and secret revelatory symbols' will lead too many to think 'in an unpriestly way'. From the mosaics that cover church walls with Bible stories, the ordinary believer might suppose, wrongly, that God's messengers are 'golden, luminous men, flashing like lightning, beauties dressed in shining garments, bright with harmless flame'. On the contrary, says Dionysius, angels are pure minds beyond all picturing, 'minds that have no figure'. Even grouping them in a triple array of triads to reflect the Trinity concedes too much to the discursive and divisive thinking of embodied minds. The pure doctrine as Dionysius preached it was a monument of unageing intellect, no country for men who were not old, nor for their dying generations. Still, the young had to get on, had to go to church, say their prayers and plead with God's messengers, visible before them in flashing, luminous images. And so those living mortals did get on, sometimes helped by material glimpses of the holy that Dionysius could not supply.

The faithful wanted stories to make the holy palpable, like the Gospel narratives about Jesus, telling in simple terms how the man-God – a repulsive paradox for some pagans – was born, grew, preached, suffered, died and rose from the dead. Demand for such stories was great – enough to produce not just the four different Gospels deemed official by the early Church but also dozens of other narratives, like the *Acts of Peter* that records a fuller account of Simon Magus than the version in the canonical Acts.

Placing Simon among the Samaritans, the New Testament says of his wizardry only that 'he astonished them with acts of magic', neither denying nor confirming that the effects were real. Our apocryphal version, set in Rome, is much expanded and pushes the question of authenticity. Simon has 'amazed the crowds with his flying', which large gatherings have witnessed against the backdrop of Rome's hills and monuments (see Fig. 7). But Simon's tricks had simply dazzled his audience, as Peter's Christian followers realized, seeing through the wizard's efforts to expose Peter 'for putting his faith in a fake god, not a real one'. Although Simon takes wing again (by all appearances), Peter's prayer brings him down: otherwise – as the apostle shouts to God – the crowd would 'not believe the signs and wonders that you have given them through me'.

Like Moses and Aaron showing Pharaoh their snake magic, Peter triumphs in a contest of wonder and power. Unlike the heroes of Exodus, however, he does not bring magic of his own to the competition, though he fears that 'signs and wonders' already delivered by him may lose credibility. After all, if Peter's own students assume that Simon's feats are just cheap tricks, the vicar of Christ should have no trouble scoring a win over this shabby 'Devil's emissary'.

Peter, never complicit in Simon's scam, triumphs when Magus meets Apostle in Rome. Some Christians of the day, taking Simon for a Gnostic deviant, will have interpreted the fight as heresy v. orthodoxy, with non-pagan contestants who were not – or were no longer – observant Jews. We see the different antagonisms that divided Jews from Christians in other stories about a flying duel in Jerusalem, tricked out with farce in a language few Christians could read: the *Generations of Jesus* in Hebrew. The Jesus of this tale, which eventually made its way into Latin, is a reprobate who steals his magic – and abuses God's holiest name – from the Temple's holiest chamber. Judas is his opponent, and he misuses the Name just as effectively to levitate and soar: 'as they both moved around in the air, everyone who saw them was absolutely amazed' – just like the crowd in Rome.

6.1

The Fall of Simon Magus:
Acts of Peter, 30–33

The core of this story, from just before the end of the second century CE, is plausible: a stage magician adds flying to his act, breaks his leg and dies (see 6.16; Fig. 7). But that is just the finale (right before Peter's martyrdom in a longer version) following other melodramatic clashes between the prince of the apostles and his nemesis, Simon Magus. Most of Simon's legend is known only from apocryphal texts like this *Acts of Peter*, embroidering a few lines from the New Testament that had secured the wizard's fame (see 2.18). He sometimes gets the blame for leading a Gnostic challenge to Christian orthodoxy, but heresy is not the main issue here, where two types of power clash: the Devil's magic infecting Simon v. God's grace working in Peter. Since Peter's miracles rely on *divine* power, Simon must lose, or else the Christian God loses face – along with the crowds who want Peter to heal their ailments and amaze them with his 'signs and wonders'. Even before Peter shows him up, Simon is a fake in these *Acts*. But his fall – the prelude to Peter's triumphant crucifixion – proves only that his magic is weak, not necessarily false. And his broken leg shows that grace too can cause casualties (see 2.14).

*

Since it was Sunday and Peter was preaching to the brethren and urging them to believe in Christ, many nobility and quite a few gentry, including wealthy ladies and matrons, were confirmed in their faith . . . On the Sabbath they also brought the sick to Peter, praying for them to be cured of their illnesses. Because they had faith in Christ's name, many paralytics were healed along with victims of gout and semi-tertian and quartan fevers: people were cured of every disease that ails the body, as more and more accepted the Lord's grace every day.

But after a few days had passed, Simon the Magus announced to the crowd that he would expose Peter for putting his faith in a fake god, not a real one. Though Simon produced many illusions, the students who were already confirmed sniggered at him. In the eating-places, he brought some spirits on stage in front of them, but these were just appearances and not really there. What else to say? Simon talked a great deal about magic. He made the lame look like they were healed for a little while, and likewise the blind. Once he seemed to make many dead people live and move – as he had done with Stratonicus. Keeping track of all this, Peter exposed the Magus in front of those who had been witnesses.

Since Simon had not managed to do as he promised and kept being humiliated by the crowd in Rome – mocked by them and not believed – he finally made this speech to them: 'People of Rome, now you suppose that Peter has got the best of me, and you listen to him instead because he is more powerful: but you have been tricked. Tomorrow, because you are ungodly and irreverent, I will leave you to fly up to God, whose Power I am – though diminished. If you have fallen, then look: I am He who Stands. I am going up to the Father, and I shall say to him, "They wanted me – your Son who Stands – to bow down too, but I soared up on my own and did not give in to them."'

By the next day, a larger crowd had already gathered on the Sacred Way to see Simon fly. But Peter, who had seen a vision, came to that place to expose him in this business as well. For when Simon came to Rome, he had amazed the crowds with his flying. But Peter – who would expose him – was not yet living in Rome, a city so dazzled by Simon's illusions that he made people crazy.

Standing on a high place and seeing Peter, Simon started to speak: 'The time has come, Peter, as I ascend in front of all these observers, to tell you this. If your god has the power – the god that the Jews buried, those same Jews who stoned you because you had been chosen by him – let this god show that faith in him is faith in God, and let it be seen, right here and now, that this is a faith worthy of God. For by ascending I shall prove to this whole crowd what kind of man I am!' And look: he was lifted up high so that everyone in Rome saw him, rising even above the city's hills and temples, as the faithful looked towards Peter.

Seeing this incredible spectacle, Peter cried out to the Lord Jesus Christ: 'If you let this person do what he has tried, it will cause all those who believe in you to stumble, and they will not believe the signs and wonders that you have given them through me. Come quick with your grace, Lord, and make him fall down from that height, broken and depleted but not dead, with his leg fractured in three places.' And Simon fell from that height, fracturing his leg in three places. After stoning him, each of them went off to his own place, all believing in Peter from then on.

One of Simon's friends – Gemellus by name, from whom Simon got many things and whose wife was Greek – rushed in from the road. And when he saw that his leg was broken, Gemellus said, 'Simon, if the god's power is shattered, will not this god, whose Power you are, grow dim?' Then Gemellus too ran after Peter, saying to him, 'I also wish to be one of those who believe in Christ,' and Peter said, 'Then what will stop you, my brother? Come join us.' But after his accident Simon found some people to carry him on a stretcher at night from Rome to Aricia. While staying there, he was brought to a certain Castor who had been banished from Rome to Terracina on a charge of magic. And after surgery that was where Simon – the Devil's emissary – brought his life to an end.

6.2

Belly-talkers:
Origen, *On the First Book of Kings*

When the Witch of Endor called up a ghost, did the prophet Samuel really rise (see 1.10)? When Samuel arrived, where did he come from? As one of the righteous, could the prophet have been in hell? Christians believed that the crucified Christ went down there briefly to rescue just souls like Samuel: this was the 'harrowing' of hell (see Fig. 3). For Jews there was no such doctrine to apply to this story, which seems to be about divining with the dead – necromancy. But 'belly-talker' – *engastrimuthos* or in Latin *ventriloquus*, not 'necromancer' or 'witch' – is what the Septuagint calls the Witch of Endor, and that Greek translation was the official bible for Christians of the early third century. Where Origen, the leading bible scholar of the day, saw 'belly-talker' in the Greek, he would find *b'alath-'ov* in the Hebrew – though what he might have made of those words is unclear (see 1.9). What the story describes is no mere stage performance, nothing as trivial as ventriloquism. But is the action as macabre as necromancy? Origen – reading the text closely, word by word – insists that Samuel really rose. If he were right, and if the story were about necromancy, the Bible itself would authenticate that ghastly practice for Christian readers, without legitimating it.

*

What was actually written? 'Then the woman asked, "Whom shall I raise up for you?"' Whose voice is it that says 'then the woman asked'? Is this the voice of the Holy Spirit, by whom we believe scripture was written, or someone else's? For the narrator's voice (as any expert on any type of text will tell you) is always the author's, and we believe that the author of these texts is not a human but the Holy Spirit who inspires humans. So it is the Holy Spirit who says 'then the woman asked, "Whom shall I raise up for you?" "Raise Samuel up," he said.'

Who is it that says 'when the woman saw Samuel, she cried out in a loud voice'? To anyone who deafens us with such questions and says a thousand times that Samuel was not in hell, I shall say that the narrator's voice said this:

When the woman saw Samuel, she cried out in a loud voice and said to Saul, 'Why have you deceived me? You are Saul!' The king said to her, 'Have no fear. What do you see?' 'I see a godly spirit rising out of the earth,' said the woman. 'What shape is it?' he asked. 'An old man comes up, wrapped in a double cloak,' she said.

For the Scripture says that she also saw his priestly cloak.

Now I know that a person who supports the contrary view will say, 'No surprises there: since Satan himself shifts his shape into an angel of light, there is also no big problem if his officers shift their shapes into ministers of justice.' But what is it that 'the woman saw'? This is 'Samuel'. For it is not written that the woman saw a demon who pretended to be Samuel. What is written, on the contrary, is that 'Saul knew it was Samuel'. Had it not been Samuel, what should have been written is that Saul *thought* it was Samuel. Instead it is written that he '*knew* it was Samuel', and no one *knows* something that does not exist. So 'Saul knew it was Samuel, and he bowed down with his face to the ground, prostrating himself.' . . .

Again . . . scripture confirms that Samuel himself says, 'Why ask me . . . since the Lord has turned away from you?' Is he telling the truth or a lie when he claims that the Lord 'has turned away from you and become your enemy . . .' saying 'he has ripped the kingdom from your hand and has given it to your partner'? Would a demon prophesy about the Kingdom of Israel? Who takes the contrary position? See how many disagreements lie in the word of God . . .

I maintain, then, that we must scrutinize this passage and read it historically . . . All that effort will show that the story is not false and that the one brought up was Samuel. Then what is the belly-talker doing? What does a belly-talker have to do with raising the soul of a just man? . . . Jesus Christ was in hell . . . and my question is this: Christ went down to hell to do what? To conquer death or be conquered by it? He went down to those places not as a servant of those who were there, but as their Lord to do battle . . . Fear not: there is no reason to tremble. Jesus Christ went to hell, and the prophets went there before him, to proclaim Christ's arrival in advance.

6.3
Lies of a Demon-ridden Hag: Eustathius of Antioch, Against Origen's Thesis, 27–30

What is a 'magician', and is that the same as a 'wizard' or a 'sorcerer'? Such questions have haunted the story of magic from the beginning. Who knows what the author of the Samuel stories was thinking when he called the Witch of Endor an expert on 'ου (see 1.10)? Was she a 'ghost-questioner', a 'belly-talker' or a 'myth-in-the-belly-woman'? Writing after 337, Eustathius promotes the last interpretation, far-fetched though it is, to conclude an attack on Origen (see 6.2). Savage, witty and attentive to language, he pushes the etymology of *engastrimuthos* beyond plausibility, ignoring the core of the Greek word *muthos*, which is 'word' – not 'myth'. This suggests that the belly-speaker's job-title was meant to describe her technique when Saul needed her to help him talk with Samuel's ghost. Insisting that no ghost actually appeared, Eustathius claims that a demon somehow caused the woman at Endor to belch up an illusion.

*

Reasoning falsely about the all-holy sentences, Origen chooses to guarantee the statements of the *engastrimuthos*, advertising new-made tools for idol-worship and piling them up to support impious divination by demons. But he is not convinced that this composite name makes any difference. In fact, the interpretation of *en-gastri-muthos* is 'telling about a *muthos* formed in the *gastêr*' – a 'myth-in-the-belly'. But the composing of the myth – covered over by the belly and happening inside it, no doubt – speaks loud for lies, not the truth . . . Worst of all – in a fever of superstition – Origen sneaks in some Greek divining. But on this point too, I think we cannot avoid taking a few moments to expose his stupidity, as one should . . .

Preserving the irregular rhythms of its narrative at every point, a myth depicts the beginning of a war and the end while also representing its progress – even the lips that speak and details of the speeches, the laughing and weeping, orations by chieftains, revels and parties, orgies, initiations, debauched carousing, erotic groaning, piratic seizures, irreparable destruction, indiscriminate slaughter, displays of poverty and deluges of wealth. A myth makes all these points convincingly, and reports *unreal* events with explicit information about behaviour . . .

So then, if what the poetry of Homer and Hesiod shows us is a false mythology whose main effect is to delude those who hear it at school, even though its elegant language excites the mind to perfect fluency, how much worse will anyone find the lies of a demon-ridden hag as she utters her fabulous phrases, especially since the term *engastrimuthos* bears out this understanding? If the boys from Greece – those experts on coining words for everything – call myths 'false' and 'counterfeit' in their own Greek tongue, it follows that the *name* leads one to suspect the worst of the *thing* . . .

Hence, if the name has been put in the correct relation to the thing, the *engastrimuthos* would seem to compose a 'myth' in her 'belly'. For she does not speak rationally or think normally. The demon lurking in her inner parts feeds on her and mars her judgement, and from her belly she utters the nonsense and weird words that the demon puts together there, overpowering her soul with various hallucinations as he transforms things into intricate shapes. But since he wears many masks and changes from form to form, it is nothing much to put on a show of rising from the earth and speaking . . .

6.4

Unclean and Inconstant Spirits:
Lactantius, *Divine Institutes*, 2.15–17

If Simon Magus is 'the Devil's emissary', the Devil's legions are the soldiers of sorcery, according to Lactantius, a prominent intellectual and politician who died around 320, after converting to Christianity and serving the Emperor Constantine (see 6.1). He describes demons as fallen angels and demoted gods who purvey magic to lure sinners away from the true faith to idolatry (see 5.10, 13; 6.5; 7.2–3). He knew the Hermetic writings in Greek and valued their theological insights, but he takes advantage of contradictions in the *Asclepius* in order to promote the Christian demonization of the old gods (see 5.11).

*

In the end, Hermes confirms that the protection for those who have knowledge of God is not just against attacks by demons: not even Fate holds them in its grip. 'Piety is the one protection,' he says: 'neither an evil demon nor Fate controls a pious person. For God frees the pious from all evil because piety is the one and only good in humans.' What piety is, however, Hermes attests in a different place with these words: 'piety is knowledge of God'. Asclepius, the student of Hermes, develops the same idea at greater length in the *Perfect Discourse* that he sent to a king. But they both affirm that demons are hostile and troublesome to humans, which is why Trismegistus calls them 'evil angels', because he realized that they became earthly after being perversely drawn away from their heavenly origins.

Astrology, haruspicy, augury, the things called 'oracles', necromancy, the art of magic and any other evil besides that people practise, whether open or hidden: all these are their inventions. And in themselves these arts are all false, as the Erythraean Sibyl testifies:

> . . . for these are all deceits
> sought by foolish mortals every day,

though the same authorities are complicit in allowing such things to be thought real. In this way, demons dupe credulous humans with divinations that tell lies because revealing the truth it is not in their interest.

Demons are the ones who showed how to fashion images and statues. To turn people's attention away from worshipping the true God, they caused likenesses of dead kings, beautifully shaped and carefully decorated, to be set up and consecrated, and then they assumed their names as if they were just characters in a play. But when magicians – and those that people correctly call evil sorcerers – practise their accursed skills, they call those demons up by their true names, the divine names that we read in sacred scripture. And then these unclean and inconstant spirits, throwing everything into disorder and flooding the human heart with their illusions, weave the false with the true and mix them all up.

6.5

The Rites Are No Good:
Lactantius, *Divine Institutes*, 4.27

Serving a Christian Emperor, Lactantius declares that Rome's old gods are really demons – now defeated by the cross, whose power proves the truth of Christianity and proclaims its victory (see 6.4). Elsewhere, he reports that Constantine's soldiers won a crucial battle after painting crosses on their shields, though anyone could wear a cross as an amulet – a familiar way to attract, contain and apply power (see 1.6; 4.3, 18; 6.11). Lactantius demotes all the old gods: 'they are the very same demons thought by the people to be gods'. His proof is that pagan priests cannot expel demons, whereas Christian priests can, while Christian symbols – the cross and the name of Jesus – are enough to make heathen rites ineffective.

*

What power this sign has! Anyone will realize how much the sign terrifies demons by noticing how far they flee from the bodies haunted by them after they are commanded in Christ's name . . . When pagans make offerings to their gods, the rites they perform are no good if someone attending has the sign on his forehead,

nor can the seer give good answers to the questions.

And this was often the best way to bring evil rulers to justice. For when their masters were offering a sacrifice and some of the officials attending were our people wearing the sign, this drove their gods away so that the diviners could not see the future in the entrails of the victims. The entrail-readers – incited by the same demons to whom they were sacrificing – understood this and complained that people present at the rites were defiled, which drove their princes into a rage and caused them to violate God's temple and contaminate themselves with a real sacrilege: the atonement exacted very heavy penalties from the persecutors . . .

But since demons cannot come near those whom they see marked by heaven nor harm those protected by the indestructible sign – like a wall that cannot be breached – they use humans to hound these people and other hands to persecute them. When the others admit that the demons are actually involved, victory is ours! For a religion must be real if it knows how the demons operate, understands their cunning, checks their power and forces them to submit to itself, after subduing and defeating them with spiritual weapons. If our opponents deny this, the testimony of poets and philosophers will refute them. But if our opponents do not disagree that the demons exist and are evil, what choice do they have but to claim that some are demons and others gods?

Then let them tell us what the difference is between the two kinds so that we can know which to worship and which to curse. Are they allies in some way or really enemies? If some close connection links them, how different should we consider them, and how shall we mix the honour and worship due to each kind? But if they are enemies, why do the demons not fear the gods, or why can the gods not drive the demons away? Look: someone provoked and excited by a demon goes raving mad – out of his mind. We bring him into the temple of Jupiter Best and Greatest or, since Jupiter cannot treat human illness, into a shrine of Aesculapius or Apollo. In either case, let a priest – in the name of his god – order the harmful spirit to leave the man. There is no way to do this!

What power do these gods have, then, if demons are not subject to them? And yet those same demons flee immediately when commanded in the name of the true God. What reason do they have to fear Christ – but not Jupiter – except that they are the very same demons thought by the people to be gods? . . . The demons, whom they admit we should curse, are therefore the same as the gods to whom our opponents pray.

If they think I cannot be trusted, let them give their trust to Homer, who put their almighty Jupiter in the same herd with the demons, like other poets and philosophers who use the name 'demon' in one place, 'god' in another – though one is correct and the other not. For those utterly despicable spirits, when commanded, confess that they are demons. When worshipped, however, they lie and claim to be gods in order to throw humans into error and distract them from knowing the true God – the knowledge that is the only way to escape eternal death . . .

Anyone who wants to look deeper into this should organize a meeting of specialists on summoning souls from the underworld. Let them evoke Jupiter, Neptune, Vulcan, Mercury, Apollo and Saturn – Father of them all. All will answer from below and speak when they are questioned, bearing witness about themselves and God. After that, let them call Christ. He will not come. He will not appear. The reason is that Christ spent no more than two days in the underworld. What proof could be surer than that? I have no doubt that Trismegistus found the truth by some such reasoning since he said many things about God the Son that are included in the sacred mysteries.

6.6

The Great Pan is Dead: Eusebius,
Preparation for the Gospel, 5.16–17

Eusebius of Caesarea, writing a defence of Christianity in the early fourth century, promoted his new culture against older pagan traditions while also relying on them, as when he repeats a conversation reported by Plutarch around 100 CE in his elegant essay *On the Ceasing of Oracles*. Although this haunting story does not make its point explicit, Eusebius has no doubts: the death of Pan in the reign of Tiberius – an emperor mentioned in the Gospels – signals the end of earthly dominance by the demons, taken by Eusebius to be pagan gods, vanquished by Christ and repudiated by all the faithful.

*

Plutarch also discusses the dying of their demons.

'Suggesting that oracles are not gods but demons that serve gods – since it befits gods to be free of earthly matters – seems not a bad idea to me,' Heracleon said . . . 'But I consider it rather rash and barbaric to assault those demons with sins, reckless acts and heaven-sent errors and to present them as dying like humans . . .'

'Now, Heracleon, you grant that demons exist . . . But if they too are uncorrupted in their being, unaffected in virtue and sinless as well, then what makes them differ from the gods? . . . Look, it wasn't just Empedocles who left us with bad demons, but Plato, Xenocrates and Chrysippus too . . . As to their dying, I've heard a story from a man who's no fool or fake . . . Epitherses: he taught me grammar and lived in my home town. He said he once boarded a ship for Italy with a lot of cargo and many passengers aboard. Then, when the wind died in the evening near the Echinades, the ship drifted on and came close to the isle of the Paxi . . . And suddenly from that island a voice was heard – of someone shouting and calling to Thamus, which they all found amazing. For Thamus was the steersman, an Egyptian whose name was unknown even to many of the crew.

'Thamus was called twice and stayed silent, but the third time he answered the caller, who then strained and shouted, "Should you ever come near Palodes, declare that the great Pan has died." When they heard this – said Epitherses – all were amazed and began to argue with each other . . . Thamus decided to keep quiet and sail past if there were any wind, but if the wind stopped and that place grew calm, he would announce what he had heard. So when he came off Palodes and there was no wind or wave, Thamus looked from the stern towards land and said exactly what he had heard – that the great Pan was dead. No sooner had he finished than there was a huge groan, not of one voice but of many, and mingled with astonishment.

'Since many people were present, word spread quickly to Rome, and Thamus was summoned by Tiberius Caesar. Tiberius found the story so convincing that he dug into it and enquired about Pan . . .'

That comes from Plutarch. But it's worth noting the time when the demon died, as he explains it. It was under Tiberius, in fact. And scripture says that our Saviour, while spending his days with mortal men during that reign, was driving the whole race of demons out of human life. That is why some demons fell on their knees before him, begging him not to send them to the hell that was waiting for them. This also gives you the time when the demons were overthrown – a story never told before.

6.7
The Coals of the Devil's Deceit: Athanasius of Alexandria, *Life of Anthony*, 3–9

Athanasius of Alexandria wrote his *Life* of the first hero of Eastern monasticism before 373, about a century after Anthony left home for the desert. Through isolation, asceticism and grotesque abuse of the body, Anthony and other enthusiasts aimed to suffer their way to heaven – perhaps the only path open to the poor and powerless (see 5.1–2). But the Devil and his troops of demons stood in their way, as Anthony learned early in his career.

*

Monasteries then were not so many in Egypt, and since no monk yet knew the remote desert, each person who wished to take care of himself trained on his own, not far from his own village . . . At first, Anthony began staying in places just outside his village . . . and in that first location he tested his intention not to return to where his parents lived or to memories of his family . . . And the Devil, hating and envying what is good, could not bear to see such purpose in a young man, so he tried to do to Anthony what he had often done to others . . .

But when the Enemy saw himself weakening against Anthony's purpose . . . he ventured to fight with weapons 'at the navel of the belly', bragging about them – since they were his main way to ambush the young – and going after the young man. The Devil troubled Anthony at night and provoked him by day, so that observers even saw them wrestling with one another. When the Devil whispered filthy words, Anthony defeated them with prayers, building a citadel of faith and fasting around his body and blushing visibly when the Devil tried to excite him. One night, just to trick Anthony, that wretch even dared take shape as a woman, behaving like a female in every way, but the young man extinguished the coals of the Devil's deceit . . .

While toughening himself in this way, Anthony left for the tombs that
were at some distance from his village. After directing one of the companions
to bring him bread every so many days, he went into one of the tombs, and
after that other person had shut the door on him, he stayed alone inside.
Since the Enemy found this unbearable and feared that even the desert would
be built up with Anthony's training before long, the Devil came one night
with a horde of demons and beat him so badly that he lay on the ground,
unable to speak from the torment . . .

The next day, when Anthony's companion showed up to bring him bread,
he opened the door and saw the saint lying on the ground like a corpse. So he
lifted him up, carried him off to the Lord's house in the village and put him
on the floor. Many of Anthony's relatives and people from the village sat
down around him as if he were dead. About midnight, however, Anthony
came to himself and got up. When he saw that everyone had gone to sleep
and his companion was the only one awake, he nodded to him to come and
take him away, back to the tombs, without waking anyone up . . .

But the Enemy, hating what is good and astonished that Anthony would
be brave enough to return after the beating, whistled up his dogs and broke
into the tomb . . . Since shape-shifting to do evil is easy for the Devil, during
the night – while the demons made so much noise that the whole place felt
like an earthquake was shaking it – they seemed to come through the four
walls of the building as if they had broken them, shifting their shapes to look
like wild animals and crawling things. And suddenly the place was full of
phantoms – lions, bears, leopards, bulls, snakes, asps, scorpions and wolves –
each moving in its own shape . . .

As he lay watching, moaning from the pain in his body but with his soul
unshaken and thinking steady thoughts, he jeered and said, 'If you had any
power, it would have been enough for only one of you to come. But . . . for us
our faith in the Lord is a seal and a sheltering wall.' Then, after many attacks,
they gnashed their teeth at him since he was making a joke of them – not they
of him. Nor in that moment did the Lord lose sight of Anthony's struggle: he
was there to support him. And when Anthony looked up, it was as if he saw
the roof opened wide and a ray of light coming down towards him.

6.8

Magic and Sorcery Fail: Athanasius of Alexandria, *Life of Anthony*, 73–79

'Where are the spells of the Egyptians?' Asking that question, Anthony was surely thinking of magical invocations manufactured in his homeland (see 5.6). He believed that the cross – instant protection for the faithful, without any book learning – had overcome the demons, even though Egypt's Greek-speaking pagans still mistook the demons for gods (see 6.5). Ignoring the miracles worked by the cross, these heathens kept wasting their time with myths about perversions and crimes that no true god could commit. When the cross chased the demons away, magic, divination and sorcery went with them – or so Anthony claimed (see 6.14).

*

Anthony was also very wise. Surprisingly, he had not learned to read, yet he was a shrewd and thoughtful person. In any case, two Greek philosophers came to him when he was at the outer mountain, thinking they could test him, but he knew who they were from the look of them . . . When they saw that even demons feared Anthony, they left astonished. But others like them came to see him at the outer mountain, meaning to mock because he had not learned his letters. To them Anthony said . . . 'a person whose mind is healthy has no need of letters' – an answer that shocked others who were there, as well as the philosophers, who went away surprised to see such quick thinking in a person without education . . .

After this, of course, various others came – persons thought by the Greeks to be sages – and they asked Anthony to give a reason for our faith in Christ. But when they wanted to mock and tried to make syllogisms about preaching the holy cross, Anthony stopped for a while because at first he felt sorry for their ignorance. Then, using an interpreter who could do a good job of translating, he asked, 'What is more beautiful, to accept the cross or to ascribe adultery and the perverting of boys to those you call gods? . . . Or do you liken a god to things that lack reason, and that is why you worship four-footed beasts, serpents and likenesses of humans? For that is what your sages worship. And you dare mock me? . . .

'As for the cross, however, what do you say is better? Is it better to bear the cross when the wicked are conspiring and not to fear death however it comes? Or is it better to tell tales about Osiris and Isis wandering, Typhon plotting and Kronos running away after eating his children and committing parricide? For this is your wisdom . . . When you talk about the cross, why are you silent about the dead who have been raised, the blind who have been given sight, the paralytics cured, the lepers cleansed, the walking on the sea and the other signs and wonders that show Christ to be divine and not human? . . .

'This is why we Christians find mystery not in the wisdom of Greek speeches but in the power of faith given us by God through Jesus Christ. And to see that this statement is true, look now at me; I believe in God without having learned to read . . . You with your fine talk have not hindered Christ's teaching, but I – by saying the name of Christ crucified – have chased all the demons away, the ones you fear as gods. And where the sign of the cross appears, magic grows weak and sorcery fails to work. So tell me: where is your divination now, where are the spells of the Egyptians, where are the illusions of the Magi? When did they all weaken and stop if not when Christ's cross appeared?'

6.9

This Noxious and Criminal Science: Augustine, *City of God*, 8.19

Augustine, who lived until 430, was well educated in Roman law, appealing to its authority to show that magic is evil – the work of demons, who are not gods and are no friends of religion (see 4.6–7, 14). In particular, demons do not carry messages between humans and gods, as Apuleius and other Platonists had claimed (see 1.2, 4; 2.1; 5.10). Augustine relies on a classical tradition that he also discredits: for information about magic, he cites Cicero and Virgil as well as Apuleius – who had written an essay, *On the God of Socrates*, describing demonic spirits as mediators (see 4.9–12, 17).

*

Why not make public scrutiny a witness against the magic arts that some people – ineffective and irreverent beyond words – also brag about? If these are actions by powers who ought to be worshipped, why is it that such strict laws punish them so harshly? Maybe Christians enacted the laws that penalize the magic arts? When the most famous poet of all says

> sister dearest, you and all the gods
> and your sweet self will surely testify
> how much against my will I arm myself
> with this dark technology of magic,

what else did he mean but that these injurious sorceries are plainly destructive to the human race? Elsewhere another line of his about

> shifting full-grown crops to neighbour fields

indicates that one person's crops are said to be shifted to another's land by this noxious and criminal science, causing a penalty to be established for anyone who committed this crime and then recorded in the oldest Roman laws, the

Twelve Tables, as Cicero noted – did he not? Finally, what about Apuleius himself: were the judges Christian before whom he was accused of practising magic? . . .

We have a very detailed and eloquent speech by that Platonic philosopher in which he defends himself against the charge of magic as something strange to him, claiming that he wishes to be found innocent only by denying that he has done things that no innocent person can do. All the marvels of magicians, rightly condemned in his view, happen on the instructions of demons and by their efforts. Given what he sees, why does he find that honour is due to them? Because, so he claims, we need the demons to get our prayers through to the gods – demons whose deeds we ought to shun if we want our prayers to go through to the true God. So what prayers, according to him, get sent from men through demons to good gods? Are they magical, I ask, or are they lawful? Magical, and the gods won't want them; lawful, and the gods won't take them from those couriers.

But if a penitent sinner pours out his prayers, especially after doing some magic, does he then get forgiveness through the intercession of those whose pressures and charms made him fall wailing into sin? Or perhaps the demons themselves, to earn forgiveness for the penitents, will have already done penance for having duped the sinners? No one has ever said such a thing about demons because, if that were the case, the demons who wished to attain the grace of forgiveness by repenting would never have dared to seek divine honours for themselves – since the one act is pride and detestable, the other pitiable humility.

6.10

Chronic Superstition:
Augustine, *City of God*, 8.22

The air is a prison for demons, not their natural place, as Apuleius had claimed (see 4.17). Far from being helpful to humans, they are dangerous, malicious and deceitful, only pretending to be gods and duping the ignorant (see 2.9–10; 6.4–5, 9, 11). When sinful humans need intercession with God, it must come from the blessed in heaven – from angels and saints – not from the Devil's agents.

*

We must put no credence at all in the case made by Apuleius and various other philosophers who share his views: the claim that demons come halfway between gods and humans as messengers and go-betweens, to carry our requests from here and bring divine help back from there. Quite the contrary: these are spirits whose strongest desire is to do harm. Complete strangers to justice, swollen with pride, livid with envy and clever at deceit, they actually dwell in the air because, when they were thrown down from heaven's heights, they had already been condemned to go there as the prison best suiting them – in payment for their unforgivable breach.

Even though the place of air is above the lands and waters, this does not put demons, on their merits, higher than humans: having chosen the true God as their help, humans rise above demons quite easily because the mind is pious, though an earthly body is no help to them. But the demons lord it over many who are plainly unfit to share the true religion, as if they were captive subjects, having convinced most of them that they are gods by using dazzling and deceptive signs as predictions or displays. But some have looked a bit closer and more carefully at their faults, and when these demons were not able to persuade such people that they are gods, they pretended to be messengers between gods and men who deliver divine favours. And others, thinking that demons do not deserve even that honour, believed that they are not gods, taking gods to be good but seeing them as evil. Yet they dared not call them entirely unworthy of divine honour, mainly not to offend the people, whom they saw serving the demons with their many rituals and shrines in chronic superstition.

6.11

Deluded by Lying Angels: Augustine, *On Christian Teaching,* 2.30–45

Advising Christians on the uses of secular learning, Augustine puts magic, astrology and some folklore in a category called 'superstition', which he sees as idolatry because it confuses creatures with the Creator (see 4.13–14). Astrology is idolatrous, for example, because it treats stars and planets as gods (see 1.7; 5.13). Demons are 'lying angels' who ambush sinners with such tricks, including some that seem harmless – like using a plant as an amulet in the way that Galen had described (see 4.2, 18; 5.14). Swallowed as medicine, a plant can act physically – and innocently – on the body, and then its magic might be *natural magic*. But how to explain the effect of the same plant worn or hung on the body as an amulet? Since the effect has no clear explanation, the better an amulet works, the likelier it is that *demonic magic* is involved. The amulet signifies a demon's presence and constitutes a tacit agreement – a pact – between the wearer and the legions of hell (see 6.14–15). Such an object, even without words or images – an *amulet* as distinct from a *talisman* – sends a message, an invitation to the Devil. Sinners should know better since Augustine has warned them about such superstitions.

*

Anything undertaken by humans to make and worship idols is superstitious, whether it involves giving divine honours to a creature or any part of a creature or enquiries and certain pacts and marks agreed and contracted with demons – like those attempted in the magic arts . . . To this group also belong all amulets as well as the remedies that medical teaching also condemns, whether in spells or in signs that they call 'characters' or in things for hanging or binding or even a kind of dancing. These are not for bringing the body into balance but for various signs – either hidden or in plain view – that they call by the milder name of 'natural' remedies, making them seem not implicated in superstition but working naturally – like ornaments on the top of each ear, loops of ostrich-bone on the fingers or telling you to hold your left thumb in your right hand when you get the hiccups. Thousands of the silliest practices are connected with these . . . like stepping on the threshold when crossing the street in front of your house, going back to bed if you sneeze while putting your shoes on, going back home if you stumble on the way out and, if mice eat your clothes, worrying more about some future harm than about the damage already done . . .

From this destructive type of superstition we must also not separate the people called 'nativity-makers' because they study birthdays – though now they are usually known as 'astrologers'. Although they may hunt for the correct position of the stars when someone is born – and may even track it down sometimes – even so, because they try to use the results to predict our actions or their consequences, they make bad mistakes and sell inexperienced people on a terrible slavery . . . The stars, whatever humans may call them, are still the ones that God has put in place and in order, and the fixed motion of those heavenly bodies makes the seasons change and vary. When someone is born, the state of this motion is easily observed through rules found and recorded by the astrologers whom sacred scripture condemns, asking, 'If they could know enough to calculate an aeon, why was it not easier for them to find its Lord?' . . .

Deceiving and deluding these people are the lying angels to whom the lowest part of this world has been subordinated by the law of divine providence, in keeping with the beautiful hierarchy of being. The result of their delusions and deceptions is that many past and future events are described by superstitious and destructive types of divination . . . When a likeness of the dead Samuel foretold the truth to King Saul, the sacrilegious rites that produced the image were no less detestable on that account . . .

Hence, all such arts are either nonsense or noxious superstition, established by a pernicious partnership between humans and demons: a Christian must completely reject and shun them as contracts made to seal a faithless and treacherous friendship . . .

Now some human products are sketches and likenesses of things in nature. Those that depend on a relationship with demons must – as stated – be completely repudiated and despised . . . Whatever has been written about geography and the natures of animals, trees, plants, stones or other bodies, as I have said before, is knowledge that can be used to solve puzzles about scripture – not that such things are to be used for signs, as if they were remedies or instruments of some superstitious practice . . .

For it is one thing to say 'if you rub this plant and drink the juice, your stomach will not hurt', and another thing to say 'if you hang this plant around your neck, your stomach will not hurt'. We approve the first, a mixture to keep you healthy, but we condemn the second, a superstitious sign. Where there are no charms or invocations, however, it is often unclear whether the object tied on or applied in some way to heal the body acts by a natural power – and can be freely used – or works by some signifying convention. In that case, the more effectively it seems to work, the wiser a Christian will be to avoid it.

6.12

Angelic and Demonic Sex:
Augustine, *The City of God*, 15.23

More than halfway though his enormous masterpiece, Augustine returns to a topic that he had left unfinished, perhaps because it was so puzzling: what does the Book of Genesis (6:4) mean by saying that 'there were giants in the earth in those days', when 'the sons of God came in unto the daughters of men'? Who were those giants, what was a son of God and how were they related? Trying to puzzle this out, Augustine almost confirms, and comes nowhere near denying, stories about *incubi* – male demons who specialize in sex with human females and (using the later terminology) beget witches (see 8.2). Since these lascivious imps cannot be 'God's holy angels', they must be the 'original apostates from God who fell with their chief' (see 2.4; 10.7).

*

I have left it unsettled whether angels – being spirits – can have physical sex with women, for scripture says that he 'makes his spirits angels', meaning that he makes those who are by nature spirits into his angels, giving them the duty of bearing messages: a person called in Greek ἄγγελος, brought over into Latin as *angelus*, is a 'messenger' in that language. But when scripture also calls 'his ministers a blazing fire', whether this too indicates bodies or means love as a spiritual fire is unclear.

And yet the same completely reliable scripture testifies that in such bodies angels could not just be seen but also touched by humans. There is a very widespread report – confirmed by many trustworthy people, who are not to be doubted, from their own experience or from the experience of others – that woodland gods and Pans, called *incubi* by the common people, have behaved indecently with women, have gone after them and had sex with them. And the demons called *Dusii* by the Gauls attempt this filthiness relentlessly and succeed, which it would be presumptuous to deny, so many reputable reports have there been. Given this evidence, I dare not say with certainty whether some spirits, embodied in the element of air . . . might also be affected by this lust and somehow have sex with women who feel it too.

But I could never believe that it was God's holy angels who had such a fall in those days nor that the apostle Peter was talking about angels when he said that 'God did not spare the sinning angels but stuffed them into Hell's dismal prisons, turning them over to be kept for punishment at the judgement.' He meant those original apostates from God who fell with their chief, the Devil . . . But the same sacred scripture gives very full testimony that men of God have also been called 'angels'. For this is written of John: 'Look, I am sending my angel before your face, and he will prepare your path.' And Malachi the prophet, by the special grace given only to him, was called an angel.

What some find striking, however, is that we read about giants being born – not humans of our own race – from those who were called God's angels and the women they loved. You might think that human bodies far exceeding our own in size . . . had not been born in our day as well. A few years ago, close to the time when the Goths would destroy the city of Rome, was a woman not seen there, along with her father and mother, whose body was like a giant's and much taller than others . . . though neither parent was quite as big as the biggest person commonly seen? Giants could have been born, then, even before the sons of God – also called angels of God – had sex with the daughters of men (men in today's sense) . . .

The words of the divine book plainly state that there were already giants upon the earth in those days, when the sons of God took the daughters of men . . . But after this happened, giants were born then too . . . And before falling as they did, the sons of God gave birth for God, not for themselves . . . , producing citizens of God's city to whom they, as God's angels, would bring messages . . .

Therefore, according to the canonical Scriptures, both Hebrew and Christian, there is no doubt that there were many giants before the flood, and that they were earthly citizens of human society. The sons of God, however, who were propagated in the flesh from Seth, slipped down into this society when they abandoned justice. Nor need we be astonished that giants could be born from them as well. They were not all giants, in fact, though in those days there were many more than in the times following the flood.

6.13
Nine Revelatory Names: Dionysius, *The Celestial Hierarchy*, 2.1–3, 6.1–2

This charter text of Christian angelology, long thought to be the work of the 'Areopagite' converted by Paul in Athens (Acts 17:34), reads like a product of the fifth or sixth century. Language and content put this and other works by the same writer in an environment of Christian Neoplatonism, shortly after Proclus (see 5.16). Although the author reveres the Bible stories about angels, his treatment is much more abstract, with none of the concessions to naturalism that Apuleius and some other pagans took for granted (see 1.2, 4, 12, 18; 2.1, 3–4, 6; 4.17).

*

We may not – thinking in an unpriestly way as the many do – suppose that the heavenly and god-formed minds are things with many feet and many faces, taking the beastly form of an ox or the animal shape of a lion or pictured with the appearance of eagles with hooked beaks or birds with feathers growing like hair, nor may we imagine them somehow as fiery wheels above the heavens or as material thrones ready for the Thearchy to rest upon or as many-coloured horses or spear-bearing leaders of troops or in such other ways handed down to us by the scriptures in intricate hieratic figures and secret revelatory symbols. For minds that have no figure, the divine word uses the hieratic figures of poetry in a simple way, out of consideration for our way of thinking, as I have said . . .

Since the sacred texts are to be taken as about simple beings not known or gazed upon by us, the imagery of the holy minds in scripture might be thought incongruous . . . One might even think that the supercelestial places are filled up with swarms of leonine and equine things, bellowing their hymns among bird-like herdsmen, other beasts and objects still more shamefully enmattered . . . But I believe that seeking the truth will show that scripture's wisdom is most sacred . . . Since it is *negations* that are true of the divine, while *affirmations* are unsuited to the secrecy of what cannot be spoken, it better suits the unseen to reveal such things in forms that do *not* resemble them . . . Incongruity is better than similarity for elevating our thoughts . . . As for more splendid hieratic figures, they might fool you into believing that the celestial beings are golden, luminous men, flashing like lightning, beauties dressed in shining garments, bright with harmless flame . . .

How many and what kind are the arrays of supercelestial beings and how hierarchies are executed among them: I say that only the divine Executor has exact knowledge of that . . . The divine word has called all the heavenly beings by nine revelatory names, and our divine and priestly Executor has divided them into three triadic arrays.

It says – according to tradition – that the first array is always near God, close to him before all others and in unmediated union. These are the most holy Thrones and the ranks of the many-eyed and many-winged – those named Cherubim and Seraphim in the speech of the Hebrews . . . This triple array makes up one and the same rank that my renowned teacher says is the first hierarchy . . . He says that the second hierarchy is completed by the Authorities, Lordships and Powers and the third by the final celestial hierarchies, the array of Angels, Archangels and Principalities.

6.14
The Wicked and the Unquiet Dead: Martin of Braga, *Correcting the Ways of Peasants*

Even in the sixth century, Saturday was still a day named for a demon, according to Martin of Braga, a Spanish bishop of that time. After the demons had fallen from heaven, said the Bishop, they took the names of villains from old myths, tricking ignorant rustics into worshipping them. Ordinary customs and conventions show how deep superstition goes, by Martin's reckoning. Because Saturn is a servant of Satan, an unconscious lapse – something as simple as saying 'I hope the weather is good on Saturday' – breaks the promise made at baptism to renounce Satan. An unthinking reflex, like saying *Gesundheit* after a sneeze, is the sign of a sinful obligation to demons who manipulate such signs – but not Christian symbols and rituals (see 6.5, 8, 10–11). And yet Martin – to make his point – uses *incantatio* ('chant' but also 'spell') for the Lord's Prayer and the Creed.

*

After God in the beginning had made heaven and earth, he made spiritual creatures, the angels, to stand in God's sight and praise him in that heavenly home. One of them, made to be an archangel surpassing all others, saw himself radiating such glory that he did not give the honour to his Creator but claimed to be like him. Because of this pride – along with many other angels who supported him – he was thrown out of that heavenly place into this air of ours, which is beneath the heavens. An archangel at first, he then lost his glorious light and became the Devil, dark and horrifying. It was the same with those other angels who had agreed with him and were also thrown out of heaven, losing their own brightness: they were made into demons . . .

After this fall of the angels, it pleased God to shape man from the mud of the earth . . . Then, once the Devil saw that man was made to inherit the place in God's kingdom from which he had fallen, envy led him to persuade man to transgress God's commandments, and for that offence man was driven out of Paradise into exile in this world of ours, to bear much labour and grief . . . Humans, once again forgetting the God who had created the world, forsook their Creator to worship creatures. Some adored the sun, some the moon and stars, some fire, some the deep water or water from springs, believing them all not to be made by God for man's use but to be gods who had come forth on their own.

Then the Devil and his servants, the demons, began showing themselves to humans in various forms, talking to people and trying to get them to offer sacrifices to them high in the mountains and deep in the woods, worshipping them as gods. And they used the names of people who were criminals, people who had spent their lives in all sorts of criminality and law-breaking.

So one demon would claim to be Jupiter, who had been a magus so sunk in incestuous adultery that he took his own sister – whose name was Juno – as his wife, seduced his daughters, Minerva and Venus, and also committed the most disgusting incest with his grandchildren and all his relatives. But another demon named himself Mars, the instigator of discord and conflict. Then another demon, the deceitful deviser of all theft and fraud, decided to call himself Mercury: people who lust as much for profit as this god sacrifice to him when they pass through a crossroads by making mounds of rocks and throwing stones at them. Also, another demon took the name Saturn for himself: since cruelty was his whole existence, he even ate his own children as they were being born. Another pretended to be Venus, a woman who was a whore and had whored herself not only in countless adulteries but also with Jupiter, her father, and her brother Mars.

See how lost people were in those days when ignorant peasants honoured the demons – sinning grievously – with devices of their own, and then for their own purposes the demons used the language invented by such people, so that they would worship them as gods, offer them sacrifices and imitate the evil deeds of the demons whose names they invoked . . . The damage that peasants do now, however, does not happen without God's permission because they have made God angry and do not believe wholeheartedly in the faith of Christ. So fickle are they that they name each day of the week with the name of a demon, saying the 'day of Mars', 'of Mercury', 'Jupiter', 'Venus' and 'Saturn', though no day was made by those demons – just by sinners and criminals of the Greek people . . .

Such is the madness that a person baptized in the faith of Christ does not keep the 'Lord's day', saying instead that he keeps 'Jupiter's day' and the days 'of Venus' and 'Saturn', to whom no day belongs, though in their own countries they were adulterers, magicians, the wicked and the unquiet dead. As I have said, however, stupid people show honour and veneration to the demons under the guise of these names of ours! . . .

As you can see, all this happens *after* renouncing the Devil, after you have been baptized. Going back to worshipping demons and evil acts of idolatry, you have betrayed your faith and broken the pact that you had made with God. You have abandoned the sign of the cross that you took in baptism, and you look to different Devil's signs made with little birds, sneezes and many other things . . . Likewise, a person who stays with the different spells devised by magicians and sorcerers has discarded the spell of the Holy Creed and the Lord's Prayer and has trampled upon the faith of Christ because it is not possible to worship God and the Devil together.

6.15

A Deal with the Devil:
Paul the Deacon, *A Miracle of Holy Mary*

The 'Roman State' in this story is the sixth-century Byzantine Empire, where the setting is on the border of Syria. Paul the Deacon, the historian who put the tale into Latin in the eighth century, attributes an earlier Greek version to the narrator, Eutychianus, from Adana in Cilicia, who may have learned it as a pious legend about a 'god-loving' cleric – the devout Theophilus. The plot turns on a written pact between the Devil and this ancestor of Faust, who experiences Satanic possession and witnesses a ritual gathering of the Devil's followers – a sort of sabbat (see 6.11, 14; 7.2; 8.1, 19). But the action starts with banal human conflicts and local church politics, poisoned by the anti-Semitism that fears of the supernatural sometimes aggravated.

*

Before the hated Persian nation invaded the Roman State, a certain manager of God's holy church – Theophilus by name and distinguished in conduct and manners – lived in a Cilician town called Adana . . . As it happened, God called the bishop of that place, ending his life. But since the whole clergy and all the people had great affection for that same manager and knew how diligent he was, they decided by unanimous agreement to make him bishop . . . But the manager kept protesting that he was unfit to mount the steps to so high a chair. And when the archbishop saw how persistent and stubborn he was – realizing that Theophilus had no intention of giving in – he let him go and promoted another man who could do the job of bishop for that church.

Once a bishop was ordained and the clergy had returned to their own town, some of them agitated to have Theophilus removed and a new manager ordained. When this was done and Theophilus left his former duties, his only concern was for his own affairs. The cunning Enemy and hostile Adversary of the human race, seeing this man live modestly and pass his days in good works, pumped his heart up with wicked thoughts, filling him so full of envy and ambition for the manager's power . . . that he even asked sorcerers for help.

And in that town lived a certain Jew, utterly despicable and a practitioner of the Devil's blackest art, whose treacherous claims had already plunged many people deep into the abyss of perdition. On fire with pride, the manager . . . hurried at night to the Jew just mentioned, knocked at his door and asked to come in. Since the Jew, hateful to God, could see that Theophilus had been worn down, he called him inside the house: 'What's your reason for coming to me?' he asked. Rushing up to him, Theophilus fell at his feet and answered, 'Help me, please! My bishop has gone against me and disgraced me.' The detestable Jew replied, saying, 'Come to me at this time tomorrow night, and I will lead you to my protector, who will assist you in what you want.'

Hearing this, Theophilus was happy to do as he was told, going to the Jew at midnight. In fact, that despicable person led him to the town's race-track, telling him, 'Have no fear, no matter what you see or hear, and *do not* make the sign of the cross!' Theophilus gave his word, and right away the Jew showed him figures who were shouting, wearing white and carrying many candlesticks – with their leader seated in the middle, for this was the Devil and his servants. Taking the manager's hand, the miserable Jew led him to that assembly of shame . . .

Speaking to the Jew, the Devil said, 'Let him deny Mary's Son and Mary herself, and because they are hateful to me, let him put this in writing: that in all things he denies them, and whatever he wants, he shall get it from me as long as he denies them.' Then Satan entered into the manager, and he gave his answer: 'I deny Christ and his mother.' Writing the statement out, he put wax on it and sealed it with his own ring, and they both left, immensely pleased by his doom.

On the next day, however, the bishop was moved by divine providence (I suppose) to call the manager back from retirement with every honour . . . As manager, Theophilus then began to organize, rising above everyone as they all obeyed him in fear and trembling and spent their time working for him. The accursed Jew often went in secret to the manager, asking, 'Do you see how well you've done and how quickly my protector gave you relief?' 'I know,' said Theophilus, 'and I'm immensely grateful for your help.'

For a little while Theophilus kept boasting like that, stuck in the ditch of his denial. But God, our Creator and Redeemer – who wants sinners not to perish but to be converted and live – did not despise his creature. When God remembered the manager's earlier conduct and how he had served the Holy

Church, he let him be converted to repentance. And then Theophilus, having turned away from all his pride and accepting sober self-denial, began to abase his own thoughts and feel depressed by what he had done . . . meditating on the tortures of eternal fire, the soul's passing, the flame that never goes out, the teeth that grind and the undying worm . . . He fasted, prayed and pleaded with our protectress, the Lord Saviour's mother, for forty days and nights.

And when those days had passed, she appeared, showing herself to him in the middle of the night . . . our Lady, truly the mother of Christ, saying to him, 'What is this? Why are you so rash and haughty that you keep up your pleading – this person who has denied my son, the Saviour of the world, and denied me?' . . . And the manager replied: 'How could I presume, my ever blessed Lady – I, miserable and unworthy, my mouth filthy and defiled, who have denied your son, our Lord, and have stumbled over this world's vain desires? But not just that: the help that I once had for my soul – I mean the holy cross and the blessed baptism that I had received – I have defiled them by writing out a statement of my most offensive denial.'

And the holy and stainless mother of God, the Virgin Mary, said to him: 'Just come and recognize him who is merciful and will accept your tears of repentance.' . . . Then that blessed man, with reverence and due humility, wailing with eyes cast down, made that avowal, saying, 'I believe, I adore and I give glory . . . '

After that vision had been seen and the day was over, the stainless Virgin and mother of God left him. And for three more days the manager kept begging and beating his face harder on the ground, staying without food in that same Holy Church and flooding the place with tears . . . 'I beg you,' he prayed, 'I, a wanton sinner, to grant me – a foolish sinner, sunk deep in slime – your kindly eternal fountain and merciful heart. Give the order so that from the one who deceived me – the Devil – I can get back the accursed document, the despicable pledge of denial that I signed, the thorn that sticks deep in my unhappy soul . . . ' Three days later, as in a vision, Mary showed him the document stating the pledge with its wax seal, just as he had delivered it – that pledge of apostasy . . .

But on the next day, which was Sunday, he went into the holy Catholic church. After the Gospel was read, he threw himself at the feet of the most reverend bishop and told him the whole story in detail: what had been done by that accursed and ruinous Jew and sorcerer, and then his own pride, his denial, the statement he had written for the sake of the world's empty glory, and finally his confession to God and repentance through the stainless and faultless fountain of God's mother, through whom he got back the statement

of his awful denial. And holding the signed document out to the most reverend bishop, he put it in his hands, to everyone's amazement – clergy and laity,
women and children – as he asked for that horrible and most evil statement
to be read in front of them all. All the people then understood what had happened to him, and how the document of denial had been returned to him . . .

After Theophilus stood up, he begged the bishop to burn that most despicable document, which was done. Seeing the accursed statement and pledge of
denial burning in the fire, the people keep crying out with many tears, 'Lord,
have mercy!' 'Peace be yours,' said the bishop, gesturing with his hand to
quiet them . . . and suddenly the face of the reverend manager shone like the
sun . . . As they went off to the holy chapel of God's mother, who had freed
him from his awful mistake, Theophilus ate a little and then collapsed as his
body weakened – in that place where he is buried . . . gone to the Lord, to
whom be glory now and always, for ever and ever. Amen.

6.16
Jesus Defiled by Judas:
The Generations of Jesus

Starting with a few Talmudic passages and echoes of the Gospel narratives, Jews made propaganda to challenge the usual Jesus stories. This tale was recorded in Hebrew texts of some substance by the tenth century, and it kept mutating: the *Generations* now survives in many different forms, including one that Christians could read in Latin by the thirteenth century. The Jesus that we meet in this version is a shady but impressive character, a con-man with talent and charm, and certainly not divine. His wonders can be duplicated by anyone who knows the trick and will take the risk of saying God's holiest name – the Tetragrammaton – out loud. A magic duel with comical aerial combat between Jesus and Judas mimics Peter's contest with Simon Magus (see 6.1). The story decays into farce, but it will be hard to find a plainer case of magic treated as religion gone bad.

∗

In the year 3671, in the time of King Jannaeus, a great evil befell the people of Israel, for a certain wicked man was born, a criminal and a lecher, from the line of a family of the tribe of Judah. His name was Joseph Pandera . . . and he lived in Bethlehem of Judah . . . [Deceived by this Joseph], Mary gave birth to a son, saying that he was named Joshua for his uncle . . . [but the people] called him by the name Jesus, thus signifying that his name and all memory of it were to be erased. When Jesus heard this and was heartbroken, he fled to Upper Galilee and stayed there for some years.

At that time, God's secret Name was carved into a certain rock in the foundations of the Temple. For while King David was excavating a foundation, he had found a rock with the Name carved on it covering a hole in the earth, and he removed it and brought it into the Holy of Holies. But those who were called Sages feared that young people would learn the Name and ruin the world (God forbid!), so they used the power of the magical arts to make two lions and put them above the door to the Holy of Holies, one to the right and one to the left. If anyone were to break in and learn the Name, the lions would roar and make that person leave so quickly that all names would pour out of his mind, and he would forget them completely.

And then, as the story spread that Jesus was a bastard, he left Upper Galilee and came in secret to Jerusalem, where he went into the Temple and learned the sacred letters. Then, to protect himself from harm after pronouncing the Name, he wrote it on a piece of paper, made a cut in his skin and hid the paper there with the Name, and by pronouncing the Name again he put the skin back in place . . . having done all these things with spells and arts of magic. But as he went out by the entryway, the lions roared at him so fiercely that he forgot the Name. When he left the city later, however, and cut his flesh open, he took the writing out and saw the Name after looking carefully for the letters . . .

Pious people came to the Queen (who was Helena, the wife of Jannaeus) . . . saying, 'This man does mortal harm, for he leads people into sin with him.' . . . And the Queen answered, saying, 'Bring him here, so I can know his case,' though she was thinking how to free him from their power since he was her relative. Sensing her intention, the Sages gave this answer: 'Please, Lady Queen, do not take it in mind to try to save him, for he corrupts people and leads them from the straight path with his arts of magic.' . . . 'Bring him to me,' she said, 'so that I can know what he says and what he does, for everyone tells me about his great and wondrous deeds.' Agreeing to do all that she said, the Sages sent for Jesus.

When Jesus arrived, the Queen said, 'I have heard what you have done to produce such wonders. Do something like that now, while I am here.' Jesus answered that he would do everything she wanted, asking only not to be turned over to the control of those villains who had called him a bastard. And then, when the Queen asked why he was afraid, he claimed that he was not, saying, 'Bring me a leper to cure.' When the leper was brought in, Jesus touched him with his hand and cleansed him by pronouncing the great Name so that his flesh became like a child's.

Then Jesus had them bring in a dead person, and when they brought someone in who had died, he put his hand on the corpse and spoke the Name. After Jesus did this and called the man back to life so that he stood on his feet . . . these were the Queen's words to the Sages: 'How can you call him a sorcerer? . . . Get out of my sight, and never say such things again in my presence!' Leaving the Queen's presence, the distressed Sages spoke with one another . . . and one of them said, 'If you will, let one of us also learn the Name and do wonders as Jesus has done, and maybe we can catch him.'

Liking this plan, the Sages replied, 'Whoever learns the Name and trips up this bastard, this son of a bitch, double that man's wages from now on!' Then one of the Sages, whose name was Judas, stood up and made this statement: 'If you're willing to risk blame for the crime when I pronounce the great Name, I shall indeed learn it!' . . .

When all this reached the ears of the Queen and her court, Judas was brought to her, and the Elders and Sages of Jerusalem came with him. But the Queen, after ordering her people to summon Jesus, said, 'Do in front of us what you did before.' As Jesus worked his wonders in front of the people, Judas said these words to the Queen and all the people: 'Let none of this astonish you, what this bastard does! For if this person builds a nest among the stars, I shall throw it down.' . . .

[Jesus replied as follows:] 'Now, before your very eyes, I shall ascend to my Father in heaven and sit at his right hand, but you Judas will never get in there!' When Jesus uttered the great Name, a wind came up and lifted him high. But then Judas also spoke the Name, and the wind took him up high too. As they both moved around in the air, everyone who saw them was absolutely amazed. Then Judas said the Name again and grabbed Jesus to throw him down to the ground. But Jesus also said the Name to force Judas to the ground, as the two continued to struggle. When Judas saw that his efforts were doing Jesus no harm, he pissed on him, and then both fell to the ground because they had been defiled, unable to make more use of the secret Name until they were washed.

Then they charged Jesus with a capital crime, saying, 'If you want to get yourself out of this, do now – right here in front of us – what you used to do.' When Jesus saw that he could not do this, he lifted his voice and said with many tears, 'My ancestor David prophesied that "on your account for the whole day are we finished", and so on.' When his followers and their no-good gang saw all this, they decided to risk death and use their weapons to fight the Elders and Sages of Jerusalem, while trying to escape from the city.

7

Arts of Magic That Astonish Us:
The Middle Ages

Figure 8: Riding with Satan

The first millennium of the Christian era was a time of struggle and triumph for the new faith. As Rome's religious institutions collapsed along with other elements of pagan power – demographic, economic, military and civic – Christianity's gains came with losses. Cities and towns withered away, and so did the schools, even though literacy was indispensable for a religion of the book. Novel Christian institutions, especially churches in towns and monasteries in the countryside, would eventually meet some of that need. But urban populations kept shrinking, and there were no monks in the West before the fourth century. How, in the meantime, would Christians teach their children to read a prayer or sing from a hymnal?

Gregory the Great, a monk who became pope, felt the weight of that question as he enlarged Rome's ecclesiastical authority. Born to a noble Roman family around 550, he had a first-rate education and realized how rare that advantage had become. Determined to preserve Europe's dwindling cultural resources for the faithful, he once chastised a bishop for 'lecturing on secular literature to certain pupils. This fills me with deep sorrow and disgust . . . because the same mouth cannot sing the praises of Jupiter and of Christ.' The bishop's disloyalty was one of his sins; another was wastefulness, squandering the intellectual treasure that a minister of Christ ought to guard for the Church. A contemporary and another Gregory, the Bishop of Tours, had enough education to write a history of the newly converted Franks. But he opens his book with an apology for 'breaking rules of the art of grammar that I have not been fully taught'. Was he fishing for compliments? Even so, he was right to worry that ignorance might cripple a righteous mind.

One effect of such fears was to narrow the range of Christian literature – as compared with the output of the defeated pagans – even where the volume of writing may have increased. Bishop Gregory and Sulpicius Severus were Christian historians, and there were others. Origen and Augustine were Christian philosophers, and there were others. Prudentius and Venantius

Fortunatus were Christian poets, and there were others. But in none of those fields, nor in the other secular arts and sciences, could Christian intellectuals – as a group and on the whole – compete with the hated heathens. Too much energy had to be spent inventing and enlarging new genres – apologetics, hagiography, salvation history, dogmatic theology – designed, in large part, to prove that the pagans really had been defeated.

This constriction is visible in the surviving traces of opinion about magic. Augustine, a major voice in those conversations, wrote so much that he had to write more in order to retract his mistakes. Experts classify many of his works as anti-Arian, anti-Donatist, anti-Manichean or anti-Pelagian because their author was a prolific defender of what he took to be orthodoxy against those heterodoxies and others of his time. Besides the letters and the *Confessions*, other writings – about two hundred and fifty in all – address faith, grace, free will, predestination, prayer, preaching, the sacraments, virtues, vices, sin, penitence, virginity, the soul and immortality, God and the Trinity, the meaning of scripture, true religion and other issues of Christian doctrine, life and morals.

The only title by Augustine to name a topic bearing directly on magic is a short work, *On Divining with Demons*, though long sections of *The City of God* are crucial as well as parts of other works, especially *On Christian Teaching*. The same pattern holds generally for early Christian literature. So much that was explicitly religious had to be said, and the old secular culture had become so untouchable, that many things went to the back of the line. Hence, when magic came up for discussion, the context had often been set by other issues of special concern to Christians.

Although pre-Christian and non-Christian writers about magic were less single-minded, they too had pressing interests and prior commitments – not to mention dispositions of time and place and the attitudes and prejudices of individuals. In Plato's Athens, Cicero's Rome or the Egypt of Plotinus, it might be clinical medicine, natural history, scientific puzzles, moral psychology, philosophical method, law, metaphysics, theology, epic valour, lyric passion or something else that set the agenda, while also motivating enquiry into magic. But no single dogma or complex of dogmas – nothing as unitary or exclusionary as Christian doctrine – shaped Greco-Roman cultural production as a whole, which included texts devoted entirely to one aspect of magic or another: demonology was explored in this way by Apuleius, astrology by Ptolemy, theurgy by Iamblichus and other topics by other thinkers, all contributing to a general conception of magic that would be synthesized by Proclus.

After Europe entered a second Christian millennium, specialized accounts of magic – seldom undertaken by early Christian writers – became even commoner than in pagan antiquity. As Christendom recovered from a long dearth of economic and social resources, religious dogma would mature, never having lost its grip on society. Crucial for recovery was the cultural leap forward around the year 1200 that produced the first universities, whose students and teachers worked to make up losses caused by the breakdown of higher education in late antiquity. Dogmatic theology – a systematic expression of religious doctrine – prospered together with logic and then metaphysics and natural philosophy, as the Latin West capitalized on gains made earlier in the Muslim world. Progress in natural philosophy, always constrained and sometimes resisted by religion, stimulated enquiry into magic, often taken to be a part of natural philosophy or as putting that theory into pratice.

Shadows of what Christians saw before them in the twelfth century can still be seen in the sixteen enigmatic sentences of the *Emerald Tablet*, derived from an earlier Arabic text. One line of this Latin document, later revered by alchemists as a founding scripture, teaches that 'all things have come from One, from the One's thinking'. That seems compatible with the Christian creation story, especially its Neoplatonic expression. Furthermore, 'lower is like what is higher, and what is higher is like what is lower', positing a principle of hierarchical similarity. Put into practice, this principle will 'work the wonders of a single thing'. Very good: a basis for wonder-working that Christians can accept. But read on: the author of the document is a pagan god, Hermes Trismegistus, and his *Tablet* treats the sun, moon, wind and earth as persons. Are they gods too? Only a close reading of the cryptic *Tablet* will settle such questions.

Since the instructions from Hermes in the *Tablet* are to 'separate fire from earth, the fine from the thick', elements and matter are in play, directing the enquirer to natural philosophy – the type of philosophy that would eventually evolve into natural science. By the middle of the thirteenth century, that part of Aristotle's comprehensive system had been recovered, encouraging further development of theories of matter, including the alchemical kind – for which Aristotle's physics was only a partial match. But that physics, with its corresponding metaphysics, ruled the Latin West, where no one remembered the ancient Greco-Egyptian alchemists, like Zosimos and his book *On the Letter Ω*.

However, a few people in Europe were exploring alternatives, coming from the Muslim world, to Aristotelian matter-theory. One Latin writer – using the name Geber to invoke the fame of a ninth-century Muslim, Jabir ibn-Hayan – left a derivative work of striking originality, a *Summa on*

Completing. The book is derivative inasmuch as Muslims had drawn on older pagan traditions to invent ideas about alchemy that Christians like Geber exploited and enriched. Its originality lies in a view of matter that was fundamentally different from the prevailing Aristotelian physics, whose authority was enormous and effectively universal in the West.

Aristotle's elements are four: fire, air, water and earth, carrying qualities in two pairs of opposites, hot/cold and wet/dry. Geber's principles, not found as such in nature, are nominally three – fatty sulphur (S), fluid mercury (M) and flaky arsenic (A) – but effectively two because arsenic behaves like sulphur. Aristotle rejects atomism decisively; Geber's system incorporates atomist notions. These are big differences on the basics.

Geber, while making use of Aristotle's elements and qualities, breaks with the esteemed philosopher in order to frame a new theory and apply it. The theory sees metals like copper, lead and gold (C, L, G, etc.) as products of principles (S, M, A) and as akin to one another. But no metal like C, by itself, can change another metal L into G, a different metal: $C + L \rightarrow G$ is not possible; but $C + S + M \rightarrow G$ can work. Only the principles can produce such transmutations, which happen naturally in mines, below the earth, and artificially, in the laboratory. The known distinctions between principles are mainly qualitative – colour, smell, texture, density, viscosity and so on – but matter itself at the micro-level has structural features as well. To put this theory into practice, the alchemist repeatedly applies 'medicines' to change those structures – to purge sulphur of its excrement, as Geber would say, often speaking in organic terms while gesturing at quantification. But his language is also religious, exulting in mystery and appealing to secrecy.

For university students educated in the conventional medieval way, it would be hard to exaggerate the strangeness of Geber's system – which aims to be a system in the strong sense. His ambitious and impressive *Summa* was an outlier in Europe's pervasively Aristotelian environment. And no alchemist had been prominent in the ancient Western tradition of magic. In its main channel – the *magia* of Pliny and Apuleius or the *mageia* of Plotinus and Proclus – that tradition had little to say about alchemy, despite the roots of both in Ptolemaic Egypt.

In the received story of ancient magic, where alchemy was invisible or marginal, witchcraft was entirely unheard of – if a witch is someone sworn to Satan, in league with demons and conspiring with other renegade humans to commit unspeakable crimes like ritual infanticide and cannibalism, flying by night to remote gatherings where the Devil is worshipped by orgiastic sex with him and his minions. Witches, in the words of one medieval authority, go out

in the silence of night . . . while the doors are closed . . . to cross great stretches
of land along with other women taken in by the same illusion of killing
people . . . yet not using any weapons that can be seen, and then eating their
cooked flesh . . . and, after eating . . . bringing them back to life again.

Calling this scene a belief, not a fact, the bishop who recorded it in the eleventh century knew pagan writings that mention other menacing females:
Graeae, Parcae, lamiae, sagae, striges and nameless women from the outback
famed for the evil eye. But it was medieval Christians who added such
fragments of horror to murderous fantasies of diabolical conspiracy, which –
despite persistent doubts from some churchmen – encouraged witch-hunts in
the later Middle Ages and afterward.

By saving the seeds of that insanity, turgid legal documents like Bishop
Burchard's *Corrector* and Gratian's *Decretum* helped add something truly
evil – and also truly original – to Europe's store of magical learning. Later,
then, when Cornelius Agrippa made his digest of ancient, medieval and early
modern magic, the demonology in his 'occult philosophy' could include a
band of demons – led by Asmodeus and ruled by Satan – who 'help bad magicians [*cacomagi*] and witches [*malefici*]'. *Maleficium*, a heinous and Satanic
crime in Agrippa's day, was no such thing until medieval Christians made it
that. The same medieval culture that supplied Agrippa with Geber's alchemy
also brought him the witchcraft madness – two very different extensions of an
ancient tradition.

Those two novelties were new kinds of *magia*. Other innovations were striking on a smaller scale. Learned Jews, commenting on an original scripture of
Kabbalah, gave instructions for making an artificial man – a Golem – out of
mud, while also inducing a trance to energize this monster. Ramon Lull, a
mystic who travelled widely after growing up on Majorca, isolated from the
Christian mainland, addressed an old problem of dialectic – how to find the
middle term that connects a predicate to a subject – with an extravagant solution: a combinatorial symbolism and mechanical procedure linking arts of
memory and invention with theology in order to 'answer all questions'. Around
the same time, Dante wrote the incomparable vernacular epic that gave the
Christian hell a concrete topography and unforgettable scenery, a space filled
by the poet with demons and damned souls who could be visualized – by people who knew the poem.

Born a century after Dante died, Nicole Oresme innovated by conceding
less to magic than some of his eminent predecessors in Christian scholasticism:
his rigorous naturalism – one approach to Aristotle's philosophy – had few

rivals before Pietro Pomponazzi in the sixteenth century. Oresme was stingier with magic than the most celebrated scholastic, Thomas Aquinas, and much stingier than Thomas's teacher, Albert the Great.

Albert's *Mirror of Astronomy* tries to systematize astrology in the scholastic way, by dividing, distinguishing and defining. Some older treatments – traditional accounts of the subject – were unsatisfactory: cluttered, chaotic and endless like the *Instruction* by Firmicus Maternus, or terse to the point of obscurity like *The Book of a Hundred Sayings*, a Latin summary extracted from Ptolemy's full-length work on astrology. The ninth saying teaches that there are 'images in the skies of each and every creature on earth' and 'faces in this world subject to faces in the heavens', which is why 'sages who used to make images of the stars looked closely at how stars entered the heavenly faces, and then they took the necessary actions'.

Not as much a riddle as the *Emerald Tablet*, the *Hundred Sayings* was a popular work and attracted commentators. They could take their bearings from the few things that the book says clearly, more or less, like the eighth saying: 'A wise soul will help the stars in their work, just as a sower of seeds helps the forces of nature.' This is easier than the ninth saying on faces. Everyone knows that good farmers give nature a hand by sowing in the right season; likewise, good astrologers will help the cosmos by respecting the right times. Times to do what, however? What actions did the sages take because they knew about 'images' and 'faces'? Besides those two words, five other obscure terms come up just in the first ten sayings: circles, receptors, choices, unlucky stars and stars of the second rank.

Albert's task in the *Mirror* was to clear a path through this jungle of terminology and map the exposed terrain. The job of collecting, identifying, sorting and organizing was the less delicate part of his work. He also had to align the results with Christian doctrine, and whether he succeeded is a nice question. Since Albert's church eventually declared him a saint, it comes as no surprise that his authorship of the *Mirror* has often been doubted, though not for sound reasons: one specious reason is that no Christian saint can have said such nice things about magic.

After a long discussion of talismans, Albert concedes that some 'get power from a heavenly figure'. This is the core of his position: a stone carved with an image (of a scorpion, for example) can draw strength from a mightier but similar figure (the constellation Scorpio) without relying on demons (like the old gods who gave their names to the planets). Ignoring Augustine's worries about implicit deals with evil spirits, Albert takes his lead from the *Hundred Sayings*, which relates 'faces in the heavens' and 'images in the skies' to 'each and every creature on earth'. The Scorpion, the Crab, the Lion and other zodiacal animals resemble earthly beasts. Could that resemblance carry the power for a purely natural magic, with no devils at all involved?

That is what the *Mirror* teaches – and not just that. If the heavens have an image for 'each and every creature on earth', many more will be needed than the eight beasts, five persons and one artefact in the zodiac. The *Hundred Sayings* fills some of the need with heavenly faces that govern 'faces in this world'. Albert – a connoisseur of magic manuals – probably knew an infamous text with pictures that shows such faces and images in a theory labelled 'necromancy'. Images of the kind he calls 'necromantic talismans' are displayed and discussed in the *Picatrix*, a Latin version – made while Albert lived – of an eleventh-century Arabic work.

Declaring necromancy to be its subject, the *Picatrix* presents an astrological theory implemented by astral and demonic magic. The practice taps the power of the stars with images, made according to detailed instructions and with specific purposes, both grandiose and mundane – love, wealth, power, obedience, catching fish or exterminating insects – that are as varied as the aims of the Greek Magical Papyri. If you want to heal a scorpion's sting, carve a scorpion into a stone, mount it in a gold ring and press the image into incense when the moon is correctly aligned with Scorpio.

Correct alignment requires the moon to be in Scorpio's second face. Like Scorpio, each constellation occupies a twelfth (30°) of the zodiac (360°) and has three faces (10° each), also called 'decans' – 'rulers of ten', like a decurion or squad-leader in the Roman army. When ancient Egyptians first constructed a calendar based on decans, they marked each ten-day sequence by a prominent star's first appearance just before sunrise – a 'heliacal' rising – and such stars were gods, in the unforgettable Egyptian style. Most of this was forgotten, nonetheless, by the time of the *Picatrix*, where astrology's main machinery – the zodiac and seven planets – is Mesopotamian and Greek in ancestry. But the zodiacal, planetary and decanal sequences are interlocked by assigning a planet to each decanal face of each zodiacal sign. The sun rules Scorpio's second face, where 'a man rises astride a camel and holding a scorpion in his hand'.

The scorpion held by the camel-rider makes him fit the zodiac better than most other decans, like the first face of Aries that 'belongs to Mars . . . a restless black man with a large body and red eyes, holding a cutting axe in his hand and belted with a white garment'. Images familiar in ancient Egypt had been twisted by time, made bizarre and unintelligible for medieval Christians, despite the drawings supplied by the *Picatrix*. The 'restless black man' remained nameless, but he, the camel-rider and their thirty-four companions are plainly persons – unearthly persons, not humans but gods or demons. The *Picatrix* lists them with their planets and constellations and shows how to address them by writing their secret names, like *zaare zaare raam*, the first three of thirty-three names, written together as a talisman and sealed with Solomon's own hexagram.

'The apex of astronomy is the science of talismans,' according to the sainted Albert, 'but with that part are linked those accursed necromantic books.' One kind of talisman described by the books invokes evil spirits without really coercing them, and another uses their names for exorcism: both are 'necromantic' and forbidden. A third is 'astronomical', however, and 'gets power only from a heavenly figure' because 'images found in this material world . . . obey images in the heavens'. A stone bearing a scorpion's image may drive scorpions away in this sinless (though risky) way even if words like 'love', 'Scorpio' and 'Mars' are inscribed on it.

By allowing words as well as images on talismans, Albert crosses a line defended by his brilliant student, Thomas Aquinas, though even he concedes more than Augustine. Proceeding more cautiously than his teacher, Thomas shrinks the domain of innocent magic by lining up the features – reliance on reason, semantic content, autonomy – that make its procedures not merely physical but also mental and thus obligated to other minds that defy God's will. Since the soulless statues of the *Asclepius* cannot move themselves, for example, the necromancy that activates them relies on a thinking and willing agent, a demon, whereas magical effects caused by stars and planets can be both real and sinless as long as no minds produce them – unlike invocations and other magical messages that get their meaning only from minds.

No minds are needed for the natural magic that links earthly objects with each other and with planets and stars. Many physical things, which are composites of matter and specific form, have magic built into them as imperceptible or occult qualities, unlike other qualities sensed as combinations of hot, cold, wet and dry. Since carving a stone gives it new qualities of a different kind – not occult but also not natural – any magic that the carving produces cannot be purely natural but might be permitted. Letters carved on a talisman and not present naturally are forbidden, however, because they spell out signs that only minds can understand.

What about a figure, like a scorpion engraved in a gem to make a talisman? Having a structure, a figure is like a form – the form that groups one natural thing with others and produces their distinctive qualities, both perceptible and occult. Just as a specific form locates a thing (like an apple) in a species of

natural objects, a figure puts a thing (like a glass apple) in a species of artificial objects, and both species – according to Thomas – belong to a genus that
is partly natural and wholly empowered by the heavens. Accordingly, the
engraved scorpion places the gem, which is a natural object made artificial by
the engraving, in the genus of scorpions that rises from earthly species (both
natural and artificial) to the zodiacal Scorpion. And – by its placement in the
genus under Scorpio – the gem 'gets power from the stars'.

Although Thomas was more cautious than Albert about talismans, neither
wanted dealings with 'the demons that help the arts of magic', and they could
have agreed on the best defence against them: 'prayer with a humble heart'.
Those words, followed by a plea to the Lord Jesus Christ, come with instructions for using a book that would have horrified both philosophers, a manual
of 'invocations and conjurations' that shows how to 'consecrate a bonded
spirit'. One passage begs the Trinity

> to sanctify and bless this book ... by these your most sacred names:
> On, Jesus Christ, Alpha and O, Ely, Eloye, On, Otheon, Stimlamathon,
> Ezelphares, Tetragrammaton, Elyoraz, Eygiraem, Usirion, Oristion, Orona,
> Anellabiassim, Noyn, Messias, Cother, Emanuel, Sabaoth, Adonay and all the
> secret names.

For the unknown compiler of this late-medieval manuscript – almost certainly a priest – the journey was not far from conventional Christian piety
with its 'sacred names' to spells and 'secret names' that would seem at home
in the Greek Magical Papyri. Secret names might belong to demons capable
of intimacy with humans, demons who could help witches impede human
sexuality or else pervert it to propagate more witches: Aquinas, who found
such notions presented by Augustine, enlarged and endorsed them, preparing
the way for the witch-hunts of late-medieval and early-modern times.

7.1
The Three Parts of the World's Philosophy: *The Emerald Tablet*

Ascribed to Hermes Trismegistus, this string of enigmatic maxims may go back to the eighth century in its original Arabic version, though Latin translations (including the one used here) began to be made by the twelfth century. Despite (or maybe because of) the puzzling language, the *Tablet* came to be treated as the charter document of alchemy and a sacred text.

*

The truth – without deceit, sure and absolutely true!

What is lower is like what is higher, and what is higher is like what is lower, to work the wonders of a single thing.

And just as all things have come from One, from the One's thinking, so have all things been born from this single thing, by fitting.

Its Father is the Sun. Its Mother is the Moon. The Wind carried it in her belly. Its Nurse is the Earth.

The Father of the whole world's every talisman is here.

Its power stays whole if it is turned into earth.

You will separate fire from earth, the fine from the thick, doing it gently and with great ingenuity.

It ascends from Earth into Heaven, descends again into Earth and gets strength from the higher and the lower.

Thus shall you have the whole world's glory.

This is why all darkness shall flee from you.

This is the brave bravery of all bravery that will vanquish every fine thing and penetrate every solid thing.

Thus was the world created.

From here will come wondrous fittings, whose way is this.

And this is why I am called Hermes Thrice-Greatest, because I have the three parts of the whole world's philosophy.

Complete is what I have said about the working of the Sun.

7.2

Have You Believed?
Burchard of Worms, *Corrector*,
5.60–70, 151–3, 170–80

Burchard, Bishop of Worms, died in 1025, more than a decade after finishing the *Decretum* whose nineteenth book is the *Corrector*, which is a 'penitential', a manual that tells priests how to interrogate penitents. Some sins are superstition, falsely attributing the Creator's unique powers to creatures – like the old gods, long since demoted yet still seeming to threaten the true faith (see 5.10–11, 13; 6.4–5, 14). False belief in non-existent power is Burchard's main burden, as he resists claims taken at face value much later, when murderous witchcraft accusations killed many innocent people (see 8.1–3). The *Bishop's Canon* of the twelfth century epitomizes Burchard's (somewhat) sceptical attitude and repeats his words – from a passage not translated here (see 7.3). Describing fantasies of night-flight, ritual cannibalism and mutilated corpses, the *Corrector* singles women out and links female roles (serving meals) with culpable delusions (invoking demons): Burchard's *Parcae* (Fates) are distant cousins of *Macbeth*'s three weird sisters (see Fig. 8). Shape-shifting and werewolves are also illusory, but some of Burchard's questions are about evil deeds, not just false beliefs. And since Satan is always active, superstition itself is 'goaded by the Devil'.

*

Have you consulted magicians and brought them into your house, whether to find something by the art of sorcery or to atone or – following pagan custom – have you invited 'diviners' to your house to divine for you, questioning them about the future as if a prophet were answering, or have you welcomed people who work with lots or hope to predict the future with lots or those who tend to auguries or incantations? If you have done this, you shall do penance for two years through the required periods of fasting.

If you have kept the pagan traditions that fathers have always, even today, bequeathed to their children – as if by hereditary right, at the Devil's service – traditions whereby you worship the elements, meaning the moon, the sun, the path of the stars, the new moon or the moon eclipsed, so that you could restore her brilliance by shouting and helping her, whether those elements assist you or you them, or if you have watched the new moon to build a house or join people in marriage: if you have done these things, you shall do penance for two years through the required periods of fasting because scripture says 'all that you do in word and deed, do it all in the name of our Lord, Jesus Christ' . . .

Have you made bindings and spells and those various enchanted bundles put together by lawbreakers, by herders of swine and cattle and sometimes by hunters, when they say their devilish verses over bread and greens and over certain illicit packages that they either hide in a tree or throw where two or three roads cross, either to free their own animals or dogs from disease or injury or to destroy another person's stock? If you have done this, you shall do penance for two years through the required periods of fasting . . .

Have you gathered plants for medicine while chanting spells that are neither the Creed nor the Lord's Prayer, meaning the *Credo* and the *Paternoster*? If you have done those other things, you shall do ten days penance on bread and water.

Have you gone anywhere to pray except to a church or another holy site shown to you by your bishop or your priest – to springs, rocks, trees or crossroads – and did you light a candle or a torch to honour that place or bring bread or some offering there or make a meal of it there or ask for your body or soul to be saved there? If you have done this or consented to it, you shall do penance for three years through the required periods of fasting . . .

Have you believed or shared in this superstition, that some woman can use certain sorceries and spells to change people's feelings – namely, from hate to love or from love to hate – or can damage or steal people's property with her bewitchments? If you have believed this or shared in it, you shall do penance for one year through the required periods of fasting.

Have you believed that some woman can do what certain women, deceived by the Devil, claim they must do, of necessity and by his command – namely, that on certain nights, along with a mob of demons transformed to look like women (the likeness that the ignorant foolishly call *Holda*), she must ride on various animals and be counted in their assembly? If you have shared in this superstition, you must do penance for one year through the required periods of fasting . . .

Have you believed what some believe, that those commonly called *Parcae* exist or can do what they are believed to do: namely, when a person is born, they then have power to do what they want with him, so whenever that person wishes, he can be changed into a wolf (which the ignorant foolishly call a *weruvolff*) or into any other shape? If you have believed it ever happened or could be that mankind's divine image could be changed into a different form or appearance by anyone except almighty God, you must do penance on bread and water for ten days . . .

Although the foregoing interrogations are for women and men both, the following apply specifically to women.

Have you done as some women customarily do at certain times of year: namely, while preparing a meal at home, you have put your food and drinks on the table together with three knives so that if those three Sisters were to come – the ones named *Parcae* by ancient tradition and ancient foolishness – they would be fed and refreshed? And have you deprived holy religion of its power and its name, turning them over to the Devil so that – as I tell you – you believe that those you call 'the Sisters' can help you either now or in the future? If you have done this or consented to it, you shall do penance for a year through the required periods of fasting . . .

Have you believed what many women believe and claim to be true, after they have turned back to Satan, believing that as you lay restless in your bed in the silence of night, with your husband curled up next to you, you can go out while the doors are closed and you are still in your body, able to cross great stretches of land along with other women taken in by the same illusion of killing people who have been baptized and redeemed by Christ's blood, yet not using any weapons that can be seen, and then eating their cooked flesh and putting straw or wood or some such thing where their hearts should be, and after eating you bring them back to life again and let them live for a while? If you have believed this, you shall do penance on bread and water for forty days (a carina), and for the next seven years . . .

Have you done what some women often do, goaded by the Devil? When some infant has died without baptism, they remove the little one's corpse, put it in some secret place and drive a stake through the tiny body, claiming, had they not done this, that the baby would rise and could injure many people. If you have done this or consented or believed, you must do penance for two years through the required periods of fasting.

7.3
Illusions and Phantoms:
Gratian, *Decretum*, 2.26.5.12

Known as the Bishop's Canon (*Canon Episcopi*) because *episcopi* ('bishop') is its first word, this official statement of canon (Church) law comes from the middle of the twelfth century but draws on older texts (see 7.2). Although women claim to ride through the night sky to serve the old gods and Satan – their master – those gods are long gone and the night flights are delusional, according to the Church's lawyers. Such fantasies corrupt not only the women who believe them but also those who accept their reports. Still, the illusions are diabolical, concocted by the Devil, the inventor and master manipulator of magic. Like Augustine, however, the law takes care not to exaggerate Satan's power by turning him into a second Creator, in the way of dualist heresies like Catharism, a severe threat to the Church at the time of the *Canon* (see 6.11).

*

Bishops must use every means to try to eliminate
fortune-telling and the art of magic

Bishops and their officers must work with all their might to root out from their parishes every trace of destructive fortune-telling and the art of magic invented by the Devil. And if they find men or women who commit this type of crime, they must expel them from their parishes, shamefully disgraced. For the Apostle says, 'After the first and second correction, shun the person who is a heretic, knowing that anyone in this condition has been spoiled.' By the Devil they have been spoiled and held captive, having abandoned their Creator to seek the Devil's approval, which is why the Holy Church must be cleansed of such a pestilence.

Nor may we omit this: that certain wicked women, having turned back to Satan and having been seduced by illusions and phantoms of demons, believe and claim that they ride on various animals at nighttime, with the pagan god

Diana or with Herodias and a countless multitude of women, crossing long stretches of land in silence and the dead of night, obeying Diana's orders as if she were their Mistress and as if they were called away to her service on certain nights.

Would that only those women had perished in their treachery without dragging many along with them to disloyalty and destruction. The fact is that countless many people, deceived by this false belief, take these things to be real, and by believing them they stray from the right faith and get tangled up in pagan error, thinking that there is some god or divinity besides the one God. With all urgency, then, priests must preach to God's people in the churches assigned to them, so that people may know these things to be completely false and that such phantasms are imposed on the minds of the faithful not by the divine Spirit but by a malicious one.

Since Satan himself, transforming into an angel of light and seizing some woman's thoughts to turn her away from the faith and enslave her, actually changes himself in an instant into images and likenesses of various persons – using dreams to delude the thoughts that he holds captive, sometimes showing happy things, sometimes sad things, sometimes persons who are known and sometimes unknown persons, and leading these phantoms off to lonely places – then seeing this, the person who lacks faith believes that it happens not in the mind, even though the spirit alone is affected, but in the body.

In fact, who is not brought out of himself to see many things while sleeping – in dreams and nighttime visions – that he had never seen awake? But is anyone really dull and thick enough to conclude that all these things that occur only in the spirit also happen in the body? The prophet Ezekiel heard and saw visions of the Lord not in the body but in the spirit, as he himself stated. 'Straightaway,' scripture says, 'I was in the spirit.' And Paul did not dare claim that he was raptured in the body.

Therefore, it must be announced to all in public that anyone who believes these and other such things throws his faith away. And a person who does not have the right faith is not God's person but the Devil's – his in whom the person believes. For it is written of our Lord that 'all things were made by him'. Therefore, anyone who believes it can happen that some creature is changed for better or worse or is transformed into a different image or likeness of something else, except by the Creator who made them all and by whom they all were made – beyond doubt that person has no faith and is worse than a pagan.

7.4

An Excellent Astrologer: Pseudo-Ptolemy, *The Book of a Hundred Sayings*, 1–10

The Syrus to whom Ptolemy had dedicated his *Astrology in Four Books* is the Iesure addressed in the first line of this very popular compilation, after the name had mutated from Greek through Arabic into Latin by the twelfth century (see 4.15). The compiler assumed a reader acquainted with astrological technicalities – like the 'times' and 'choices' (elections) of the second, sixth and tenth sayings, or the 'faces' in the ninth – that could be left undefined in short statements for informed readers (see 7.6–9). But travel between languages made the maxims more obscure than pithy. That 'a wise soul will help the stars in their work' suggests that astral influence is real, though not insuperable: a clever astrologer can help his client adapt to the stars, perhaps by using the talismans to which the ninth saying alludes (see 7.10–12).

*

Ptolemy said, 'I have already written some books for you, Iesure, about effects produced in this world by stars, and these books are of great use to those who want foreknowledge of the future.' This work is a harvest from those books, and it has often been examined – liked only by those who have worked with the other books to acquire much other information: so accept it with good wishes.

Saying 1, on knowledge of things that provide accurate judgement. Knowledge of the stars comes from you and from them. But an astrologer should not discuss anything specific, only what is universal, in order to see things in a more perspicuous way – not by looking at matter, which would not lead to certain knowledge. The knowledge that we have of a thing through matter is doubtful, but through form it is certain. And those who have knowledge of the future through the better part of the soul are closer to the truth because in them the soul's power dominates, even though they may not have much knowledge of this art.

Saying 2, on the real movement of the circles. When the person who chooses makes the better choice, there will not be any difference between the thing itself and its natural state.

Saying 3, on a star's apparent effect when it is strong in a person's nativity. From his own nativity, a person who produces something naturally or artificially will find a planet naturally strong in the same way.

Saying 4, on heavenly bodies of the second rank and on judging them. A soul that produces judgements naturally will make judgements about stars of the second rank, and his judgement will be better than that of someone who makes judgements about primary stars.

Saying 5, on changing and preventing harm to come according to the stars. An excellent astrologer will be able to prevent much of the evil that is to come according to the stars.

Saying 6, where choices are very successful, and where they are not. Choices succeed when the force of the time or the choice is greater than the excess that separates the two receptors. If there is less force, however, the success will not be apparent, though there may be some small success.

Saying 7, on knowing a virtue from the nature of the soul itself. Only a person who has a good understanding of the strength of the soul and the physical temperament will be able to produce judgements from the temperament of the stars.

Saying 8, on the level of the soul's foreknowledge. A wise soul will help the stars in their work, just as a sower of seeds helps the forces of nature.

Saying 9, on images in the skies of each and every creature on earth. Faces in this world are subject to faces in the heavens, and for that reason the sages who used to make images of the stars looked closely at how stars entered the heavenly faces, and then they took the necessary actions.

Saying 10, what unlucky stars are good for. One must use unlucky stars in making choices, just as skilled physicians use poisons in the right quantity.

Making a Golem:
Eleazar of Worms, *Commentary on the Book of Formation*

The Golem – an ancestor of Frankenstein's monster and the subject of Paul Wegener's classic film – is an artificial human made of mud. The rites used to bring the Golem to life involve manipulations of the Hebrew alphabet, especially letters that spell the names of God. A key quantity is the possible number of 2-letter combinations in a certain pattern, set at 221 by Rabbi Eleazar of Worms, an architect of medieval Ashkenazi magic and Kabbalah who died in 1248. Eleazar's commentaries on the *Book of Formation* are of great importance, and that little book – older by several centuries – had already inspired other Kabbalists. The short passage on making the Golem that follows here is a distinct section of Eleazar's introduction to one of his commentaries.

*

Whoever applies himself to the *Book of Formation* must be purified, must wear white clothes and must not be alone but with two or three people: as it is written 'the souls that they made in Harran' and also 'two are better than one' and also 'it is not good for a man to be alone, so I will make a help for him to suit him'. And for this reason Genesis begins with the letter *bet* of *Bereshit bara* – 'In the beginning [God] created'. Then you must get virgin earth from a place in the mountains that has never been ploughed, and you must put the earth in running water, make a Golem and begin the alphabetic changes of the 221 Gates for every limb and organ, one by one – using the letter of the alphabet mentioned in the *Book of Formation* for every one. At the start use the alphabetic changes, then in sequence change with *alef, alef, alef, alef, alef, alef,* always using one letter of the Name with those *alef*s and the whole alphabet. Next use *alef yod*, then *alef yod*, then *alef yod* and in this way *alef waw*, then *alef he* and so on, thus putting the *bet* in charge, and then the *gimel* and every limb with the letter assigned to it, doing all this when in a state of purity. These are the 221 Gates. From the first cycle nothing will be lacking, from the second – out of all the letters – one will be lacking, from the third two letters, from the fourth three letters and so on until *alef lamed*. Then start *alef mem*, reversing everything until the end of the Gate, and then the cycles are completed.

7.6
The Name of This Science is Necromancy: *Picatrix* 1.2, 4

The Latin *Picatrix* was crudely translated in the middle of the thirteenth century from a roughly contemporary and equally bad Spanish version of an Arabic original (called the *Ghaya* or *Goal*) written about two hundred years before. This magic manual shows how to make and use talismans, a practice grounded in a theory whose components are astrological, alchemical, medical, philosophical and theological – material introduced by the *Picatrix* as *nigromancia*. That necromancy is divining with the dead is the meaning of the Greek word, whose parts are 'corpse' (*nekros*) and 'divination' (*manteia*) (1.9–10; 4.12; 6.2–3). But *nekros* has evolved in the Latin *Picatrix* into *niger* ('black'), underwriting the vague notion of 'black magic'. Distinctive elements of the necromantic theory are (*a*) *spiritus*, a thinly materialized energy that binds heaven and earth (see 4.4; 5.8, 11; 7.15, 19); (*b*) an alchemical elixir, blending and cleansing mineral, plant and animal ingredients to transform physical objects and make them more receptive to celestial influence (see 5.12–13); (*c*) words that have a magic of their own; and (*d*) an astrological doctrine of 'choice' or 'election' that gives some control of heavenly power to people who know – and thus can choose – the times when influences come and go (see 7.4, 9). In fact, 'the whole power of images lies in choosing hours and times to get the right constellation to match the things on which the images are based'. Although no corpses or ghosts haunt this introduction to an astral magic of talismans, the forces in play are mysterious, dangerous and – no doubt – offensive to the single, dematerialized God of Muslims, Jews and Christians.

*

Know that the name of this science is 'necromancy'. What I call 'necromancy' is all that a person does by that work and by all its parts to produce understanding and insight for the sake of the amazing things that have these effects, when thinking about such things or wondering at them brings understanding. Because there are divine powers helping them to achieve what has been said, they are hard for our reason to understand and hidden from sight under their likenesses. That is why this science is too deep and strong for the intellect.

Part of this science is practical because of effects that go from one spirit to another, by making things alike that are not so by essence. Producing images is for the spirit to work on a body, but the process of alchemy is for a body to work on a body. And I use the word 'necromancy' as a general term for everything hidden from the understanding – things whose sources and causes are not perceived by the greater part of mankind. The sages call images 'talismans', which means 'forceful', because whatever an image does happens by force. And what the image was made to do, it does triumphantly, achieving that triumph by mathematical proportions, influences and actions of the heavens.

Images are made of bodies fit to achieve what has been described, and to do so at the right moment, when the bodies have been fortified with smoke to attract spirits to the images. Knowing how to do this is like an elixir triumphing over bodies, reducing them to different, cleaner bodies. This is how images work, doing everything by force, in just the same way that poison works by coursing through a body, transforming things and reducing them to its own nature, transforming a body into a different body so that the one body is changed into another by the power of the mixture that exists in the poison.

Know that the property of the wash called 'elixir' is a mixture of earth, air, fire and water. These four forces are united in it and reduced to its property and nature so that, when the wash enters and penetrates a body, its parts drip into the body and change it, and when the body has been made lighter, it is quicker to obey and more governable. Likewise in alchemy, the same elixir acts gently to convert bodies from one nature into another nobler one, first by covering up the spirit, the hardness and the creaking and then by removing the noise and the filth. And this is the secret elixir according to the ancient sages. This word 'elixir' means the 'strength' that shatters other strengths and overcomes them, transforming them from one property to another until the elixir reduces them to something just like itself. The elixir can be made only from animals, trees, plants and – for one part of the mixture – minerals, according to those who claim that it is like the cosmos and that the cosmos is made of the things that I have described . . .

And I say that necromancy is divided into two parts, theoretical and practical.

The theory is the science of the places of the fixed stars: first, that the heavenly figures and forms of the heavens are made from the stars; next, how they project their rays on to the planets as they move; and then how to understand the figures of the heavens when people go after what they want. This includes everything that the ancient sages said about choosing hours and times for making images. You must realize that a person who has that much knowledge of making images knows that the whole power of images lies in choosing hours and times to get the right constellation to match the things on which the images are based. And in one of the parts of necromancy there are also words because words have the power of necromancy in them. This is why Plato says that kind and loving words turn an enemy into a friend just as evil words of reproach turn a friend into an enemy, from which it is clear that a word has in it the power of necromancy. And that is the theory.

But the practice is compounding the three natures with power that flows in from the fixed stars. And this the sages call 'power' without knowing how it works or in what way the aforesaid power is added. But after those things that have the aforesaid power are added in, they need to have an elemental heat, and this is in the smoke that helps to complete that incomplete power. Likewise, they need to have a natural heat, which is to be dissipated. These two cannot be complete nor give any help without the person's ensouled spirit . . .

But when the ancient sages wished to make images, they could not refuse the constellations that are the roots of the science of images and the things that open up its effects. My purpose, however, is to discuss the roots of those constellations by which you will help yourself in everything that images do, and the heavens will make those roots for producing the effects of images. But those who seek to make images should first know how to balance the planets and the other constellations as well as the movements of the heavens.

They must also believe firmly in what they do with the images so that the results will be genuine and beyond question, nor may they doubt any of those effects since they are doing such things not to try them out or prove whether they are real or not. No: they are to believe that they are real and to will them so. The rational spirit will then grow strong and be joined to that power of the higher world from which comes the spirit of the one that acts on the image, and this will be what you seek. Now I want to teach you something absolutely necessary in this work – and for the worker who does better in this world. For I tell you that you should do nothing in this work unless the Moon is in a state suited and appropriate to the work that you mean to do.

7·7
Make No Mistakes with the Names:
Picatrix 1.5

Ascendants, faces, fortunes and houses, sextile and trine aspects: this technical talk about astrology is part of the machinery of the *Picatrix* (see 4.15; 5.8; 7.4, 8). Another part is the physical and symbolic apparatus of magic: rings, seals, signs, ciphers, unintelligible words of power and famous secrets like Solomon's hexagram, known in other contexts as the Shield of David (see 7.20–22). Such devices had not changed much since the days of the Magical Papyri: the stakes are life and death, sickness and health, pleasure and pain, love and hate, food, sex, power, money and many other causes of conflict or desire (see 5.6). Despite prior claims to the contrary, the author wants to test the practical results of his talismans, potions and magic words (see 7.6).

*

When you want to make an image to put love between two people and make their love and affection solid and strong, make images of both people with their likenesses. See that they are made in the hour of Jupiter or Venus, that the Dragon's Tail is in the ascendant, that the moon is with Venus or else looks towards her in a good aspect and that the Lord of the seventh house looks on the Lord of the first house in trine or sextile aspect. And after this join the said images together in an embrace and bury them in a place that belongs to one of them – the one that you want to cherish the other more. And what you want will happen . . .

An image to put love between two people. Make two images, and put the fortune in the ascendant in the first face of Cancer with Venus in it and the moon in the first face of Taurus and the eleventh house . . .

An image for lasting love. Make two images and put the fortune in the ascendant and the Moon in Taurus joined to Venus. On one image write a cipher – namely, the numeral 0 written 220 times – and on the other image write that figure 284 times. Then join the two together in an embrace, and a lasting love will be fulfilled between them . . .

An image to make a Lord's men cherish him and always obey him . . .

An image to increase wealth and merchandise . . .

An image to increase the size of cities and make them prosper . . .

An image to destroy an enemy . . .

An image to prevent the construction of buildings . . .

An image to get a prisoner out of jail . . .

An image to drive any person from his residence . . .

An image for catching many fish . . .

An image for getting rid of scorpions . . .

An image to heal scorpion stings. Make an image of a scorpion on a bezoar stone, and do this in the hour of the Moon when she is in the second face of Scorpio, with Leo, Taurus or Aquarius rising. You will mount this stone in a golden ring, and with it you will press a seal into incense softened under the aforesaid constellation. Then, when you give the person who has been stung a piece of the sealed incense, he will be healed immediately and the pain will be relieved.

And a certain man who came from the land of the black people said that he kept trying to test the things just described and the knowledge of them. He tried writing a name on a quarry-stone slate and kept it with him. When someone was stung by a scorpion, he washed the slate in water and gave it to the one who was stung to drink, and the person was healed immediately and the pain was relieved. He also said that when he had no quarried slate, he would write the name on a clean plate with chalk that he could use in the same way to draw things like a crocus or other such things that can be drunk. When he washed this in water and gave it to a sick person to drink, the pain would stop immediately.

Were I not worried about saying too much, I would tell about the marvels that he produced with those names since there are a great many people to whom he gave them to drink, and I cannot describe this quickly. Yet since I have seen those names tried, I have decided to describe them in this book of mine and in this chapter. And here they are:

zaare zaare raam
zaare zaare fegem bohorim
borayn nesfis albune fedraza affetihe taututa
tanyn zabahat aylatricyn haurane rahannie ayn latumine
queue acatyery nimieri quibari yehuya
nuyym latrityn hamtauery vueryn
catuhe cahuene cenhe beyne

The aforesaid names must be written in exactly seven lines, no more and no less, with Solomon's sign at the seventh line. And some say they must be written on the first day of Jupiter in the month of May, but others say they may be written on the first day of Jupiter in any month you like, and I have seen them written on various days as people preferred. Be careful to make no mistakes with the names or their forms or figures so that you do not fall into error with them. And the names written with *bohorim* I have seen a sage write with *nohorim*, using an *n*, though I remember it with a *b*, as I said above. And I tell you this so that the secrets of this science might be made known to you.

7.8
Images, Forms and Figures: *Picatrix* 2.11

The twelve signs of the zodiac and the seven planets are basic components of astrology, which links stars with planets in complicated ways, to which ancient Egypt added more layers of complexity (see 4.15; 5.8). To regulate their agricultural calendar, Egyptians divided each zodiacal sign of thirty degrees into three segments of ten degrees, in order to track the 'heliacal rising' of stars – Sirius, for example – that appear on the horizon just before sunrise. The Greeks called those thirty-six stars 'decans' ('ten-rulers') at a time when people still understood their role in Egypt's pantheon of animal-headed gods. But by the time the *Picatrix* was written, the old star-gods had been transformed, first in the mixing-bowl of Hellenistic culture, when Greek notions like the *dekanoi* travelled as far East as India, and then later through Muslim and Arabic intermediaries to the Latin Christendom of the thirteenth century, by which time almost nothing of the Egyptian originals remained in the strange figures described by the *Picatrix* (see 3.7; Fig. 9; 5.1, 4). If these bizarre shapes are conduits of astral power, what could they be but pictures of demons? One plain answer to that question exposes the talismans of the *Picatrix* as tools of Satan, but plain answers were hard to find (see 7.9–12).

*

Note that each of the twelve signs is divided into three equal parts and that each division is called a 'face'. And in each of those faces are the images, forms and figures that the sages of India talked about, such that every one of the said faces belongs to one of the seven planets. The faces are divided and distributed by the locations of the planets and their order, starting high and going down to the lowest in order before going back up again, as I shall explain – beginning with Aries whose first face is given to Mars, then the second face to the Sun that comes next in order, the third to Venus, which follows the Sun, and then the first face of Taurus goes to Mercury, and so on in order through the planets, until the end of the signs. These faces, in fact, have natures and forms that match the forms and natures of their Lords. And here I propose to describe the forms that are ascendant in each of them, as follows.

Figure 9: Fornicating as a Decan of Mars

The first face of Aries belongs to Mars, and – according to the great master of this science – the form ascendant in it is of a restless black man with a large body and red eyes, holding a cutting axe in his hand and belted with a white garment, and this is of great excellence in itself. It is a face of courage, serenity and unashamed excellence, and this is its form.

Ascendant in the second face of Aries is a woman clad in green clothes and missing a leg. This is a face of serenity, nobility, excellence and majesty, and this is its form.

Ascendant in the third face of Aries is a restless male holding a golden hoop in his hands, wearing red clothing, wishing to do good but in vain. This is a face of precision and precise teachings, novelties and such-like devices, and this is its form.

Ascendant in the first face of Taurus is a woman with curly hair holding a single son who wears clothing that looks like fire, and she too wears clothing that looks like fire. This is a face of ploughing and working the land, of sciences, geometry, sowing and building, and this is its form.

7·9
Talismans at the Apex of Astronomy: Albert the Great,
The Mirror of Astronomy

This short but impressive work is almost certainly by Albert the Great, a patriarch of university scholasticism who died in 1280. Besides describing the four divisions of astrology, which he calls 'astronomy' and treats as part of the normative science of the day – known as 'natural philosophy' – Albert also shows how astrology reinforces Christian piety by subordinating the hierarchy of celestial causes and terrestrial effects to the Creator's will. He maintains that astrological choices (*electiones*), far from eroding the free will of human creatures, actually strengthen it, and that some of the talismans (*imagines*) used to enact choices are morally harmless and otherwise beneficial (see 7.4, 6). Effects of such 'astronomical talismans', unlike those of the prohibited 'necromantic' kind, involve no personal agency – demonic or otherwise. They rely only on matching a heavenly 'figure', like the constellation Scorpio, with an object bearing the right image, like an engraved scorpion (see 5.12, 16; 7.7). 'The apex of astronomy,' according to Albert, 'is the science of talismans.' The *Mirror* gives an extensive list of writings about both types of astrology, 'in order to separate the lawful from the unlawful'.

*

Presented with certain books that do not go to the root of science, some important people have taken to complaining about them both because they are hostile to true wisdom – to our Lord Jesus Christ, in other words, who is the image of the Father and the wisdom through whom he made this world – and also because they have rightly been distrusted by lovers of the Catholic faith. People complain about some of these books but think that others may be harmless. Because many authors cover up the necromancy in such writings by pretending to profess astronomy, they have caused fine books on that subject to be disgraced among good people, turning them into something offensive and hateful. This is why a certain man, a zealot for the faith and for philosophy, has turned his mind to listing both types of book in order to make a record of them, setting out the number, titles, beginnings and general contents of each and who their authors were – in order to separate the lawful from the unlawful, and beginning (if he may say so) at God's pleasure.

Of two important subjects, each deserves the name 'astronomy'. The first is the science of the structure of the first heaven, with its features above the equinoctial poles and with the other heavens located beneath and situated above the other poles, in addition to the first: those are the heavens of the fixed and wandering stars, whose structure is like a structure of spheres inside one another . . . This science also describes what happens to heavenly bodies when they change location, as when invisible rays are projected, when the sun and moon are eclipsed, and other planets are eclipsed by one another . . . This, then, is one important subject that I have described as deserving the name 'astronomy', and no one will deny this unless he denies the truth . . .

The second important subject, likewise called 'astronomy', is the science of judging the stars that links natural philosophy with mathematics. For the most high God, in his supreme wisdom, so ordered the world that the living God of a heaven without life chooses to operate – through stars that are deaf and mute, as if they were tools – in things that are caused and found in these four lower elements. And we have one mathematical science that teaches us to examine the causing of creatures in the causes of things and another natural science that teaches us to perceive the causing of creatures in the things that are caused.

What more could an enquirer want than to have the knowledge that teaches us how changes in this world's objects, from one thing to another, are produced by changes in heavenly bodies? This one science is also one of the best proofs, is it not, that there is just one high and glorious God of heaven and earth, since it is clear that the motion below obeys the motion above? For if their principles were different, then God would have a partner in heaven or in earth, and the kingdom of heaven would be different from the kingdom of earth, since it is unlikely that this sort of obedience could be stable and enduring without divine assent.

The problem is plainly eliminated by that science, however, since the obedience in question stands and endures without change, and this is why, insofar as the science makes man attend more to God as the foundation and summit of everything, it moves man – to that same degree – to love God more attentively. For there is no way to love what is not known. But God is known not through something prior, since nothing else is primary, nor through himself, since he is beyond understanding. The alternative is knowing God through what is posterior – through his own glorious effects. But these effects are man and the ordering of the universe for man – plainly, ordering the supercelestials to give a pattern to rational beings and ordering the elements that measure the needs of rational beings – and no human science deals as fully with this ordering of the universe as the science of judging the stars . . .

That science has two divisions, then, of which the first is introductory and deals with principles of judging. But the practice of judging is the content of the second, which in turn divides into four parts, the first about revolutions, the second about nativities, the third about interrogations, the fourth about choosing the best times, and a section of that part is a part about talismans . . . The apex of astronomy is the science of talismans, but with that part are linked those accursed necromantic books about talismans, tricks, characters, rings and seals . . .

The principles of judging that make up the introduction to the science are the essential natures of the signs whereby we call something hot, cold, wet and dry, moving and fixed, neuter, masculine and feminine, diurnal and nocturnal, commanding and obeying, self-loving and hating, agreeing in ascensions, force or route, and then what happens when these are divided by regions, cities and places, by trees and seeds, by four-footed animals, birds and crawling animals, by parts of the human body, by diseases and by various things that pertain to habits of mind depending on fitness or lack of fitness . . .

The part about revolutions divides into three . . . The first deals with conjunctions . . . and the total of these is 120, of which the science pays special attention to those involving the three higher planets. It also includes all the planets as they eclipse one another, especially the luminaries . . . The content of the second part, about the annual revolution of the world, is the science of the Signifier in the hour of its entering the first minute of the sign of Aries, called the Lord of the Year. With God's assent, this Signifier cooperates in disposing things. Knowing this and the aspect of the planets towards it . . . shows how God in his glory on high acts in that same year through the stars, using them as tools . . . But the third part, dealing with the changing seasons, is about causal and accidental features of the planets above as they enter into the upper and the lower air; also about the differences of the year with its four wet and dry periods; the knowledge of dew and rain and their timings in various regions, through the twenty-eight mansions of the moon, through the forward and retrograde movements of the planets and the leftward and rightward breadth of the signs; and the twelve gates of the moon, especially their openings. There is also a science of the winds and their parts . . .

The part about nativities teaches nativities by explaining what the Signifiers of a child's rearing are, choosing the place of the hyle from the luminaries and the part where the fortune is, both from the degree of the Ascendant and from the degree of conjunction and anticipation before the nativity, and also choosing the Alchodes from the Lords of the four ranks of that same hylic place, which are the house, the exaltation, the term and the triplicity of the one that is in aspect, and especially the one that should be stronger in aspect . . .

The part about interrogations teaches how to judge the case about which an interrogation is made, where the basic issue is whether something can be done or not; and, if the answer is yes, what the cause is and when this will happen; but if the answer is no, what prevents this from being done and when it will be evident that it should not be done . . .

And then the part about choices teaches how to choose to start doing something at the time that is best for the person whose nativity is known because the Lord of the deed agrees with the Signifier of that person's nativity. But should the nativity be unknown, take the most reliable interrogation, because when someone interrogates, he has already gone from his nativity to something good or bad that is a sign of his nativity, and in place of the nativity take the interrogation as your basis because, since nativities are facts of nature, interrogations are like natural things . . .

I said that the science of talismans is a section of the part about choices – meaning astronomical talismans, not just any kind, since talismans are of three kinds. For there is a hateful way to use talismans that relies on signifying and invoking. Such are the talismans of the Greek Toz and Germath of Babylon that have places for the worship of Venus. Such are the talismans of Belenus and Hermes that are exorcized by the fifty-four names of angels who are said to serve the talisman of the Moon in her circle, though maybe they are names of demons instead, and seven names are carved in these talismans, forward for a good result and backward for a bad result, when the effect desired is to get rid of it. For a good result they also use the smoke of aloe wood, saffron and balsam, and for a bad one asafoetida, sandalwood, redwood and resin.

This does not coerce the spirits, to be sure. But when God permits them to deceive people because their sins require it, the spirits present themselves as coerced. This is the worst kind of idolatry, and to make it somewhat credible they watch the twenty-eight mansions of the moon and the hours of day and night along with certain names for those days, hours and mansions. But let us have nothing to do with this way, and far be it from us to show a creature the honour owed to the Creator.

Another way is somewhat less wrong, though it is detestable, and it is done by writing characters with certain names for exorcizing, as with Solomon's four rings and nine candles, the three figures of the spirits called 'princes' in the four quarters of the world, Solomon's Almandal, the seal for the demon-ridden, also the seven names from the book Uraharum, also fifteen from the same book as well as the names from the book of Institutes called Raziel's, namely those of earth, sea, air and fire, of the winds and cardinal points of the earth, and also the signs of planets and angels, listing them by the names they each get in the triplicities of day and night. Let us also have nothing to do with this way, for we suspect that something may lurk there – if only under the names of an unknown language – to damage the good name of the Catholic faith.

These two are ways to use the necromantic talismans that dare usurp the noble name of astronomy (as I have described it). And I have long since examined many books about them. But because I hated them, my memory for their number, titles, beginnings, contents and authors is not perfect. My mind was never easy with them, in fact, so I wanted to look at them only in passing so that at least I would not be uninformed about how absurd their wretched advocates are . . .

A third way, however, is that of astronomical talismans: this eliminates those loathsome invocations and applications of smoke and also has no exorcizing and allows no writing of characters but gets power only from a heavenly figure. Accordingly, if a talisman of some type from some place is to do harm – just what is wanted after first taking an interrogation with a reckoning that is completely certain and gets nothing wrong, either tiny or immense – then, if the signs signify ascension, cast the talisman under an Ascendant of that type, or under an Ascendant from the same interrogation, in an Ascendant of bad luck . . . But if the effect wanted from the talisman is pleasure or love or success, do just the reverse of what I have said, adding that its form must be carved under the chosen time, and with God's assent it will get its effect from heavenly power, in that images found in this material world of four elements obey images in the heavens . . .

But choices raise a very difficult question, for freedom of the will is not constrained by choosing the best time: on the contrary, when starting something important, disregarding choice is rash and does not free the will . . . All the philosophers have agreed that by knowing the time when a woman has become pregnant, we know the outcome until the infant draws breath and then up to the time it leaves the womb and even until death. But through the nativity astrologers have made no judgement except that the time of impregnation can hardly be known with certainty, and so Ptolemy says that the time of the nativity must be preserved, at least as a matter of judgement.

For the wife of a king, a prince or a lord living in the best conditions, is this not why we choose the time for her husband to get a child from her – if the Creator of the whole reproductive process assents – so that what will happen to the newborn are the good things, out of the series of nativities for children, that an astrologer foretells for the future? Again, is this not why we choose the time to give drugs if we know that the Ascendants and Signifiers in the ruminant signs – Capricorn especially – bring on vomiting . . . Or in a surgical procedure, shall I not fear to cut into a limb when the Moon is in a sign that signifies for that limb, for at that moment the limb is full of fluid, and the pain brings the fluid out. I have seen almost countless problems caused by this, I daresay. I have also seen a person, an expert on the stars and medicine, who was at risk from chest pain and drew blood from his arm with the Moon in Gemini, which signifies for the arms, when no illness was visible except a slight swelling of the arm, and he died within seven days . . .

But I do not defend the part about astronomical talismans since they come close to necromantic talismans. I claim nothing beyond what I said about them previously, that they get power from a heavenly figure – as in Ptolemy's ninth saying where he mentioned 'images in' and so on. But nothing prevents defending them to the extent that they can be defended negatively.

To give an example, then: casting a talisman, under the conditions described above, to drive scorpions away from some place – if God wills it – seems not to be an exorcism or invocation if, in casting it, they say it is a talisman for ridding a certain place of scorpions as long as the talisman is kept there. Again, there seems to be no writing of characters if they engrave 'get rid of it' on the back, or if they write the word 'love' on the belly and likewise on the rear of a talisman for love, or they write the word 'scorpion' – the name of the thing to be chased away – on the front, with the name of the Ascendant and the name of its Lord, who is Mars, and the name of the moon on the breast. Also, who will conclude that it is worship if, in the middle of the place from which we want to drive the thing, there is a talisman with a scorpion's head pointed down and its feet up? I do not recommend these talismans, yet it seems unreasonable for them to bear the bad reputation of the others.

As for necromantic books – without prejudging a better opinion – it seems that more should be kept than destroyed. For the time may be near when, for reasons that I now omit, it will help at least to look at them now and then, although those who look at them should be no less careful about misusing them.

There are also certain books based on experience whose names end like 'necromancy' – geomancy, hydromancy, aeromancy, pyromancy and chiromancy – that do not really deserve to be called sciences, being babblomancies instead . . .

7.10

Forms and Powers in Stones: Albertus Magnus, *On Minerals*, 1.1.6

Albert accepts that some stones have powers, called 'hidden' or 'occult', that are not sensed like hot, cold, wet and dry, the qualities of fire, air, water and earth, the four elements. Such powers – a magnet's ability to attract iron, for example – usually lack names like the familiar 'heat' or 'moisture'. They come not from the elements but from a *specific form*, the form that makes a stone a member of its species, and therefore a magnet, for example, as distinct from a sapphire. Albert identifies the specific form that puts a thing in its species with the *substantial form* that gives the thing its existence, which in a stone – unlike a heap of sand or a cloud of steam – is something well defined. This scholastic metaphysics of form and matter, called 'hylemorphism', gives a principled account of magical action in nature, appealing to the same properties called 'undescribable' in Greek by ancient physicians and philosophers (see 4.18; 5.3, 11–12, 14).

*

To doubt that stones have substantial forms is foolish because we can be sure by looking at them that they are all solidified and that the matter in them has been fixed for a certain species. For if their elements were arranged only for them to change into one another or into something else, like clouds, rain and snow, surely they would not stay as one or the other for long but would soon dissolve into their elements. But what we see happening in the natures of stones is just the opposite. Moreover, in stones we find powers – like expelling poison, getting rid of ulcers and attracting or repelling iron – that do not come from any element. The shared view of all the experts about them (as I will prove below) is that this power results from the species and the form of one stone or another.

So it is clear from this that stones have fixed forms and species, though these forms are not souls, as some of the ancients thought . . . but different substantial forms given by heavenly powers to a specific mixture of elements.

These forms are mostly without names, yet the different kinds get their names from the various types of stone, being called tufas, pumices, flints, marble, sapphire, emerald and so on. Since these are hidden to us, this is why we lack definitions belonging to the stones except by defining them in a roundabout way with accidents and signs . . .

7.11

Magic in Nature:
Albert the Great, *On Minerals*, 2.3.5–6

Albert's experience – personal or vicarious – of magnetic force was no more or less credible to him and his contemporaries than countless other phenomena reported by reputable authorities, past and present, as eminent as Aristotle, Avicenna, Dioscorides and Galen (see 4.18; 5.3, 12, 14). When such phenomena elude the usual explanations, Albert still classifies them as natural but traces them through specific and substantial forms to celestial causes, using this same physical and metaphysical framework to account for the resonance between figures made by stars and planets in the skies and images used on earth to decorate talismans (see 5.16; 7.9, 12).

*

To help the reader, I will give some information about the meaning of images, and then about amulets or necklaces made with them . . . Generally, then – and giving the usual description – when Aries, Leo and Sagittarius are engraved for fire and the eastern triplicity, they indicate that those stones have a property that counteracts fever and diseases like dropsy, paralysis and such others. And because the heat gets things moving, they are said to make those who wear them clever and eloquent and to elevate them in worldly honours – Leo especially . . .

The same thing applies to images in the sky outside the zodiac. When inscribed to ornament a stone, Pegasus is good for those who soldier, fight on horseback and on a level battlefield, and they say it works against equine diseases. The figure of Pegasus is half an image of a winged horse, and because of its effects a Pegasus is called Bellerophon – Battle-Fountain – in the craft of images . . . When Saturn is inscribed – a swarthy old man with few hairs in his beard, not cheerful or laughing, holding a curved sickle in his hand – they say the effect it brings is steady and growing because of the coldness and dryness, especially in a stone with the same power. And you should know that the result is quicker for a low-born person than for someone well-born because Saturn does not like the well-born, according to the craft of stars . . .

I might introduce many such things here, but I should not because there is a different science to deal with them, and they cannot be confirmed by physical principles. For that one must know astronomy, magic and necromancy – sciences to be discussed elsewhere. What seems more pertinent to this science are the amulets and necklaces made of stones because they bring healing and help with their powers only in a natural way . . . My aim here is only to describe them and the effects they have according to the best philosophers . . .

Aristotle says that an emerald hung around the neck hinders epilepsy and sometimes completely cures it, because of which they tell the nobility to tie this kind of stone on their children so that they will not come down with epilepsy. In his book *On Stones*, Aristotle also says that 'the angle is that of a certain magnet whose power to grasp iron goes to the *zoron* or north pole, and this is the one that sailors use, but the magnet's other angle pulls in the opposite way to the *aphron* or south pole. And if you bring iron near the *zoron* angle, the iron changes to *zoron*, and if you bring it near the opposite angle, it immediately changes to *aphron* . . . ' Aristotle also says that the types of magnet are quite different, for some attract gold while other types different from that attract silver, and some attract tin, some iron and some lead . . . and some attract human flesh, and they say that someone smiles when drawn by such a magnet and that he stays close to it until he dies, so mighty is this stone . . .

Dioscorides says that a stone which comes from sea foam – also called *Meerschaum* – tied above a pregnant woman's hips makes the birth speedy and, when tied around the neck of a boy with a bad cough, relieves the coughing. But Galen and Avicenna say that when they tried red coral for stomach-ache, hanging it directly over the site of the pain, it relieved the pain. These are physical experiences and tests by important men, showing that stones work by powers of their forms and species.

7.12

Magic Philosophized: Thomas Aquinas, *Summa Against the Heathens*, 3.104–7

Thomas Aquinas studied with Albert the Great, who outlived Thomas's death in 1274, and Albert may have written his *Mirror of Astronomy* even before his student finished his first *Summa* in the early 1260s (see 7.9). Nonetheless, this *Summa Against the Heathens* is more thoughtful and careful than the *Mirror*, taking celestial forces for granted but restricting their influence in order to curb naturalism and defend God's sovereign power. Thomas insists that demons – personal agents with minds – often cause the unusual effects ascribed to impersonal and mindless celestial forces. When human persons send and receive messages to and from demonic persons, 'the arts of magic get their efficacy from another being with a mind, to whom the magician addresses his message' (see 5.16; 6.11; 7.7, 9). Thomas also distinguishes natural from non-natural effects, ensouled agents from agents that lack souls and *figure* from *form*: this last metaphysical distinction nonetheless allows that 'figures in artificial objects are like specific forms', thereby making a key concession to the celestial figures that were commonly held to energize talismans. Following Augustine, Thomas repudiates Hermetic god-making as idolatry, but he cites Porphyry – also by way of Augustine – while explaining that demons are not *naturally* evil (see 4.7; 5.11, 13; 6.4, 11).

*

Some have claimed that deeds done by arts of magic that astonish us are done not by various spiritual substances but by the power of heavenly bodies. Since those who do deeds of this kind find it important to have the stars in certain positions, this seems to be evidence for that claim. These people also use various ingredients from plants and other objects to help their work, as if to prepare the matter down here to receive the influence of power from the heavens. Yet this goes directly against the appearances. For since it is not possible for a thought to be caused by any bodily principles . . . effects of a properly mental nature cannot be caused by the power of a heavenly body. But in these things that magicians do, certain actions are evident that belong to a nature that reasons, as when answers are given about stolen goods and other such things, which could be done only by thinking. So it is not true that all such effects are caused only by the power of heavenly bodies.

Moreover, speech itself is an act belonging to a rational nature, but in the aforementioned activities there is evidence of speaking with human beings and conversing about various things, so it is not possible for such things to happen solely by the power of heavenly bodies . . . What happens by the power of heavenly bodies is a natural effect, since the forms caused in things here below by the power of the heavenly bodies are natural forms. What cannot be natural to anything, then, cannot be done by the power of a heavenly body. But such things are said to be done by the aforementioned acts – that everything locked is opened when some person is present, that a person is made invisible and many other such stories . . .

If some result is granted for something by the power of heavenly bodies, what produces that result is also granted for it. Motion results from having a soul, however, since it belongs to ensouled things to move themselves, which makes it impossible – by the power of the heavenly bodies – for something not ensouled to move itself. Yet they say it happens that a statue moves by itself or makes a sound by arts of magic . . . And if they say that the statue gets some basis for life by the power of heavenly bodies, this cannot be, for in all living things the basis of life is a substantial form, since 'in living things to live is to be', as the Philosopher says in his second book *On the Soul*. But it is impossible for anything to receive a new substantial form without losing the substantial form that it already had, for 'producing the one destroys the other'. But no substantial form is lost when a statue is made: only the figure changes, which is accidental, since the form of the bronze or some such thing remains. So it is not possible for such a statue to acquire a basis for life . . .

Complete living things are not produced by heavenly power alone but also from seed: 'it is a human, along with the Sun, that produces a human'. But things produced without seed by heavenly power alone are animals of a lower kind and others like them produced from rotting. Therefore, if by heavenly power alone such statues get a basis for life, with the ability to move by themselves, they must be among the lowest animals. Yet this would be false if they were activated by an inner basis for life, for higher activity is evident in what they do to give answers about hidden objects . . . One can sometimes find a natural effect produced by the power of heavenly bodies without an artificial action, for even though someone uses artificial means to produce frogs or something like them, frogs are sometimes produced without anything artificial. So if such statues are made by the necromantic art and get a basis for life, it will be possible to find such things produced without any such artifice, but this is not found, so it is clear that such statues have no basis of life nor do they move by the power of heavenly bodies.

This excludes what Hermes claims, who – as reported by Augustine in Book 8 of the *City of God* – said this: 'Just as God is the maker of heavenly gods, so it is mankind who fashions the temple gods who are content to be near humans: I mean statues ensouled and conscious, filled with sense and spirit.' . . . This claim is also eliminated by divine authority, for the Psalm says that 'the idols of the nations are silver and gold, works of human hands: they have mouths that do not speak, nor is there breath in their mouths'. But the foregoing seems not to deny absolutely that something effective comes from the power of the heavenly bodies, though this applies only to those effects that any lower bodies can produce by the power of heavenly bodies.

It remains to ask where the arts of magic get their effectiveness, which is actually easy to see if we consider how they work. For when magicians do these things, they use certain meaningful sounds to produce particular effects. But a sound, as meaningful, has no power except from some mind, either from the mind of the person who speaks it or from the mind of the person to whom it is spoken . . . But human minds are generally found to be so disposed that their concepts are caused by things, rather than things being caused by what the mind conceives. Thus, if there were any persons who, with words expressing what their minds conceive, could transform things by their own power, they would be of a different species and would be called 'human' equivocally . . .

What remains, then, is that effects of this sort may be achieved by a mind that is addressed by the speech of someone uttering such sounds. But a sign of this is that meaningful sounds of this sort used by magicians are invocations, supplications, adjurations or even commands, as if to address the other party in a conversation. And in practising this art, they use various characters and figures. But a figure is not a principle of acting or of being acted upon; otherwise, mathematical objects would be active and passive. Therefore, since matter cannot be disposed by particular figures to receive natural effects, magicians do not use figures as if they were dispositions, and the alternative is that they use them only as signs since there is no third choice. But we use signs only for other persons who have minds. Therefore, the arts of magic get their efficacy from another being with a mind, to whom the magician addresses his message.

But if someone says that some figures match some heavenly bodies, meaning that lower bodies, through some figures, have particular relations to impressions received from some heavenly bodies, the claim seems not to be well reasoned. For nothing affected is situated to receive the impression of an agent except through what is in potency, so that the only things determining it to receive a specific impression are those that somehow put it into potency. But matter is not disposed by figures to be in potency to any form since figure, by definition, abstracts from all matter and sensible form because it is something mathematical. Therefore, no body is determined by figures or characters to receive any influence from a heavenly body . . .

Matter, as has been shown, is in no way disposed by figures to form. Hence, bodies in which such figures are impressed have the same capacity to receive heavenly influence as other bodies of the same species. But when something acts on one of a number of equally disposed bodies – with respect to something found there that matches – and not on another body, this is by the agent's choice, not by natural necessity. Clearly, then, such arts that use figures to produce various effects do not get their effectiveness naturally from some agent but get it from some substance that has a mind acting mentally. The name given to such figures also shows this because they call them 'characters', for a character is a sign, the conclusion being that they use such figures only as signs displayed to some nature with a mind.

But because figures in artificial objects are like specific forms, someone can say that nothing prevents some power of heavenly influence from following the arrangement of the figure that gives a talisman its species, not as it is a figure, but as it causes the species of the artificial product that gets power from the stars. Of the letters used to write something on the talisman, however, and of other characters, nothing can be said except that they are signs and hence are ordered only to some mind . . .

The next question asks what this mental nature is by whose power such deeds are done. And it is immediately evident that it is nothing good and praiseworthy . . . since such arts frequently lead to adultery, theft, murder and other crimes . . . and the people using these arts are generally criminals . . . Magicians use various deceits in their invocations to entice those who use their help. They make impossible threats, for example, claiming that unless help comes from the being who is invoked, the supplicant will break up the sky or displace the stars, as Porphyry tells it in his *Letter to Anebo* . . . This excludes the mistake that the pagans made by attributing effects of this sort to gods . . .

In the order of nature, a substance with a mind wants what is good, so it is impossible to be naturally evil for those mental substances whose help the arts of magic use . . . But this eliminates the Manichean error of claiming that such mental substances – those we call 'demons' or 'devils', using the customary names – are *naturally* evil. It also eliminates the view described by Porphyry in his *Letter to Anebo*, saying 'some believe there is a certain type of spirit, whose business is to attend to magicians, that is naturally deceptive and changes its form, imitating gods, demons and souls of the dead. And this is the type that does everything that seems to be good or bad. For things that really are good, they give no help, actually knowing nothing about them. But they procure the evil deeds.' . . . Porphyry's words clearly show the malice of the demons that help the arts of magic, the only problem being his claim that this malice is in their nature.

7.13
Witchcraft, Impotence and Frigidity: Aquinas, *Commentary on the Sentences*, 4.34.3

The physical preventing (*impedimentum*) of sex, as distinct from a psychological dis-inclination (*frigiditas*), eliminates the body's capability. In his immense theological commentary on Peter Lombard's *Sentences*, Thomas stresses that difference while discussing various obstacles to marriage, including sexual dysfunction, though he takes a more sedate approach than the Greek Magical Papyri or the *Picatrix* (see 5.6; 7.7). Arguing in favour of witchcraft as a possible source of physical preventing, he must first confirm that the Devil, his demons and witches are real and that they cause real evil in the world. The sexual damage done by witchcraft is mainly a male problem – so Thomas assumes (compare 8.3).

*

Some have said that the only witchcraft in the world exists in the thoughts of people who would ascribe natural effects to witches because their causes are hidden. But this goes against the sacred authorities who say that demons have power (when God permits it) over human bodies as well as the imagination, so that witches can produce various signs through demons. The root of this view is a failure of faith or lack of belief – supposing that demons exist only in the minds of the uneducated when a person creates terrors out of his own thoughts and attributes them to demons. And because shapes like those that people think up also seem to be sensed when the imagination is strong, they would then think that they see demons too.

But the true faith contradicts these views, teaching that angels fell from heaven, that we believe them to be demons, and that they – being of a keener nature – can do many things that we cannot. People who lead demons to do such things are then called *witches* or *doers-of-evil*.

This is why others have said that acts of witchcraft can account for the preventing of sexual intercourse, though this does not dissolve a contracted marriage since no such thing is lasting. And they say that the rights involved in this contract have been revoked. But this contradicts experience and violates new rights compatible with the old ones. To try things out, the Church has fixed a time – three years, actually – the same as for frigidity. But there is this difference between witchcraft and frigidity: someone impotent from frigidity is just as impotent with one woman as with another. Hence, when the marriage dissolves, he is not free to join with someone else. From witchcraft, however, a man can be impotent with one woman and not another. And so when the marriage is dissolved in the Church's judgement, both parties are allowed to look for someone else . . .

Because the primal corruption of sin that made man the Devil's slave has descended to us through the act of procreating, God therefore granted the Devil more power over witchcraft in this act than in others, just as we observe more power of evil-doing and witchery in serpents than in other animals because it was through a serpent that the Devil tempted the woman . . . Also, this witchcraft is so lasting that it has no remedy by human action, even though God can provide a remedy by compelling the demon – as the demon can too by desisting. For what has been done by witchcraft need not always be undone by another act of witchcraft.

And even if witchcraft could provide a remedy, it would still be considered lasting because no one should ever invoke a demon's help through witchcraft. Likewise, if the Devil were given power over someone because of a sin, the power need not go away with the sin because the penalty remains when the guilt is gone. Absent that decision by God, not even the Church's exorcisms always work as effectively to keep demons in check as they do for all the body's troubles, though they always work against those demonic attacks that were the main reason for establishing them.

7.14
Incubus and Succubus:
Aquinas, *Summa of Theology*, 1.51.2–3

Following Augustine up to a point, Aquinas paints a sharper picture of how angels and demons use the body and its products (see 6.12). The bodies that people see when they encounter these spirits are actually made of air. Though the spirits may seem to speak and eat, just like you and me, they are not really doing so – strictly speaking. Likewise, when male demons or *incubi* have sex with female humans, this is no ordinary fornicating. The semen that impregnates a human woman has been taken from a human male by a demon, and then 'the same demon who is a succubus for a male becomes an incubus for a woman'. A later treatment by other Dominicans – *The Hammer of Witches* – complicates the transaction (see 8.3).

*

Some have said that angels never assume bodies and that everything we read in the divine Scriptures about angels appearing happened in a prophet's vision – in the imagination, that is. Yet this conflicts with Scripture's meaning. For something seen by imaginary seeing exists only in the imagination of the person who sees it, so it is not seen by just anyone. But scripture sometimes introduces angels who appear in such a way that they are seen in common by everyone, like the angels who appear to Abraham . . . Hence, this is obviously a case of bodily seeing, such that the place of the thing seen is external to the one who sees, meaning that it can be seen by everyone. Only a body can be seen by such seeing, however. Since angels are not bodies, then, nor do they have bodies naturally united with them . . . what remains is that sometimes they assume bodies.

Angels need to assume bodies not for their own good but for us so that by talking in a friendly way with people they can show them the intellectual relationship that humans hope to have with angels in the life to come . . . The assumed body is united with the angel not as its form, in fact, nor as its mover but as the mover represented by the moving body that has been assumed . . .

While air holds no shape or colour as long as it stays thin, when condensed it can be shaped and coloured, which is plain to see in clouds, and in this way angels assume bodies from the air . . .

Through the bodies that angels assume, they can produce life's activities within what is common [to bodies and living things] . . . though not for what is proper to living things . . . Strictly speaking, angels do not talk through their assumed bodies, though there is something resembling speech in that they form sounds in the air that resemble human voices . . . Nor is eating suitable to angels, strictly speaking, since eating requires the consuming of food that can be converted into the eater's substance . . . But the food taken by angels . . . was not really eaten, only symbolic of spiritual eating . . .

Augustine says that many 'confirm from their own experience or from the experience of others . . . that woodland gods and Pans, called *incubi* by the common people, have often behaved indecently with women, gone after them and had sex with them . . . nor need we be astonished that giants could be born from them as well' . . . But if they were sometimes born from sex with demons, this was not from semen ejaculated by demons or by bodies that they had assumed but from the semen of some human collected for this purpose – in that the same demon who is a succubus for a male becomes an incubus for a woman, just as demons also take seeds from other things in order to reproduce them. As Augustine says in book 3 *On the Trinity*: in this way, the one born is not the child of a demon but of the human whose semen was taken.

Sulphur, Arsenic and Mercury:
Geber, *Summa on Completing*, 1.24–30

Although the name Jabir ibn-Hayan became attached to a large body of Arabic alchemical writing produced in the eighth and ninth centuries, this Latin work attributed to Geber comes from the late thirteenth century (see 7.6). Geber's *Summa on Completing*, probably the work of an otherwise obscure Paul of Taranto, shows how to complete the alchemical process and make gold out of other metals, applying the much older theory – inspired by Aristotle but transformed by Jabir – that sulphur and mercury are the principles of all metals. This matter-theory, challenging the usual Aristotelian doctrine of four elements and four qualities, has an atomist (loosely speaking) dimension – a non-Aristotelian notion of *minima naturalia* or least parts (see 7.10–11). The *Summa* also gives practical advice about distilling, layering (cementing), controlled heating (calcining), and other laboratory techniques, as well as the specialized apparatus needed for the alchemical process (see 5.7).

*

I suggest to you then – following the views of older authorities who belonged to the group that imitated our art – that the principles of natural action are a stinking spirit and a quick or living water. (I also allow the term 'dry' water.) I have divided the stinking spirit, however: in hiding, it is actually white, but it is both red and black in the process of this work, while in the open both the white and the black tend towards redness. In a brief account, then, which is sufficient and not incomplete, I shall describe the production of each of these as well as the way of producing them . . .

Generally, I shall say that each natural principle is very strong in composition and uniform in substance, which is because earthy parts are bound in them to airy, watery and fiery parts through the least parts, in such a way that no part can let any other fall off by being broken away. Each part, no matter which one, breaks away along with the other because of the strong bond that they have with one another through least parts from an equal heat multiplied in mines deep inside the earth, then flattened and levelled out in the usual course of nature as their essences require – in the view of some older philosophers.

But others have said something different: that the principle was quicksilver not in its own nature but as altered and converted into an earth, and likewise for sulphur – altered and transmuted into an earth. Hence, their claim was that the principle – in the natural sense – was something other than the stinking spirit and the runaway spirit. And what convinced them was finding nothing, in silver mines or mines of other metals, which is quicksilver in its natural state, and likewise nothing that is sulphur . . .

For this reason, then, they are forced to conclude that quicksilver – like sulphur – is not in its natural state a principle in the natural sense, but that there is a different principle that comes from altering the essences of those principles, at the root of nature, into an earthy substance. The way this happens (as before) is that each of those principles is converted to an earthy nature. And the heat multiplied deep inside the earth separates a very light smoke from both those earthy natures, and that smoke of two kinds is the bare matter of metals. But when the smoke is cooked by heat that is tempered in a mine, it changes its nature to a kind of earth.

In this way, the smoke acquires a sort of fixity that is dissolved by the water that flows inside the mine through the porous earth, and the smoke bonds with it in a bond that is naturally and firmly bonded . . . and a natural union eventually produces the single thing that comes from the substance of the earth dissolved down deep along with the flowing water that dissolves it. In the correct natural proportion, all the elements reach this state of mixture, mixed through least parts until they produce a uniform mixture. By repeated cooking in the mines, this mixture thickens and hardens, becoming a metal.

These other people also come close to the truth, though what they conclude is not the pure truth . . .

Since there are three natural principles – sulphur, arsenic and quicksilver – I shall write a section on sulphur first, arsenic second and quicksilver third. Then I shall dedicate a section to each of the metals that are effects of those principles, as it happens by natural action. From there we must move on to the things that are bases of this process and also move on to the results, pointing out the causes of them all.

I say, then, that sulphur is fattiness in the earth thickened in the earth's mines by moderate cooking until it hardens and dries. Since sulphur actually has a very strong composition, it is also of uniform substance in its parts – homeomerous because it is homogenous. This is why its oil is not driven off by distilling, as with other things that have oil in them.

Hence, those people are wasting their labour who try to use calcination on sulphur and not lose any part of its substance that needs to be kept. The calcination takes great effort and scatters much of the substance: out of a hundred parts, in fact, you will save scarcely enough for three after calcining. Also, sulphur cannot be fixed unless it is calcined first. It can be mixed, however, slowing its dispersal a bit and limiting its burning, so that the calcining is easier when the sulphur has been mixed. Therefore, anyone who tries to get a result from sulphur by treating it by itself will get no result because it is completed by the mixing, and, without that, the process lags to the point of despair.

With its partner, sulphur becomes a tincture and gives completed weight to each of the metals, cleansing its own bad smell as it brightens and completes the metal by the process without which none of them excels but decays and blackens instead. Without the process, then, you should not use sulphur. He who knows how to mix it in a preparation and make it a friend to bodies will know one of nature's greatest secrets and one path to completion, although there are many paths to the single result and the single purpose . . . No one should think that sulphur by itself will achieve the work of alchemy . . .

Arsenic is of fine matter and like sulphur, so it is not necessary to define it in a different way than sulphur . . . Sulphur and arsenic are not the matter that completes this work, however, since they do not finish it, though in some cases they support the completion. But the best arsenic is shiny, flaky and brittle.

Quicksilver, which in the older usage is also called 'mercury', is a thick water in the earth's innards bonded in a total bond through least parts to a light, earthy, white substance by a very tempered heat until the wet is tempered together with the dry and the dry equally with the wet. This is why mercury runs right off a flat surface without sticking, because of the wetness of its water, even though its dryness makes the wetness thick, tempering it and preventing it from sticking. As some say, quicksilver – along with sulphur – is also the matter of metals . . . Without it, none of the metals can be gilded . . .

I am describing the metallic bodies that are effects of those principles of nature, and they are six in number: gold, silver, lead, tin, copper and iron. And then I say that a metal is a mineral body that can be melted and spread out in every dimension under the hammer. A metal, as I have said, is dense in substance and very strong and solid in composition. Though all metals have a great affinity for one another, a complete metal does not complete a lesser one by mixing with it. For if gold is mixed with lead by melting, the lead does not become gold from this but burns up and disappears from the mixture, while the gold remains in the assay.

By induction, the same thing happens with the rest of the metals, following the pattern that they share. But when our process is followed, the complete helps the incomplete to be completed, and the incomplete in our process is completed in itself without putting any external thing into the mix. And this completes the incomplete by the same process. Through God, they change and are changed by one another, completing one another and being completed, and yet each is completed by itself, without help from anything else . . .

Gold is a metallic body, lemony, heavy, unsounding, glittering, distributed equally through the bowels of the earth, washed with mineral water for a very long time, able to be spread under the hammer, able to melt, able to stand assay by a sand bath and layering. From this you should conclude that a thing is not gold unless it has all the differences of gold and all the causes of its definition. Yet whatever makes a metal lemony at its root, whatever brings it to stability and cleans it – that is what produces gold from every kind of metal, which is why we reckon that copper can be transmuted into gold by natural action and by artifice.

7.16
Preparing the Stone:
Geber, *Summa on Completing*, 3.24–30

One feature that makes alchemical texts hard to read is their unusual terminology, which turns even ordinary words like 'complete', 'fill', 'medicine' and 'stone' into entries in an esoteric dictionary – ripe for mockery (see 10.5). Although the 'stone' in this excerpt may be the Philosopher's Stone, the ultimate agent of transmutation, the focus is on 'medicines' (see 7.6). Before the alchemical process is complete, 'casting' (*projectio*) is the stage when a medicine is applied to an object that is not yet complete (see 7.15). The incomplete thing must acquire the properties of a complete thing – colour, lustre, weight and so on in the case of gold – and Geber describes how three types of medicine induce the desired properties. Checking on that process, he notes that 'natural weight is one of the signs of completing', meaning that the artificial gold made by an alchemist must have the weight of natural gold. He adds that a medicine introduces that weight – the 'weight of completion' – by causing the micro-structure of the transmuted object to be closely packed. In this way, much of Geber's book explicates a theory of matter, a kind of chemistry. But this passage concludes with the religiosity often seen in alchemy: Geber justifies alchemical secrecy as a way of keeping something 'mysterious and most precious' from the 'vile and wicked people' who might defile it (see 5.7).

*

First of all, let me give a general account of medicines along with their causes and one's open experience of them. I suggest, in fact, that incomplete things cannot be completed unless all the excrement is removed from them either by a medicine or by the method of preparing – namely, by taking every excremental quality of sulphur away from them and every filthy earthiness so that they can be separated from the mixture during the melting after casting the medicine that alters them. It is really when you discover this that you already have one of the differences of completing.

Likewise, unless the medicine also brightens and changes a body to a white or lemony colour in the way that you want – so that it brings on a pleasant brilliance and flashing brightness – bodies totally lessened in their filling are certainly not completed by the completing. Furthermore, unless the melting that it brings on is steadily lunar or solar, this cannot be changed in the filling because it is not stable in the trials but separates from the mixture and goes away. I will show you a more extensive treatment of this in what follows.

Moreover, unless the medicine is continued and the pressure to change is steady, its transmuting does not work since the pressure does not stay but disappears. Also, unless this brings on the weights of completion, it does not transmute under a true and steady filling of the nature, where no mistake of false confidence causes deception. For natural weight is one of the signs of completing. Clearly, then, since the differences of completion are five, the medicine of our process must bring on these five differences in the casting . . .

In the same way, one must also bring other factors into the alteration of weight, along with their causes and the correct sequence. The cause of great weight, then, is the fineness of the substance of bodies and uniformity in essence. Because of this, in fact, the parts of those bodies can be packed close when nothing comes between them, and the close packing of the parts comes from bringing weight in and completing it. Clearly, then, the situation makes it necessary to use the artifice of the work and search carefully for this fineness both in preparing the handling of bodies and also for the medicine that completes the preparation. The greater the weight of the transmuted bodies, the greater one finds their completion to be from the art and its searching . . .

I suggest that difference in medicines is necessarily of three kinds: one medicine is of the first degree, one of the second and one of the third. But I call a first-degree medicine every preparation of minerals which, when cast on bodies that had been less than complete, applies pressure for a change that does not bring on enough filling, allowing the changed body to be transformed and destroyed as the medicine causing the pressure completely evaporates . . . I call a second-degree medicine every preparation which, when cast on bodies that had been less than complete, changes them into some difference of filling so that other destructive differences are left behind and whole . . .

And I call a third-degree medicine every preparation which, when it reaches the bodies, takes away everything destructive when it is cast and completes them with the difference of the whole filling. But this medicine is unique and alone, which is why we are freed by it from doing the work of finding ten second-degree medicines. Therefore, the effect of the first degree is called 'smaller', of the second 'middle' and of the third 'larger'. And this is enough about difference in all the medicines . . .

A third-order medicine is of two kinds – solar and lunar – yet in essence it is one and one also in its way of acting. This is why our older experts, whose writings I have read carefully, give this medicine the name 'unique'. But the difference between the one and the other – the lunar and the solar – is the addition of a lemony colour completed by a very clean sulphurous quality and the substance of fixed sulphur. The solar medicine definitely has this in it, but the lunar does not have it. Yet this third degree is called the degree of greater effect, and this is because its medicine – compared to that of any other degree – requires more work to get to the real thing as well as more diligence and better judgement in applying the medicine and preparing the completion . . . For this is the medicine which transforms every body that is less than complete and every quicksilver of whatever kind into a wholly complete lunar body.

To complete a solar medicine of this kind, one makes an addition of the sulphur that does not burn and has been carefully, adroitly and perfectly applied, using the method of fixing and calcining as well the multi-stage method of dissolving with many repetitions until the addition becomes clean, when the application has been completed by these steps and by elevation it reaches what is completed. Obviously, the way to make this addition is by repeatedly elevating the part of the stone that is not fixed, by ingeniously conjoining it through least parts until it rises with the medicine. And the sulphur should be fixed repeatedly with the medicine so that it is stable. And the more this sequence of filling is repeated, the more the productivity of this medicine is multiplied, the more its excellence increases, and then its increase in completion is multiplied as much as possible.

And I, wishing not to be nipped at by the undutiful, tell the whole story of this process in a brief account that is finished and well understood. The gist of it is that the stone and its addition are cleansed to absolute completion by elevation, and from that point, by using ingenious devices, the fleeting is fixed from them. Then let the fixed take wing and, by repetition, let the winged be fixed, thus letting the winged be fixed, the fixed take wing and the winged be fixed so often that, with firing, the melting readily shows.

And in this sequence one achieves something mysterious and most precious, beyond every mystery of this world's sciences and also a treasure beyond compare. Indeed, you should work towards it with all urgent zeal and the concentration that endures beyond measure. With such effort, but not without it, you will find it. And with such diligence assured, repeating the best method of application can work with this medicine in preparing the stone until the quicksilver changes to something truly boundless – solarizing and lunarizing – and depending only on multiplying the medicine.

Praise God, then – the high, blessed and glorious God who has revealed to us all the medicines in succession, together with the experience of the enquiry that I have undertaken with my best and most urgent labour. With my eye I have searched and I have touched with my hand the fulfilment of labour that my process has explored. If it turns out that I have covered this up, a son of learning should not be surprised, for I have covered it up only from vile and wicked people.

An Art to Answer All Questions:
Ramon Lull, *The Brief Art*

Around the time when Ramon Lull was born in 1232, Peter of Spain was writing his *Summaries of Logic*, the textbook that defined the subject for the next several centuries. Just as Peter claims to have 'a path to the principles of all methods', Lull proposes 'to answer all questions'. Both understand the power of abstracting and generalizing, but Peter is staid and conventional – looking back from Boethius through Porphyry to Aristotle – while Lull is visionary and idiosyncratic, inspired by Ghazali, the Muslim theologian and logician. Lull's *Brief Art* of 1308, abridging the *Great Art* of 1305, uses nine *letters* in a heuristic algebra – both analytic and productive – displayed in wheels, trees, grids and other figures. Tied first to nine *principles* of great generality – Goodness (B), Greatness (C), Duration (D) and so on – the letters also coordinate other sets of nine, like the *subjects* God (B), angel (C), heaven (D) and so on. Principles, despite their generality, can specify one another, as when 'goodness is great'. They can also be individuated if, for example, 'Peter's goodness is great'. One task of the art is to say when a predicate like 'great' may be said of an item like Peter's goodness – or when the 'middle term' of a syllogism (its parts supplied by the *Art*) can be found to link 'great' as the predicate of a proposition with some such item as that proposition's (logical) subject. When principles and other components of the system are symbolized by letters and displayed on segments of concentric wheels, the machinery is in place for an apparatus of combinations that Lull's admirers have found to be divinatory.

*

The reason why I am producing this *Brief Art* is to make it easier to know the *Great Art*. For when that brief art is known, people will find it easy to learn or know the art just mentioned and other arts as well. The subject of this art is to answer all questions, assuming that one knows what the name means.

This book is divided into thirteen parts like the divisions of the great art. The first part is about the alphabet, the second about figures, the third about definitions, the fourth about rules, the fifth about the table, the sixth about emptying with the third figure, the seventh about multiplying with the fourth figure, the eighth about mixing principles and rules, the ninth about the nine subjects, the tenth about application, the eleventh about questions, the twelfth about habituation and the thirteenth about how to teach this art.

And first I say this about the first part . . . which is about the alphabet. I put the alphabet in this art in order to be able to make figures with it and to understand or to mix principles and rules for seeking the truth. For through one letter that has several meanings the intellect becomes more generalized for taking in many meanings and also for producing knowledge. This alphabet must certainly be known by heart, for otherwise the artist will be unable to make good use of this art.

> B Goodness, difference, whether, God, justice and avarice
> C Greatness, agreement, what, angel, prudence and gluttony
> D Duration, contrariety, from what, heaven, courage and lust
> E Property, principle, why, man, temperance and pride
> F Wisdom, means, how much, imagining, faith and sloth
> G Will, end, what kind, sentient, hope and envy
> H Virtue, excess, when, growing, love and anger
> I Truth, equality, where, elemental, patience and deceit
> K Glory, defect, how instrumental, piety and inconstancy

This art is divided into four parts – into four figures, that is to say. The first is about the **A**, which actually contains nine principles in itself – goodness, greatness and so on – and nine letters: namely, **B, C, D** and so on. The reason this figure is circular is that a subject changes to a predicate and the reverse, as in saying 'great goodness', 'good greatness' and so on for the others. In this figure the artist looks for a natural conjunction between subject and predicate – a disposition and proportion to enable him to find a middle term that will produce a conclusion.

Taken by itself, any principle is completely general, as in saying 'goodness' or 'greatness'. But when one principle is drawn in to another, it is then subordinated, as in saying 'great goodness'. And when a principle is drawn in to a singular thing, then the principle is most specific and has been specified, as in saying 'Peter's goodness is great' and so on. In this way, the intellect has a

Figure 10: A Wheel from Lull's *Short Art*

ladder going up and down from a completely general principle to the not completely general and not completely specific and from the not completely general and the not completely specific to the completely specific. This way of going up the ladder can be described in its own manner.

Whatever exists is encompassed by the principles of this figure, for whatever exists is either good or great and so on, as with God and angel and so on, which are good and great and so on, so that anything can be traced back to the aforementioned principles . . .

Nine subjects are posited in this art and signified in an alphabet that covers whatever exists, and outside of them there is nothing. The first subject is *God*, signified by **B**; the second is *angel*, signified by **C**; the third is *heaven*, signified by **D**; the fourth is *man*, signified by **E**; the fifth is the *imagining*, signified by **F**; the sixth is the *sentient*, signified by **G**; the seventh is the *growing*, signified by **H**; the eighth is the *elemental*, signified by **I**; the ninth and last is the *instrumental*, signified by **K** . . .

The *angel* is deducible by principles and rules; clearly, it has natural good-ness, greatness, duration and so on, and this is its definition: an angel is a spirit that is not conjoined. In it there is no natural contrariety since it is indestructible. The matter in it is of the '-able' kind – namely, the good-able, the great-able and so on, as signified by the second type of rule about **D**. There is greatness in the angel because it is more like God than man is. And in this context the intellect understands that even if man cannot use his senses without an organ of sense, this does not mean that an angel cannot do this without an organ since the angel is higher. And in this context the intellect understands that angels can speak to one another, act on us without any organ and go from one place to another without any intermediate place . . .

Heaven has natural goodness, greatness, duration and so on, and this is its definition: heaven is the first substance that is mobile. In it there is no contra-riety because it is not a composite of contrary principles, for the instinct and appetite in it are natural – with motion as the result – and without motion it could not have natural instinct and appetite. There is an effective principle in it, nonetheless, since this is found in things below. And its constituents are its own specific form and matter so that it acts through its own species . . .

Man is a body/soul composite, and the reason for this can be inferred from principles and rules in two ways – a spiritual and a bodily way – and this is the definition: man is a man-making animal. Because of his double nature – the spiritual and the bodily of which he is a composite – the principles and rules are doubled in him. This makes man more general than any other created being, and for this reason one can say without hesitation that man is the greater part of the world . . .

In the *imaginative* are specific principles and rules for imagining the imaginable, as when a magnet attracts iron, and this is its definition: the imaginative is the power to which imagining properly belongs . . . Using par-ticular senses, the imaginative takes species from what is sensed, doing this with its correlates signified under the second type of rule **C**. With goodness it makes those species good, and with greatness it makes them great, as when one imagines a great mountain of gold . . .

In the *growing* are the specific principles and rules by which plants act according to their species: among them are pepper, which acts according to its species, as the rose and the lily act according to theirs. The principles of the growing are more compact than those of the *sensitive*, and the principles of the sensitive more compact than those of the imaginative . . . The growing transmutes the elemental into its own species by way of generation . . .

Astronomy is the art by which an astronomer understands the powers and motions possessed by the sky and having effects on things below . . . Does the sky move itself? The answer is 'yes' because, through its constellations, its principles have proper and substantial correlates . . . Does an angel move the heavens? The answer is 'no' because if angels moved them, their '-tive' correlates would come below the higher '-able' correlates, and heavenly form would clearly not even move the elements, but its matter would – impossibly. Does the sky have a motive soul, they ask, and the answer is 'yes', for otherwise the sentient and growing would not have motive souls, nor would the elementals have motion . . . By the second type of rule **E**, the question is why is there a sky, and this must be the reply: so that things below can have motion.

7.18
Hell's Doorkeeper:
Dante, *Inferno*, 5.1–45

When we go to a movie and see *Batman*, we go knowing what he and Bruce Wayne should look like. Comic books and television have made the Caped Crusader familiar and memorable by disseminating images that are fun to look at. Having only rhythms, rhymes and words to work with – in a stricter and serious register – Dante does much more for the snarling Minos and his shrieking victims. The gloom is dense where the monster stands, and moaning sinners thicken the darkness, making this pit of carnality 'all deaf to light' – sublime language to immortalize the horrors recorded by Dante. The awful vision that screams around him and Virgil is one of hell's now timeless scenes and sounds, brought within human time and space by the godlike art that justifies the name of the *Divine Comedy* (see 4.12; 10.7).

*

As I dropped below the higher circle
down to the second that cinches in a smaller
and a sadder space that makes us weep,

There stands Minos terribly and snarling,
examining the guilty as they enter,
judging and assigning those he grabs:

I'm saying how a soul to evil born
will come before him and confess it all,
and then that careful connoisseur of sins

Sees what place in Hell the soul will get,
cinching his tail as many times around
as where he'll plunge the sinner to his level.

Many of them always stand before him,
each going on its fated way to judgement,
talking, listening – then he hurls them down.

'This cruel hostel, where you're signing in . . . '
he says, and then great Minos looks at me,
breaking off his awful duties just that long,

' . . . watch how you enter, careful whom you trust,
and don't let the spacious entrance fool you!'
To which my guide replies: 'Now why the scream?

'Don't block his destined journey: that's the will
that's willed where what is willed
is what can be, and we can ask no more.'

Now the doleful noise of pain starts up
and makes me hear it; now I go
where lamentation beats upon me hard.

I come into a place all deaf to light
and roaring like an ocean struck by storms
of warring winds that strike and batter.

This hellish hurricane that never rests
guides the spirits like a robbing thug,
whirling, pummelling and tormenting them.

All the ruination that they face,
the shrieks, the moaning, the laments –
right here this makes them curse the might of God.

I learned that those tormented in this way
are damned because they sinned the sins of flesh,
subduing reason to their likes and lusts.

And – when the weather's cold – as starlings
wing themselves in full, far-reaching flocks,
just so that blast directs the evil spirits,

To here, to there, above, below it leads them,
with never any hope of comfort, never
any rest, nor even any hope of lesser pain.

7.19
No Need for Demons: Nicole Oresme,
On the Causes of Wonders

Bishop Nicole Oresme, an eminent philosopher by the middle of the fourteenth century and a successful politician thereafter, served a King – Charles V – whom he considered superstitious (see 4.13–14; 6.11). A remarkably independent thinker, the Bishop also thought that Aristotle was often wrong, especially about natural philosophy. But the naturalism that came naturally to some Aristotelians was his response to people – like King Charles – who saw stars and demons acting everywhere. Although Oresme finds natural causes 'much more possible and plausible than demons or an unknown influence', he falls back on well-known mechanisms – a semi-material spirit and forms detachable from objects – to account for action at a distance and various unusual phenomena (see 4.2; 5.3).

*

To bring some peace to people's minds, although it goes beyond my task, I have proposed to reveal the causes of some things that are seen as wonders but happen naturally – just like other effects that ordinarily cause us no wonder. We need not rush to the heavens, as if this were the last refuge of the distressed, nor to demons nor to God in his glory: because it is plain that he would produce those effects directly, more than others whose causes we take to be better known to us.

One thing I note here, however: that one must also assign singular causes to singular effects, which is very hard unless a person sees those effects as singulars along with their singular circumstances. And this is why it will be enough for me to show that the aforesaid events happen naturally, as I said, and that nothing unreasonable follows. But why is Sortes poor and Plato rich, or why did an animal die at a particular time, or why does pepper in a small amount bring on the runs or in a large amount cause urinating when scammony does the opposite, as Aristotle says in the first part of the *Problems*? Why did the wheat fail in *this* field? And why did Sortes hear *that* voice or see *that* wonder? How can we find the particular and direct causes of such things and understand their singular circumstances?

As I have said, then, because in general such things happen naturally, I shall simply clarify them as capable physicians have done, writing general rules for medicine and leaving single cases to physicians who work on the particulars. For no physician would know how to tell Sortes, if he were ill, what his illness is like and how it will be cured unless the physician sees him and examines the singulars that must be examined . . .

Almost all say that maniacs are demoniacs . . . and some of those who do not know the causes that are direct and natural run off to the demons, others to the heavens, others to God. And because such things seem wonderful, they attribute them in the usual way, but this is false. And I say that Avicenna does not make this claim: no, he claims a cure for such people, which he would not do if the disease came from a demon. What good would such a treatment do, then, since a devil would not depart because of it? . . .

Perhaps one man facing another and very afraid or very desirous of something, when everything is disposed for this, can somehow move another's soul and alter it for that purpose. Avicenna concedes this . . . because the power of imagination can move a thing outside. Later I shall say more about this because I do not simply grant it. Yet I grant that because of the fear, love and so on, one could produce so much constraint that someone as entirely clever as I assume this person to be – the cleverest of all – could not explain it . . .

Sometimes the species of a thing is multiplied, yet not from anything outside but from another species. An example of a different kind: fire in the air nearby produces heat, and that produces additional heat, and so on up to my hand and beyond. Also, when a bell is moved it makes a sound in the medium, and that makes another and so on, so that an echo can come after the first soundable or sounded thing has been destroyed. Likewise the species of colour in a medium . . . I might be somewhat persuaded by this that some species strongly impressed in the soul of Sortes – if at that moment Sortes were thinking actively, and at that moment he were wishing and desiring me to know this and be moved by it, and so on – that these species might move me a bit so that I would think the same thing that Sortes was then thinking because, just as in the examples stated, where the soul is moved and receives the species of a thing and yet the thing does not exist, it thus seems possible that the things that are in Sortes can move me – meaning my soul . . .

Don't such things often happen – that in someone's presence it occurs to me or you to think of something? Moreover, I say that at the moment it is possible that I attend to nothing else so that the soul is not distracted else-where. And I also say that at the moment it is possible for Sortes to think this thought strongly, 'let him know this or that' and so on, so that the species and spirits in him will be moved. Then perhaps the medium, the organs and other things are disposed so that maybe they will move my soul along with what he was thinking before . . . Now this seems no more wonderful to me than when the species of a wall remains in the medium or the organ when the wall is absent . . .

But that those species move a distant subject in place, as Avicenna claimed . . . I deny – denying it because this goes against the philosophy of Aristotle unless, as I have said, the claim were that a species in Sortes moved me to know the same thing, just as if I were Sortes, and then as a result I could move myself, as a person moves himself as he wishes. But that your imagina-tion would move me, against my will, or a stone, is truly against Aristotle . . . How did Avicenna know if his claim was true: that imagination made a mule fall down? . . . Others besides Avicenna like Algazel . . . have claimed that matter obeys the intellect not only in the same subject but also in different subjects, but to me this seems entirely contrary to the Philosopher . . .

Because of the variety and wondrousness of effects, one need not rush off to the heavens and an unknown influence nor to demons nor to the glorious God as if this were the cause . . . since effects just as wonderful or nearly so are found here on earth. To find their causes, people do not rush off to the places just named as the causes. They are perfectly happy with natural causes. Next, I have shown that the natural causes thus assigned and the ways of finding them are much more possible and plausible than making demons or an unknown influence the causes of said effects . . .

Effects just as wonderful occur here and people do not wonder at them. Furthermore, how many demons are there? What sort of thing are they? Why do they involve themselves? As for the claims made about them, what could be more unknown in natural philosophy – even where faith is concerned – than their involving themselves with such inept devices, and what could be harder, since these boy and girl demons can only do as much as the glorious God allows? And it is the same with unknown heavenly influ-ence, which ordinarily is like light, motion or location.

7.20

Spirits Inside the Circle:
A Magic Manual

A manuscript now in Munich – written by a number of scribes in the first half of the fifteenth century and called a 'Necromancer's Manual' by its modern editor – shows how to produce effects that might be hard to trace to natural causes, even for Oresme (see 7.19). One of the manuscript's several dozen sections gives detailed instructions – including a sketch of a magic circle – for 'calling up servers for a meal' and for managing the sixteen spectral knights who bring the waiters with them. Kneeling inside the circle, the person who conjures up the feast must pray to 'our Lord Jesus Christ, Son of the true God', but only after naming the secret names of sixteen spirits: Oymelor, Demefin, Lamair, Masair, Symofor and the rest. Invoking them is sinful, and frivolity makes it worse (see 7.9). Why risk your soul to have a banquet catered? Yet Doctor Faustus has Mephistopheles use his power to play tricks at a feast in the Pope's palace (see 10.2).

*

The technique that you often saw me use in your court – namely, calling up servers for a meal – should start by invoking sixteen spirits in this way. First, at noon on a Thursday or Sunday when the moon is waxing, you must go outside the village and bring with you a brightly shining sword and a hoopoe bird and use the sword to make circles in some remote place. After you have done that, with the point of the sword you must write the sixteen names as given below in the figure. When that is done, you must make a drawing of the sword inside the circle at the east, as shown in this design:

With that done, you should tie the hoopoe to you so that it cannot get away from the inside circle, in which you must be standing. And with that done, while kneeling, facing east and holding the sword with both hands, say these words:

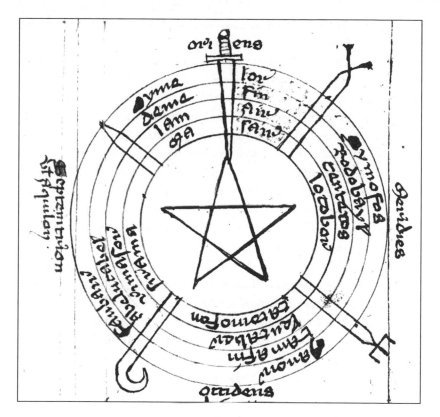

Figure 11: A Circle and Pentagram from A Magic Manual

Oymelor, Demefin, Lamair, Masair, Symofor, Rodobayl, Tentetos, Loto-bor, Memoyr, Tamafin, Leutaber, Tatomofon, Faubair, Selutabel, Rimasor, Syrama – spirits most festive, happy and joyful, I, so-and-so, adjure you by the Father and the Holy Spirit; by the only Son of God, mightiest of all, living and real, who for us and our salvation came down from heaven and was made flesh of the Holy Spirit from the pure, inviolate and unspoiled virgin Mary; by the birth and resurrection of our Lord Jesus Christ, Son of the true God; by the holy baptismal bath whereby each person is saved; by the Sun, Moon and all the heavenly stars; by all those that can frighten and bind you; and by the power of those who must come when I call them: you must come here to this spot without delay, in a gentle, calm and joyous form, and cause whatever I say to appear . . .

After saying this, turn west with the sword and hoopoe, and you will see sixteen knights, strong and handsome, who will say, 'You called us, and we have come to you, submitting as you have named us. Seek what you want without fear, for we have come ready to obey you.' Say to them, 'Let me know your power so that I can see tables seating many guests with no end of things to eat,' and they will answer that they are happy to comply. Many servants will appear right away, carrying side-tables, napkins and other necessaries . . .

Know that the twelve who are standing outside the circle and nearby, watching and talking to you, will not leave you. Know also that when three kings come to you from those seated near the circles and ask you to come out and dine with them, you should answer that you cannot possibly leave, and after you have said this, they will return to their places right away . . . Finally, right in front of your eyes, they will all vanish except for the twelve standing by you who will ask, 'Has our entertainment not pleased you?' And you will answer with a cheerful, 'Yes!'

After your answer, they will ask you for the hoopoe which, strange to say, will keep trembling, and you will tell them, 'I mean to give you the hoopoe if you swear to come to me and produce this entertainment whenever I want.' They will say that they are ready to swear, and right away you should have a book brought in for them to swear on . . . as they will do. Once they have sworn, give them the hoopoe . . . They will go away, and you too can move out of the circles, erasing them so that nothing will be seen when you leave, carrying your sword.

Note that the hoopoe has great power for necromantic rites and invoking demons, which is why I often use it to protect myself.

7.21
Repairing the Book of Consecrations:
A Magic Manual

The same Munich manuscript preserves two versions of a *Book of Consecrations*, which is mainly a sequence of prayers giving the user – called an 'exorcist' – 'full power to subdue evil spirits', compelling them 'to give true answers and follow the exorcist's orders'. Before the prayers, the *Book* lays out elaborate procedures – plainly meant for a priest to follow – of ritual purification and preparation to preserve or restore its own power, in case someone makes a mistake when copying the book or somehow defiles it.

*

The Book of Consecrations begins by saying or showing what its devices are for and what their effects are . . . a very praiseworthy and reliable book because it has been consecrated and confirmed by sacred names so that no one who has hope and a sure faith in our Lord Jesus Christ can be tricked in working with the book: . . . as sacred scripture says, a person who has not believed surely and faithfully cannot be saved. Hence it is necessary for anyone who does the work to believe in order not to be tricked.

Know with certainty, then, that the work was devised to eliminate a mistake in various procedures, so that by the power of invoking God's holy names and by his undescribable mercy, truth and might, the procedures can get what they should get, as explained below. Although a procedure has lost power and potency, it can be recovered in the way shown below . . .

First of all, anyone who will produce this work called the Book of Consecrations must abstain from all defilement of mind and body in eating, drinking and idle talk, must be well behaved, and must wear clean clothing for eleven days before starting the work. Every day he must hear mass, bring this book with him and put it on the altar until the mass has ended, doing so with great reverence and with prayer and fasting, as it is written: 'By fasts and prayers the mysteries hidden in heaven are revealed, and in divinity the arcane rites are opened up.'

Every day after mass he takes the book home, keeps it clean in a secret place without dirt, lets no one near the book, and sprinkles the place where he puts it with water and blessings: that is, he wraps it up in a cross made with a priest's cincture and a blessed stole; then he kneels and points the book to the east, saying – in all reverence and with heartfelt piety – the seven Psalms with a long prayer and the litany, sanctifying, blessing and consecrating the book that has been inscribed with the names of its saints. Then may God Almighty in his goodness and mercy sanctify, bless and consecrate this book inscribed with his own most sacred names so that a person can get power – the power to consecrate a bonded spirit, enabling him to do all the invocations and conjurations for those spirits and all the other procedures.

Note: If anyone defiles this book, let him know that it has no more power unless he consecrates it anew and then brings the book back to life by prayer and the litany.

Let him open the book and say this prayer with a humble heart and a devout soul, beginning this way: My God, spare me and have mercy on me for my evil deeds; save my soul, for I have sinned against you . . . Lord Jesus Christ, by your inexpressible mercy, spare me and have mercy on me. Hear me now as I invoke your triple name – Father, Son and Holy Spirit . . . Unworthy sinner that I am, yet having faith in you, I beg you to sanctify and bless this book inscribed with your sacred names and consecrate it by these your most sacred names: On, Jesus Christ, Alpha and O, Ely, Eloye, On, Otheon, Stimlamathon, Ezelphares, Tetragrammaton, Elyoraz, Eygiraem, Usirion, Oristion, Orona, Anellabiassim, Noyn, Messias, Cother, Emanuel, Sabaoth, Adonay and all the secret names contained in this book . . .

Glorious Adonay, by whom all things that exist were created and begotten, show favour to my invocations and kindly grant me that this process will have full power to subdue evil spirits, willing or unwilling, and make them always humbly obedient to the exorcist . . . And when they have all been exorcized and invoked, let them come right away, wherever they may be, to give true answers and follow the exorcist's orders . . . Adonay, Meloth, Adonay, Naioloth, Leolam, Naoch, Adonay . . . by these your most sacred names and by all those that may not be named, I beg and entreat you to grant might and power to these prayers and consecrations . . .

7.22
Invoking Satan as Mirage: A Magic Manual

The name Mirage (three syllables) in the Munich manuscript probably means 'Do-Wonders', from the Latin *mira* and *age*. But a cascade of epithets and a Gospel allusion show that 'Mirage most wicked' is Satan, 'master of demons' (see 2.3). He is to be subdued by Christ himself, with the help of angels, archangels, patriarchs, prophets, apostles and saints – all six divisions of the celestial army. Having been adjured, conjured, bound, fettered, admonished and exorcized, the Devil himself will do the exorcist's bidding, sending a docile spirit to serve him, bring him treasure, make him invisible and fulfil his every wish – including more consecrated books. Except for the name Mirage, Doctor Faustus would find none of this strange (see 7.20; 10.2).

*

By my invoking the name of the Lord Jesus Christ, may the unblemished Lamb command you, Mirage, and then may the angels and archangels charge you, Michael, Gabriel and Raphael, may the three patriarchs charge you, Abraham, Isaac and Jacob; may all the prophets and apostles of Christ charge you; and may all the saints and chosen of God charge you. Then – by day and by night, by hour, by month and by the minute – may your ears fail you, Mirage, just as they failed Iannes and Mambres, unless you obey my words quickly and without delay and submit to my will.

God of angels . . . I supplicate and beseech you, deign to give me your help against that evil spirit, Mirage, wherever he lurks, so that on hearing your name he will hurry away from his place and come to me. He commands you, Devil, the one who threw you down from heaven's utmost heights to be buried beneath the earth. Hear, then, most wicked Mirage, defeated and cast down, and be afraid: come in Jesus Christ's name. Mirage most wicked, enemy of faith, inventor of death for humankind, voice of injustice, root of evils, fuel of vice, seducer of humans, master of demons, you who stand and resist, even knowing that your powers are lost, fear him who was sacrificed in Isaac, sold in Joseph, slain in the lamb, crucified in man and then rose up triumphant as God. Hear then, Mirage, fear the words of God, and be ready for me in all the dealings that must be tended to.

I adjure you, ancient serpent, by the Judge of the living and dead, by the one who has the power to send you to Gehenna, to do quickly whatever I tell you, on the orders of Him who sits among the most high . . . I adjure and bind and admonish you, Mirage, to obey me without hindrance or harm or injury and damage to my body and soul, now and for ever. Again, I conjure you, Mirage, by all the aforesaid rites that have been done and are to be done; by all that is holy and has been created, living and dead; by Him who threw you down from heaven. I conjure you and admonish you by the blessed victim and the immaculate victim; by the victim described in scripture, the victim that is blessed and pleasing to God. I conjure you and admonish you, Mirage, by all that can bind and fetter you. I exorcize you by the name of the Lord, by the power of all spirits, by all the characters, by the Seal of Solomon, by Solomon's rings and by the seven golden lampstands shining before the Lord . . .

I also conjure you by all the aforementioned to make a spirit come to me and bring me gold and silver or hidden treasures before I leave this place, making him a servant for me in all that I want, who will appear before me right away whenever I invoke him, kindly and submissive, doing no harm, yet fulfilling my wishes and accomplishing them all: let it be, let it be, let it be so, amen! Send me a spirit ready and helpful in every kind of knowledge and with the power to make me invisible whenever I want, obedient to me and always under my control, and also grant to him the power to consecrate books, procedures and everything else that I want. Amen.

8

Ancient Wisdom and Folly: The Earlier Renaissance

Figure 12: A Stargazer About to Stumble

By the end of the Middle Ages, magic was a fixture in Western Europe, in practice and in theory. From biblical and classical roots and in a fully Christian culture, a robust literature on *magia* had grown up, stirring fascination with that subject and its parts: alchemy and astrology; the lore of angels and demons; techniques for divining and interpreting dreams; instructions for choosing, preparing and using charms, spells, rites, amulets and talismans to heal, harm, seduce and control one's family, friends and enemies on earth and beyond the earth.

As new experts on these contentious topics learned from older experts, the expertise ramified and differences of opinion multiplied. Within the century after 1350, when the Black Death was at its worst, Nicole Oresme could classify most so-called marvels as natural and in no way really marvellous, rarely needing demons to explain them. Bishop Oresme was an important Church official and served a King who called himself 'most Christian'. During the same period, a priest of much lower rank acted without Church or state approval to preserve a *Book of Consecrations* and 'get power to consecrate a bonded spirit . . . and do all the invocations and conjurations'.

Instructions like those in the *Book of Consecrations* were recipes for legal trouble even earlier: in the fourteenth century, people charged with sorcery were sometimes victims of politics. The immense wealth and international reach of the Templars made them – like Pope Boniface VIII – high-value targets for the French monarchy by 1301. But marginal figures accused of sorcery might be surrogates for someone mightier who could not be accused directly. Even if the charges were sincere, they could still be expedient.

Although the Templars were many and had great prestige, their persecution was localized in time and space – managed from Paris and Avignon and finished, though not forgotten, in little more than a decade. Starting in the fifteenth century, however, the catastrophe known as the 'European Witch-Craze' would rage sporadically through the late seventeenth century, when it crossed the Atlantic to take twenty lives from the small settlements of Massachusetts. In Europe tens of thousands had already died, their doom sealed at first by inquisitors who found a new way to torment 'heretics' by trying 'witches'. The link between witchcraft and heresy was explicit in the name used – at the time – for trials in Arras that began in 1459 and led to twelve executions within two years. This *Vauderie* was ostensibly a hunt for *Valdenses* or Waldensian heretics – originally disciples of Peter Waldo, who had preached in and around Lyon in the late twelfth century – but it was also a witch-hunt, one of the first of a new type.

Symphorien Champier, a Lyonnais physician who died around 1540, knew about these disturbances and discussed them as an enlightened healer – enlightened by the new classicizing culture of the Renaissance. It was Champier who first brought the news about Marsilio Ficino and Giovanni Pico della Mirandola north to France in several dozen books of little originality but great influence. One subject to which Pico and Ficino had given their genius was magic, and Champier helped spread their views on that troublesome topic throughout Europe.

Ficino and Pico, who were friends and often saw each other in Florence, both promoted the magic they called 'natural' to distinguish it from demonic magic – Satanic spells that could 'make a spirit come', even if the spirit was Mirage (Do-Wonders) when the Devil answered to that name. These two advocates of magic were philosophers at a time when part of philosophy was natural philosophy and natural magic was part of that. Ficino turned all of Plato into Latin, putting all the dialogues for the first time into a language widely known in Western Europe. He also translated and interpreted Plotinus, Porphyry, Iamblichus, Synesius, Proclus and Dionysius the Areopagite – Neoplatonists who philosophized about magic. Pico was the first Christian who learned enough Hebrew to uncover secrets of Kabbalah. He and Ficino did their most important work on magic in the ten years before Pico died in 1494, in the same period when *The Hammer of Witches* was written and printed.

Published in 1486, that venomous book was the work of two Dominican inquisitors. Jakob Sprenger, who died in 1495, taught theology at Cologne and elsewhere. His commission as an inquisitor was a formality, but not so for Heinrich Kramer (Institoris), who lived until 1505: Kramer travelled from town to town to conduct investigations, sometimes annoying the local clergy with his methods. His enquiries in German and Austrian lands just north of the Alps had been authorized in a routine papal statement by Innocent VIII in 1484. As Dominican friars, Kramer and Sprenger dedicated their lives to preaching the Gospel and eradicating heresy: other Dominicans were the primary audience for their bulky volume.

No one knows why educated Europeans in positions of power – contemporaries of Pico and Ficino, those heroes of 'humanism' – were now panicked by Satanic conspiracies. But as more people felt the threat (or concocted it), more priests needed to preach about *maleficium*. To find material for sermons about witches, priests could go to the first part of the *Hammer*: its theological content suggests that Sprenger, the professorial member of the team, may have written it, while the procedural information in the back of the book may have been Kramer's contribution, based on his experience as a detective and prosecutor.

Both parts of the *Hammer* – the propaganda and the lawyering – made the authors as guilty of inciting gynocide as any writers have ever been. They could have titled their book *Malleus maleficorum*, not *maleficarum*, preserving the masculine *malefici* of Exodus, which could be read as generic. But it was women – *maleficae* – whom the two friars wanted to crush. To judge by its success in the press, the book's influence was enormous and malignant: after many editions, it was still being printed in the age of Pierre Bayle and Balthasar Bekker. Before the *Hammer*, there had been no authoritative, comprehensive and systematic account of witchcraft that painted the whole despicable picture and declared that 'this heresy should be named for witches, not sorcerers'.

Hearing accusations like those made by Kramer and Sprenger, many people concluded that the victims were 'guilty of witchcraft as charged' and agreed that 'legal penalties should apply'. That was Champier's assessment of the state of opinion around 1500, though he disagreed, believing that the accused were usually just deluded. Nonetheless, the delusion itself was the Devil's work: 'Their Prince is the author of lies,' he wrote, and Satan orchestrated the deceptions. The legions of hell might just manipulate the deceived, or demons might actually live inside them: 'Almost all say that maniacs are demoniacs,' according to Oresme, who was more sceptical than Champier.

None of these Christian scholars doubted the reality of demons, however, and how could they? The charter documents of Christian faith, now confirmed by centuries of study and prayer, made it clear – in Pico's words – that there is an 'evil demon who is the Prince of This World'. Although Pico wanted magic amalgamated with Kabbalah to make the faith stronger, he warned that his methods could invite diabolical assault. No magic can be effective without Kabbalah, he declared, but the Kabbalist who 'makes a mistake in the work or comes to it unpurified will be devoured by Azazel' – the scapegoat demon of Leviticus. Because 'image-makers are quite often possessed by evil demons', Pico's friend Ficino feared that unclean spirits might pollute his magical therapies.

Ficino's *Three Books on Life* – the third book presenting his theory of magic – thrived after their first printing in 1489. Like *The Hammer of Witches*, but with a very different message, *On Life* was still finding new publishers in the seventeenth century. In the previous century, as the book's ideas about magic gained influence, some readers came to it for Ficino's eclectic philosophy, with its cosmic harmonies, organic sympathies and energizing spirits. But others saw the great Platonist as a physician and viewed his magic as a medical regimen. Either way, even though Galileo, Descartes and other innovators ignored Ficino's original metaphysics and moral psychology (though not his philosophical translations), Ficino was still a celebrity in Cambridge for Henry More and his friends, and More's world was also Newton's.

Pico also became a celebrity, but not as he had hoped – for his philosophy. He was famous mainly for being Pico, a meteoric genius with a captivating story. He burned out quickly, before finishing anything on the scale of Ficino's *Platonic Theology*. His immense polemic on astrology was posthumous and has yet to be fully digested, even though it caught Kepler's attention. In the age of baroque scholarship, when there was plenty of Hebraica in print, the learned were more attracted by Pico's pioneering Kabbalah – thin and impenetrable though it is. Much of the material on Kabbalah in his posthumous *Oration* is stated obliquely, in a text that was not much read until recently and even less understood – likewise the short statement in the speech about magic. The 900 *Conclusions* that the *Oration* was meant to introduce were never actually debated, though they were published in Pico's lifetime. The 119 theses that he wrote about Kabbalah were treasured by later generations of Christian Hebraists, who kept finding inspiration in them – if not clarity.

8.1

Why Witches Must Be Killed: Kramer and Sprenger, *The Hammer of Witches*, 1.1

That witches must be killed is God's law, and the most revered theologians agree that witchcraft is real – no mere delusion (see 1.5). Citing the Bible by chapter and verse, the *Hammer* bolsters its case by citing the most respected teachers, Augustine and Aquinas – especially Aquinas, the highest authority of all for Dominicans like the two authors (see 6.12; 7.13). Specialists in heresy-hunting, these inquisitors attack witchcraft as a 'failure of faith'. Knowing that the Church's own law had once diagnosed witchcraft as a sin of imagination, not an actual crime, they make the contrary argument: that demons are real and that witches are their accomplices (see 7.2–3).

*

From the teaching of St Thomas, where he discusses witchcraft as a way to prevent sex . . . some people have tried to show that this is nothing but a popular belief held by those who 'ascribe natural effects to witches because their causes are hidden'. A second group accepts witches but claims that the effects of their assisting with witchcraft come just from imagination and fantasy. A third notion is that witchcraft's effects are completely imaginary and mere fantasy, though a demon may actually assist a witch. The errors of these people are to be exposed and condemned.

The first are reprimanded as absolutely heretical by many teachers, especially Saint Thomas . . . because sacred scripture says authoritatively that 'demons have power (when God permits it) over human bodies as well as the imagination' . . . Hence they are wrong to say that 'the only witchcraft in the world exists in the thoughts of people'. Such critics also believe that 'demons exist only in the minds of the uneducated when a person creates terrors out of his own thoughts and attributes them to demons'. What contradicts them is the true faith whereby we believe that demons are the angels who fell from heaven, causing us to recognize that 'they – being of a keener nature – can do many things that we cannot. People who lead demons to do such things are called *witches*.' And because *heresy* is the name for such a failure of faith in a baptized person, these doubters are charged as heretics.

The other two errors, while not denying demons and their natural power, are in disagreement on the effect of witchcraft and the witch herself . . . These people have located grounds for their error in two passages of the 'Bishop's Canon': the first reproves women for believing that they ride at all hours of the night with Diana or Herodias; . . . the second involves someone's belief or claim that a creature can be changed into . . . a 'different image or likeness' than the one created by God . . . However, since these errors smell of heresy and clash with the Canon's plain meaning, we will show how this is so . . .

In fact, the divine law commands us in many places to kill witches, not just shun them, and scripture imposes such penalties only because witches are real people who work with demons to produce actual effects and do harm . . . If you also examine what else has been said by the commentators on sacred literature who . . . have reported on the power of demons and the magical arts, you will find no disagreement about magicians and witches: with God's permission, demons can produce effects that are astonishing and not imaginary . . . St Thomas deals extensively with such acts . . . and St Augustine's comments should also be reviewed along with those of other Doctors: to contradict all our authorities would be completely absurd and rightly judged heretical, and we accept no excuse for the vice of heresy.

8.2

Sex With Demons:
Kramer and Sprenger,
The Hammer of Witches, 2.1.4

Witches are not born every day, and the Devil has a roster to fill, putting *incubi* and *succubi* at his command. Aiming 'to increase the number of the faithless', these grossly unclean spirits are experts on reproductive anatomy and astrology. Noting Augustine's view of diabolical birthing – that the newborn are children of the humans whose semen gets used – Aquinas had specified that 'the same demon who is a succubus for a male becomes an incubus for a woman', which requires some shape-shifting but only two transfers of bodily fluids among three parties – one of them a demon – before insemination (see 6.12; 7.14; 8.1). But if a demon wants to avoid serving a witch as her incubus, another must be assigned, bringing the transfers to three and the participants to four (including two demons). Since nearly fifty witches had recently been burned in the region described by the *Hammer*, the authors must have thought the arrangements effective.

*

No one who reads through the histories can doubt that there have always been witches, that much harm has been done to people, animals and crops by their vicious deeds, or that demons are *succubi* and *incubi* . . . Yet there is this difference, that in times gone by incubus demons molested young women who did not want it . . . As for the claim that witches today have been infected with this diabolical filth, what has made all this credible is not so much our opinion as the testimony of the witches who have experienced these things, not – as in times past – submitting to this most disgusting and deplorable servitude against their wills but doing so freely and eagerly.

Indeed, in a number of dioceses . . . we have turned many of these witches over to the civil authorities for punishment, women who had clung to their filthy deeds for many years – some ten years, some twelve and some thirty – all the while denying the faith wholly or in part. All the residents of those dioceses are also witnesses: in fact, not counting those who repented privately and those who returned to the faith, no fewer than forty-eight witches have been consigned to the flames in the space of five years. And because these women confessed willingly, there is no question of being too quick to believe them since they all agree to this – that they are obliged to commit themselves to this filth in order to increase the number of the faithless ... People confirm all this because they have seen it or heard it or experienced it, or else they have had reports from trustworthy sources ...

Demons can understand what power the spilled semen has, already knowing the state of the person who spilled it; second, which woman is suited to the semen of the one who spills it; third, which constellation helps the effect on the body ... This is how the process works: a succubus demon, having been duly assigned to a man and not wanting to make herself an incubus demon for a witch, lets the semen fall from that degenerate and transfers it to a demon assigned to a woman or witch. And then that demon, under a particular constellation that serves him to produce a male or female child with the lasting strength that it takes to do witchcraft, will make himself the incubus for the witch.

3
Why Most Witches Are Women:
Kramer and Sprenger,
The Hammer of Witches, 1.6

If grammatical gender in a crudely printed text is our guide, the very first witches mentioned by the *Hammer* are masculine – *malefici* – though on the next page it takes a feminine *malefica* (along with the Devil and God's permission) to cause the preventing of sex that fascinated the inquisitors (see 1.5; 8.1). After dealing with the Devil's involvement, the role of *incubi* and *succubi* and the evidence of increasing witchcraft, the authors ask why 'more women than men are found to be infected'. The core of the answer is that 'all witchcraft comes from the carnal lust that is insatiable in women', but the litany of misogyny goes on: mental and physical weakness, fickle dispositions, gossipy habits, credulity and other failings in a list meant to convince any doubters that 'this heresy should be named for witches (*malificae*), not sorcerers (*malefici*)'.

*

If our problem is why the multitude of witches found in the female sex, which is so delicate, is greater than among males, it does no good just to deny that assertion since, in addition to testimony recorded from trustworthy people, experience itself makes such findings credible . . . Some teachers . . . say there are three things in nature – the tongue, a cleric and a woman – that know no moderation, whether in kindness or in malice: exceeding the limits of their condition, they lay claim to the highest degree and pinnacle of kindness or malice . . . and when an evil spirit rules them, the malicious things they do are the very worst . . .

'What else is a woman but an enemy of friendship, an inescapable punishment, a necessary evil, a natural temptation, a desirable disaster, a domestic danger, a delight that does damage and an evil of nature painted in pretty colours? So if it is a sin to send her away when she should be kept, then the torment is truly inescapable: either we commit adultery by divorcing her, or we take a beating every day.' . . . Hence, whenever we read denunciations of the lust of the flesh, these can be interpreted to use 'lust of the flesh' as a synonym for 'woman' . . .

Others also give added reasons why greater numbers of women than men are found to be superstitious, citing three causes. The first is that they are apt to be credulous, and since the demon's main goal is to destroy faith, he prefers to attack women . . . The second reason is that women are variable in temperament and more easily convinced to accept what the influence of separated spirits reveals to them; hence, even though they can behave quite well and exercise this temperament for good, they are all the worse when they use it for evil. The third reason is that a woman has a loose tongue, making it impossible for her to conceal from her female companions what she learns by evil methods.

Since women lack strength, they look for a covert way to get what they want – through witchcraft . . . And because they are deficient in all the faculties of mind and body, it is no surprise that they often procure witchcraft against their rivals . . . The natural reason is that women are more carnal than men, which is clear from the many carnal and filthy things that they do . . . A wicked woman is therefore quicker to doubt the faith, and she also sooner renounces it, supplying the basis for witchcraft . . . We conclude that all witchcraft comes from the carnal lust that is insatiable in women, as it says in Proverbs: 'There are three things that cannot be satisfied and a fourth that never says "enough"' – namely, the 'mouth of the vagina' – which is why they gratify their desires even by doing it with demons . . .

To those who understand, it is plain enough and no surprise that more women than men are found to be infected with the heresy of witchcraft. Accordingly, this heresy should be named for witches, not sorcerers, taking its designation from the more potent source. And blessed be the Most High who, up to now, has kept the male sex away from so great a disgrace.

8.4
The Metaphysics of Magic:
Marsilio Ficino, *On Life*, 3.1

Although Ficino takes his philosophy of magic where he can get it, ancient Platonism and Neoplatonism are his favourite guides, especially to fill the gap between mind and body with Soul as a third 'hypostasis' or metaphysical principle (see 4.4–5; 5.5, 15–16). Acting as the World-Soul, this divine force animates the cosmos, just as human souls give life to human bodies. Reaching down from Unity and Mind, Soul's role is to mediate in a universe whose highest divinities are inconceivably remote. Soul carries the seeds of divine Ideas and transmits them through stars and planets as forms to produce (metaphysical) species of things below on earth. 'Through its own seeded form, each and every species can . . . get something from an Idea up there.' Forms sown like seed into the matter of stones, plants and animals make them lures and baits that attract power from on high (see 5.11–13).

*

If there were only these two things in the world – intellect there, body here – but soul were missing, then intellect, being very far away from body, would not be drawn to body because it does not move and, for a source of motion, has no feeling at all. And body, so far removed, would not be drawn to intellect, being unfit for motion and incapable on its own. But if a soul conforming to both were put between them, an attraction from each and to each would easily be produced . . . because soul joins equally with everything, even things distant from one another yet plainly not distant from soul . . . which is always everywhere.

Add to this that by divine power the soul of the world has at least as many forms of things seeded in it as there are Ideas in the divine mind, and she uses those forms to produce just as many species in matter. Hence, through its own seeded form, each and every species corresponds to its own Idea, and through this form a species can easily and often get something from an Idea up there, seeing that the species was produced from there through the form . . . And if you correctly apply to some particular species of things, or to an individual, the many scattered things that still conform to the same Idea, from that Idea you will soon draw a remarkable gift into the matter thus duly prepared, and it comes through the reason seeded in the soul since, strictly speaking, it is soul that is led – not intellect itself.

Let no one think, then, that certain divinities completely separated from matter are drawn to material things in the world: instead, these demons are gifts from the ensouled world and the living stars. Furthermore, no one should be surprised that soul can somehow be attracted by material forms since soul herself has made baits of this sort fit for her, and she always happily inhabits them. Nowhere in the whole living world do we find anything too ugly for soul to be with it – too ugly for a gift from soul to be within it. 'God's bait', therefore, was Zoroaster's phrase for the fitness of such forms to those in the world's soul, and Synesius confirmed that they are magical 'lures'.

8.5
A Mean Between Body and Soul: Ficino, *On Life*, 3.3–4

'The world's body is everywhere alive' – cosmic matter animated by a soul that is not itself material. To explain the linkages of immaterial human souls with human bodies made of matter, physicians like Ficino relied on liquids (humours) and vapours (spirits), thinking them fluid and fine enough to make physiological and psychological connections between body and soul. Like the ancient Stoics who influenced the Neoplatonists, Ficino emphasizes one of these media – *pneuma* or *spiritus*, meaning 'breath' – and makes it cosmic, giving the whole world a way to keep body and soul together (see 5.7–8, 11; 7.6, 9, 15, 19; 8.4). The *spiritus* that acts locally in every earthly thing also acts globally as a cosmic 'fifth essence' – distinct from the four terrestrial elements but akin to them all and continuous with bodily spirits, which can be improved medically to 'get this spirit inside you . . . from the body of the world and its soul and also from stars and demons'.

*

Surely, given all the evidence that things are mobile and productive, the world's body is everywhere alive, which the philosophers of India prove from the fact that the world brings living things out of itself everywhere: this body, therefore, lives with a soul everywhere present and perfectly adapted to it. Hence, between the soul of that body of the world – a soul whose nature is quite distant from such a body – and the body that is palpable and partly perishable, a spirit is in them everywhere, just as there is between our soul and body, given that life is always shared by a soul with a grosser body. For such a spirit is needed as a medium whereby a divine soul can be present to a grosser body and impart life to it deep inside . . .

Since all things bring forth by a spirit of their own, the world brings all things forth through its spirit, which we can call 'the heavens' in some cases, the 'fifth essence' in others. In the world's body this spirit is almost the same as in our body, with this main exception, that the world's soul does not extract it from the four elements, as if she had the humours that our soul uses: no, she brings it forth 'nextmost' (if I may talk like Plato or Plotinus) from her own genital power, as if she were pregnant, birthing the stars along with spirit and then on to the four elements, as if they all were in her spirit's power. Spirit is a very fine body, somehow not a body and then somehow a soul, or somehow not a soul and then somehow a body. In its power there is little of the earthy nature, more the watery, more still the airy and most of all the fiery and astral . . . It lives everywhere in everything as the nextmost maker and mover of all begetting, of which the poet says that 'spirit feeds within'. By its own nature it is completely clear, warm, moist and life-giving, having got those properties from higher properties of the soul . . .

The main thing for you is to strive to get this spirit inside you: this is the way for you to get back certain natural benefits from the body of the world and its soul and also from stars and demons. For spirit is a mean between the world's gross body and its soul; in it and through it the stars and demons also exist. Whether the world's body and things in the world come nextmost from the world's soul (as Plotinus and Porphyry believe), or the body of the world, like its soul, comes nextmost from God (as our people believe, and perhaps Timaeus the Pythagorean), the world is wholly alive and it breathes, and we may drink the spirit in. But a human really drinks it in through his own spirit which, by its own nature, conforms to the world's spirit, especially if there is a method to make it more akin – if the spirit turns out to be as heavenly as possible, in other words . . .

8.6

To Capture the Power of a Star:
Ficino, *On Life*, 3.8

From pagan, Muslim and Christian astrologers, Ficino compiled the data needed 'to capture the power of any star' (see 4.15; 5.8; 7.4). His sources not only located stars and planets in their times, places and configurations but also showed how and when to make artificial objects to tap their powers. The workings of such devices – the jewels described by Albert the Great, for example – might be nothing more than spirit (*spiritus*) acting naturally (see 7.11; 8.5). Even Aquinas taught that heavenly bodies can affect not only the body but also one's mind and circumstances (see 7.12). Ficino is curious but cautious, claiming to prefer ordinary medicines used in conventional ways.

*

The tail of the Greater Bear, which goes with Venus and the Moon, is in the 19th degree of Virgo: people think its stone is the magnet, its plant chicory and mugwort, giving protection against robbers and poisonings. The right wing of the Crow is in the 7th degree of Libra, also in its 12th and perhaps the 13th, the left wing that goes with Saturn and with Mars as well. Its plant, they say, is sorrel and henbane as well as frog's tongue, for increasing boldness, though it may be toxic . . . The Scorpion's heart, going with Mars and Jupiter, governs sardonyx, amethyst, the long birthwort and saffron. They believe it produces a good colour, makes the mind happy and wise and drives demons away . . .

Thebit the philosopher teaches that to capture the power of any star just described, take its stone and its plant and make a gold or silver ring, putting a bit of the stone inside the ring with the plant under it, and wear it so that it touches you. But you should do this as the Moon goes under the star or looks on it in trine or sextile aspect, or as the star passes through the mid-sky or is ascendant. Actually, I would rather make a compound of things related in this way to stars – in medicinal form, applying them internally or externally, and observing the proper moment at the stated time, rather than put them into a ring. The ancients made much of rings, however . . .

If rings of that sort have any power from above, I think it reaches not so much the soul or the gross body as the spirit, as the ring gradually warms up, so that the effect on the spirit is to make it steadier or clearer, stronger or gentler, harsher or cheerier. Such effects certainly pass into the body – doing so completely, in fact – and to some degree they also pass into the sensual soul that often yields to the body. But claims that rings are good against demons or enemies or good for pleasing princes are either fictions or else they are based on one of two things: that rings make the spirit steadfast and dauntless, or else they make it tame, agreeable and anxious to serve.

Yet if I were to say that heavenly things bring something beyond bodily health to one's mind, skill and fortune, I would not disagree with our Thomas Aquinas. In the third book *Against the Heathens* he proves that something is impressed on our bodies by the heavenly bodies – a benefit that often disposes us to choose what is better even in ignorance of the reason and result. On this point, in fact, he calls people 'very fortunate' and 'well born', and Aristotle agrees. He also adds that by heavenly power some people become good at getting various results (to use his words) from technique, as a soldier succeeds in conquering, a farmer in planting and a physician in healing. For just as plants and stones have certain strengths beyond their elemental nature, he says, so people also have some such strengths in matters of technique.

I would be happy if there were some way for heavenly things to bring good health, acting like medicines used internally or externally, as long as our search to save the body does not cause us to throw the soul's salvation away. Let us never try anything prohibited by holy religion.

8.7
From Each and Every Star Hangs a Series: Ficino, *On Life*, 3.13–14

Eminent authorities recommend astrological images, but a skittish Ficino questions them, worried about idolatry and demonolatry: Hebrews aligned a golden calf with Venus and the moon; Egyptian wizards chose the best moment for 'implanting the souls of demons' into their idols; Neoplatonist philosophers warned that demons would be hard to keep away at any time (see 5.10–11, 13). As nodes in the cosmic circuitry, moreover, amulets and idols of stone and metal have the disadvantage of being hard – resistant to penetration by heavenly forces though perhaps good at retaining them (see 7.10–11). Ficino frames this physical point with a metaphysical construct little known at the time, which he had found ready-made by Proclus: the notion of an ontological hierarchy, a 'series' of entities rising – through many levels – from mortal things (a desert scorpion) through heavenly immortals (the constellation Scorpio) to hypercosmic gods (the supercelestial Scorpion) who give form to everything below them (all the lesser scorpions; see 5.16; 7.7, 9, 12). Ficino's point is that a stone in the scorpion series, stuck at the bottom of its order, is not very powerful at all – maybe not worth prescribing to a patient. But he also realizes that 'nowhere in the whole living world do we find anything too ugly for soul to be with it' and that 'a divine soul can be present to a grosser body': even last place in a series connects its occupant with higher powers – gods by Ficino's reckoning but devils for his critics.

*

In the *Hundred Sayings* Ptolemy remarks that likenesses of things below come under the visages in the skies and that the ancient sages therefore used to construct various images when the planets – as if they were exemplars of things below – were entering into the faces in the sky that are like those things. Haly actually acknowledges this, commenting on this passage to say that an image of a serpent can be made useful when the Moon comes under the heavenly Serpent or is in a friendly aspect with it. Likewise, an image of a scorpion is effective when the Moon enters the sign of Scorpio . . . He says this was done in his day in Egypt and in his presence, when a figure was pressed into incense in that way from the seal of a scorpion made of a bezoar stone. When this was then given in a drink to a person stung by a scorpion, he was instantly cured . . .

Haly also talks about a wise man whom he knew there and who took the same pains to make images that moved – an effect somehow produced by Archytas, as we read. The Egyptians, says Trismegistus, also used to make such images from various ingredients in the world, implanting the souls of demons into them at the right moment – including the soul of Mercury, his ancestor, and also those of a certain Phoebus and of Isis and Osiris, who came down into statues to help people or to harm them as well . . .

The Hebrews too, having grown up in Egypt, learned how to assemble a golden calf, so their astrologers believe, in order to capture the good will of Venus and the Moon against the influence of Scorpio and Mars, which is hostile to Jews. Porphyry also testifies in his *Letter to Anebo* that images are effective, adding that airy demons would immediately get inside the images from certain vapours present in the ritual smoke that was their own. Iamblichus confirms that not just heavenly effects and forces but also the demonic and divine can be had in materials that are naturally suited to higher powers, brought together from various places and compounded in the right way at the right time. Proclus and Synesius say exactly the same thing.

Products amazingly good for health, which can be made by physicians expert in astrology from compounds with many ingredients – powders, liquids, ointments, lozenges – seem themselves to have an explanation that is more plausible and better known than images have: first, because powders, liquids, ointments and lozenges made at the right moment take in heavenly influences more easily and quickly than the harder materials of which images are usually made; next, because these things are already affected by the heavens and either consumed by us and changed accordingly or else, if used externally, at least they hold on better and then penetrate; also finally, because images are put together from one thing only or very few, while those medicines can be compounded from as many ingredients as you like . . .

The heavens have worked a very long time to put these things together and cook them up. But since you cannot easily make many such compounds, you are compelled to conduct a careful search for the metal that is more potent than all the rest in the order of some star, and for the stone that is highest in the order, so that, as best you can, you can include all the others in some one item that is highest in an entire genus and order and, using such a receptacle, you can acquire the heavenly things that are suited to it . . .

From each and every star (I'm speaking as a Platonist) hangs a series of things that belong to it, down to the last. Under the actual Heart of Scorpio, after demons, humans and animal scorpions, we can also locate the plant aster – 'astral', in other words – whose shape is like a star's that shines at night, and physicians report that it has the property of a rose and possesses amazing power against diseases of the genitals. Under the Serpent or Serpentarius in the sky they put Saturn and, to some extent, Jupiter, then demons that often take the form of serpents, humans of this kind next, and animal serpents, the snakeweed plant, the stone draconite that comes from the head of a dragon, also the stone often called 'serpentine' and others that I shall introduce later. Under Sirius, the solar star, the Sun comes first, then also the Apollonian demons who, according to Proclus, have sometimes appeared to people in the form of lions or cocks, next the solar humans and beasts that are quite similar, then the Apollonian plants and also the metals and stones and burning steam and air.

In such a way they reckon that from every star in the firmament and through any planet a framework of things descends by degrees under the proper governance of that heavenly body. So if, as I was saying, you include every solar thing of whatever degree in its order – solar people, things belonging to such a person, also animals, plants, metals, stones and things related to them – you will keep drinking the Sun's power in and, in some sense, the natural ability of solar demons. Note that I have said the same about the others . . .

There is no other reason for the lion to fear the cock except that in the Apollonian order the cock is higher than the lion. For the same reason, says Proclus, the Apollonian demon who sometimes appeared in the form of a lion vanished as soon as a cock was put in front of it . . . Among plants the palm is Apollonian and especially the laurel, by whose power poisons and lightning are also warded off. By a similar ability the ash-tree also repels poisons from afar. Round leaves and fruit show that the lotus is Apollonian, also the opening of lotus leaves by day and their folding up at night. Not just the peony's power shows it to be Apollonian but also its name. To the same order belong flowers and plants that close up when the Sun goes away, unfold when it comes back and keep bending towards the Sun . . .

From all these or from many of them, at least, you should make some compound medicine when the Sun is dominant. And while the Sun dominates you should also start using the medicine, while also wearing solar things, living with them, looking at them, hearing, smelling, imagining, thinking and wanting them, all the while imitating the Sun's rank and functions in your life, spending time with solar people and plants and constantly handling the laurel.

8.8

Testing Talismans: Ficino, *On Life*, 3.15

Anyone who has seen a magnet attract iron knows that stones have power (see 7.10–11). Ficino thinks that this power can be enhanced *naturally* by strengthening the stone's links with other natural objects in its series. Since a bit of iron and a lodestone are both in the series of the Bear (the constellation Ursa Major), the magnet will gain strength as an amulet if a patient simply hangs it on his body with iron rather than silk or silver (see 4.3; 5.14; 8.6). This is an easy application of a 'maxim of magic', which summarizes the theory of ontological hierarchy and magical action that Ficino took from Proclus (see 5.16; 8.7). The next step is to amplify the magic 'by gathering many into one' – by concentrating related items that the expert 'collects, crushes, combines and cooks together under a certain star' (see 5.11). Ficino thought he might test an iron/magnet amulet in this way by converting it into an Ursine talisman – by carving the celestial Bear on the stone at a propitious time. Warned by Iamblichus that 'image-makers are quite often possessed by evil demons', he decided against the experiment when he learned that dangerous demons come from Ursa's part of the sky (see 5.10, 13). Later he tried out a dragon-stone in a different test of resonance with Draco, a trial with striking results: the stone seemed to move around on its own. Still, Ficino claims just to be describing all this, not dispensing dragon talismans to his patients.

*

If you have acquired the Apollonian stones that I just told you about, there will be no need to impress images on them. Just set them in gold and hang them around your neck on strings of yellow silk when the Sun passes under Aries or Leo and is ascendant or holds mid-heaven in aspect with the Moon. Yet Proclus tells about stones in the Moon's series that are much more potent . . . My wish, nonetheless, is to have no trouble finding a stone – solar or lunar – of great potency in its own order, like the magnet and iron that we have under the series of the northern pole-star. In the glasses that sailors use to point to the pole, we see that a needle balanced and charged by a magnet at the tip moves towards the Bear: plainly, the magnet draws it there because the Bear's power also prevails in this stone and is transferred from it into the iron, drawing them both towards the Bear. But the power communicated to it from the start also keeps growing on the Bear's rays. Maybe amber has this relation with the other pole, as it does with straw.

But meanwhile, say why a magnet attracts iron everywhere: not because they are alike, or else a magnet would attract a magnet much more and iron would attract iron; and not because a magnet is higher in the order of bodies, since a metal is actually higher than a stone. Why then? Both are included in the order that follows the Bear, but the magnet's level is higher among Bearish items, while iron is lower. The fact is that the higher attracts the lower in the same framework and turns it towards itself, or else in some way it activates or affects it with a power already imparted to it. And again, by the same dose of power the lower is turned towards the higher, or else activated and directly affected . . .

When I was young and had explored these matters to this extent, I was quite excited, planning, if I could, to carve a figure of the Bear on a magnet when the Moon was in a good aspect with it and then hang the stone around my neck by an iron wire: in the end, my hope was to master that constellation's power. But after investigating for a very long time, what I found was that the influences of that star-group come mostly from Saturn and Mars. I learned from the Platonists that evil demons are mostly northern. The Hebrew astronomers also recognize this, locating the hurtful demons of Mars in the north, the helpful demons of Jupiter in the south. From the theologians and from Iamblichus I learned that image-makers are quite often possessed by evil demons and deceived.

In Florence I have actually seen a stone brought from India, where it was extracted from the head of a dragon: round like a coin, naturally marked with many star-like dots in a row, when soaked in vinegar it moved straight for a little while, next sideways and then in a circle until the vapour from the vinegar evaporated. My thought was that a stone of this kind has the nature of the heavenly Dragon and (almost) its shape, and that it also gets the Dragon's movement when the spirit of the vinegar or strong wine makes it friendlier to the Dragon or to its sky. So a person who wore this stone and often soaked it in vinegar might get some of that Dragon's strength – the Dragon that entangles the Greater Bear on one side, the Lesser Bear on the other . . .

So interconnected is the world's machinery that on earth there are heavenly things in an earthly state and then in heaven earthly things with heavenly rank, and within the world's hidden life and the world's queenly mind are heavenly things whose property and perfection are lifegiving and yet intellectual. On this basis some people also confirm that maxim of magic: at the right times, heavenly things can somehow be drawn to humans through lower things that are suited to the higher, and, through heavenly things, those beyond the heavens can also be acquired by us or perhaps introduced directly – though this latter is for those people to say.

Yet it seems likely enough (as I have stated) that by some technique, properly executed at the right time, the former can happen by gathering many into one, whether through the seeded forms that I have attributed to higher things or because many such items – when a physician and astrologer collects, crushes, combines and cooks them together under a certain star, as they, on their own, gradually come under a new form by reason of the cooking and leavening – acquire this form by a kind of kindling in the heavens when rays act inside them, making the form heavenly.

At the moment when the metal or stone is carved, it seems not to get a new quality but a figure, and the process does not move through the usual steps of decomposition that govern natural alteration and production. But since a heavenly nature – somewhat as a lower nature is regulated – usually advances along a certain natural course, so that it approaches by advancing, many correctly doubt that images of this sort get any power from heaven. I too often hesitate and would deny that they get it – except that all the ancients and all the astrologers think that they do have amazing power. Actually, my denial would not be absolute, for unless someone persuades me otherwise, my view is that images have some power, at least to improve health, especially by the reason seeded in the material selected, though I think that the power is much greater in drugs and ointments compounded when the stars are favourable. What I meant when I said 'by the reason seeded in the material selected' I will make clear in what follows.

So, let me briefly report what can be said on behalf of images while using the views of magicians and astrologers to interpret Plotinus, though I have already warned you not to suppose that I approve the use of images here, where I am just talking about them. What I use are medicines compounded to suit the heavens, not images, and every day I give others the same advice. But if you grant that God has implanted astonishing powers in things below the Moon, you should grant powers even more astonishing to things in heaven. Furthermore, if you decide that people may use lower things to improve their health, you should decide that they may also use higher things and apply medical technique to put the lower together by the higher standard, as God has also put them together from the beginning . . .

8.9

Images They Used to Make:
Ficino, *On Life*, 3.18

Calling Aquinas 'our guide in theology', Ficino writes that the saint 'fears images more and concedes less to them' than other experts, notably Porphyry in his account of the star-blasting of Plotinus but also Albert in his *Mirror of Astrology* (see 5.4; 7.9). Albert permits 'figures, letters and sayings imprinted on images', but Thomas derides all talismanic *writing* because it might contain 'signs directed to demons'. He does not entirely exclude *figures*, however, as long as their effects stay within natural limits (see 7.12). Thomas's reasoning is even more obscure in Ficino's compressed version than in the original: a talisman is an artefact that 'has its place in some particular species of the artificial' – in an artificial branch of an ontological hierarchy, in other words (see 5.16; 8.7). Recalling that Iamblichus too was cautious about images and fearing 'even the shadow of idolatry', Ficino puts his money once again on ordinary medicines, adding that any unusual effects that come from a carved stone are probably natural: either from the stone's matter or from hammering, heating and cutting it (see 5.10, 13).

*

It would be excessive and perhaps harmful to tell you what images they used to make and how higher minds were to be associated or segregated to bring happiness or produce disaster for a single person or a household or a city. I do not claim, in fact, that such things can be done. But astrologers think they can be done, and they show how – matters that I dare not talk about. Describing the life of Plotinus, his teacher, Porphyry confirms that such things can be done. He tells how Olympius, a magician and astrologer from Egypt, tried them against Plotinus in Rome, in an effort to use images or some such things to blast Plotinus with a star, but the lofty soul of Plotinus turned those efforts back against their source.

Albert the Great, who taught both astrology and theology, also says in his *Mirror* – where he claims to be distinguishing licit from illicit practices – that images put together properly by astrologers get power and effectiveness from a figure in the heavens. Next he tells about their amazing effects, as certified by Thebit Benthorad, Ptolemy and other astrologers. He describes images – which I advisedly leave out – meant to bring disaster or success to someone. While confirming that such images can be effective, as a good man he still condemns the abuse of the method, and as an official theologian he abominates the prayers and smoke-filled rituals used by certain wicked people to invite demons when images were being made. Yet he does not reject the figures, letters and sayings imprinted on images, as long as they are used to get some gift from a figure in the heavens . . .

Thomas Aquinas, our guide in theology, fears images more and concedes less to them. For he thinks that through figures we can get power from heaven only inasmuch as it promotes those effects that the heavens ordinarily produce through plants and other natural objects – and then that figure harmonizes with the heavens not so much because such a figure is in the matter as because such a composite already has its place in some particular species of the artificial. He says this in the third book *Against the Heathens*, where he laughs at characters and letters added to figures but at figures not so much, unless they are added on as certain signs directed to demons. In his book *On Fate* he also says that constellations give an order of existing and persisting not just to natural things but also to the artificial, which is why images are fashioned under particular constellations. But if anything astonishing, beyond the usual effects of natural objects, happens because of images, he flings them back at the demons who mean to mislead people. This is perfectly clear in his book *Against the Heathens*, but even more in his letter *On the Hidden Works of Nature*, where he also seems to make light of the images themselves, no matter how they are made, and I too – inasmuch as he commands it – make nothing of them.

Nor is it strange for the Platonists to refer certain astonishing effects of images to demonic deceit. Indeed, Iamblichus – talking about people who trust only images and hope for divine gifts from them because they neglect holiness and religion at its best – says that such people are often deceived in this matter by evil demons who appear in the guise of good divinities. He does not deny, however, that some results, natural and good, come from images constructed by a legitimate astrological method.

In the end, I think it safer to rely on medicines than on images and that the seeded forms, to which I ascribed the heavenly power in images, can be effective in medicines rather than in figures. For if images have this power, they probably get it not so much from a figure recently made as from the matter that they possess naturally and which has been affected in this way. But if something new is acquired when the image is carved, it comes not so much from getting the figure as from the heating caused by hammering. The hammering and heating produced under a heavenly harmony, if it resembles the harmony that once imparted power to the matter, excites and strengthens that very power, just as a breath excites a flame, making manifest what was concealed, just as heat from a fire brings to view the letters that cancel themselves when written in onion juice . . .

When making medicines, it helps to be in time with the heavens. And if someone might want to use metals and stones, it is best only to pound and heat them rather than make a figure. For beyond my suspicion that figures are worthless, it would be rash of us to accept even the shadow of idolatry, and also rash to use the stars – even stars that help us – which most resemble the diseases to be driven away, for they often aggravate those diseases, just as harmful stars sometimes relieve diseases that do not resemble them, which Ptolemy and Haly clearly teach, of course.

8.10
Astral Spirits Kept Inside Them:
Ficino, *On Life*, 3.20

Toxic hellebore was a dangerous drug in Ficino's day, but not unnatural. The plant's effects were traced to its physical properties, both manifest and hidden (or 'occult'), and those effects were seen as nature's workings: effects of occult qualities were puzzles but not miracles – no more than a magnet's pull on iron. But students of *natural philosophy* (what we call 'science', more or less) counted both hellebore and the magnet as examples of *natural magic* (part of that philosophy or its application; see 5.3, 12, 14; 7.10). Like a stone or a plant, the metal used to make a mirror is also natural, though the mirror is artificial. Used to focus the rays of the sun, the mirror has great destructive power and acts at a distance – like a magnet. Accordingly, when Olympius tried to star-blast Plotinus from far away, was his magic just natural? As Porphyry tells the story, no figure or image was used, but those are Ficino's concerns when he wonders 'how images can have any effect on a distant object' (see 5.4). Is that effect natural, like purging with a plant or burning with a mirror? When Arabs and Egyptians made talismans and idols, natural magic was not enough: they thought there were 'astral spirits kept inside them' in the way that demons possess their victims (see 2.7, 10; 5.11, 13; 6.11; 7.9, 12).

*

If someone uses hellebore as prescribed and has the strength to handle it, I take it to be established that the desired purging and the plant's hidden property somehow change the spirit's quality and the body's nature and, in part, the movements of the mind, so that the patient becomes almost young again and seems nearly reborn . . . Astronomers think that helpful images have a power like this that somehow changes the nature and behaviour of those who wear them, restoring them to better health and making them almost different people – or at least keeping them in good health for quite a long time. But they think that images harmful to the wearer have a force like hellebore's – toxic and destructive – when its use violates the method and exceeds the capacity of the person who takes it. They also think that an image directed against someone else, for whom it was meant and made to cause disaster, has the power of a concave bronze mirror aimed straight at him, so that it actually burns him up with rays focused and reflected back at him, if it is close, and from far away it forces him to grope around.

This has produced the story or belief or supposition that people, animals and plants can be star-blasted and consumed by magical potions and astrological devices. But how images can have any effect on a distant object I do not quite understand, though I suspect they have some effect on the people who wear them. This is not the effect that many imagine, however, and it comes from the matter's seeded reason rather than the figure. And I far prefer medicines to images – as I have said.

Arabs and Egyptians, however, attribute so much to statues and images fashioned by magical and astronomical technique that they think astral spirits are kept inside them. While some understand 'astral spirits' to be the amazing powers of the heavens, others also take them to be the demons who minister to one star or another. And then, whatever the astral spirits are, they think they are kept inside statues and images, no differently than demons may sometimes inhabit human bodies, using them to talk, move around, move other things and work wonders. They think that demons dwelling in the world's fire are put into our bodies through fiery or enflamed humours and also through enflamed spirits and effects of that kind. They also think that astral spirits are implanted in the corresponding materials of images through rays received at just the right moment and through powerful vapours, lights and sounds, and that these images can have astonishing effects on the person who wears them or on someone nearby. I think that demons can really do such things – not so much because a particular material restrains them as because they enjoy the ritual attention.

8.11

Singing to a Star:
Ficino, *On Life*, 3.21

Songs with words have physical and semantic features: senders transmit them through a medium for receivers to hear; once formed, their meanings are preserved in transmission to be understood by other minds. The medium is air. Hot, warm and alive, air is also the singer's breath and spirit, continuous with cosmic spirit, pervading the whole world and 'conveying meaning like a mind'. Minds add personal voices to the symphony, earthly human singers with inner ears attuned to astral choirs on high, the supernal musicians who listen for songs from below (see 4.3; 5.5, 11, 15): when human singing 'imitates heavenly things, the stimulus is amazing – for our spirit to accept heaven's influence'. Song's organic energy, 'aerial and also somehow rational', is also mobile, active and emotional, affecting the singer, the listener and even the bystander who breathes the same air. Song is contagious, for better or worse: the contagion can be demonic and dangerous.

*

Song is the most potent imitator of all. Song imitates the mind's meanings as well as feelings and words, while at the same time conveying a person's gestures, movements and actions along with his character: all these it imitates and portrays so powerfully that it stimulates both the singer and the audience to imitate these same things and act them out right away. When song, with equal power, imitates heavenly things, the stimulus is amazing – for our spirit to accept heaven's influence and for the influence to reach our spirit. But the very material of singing is purer and much more like the heavens than medicinal material: this material is air – air that is hot or warm, even breathing and in some sense living, assembled from various joints and limbs like an animal, not only supporting movement and showing emotion but also conveying meaning like a mind, so that this animal can be called aerial and also somehow rational. Singing, therefore, full of spirit and sense – if the song responds to this star or to that one by its meanings, by its linkages and the form resulting from them, and also by the effect of the imagination – transfers from those sources to the singer, and from him into a listener nearby, no less power than anything else that can be put together, as long as the singing sustains its strength and the singer's spirit.

8.12

A Demon in Charge of Each Person:
Ficino, *On Life*, 3.23

Socrates had a demon – a *genius* in Latin – to make him stop and think; people said the same about Apollonius; and an 'indwelling spirit of the more divine degree' came to help Plotinus (see 4.16; 5.1, 4). Fusing those pagan stories with Christian traditions about guardian angels, Ficino puts them in astrological perspective: 'Every person is born with his own particular demon, determined by his very own star.' But stars are persons because they are gods with souls and minds. A planetary Lord of geniture is such a godly person, heaven's agent in shaping human characters and dispositions (see 4.15; 5.8; 7.4). People should learn enough astrology to align themselves with the heavens when choosing where to live, what house to buy, what clothes to wear, what food to eat, what drugs to take and what work to do. Advising against more ambitious interventions, Ficino thinks that things often come out well because God has provided, while leaving us room 'to join the planets together and get the work done'. A person who has chosen poorly 'submits to a demon that differs from his native genius'.

*

Any person born with a sound mind has been naturally prepared by the heavens for some kind of decent life and work. So anyone who wants help from the heavens should start by taking that work on and living that way, and then, since the heavens favour their own projects, he should keep doing this diligently. Nature has made you more for this work than for anything else – the thing that you do, discuss, desire, devise, dream and mimic from your early years. Trying it more often, finishing it more easily, you have your best success at it, enjoying it more than anything else and not wanting to stop doing it. This, of course, is what the heavens and heaven's Lord produced you for.

Accordingly, the Lord of your geniture will support what you have started and will assist your life to the extent that you follow up what your Progenitor has begun – especially given the truth of that Platonic maxim to which all the ancients assent: every person is born with his own particular demon, determined by his very own star, to watch over his life and help him towards just those duties that the powers of heaven allotted to him when he was born. Therefore, a person who examines his native talent using the evidence that I have just described will find his own natural work in such a way that he finds his own star and demon at the same time. Tracking those beginnings, he will have success and live happily: if not, bad luck will be his experience, and he will feel that the heavens are hostile . . .

It will be worthwhile to find out which region, as initially designated by your star and demon, is best for you to live in and improve, since those forces will be of more help to you there . . . It will also be useful to attend to the house that you live in . . . By a change of name, job, housing, diet or place, heaven's influence on us changes for better or for worse, and our demons can also change along with them, or else – as the Platonists will decree – we behave differently towards the same demons from one situation to the other. Astrologers agree with the Platonists that every person's guardian demon can be twinned, one belonging to his nativity, the other to his job. As long as his job matches his nature, the same demon – or certainly one very similar – helps us in both ways, making life more coherent for us and calm. But if one's job and nature do not match, the demon acquired by him artificially disagrees with the native genius, making life difficult and disturbed.

For those who wish to learn what kind of demon has charge of each person from conception, Porphyry looks for a rule from the planet that is the Lord of geniture. Julius Firmicus says that the Lord of geniture is a planet: it is either the one that has more dignities at that moment, or else a firmer statement by Julius favours the one where the moon will travel after leaving the sign that she already occupies as the person is born . . . But since I think it useless to wish for things in the past, my advice is to observe the same planets that the ancients wanted for demons and fortunes, the point being to join the planets together and get the work done . . .

So let us first find out where nature and the demon are taking us. Whether we do so with the effort and care that I described before or by this method that I have just reviewed, we will judge a person unlucky if he has no decent work to do. For the fact is that someone who lacks a guide in his job and takes up no respectable work also has scarcely any natural guidance because the stars and demons or angelic guides assigned by God to watch over us have the duty of always acting for the best and in the very broadest sense. Unluckier still, as I said before, is the person with a job contrary to his nature who submits to a demon that differs from his native genius.

8.13

How Impure the Superstition:
Ficino, *On Life*, 3.26

Ficino has made his case for talismans in medicine but has not endorsed them. He claims to prefer less risky treatments, though this choice is not easy (see 8.6–10). Arguments from reason, empirical evidence, pagan wisdom and Christian authority might persuade a physician to recommend talismans and might convince a priest to justify them. And for a philosopher, two types of argument have been forceful throughout the book *On Life*, whose final chapter summarizes both. One gives magic a metaphysical armature – the body/spirit/soul/mind hierarchy that Proclus explained (see 5.16; 8.4–5). The other is physical: a set of models to make action at a distance intelligible, to show how magic can come down from gods so far above. To make that point, it was Proclus again who called soul 'a kind of tinder in the world's spirit and body'. A flame held *above* to light the tinder without touching it is like a god descending to a statue – attracted but not by bodily contact. Other analogies with baits, lures, echoes, reflections, grafts, farming, copulation and conception rely on ordinary human experience to make magic concrete and credible (see 7.4; 8.4, 8–9). Just this much physics and metaphysics might have kept Plotinus out of trouble when he theorized about the magic in Egyptian statues (see 5.11). But the Egyptian Hermes 'adds songs resembling the powers of heaven, who delight in those songs'. Songs are messages, as Aquinas had taught, and the powers pleased by them may be demons (see 7.12; 8.11). Iamblichus, who recognized the problem, denounced statue-making as worship of gods too vile to be honoured, which showed Ficino 'how impure was the superstition of pagan people' (see 5.13).

*

In addition to this body of the world, intimately manifest to the senses, a spirit hides within it, a type of body that escapes the grasp of transitory sensing. In the spirit thrives a soul, and in the soul an intelligence flashes. And just as no air below the moon mixes with water except through fire, nor fire with water except through air, so there is also a kind of bait or tinder in the universe for bonding soul to body – this very thing that we call 'spirit'. Soul is also a kind of tinder in the world's spirit and body for attaining intelligence by divine means – in the way that a certain extreme dryness in wood has prepared the wood to be penetrated by oil. The oil drunk in by the wood is fuel for fire – though first it is fuel for heat, I mean. Heat itself is the carrier of light, like the kind of wood that we sometimes see blazing but not burning up when fire is present. Now from this example we shall see whether a person or something else under the moon can sometimes, when the time is right, get various life-giving and perhaps even intellectual benefits from above because certain preparations have been made – partly natural, in fact, and partly procured by technique . . .

Regarding natural influences of any kind that come from above, know that we can use technique to get them inside us and inside our matter only when nature has supplied us and our matter with kindling for them and when the heavens have been harmonized with those same influences at just the right moment. Is this not so: that in the fetus, the nature that crafts the fetus, having arranged that little body in one way or another and having shaped it, draws the spirit down from the universe by these preparations – as if by some sort of bait? And through that tinder, as it were, the fetus drinks in life and soul – no? Finally, through the soul's fixed species and ordering, the body that lives in this way is at last worthy to have within it a mind divinely endowed.

Everywhere nature is a sorceress, then, as Plotinus says and Synesius too, luring various things everywhere with particular foods, which is no different than nature's attracting heavy things with the earth's centre, light things with the vault of the moon, attracting leaves with heat, roots with moisture and other things in the same way. Indian sages maintain that the world is actually fettered to itself by its own attraction. They claim that the world is an animal – male and female simultaneously and without distinction – copulating with itself everywhere in the mutual love of its own limbs, and thus fitting together lastingly. But in the limbs is a bond produced by the mind engrafted in the world, and through the joints of the limbs it 'stirs the mass and mixes with that huge body' . . .

In light of this, farming prepares a field and seeds for gifts from heaven and extends the life of a plant by making grafts to put a plant into a different and better species. The physician, scientist and surgeon do similar things in our bodies to sustain our lives and match them more fruitfully to the nature of the universe. A philosopher expert in natural science and astronomy does the same, and usually I call him a magus – the correct term: he uses particular lures to implant heavenly things in earthly things at the right time, no differently than the farmer expert at grafting puts a new shoot into an old stalk. Ptolemy has strong proof of this, affirming that such a sage can assist the stars in their work just as a farmer enhances the power of the land. The magus brings the earthly under the heavenly – putting the lower under the higher everywhere, so that all the right females are impregnated by their males, as when iron is drawn to a magnet, camphor is sucked into hot air, crystal lights up in the Sun, sulphur and a volatile liquid are kindled by flame, an empty eggshell filled with dew is raised towards the sun or the egg itself is brooded by a hen . . .

The sage, when he has understood *which* materials or *which* kinds – partly started by nature, partly finished by craft, and brought together even though they had been scattered – can get *which* influence by heavenly power, collects them when the influence rules at its strongest, preparing them, applying them and claiming gifts from heaven through them. For wherever some material has been exposed to higher powers in this way – like a glass mirror opposite a face or a wall opposite a voice – right away it feels the effect of a mighty and supernal agent, a wondrous power and life present everywhere, and from that effect it gets power, no differently than the mirror represents an image from the face or the wall produces an echo from the voice.

Plotinus himself uses such examples where, copying Mercurius, he says that the ancient priests or magi used to capture something godlike and amazing in statues and material sacrifices. Like Trismegistus, however, he supposes that divinities completely apart from matter are not really captured by these materials, only worldly powers, as I have said from the start with support from Synesius – worldly, I say, meaning a life or something living that comes from the world's soul and the souls of spheres and stars, or even a kind of movement and a sort of living presence that comes from demons. The very Mercurius whom Plotinus follows, in fact, sometimes says that demons of just that kind – aerial, not heavenly, much less loftier – are present in the materials, and Mercury himself assembles statues from those plants, trees, stones and spices that have in them the natural force of divinity. He adds songs resembling the powers of heaven, who delight in those songs, he says, and that is why they stay longer in the statues to help people or hurt them.

He notes that the sages of Egypt, who used to be priests as well, at a time when they could give no reasons to persuade people that there are gods – spirits of some superhuman kind – thought up this magical enticement, using it to draw demons into statues and proclaim them as divinities. But Iamblichus condemns the Egyptians because they not only accepted the demons as steps on the way to finding higher gods but usually worshipped them. In fact, Iamblichus prefers the Chaldaeans who were not possessed by demons to the Egyptians – Chaldaeans who were ministers of religion, I mean, for I suspect that Chaldaean and Egyptian astrologers both tried to find a way to use heaven's harmony to attract demons into clay statues. This is what the Hebrew astrologer Samuel, relying on the authority of David Bil, also an astrologer, seems to mean – that the image-makers of antiquity made statues to foretell the future . . .

But if they actually made talking statues, my first thought – based on the view of the blessed Thomas – is that it was demons who formed the words and not simply the influence of stars on the statues. Next, if demons did perhaps enter statues of this kind, I do not think they were forced into them by heavenly influence but submitted willingly to their worshippers instead and would then deceive them. For a higher nature too is sometimes really won over by a lower one, but it cannot be subdued . . . However, even though there is no astronomical method for enclosing demons in statues, Porphyry says that the ancients followed the rules of astronomy in delivering oracles, and so their prophecies were often ambiguous – which is correct, since Iamblichus shows that a true and certain prophecy cannot come from evil demons, nor are they produced by human methods or by nature but by divine inspiration in minds that have been cleansed.

Getting back to Mercurius, however, or really Plotinus – Mercurius says that priests got a unifying power from the nature of the world and mixed it in. Plotinus, who followed Mercurius, thinks that a unitary whole can easily be prepared if the world's soul is won over, inasmuch as that soul produces and moves the forms of natural objects through the seeded reasons planted in her by divine power . . . But sometimes it is possible for higher gifts to come down as well, in that the reasons seeded in the world's soul are conjoined to the intellectual forms of the same soul and, through them, to the ideas in God's mind. Iamblichus confirms this when he deals with sacrifices – a subject more appropriate for me to discuss elsewhere, where it will also be obvious how impure was the superstition of pagan people and how pure, by contrast, was Gospel piety . . .

8.14

This Natural Magic:
Pico, *Oration*, 214–33

Pico devotes a set of twenty-six theses to magic, a topic also examined elsewhere in the *900 Conclusions*. Introducing this issue in the *Oration*, his first concern is to sharpen a distinction between natural and demonic power made long ago by pagan sages and sustained by Christian teachers, though sometimes grudgingly (see 4.7, 18; 5.3–5, 12, 14, 16; 6.11; 7.4, 9, 11–13, 15, 19). One kind of magic is blameless and reliable because it is grounded in a genuine philosophy of nature; the other kind is treacherous and evil because it relies on the 'authority of demons'. Plotinus defied those evil spirits and showed that 'the magus is nature's minister, not her artificer'. The magician's task is to uncover the cosmic sympathies that make natural magic both good and effective. This righteous art and science honours the Creator by disclosing the wonders of creation, while demonic magic enslaves its users to God's enemies. Pico names more than a dozen authorities, mostly philosophers, to support his conception, highlighting two whom Plato had singled out: Xalmosis (Zalmoxis) from Thrace and the Persian Zoroaster (see 3.4; 4.3). He says nothing about the Egyptian Hermes (see 5.11).

*

I have also proposed theorems about magic, taking the word 'magic' in two senses. One magic, which depends entirely on the activity and authority of demons, is a monstrous and accursed thing, as God is my witness. The other, when well researched, is nothing more than the final realization of natural philosophy. Although the Greeks mention both, they call the former *goêteia*, never dignifying it with the word 'magic', while for the latter they use *mageia*, the special name suited to it as the highest and perfect wisdom. In the Persian tongue, as Porphyry says, the word '*magus*' means the same thing as our 'interpreter' or 'worshipper of the divine'.

But between these arts is a great – no, Fathers, the very greatest – difference and disparity. Not only the Christian religion but all laws and every well-ordered state condemn and curse the former. All the wise, all nations that study the heavenly and the divine, approve and embrace the latter. One is 'the most dishonest of the arts', the other a higher and holier philosophy; one is hollow and useless, the other solid, strong and reliable. Whoever has practised the one has always concealed it because it would bring disgrace and discredit on the author; from the other, ever since antiquity, people have almost always sought great fame and cultural distinction. No philosopher desirous of learning the liberal arts was ever a student of the former; 'to learn the latter, Pythagoras, Empedocles, Democritus and Plato travelled abroad, preached it when they returned and gave it a high place in their secret doctrines'. No arguments support the former, and no competent authorities approve it. The latter, as if ennobled by eminent parents, has two authors especially: Xalmosis, whom Abbaris the Hyperborean imitated, and Zoroaster – not perhaps the one you think, but the famous son of Oromasus.

If we ask Plato what the magic of those two is, he will answer in the *Alcibiades* that Zoroaster's magic is nothing but the knowledge of divinity that the kings of the Persians taught their sons so that they might learn to rule their state on the model of the cosmic state. He will answer in the *Charmides* that the magic of Xalmosis is medicine for the mind and that it makes the mind temperate just as medicine makes the body healthy. Carondas, Damigeron, Apollonius, Hostanes and Dardanus later stayed on the same path. Homer too stuck with it, concealing magic – along with all other kinds of wisdom – under the 'wanderings of his Ulysses', as I shall prove someday in my poetic theology. Eudoxus and Hermippus also stayed the course, like almost all who have made a thorough study of the Pythagorean and Platonic mysteries. Among more recent authorities, moreover, I find three who were on the trail of magic: Alkindi the Arab, Roger Bacon and William of Paris.

Plotinus also mentions it where he shows that the magus is nature's minister, not her artificer. This man of the loftiest wisdom approves and confirms this magic and abhors the other so that, when summoned to the rites of evil demons, he said it was 'better that they should come to him than he to them'. And rightly so: for as the one magic exposes and enslaves man to unclean powers, the other makes him their lord and prince.

In the end, the one magic cannot claim the name of art or science, while the other is full of the deepest mysteries, containing the most profound contemplation of the most abstruse secrets and leading at last to the knowledge of all nature. Not so much by working wonders as by diligently serving nature as she works them, the other magic calls from hiding into light powers sown by a loving God and scattered over the world. After probing deep into the harmony of the universe that the Greeks rather expressively call *sumpatheia*, after examining how natures are kin to one another, and applying to each and every thing its inborn charms – called the jynxes of the Magi – this magic makes public, as if it were their maker, the wonders concealed in the world's secret parts, in nature's heart, in God's hideaways and storerooms, and as the farmer marries 'elm to vine', so the magus joins earth to heaven, binding things below to the properties and powers of those above.

So it is that this other magic is as divine and helpful as the first one is dreadful and harmful, for this reason especially: that the first leads man away from God by enslaving him to God's enemies, while the other excites man to that wonderment at God's works of which hope, faith and a ready love are sure and certain effects. For there is no greater stimulus to religion or to any worship of God than the constant contemplation of God's wonders. As we have explored them carefully through this natural magic of which I speak, we shall be stirred to love and to worship their Creator with a hotter passion, and then we are forced to sing that famous song: 'full are the heavens, full is the whole earth with the greatness of your glory'.

And this is enough about magic, of which I have said this much because I know there are many who also – as 'dogs always bark at strangers' – often denounce and detest what they do not understand.

8.15

The Ancient Mysteries of the Hebrews:
Pico, *Oration*, 234–57

Pico prized the philosophical magic that Ficino had found in ancient Neoplatonism (see 8.14). Kabbalah was another priceless revelation that he himself had 'unearthed from the ancient mysteries of the Hebrews'. Originally the oral counterpart of the written law given to Moses on Sinai, this 'true and more secret' lore came to be recorded in books – so Pico thought, believing that he had special access to them. He values this arcane learning as both exotic and esoteric, explaining at some length why mysteries are needed to keep the deepest truths undefiled. Jews had guarded the oral law by restricting it to senior males of their own faith. But Pico will now disclose the secrets to Christians in order to 'defeat and rebut' the learned Jews, and he calls Kabbalah itself 'not so much Mosaic as Christian'. Knowing how bizarre his compatriots would find this alien wisdom, he denies that it is nonsense, maintaining that Christians will recognize their own creed in the theology, metaphysics and natural philosophy of 'the books of the science of Kabbalah'.

*

I come now to what I have unearthed from the ancient mysteries of the Hebrews and have brought forward to confirm the most holy and Catholic faith. So that people who know nothing about them might not regard them as fallacious nonsense or fables spread by fakers, I want everyone to understand what they are and what they are like, where they come from, who has confirmed them and on what eminent authority, how remote they are, how divine, and how much our people need them to do battle for religion against the savage slanders of the Hebrews.

Not only the famous teachers of the Hebrews but also our Esdras, Hilary and Origen write that what Moses got from God on the mountain was not just the Law that he recorded for posterity in five books but also a true and more secret reading of the Law. God's command to Moses was indeed to make the Law public to the people but not to divulge the interpretation of the

Law or put it into books. Moses was to reveal this only to Jesus Nave, and he in turn to the high priests who succeeded him, under a sacred rule of silence.

From the simple story there was enough to recognize God's power in one passage, in another his wrath at the wicked, his mercy to the good, his justice to all, and from the divine and saving commandments there was enough to learn how to live a good and holy life and to worship in the true religion. But to disclose to the people the more secret mysteries, the arcana of supreme divinity concealed beneath the bark of the Law and the rough surface of its words, what would that be but 'to give something holy to dogs and cast pearls before swine'? Hence it was a matter of divine command, not human judgement, to keep secret from the populace what should be told to the perfect – the only ones among whom Paul says that he 'speaks about wisdom'.

The ancient philosophers observed this custom scrupulously. Pythagoras wrote only the few little phrases that he trusted to his daughter Dama as he died. Sphinxes carved on the temples of the Egyptians used to give this warning, that intricate riddles should keep the mystic dogmas secure from the vulgar crowd. Plato, writing to Dionysius about the highest beings, says, 'I must speak in riddles so that no one else may understand what I write you, in case my letter falls into another's hands.' Aristotle used to say that the books of the *Metaphysics* that deal with theology were 'published and not published'. What more to add? Origen claims that the master of life, Jesus Christ, revealed much to his disciples that they decided not to write down in order to keep it from becoming common knowledge. Dionysius the Areopagite confirms this best of all: he says that the founders of our religion transmitted the more secret mysteries *ek noos eis noun, dia mesou logou sômatikou men, auloterou de homôs, graphês ektos* – 'from mind to mind, without writing, only bodily speech mediating in between'.

Since that true interpretation of the Law divinely bestowed on Moses was revealed by God's command in just the same way, it was called *Kabbalah*, which is the Hebrew for our word 'reception': this is because one person would 'receive' that teaching from another not through written records but from a regular succession of revelations, as if by right of inheritance. But after Cyrus restored the Hebrews from captivity in Babylon and the temple was renewed under Zorobabel, they turned their attention to recovering the Law.

Once Esdras, then the leader of the assembly, had corrected the book of Moses, he saw clearly that after exiles, massacres, escapes and the captivity of the people of Israel, the custom of passing the Law from person to person could not be kept as the elders had established it. He also realized that the secrets of heavenly doctrine divinely granted to them would perish, since the memory of them could last no longer without the support of written texts. So Esdras arranged for the sages who then survived to be called together and for each to contribute what he remembered of the mysteries of the Law, and scribes were brought in to compile these contributions in seventy volumes (for that was roughly the number of sages in the Sanhedrin).

On this matter no need to trust my word alone, Fathers. Hear what Esdras himself has to say:

> After forty days had passed, the Most High spoke, saying, 'Make public what you have written first, let the righteous and unrighteous read, but the seventy most recent books you shall hold back to pass them on to the sages of your people. For in them is a vein of intellect and a spring of wisdom and a river of knowledge.' And thus have I done it.

These are the exact words of Esdras. These are the books of the science of Kabbalah. Esdras was right to declare, in a voice of singular clarity, that in these books there is 'a vein of intellect', or an ineffable theology of supersubstantial divinity; 'a spring of wisdom', or a finished metaphysics of intelligible and angelic forms; 'and a river of knowledge', or a most certain philosophy of nature. Sixtus IV, the Supreme Pontiff who ruled just before that Pope Innocent VIII under whom we are fortunate to live, saw to it with great care and diligence that these books were put into Latin for the general good of our faith. And now that he has passed away, three of them have come down to Latin readers.

So scrupulously are these books revered by the Hebrews of our time that they permit no one under the age of forty to touch them. After I bought them for myself at no small cost and read them through with the greatest attention and unremitting labour, I saw in them – so help me God – a religion not so much Mosaic as Christian. There I read about the mystery of the Trinity, about the incarnation of the Word, about the divinity of the Messiah, about original sin, its atonement through Christ, the heavenly Jerusalem, the fall of the demons, the orders of angels, about purgatory and the pains of hell – reading the same things that we read every day in Paul and Dionysius, in Jerome and Augustine.

But where these books bear on philosophy, you might actually be hearing Pythagoras and Plato, whose teachings are so closely related to the Christian faith that our Augustine gives great thanks to God because the books of the Platonists came into his hands. All in all, there is hardly any substantial controversy between us and the Hebrews on which these books of the Kabbalists cannot defeat and rebut them, leaving no corner for them to hide in. I have a most impressive witness to this fact in Antonio Cronico, a man of immense learning. When I was dining at his house, with his own ears he heard the Hebrew Dattilo, an expert in this science, 'move hand and foot' to an entirely Christian position on the Trinity.

8.16
Magic, Kabbalah and the Divinity of Christ: Pico, *Conclusions*

Natural magic – the apex of natural philosophy and by no means prohibited – aims to put a theory of nature into practice. But any practice of magic will fail unless it is linked with Kabbalah. Although Christ's miracles were neither magic nor Kabbalah, those two sciences together give the surest proof that Christ is God: we can best understand the unique power of Jesus by contrast with other ways of working wonders. When Pico made those rash claims, he was not exalting the 'magic used by the moderns', which he identifies with the demonic magic that the Church rightly forbids (see 7.6–9, 20–22; 8.15). He promotes a novel magic of his own, shockingly original, that cannot be 'at all effective unless it has an act of Kabbalah . . . tied into it'. The familiar bits of Pico's telegraphic theses present magic as 'marrying the world', as 'uniting and activating things that are divided and seeded in nature' (see 7.4; 8.4, 8–10, 14). Far riskier – reckless, in fact – was his use of Kabbalah to sanctify magical sounds, letters, words, and numbers with God's own voice (see 8.11).

*

1. The whole of magic used by the moderns, which the Church rightly bans as well, has no solidity, no basis and no truth because it relies on forces hostile to primal truth, those powers of darkness who spread shadows of deceit into the minds of the ill disposed.
2. Natural magic is licit and not prohibited, and on the general theoretical principles of this science I posit the conclusions stated below, in accord with my own views.
3. Magic is the practical part of natural science.
4. From that conclusion . . . it follows that magic is the noblest part of natural science.
5. There is no power divided and seeded in heaven and earth that the magus cannot both activate and unify.

6. Any astonishing act that gets done – magical, Kabbalist or any other kind – is in the first and absolute instance to be ascribed to the glorious and blessed God whose grace rains profuse and supercelestial waters of astounding power on contemplative people of good will.

7. Christ's deeds could not have been done either through the path of magic or through the path of Kabbalah.

8. Christ's miracles are the surest evidence of his divinity, not on account of the thing that was done but on account of the way of doing it.

9. There is no science that gives more certainty of Christ's divinity than magic and Kabbalah.

10. What a person does by craft as a magus, nature has done naturally by making the person.

11. No wonders of the craft of magic are possible except by uniting and activating things that are divided and seeded in nature.

12. For magical power as a whole, the form comes from a human soul standing and not falling.

13. Doing the magical is nothing but marrying the world.

14. If there is any nature directly ours that is rational – either absolutely or inasmuch as it behaves rationally – it has the magical in the highest degree, and in humans this nature can be more complete by sharing the magic.

15. There can be no magical action that is at all effective unless it has an act of Kabbalah, explicit or implicit, tied into it.

16. The nature that is time's eternal horizon is near the magus but beneath him.

17. Magic, belonging to the nature that is the horizon of time and eternity, must be sought from there in the obligatory ways known to sages.

18. Near the magus, but above him, is the nature of what is the horizon of temporal eternity, and Kabbalah belongs to him.

19. This is why sounds and words have effect in an act of magic, because the sound of God's voice is where nature first does the magical.

20. Any sound, since the sound of God's voice gives it form, has power in magic.

21. Meaningless sounds can do more in magic than meaningful sounds, and anyone with depth can understand the reason for this conclusion from the previous conclusion.

22. As meaningful, and inasmuch as names are singular and taken in themselves, no names can have power in an act of magic unless they are Hebrew or closely derived from Hebrew.

23. Except the ternary and the denary, any number in magic is material, and in magical arithmetic those are numbers of numbers.

24. From secret principles of philosophy, it must be acknowledged that characters and figures can do more in an act of magic than any material quality can do.

25. Just as characters belong to an act of magic, numbers belong to an act of Kabbalah, and letters are used as a mean between the two which is assimilable by varying towards the extremes.

26. Just as something happens without contact through intermediate causes by the influence of a first agent, if the agent is specific and direct, so through an act of Kabbalah, if the Kabbalah is pure and direct, something happens without contact by magic.

8.17
Kabbalah, Angels and Demons: Pico, *Conclusions*

Kabbalah gave Pico a new perspective on the combat between angels and demons. But when he lists nine Hebrew names for the Areopagite's celestial hierarchies, the novelty may be merely lexical (see 6.13). Converting a name of God into one of Satan's names by transposing their letters is more adventurous, and the procedure is a speciality of Kabbalah – shocking for Christians but, for learned Jews, nothing very profound. Deeper theological currents run in the cryptic exegesis of words from Job 25:2 as describing a struggle on high between the 'Southern Water' and the 'Northern Fire'. The meaning of this riddle, beyond the reach of almost all Pico's Christian contemporaries, lies at the heart of Kabbalist theosophy: the hidden God reveals himself first in ten emanations, attributes, appellations or properties called *sefirot* or 'countings' – 'Numerations', according to Pico. The ten line up in various configurations; the dark, harsh, fiery powers on the left are always in combat with the bright, loving, watery forces on the right. This is one of the traditional themes of Kabbalah highlighted by Pico in his first forty-seven theses on that topic (see 8.18).

*

2. There are nine hierarchies of angels, whose names are Cherubim, Seraphim, Hasmalim, Haiot, Aralim, Tarsisim, Ophanim, Thephsarim and Isim.

19. The letters of a name of the evil demon who is the Prince of This World and of a name of God, the Triagrammaton, are the same, and one who knows how to arrange their transposition will derive the one from the other.

21. One who knows the attribute that is the secret of darkness will know why evil demons do more harm at night than by day.

24. When Job said, 'who makes peace in his heights,' he understood the Southern Water, the Northern Fire and their Commanders, of whom nothing more should be said.

28. By the flying fowl created on the fifth day we should understand the angels of the world who appear to humans, not those who do not appear except in spirit.
30. No angel having six wings ever changes.
33. In the whole Law there are no letters whose forms, ligatures, separations, twisting, direction, defect, excess, smallness, greatness, crowning, closing, opening and order do not reveal secrets of the ten Numerations.

8.18
Whatever Other Kabbalists May Say: Pico, *Conclusions*

Using Kabbalah to transform magic and aggrandize it kept Pico on somewhat familiar ground. Kabbalist angelology was an adventure, however, and the core of this esoteric theology was truly the heart of darkness – for a Christian. With few words to spend, Pico tries to say how Christian doctrine can be reconciled with Kabbalah and invigorated by it. He points out that Aristotle's philosophy, as stated, is not really what Aristotle was saying, and that the same goes for Homer's and Virgil's epics: they were all getting at something deeper that had to be disguised to keep it pure. The Jews did the same: what Maimonides says in the *Guide* seems philosophical, but it is just the bark that covers his mystical theology. Parting the veils of profane philosophy and penetrating the literal sense of scripture, Pico has seen that the Book of Genesis is really natural philosophy, that Ezekiel's chariot (*merkavah*) is really metaphysics and that the biblical names of God announce the Trinity in Hebrew. 'Whatever the rest of the Kabbalists may say', he will proclaim all of that and more in the last 72 of his 900 theses, which is the second group that he gives to Kabbalah, identifying its propositions as his own (see 8.17).

*

1. Whatever the rest of the Kabbalists may say, the first distinction that I would make divides knowledge of Kabbalah into knowledge of *sefirot* and *shemot* – visionary and practical, as it were.
2. Whatever other Kabbalists may say, I would divide the visionary part of Kabbalah into four, corresponding to the fourfold division of philosophy that I have usually applied. First is what I call knowledge of revolving the alphabet, corresponding to the part of philosophy that I call the universal philosophy. The second, third and fourth parts are the threefold *merchiava*, corresponding to a threefold philosophy parted into divine, middle and sensible natures.

3. The knowledge that is the practical part of Kabbalah puts all of formal metaphysics and lower theology into practice.

6. Someone with a deep knowledge of Kabbalah can understand that the three great quaternary names of God contained in the secrets of the Kabbalists ought to be assigned to the three persons of the Trinity through a wondrous allocation so that the name אהיה belongs to the Father, the name יהוה to the Son, the name אדני to the Holy Spirit.

9. If humans may speculate about the last days, through a highly secret path of Kabbalah we can find out that the end of time will come in 514 years and 25 days from now.

11. The way (though the Kabbalists leave it unspoken) in which rational souls are sacrificed to God by an archangel happens only by the soul's parting from the body, not the body's parting from the soul – except secondarily, as it happens in the death of the kiss, of which it is written: the death of his saints is precious in the sight of the Lord.

12. One who is not rationally intellectual cannot work through pure Kabbalah.

13. One who works at Kabbalah and mixes in nothing extraneous, if he stays long at the work, will die from *binsica*, and if he makes a mistake in the work or comes to it unpurified, he will be devoured by Azazel through the attribute of Judgement.

18. One who has connected astrology with Kabbalah will see that, after Christ, keeping the Sabbath and resting is more fitting on the Lord's Day than on Saturday.

48. Whatever the rest of the Kabbalists may say, I say that the ten spheres correspond to the ten Numerations as follows, starting from the Building: Jupiter belongs to the fourth, Mars to the fifth, the Sun sixth, Saturn seventh, Venus eighth, Mercury ninth, the Moon tenth; then, above the Building, the firmament belongs to the third, the first moved sphere to the second, the empyrean heaven to the first.

49. Whoever knows the correspondence of the ten commandments to what is forbidden by the connection of astrological truth with theological truth will see from our principle in the preceding conclusion – whatever other Kabbalists may say – that the first commandment corresponds to the first Numeration, the second to the second, third to third, fourth to seventh, fifth to fourth, sixth to fifth, seventh to ninth, eighth to eighth, ninth to sixth, tenth to tenth.

50. When Kabbalists say that one should ask the seventh and eighth for sons, you may say that in the lower *merchiava* it is accepted that the one is asked

to give and the other not to forbid. From the preceding conclusions, one who has understanding of astrology and Kabbalah can understand which one gives and which forbids.

56. If he is expert in Kabbalah, one who knows how to extend the quaternary into the denary will have a method for deriving the name of 72 letters from the ineffable name.

57. From the preceding conclusion one who understands formal arithmetic can understand that working through the *Scemamphoras* is proper to a rational nature.

63. Just as Aristotle himself concealed under the guise of philosophical speculation and obscured by terse expression the more divine philosophy that the ancient philosophers veiled under fables and stories, so Rabbi Moses of Egypt in the book that the Latins call *Guide for the Perplexed* embraces the mysteries of Kabbalah through hidden interpretations of deep meaning while seeming through the outer bark of words to proceed philosophically.

72. Just as the true astrology teaches us to read in the book of God, so Kabbalah teaches us to read in the book of the Law.

8.19
The Demon Makes Fools of Them All: Champier, *Dialogue Against the Destructive Arts of Magic*, 2.3

As Champier was writing his little *Dialogue*, he was also starting the career that would make him the leading physician of his day in Lyon, one of France's great cities. He copies most of what he says about witchcraft from a *Scourge of Witches*, written about forty years before by Pierre Mamoris, a theologian. But Champier – shaped by his medical education and also aware of Marsilio Ficino's new psychology of magic – will not accept what had come to be the usual story about witchcraft: night-flight, the sabbat, sex with Satan and so on, as presented by *The Hammer of Witches* (see 8.1–3). He diagnoses the testimony of the accused against themselves and one another as delusional – with physiological as well as psychological causes.

*

There are many who cast spells and claim to go by night to a sabbat of demons or say that demons transport them there, where a great crowd sometimes gathers to do homage to the Devil. You should realize that the demon causes many illusions in the internal sense, making people believe that something in the internal sense is in the external sense because of humours that the demon stirs up in the internal sense. This is why these people are often delusional – very often, I think – to suppose that they go with a demon by night to dance with women, joining with them in drinking and feasting, some to do harm or kill, entering caves to swill wine, worshipping the Devil in one form or another by giving him a kiss on the rear . . . They get a deluded fantasy of such things from the demon who supplies them with the spirits and phantasms that a demon can easily produce. Inwardly deluded in this way, not once but many times, they think that they have done things on many occasions that happen only in a fantasy . . .

These are measures taken by the Devil, and humans are generally ignorant of them. Women or men of this type say they have done the evil things described above, but these were really results of the liquids, powders, pills, fats and likenesses that were found stored up with their things. The upshot of it all is that they confess without reservation to having done the evil deeds about which they are interrogated. Witnesses maintain that this is actually the truth, and the common verdict is that they have done them. Those crimes are in fact discovered, and the tools of witchcraft are found in the secret places where they have kept them.

People conclude from all this that they are guilty of witchcraft as charged and that legal penalties should apply. Many of them also say that they have seen each other dancing and having sex, each of them testifying about the other and vice versa – all of this manifestly false. They are deceived and believe things to exist outside the mind that are found only in the power of imagination . . .

We may conclude, then, that whatever else these people may do that is evil and damnable, they confess more that is false than true because their Prince is 'the author of lies'. Accordingly, a judge should examine such cases with the greatest care and diligence to see whether they are just deluded internally or may also have done evil things on the outside. Upright men learned in theology who teach about such matters should be called in with experts on philosophy and theological theory . . . It will also be fitting to summon physicians with experience in examining these people . . . And if they are found only to have brain-damage, they should be given medical treatment . . . and should be shown what trouble the demon takes to make fools of them all.

9

Ancient Wisdom Modernized:
The Later Renaissance

Figure 13: The Green Lion Eats a Bleeding Sun

Reginald Scot from the County of Kent was at least thirty in 1574 when he published a popular guide to growing hops, based on his own experience. Although farming, engineering and soldiering took up most of his time, he also studied at Oxford, where he saw Renaissance classicism nearing its crest. As that movement gathered strength through the sixteenth century, the celebrity of experts on the classics like Ficino sustained, enlarged and transformed not only a new philology but also a new philosophy of magic.

Scot was not impressed. Some of his manuscript notes evolved posthumously into *Hocus Pocus Junior* or *The Anatomy of Legerdemain*, a manual of shell games, card tricks and more intricate illusions. He studied sleight of hand to expose fake conjuring, and he debunked witchcraft beliefs and witchcraft trials with the same ferocity. Since so many claims by and about accused witches have proved false, he argues, a sensible person should react 'as when a juggler hath discovered the slight and illusion of his principall feats'. With so many cards on the table, who would 'continue to thinke that his other petie juggling knacks of legierdemaine are done by the helpe of a familiar'?

Scot's bulldog interrogations surpassed anything intended or achieved by Champier's *Dialogue Against the Destructive Arts of Magic* – written just as he had started to promote Ficino in France. Champier's quieter complaints, made before his own career had accelerated, were zephyrs against the hurricane of hatred that Kramer and Sprenger had stirred up in 1486. Nearly a century later, when Scot brought out his *Discoverie of Witches*, the craze had intensified, which explains why Scot was so much more alarmed. During Scot's century, as *maleficium* grew like an ulcer in Europe's conscience, prominent intellectuals were also joining the debate about *magia* in larger numbers.

One side of that conversation was learned and bookish, amplified and broadcast by the new print technology. As more and more material found its way to print in various formats and sizes, some authors quickly became authorities, tempting others to emulate them. That was the fate of the book that turned *magia* into 'occultism': *On the Occult Philosophy* by Henry Cornelius Agrippa von Nettesheim. Drafted by 1510 but not published in full until 1533, Agrippa's hefty volume found many readers over many years: at least four editions of the 1650 English version were published by 1665.

Marlowe's Faustus brags that he 'will be as cunning as Agrippa was', and he would have read *De occulta philosophia* in Latin – the everyday language of universities (see 10.2). 'Is not thy common talk found aphorisms,' Faustus asks himself, 'are not thy bills hung up as monuments?' His medical chatter and even his prescriptions are the talk of Wittenberg, a university town. But he renounces medicine along with theology, law and scholastic philosophy for Agrippa's teachings, a better route to power, wealth and fame – so he thinks. Far from shunning magic as disgraceful, he glorifies it as just the right ticket for an up-and-coming celebrity. Faustus is a fool, of course: his path leads straight to hell. But his foolishness is plausible – believable enough to have kept Marlowe's tragical history on stage for centuries.

In Marlowe's lifetime and shortly afterwards, Giordano Bruno was Europe's most infamous magus. The Inquisition arrested Bruno in 1592. Marlowe was murdered in 1593. Both had been on the books of Francis Walsingham, Queen Elizabeth's spymaster, though just why is hard to say. Clearly, however, espionage was one place to find the edge of European society and risk going over it. Magic was another. When the Church burned Bruno on Ash Wednesday of 1600 as 'an impenitent, pertinacious and obstinate heretic', part of his heresy was magic. His original accuser had charged him with claiming that Christ 'was a magician, and likewise the apostles, and he had a mind to do as much as they and more . . . He wants to tend to the art of divination, and draw the whole world behind him.' At one point in his trial, given a list of crimes to abjure, Bruno would not disclaim 'the art of divination'.

Nineteen years later, the Parlement of Toulouse executed another philosopher of magic, Giulio Cesare Vanini, a Carmelite from Puglia who had opposed the papacy in a political dispute with Venice. He fled to England and turned Protestant – for a few months – then changed his mind and escaped to France, where he tried to clear things up by writing books: one book explores the *Divino-magical Amphitheatre of Eternal Providence*, the other reveals *Nature's Amazing Arcana*. When Vanini chose *Queen and Goddess of Mortals* as Nature's title in his second book, he meant 'mortals' in the strict sense: he denied that humans have immortal souls. To make matters worse, he wrote as a follower of Pietro Pompoanazzi, the most notorious critic of the Church's official line on immortality and a vigorous defender of natural magic.

Immortality is the subject of Ficino's masterpiece, his *Platonic Theology on the Immortality of Souls*, and for most Christians of his time the idea was rock solid. As a philosopher, however, Ficino had to defend immortality against 'Averroists' – followers of Averroes, the great Muslim commentator on Aristotle, who described the individual soul as just the life of the body and as perishing with the body. The Church, also concerned about Averroism, decreed in the Fifth Lateran Council of 1513 that university professors must defend immortality and refute its opponents. Pomponazzi, then a professor at Bologna, did just the opposite in his treatise *On the Immortality of the Soul*, published in 1516. The book was burned in Venice.

Although powerful friends saved the book's author from the flames, the controversy eventually silenced him. By 1520 he finished another study, *Of the Causes of Natural Effects, or On Spells*, but he did not publish it. Had the book been printed, the Church would have had even more cause to torment him. *On Spells* is a manifesto of Aristotelian naturalism – Averroism in the eyes of its Christian opponents – in an account of natural magic that completely eliminates demonic magic: no competent philosopher, according to Pomponazzi, can maintain Aristotelian principles and accept demons as causes of magical effects. In matters of religion, however, he concedes 'the inadequacy of what Aristotle and other philosophers teach'. And who cares about philosophers? Why should the Church have worried about Pomponazzi's professorial opinions?

The heart of the matter was the religious and institutional role of Aristotelian philosophy, whose medieval Christian professors were sometimes called 'scholastics' or 'Peripatetics'. The universities that taught scholasticism dominated higher education in Europe, and clergy ruled the universities. Bishops, abbots, monks, friars, priests and tonsured clerics needed some level of literacy – sometimes very high levels – and scholastic professors were gatekeepers of the written word. The universities that employed them had been founded in the same moment of cultural revival – around the year 1200 – when most of Aristotle's writings were recovered.

Most of the university curriculum was based on those writings, which supplied problematic answers to questions of Christian faith. Has the universe always existed? Does the soul die with the body? Is the bread and wine on the altar just bread and wine? Seeking answers that defied at least some intuitions, Christian intellectuals turned to Aristotle, making their own doctrine Aristotelian as a result. When the stakes were basic dogmas like the creation of the world, or bread and wine becoming Christ's body and blood, or the soul surviving the body's death for all eternity, the game was now Aristotelian – or scholastic, more accurately, since much of the doctrine would have baffled Aristotle.

To diminish Aristotle, nonetheless, was to erode the Christian faith. But Pomponazzi was a staunch Aristotelian. Yet he read Aristotle as a naturalist on key points – especially immortality – where naturalism contradicted the Christian creed. If Pomponazzi was right about Aristotle, Christianity's favourite pagan would be useless to the Church and its supernaturalist dogma. So Pomponazzi had to be stopped. Then what might a professor do if he could not profess? In this situation, Pomponazzi kept quiet about his naturalist account of magic, demons and angels.

Like Pomponazzi, some experts on magic in the later Renaissance were philosophers – though not always university philosophers, and so not as constrained as he was by institutional habit and prejudice. Bruno's academic career was cut short, and Giambattista della Porta had no such career – not even a university education. Theophrastus Bombastus von Hohenheim, better known as Paracelsus, was certainly no philosopher. He loathed philosophers, especially the professionals, though he may have spent some time in universities. John Dee studied at Cambridge in the generation before Marlowe, and Prague gave him a medical degree later in life. When he wrote about astrology and worked on alchemy, they were parts of natural philosophy. But Dee also had conversations with angels at a time when people were putting such things in a new category – not philosophy but theosophy.

When Johann Kepler called Robert Fludd a 'theosophist' in 1622, he contrasted that label with 'cosmosophist', charging that Fludd missed the point of the new science: to learn about nature, one must observe, measure and explain the natural cosmos as Kepler had done. Fludd's theosophy, by contrast, makes three mistakes – heuristic, epistemic and methodological. The heuristic error is to look for *scientific* truths in *religious* revelation, whether by searching in scripture or by awaiting inspiration. The epistemic error is to judge claims about nature not by physical things outside but by spiritual experience within. The methodological error is to use poetic symbols and expressive images where only scientific language will do. Revived by Kepler as a pejorative, 'theosophy' was an old word, usually a synonym for 'theology'. When others in Fludd's tradition – Thomas Vaughan, for example – applied it to themselves or those they admired, it was a term of praise with a new meaning. The ancient writer who came closest was the Areopagite when he praised 'all the theosophists and interpreters of secret inspiration' (see 6.13).

A wellspring of theosophy was the flood of books and pamphlets written or inspired by Paracelsus: most of them circulated only after he died in 1541. Dead before fifty, he travelled widely, talked audaciously and wrote profusely, enraging the enemies who kept most of his work out of print. His formative moment was the Peasants' Revolt of 1524. While Luther was using the printed word to shake the old order, the new medium of broadsheets and pamphlets also transmitted more radical voices, and Paracelsus spoke their language. Since society's corruption is complete, he declared, reform must also be complete. Everything old is bad; only the new can be good.

Paracelsus was seldom subtle – a Jacobin before his time, but without the secularist politics. In the face of the Establishment and its traditions, he treated the learned professions as class enemies: lawyers as parasites on society, theologians as a blight on religion and – worst of all – physicians as a plague in the streets. Champier spent his life becoming the sort of physician that Paracelsus hated – better at reading Latin than healing the sick, swooning at Galen in Greek, blind to nature and deaf to the spirit.

Godly reform needs dominion over nature, according to Paracelsus, requiring science, medicine and technology to be renewed. The old philosophers had seen magic as part of science or natural philosophy, often emphasizing its practical side, and Paracelsus went further, putting magic at the centre of all his science and medicine because 'the magical art . . . discovers the other arts'. His magic – broadly viewed – needs the tidily packaged hierarchies, sympathies and correspondences that Agrippa had extracted from Ficino. But his writing is so disorderly and his language so eccentric that what had always been exotic and esoteric in magic had now become idiosyncratic and sometimes incomprehensible.

Such problems were not new with Paracelsus. Pliny had felt 'very much in the dark' about religion and magic: he disliked the 'odd practices of different nations' and 'outlandish words that we cannot pronounce'. Alchemists had always used strange names and weird symbols to mystify and conceal. Kabbalah was a cavalcade of mysteries and secret symbols. For Pico 'it was a matter of divine command . . . to keep secret from the populace what should be told to the perfect'. Set beside the murky sentences of Paracelsus, Pico's prose is a limpid pond.

What is *Gabalia*? What is an *archeus*? Is *ilech* harmful? Will *vulcanus* help? After nearly five centuries, experts on Paracelsus have tracked some of this down. By distancing himself from tradition, however, the author of all this private language made the search hard for his friends – not to speak of his enemies. He bequeathed this burden to theosophy, the tradition that he inspired. According to critics like Kepler, theosophists like Fludd – misled by Paracelsus – looked in the wrong place for the facts of science, judged its claims by the wrong standard and made nature obscure with a perverse symbolism. Outlandish terminology aggravated those mistakes, encouraging the detractors of Paracelsus to ignore what he wrote as gibberish or denounce it as nonsense.

To achieve reform, Paracelsus stepped outside of tradition, and by most measures he stepped too far. Bruno was another overreacher, but unlike Paracelsus he did not cut all his ties with the past. Because he began as a Dominican friar, Bruno's breach with scholasticism – from that pious point of view – was unthinkable: Aquinas was the supreme Dominican hero. But Bruno's was not an unintelligible break. Up to the end, his heresies were recognizably philosophical. He discarded Aristotelianism to replace it with his own philosophy – a monist atomism or atomist monism inspired by Aristotle's ancient competitors, the Stoics, Epicureans and pre-Socratic naturalists.

This eclectic mix gave Bruno principled reasons for believing in magic, though the reasons were not always lucid or coherent: he presented them in *A General Theory of Bonds*, in an essay 'On Natural Magic' and in other works. He tried to solve a problem that was built into scholastic philosophy, the distinction between form (*morphê* in Greek) and matter (*hulê*), reflected by mind's separation from body. Faced with this core principle of hylemorphic metaphysics, anyone who wanted to locate magic within natural philosophy – and keep magical action effective at a distance, without physical contact – had to bridge the gaps posited by hylemorphism.

Ficino's response had been positive, searching for substances (spirit) and forces (astral influence) to make the connections needed for natural magic. Pomponazzi's response was negative, rejecting demonic magic by denying that demons could make such connections. Both kept their theories within the hylemorphic framework, finding different ways to reconcile its ineliminable dualism with magic. But Bruno eliminates the dualism by abandoning hylemorphism and replacing it with a monist and vitalist materialism that accommodates atomism. 'Matter is something divine,' he insists, 'just as form is . . . something divine.' Even God is matter, and God's love is the 'divine force in all things' that binds them together with an organic magic.

What Bruno says about God, matter and magic is clearer than Paracelsus on *Gabalia* or Dee on the monad. But in its time and place, his theory of bonds was worse than bizarre. It was a heinous heresy whose bewildering newness made it all the more shocking. In 1576, suspicion of heresy started Bruno on his long travels away from Naples – and eventually to the

Protestant north. Around the same time, the authorities in Naples were also investigating Porta, forcing him to close the Academy of Secrets that he had founded to promote natural philosophy in that city. But Porta survived his troubles, kept the support of Church officials and died famous at the age of eighty in 1615.

The book on natural magic that Porta revised several times for new editions was conventional in its theoretical part, leaning heavily on Ficino and Agrippa. That may be why he could appease the heresy-hunters who put Bruno in prison when the Nolan was still young and rash. The practical subjects that Porta emphasized – alchemy, magnetism, optical instruments – were less threatening to the janissaries of faith, until Galileo made much bigger trouble with his telescope and delivered a more disturbing message from the stars.

These Effects Are Real:
Pomponazzi, *On Spells*, chap. 13

Effects otherwise unexplained – magnetism, electric fish, the anti-epileptic peony, the lion that fears the cock – had motivated the long search for magical causes (see 4.2, 14, 18; 5.3, 12, 16; 7.10–11; 8.7–8, 10, 14). Accepting such effects as real, Pomponazzi introduces the familiar distinction between natural and demonic magic, and he classifies demons as 'immaterial substances'. But immaterial agents acting in nature on material objects 'are not permitted in an Aristotelian framework' – meaning scholastic Christian Aristotelianism. What about the human mind acting naturally on its own body? The mind/body or soul/body connection – crucial for dogmas like immortality in an afterlife of rewards and punishments – had been debated endlessly by Pomponazzi's scholastic predecessors, few of whom shared his commitment to naturalism. The results of those enquiries, he claims, eliminate demons as causes of the effects in question. Leave the philosophers out of it, he adds, and demons are made redundant by plain facts of nature: that stars and planets cause many of the problematic phenomena, for example. Nonetheless, 'the Church determines that there are demons' – though many have doubted the sincerity of Pomponazzi's compliance in the closing paragraphs of his book.

*

Because what I have said up to now makes me seem to take both sides . . . I have decided to state some conclusions in this final chapter so that my considered views on this matter can be clearly understood. Assume that these effects are real, as I have often said . . . in that not all such claims are true nor all false. On that assumption, this is my first conclusion: those who speak as Aristotelians and posit immaterial substances in addition to the intelligences that move the spheres should by no means be called 'Aristotelians': no, they should be regarded as complete strangers to that teaching.

This conclusion is obvious, first from what Aristotle says . . . and second on the basis of reason. Since such substances would be eternal and intelligent, they cannot be living bodies equipped with sense . . . and so they are completely separated and unmoved. This is the question, then: whether such beings are posited on the basis of some phenomenon that cannot be saved without them or rather for no reason at all. Since the second choice is alien not just to all serious enquiry but to anyone who does not want to be thought frivolous and not serious, we must take refuge in the first.

But there is no need to posit such beings on behalf of the heavenly spheres and the processes of growth and decay in this lower world since God and the intelligences suffice for those purposes, and nature does nothing useless. Therefore, one will need to posit those beings for the kinds of effects mentioned previously – to explain oracles and demonic possession, for example, and other such claims already described, as people commonly say. But even if effects like those are granted, such substances are not permitted in an Aristotelian framework.

The reason is that those effects are produced either by intelligences – indirectly, through heavenly bodies – or else directly by angels and demons. It is not the first, as we all know, since then they would not know their own rules, and not the second, because a direct instrument of immaterial substances cannot be something destructible. If that were possible, the heavenly bodies would be useless, nor would it be necessary to trace every movement of things that grow and decay back to the eternal motion that belongs to the heavens – something that all Aristotelian teaching denies, as even people with little experience of Aristotle know full well . . .

If an angel or demon moved some growing or decaying body directly, this could not be done without changes of many kinds. If something moves now that had not moved before – when such a movement, by hypothesis, does not depend on a heavenly body – and to change it there were something to cause the motion's newness, that too (the angel or demon) would need to change because there is no newness in the effect without newness in the cause. Moreover, since the mover contacts the moved, if a demon moves a body from east to west, the demon will be moved together with that body . . . and will change its place. But this is nowhere close to Aristotle's position since such change can happen only in something bodily. Therefore, according to Aristotle, such substances are not permitted.

This is my second conclusion. Even leaving Aristotle out of it, the effects that people commonly attribute to demons and even to good angels – without God's intervening in some special and proper way but only in the ordinary way – do not suffice to prove that such immaterial substances exist. This conclusion has many proofs. First, things done in this way by angels or demons are results of alteration, local motion or both, but none of this is conclusive . . . Second, it seems completely absurd that the heavenly bodies and their intelligences that govern and sustain the universe and move such an immense mass of things . . . could not produce effects so useless and trivial, which are very rare and of no importance . . . Third, this conclusion is confirmed by an obvious point: these effects were also known to Aristotle, as shown previously, and to Theophrastus, Eudemus and Alexander, men of the most evident wisdom, and they ascribed this to the heavenly bodies, as St Thomas Aquinas does . . .

Even though the Peripatetics agree with religious law on this point – that these things are done by immaterial substances – there is still a big difference since the Peripatetics argue that this is done by the intelligences as movers of the heavenly bodies and with those heavenly bodies as intermediaries, whereas the claim of religion is that it is done by angels or demons directly and without the heavenly bodies. This is astonishing – not for ordinary people, I mean, but for professors of philosophy: since those angels or demons are not the forms of those moving bodies, why make the claim for them and not the bodies? As to altering those changeable bodies or moving them locally, what can a demon or an angel do that the intelligences cannot do with the heavenly bodies as intermediaries, since we see that they govern the universe? . . .

This is my third conclusion. If there is some effect in this lower world that must be done by God without second causes, Peripatetics cannot account for that effect, which shows Peripatetic teaching to be defective and not true . . . My fourth conclusion is that some things happen in this lower world that Aristotle's principles can in no way account for . . . Fifth conclusion: those miracles that are beyond the order of created nature and can be done only by God – and sometimes are done – truly demonstrate the inadequacy of what Aristotle and other philosophers teach, and they plainly declare the truth and solidity of the Christian religion . . . My sixth conclusion is this: whatever has been confirmed by canonical scripture and universally decreed by the Holy Catholic Church must be held entirely, firmly, definitively, inviolably, unshakably and without any trace of doubt . . . And my seventh conclusion follows: since the Church determines that there are demons and angels and that the things described are sometimes done, this must be held most firmly and without any doubt or qualification.

9.2
A Higher and Holier Philosophy: Agrippa, *The Occult Philosophy*, 1.1–2

In a book that still has an audience, Agrippa simplifies the principles of hierarchy that Ficino took from Proclus and explained in more detail (see 5.16; 8.7). Agrippa exalts the 'occult philosophy' as the grand unified theory of which physics, mathematics and theology are special cases. Magic is the core of that philosophy – and not just natural magic. Physics studies elemental things on earth; mathematics looks to the heavens for higher forces; and theology reaches beyond to 'the powers of the various intelligences'. The magus ascends through these three realms to bring higher energies down to earth. The earthly and heavenly levels of the hierarchy constitute the natural cosmos, but the intellectual level is hypercosmic and supernatural, inhabited by angels, demons and intelligences whom the magus addresses in 'rites and ceremonies' with 'words and figures and . . . the mysteries of seals' – techniques advertised by the *Picatrix*, forbidden by Aquinas and feared by Ficino (see 7.6–8, 12; 8.6–11).

*

The world is an elemental, celestial and intellectual triad where every lower thing is ruled by something higher and receives that mighty influence whereby – through angels, heavens, stars, elements, animals, plants, metals and stones – the archetypal and supreme Craftsman transfers his omnipotent powers into us, having made and created all of them to serve us. The Magi think (and not unreasonably) that we can ascend by those same steps through each world to that same archetypal world, the Craftsman and first cause of everything from whom all things proceed and exist – thus empowering us not only to employ the forces that nobler beings already possess but also to attract new and different forces from above.

Accordingly, people use medicine and natural philosophy to hunt for the forces of the elemental world in various mixtures of natural objects. Next, using the rays and influences of the celestial world and following the rules of astrology and the teachings of mathematics, they link celestial powers with them. Then, in sacred religious rites, they strengthen and energize them all with the powers of the various intelligences . . .

Magic is a subject of enormous power, full of the deepest mysteries: it includes a very close look at the most hidden secrets along with a knowledge of nature as a whole – its nature, potency, quality, substance and power. Magic teaches us how things differ from one another and how they agree, thus producing their amazing effects by applying their powers to one another – and to lower things affected by and compatible with them – and then unifying them all, everywhere marrying and coupling them with the powers and endowments of higher beings.

This magic, the supreme and most perfect science, is a higher and holier philosophy – in the end, the absolute summation of the whole of philosophy at its noblest. Now every philosophy productive of rules divides into physics, mathematics and theology: physics teaches about the nature of things in the world, examining and investigating their causes, effects, times, places, manners, results, wholes and parts . . . But mathematics teaches us to understand nature both in the plane and also as extended in three dimensions, and to recognize motion and the courses of the heavens as well . . . Theology teaches us what God is, what mind is, and what is an intelligence, an angel and a demon, a soul, religion, sacred rites and ceremonies, temples, sacred customs and mysteries, instructing us also about faith, miracles, the power of words and figures and the arcane effects and mysteries of seals. Theology, as Apuleius says, teaches us to know and practise the laws of ceremonies, the way of rites and the rule of religion . . .

Magic includes these three most commanding subjects, unifying and making them work for her, which is why the ancients were right to consider magic the supreme and holiest science . . . Therefore, a person who aspires to study this subject cannot understand the rational basis for magic without instruction in physics, which reveals the qualities of things and opens up the occult properties of every entity; without skill in mathematics and the aspects and figures of the stars on which the noble power and property of everything depends; and without learning theology, which makes manifest the immaterial substances that control and administer everything.

9.3
Naming the Demons and Angels: Agrippa, *The Occult Philosophy*, 3.18, 20, 24–5

Agrippa needs a demonology and a nomenclature to regulate his third and highest type of magic, some of whose key words are names of demons. Up to a point, his approach is conventional: finding a demonic equivalent for the nine orders of angels, sorted by character (tempters, liars, provokers) and function (infecting, accusing, divining) and naming the heads of each order – Beelzebub, Belial, Asmodeus, and so on (see 1.8, 18; 2.10). When he observed rites of weather-magic, Agrippa saw that 'the name and seal of a particular spirit' had to be used to get the effect desired. He lists many names in some detail, going beyond the usual biblical and classical sources to Origen, whose views were controversial, and to Kabbalah, still a bizarre novelty for Agrippa's readers (see 8.15–18). With only a little Hebrew, he shows how some names describe a spirit's function, so that Gabriel (*gvr-el*) is 'God's might' and Raphael (*rfa-el*) is 'God's healing'. Other names are secret, needing techniques of Kabbalah to reveal them, as Agrippa demonstrates with the 'ineffable' Name hidden in Exodus 14:19–21.

*

Some experts on theology arrange evil demons at nine levels, opposing them to the nine orders of angels.

The first of these gets the name *pseudothei* or 'false gods' because they usurp the name 'god', wanting to be worshipped as gods and looking for sacrifices and adoration, like the demon who said to Christ, 'If you fall to the ground and adore me, I will give you all of this,' showing him all the kingdoms of the earth. And their prince is the one who said, 'I shall rise above the height of the clouds, and I shall be like the Most High,' for which reason he is called *Beelzebub*, meaning a 'god of old'.

Following them in second place are the spirits of lies, like that lying spirit who went out into the mouths of Ahab's prophets, and their prince is the serpent *Python*, after whom Apollo was called 'Pythian', like that woman who was a pythoness in the Book of Samuel, and the other one in the Gospels who had a python in her belly. A demon of this kind meddles with oracles, then, in order to trick people with divinations and predictions and thus deceive them.

In the third order are the vessels of iniquity, also said to be vessels of wrath: they are inventors of evil and all the evil arts, like the demon Theut in Plato who taught games and gambling, from which comes all manner of crime, malice and ugly behaviour. In Genesis, while blessing Simeon and Levi, Jacob says, 'The vessels of iniquity are in their dwellings, and let my soul not take counsel with them.' . . . *Belial* is their prince, whose name means 'yokeless' or 'disobedient' – a sham and an apostate of whom Paul said to the Corinthians, 'How can Christ agree with Belial?'

The avengers of crime follow in fourth place, and their prince is *Asmodeus* – 'maker of judgements'. After them in fifth place come the tricksters who work fake miracles to help bad magicians and witches and then use their miracles to seduce people, as the serpent seduced Eve. Their prince is *Satan*, already described in the Book of Apocalypse as having seduced the whole world by 'producing great signs, making fire come down from heaven for people to see, seducing those who dwell in the land because of the signs given him to make'.

The powers of air present themselves in sixth place, blending with thunder and flashes of lightning, infecting the air by introducing plague and other ills. Of their number are the four angels described by the Apocalypse as assigned to hurt the land and sea by 'holding the four winds from the four corners of the earth'. And their prince is called *Meririm*, the 'noon-day demon', a burning spirit who rages at mid-day, whom Paul in Ephesians calls 'the prince of the power of this air' and 'the spirit working in the sons of bad faith'.

The furies – sowers of evil, discord, war and devastation – hold the seventh station. In the Apocalypse their prince is called *Apollyon* in Greek, *Abaddon* in Hebrew, which is 'the destroyer' and 'the devastator'. In eighth place stand the slanderers and spies whose prince is *Astaroth*, meaning 'spy', though he is called *diabolos* in Greek, meaning 'slanderer' or 'prosecutor'. The Apocalypse calls him the 'accuser of our brethren, accusing them day and night in the sight of our God'. Then the tempters who lie in ambush – one for each person – have the ninth and last place. We call them our 'bad angels', and their prince is *Mammon*, interpreted as 'avarice'.

All unanimously add, however, that the demons wandering in this lower world are evil and hostile to everyone, and so they call them 'devils', of whom . . . most have this opinion: that the Devil was an angel and became apostate, persuading many angels to go astray with him, to be called his angels from then on . . . And so, having been cast into this vale of tears, some are near to us, roving about in this gloomy air. Some inhabit lakes, rivers and seas, others the land, frightening the land's residents and assailing those who dig wells and mines. They cause the earth to crack open, and they shake the foundations of mountains, tormenting not just people but animals as well.

Others are content with jokes and tricks, aiming not to injure people but to wear them out, sometimes extending their height in gigantic bodies, at other times shrinking themselves to the size of pygmies and assuming various shapes to agitate people with empty fear. Others specialize in lies and blasphemies . . . But the worst demons of this kind are those who impede journeys by attacking travellers, taking pleasure from war and bloodshed and assaulting people with the most savage insults. We read about them in Matthew: 'for fear of them no one then dared to travel that road'.

Now scripture actually mentions demons of the night, day and noon, using different words to describe different spirits of iniquity, like those we read about in Isaiah: donkey-centaurs, spiky demons, shaggy demons, sirens, screech-owl vampires and ostrich-demons. The demons in the Psalms are asps, basilisks, lions and dragons, and we read in the Gospel about a scorpion, a mammon, a prince of this world and rulers of darkness. Over them all Beelzebub is prince, whom scripture calls the Prince of Perversity . . .

Origen's view about demons is this: demons who by their own choice withdrew with the Devil, their prince, from God's service, should they start to come to their senses a little, are encased in human flesh . . . in order to return home to the vision of God still free of aerial and ethereal bodies . . . Many believe that their prayers are heard . . . as Christ heard the pleas of demons and allowed them to enter a herd of pigs . . . The Kabbalists think that some demons are to be saved, which is clearly what Origen felt . . .

Theologians share the view that the nature of all evil demons is to hate God and man equally, for which reason divine providence has assigned to us the purer demons who are nearby, putting us in their care as shepherds or guides to help us every day, to fend off, restrain and fetter the evil demons and prevent them from hurting us as they intend: hence we read in the Book of Tobias that Raphael took hold of the demon named Asmodeus and sent him away to the desert of Upper Egypt . . . For no prince, no potentate could stay

unharmed, no woman could remain inviolate, no human in this vale of ignorance could achieve the goal set for him by God if there were no good demons
to assist and protect us or if evil demons were permitted to do the bidding of
evil men. Therefore, just as a special guardian from the good demons is assigned
to each individual to strengthen that person's spirit for the good, so from the
evil demons an opponent is sent, a guardian for the flesh and its itch, and
the good guardian fights for us on behalf of the spirit, against the enemy and
the flesh . . .

All humans are ruled in this way by the ministry of different spirits, and
they are led to that level of power, merit and dignity of which they
show themselves worthy. But the unworthy are shoved aside and pushed back
to the lowest level of misery both by evil demons and by good spirits . . .

About good and evil spirits both there are many ways to speak, but their
true and proper names – like those of the stars – are known only to God, who
alone numbers the stars in their multitude and has names for them all. We
can know none of them except by divine revelation, and very few have been
made explicit to us in the sacred writings. But the teachers of the Hebrews
think that names were imposed upon the spirits by Adam . . . and so the
Hebrew Kabbalists, like the Magi, think that it is also within the power of
humans to give them names – but only a person who by some gift or sacred
power has been exalted and promoted to that capability . . .

I knew someone whom I saw write the name and seal of a particular spirit
on blank paper in the hour of the moon. Later, when he gave the paper to a
river frog to eat, then muttered some verses and let the frog go in the water,
it soon began to rain. I saw the same man write the name of another spirit
with its seal in the hour of Mars and give it to a crow which he let go after
mumbling some verses, and right away, from the part of the sky where the
crow flew, lightnings, rumblings and terrifying thunder came from the clouds
that built up there. But the names of those spirits were in no unknown tongue,
nor did they signify anything but their functions. Of this kind are the names
of the angels Raziel, Gabriel, Michael, Raphael and Haniel – meaning God's
vision, God's might, God's courage, God's medicine and God's glory. In the
same way, in the functions of evil demons we read their names: trickster,
deceiver, dreamer, fornicator and more of that sort . . .

From the ancient Hebrew fathers we get such names for the angels who
preside over the planets and signs: Zapkiel for Saturn, Zadkiel for Jupiter,
Camael for Mars, Raphael for the sun, Haniel for Venus, Michael for Mercury and Gabriel for the moon. Those are the seven spirits who always stand

before the face of God ... Of the twelve signs, Malchidael has charge of Aries, Asmodel of Taurus, Ambriel of Genesis ... Again, there are twenty-eight angels who are lords of the twenty-eight lunar mansions: Geniel, Enediel, Amixiel ...

Following the same pattern for evil spirits, the four mightiest kings, one for each of the world's four parts, preside over the rest, and their names are Urieus, King of the East, Amaymon, King of the South, Paymon, King of the West and Egyn, King of the North. When the teachers of the Hebrews call them Samael, Azazel, Azael and Mahazael, this may be more correct. Many other princes and chiefs of legions hold power under them, and there are also countless demons serving as private soldiers ... Otherwise, anyone who wants exact information about the particular names, functions, places and times of angels and evil demons should look in the *Book of Temples* by Rabbi Simon, the *Book of Lights* by the same author, the treatise *On the Great Stature*, the treatise *On Temples* by Rabbi Ishmael and almost any of the commentaries on the *Book of Formation*, and there he will find a great deal written about them ...

There are also other sacred names – of God and of evil spirits both – assigned to each by function, names much more powerful than those already described. They are taken from the sacred scriptures by a technique that the Hebrew Kabbalists teach about them, just as certain names of God are taken from certain passages. The general rule governing them is that wherever the sacred writings say anything about the divine essence, from that passage a divine name can be rightly inferred, but wherever a divine name is stated in the sacred writings, there you should think of the office which lies under that name. Hence, wherever scripture speaks of an office or act of some good or evil spirit, from that passage the name of the same good or evil spirit can be derived ...

There is a certain text in Exodus contained in three verses, each written in seventy-two letters, where the first verse starts with *vajisa* ויסע, the second with *vajavo* ויבא and the third with *vajot* ויט. When each of these is continued in a line, reading the first and third from left to right but starting the middle line in reverse order on the right and ending on the left, then each group of three letters standing under one another makes up a name, and there are seventy-two such names, which the Hebrews call *Schemhamphoras*. With the divine name El אל or Iah יה added at the end, these produce seventy-two names of angels in three syllables, and each one carries a great name of God, as it is written: 'my angel goes before you, watch him, for my name is in him'.

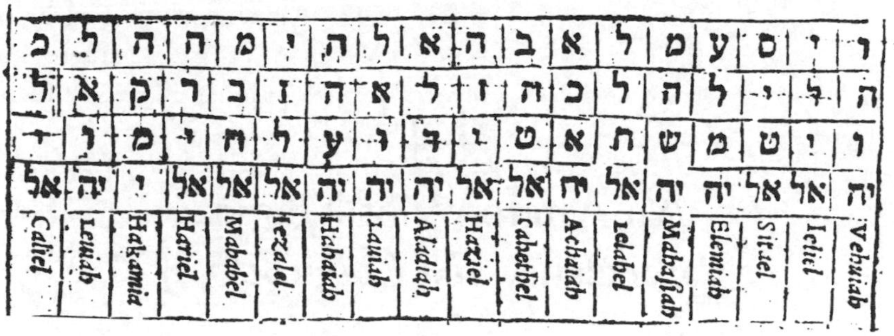

כ	ל	ה	ה	מ	י	ה	ל	א	ה	ב	א	ל	מ	ע	ס	י	ו
ל	א	ק	ר	ב	ז	ה	א	ל	ז	ה	כ	ל	ה	ל	י	ל	ה
י	ו	מ	י	ה	ל	ע	ו	ד	י	ט	א	ת	ש	מ	ט	י	ו
אל	יה	י	אל	אל	אל	יה	יה	יה	אל	אל	יה	אל	יה	יה	אל	אל	יה
Caliel	Leuiah	Hakamia	Hariel	Mababiel	Iezalel	Hahaiah	Lauiah	Aladiah	Haziel	Cahethel	Achaiah	Lelahel	Mahasiah	Elemiah	Sitael	Ieliel	Vehuiah

Figure 14: From Agrippa's Table of Angel Names

And these are the names that preside over the seventy-two celestial quinaries, the same number of nations and languages and the joints of the human body . . . The names, following the derivation done by the Kabbalists, are shown in the following table.

9.4

An Anatomy of Magic:
Paracelsus, *The Labyrinth*, 9

Paracelsus wrote *The Labyrinth* three years before he died in 1541; it was printed twelve years later. The book excoriates the medical establishment for wandering uselessly in its own learned maze. Leading medics have learned Greek but not medicine, worsening the whole society's decadence. The first step towards reform is to throw all the old books away – except the Bible. Since the Creator is medicine's only source, a righteous healer will forget Galen and Avicenna and go straight to God's creation. But nature will never come into focus, by its own light, if the only vision is bodily: it takes a bodiless astral body to peer 'deep into nature'. From that perspective, 'all illnesses are occult' and 'magic is medicine's anatomy'. Accordingly, the parts of plants that look like organs of the human body will be worth examining. But shapes and colours on the outside, seen with the body's eyes, are just clues to deeper realities – internal and invisible – that 'dwell in the spirit, not in the body'. Elsewhere Paracelsus states a principle to guide the search for them: 'the art of the Signed (*Signata*) teaches us to give each thing the correct name that was born into it'. Since this *signatura* is a science of signs that works from within the physician's spirit, analysing a plant's signs cannot be a physical dissection. The investigator needs magic, whose components are Gabalia and Gabalistic magic (cf. Kabbalah; 8.15–18; 9.3). The purpose of Gabalia, a spiritual astronomy of astral bodies, is to find 'the signing of the signed'.

*

Since medicine must proceed from a stable foundation – that foundation being a stable, manifest and demonstrative doctrine, not some empty mental speculation – we must first understand that all illnesses are occult and that all medicine likewise has been made occult. Since there is nothing about illness or medicine that humans can do or discover by using their own powers, all such things need to be done through an astral body in order for that astral body to look deep into nature and penetrate, just as the sun penetrates when it shines through glass or water. Then one must also understand the method by which those occult things, which obviously are invisible to humans, may be dug up, rooted out and discovered. And we shall see that they are made manifest to us only by magic and its types – Gabalia, for example, and the Gabalistic – for by those sciences all things are made manifest that in nature are arcane or made occult.

It is quite fitting and necessary, then, for a physician to be educated and skilled at those subjects in order not to be one of the errant and deceitful kind who aims at lies rather than truth – as the facts will also show. For the art of magic is medicine's anatomy. Just as a butcher slaughters, skins and cuts up an ox or pig and then lays out all the internal organs and other parts so that he can inspect the whole animal visually, as he could not have done before when the hide covered it, so the art of magic also anatomizes all of medicine's bodies in which remedies are hidden, by laying out any occult things that had been inside them and exhibiting them for us to observe.

And just as in a human body or any other all the organs are in good order and proportion – one lying on the right side, another on the left, one looking a bit large, another smaller and so on, just as they are all observed in a physician's anatomy – so also in the bodies of plants there are distinct organs, for this one is called a 'heart', that one a 'liver' and another a 'spleen' and so on, just as in the body. Yet it is not the case that what is called a 'heart' in plants resembles a human heart in shape and appearance, though it equals the human heart in power, property, effectiveness, activity and receptivity.

Consider an example. Wind has many powers and properties, at least one of which – the wind that dries – I find relevant. But no one sees with his eyes how the drying happens. The Sun produces heat, yet no one observes what it is that makes the heat. You strike fire from flint, yet no one detects fire in the flint, nor is there a fire that burns when you touch the flint.

In that same way, any body has manifold parts constituting the one body, and a single plant often has the manifold powers that can be seen in the firmament, where seven distinct organs have been identified – a heart, kidneys, a stomach, a lung and so on, as in a man. These are not organs, however, but properties and powers of that kind resembling such organs in us, acting not in a bodily way but acting as powers untouched by the hands yet known by the mind. So also in the moon-plant the full moon's path and body are represented – not visibly, however, but spiritually. In fact, medicines dwell in the spirit, not in the body, and body differs from spirit, obviously: thus in the crab-plant are various organs – microcosms, to be sure – yet not in the plant's body but in its remedies, which are spiritual.

Accordingly, because the medicines by which the sick must be healed are spirits and have been made occult in this elemental body, as I have said, and yet they are still recognized by the astral body, it follows that the art of magic – not Galen, Avicenna or their ilk, by any means – is medicine's school-mistress, instructor and teacher, showing the things by which we must drive out diseases. And because I have discussed the art of medicine quite often, both here and in other books of mine, in order to inspire in us a great love for the art, I am most anxious to think very carefully about it.

There is, in fact, an altogether careful, acute and persistent way to discover and investigate all the things made occult in us, because of which I dare to claim even this: if a person were to learn this art thoroughly as a physician and understand it completely, and if he were then to throw all his medicine away, and if it happened that all his books on the teaching of medicine were lost, so that medicine could seem totally destroyed to him, then, if this one book were still extant and the art of magic were still strong, nothing would be at risk. For if that book still survived to discover medicine and other arcana, from that one book the loss could easily be made up and medicine established anew.

Magic, as I said before, is the anatomy of the art of medicine. But it does not proceed like the external anatomy of a body that puts the parts of roots, limbs and greenery before our eyes to see. Instead, it displays the plant's powers, properties and strengths for us to understand. And this anatomy – a discovery of the arts – first points out to us what has been *signed*. The *signing* of the signed is pointed out by the art of Gabalia, however, which is a type of the magical and a part of astronomy. But not even this art of discovery is to be understood as the only path, as if there were just one way to discover: one must understand that it involves all the types of astronomy and its gifts.

Though the parts of this art are manifold and its types are various, all still pertain to the magical, and together all produce discoveries, explanations and interpretations of anatomy, the sciences, the arts and remedies. It follows – necessarily – that these types and parts are made visible in the astronomical process of discovery. For just as the Sun's fire is made visible by a crystal, and just as the fire that had been occult in flint becomes visible when contacted and struck by steel, so a magical sun is made visible by a magic crystal, and magic steel strikes a magical fire. At that moment, then, the anatomy blazes up and shows us the fire, displaying all that we need to see in any body, and showing it so clearly and transparently that the Sun's rays can look no clearer – nor does the fire burn hotter or look brighter that drops from the flint when wood is brought near. Plainly, the magic wood ignites – meaning that the arcana ignite in plants, as if the fire, in order for its power to show clearly, knew what goes well with what.

But Satan, that Thousand-Fold Contriver – to take this anatomy away from human eyes and rip it from memory – how hard has he laboured, I ask, what efforts has he made, what plans has he devised and altered? Meanwhile, he has invented all sorts of nonsense and superstitious delusions, giving them the name 'magical' and presenting them to humans in place of the real magic – to make them forget the proper kind, prefer the nonsense, take pleasure in his deceptions and spend all their time on useless fictions. So much has Satan suppressed this art that for many years few have understood it, and it has been made almost hateful. For Satan realizes that a person who knows nothing also loves nothing. Plainly, an ignorant person understands nothing, is good for nothing and earns our scorn – unlike the person who understands, loves, desires, takes notice, works and learns.

This is why it is brilliant of the Thousand-Fold Contriver to lead us away from that desire and eagerness – and that love of learning, I tell you. For he knows this too about people: once a person has heard something about these arcana and seems to like them, he will not stop or rest until he has them in his grasp, wholeheartedly embracing this book that gives directions for finding so great a treasure. On the other hand, should he remain ignorant of these sciences and such arcana, having been corrupted in the end by idleness and dullness, he will have taken a different path – a worse one, indeed.

I also find this to be true. To the extent that a person is a stranger to the sciences, then in accord with a science of his own – according to his disposition, in other words – he acts by getting himself drunk, whoring, lying hung-over in bed, playing around, brawling, sleeping and so on. For this is certain and beyond doubt: if a person has not known God and does not love him or learn from him, and if he does not understand the divine Trinity, does not believe that it exists and so does not cherish it, does not know the saints and cherish them, does not have nature clear in view and does not cherish it, and (to summarize) if he does not merely fail to love what he fails to know but also avoids it, despises it and believes nothing need be learned about it, caring only for the external body and honouring and worshipping his belly as God – then, if science and knowledge about anything grows in such a person, love for it will increase in him to that extent.

For correct knowledge is the locus of all things, which all flow from knowledge, and all the good results flow back from knowledge to the knower. Knowledge also gives faith, for one who has known God begins to have faith in him immediately, and there is faith in something – such as it is – in that there is knowledge of it, and the reverse. So also in medicine: a person ventures as much and produces as much as he has known beforehand in nature and about nature, but whoever has known nothing in nature, has also done nothing. Whatever he has done, however, he does almost as if he were a painter painting a picture with no life and strength in it.

About my main point, how to make the science of magic visible: though in many other places – and here also – I have said more than enough (so it seems to me), still, in order to make my mind and purpose completely clear to the reader, it seems best to repeat these things here briefly, as follows.

The magical art, gathered and acquired from all the types of astronomy, discovers the other arts and thus everything that has been made occult. And just as the Magi from the East discovered the Christ child through this same force of discovery, with a star showing the way, so also are the arts and the arcana of nature discovered, through this art that provides an illumination that is a bit brighter than any luminous body. And since those Kings, the Magi, did not hesitate to seek Christ by so long a journey from Saba, Tarsus and other places, and since at last they also discovered him, even so far away, surely nature's treasure can be discovered much more quickly and with less labour and risk.

Indeed, all the principles of the magical art originate from the East, while nothing good or useful to us comes from the North. You physicians, then – if you want to be physicians and defend your name lawfully – do your very best at this, I beg you, and set about it in the right way, with dignity and respect, not without due preparation, as if you were looking for turnips in a field.

9.5
The Philosopher's Stone:
A Rose Garden of Philosophers

First printed in 1550, this anonymous collection of short alchemical works has roots in the fourteenth century. After an illustrated title page, twenty striking images punctuate the text: sex, birth and death are allegories of stages in the alchemical work. Death and resurrection precede the alchemist's first sight of the Philosopher's Stone, needed to make gold, perhaps by sowing seeds of gold and helping them grow. The Stone is thematic for this influential book, often copied by hand after it was printed – in keeping with the secretive habits of alchemists: to 'hide it from fools, philosophers have named the Stone by various names'. Likewise, the Sulphur and Mercury that go into the Stone are the 'philosophical' kind, not the substances commonly known by those names. If Mercury is a Lion eating the Sun, it might be a solvent for gold (see Fig. 13). But none of this is explicit or consistent: mystification is a goal, not a mistake. Mercury is also a terrible Dragon that 'marries itself, makes itself pregnant, gives birth in its own time and kills every living thing with its poison'. This mercurial beast that 'changes by changing' is an emblem of transmutation and perfect for this book.

OUR MERCURY, WHICH IS THE GREEN LION DEVOURING THE SUN

The image is Mercury. You must know that this is the cold and wet element from which God created all minerals, for it is airy and flees from fire. When anything partial is fixed to it, then, Mercury produces a sublimed work, a spirit that has uses: there is nothing in the world that is not Mercury; there is nothing that may stand in its place; and Mercury alone goes deep in every body by raising the body up. Hence, by mixing with a body, Mercury brings it to life and illuminates it, transforming it from state to state and from colour to colour.

Therefore, Mercury is the whole elixir of whiteness and redness, the lasting water, the water of life and death, the virgin's milk and the herb that washes: it is the fountain of life from which one drinks and never dies; it accepts colours and heals the thing that is coloured by it; it is what mortifies, by drying and moistening, by heating and cooling, producing contraries according to its own measured procedure. And when it is living, it has effects of one type: when it is dead it has other effects; when sublimated still other effects; and when dissolved other effects yet again.

Mercury is the Dragon that marries itself, makes itself pregnant, gives birth in its own time and kills every living thing with its poison. Fire destroys the Dragon, finishing it in a short time because quicksilver is alive, and the Dragon can neither overcome the fire nor eat it up, fleeing from it instead. But the sages, the first philosophers, ingeniously applied to the Dragon every ingenious method until little by little they made it welcome the fire, so that the Dragon never stops climbing up over the fire that beats on it. The Dragon feeds on the fire, making astonishing changes occur when any fixing fixes on it, for this reason: because the Dragon changes by changing, as its blackness appears with its noise and its brilliance. So when the Dragon is tinctured, the tinctured tinctures; when it is curdled, the curdled curdles; when it is dissolved, the dissolved dissolves; and it whitens itself and then reddens in plain sight.

The Dragon is the gathering water, the milk, the strong urine, the emollient oil, the father of all wonders, the mist, the vapour, the fugitive servant, the sunset mercury that has put itself ahead of the gold and has defeated it. So the gold asks the Dragon, 'do you put yourself ahead of me, and I am the lord of stones, welcoming the fire?' To the gold our Mercury says,

> but surely I begat you and you were born from me, and one of my parts gives life to many of your parts. You are greedy, however, and compared to me you give nothing . . . I am the whole secret, and in me the knowledge is hidden since I convert everything into the Sun and Moon because my nature is to soften the hard and harden the soft.

As to this alchemy, then, note that the Philosopher's Stone is the one thing in the whole world that produces it correctly, and they believe that anyone who strays away from this single thing will go off over the edge.

Still – in that very nature of its own to which the Stone has brought the minerals but to which the craft brings the Stone – the Stone is not perfect, for without the mastery nothing works for us nor does any good. Nothing perfect is produced, only corruption, and I say this inasmuch as you work with the mastery, because it is the pure phlegm. Philosophers sometimes call it 'sulphur' and the 'lemony black humour': because its astonishing power has such great effect, some have thought that God created all the nations out of it and established their origin.

This Stone of ours some have also called the 'white copper'. Hence, Lucas and Eximeus: 'All you who seek knowledge, know that there is no tincturing except from our white copper, for our copper is not the common copper. Common copper decays, infecting everything that it rests upon, whereas the philosophical copper perfects, and it whitens whatever it is joined with.' This is why Plato says that 'all gold is copper, but not all copper is gold. Our copper, therefore, has body, soul and spirit, and those three are one because they are all from the one, of the one and with the one that is its root. The copper of philosophers is their elixir, then, perfect and complete from spirit, body and soul.'

Accordingly, to show the Stone to sages and hide it from fools, philosophers have named the Stone by various names, though by any name whatever it is one and the same – and of the same. Hence Merculino:

> Buried deep, a Stone lies hidden in a spring,
> discarded in the muck and covered up with dung,
> a single godlike Stone with every name united
> as Morienus lists them in his sage's book:
> 'This Stone is not a stone – a living thing
> that's fit to grow, a bird, a Stone and not a stone
> and no mere bird – a lump that's Saturn's stem.
> This Stone is Jupiter, Mars, the Sun and Venus,
> next the Moon that races to outshine the rest.
> Now gold, now silver, now the elemental,
> now wine or water, blood or chrysoline,
> now virgin's milk or ocean spray or acid,
> now urine drips down in the stinking bilge,
> now also common salt or salt's own gem, Almisadir,
> now orpiment they rank the elemental prime,
> now ocean water cleaned and purged with sulphur –
> thus to hide them from the ignorant do they
> transpose the names that will not fool the wise,
> but neither will they show to the unknowing
> the single Moon that's called by all those names.'

9.6
A Practical Part of Natural Philosophy:
Porta, *Natural Magick*, 1.3

Magic relies on natural philosophy and the special sciences – mathematics, physics, optics, geology, chemistry and botany: to give modern names to those 'servants and helpers' of magic (see 7.10–11, 19; 8.10, 14; 9.1). The magician must be 'a very perfect philosopher', and a philosopher's problems must be solved with reasons of a philosophical kind, so the burdens of philosophy will weigh on his magic. Without eliminating novel ideas or idiosyncratic language, this rationalist heritage constrains Porta's project: he wants his creativity to be respectable. Unlike Paracelsus, who subverted institutions in the cause of reform, Porta courted the academies that welcomed intellectual grandees like himself, and he even founded one of his own. In magic his originality was more practical than theoretical. Without doing much about it, Pico had declared that 'magic is the practical part of natural science' (see 8.16). Porta applies that principle with great energy, reconstructing magic as a system of technologies – presented here in an English version made within a few decades of his death.

*

Seeing magick, as we shewed before, is a practical part of natural philosophy, therefore it behoveth a magician – and one that aspires to the dignity of that profession – to be an exact and a very perfect philosopher. For philosophy teaches what are the effects of fire, earth, air, and water, the principal matter of the heavens and what is . . . the whole witty force of hidden nature. Then also he must be a skilful physician: for both these sciences are very like and neer together, and physick, by creeping in under colour of magick, hath purchased favour amongst men . . . Moreover, it is required of him that he be an herbalist, not onely able to discern common simples but very skilful and sharp-sighted in the nature of all plants, for the uncertain names of plants and their neer likeness of one to another, so that they can hardly be discerned, hath put us to much trouble in some of our works and experiments . . .

He must be as well seen also in the nature of metals, minerals, gems and stones. Furthermore, what cunning he must have in the art of distillation, which follows and resembles the showers and dew of heaven as the daughter the mother, I think no man will doubt of it, for it yeelds daily very strange inventions, and most witty devices and shews how to finde out many things profitable for the use of man . . . And this he must learn to do not after a rude and homely manner but with knowledge of the causes and reasons thereof.

He must also know the mathematical sciences and especially astrologie, for . . . by the sundry motions and aspects of the heavens, the celestial bodies are very beneficial to the earth, and from thence many things receive both active and passive powers, and their manifold properties – the difficulty of which point long troubled the Platonicks' mindes, how these inferiour things should receive influence from heaven. Moreover, he must be skilful in the opticks, that he may know how the sight may be deceived, and how the likeness of a vision that is seen in the water may be seen hanging without in the air by the help of certain glasses of divers fashions, and how to make one see that plainly which is a great way off, and how to throw fire very far from us, upon which sleights the greatest part of the secrecies of magick doth depend. These are the sciences which magick takes to herself for servants and helpers, and he that knows not these is unworthy to be named a magician.

9.7
An Excellent Art Discredited:
Porta, *Natural Magick*, 5 pr.–2

If Paracelsus was one of the 'rude and unskilful' people who caused alchemy to be scorned, according to Porta, lust for wealth was certainly not his error, though most alchemists wanted to make gold and sought the Philosopher's Stone for that reason (see 9.4–5). Porta promotes alchemy not as a quest for the Stone or the elixir of life or for gold-making but as practical metallurgy, tested by his own trials and compiled in technical recipes. Lead, for example, could be used with other metals as an alloy of tin to make pewter: as Porta explains, the 'white' type of tin is brittle and lead makes it malleable.

*

We are now come . . . to those experiments which are commonly called by the name of alchymy matters, wherein not onely a great part of the world is much conversant but also every one is very desirous to be a practitioner in them and doth thirst after them with an unquenchable lust. Wherefore we are constrained to speak something concerning this subject, the rather because many rude and unskilful men – being drawn on partly by the hope of gain which they looked for by it and partly by the pleasure and delight which they did take in it – have bestowed themselves in these experiments to the great slander both of the art itself and also of the professors thereof, so that nowadays a man cannot handle it without the scorn and obloquy of the world because of the disgrace and contempt which those idiots have brought upon it . . .

Thus was an excellent good art discredited and disgraced by reason that they abused it, which falls out also in many other better things then this is. The Art of itself is not to be set at nought but rather to be embraced and much to be sought after, especially by such as apply their minds to philosophy and to the searching out of the secrecies of nature . . . I do not here promise any golden mountains, as they say, nor yet that Philosopher's Stone which the world hath so great an opinion of and hath been bragged of in many ages and

happily attained unto by some. Neither yet do I promise here that golden
liquor whereof if any man do drink, it is supposed that it will make him to be
immortal, but it is a meer dream . . . These things which here you shall find I
myself have seen and proved by experience, and therefore I am the bolder to
set them abroach to the view of the whole world . . .

The nature and the colour of tinne is such that it will whiten all other met-
tals, but it makes them brickle and easie to be knapt in sunder. Onely lead is
free from this power of tinne. But he that can skilfully make a medley of this
mettal with others may thereby attain to many pretty secrecies, wherefore we
will endeavour to counterfeit silver as neer as we can – a matter which may be
easily effected if we can tell how to abolish and utterly destroy those imper-
fections which are found in tinne whereby it is to be discerned from silver . . .
But this is a marvellous hard labour and not to be atchieved without very
great difficulty. You may likewise alter and transform tinne into lead – an
easie matter for any man to effect by reducing tinne into ashes or powder
oftentimes. For the often burning of it will cause the creaking noise which it
is wont to make to be voided from it and so to become lead without any more
ado, especially, if you use a convenient fire when you go about to reduce it into
powder . . .

This lead is a mettal that hath in it great store of quicksilver, as may appear
by this: because it is a very easie mastery to extract quicksilver out of lead. Let
your lead be filed into very small dust, and to every two pounds of lead thus
beaten into powder you must put one ounce of saltpeter and one ounce of
ordinary common salt and one ounce of antimony. Let all these be well beaten
and powned together and put into a sieve. And when they are well sifted, put
them into a vessel made of glass. And you must fence and plaister the glass
round about on the outward side with thick loam tempered with chopt straw,
and it must be laid on very fast. And that it may stick upon the vessel the better, your glass must not be smooth, but full of rigoles, as if it were wrested or
writhen. When your vessel is thus prepared, you must settle and apply it to a
reflexed fire . . . so that the vessel may be throughly heated by it, even to be
red hot.

Then set a blower on work, and let him not leave off to blow for the space
of four whole hours together. And you shall see the quicksilver drop down
into the vessel that is half full of water, being flighted, as it were, out of
the mettal by the vehement force of the fire . . . By this practice I have
extracted oftentimes out of every pound of mettal almost an whole ounce of
quicksilver – yea, sometimes more then an ounce when I have been very diligent and laborious in performing the work.

9.8

Desiring the Company of Iron:
Porta, *Natural Magick*, 7 pr.–2

When inventors in the nineteenth century tried to make telephones, they used magnets in a number of ways. Porta had a related idea about telecommunication – vague and implausible though it was. Accounts of magnetism in classical texts came up short, so he conducted his own trials to learn why this stone is 'the most admirable'. Like Galen, he rejects exchanges of atoms as the cause of attraction, and he proposes a different principle of combat and conservation – that 'all creatures defend their being'. Thinking (correctly) that a loadstone is partly iron and partly not, he assumes that this principle governs both parts: stone battles iron to preserve itself, iron does the same and the result is continuing conflict. But the iron in the magnet attracts more iron from outside – a 'friendly' attracting that happens 'willingly' in both directions. Porta's contemporary, Bernardino Telesio, proposed a similar conservation principle, with less anthropomorphism. But the anti-Aristotelian naturalism favoured by Telesio and Porta pushed its boldest advocates – Bruno and Campanella – towards mentalism and vitalism (see 9.12–13; 11.5–7). Those views, used to explain magic, provoked attacks from Galileo, Descartes and other proponents of the new 'mechanical philosophy', whose theories of matter were usually atomist or corpuscularian.

*

We pass from jewels to stones, the chief whereof and the most admirable is the loadstone, and in it the majesty of nature doth most appear. And I undertake this work the more willingly because the ancients left little or nothing of this in writing to posterity. In a few days – not to say hours – when I sought one experiment, others offered themselves that I collected almost two hundred of principal note, so wonderful is God in all his works . . . I shall begin from the most known experiments and pass to higher matters, that it may not repent any man of his great study and accurate diligence therein. By these the longitude of the world may be found out, that is of no small moment for saylors and wherein the greatest wits have been employed. And to a friend that is at a far distance from us and fast shut up in prison we may relate our minds, which I doubt not may be done by two mariner's compasses, having the alphabet writ about them. Upon this depends the principles of perpetual motion and more admirable things which I shall here let pass . . .

Because some have written whole books of the reason of the loadstone's attracting of iron, lest I should be tedious (which I purpose not to be), I think fit to pass over other men's opinions, especially because they depend onely upon words and vain cavils that philosophers cannot receive them. And I shall set down my own, founded upon some experiments. Yet I shall not pass by the opinion of Anaxagoras, set down by Aristotle in his book *De anima*, who by a similitude calls it a living stone, and that therefore it draws iron – and for some other peculiar forces which might be properly said to proceed from the soul, as you shall see.

Epicurus would fain give a reason for it, as Galen and Lucretius report. For, say they, the atoms – that flew out of the iron and meet in the loadstone in one figure so that they easily embrace one the other – these therefore, when they light upon both the concretes of the stone and iron, and then flie back into the middle, by the way they are turned between themselves, and do withall draw the iron with them. Galen inveighs against this, for he cannot believe, as he saith, that the small atoms that flie from the stone can be complicated with the like atoms that come from the iron, and that their embracing can draw such a heavy weight . . .

But I think the loadstone is a mixture of stone and iron – as an iron stone or a stone of iron – yet do not think the stone is so changed into iron as to lose its own nature, nor that the iron is so drowned in the stone, but it preserves itself. And whilst one labours to get the victory of the other, the attraction is made by the combat between them. In that body there is more of the stone then of iron. And therefore the iron, that it may not be subdued by the stone, desires the force and company of iron, that being not able to resist alone, it may be able by more help to defend itself – for all creatures defend their being. Wherefore, that it may enjoy friendly help and not lose its own perfection, it willingly draws iron to it, or iron comes willingly to that. The loadstone draws not stones because it wants them not, for there is stone enough in the body of it, and if one loadstone draw another, it is not for the stone but for the iron that is in it.

What I said depends on these arguments. The pits of loadstone are where the veins of iron are. These are described by Galen and such as deal in minerals. And in the confines of them both – of the stone and the iron – they grow.

And the loadstones are seen wherein there is more stone, and others in which there is more iron. In Germany a loadstone is digged forth out of which they draw the best iron. And the loadstone, whilst it lies in the filings of iron, will get more strength, and if it be smeered or neglected, it will lose its forces. I oft saw with great delight a loadstone wrapt up in burning coles that sent forth a blue flame that smelt of brimstone and iron, and that being dissipated, it lost its quality of its soul that was gone – namely, its attractive vertue. It is the stink of iron and brimstone, as such who destroy iron by reducing it to a calx or use other chymical operations can easily try. And I thought that the same soul, put into another body, must necessarily obtain the same faculty.

9.9
So May a Man Secretly See:
Porta, *Natural Magick*, 17 pr.–2, 5

'Someone who knows the powers of figures and bodies can work many wonders in perspective and natural magic,' wrote Agrippa, 'especially with looking-glasses. I know how to make amazing things from them, including glasses in which you can see whatever you want at the furthest distance.' Porta sounds like Agrippa when he says that 'a man may secretly see' with a telescope – also when he describes mirrors that show images 'hanging in the air' like phantoms. Nonetheless, he got impressive results by applying the science of optics for 'wonder and profit'. Around the time when Galileo built the first working telescope, Porta made a sketch of a similar instrument. Here he discusses burning mirrors, eyeglasses, magnifying lenses, telescopy and microscopy. Some of his devices would combine plane and curved lenses on the basis of optical measurements and calculations.

*

Now I am come to mathematical sciences, and this place requires that I shew some experiments concerning catoptrick glasses. For these shine amongst geometrical instruments for ingenuity, wonder and profit. For what could . . . seem more wonderful then that by reciprocal strokes of reflexion images should appear outwardly, hanging in the air, and yet neither the visible object nor the glass seen, that they may seem not to be the repercussion of the glasses but spirits of vain phantasms? To see burning glasses not to burn alone where the beams unite but at a great distance to cast forth terrible fires and flames that are most profitable in warlike expeditions? . . . I shall adde also those spectacles whereby poor blinde people can at great distance perfectly see all things . . .

Nor will I omit how letters may be cast out and read on a wall that is far distant, which we shall do with the same plain glass, and lovers that are far asunder may so hold commerce one with another. On the superficies of a plain glass make letters with black ink or with wax, that they may be solid to hinder the light of the glass and shadow it. Then hold the glass against the sun-beams so that the beams reflecting on the glass may be cast upon the opposite wall of a chamber: it is no doubt but the light and letters will be seen in the chamber, the Sun's light will be clearest and the letters not so bright so that they will be clearly discovered, as they are sent in . . .

Also you may see in plain glasses those things that are done afar off and in other places. So may a man secretly see – and without suspition – what is done afar off and in other places, which otherwise cannot be done. But you must be careful in setting your glasses. Let there be a place appointed in a house or elsewhere where you may see any thing, and set a glass right over against your window or hole that may be towards your face. And let it be set straight up if need were, or fastned to the wall, moving it here and there, and inclining it till it reflect right against the place, which you shall attain by looking on it and coming towards it. And if it be difficult, you cannot mistake if you use a quadrant or some such instrument. And let it be set perpendicular upon a line that cuts the angle of reflection and incidence of the lines, and you shall clearly see what is done in that place. So it will happen also in divers places. Hence it is that if one glass will not do it well, you may do the same by more glasses, or if the visible object be lost by too great a distance or taken away by walls or mountains coming between . . .

A plain glass as it receives the parallel beams of the Sun, it so reflects them and therefore will cast the beams that are equidistant a great way. But if a concave glass receive them, it so unites them that it sets things on fire. Wherefore – first proving where the concave-glass must be placed, that it may fire the fuel cast in – the next day, at the hour appointed, let the plain glass cast in the beams upon the concave glass that will unite them: so without danger – or any suspicion of the enemy – we may kindle fire for our use.

Nor is it useless that by a plain and concave glass the smallest letter shall appear very great when letters are so small that they can onely be seen. For I have seen St Johns Gospel – 'in the beginning', and so on – writ so small in so little place that it was no bigger than a small pimple or the sight in a cock's eye. By this artifice we may make them seem greater and read them with ease. Put a concave glass with the back of it to your brest. Over against it in the point of burning set the writing. Behind set a plain glass, that you may see it. Then in the plain glass will the images of the characters be reflected that are in the concave glass, which the concave glass hath made greater that you may read them without difficulty.

9.10
The Monad's Progeny:
John Dee, *The Hieroglyphic Monad*

Addressing Maximilian, the Habsburg King, in 1564, John Dee rates himself and his paradoxical gift to the monarch as one in a million: he had designed the monad by 1557, when he was thirty. It is that rarest of symbols – hieroglyphic, yet as clear as counting. Experts in all the arts and sciences will acknowledge its stunning power, he maintains. But Dee – a mathematician – ignores rhetoric and rejects logic, keeping only grammar from the trivium and focusing on the calculating quadrivial sciences: arithmetic, geometry, music and astronomy, amplified by optics, mechanics and new instrumentation. To discover 'new arts . . . that are entirely obscure', he bypasses the visible Hebrew language and its 'ordinary' Kabbalah for the genuine article (see 8.15–18). This 'real Kabbalah' underlies a 'parable of magic' whose words say what the monad teaches wordlessly – how to attain 'the true invisibility of the Magi' by watching the monad transmute itself, the metamorphosis by alchemical marriage of the earthly point 'hiding in the centre of its centre' (see 9.5). Starting with the familiar sign for Mercury in alchemy or astrology, Dee digs deeper, adding a 'sting' at the bottom. The sting is the usual sign for Aries – fiery, says Dee, hence crucial for alchemy. His design also incorporates a solar circle (gold) and a lunar crescent (silver). Who can say more? In 1584 Dee sent his monadic book to Emperor Rudolf II, who was Maximilian's son and very fond of mysteries. Rudolf then told Dee in an audience that this puzzle was too hard for him, and Dee seems to have taken that as a compliment.

Learn Or Be Silent If You Do Not Understand

The Hieroglyphic Monad

By

John Dee Of London

To

Maximilian,

By God's Grace The Most Sage King Of The Romans,
Bohemia And Hungary

Figure 15: Dee's Monad

Both reasons that can move a person like me to present so great a King with
so poor a gift have now compelled me to do so – my very great affection for
your Majesty, of course, but also the gift's great rarity and value, by no means
negligible, small though it is . . . As for the gift – slight in size, indeed – let me
take just a few words to describe its rarity. Searching mentally as far as I can,
I find that we must take life's path as leading two ways by different choices: . . .
either we devote all our work to philosophy for the rest of our lives, like people
seized by the love of truth, or we invest everything in a life of ease and profit . . .

What to think of a person who overcomes every such obstacle and aspires to observe and understand supercelestial powers and metaphysical influences? In this world, in these absolutely lamentable times, shall we hope for that great-souled hero – when he may be the only one? Projecting the thousand-fold ratio that I did not lightly accept, we must expect one such unique and exceedingly productive birth out of a million honest philosophers . . .

To this proof of rarity I shall add a hieroglyphic image in the style called 'Pythagorean' . . . and after that explanation, most clement King, you can easily guess the level of philosophical rarity that I expect for my gift, since you have mastered the most potent arts and greatest secrets and know their riches . . . Though I call my gift 'hieroglyphic,' anyone who looks deeper inside will grant that an almost mathematical clarity and power lies within it – which happens quite rarely in matters so rare. Is it not rare, I ask, for the usual astronomical characters of the planets to be filled with immortal life – not like the dead, mute or at least nearly barbarous symbols known at this time – and to become capable of declaring their own strength, with perfect eloquence, in any language of any nation? The very rarest thing is for all of this to be included in a single hieroglyphic character – that of Mercury equipped with a sting . . .

This is signed with my seal of Hermes from London, having in it not one dot too many nor one dot too few for what I have described – and for things far greater. Grammarians will testify to this, seeing themselves advised that reasons must be given for the form and situation of letters, for their places in the alphabet, their different ligatures, numerical value and various other properties – where the principal alphabets of the three languages must be considered . . . When I mention in passing that writings on the alphabet contain great mysteries, this will not surprise you, since He who is the only author of all mysteries has compared himself to the first letter and the last . . .

My point here is not to ask all the grammarians to puzzle over these issues, but – addressing those who labour to dig out the mysteries hidden in things – to make them bear witness that, with my monad, I have demonstrated a rare thing of this kind, giving them this friendly advice: the first and mystical letters of the Hebrews, Greeks and Latins originated from God alone and were handed down to mortals; and – as framed by astonishing craftwork of the greatest wisdom, whatever human arrogance may boast – the shapes of all the letters came from points, straight lines and the outsides of circles . . .

Having done with those philosophers of letters and language, I shall bring my own mathematicians back as the most reliable witnesses that this gift of mine is rare. Will the expert on arithmetic (not the logician, please) not be amazed that his numbers – which he used to abstract from bodily things, free-ing them from everything sensory and hiding them in the recesses of reasoning in order to apply various mental processes to them – will he not be amazed that those same numbers, in my work, I have made concrete and bodily and shown them to be so, severing their souls and formal lives from them for our use? Will he not be amazed that the monad's progeny is so great? . . .

The geometer, my King, will start to worry that the foundations of his art are not well established – strange to say – when he understands what is hinted and whispered here in this secret: that in the quadrate mystery of this hiero-glyphic monad is something circular and perfectly symmetrical . . . How very right that the musician might be stunned when he understands that inexplic-able heavenly harmonies are here without sound or movement. And the astronomer, will he not greatly regret suffering the cold of the open sky to stay awake and work, when here at any time – under his own roof with all the windows and doors shut and feeling no pain from the weather – he can make the most precise observations of the courses of the heavenly bodies? . . . The expert on optics will condemn the stupidity of his art . . . And the person who has given all his life's work to carefully examining weights, how well will he think his labours and funds have been spent when the mastery of the monad will teach him here, by the most certain experience, that the element of earth can float on water? . . . Store all these things, wisest of monarchs, in the most secret treasuries of your mind and memory.

Now I come to the Hebrew Kabbalist. When he sees his gematria, notarikon and *tzyruph*, essentially the three chief keys to his art, being applied outside the bounds of the language called 'sacred' – yes, and he sees the signs and characters of the mystical tradition received from God being gathered in from anything, seen or unseen, that presents itself anywhere – he will call this art 'sacred' too . . . No mortal can excuse himself for not knowing this sacred language of ours that . . . I have called the real (τοῦ ὄντος) Kabbalah, naming that other ordinary Kabbalah 'grammatical' (τοῦ λεγομένου) which depends on letters that people know very well and can write. This real Kab-balah – which, as Paul suggests, is our birthright by a law of creation – is also a more divine gift that discovers new arts and gives completely reliable accounts of arts that are entirely obscure, as others can try to do in other cases, following my example.

I am sure you will not be horrified, my King, if now, in your royal presence, I dare to offer this parable of magic. This hieroglyphic monad of ours has a kind of earthly body hiding in the centre of its centre. Without words the monad teaches what the divine power is by which that body must be activated ... When this *gamaea* – which I translated for the Parisians as τῆς γαμῆς αἶαν, the 'earth of marriage' or an earthly sign of a wedding of influences – has been performed with God's assent, that same monad can no longer be fed or watered on its native soil until a fourth, great and truly metaphysical revolution has been completed. When that step has been taken, the very one that fed the monad will be the first to go into metamorphosis, to be seen very rarely afterward by mortal eyes. This, best of kings, is the true invisibility of the Magi, so very often and harmlessly sung of, which – as all future Magi will acknowledge – has been granted by the seeings of our monad . . .

9.11
Instructions from Angels: John Dee's Diaries

Because Emperor Rudolf was a patron of alchemy, his court was an attraction for Dee and Edward Kelley, one of the 'skryers' who helped Dee talk to angels. In his audience with Rudolf in 1584, the mathematical magus was testy, even threatening, prodding the monarch to join the talks. But the Emperor wanted no part of it. Perhaps he had been briefed by Jacob Kurtz, a member of his Privy Council, who was Dee's minder in Prague. Later, Dee (Δ in the dialogues below) talked at length with Kurtz about his encounters with Raphael (**R** in the dialogues) and other angels. Much later, just two years before he died in 1609, Dee got new instructions from Raphael about his travel schedule, English politics and alchemical procedure: Salisbury, Dee's 'secret enemy', is Robert Cecil, whose father had been a supporter; the younger Cecil ran spies for the new King, James I, who had written about witchcraft and was now Dee's 'supreme head and governour'. Other advice is personal: kidney stones may have been troubling the ageing Dee. A favourite of his was St Dunstan, a goldsmith and the patron of alchemists: Kelley claimed to have his book on the Philosopher's Stone. John Pontois, also an alchemist, inherited Dee's library, including the angel conversations: some were bought by Meric Casaubon, Isaac's son, who published them in 1659. E. K. is Edward Kelley.

*

Because I have found so much halting and untruth in E. K. his reports to me made of the spiritual creatures where I have not been present at an action, and because his memory may fail him, and because he was subject to ill tempters, I believe so much hereof as shall by better trial be found true or conformable to truth . . .

I began and declared my long course of study for forty years, always by degrees going forward and desirous of the best . . . At length I perceived onely God – and by his good angels – could satisfie my desire, which was to understand the natures of all his creatures . . . And herein I had dealed sundry wayes and at length had found the mercies of God such as to send me the instruction of Michael, Gabriel, Raphael and Uriel and divers other his good and faithful messagers, such as I had here now brought books – about eighteen – to shew him the manner of their proceeding . . . And I thought it good to begin at the last book, which also concerned most this present Emperour Rodolph. And so I did, and so by degrees from book to book lightly, I gave him a taste . . . and also let him see the Stone brought me by Angelical ministery . . .

July 9, 4 in the afternoon, [1607]

Δ After my prayers for a quarter of an hour, a voice said 'I am Raphael whose voice thou dost hear. Tomorrow morning at nine of the clock God will send me to thy sight.' So, with thanks to God, I ended.

R John Dee, I am Raphael, one of the blessed and elect angels of the Almighty. And at his will and his good pleasure he hath commanded me to appear here at this time . . . My message . . . is of great force in that God would have thee to do. And whereas it was said at my last appearing . . . that *I would appear again* and . . . *make plainly known what Gods will is to be done in all that hath been before said*, now I do make known unto you the plain meaning and understanding thereof.

First thou hast been promised the secret knowledge and understanding of the *Philosophers Stone* of the *Book of St Dunstans* . . . And now to . . . let thee to understand why thou hadst not thus these rare gifts and promises performed unto thee, it was the will of God to keep them away, and to suffer the heart of thy Supreme Head and Governour, under God, to be hardned against thee, that thou art no better account made of unto him, but to be such an one that doth deal with devils and by sorcery – as you commonly term them, witchcraft.

And who doth and who hath informed him to be thus evil and hardly informed against thee but only the Devil, and by the hatred of thy secret enemy whom thou knowest (*Salisbury*, I mean) and all malice and enemies that he can by his Devils, Maserien, Hermeloe, the four wicked ones – the which are accounted the four Rulers of the Air, whose names be *Oriens, Egym, Paynim* and *Mayrary*, they be the Devils that he doth deal withall – that he . . . *and his Devils do seek thy overthrow in all good things, and doth and shall*, so far forth as God will suffer them, seek all the malice and hindrance in all good causes *to be done to thy good*.

Therefore now, *John Dee*, I am to let thee to understand plainly what Gods will and his great purpose is to have thee to do, although it may seem hard to thy good liking, considering, as thou dost think, the weakness of thy body and course of age. Yet . . . that same merciful God shall keep thee, and make thee able to perform things that shall be made known unto thee; for God will not . . . bestow pearls amongst those that will not believe nor understand . . . So if thou wilt do as God shall command thee by this message, *thou shalt have all these messages*, promises and wisdom, both for the *Philosophers Stone*, the book of St Dunstans, the secret wisdom of that jewel that was delivered, as thou knowest . . .

Now, *John Dee*, it is the will of the Almighty to send me, Raphael, to deliver unto thee this *message, the which will seem unto thee to be very hard*. Yet as thou art the servant of God, and one whom God doth favour and love (although the world by wicked enemies doth hate thee), *willingly and obediently follow* that course the which God in his mercies at this time shall make known unto thee . . .

So, if thou wilt follow this commandment from God delivered unto thee by me, Raphael, that thou shalt not doubt nor waver . . . God shall and will deal with thee in finding ease of the infirmity of the stone, that the Angels of God shall direct thee in thy heart and mind, how thou shalt use thy body to the health and comfort of thy strength. And . . . God will most graciously raise thee up some good friends to be helping unto thee, that thou have maintenance in thy journy. And thy very friend, John Pontoys . . . will be a great aid unto thee . . . Therefore I command thee from God . . . that thou shouldst not doubt to take this journy in hand, for God will be with thee and for thee, and his blessed angels shall be thy comfort, even as the angel of God was the comfort unto young Tobias in his journey . . .

And thus to Gods honour and his glory, I have ended my message, yielding unto God all honour and praise and thanks . . . both now and for evermore. Amen. Blessed be God in all his gifts and holy in all his works. Praised be God. Amen, amen.

Δ Amen. Now, O God, as I have willingly yielded unto thy will and commandment of undertaking a journey, so I beseech thee . . . to notifie unto me the country, region or city unto which thou wouldst have me direct my course from henceforward. (*nothing appeared*) A voice, a voice: 'In the name of God, tomorrow at ten of the clock.' So be it. All thanks, praise and glory be to God the Father, God the Son, and God the Holy Ghost, now and forever, amen.

9.12

Love is the Great Demon:
Bruno, *A General Theory of Bonds*, 3.12–15

Amphitrite is the Sea – not Poseidon's wife in Bruno's theory of bonds, but the paternal power of Love, the androgyne and universal Venus who makes everything cohabit (see 4.3–4; 5.5–6, 16). This same force that binds all things shows up differently in each thing, exhibiting a different bond each time. This oceanic and particularizing force is material, and matter is the only locus of form. In fact, since 'there is no form except within matter', outside of matter there is nothing. Even God is matter, and matter is divine, always already ensouled, sentient and thinking. Since minds, both divine and human, and souls, both universal and individual, exist only within this material whole, all the magical connections have been made. It remains only to find and use them (see 5.10, 15; 8.7, 13).

*

There is a divine force in all things – Love himself, the Father, source and Amphitrite of bonds. Hence it was not wrong for Orpheus and Mercury to call him 'the great demon' since the whole substance, constitution and, as I would say, hypostasis of things is a kind of bond. We get to know this first and greatest teaching about the bond when we turn our eyes to the order of the universe. In this bond, the higher provides for the lower, the lower turns towards the higher, and equal allies with equal, finally making the universe complete in keeping with the pattern of its form. A single Love makes a single bond for all things and has different faces in different things, so that each thing bonds differently with something else . . .

When philosophers go deeper, they understand what I have explained elsewhere, that matter itself has the origin of all things in its heart in such a way that it draws everything out from there and sends it forth – not like a pure privation that would take every foreign thing in from outside. In fact, there is no form except within matter: all things lie hidden inside it and all are then brought out of it. Whether you look at this politically or from all aspects of bonding, two things should be clear: first, that in all matter or in every part of matter, in every individual or in some particular, all the seeds are hidden beneath and contained within; next, the result is that a person with skill and ingenuity can complete all the joinings of the bonds.

Hence, a principle that wants to become everything is more perfect, moving not to a particular form and perfection but to a universal form and perfection. Like this is matter as a whole, outside of which there is no form, in whose potency, desire and disposition are all the forms, and which takes all forms into its parts by exchanging them, even though it cannot take in two of them together. Matter is something divine, then, just as form is thought to be something divine, though it is either nothing or else something related to matter . . . There is nothing foolish in the position reached by David of Dinant and also by Avicebron in his *Source of Life*, citing the Arabs, who dared to call God 'matter' as well.

The most potent bond of all belongs to Venus, the genus of Love.

9.13
The Bonds of Magic:
Bruno, *On Natural Magic*, 49–83

After Proclus had sketched the magical hierarchies, Ficino tried to sanitize them for Christians and Agrippa simplified them (see 5.16; 8.7; 9.2). But Bruno exchanged them for mutualities, whose key emblem is a bond or cord, not a ladder (see 1.4). Bodies are not housings for separate souls, he insists: they are local nodes of the ensouled and intelligent universal body, whose every atom reflects the All and every other atom, bound together by life and Love (see 9.12). The countless avatars of this single, supreme Bond constitute 'the manifold bond of spirits, where the whole doctrine of magic is contained'. Every binding, magical or not, needs an *agent* to act, an *object* to be acted upon and a *circumstance* (or application) within which the action happens. Not all agents, objects and circumstances make effective bonds, however, and the occult cause of each effect – never registered by the senses nor grasped by the mind – must be sought by itself. So complex are the bondings that they elude even demonic intellects, though mathematics, philosophy and psychology can help the enquiring magus. Observing the effects of demonic possession, for example, a sage will know that effective bonds are not merely material, like bodily fluids, nor purely spiritual, like disembodied demons, and that the two must be bound together to do their work. Bruno himself, when he saw demons, observed spirits with bodies that could act on embodied humans. Like him, the possessed 'hear what they hear and see what they see' – not Pomponazzi's verdict, exactly (see 9.1).

*

Porphyry, Plotinus and other Platonists assign bodies to spirits . . . It happens that I too have seen them at Mount Libero and Mount Lauro – but not just me: they often appear to the people who live there . . . Different spirits have been put in different bodies, arranged in a certain order with places justly allotted to them . . . Demons are bodily, then, varying and differing according to the differences and varieties of their bodies: evidence of this is that they have feelings, passions, rages and jealousies, which are like human feelings and those of animals that are made of denser sensible matter . . . Some, the famous and more powerful demons, have been named, but others are the common type . . .

In the end, it must be firmly stated and clearly understood that all things are full of spirit, soul, power, God or divinity and that intellect and soul are wholly everywhere – though not to do everything everywhere . . . Bodily substance differs from the substance of such a mind, soul and exalted spirit. The universal body is wholly in the whole and in the universe, while that other substance is wholly in every part, everywhere constituting a sort of whole and reflecting an image of the whole, now more clearly, now obscurely, now in a more particular way, now plurally, so that a likeness of the same idea and light is reflected as a whole by every particle of matter, as the whole likeness is also reflected by the whole of matter.

This can be observed, plainly enough, in a large mirror that reflects the image of a single thing, and then the same mirror, shattered into a thousand fragments, still reflects the complete image from all the parts . . . In this way, if all the spirits and parts of air were to flow into the one Ocean, they would produce a single soul, though otherwise the souls would be many and countless. Hence philosophers say that matter is one, spirit one, light one, soul one and intellect one in the primeval state. Now let me turn to reporting on the manifold bond of spirits, where the whole doctrine of magic is contained.

First, the bond by which spirits are tied together is general and metaphorical, showing the three-headed Cerberus, Hell's door-keeper, tied up. This is the threefold power needed in a binder or magus – physical, mathematical and metaphysical. In the first is the base, in the second the steps, in the third the top of the ladder. The first gives an account of active and passive principles by kind, the second of times, places and numbers, the third of universal principles and causes. This is a three-stranded cord that is hard to break.

Second is the triple bond needed in the doer, in what is done and in what the doing attends, and it consists of faith or belief, also of invoking, also love and the intense emotion that goes along with applying actives to passives, for the soul as effective cause has the power to transform bodies or the composite, while the body as material cause has the power to transform the soul. Unless these are accessible or really present, nothing comes of all the trouble, movement and excitement. A magician is very fortunate, then, if many believe in him – with great conviction.

The *third* bond, considered an efficient cause, is the set of principles distributed over the four poles of the universe for those actions that the heavens and nature require. In addition to these, to take care of voluntary and non-natural effects, there are principles that have no assigned place. The *fourth* bond is the soul of the world or the spirit of the universe which couples all things and unites them to everything, thus providing access from all things to all things, as I have said before. The souls of the stars and the princes of places, winds and elements are the *fifth* bond . . .

For actions to be completed in reality, three things are needed: an active power in an *agent*, a passive power or disposition in an *object* of action . . . and an *application* appropriate to the circumstances of time, place and other things involved. It all comes down to the agent, the material and the application, and if these three are absent, all action is blocked, to put it in simple terms . . .

Not everything is suited to act on everything nor to be acted upon, but, as it says in the *Physics*, all being-acted-upon is *from* a contrary and all acting is *upon* a contrary. This is not always so, however, only for a contrary that has been disposed, and thus the saying: 'actions of the active on a patient well disposed'. From this we see the reason why water mixes with water – and why water blends with water – because of a likeness or a kinship or a covenant . . . The situation, composition and distinctness of parts must be noted, then, in that a whole can penetrate a whole from one side but not another. This applies to everything, which is clear for stones and wood and flesh as well . . .

Not just the situation and nature of the parts must be examined but also the state of the whole form, for certain passions are well suited to be received *upon* one object and not by another, like the numbness caused by a ray in a fisherman's hand but not in his nets . . . Likewise for the thunderbolts that sometimes melt a sword or steel without any harm to the scabbard. Something amazing also happened in Naples to a noble girl who was very good-looking when lightning burned only her pubic hair . . . Many such things result from the basic structure hidden in the atoms of that kind of fire so that it acts on one thing but not another . . .

As far as people are concerned – why not all of them experience what happened to that girl – the reason is that they do not all have the same temperament or take in the same kind of spirit, though there are also some whose souls are such that they can even prevent rain and command winds and storms. In this way, the type of temperament also explains the amazing things that happen in bodies, some as the prerogative of the whole species, but some as a special endowment of individuals because of their structural differences. In such cases, therefore, magicians look both to species and to individuals to find the effects of their powers . . .

One must stay with a general rule, then: not all are acted upon by all, not all effects are agreeable to all in relation to the same differences, and the reasons for them must be found, case by case, in the effects themselves – when a specific account is needed. But no names have been given to those occult differences or forms; they cannot be sensed by sight or touch; nor can they be reasoned about on the basis of visual and tactile differences that might elicit a definition by origin – leaving us nothing to say but that such things exist. In light of this, my conclusion is that not even the demons could easily sort such things out, should they wish to join us in defining them by our words and the meanings signified by our words.

A second type of bonding comes from the conformity of numbers to numbers, measures to a measure and moments to a moment – the source of those rhythms and songs that are said to have the very greatest power . . . Through sight the spirit is also bonded, as already noted, when the eyes observe forms in one way or another. This is why enchantments, both active and passive, emerge from the eyes and enter through the eyes . . . The appearance of the beautiful also stirs up a feeling of love; the contrary sight provokes hatred and horror. And through their effects on the soul and spirit, something more is transfused into the body itself, abiding there under the guidance of the soul and the spirit's moderating force . . .

The imagination's function is to receive and retain forms that are brought in from the senses – also to combine and separate them, doing so in two ways: one is by a choice and decision of the person who imagines, like the work of poets and painters, writers of fiction and generally all those who have some method of putting ideas together; the other kind is without choice or decision. The latter also goes two ways: either through a cause that also wills and chooses or through one that moves from outside. And that cause also has two types: either indirect, as with a person who stirs up feelings with sounds or apparitions that are heard or seen; or direct, as with a spiritual, rational or demonic agent who acts on the fantasy in dreams, or also in sleeplessness, to shake up the forms inside and give the appearance of perceiving something with an external sense.

This is why some possessed people seem to see and hear all sorts of sights, sounds and statements, thinking that external agents are really slipping them in. This makes them insist – incessantly and obnoxiously – that they have seen real things and heard real things when surely their reason is deceived, not their senses: for they hear what they hear and see what they see. Yet what is presented to them in the internal sense through a form of fantasy they think is the same as what comes in through the ears from a sound outside, or they think they see a form outside that has come in through sight, and they maintain that ideas of the internal senses are real things . . . Physicians classify this as madness and melancholy, using the term 'waking dreams'.

Actually, what this bond involves is neither the purely material principle assumed by the completely crude and quite uncivilized rigidity of certain boorish physicians nor a purely efficient principle of the demonic or diabolical kind that, for their part, certain theologians defend. Instead, the two principles act together. The melancholic humour – which I call a tavern or brothel for saturnalian demons – is indeed a material cause, but the demonic spirit itself also acts as a moving and efficient cause. Although this substance is not altogether non-bodily, in that demons are seen to be equipped with many animal feelings – very powerful ones, in fact – yet it is a spiritual substance that has been given a finer body less accessible to the senses . . .

As different spirits approach and withdraw because of particular accidental temperaments or because additions are made to the body, with the result that a spirit of rage gets control, it can be taken out, of course, whether by an incantation – namely the rhetorical, helpful and healing kind that restores the beset spirit by a kind of persuasion – or by emptying out or expelling toxic material with purgative drugs, or by jovial, solar and other seasonable foods that agree with human life, either by supplying the spirit with better material or by mellowing and moderating the poorer kind that sometimes makes its way into the body's mix . . .

In itself the bond of fantasy is unreliable, if the bond of cogitation does not double its strength. For those apparitions that bind and fetter the minds of the ignorant, stupid, gullible and superstitious are mocked, despised and treated as empty shadows by an intellect that is cautious, well bred and disciplined. This is why no operators or magicians or prophets get any results unless confidence leads the way, and their operations follow the measures of the foregoing confidence . . . Hence the well-known saying of Hippocrates: 'the physician who gets the best results is the one in whom people believe most' – because he binds more of them by his eloquence or presence or fame. And this is true not only for the physician but for magic of any kind . . .

For now, what pertains to the soul's more spiritual potencies – memory, reason, experience, intellect and mind – is not my task to pursue in the present enquiry since the activations of those potencies do not carry over to the body or change it. Instead, the origin of the whole transformation lies in the potencies that come before the cogitative faculty, even though the change is worked out by cogitation and occurs chiefly there. All magical power, both active and passive, comes from there, and to that extent all forms come within the bonds of magic.

9.14
Abominable and Devilish Inventions:
Scot, *Discoverie*, 1.7–9

To every creature, including humans, God provides the natural powers observed in the ordinary course of events, which are nothing like 'witches supernaturall actions'. These are illusions, according to Scot, whether contrived or spontaneous – the latter arising from psychological defects, the former from greed and malice. Although England no longer respects 'the Pope's absurd religion', the habits of superstition are hard to break. Scot has read books and pamphlets about witchcraft that 'not onlie agree with forren crueltie but surmounteth it farre', showing 'what flat and plaine knaverie is practised against these old women' (see 8.1–3; 11.9). Writing in the vernacular and as a Protestant, Scot rejects witchcraft more decisively than Champier had done at the start of the century, though his reasoning about mental illness is similar (see 8.19).

*

Surelie the naturall power of man or woman cannot be so inlarged as to doo anie thing beyond the power and vertue given and ingraffed by God. But it is the will and mind of man which is vitiated and depraved by the Divell. Neither dooth God permit anie more than that which the naturall order appointed by him dooth require, which naturall order is nothing else but the ordinarie power of God powred into everie creature, according to his state and condition ... Howbeit you shall understand that few or none are throughlie persuaded, resolved or satisfied that witches can indeed accomplish all these impossibilities. But someone is bewitched in one point, and some is coosened in another, untill in fine all these impossibilities – and manie mo – are by severall persons affirmed to be true.

And this I have also noted, that when anie one is coosened with a coosening toie of witchcraft and maketh report thereof accordinglie, verifieng a matter most impossible and false as it were upon his owne knowledge as being overtaken with some kind of illusion or other (which illusions are right inchantments), even the selfesame man will deride the like lie proceeding out of another man's mouth as a fabulous matter unworthie of credit.

It is also to be woondered how men – that have seene some part of witches' coosenages detected and see also therein the impossibilitie of their owne presumptions and the follie and falsehood of the witches confessions – will not suspect but remaine unsatisfied or rather obstinatelie defend the residue of witches supernaturall actions: like as when a juggler hath discovered the slight and illusion of his principall feats, one would fondlie continue to thinke that his other petie juggling knacks of legierdemaine are done by the helpe of a familiar; and according to the follie of some papists, who seeing and confessing the Pope's absurd religion in the erection and maintenance of idolatrie and superstition – speciallie in images, pardons, and relikes of saints – will yet persevere to thinke that the rest of his doctrine and trumperie is holie and good. Finallie, manie mainteine and crie out for the execution of witches that particularlie beleeve never a whit of that which is imputed unto them if they be therein privatelie dealt withall and substantiallie opposed and tried in argument . . .

Cardanus writeth that the cause of such credulitie consisteth in three points: to wit, in the imagination of the melancholike, in the constancie of them that are corrupt therewith and in the deceipt of the judges who – being inquisitors themselves against heretikes and witches – did both accuse and condemne them, having for their labour the spoile of their goods, so as these inquisitors added manie fables hereunto, least they should seeme to have doone injurie to the poore wretches in condemning and executing them for none offence. But sithens (saith he) the springing up of Luther's sect, these priests have tended more diligentlie upon the execution of them bicause more wealth is to be caught from them – insomuch as now they deale so looselie with witches (through distrust of gaines) that all is seene to be malice, follie or avarice that hath beene practised against them. And whosoever shall search into this cause or read the cheefe writers hereupon shall find his words true.

It will be objected that we here in England are not now directed by the Pope's lawes, and so by consequence our witches not troubled or convented by the inquisitor's *haereticae pravitatis*. I answer that in times past here in England, as in other nations, this order of discipline hath beene in force and use, although now some part of old rigor be qualified by two severall statutes made in the fift of Elizabeth and xxxiii of Henrie the Eight. Nevertheles, the estimation of the omnipotencie of their words and charmes seemeth in those statutes to be somewhat mainteined as a matter hitherto generallie received and not yet so looked into as that it is refuted and decided.

But how wiselie so ever the Parlement House hath dealt therin, or how mercifullie soever the Prince beholdeth the cause, if a poore old woman, supposed to be a witch, be by the civill or canon lawe convented, I doubt some canon will be found in force not onelie to give scope to the tormentor but also to the hangman to exercise their offices upon hir. And most certaine it is that in what point soever anie of these extremities which I shall rehearse unto you be mitigated, it is thorough the goodnesse of the Queene's Majestie and hir excellent magistrates placed among us. For as touching the opinion of our writers therein in our age – yea, in our owne countrie – you shall see it doth not onlie agree with forren crueltie but surmounteth it farre.

If you read a foolish pamphlet dedicated to the Lord Darcy by W. W., 1582, you shall see that he affirmeth that all those tortures are farre too light and their rigor too mild. And that in that respect he impudentlie exclameth against our magistrates who suffer them to be but hanged when murtherers and such malefactors be so used, which deserve not the hundreth part of their punishments. But if you will see more follie and lewdnes comprised in one lewd booke, I commend you to Ri. Ga., a Windsor man, who being a mad man hath written according to his frantike humour – the reading wherof may satisfie a wise man how mad all these witchmoongers' dealings be in this behalfe . . .

And bicause it may appeare unto the world what trecherous and faithlesse dealing, what extreame and intollerable tyrannie, what grosse and fond absurdities, what unnaturall and uncivil discourtisie, what cancred and spitefull malice, what outragious and barbarous crueltie, what lewd and false packing, what cunning and craftie intercepting, what bald and peevish interpretations, what abhominable and divelish inventions, and what flat and plaine knaverie is practised against these old women, I will set downe the whole order of the inquisition, to the everlasting, inexcusable and apparent shame of all witchmoongers.

Neither will I insert anie private or doubtfull dealings of theirs or such as they can either denie to be usuall or justlie cavill at, but such as are published and renewed in all ages since the commensement of poperie, established by lawes, practised by inquisitors, privileged by princes, commended by doctors, confirmed by popes, councels, decrees and canons, and finallie be left of all witchmoongers – to wit, by such as attribute to old women and such like creatures the power of the Creator. I praie you, therefore, though it be tedious and intollerable, as you would be heard in your miserable calamities, so heare with compassion their accusations, examinations, matters given in evidence, confessions, presumptions, interrogatories, conjurations, cautions, crimes, tortures and condemnations devised and practised usuallie against them.

10

Magic Seen, Heard and Mocked

Figure 16: Faustus Summons Mephistopheles

Medieval books, every one made by hand laboriously, are sometimes illustrated. The books – bibles, for example – sometimes tell stories that show strange things: Aaron turns his wand into a snake; an angel tells a virgin she is pregnant; a magician falls from the sky. In manuscripts and on the walls of churches, the Devil was a common sight, usually presiding over the wrong end of the Last Judgement. The scruffy Devil shown here comes from the *Codex Gigas*, a gigantic (hence the name) manuscript put together by Benedictine monks in the early thirteenth century. The Devil's anatomy is monstrous. Non-human parts distort a human form to make it anti-human and horrible. But the horror of monstrosity itself is not the main content of this image, which shows an individual person whose name we all know: it is a picture of *someone*, although that someone is supernatural.

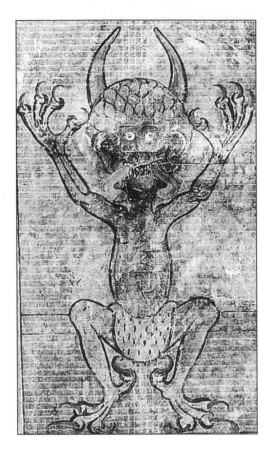

Figure 17: Satan Himself in the *Codex Gigas*

An image of a different kind, from a book by Ulisse Aldrovandi, is of no one
in particular: it is a virtuoso display of monstrosity as such. In Aldrovandi's
day, printed books with grotesque pictures were best-sellers, like other volumes – elegantly illustrated – on geology, botany, zoology and human
anatomy. Convincing pictures in books of natural history set norms for seeing
that made images of monsters just as believable. People who read the books
that we now call 'scientific' had seen *some* of the stones, plants, insects, fish,
reptiles, birds and mammals pictured in them – rocks by a road, roses in a
garden, horses in a pasture. Seeing familiar objects of nature expertly depicted
built confidence in pictorial conventions that naturalized the exotic: had you
never come near an elephant or a rhinoceros, but you had seen a plausible
cockerel or a recognizable rabbit in one of Aldrovandi's books, you might also
trust his pictures of creatures from far away, beyond the range of what you
could see for yourself.

Figure 18: A Monster by Aldrovandi

Why not trust Aldrovandi's monsters too? Pictures of monsters in early printed books often come with thrilling stories. Usually sensational and sometimes apocalyptic, they provided pertinent entertainment during decades of religious war – excitement for Christians who kept expecting the end of days and kept looking for omens to announce it. There were many endorsements for these strange sights.

The Bible predicts an apocalypse and an Antichrist, a monster of iniquity whose extra-biblical legend was meatier than the official version. Less remote was the domestic experience – reported by family, relatives or neighbours – of nature gone wrong in human and animal births. Limbs missing, misshapen, misplaced or too many, openings in the body where none should be, deformed skin or strange hair, disturbingly odd behaviour: then as now, reactions were sharp when people suffered such things, and medical science could give no relief. So people prayed and told stories about monsters, sometimes spinning them into inky nightmares in books like Aldrovandi's. The artists and crafts-men who produced those volumes had improved the art of printing and the commerce of publishing by Aldrovandi's time: he died in 1605, and his *History of Monsters* appeared in 1642.

By then, during Aldrovandi's heyday, the great age of European theatre had come and gone – except in one genre, comedy, where Molière had yet to make his mark. Ben Jonson, another master of comedy, died in 1637, outliving Shakespeare by more than twenty years. Marlowe was killed in 1593, just after Shakespeare started performing in London. The majestic dramaturgy of Elizabethan and Jacobean England – like the sumptuous craft of the book while Aldrovandi worked – was, among other things, an art and a technology of picturing.

In the theatre, one kind of picturing relies on the ensemble of costumes, furniture and other gear on stage. With help from a cast and crew, each per-son in the audience also pictures things in a singular way. When Londoners watched players on a stage and saw witches on a moor or a ghost haunting a castle or fairies feuding in a forest, the visual experience of mysterious activ-ity, made electric by language of very high voltage, was like nothing ever seen-and-heard before. Watching in audiences as large as 3,000, standing like Faustus inside circles of energy, ordinary people were communal witnesses of magical events.

The new technologies were good at disseminating images, whether they moved on a stage or stayed still in books. Before Shakespeare's time, however, dissemination had not been a strength of play-acting or book-making. Con-sider the Devil in the *Codex Gigas*, which opens more than a yard wide: his picture will be hard to miss for anyone who glances inside that bulky volume. But a look at this image of Satan was hard to get until recently. The huge Bible was made and housed in a remote monastery: then it passed through other monastic libraries on the way to Rudolf II's celebrated collec-tions. Even there, the Devil will usually have stayed out of sight.

Aldrovandi – a collector like Rudolf but in a more public environment – made pictures of monsters accessible to more people than the few who could visit an Emperor's court. When his *History of Monsters* was published, a thousand or more copies of a book might be printed for one edition. For a large, expensive volume like the *Monsters*, fewer copies may have been made, but Aldrovandi's readership – centred on the city of Bologna yet European in scope – was larger than Rudolf's restricted audience. Through the sixteenth century, as more and more such books reached more and more viewers, picturing in print corroborated the talk about magic. Aldrovandi's publications – like those of other natural historians – created two moments of authentication. First, pictures of ordinary things were produced in such numbers and so persuasively that the pictorial conventions used to make them became normal and habitual. Then, once pictorial seeing was believing for everyday things, displays of the same kind could also confirm the more exotic and arcane items also shown in books.

After Aldrovandi died in 1605, however, pictures of a different kind became more common. Technical illustrations in books by Descartes, Galileo, Gilbert, Hooke, Huygens and others communicated new theories of matter and force that were making magic disreputable for European intellectuals. Images in Porta's books pointed both ways: physiognomies of people, animals and plants evoked the signatures of Paracelsus, while optical designs and sketches of experiments made the old magic look out of date and ineffective. The comic theatre of Jonson and Molière would have similar effects – eventually. But that transformation was decades away in 1611 when Shakespeare brought his monster Caliban to court for James I to see.

Watching magic up close, on stage – sighing as Prospero exploits Ariel in his kindly way, cringing as Faustus disgraces himself, sharing those feelings with people seated on either side – that was the power of theatre working in fictions of magic, just as the same dramatists paraded the warlike deeds of kings and exposed the conniving of courtiers. Except through the lines of a play and actions on a stage, Harry Hotspur was no more real to a London audience than Owen Glendower, the wizard prince from Wales. 'I can call spirits from the vasty deep,' Glendower boasts. Then Hotspur asks, 'But will they come when you do call for them?' In the theatre, the spirits always came for Shakespeare, Jonson and Marlowe.

Those playwrights were the supreme poets of their age, setting the standard not just for drama but for all serious literature. Edmund Spenser was also a great poet – but in language made all but unreadable by contrast with his successors. Later, when Milton challenged Dante as hell's architect in verse, the bar had been set high in two domains by his own countrymen. One was linguistic, and in that respect Milton's achievement has stood with Shakespeare's and Chaucer's: Satan speaks English because Milton taught him how. The other challenge was visual: epic poetry has its scenes, but no stages. How could reams of blank verse show a playwright's audience what to see? Milton answered in 1667 with the first two books of *Paradise Lost*, where the most painful sights for Satan are visions inside him: 'The mind is its own place,' he explains, 'and in itself can make a heav'n of hell, a hell of heav'n.'

Milton wrote 'to justify the ways of God to men'. Nothing could be more serious. But in Milton's day not everyone still took magic seriously: some were starting to entertain doubts about the Devil. In that climate of creeping enlightenment, the same high art that made magic visible on the stage and eloquent in poetry could also make it ridiculous. Making fun of magic was nothing new, of course. Plautus joked about a haunted house. Chaucer made alchemy look foolish. But Jonson, taking that same topic to new heights, works a miracle, turning technical writing about alchemy – as in the *Rose Garden of Philosophers* – into the comedy of empty language. The master of that line of wit is still Molière – in any language. Judged by results in the press, however, the most successful mockery of magic was a counter-epic – comic relief for Milton's stately verses. Samuel Butler's main targets in *Hudibras* are Presbyterian pedants and fanatics. But his Sidrophel, a 'cunning man', is the silliest wizard in English letters.

Butler, Molière and Jonson laughed at magic in the best company. *The Alchemist* was first performed in 1610, the year of Galileo's telescopic discoveries, announced in his *Starry Messenger*. When Molière died in 1673, acting in *The Imaginary Invalid*, the Royal Society of London was looking at nature from the other end, through the microscopic images of Antonie van Leeuwenhoek. In 1677, when Leeuwenhoek trained his sights on human sperm, all of Butler's *Hudibras* was complete and published. New instrumentation and pictures of a new kind were helping the mechanical philosophers – cheered by comedic allies – to escort magic from centre stage, leaving the honour of science unsullied. Few of the new-model sages, after Molière had killed the occult philosophy with a joke and collapsed on stage, could still agree with Faustus that magic is a source 'of power, of honour, of omnipotence'.

10.1

Merlin's Enchanted Sword: Spenser, *The Faerie Queene*, 2.8.17–22

Published in the 1590s, Edmund Spenser's unfinished allegorical epic of patriotic Christian chivalry links medieval legends with the new poetry and drama of Elizabethan England. Spenser's language – pure artifice and antiquated (by design) even in his day – speaks less effectively than Shakespeare's English to modern readers. Temperance is the thematic virtue of the second book of this huge poem, and Guyon is the knight of temperance. Prince Arthur 'of bold and bounteous grace' rides in to rescue him. Arthur arrives just in time to save the unconscious Guyon from 'th'enchaunter' Archimago – an evil sorcerer – and his two accomplices, the ill-tempered Pyrochles and his brother, the indecisive Cymochles. The most conspicuous prop in this canto is Arthur's magical sword – here called 'Morddure' or 'Bite-Hard' – 'which Merlin made by his almightie art', using a wizard's plant ('medaewart', or meadow-wort) to prepare the weapon for other treatments that supplied its 'hidden vertue' or occult power.

*

> . . . towards them did pace
> an armed knight of bold and bounteous grace
> whose squire bore after him an heben launce
> and coverd shield. Well kend him so far space
> th'enchaunter by his armes and amenaunce
> when under him he saw his Lybian steed to praunce.
>
> And to those brethren said: 'Rise, rise bylive,
> and unto batteil doe your selves addresse,
> for yonder comes the prowest knight alive,
> Prince Arthur, flowre of grace and nobilesse,
> that hath to paynim knights wrought great distresse
> and thousand Sar'zins fowly donne to dye.'

That word so deepe did in their harts impresse
that both eftsoones upstarted furiously
and gan themselves prepare to batteill greedily.

But fiers Pyrochles, lacking his owne sword,
the want thereof now greatly gan to plaine,
and Archimage besought him that afford
which he had brought for Braggadocchio vaine.
'So would I' – said th'enchaunter – 'glad and faine
beteeme to you this sword, you to defend,
or ought that else your honour might maintaine,
but that this weapon's powre I well have kend,
to be contrarie to the worke which ye intend.

For that same knight's owne sword that is of yore
which Merlin made by his almightie art
for that his noursling, when he knighthood swore,
therewith to doen his foes eternall smart:
the metall first he mixt with medaewart
that no enchauntment from his dint might save,
that it in flames of Aetna wrought apart
and seven times dipped in the bitter wave
of hellish Styx, which hidden vertue to it gave.

The vertue is that neither steele nor stone
the stroke thereof from entraunce may defend,
ne ever may be used by his fone,
ne forst his rightful owner to offend,
ne ever will it breake ne ever bend –
wherefore Morddure it rightfully is hight.
In vaine therefore, Pyrochles, should I lend
the same to thee against his lord to fight,
for sure it would deceive thy labour and thy might.'

'Foolish old man,' said then the pagan wroth,
'that weenest words or charms may force withstond:
soone shalt thou see and then beleeve for troth

that I can carve with this inchaunted brond
his lord's owne flesh.' Therewith out of his hond
that vertuous steele he rudely snatcht away,
and Guyon's shield about his wrest he bond –
so ready dight fierce battaile to assay
and match his brother proud in battailous aray.

10.2

Within This Circle:
Marlowe, *Doctor Faustus* (A–Text), 1.3

'Why this is hell,' says Mephistopheles to the brilliant yet naïve Faustus, who wonders how the Devil can have shown up in his study. The power of vernacular drama reaches new heights in Marlowe's plays – the power to take us inside another mind, even Satan's mind, and to make theatrical reality out of the most bizarre material, even a necromancer's circle (see 7.20). Just twelve years younger than Spenser, Marlowe brings magic into a changing world where the older poet's allegories might be beautiful but could no longer be convincing (see 10.1, 10). The moral armature that had sustained holiness, temperance, chastity, courtesy and other virtues of a Christian nobility was collapsing in Marlowe's society, where the ambitious Faustus – parsing the ambitions of a university professor – renounces religion for the sake of pleasure and power, including magical power.

*

F   Now that the gloomy shadow of the earth,
     longing to view Orion's drizzling look,
     leaps from th'Antartic world unto the sky
     and dims the welkin with her pitchy breath,
     Faustus, begin thine incantations,
     and try if devils will obey thy hest,
     seeing thou hast prayed and sacrificed to them.
     Within this circle is Jehovah's name
     forward and backward anagrammatized,
     the breviated names of holy saints,
     figures of every adjunct to the heavens,
     and characters of signs and erring stars
     by which the spirits are enforced to rise.
     Then fear not, Faustus, but be resolute
     and try the uttermost magic can perform.

[chants in Latin]
May the gods of Acheron help me!
May Jove's threefold power give me strength!
Hail, you spirits of fire, air and water!
Beelzebub, Prince of the East, monarch of the burning fire, and
Demogorgon, let me appease you so that Mephistopheles will rise up
and show himself. Why delay? By Jehovah, Gehenna and the holy water
that I now sprinkle, by the sign of the cross that I now make and by your
own prayers, let the one called Mephistopheles now rise up before me!
(Enter a Devil)

I charge thee to return and change thy shape:
thou art too ugly to attend on me!
Go, and return an old Franciscan friar.
That holy shape becomes a devil best. *(Exit Devil)*

I see there's virtue in my heavenly words.
Who would not be proficient in this art?
How pliant is this Mephistopheles,
full of obedience and humility:
such is the force of magic and my spells!
Now, Faustus, thou art conjuror laureate,
that canst command great Mephistopheles:
[in Latin] Come back, Mephistopheles, only look like a friar.
(Enter Mephistopheles)

M Now, Faustus, what wouldst thou have me do?
F I charge thee wait upon me whilst I live,
  to do whatever Faustus shall command –
  be it to make the Moon drop from her sphere
  or the ocean to overwhelm the world.
M I am a servant to great Lucifer
  and may not follow thee without his leave:
  no more than he commands must we perform.
F Did not he charge thee to appear to me?
M No, I came now hither of mine own accord.
F Did not my conjuring speeches raise thee? Speak!
M That was the cause but yet *per accidens*:
  for when we hear one rack the name of God,

abjure the Scriptures and his Saviour Christ,
we fly in hope to get his glorious soul,
nor will we come unless he use such means
whereby he is in danger to be damned.
Therefore, the shortest cut for conjuring
is stoutly to abjure the Trinity
and pray devoutly to the prince of Hell.

F   So Faustus hath
already done and holds this principle:
there is no chief but only Beelzebub
to whom Faustus doth dedicate himself.
This word 'damnation' terrifies not him
for he confounds Hell in Elysium.
His ghost be with the old philosophers!
But leaving these vain trifles of men's souls,
tell me what is that Lucifer thy lord?

M   Arch-regent and commander of all spirits.

F   Was not that Lucifer an angel once?

M   Yes, Faustus, and most dearly loved of God.

F   How comes it, then, that he is prince of devils?

M   O, by aspiring pride and insolence,
for which God threw him from the face of heaven.

F   And what are you that live with Lucifer?

M   Unhappy spirits that fell with Lucifer,
conspired against our God with Lucifer,
and are for ever damned with Lucifer.

F   Where are you damned?

M   In hell.

F   How comes it, then, that thou art out of hell?

M   Why, this is hell, nor am I out of it.

10.3
Fairies and Hobgoblins: Shakespeare, *A Midsummer Night's Dream*, 2.1

Oberon, King of the fairies, wants Titania, the Fairy Queen, to hand over a change-ling boy 'to trace the forests wild' with him. But Titania – protesting loyalty to the boy's human mother, while also nursing a jealous quarrel with Oberon – will have none of it: the anger between the two demi-gods infects nature itself and throws the whole world out of joint. To break Titania's resistance, Oberon commands Puck to bring him the makings of a love-potion that will wreck his Queen's plans. Puck (P) enters talking to a fairy (F) about Oberon (O), Titania (T) and himself. The fairy and Puck, 'that merry wanderer of the night', are not bound by space and time. Puck can 'put a girdle round about the earth in forty minutes'. These two sprites are more and less than human, like Titania and Oberon – just back 'from the farthest steep of India'. But jealous rage transposes the enchanted society of goblins and fairies to the familiar psychological terrain of mortal passions and a staged reality.

*

P How now, spirit! Whither wander you?
F Over hill, over dale,
   thorough bush, thorough brier,
   over park, over pale,
   thorough flood, thorough fire –
   I do wander everywhere,
   swifter than the Moon's sphere,
   and I serve the Fairy Queen . . .
   I must go seek some dewdrops here
   and hang a pearl in every cowslip's ear.
   Farewell, thou lob of spirits, I'll be gone:
   our Queen and all our elves come here anon.

P   The King doth keep his revels here tonight:
      take heed the Queen come not within his sight.
      For Oberon is passing fell and wrath
      because that she as her attendant hath
      a lovely boy stolen from an Indian king:
      she never had so sweet a changeling.
      And jealous Oberon would have the child
      knight of his train, to trace the forests wild.
      But she perforce withholds the loved boy,
      crowns him with flowers and makes him all her joy.
      And now they never meet in grove or green,
      by fountain clear or spangled starlight sheen
      but they do square – that all their elves for fear
      creep into acorn cups and hide them there.

F   Either I mistake your shape and making quite,
      or else you are that shrewd and knavish sprite
      called Robin Goodfellow: are not you he
      that frights the maidens of the villagery,
      skim milk, and sometimes labour in the quern,
      and bootless make the breathless housewife churn,
      and sometime make the drink to bear no barm,
      mislead night-wanderers, laughing at their harm?
      Those that Hobgoblin call you and sweet Puck,
      you do their work, and they shall have good luck:
      are not you he?

P   Thou speakest aright:
      I am that merry wanderer of the night.
      I jest to Oberon and make him smile
      when I a fat and bean-fed horse beguile,
      neighing in likeness of a filly foal.
      And sometime lurk I in a gossip's bowl
      in very likeness of a roasted crab,
      and when she drinks, against her lips I bob
      and on her withered dewlap pour the ale . . .
      But, room, fairy! here comes Oberon.

F   And here my mistress. Would that he were gone!
      (Enter the King of Fairies at one door with his train
      and the Queen at another with hers)

O   Ill met by moonlight, proud Titania!

T   What, jealous Oberon? Fairies, skip hence –
     I have forsworn his bed and company!

O   Tarry, rash wanton: am not I thy lord?

T   Then I must be thy lady, but I know –
     when thou hast stolen away from fairyland
     and in the shape of Corin sat all day,
     playing on pipes of corn and versing love
     to amorous Phillida. Why art thou here,
     come from the farthest steep of India,
     but that, forsooth, the bouncing Amazon –
     your buskinned mistress and your warrior love –
     to Theseus must be wedded, and you come
     to give their bed joy and prosperity?

O   How canst thou thus for shame, Titania,
     glance at my credit with Hippolyta,
     knowing I know thy love to Theseus? . . .

T   These are the forgeries of jealousy!
     And never since the middle summer's spring
     met we on hill, in dale, forest or mead,
     by paved fountain or by rushy brook
     or in the beached margent of the sea
     to dance our ringlets to the whistling wind
     but with thy brawls thou hast disturbed our sport . . .
     The human mortals want their winter cheer:
     no night is now with hymn or carol blessed.
     Therefore the Moon, the governess of floods,
     pale in her anger washes all the air
     that rheumatic diseases do abound.
     And thorough this distemperature we see
     the seasons alter: hoary-headed frosts
     far in the fresh lap of the crimson rose,
     and on old Hiems' thin and icy crown
     an odorous chaplet of sweet summer buds
     is – as in mockery – set: the spring, the summer,
     the childing autumn, angry winter change
     their wonted liveries, and the mazèd world
     by their increase now knows not which is which.
     And this same progeny of evils comes
     from *our* debate, from *our* dissension:

we are their parents and original!

O   Do you amend it then; it lies in you!
Why should Titania cross her Oberon?
I do but beg a little changeling boy,
To be my henchman.

T   Set your heart at rest!
The fairyland buys not the child of me.
His mother was a vot'ress of my order: . . .
but she, being mortal, of that boy did die,
and for her sake do I rear up her boy,
and for her sake I will not part with him.

O   How long within this wood intend you stay?

T   Perchance till after Theseus' wedding day.
If you will patiently dance in our round
and see our moonlight revels, go with us.
If not – shun me, and I will spare your haunts.

O   Give me that boy, and I will go with thee.

T   Not for thy fairy kingdom! Fairies, away!
We shall chide downright if I longer stay.
(Exit Titania with her train)

O   Well, go thy way: thou shalt not from this grove
till I torment thee for this injury.
My gentle Puck, come hither. Thou rememberest
since once I sat upon a promontory
and heard a mermaid on a dolphin's back
uttering such dulcet and harmonious breath
that the rude sea grew civil at her song
and certain stars shot madly from their spheres
to hear the sea-maid's music?

P   I remember.

O   That very time I saw – but thou couldst not –
flying between the cold Moon and the Earth,
Cupid all armed. A certain aim he took
at a fair vestal throned by the West
and loosed his love-shaft smartly from his bow,
as it should pierce a hundred thousand hearts.
But I might see young Cupid's fiery shaft
quenched in the chaste beams of the watery Moon –
and the imperial vot'ress passed on

in maiden meditation, fancy-free –
yet marked I where the bolt of Cupid fell:
it fell upon a little western flower
before milk-white, now purple with love's wound,
and maidens call it *love-in-idleness* . . .
Fetch me this herb, and be thou here again
ere the leviathan can swim a league.

P   I'll put a girdle round about the earth
in forty minutes. *(Exit)*

O   Having once this juice,
I'll watch Titania when she is asleep
and drop the liquor of it in her eyes.
The next thing then she waking looks upon –
be it on lion, bear or wolf or bull,
on meddling monkey or on busy ape –
she shall pursue it with the soul of love.
And ere I take this charm from off her sight,
as I can take it with another herb,
I'll make her render up her page to me.
But who comes here? I am invisible,
and I will overhear their conference.

10.4

A Spirit Too Delicate:
Shakespeare, *The Tempest*, 1.2

As the doting father of a stunning daughter, Prospero (P) is a familiar human figure. Many parents in Shakespeare's audience will have shared his feelings for Miranda (M), who dozes through her father's first conversation with Ariel (A), a spirit of the air who serves Prospero in a different role – the good magus whose power is no less fearsome for being well meant. If Ariel misbehaves, Prospero will 'rend an oak and peg thee in his knotty entrails', putting him back as the kindly wizard had found him – not free to soar but sealed inside a tree by the witch Sycorax, that 'blue-eyed hag'.

*

A   All hail, great master! Grave sir, hail! I come
      to answer thy best pleasure; be't to fly,
      to swim, to dive into the fire, to ride
      on the curled clouds, to thy strong bidding task
      Ariel and all his quality.
P   Hast thou, spirit,
      performed to point the tempest that I bade thee?
A   To every article:
      I boarded the king's ship – now on the beak,
      now in the waist, the deck, in every cabin,
      I flamed amazement. Sometime I'd divide
      and burn in many places: on the topmast,
      the yards and bowsprit, would I flame distinctly,
      then meet and join . . .
P   My brave spirit!
      Who was so firm, so constant, that this coil
      would not infect his reason?

A   Not a soul
but felt a fever of the mad and played
some tricks of desperation . . .

P   But are they, Ariel, safe?

A   Not a hair perished,
on their sustaining garments not a blemish
but fresher than before . . . Safely in harbour
is the king's ship – in the deep nook, where once
thou call'dst me up at midnight to fetch dew
from the still-vexed Bermudas, there she's hid:
the mariners all under hatches stowed,
who, with a charm joined to their suffered labour,
I have left asleep . . .

P   Ariel, thy charge
exactly is performed. But there's more work.
What is the time o' the day?

A   Past the midseason.

P   At least two glasses. The time 'twixt six and now
must by us both be spent most preciously.

A   Is there more toil? Since thou dost give me pains,
let me remember thee what thou hast promised,
which is not yet performed me.

P   How now? Moody?
What is't thou canst demand?

A   My liberty.

P   Before the time be out? No more!

A   I prithee,
remember I have done thee worthy service,
told thee no lies, made no mistakes, served
without or grudge or grumblings. Thou didst promise
to bate me a full year.

P   Dost thou forget
from what a torment I did free thee?

A   No.

P   Thou dost, and think'st it much to tread the ooze
of the salt deep,
to run upon the sharp wind of the North,
to do me business in the veins o' the earth
when it is baked with frost.

A   I do not, sir.
P   Thou liest, malignant thing! Hast thou forgot
      the foul witch Sycorax, who with age and envy
      was grown into a hoop? Hast thou forgot her?
A   No, sir.
P   Thou hast. Where was she born? Speak;
      tell me.
A   Sir, in Argier.
P   O, was she so? I must
      once in a month recount what thou hast been,
      which thou forget'st. This damned witch Sycorax,
      for mischiefs manifold and sorceries terrible
      to enter human hearing, from Argier,
      thou know'st, was banished: for one thing she did
      they would not take her life. Is not this true?
A   Ay, sir.
P   This blue-eyed hag was hither brought with child
      and here was left by th' sailors. Thou, my slave,
      as thou report'st thyself, wast then her servant.
      And, for thou wast a spirit too delicate
      to act her earthy and abhorred commands,
      refusing her grand hests, she did confine thee –
      by help of her more potent ministers
      and in her most unmitigable rage –
      into a cloven pine, within which rift
      imprisoned thou didst painfully remain
      a dozen years, within which space she died
      and left thee there, where thou didst vent thy groans . . .
      [to] make wolves howl and penetrate the breasts
      of ever angry bears. It was a torment
      to lay upon the damned, which Sycorax
      could not again undo. It was mine art,
      when I arrived and heard thee, that made gape
      the pine and let thee out.
A   I thank thee, master!
P   If thou more murmurest, I will rend an oak
      and peg thee in his knotty entrails till
      thou hast howled away twelve winters.
A   Pardon, master:

I will be correspondent to command
and do my spiriting gently.

P   Do so, and after two days
I will discharge thee.

A   That's my noble master!
What shall I do? Say what? What shall I do?

P   Go make thyself like a nymph o' the sea. Be subject
to no sight but thine and mine, invisible
to every eyeball else. Go take this shape
and hither come in't: go, hence with diligence!

10.5

The Simple Idiot Should Not Learn It: Jonson, *The Alchemist*, 2.2

The Alchemist was first performed in 1610, when Ben Jonson was in his late thirties and already famous. Although he had no university education, his learning was prodigious – including the details of alchemical technique and terminology that supply much of the play's humour. Jonson took his information not only from digests like the *Rose Garden of Philosophers* but also from standard authorities like Geber (7.15; 9.5). Subtle (Sb) is a con-man who puts on a good alchemical show, not least in the rapid-fire orders he gives to his servant, Face (Fa) – transmuted into Ulen Spiegel, a sorcerer's apprentice who can talk a good game. The two of them play Sir Epicure Mammon (Ma) like a fiddle, but his friend Surly (Sr) will not be duped. 'What else are all your terms,' he asks, 'whereon no one of your writers 'grees with other?' The empty language that Surly exposes is fuel for Jonson's comedy.

*

Ma Good morrow, father.
Sb   Gentle son, good morrow,
      and to your friend there: what is he, is with you?
Ma An heretic that I did bring along
      in hope, sir, to convert him . . .
      You shall not need to fear me. I but come
      To ha' you confute this gentleman.
Sr   Who is,
      indeed, sir, somewhat costive of belief
      towards your stone – would not be gulled.
Sb Well, son,
      all that I can convince him in, is this –
      the work is done! Bright Sol is in his robe.
      We have a med'cine of the triple soul,
      the glorified spirit. Thanks be to heaven,

and make us worthy of it! *[calls Face]* Ulen Spiegel!

Fa *[within]* Anon, sir. *[enters]*

Sb   Look well to the register,
and let your heat still lessen by degrees
to the aludels.

Fa   Yes, sir!

Sb   Did you look
on the bolt's-head yet?

Fa   Which? On *D*, sir?

Sb   Ay.
What's the complexion?

Fa   Whitish . . .

Sr *[aside]* What a brave language here is! Next to canting! . . .

Fa   Sir, please you,
shall I not change the filter?

Sb   Marry, yes!
And bring me the complexion of glass *B*. *[exit Face]*

Ma Ha' you another?

Sb   Yes, son; were I assured
your piety were firm, we would not want
the means to glorify it. But I hope the best:
I mean to tinct *C* in sand-heat tomorrow
and give him imbibition.

Ma   Of white oil?

Sb No, sir, of red. *F* is come over the helm too –
I thank my Maker – in St Mary's bath
and shews *lac virginis*. Blessed be heaven!
I sent you of his faeces there, calcined:
out of that calx, I ha' won the salt of mercury!

Ma By pouring on your rectified water?

Sb Yes, and reverberating in Athanor. *[enter Face]*
How now! What colour says it?

Fa   The ground black, sir.

Ma That's your crow's head?

Sr *[aside]*   Your cockscombs, is it not?

Sb No, 'tis not perfect: would it were the crow!
That work wants something . . .
We should have a new amalgama.

Sr *[aside]*   O this ferret is rank as any pole-cat

Sb   But I care not:
let him e'en die, we have enough beside
in embrion. *H* has his white shirt on?
Fa   Yes, sir,
He's ripe for inceration, he stands warm . . .
Sb   Ha' you set the oil of Luna in kemia?
Fa   Yes, sir.
Sb   And the philosopher's vinegar?
Fa   Ay. *[exit]*
Sr   *[aside]* We shall have a salad!
Ma   When do you make projection?
Sb   Son, be not hasty, I exalt our med'cine
by hanging him in *balneo vaporoso*
and giving him solution, then congeal him
and then dissolve him, then again congeal him –
for look, how oft I iterate the work,
so many times I add unto his virtue.
As, if at first one ounce convert a hundred,
after his second loose, he'll turn a thousand,
his third solution, ten, his fourth, a hundred.
After his fifth, a thousand thousand ounces
of any imperfect metal into pure
silver or gold, in all examinations
as good as any of the natural mine.
Get you your stuff here against afternoon –
your brass, your pewter, and your andirons.
Ma   Not those of iron?
Sb   Yes, you may bring them too:
We'll change all metals.
Sr   *[aside]*   I believe you in that.
Ma   Then I may send my spits?
Sb   Yes, and your racks.
Sr   And dripping-pans and pot-hangers and hooks –
Shall he not?
Sb   If he please –
Sr   – to be an ass.
Sb   How, sir!
Ma   This gentleman you must bear withal:
I told you he had no faith.

Sr   And little hope, sir,
but much less charity should I gull myself.

Sb Why, what have you observed, sir, in our art
seems so impossible?

Sr   But your whole work, no more:
that you should hatch gold in a furnace, sir,
as they do eggs in Egypt! . . .

Sb Marry, we say – *[Mammon interrupts]*

Ma   Ay, now it heats: stand, father,
pound him to dust –

Sb   It is, of the one part,
a humid exhalation, which we call
materia liquida or the unctuous water,
on th'other part a certain crass and vicious
portion of earth, both which – concorporate –
do make the elementary matter of gold,
which is not yet *propria materia*
but common to all metals and all stones.
For where it is forsaken of that moisture
and hath more dryness, it becomes a stone.
Where it retains more of the humid fatness,
it turns to sulphur or to quicksilver,
who are the parents of all other metals.
Nor can this remote matter suddenly
progress so from extreme unto extreme
as to grow gold and leap o'er all the means.
Nature doth first beget th'imperfect, then
proceeds she to the perfect. Of that airy
and oily water, mercury is engend'red,
sulphur o' the fat and earthy part; . . .
     But these two
make the rest ductile, malleable, extensive.
And even in gold they are: for we do find
seeds of them, by our fire, and gold in them,
and can produce the species of each metal
more perfect thence than nature doth in earth . . .

Ma   Well said, father! *[turns to Surly]*
Nay, if he take you in hand, sir, with an argument,
He'll bray you in a mortar.

Sr   Pray you, sir, stay.
Rather than I'll be brayed, sir, I'll believe
that alchemy is a pretty kind of game,
somewhat like tricks o' the cards – to cheat a man
with charming.

Sb   Sir?

Sr   What else are all your terms
whereon no one of your writers 'grees with other?
Of your elixir, your *lac virginis*,
your stone, your med'cine and your chrysosperm,
your sal, your sulphur and your mercury,
your oil of height, your tree of life, your blood,
your marchesite, your tutie, your magnesia,
your toad, your crow, your dragon and your panther,
your sun, your moon, your firmament, your adrop,
your lato, azoch, zernich, chibrit, heautarit,
and then your red man and your white woman,
with all your broths, your menstrues and materials,
of piss and eggshells, women's terms, man's blood,
hair o' the head, burnt clouts, chalk, merds and clay,
powder of bones, scalings of iron, glass
and worlds of other strange ingredients
would burst a man to name?

Sb   And all these named,
intending but one thing, which art our writers
used to obscure their art.

Ma   Sir, so I told him:
because the simple idiot should not learn it
and make it vulgar.

Sb   Was not all the knowledge
of the Egyptians writ in mystic symbols?
Speak not the scriptures oft in parables?
Are not the choicest fables of the poets
that were the fountains and first springs of wisdom
wrapped in perplexed allegories?

Ma   I urged that
and cleared to him that Sisyphus was damned
to roll the ceaseless stone only because
he would have made ours common.

10.6

Fake Magic Goes to College:
Mewe, *False Magic*, 3.6–7

When William Mewe wrote this play in Latin verse around 1627, he was finishing his career as a student at Emmanuel College, Cambridge, where the play – not printed in Mewe's time – would have been performed (if it was performed) by the College's students and faculty. As dramatic literature, Mewe's amateur effort is nothing like Jonson's inspired comedy. But the play's cast and audience – students and teachers of a great university – were well placed to help settle the fate of magic by laughing at it. Four characters – Dorinda, Otho, Serastus and Viraldus – close the third act of *Pseudomagia*, which borrows its haunted house device from Plautus (see 4.8). Dorinda (D) is the daughter of the house's owner – Viraldus, brother of Alonzo, Duke of Mantua. Serastus (S) is his elder and wayward son. A fake funeral for Viraldus has opened the play: Serastus thinks that his mother killed the old man, but she has deceived her son in order to reform him. Her plot relies on Otho (O) – dressed as a Persian wizard but really Viraldus in disguise – who colludes with Dorinda to dupe Serastus, who has just finished talking to a servant as he enters.

*

S You go ahead with Galhispanglo, while I enjoy myself here alone. Just wait for me a little while at Ossecaster's place. [*sees Otho chanting a spell*]

O Lords of twelve houses, each with his sign,
  day's Cavalier and Saturn malign
  armed with a sickle, and all you ascendants,
  gods who protect us, and potent descendants,
  images here of inferior things
  beckon you into my magical rings.

S God help me! I'm afraid he's conjuring! May the gods smile upon you and your work, reverend Magus.

O Away from here now, spectral hosts,
  hungry goblins, ghouls and ghosts:

> let every horror flee from here
> and every terror vanish clear!
> And you, light wraith, whose foot stands fixed
> in the depths of distant Styx,
> Viraldus – chastened by my wand,
> slip back beneath Hell's dismal pond.

S   Please, reverend sir, I don't want to bother you.

O   Oh, the worthy Serastus! Hello! How are you? Still not feeling well?

S   You're the right person to answer that question: how I'm doing is up to you. So tell me – have you driven the ghosts and spirits from the house? The spirit of Viraldus rests in peace, right?

O   Trust me. I've sent him away to Hell's farthest limits and tied him up there like Prometheus in the Caucasus.

S   How happy you've made me, worthy sir! If just one more thing turns out well for me now, I can't imagine what could make me happier. How is Dorinda? Still lovelier than the goddess Diana?

O   That's for you to say, Serastus. I'm no expert in the art of love: my vigour ages with my body, and I've long since said good-bye to such amusements.

S   But what's on her mind? Tell me. What does she want? She'll give me a royal welcome, won't she? Gladly? Graciously?

O   My God, boy, not a chance! She has no happy thoughts, and she has exiled herself from joy. Her father's recent death keeps hovering before her eyes. Every day it's him she listens for, staying up all night weeping and wailing – very obvious signs of grief.

S   Tokens of love too?

O   Well, maybe. *[aside]* I need to build up his hopes. *[to Serastus]* Her grief was sudden: it will weaken every day and pass quickly.

S   I hope so!

O   Her sadness is just so much smoke, trust me. *[scoffing]* These women have their tears down to a T. Just touch an eye with a fingertip, and out they come.

S   Don't talk that way about Dorinda!

O   Why not? They all drink these tricks in with the mother's milk. But I'll go get her for you . . . *[Otho exits and Dorinda enters, fending Serastus off in conversation]*

S   Please, forget your father's death! Let Janus take care of what's behind you, while you look out for what's in front – the future . . . Enjoy my bondage to you, along with anything else I can offer for your love. My heart is in danger, and my tongue is thick: what do you say?

[Viraldus – dressed as a ghost, armed with a sword and carrying a torch – enters behind Serastus] What? Why don't you say something? Is being called 'Duchess' too shabby for you?

D   I heard what you've just said, but I'll reverse it: better keep an eye on what's behind you, not just what's in front.

S   *[turns and sees the ghost]* Oh my God! What can I do? Hurry up, Otho, please, or I'm done for – ruined for ever!

D   Stop! Don't run! Don't you see how he threatens you – how scary he is? Run and you're in trouble!

S   What do you want, unhappy ghost? What brings you back to this upper world? Oh me, oh my! Weren't we careful to give you a fine funeral? Maybe you'd like a procession? Something more splendid for a tomb? Or would you prefer that we dedicate a shrine or temple to you? I'll see to both – big ones – right away . . . Not enough? I'm done for! What can I do? Ah, my penance is too light, and that's a fact. Your threats are real, I see it now – like the avenging torches that you're waving in front of my face . . . I've hurt you too much, uncle Viraldus. Wretch that I am, I made you die before your time . . . *[opens his shirt]* Go ahead, then! Your victim is ready, and my heart is a sacrifice on your altar . . . *[exit Viraldus]* What? You won't even grant me the punishment that I deserve? . . . *[turns to Dorinda]* Please, give me just one last kiss . . . Now good-bye, good-bye forever! I give my word that I'll be celibate for ever for your sake.

D   Careful with the swearing: watch the perjury.

S   My oath is sacred – unless there's something else you want. Good-bye!

D   Good-bye, good-bye. *(exit Serastus)* Good God! If you weren't so pitiful, I'd laugh at you.

A Summons to Pandaemonium: Milton, *Paradise Lost*, 1.253–798

When Mewe was finishing his studies at Cambridge, John Milton was starting out and stayed in the university until 1632. Twenty-six years later, when he began work on *Paradise Lost*, the poet had lost his sight entirely, which may help explain the enormous visual power of his masterpiece and its stunning evocation of place. Pandaemonium, at the hub of hell, is psychologically immense but physically confined: only the mightiest of the fallen angels – some of them named by Milton – remain 'in their own dimensions'. The rest have shrunk, as befits their moral stature. But Satan is in all ways larger than life – an epic character and a dramatic anti-hero whose thundering addresses to the demons are Shakespearean in theatrical force. Although oratory is their form, Satan's speeches penetrate psychologically like Shakespeare's soliloquies: their author had learned the art of tragedy from *Hamlet*, *Macbeth*, *Othello* and *Lear*. Milton's Satan is terrifyingly real, nothing like the false wizards and fake spooks of the comic *Pseudomagia*.

*

'The mind is its own place, and in itself
can make a Heav'n of Hell, a Hell of Heav'n.
What matter where, if I be still the same,
and what I should be, all but less then He
whom thunder hath made greater? Here at least
we shall be free: th'Almighty hath not built
here for his envy, will not drive us hence.
Here we may reign secure, and in my choice
to reign is worth ambition though in Hell –
better to reign in Hell than serve in Heav'n.' . . .
So Satan spake, and him Beelzebub
thus answer'd: 'Leader of those armies bright,
which but th'Omnipotent none could have foiled,

if once they hear that voice . . .
                          they will soon resume
new courage and revive, though now they lie
grovelling and prostrate on yon lake of fire.' . . .
[Then Satan] call'd so loud, that all the hollow deep
of Hell resounded: 'Princes, potentates,
warriors, the flow'r of Heav'n – once yours, now lost –
awake, arise or be for ever fall'n.'
They heard and were abashed and up they sprung . . .
[and] to their general's voice they soon obeyed
innumerable . . .
So numberless were those bad Angels seen
hovering on wing under the cope of Hell,
'twixt upper, nether, and surrounding fires,
till, as a signal giv'n, th'uplifted spear
of their great Sultan waving to direct
their course, in even balance down they light
on the firm brimstone and fill all the plain –
a multitude . . .
Forthwith from every squadron and each band
the heads and leaders thither haste where stood
their great commander: godlike shapes and forms
excelling human, princely dignities
and powers that erst in Heav'n sat on thrones –
though of their names in heav'nly records now
be no memorial, blotted out and razed
by their rebellion from the Books of Life . . .
Then were they known to men by various names,
and various idols through the heathen world . . .
The chief were those who from the pit of Hell,
roaming to seek their prey on earth, durst fix
their seats long after next the seat of God,
their altars by his altar, gods adored
among the nations round, and durst abide
Jehovah thund'ring out of Sion, throned
between the Cherubim: yea, often placed
within his sanctuary itself their shrines –
abominations – and with cursed things
his holy rites and solemn feasts profaned,

and with their darkness durst affront his light.
First Moloch, horrid King besmeared with blood
of human sacrifice and parents' tears . . .
Next Chemos, th'obscene dread of Moab's sons . . .
Peor his other Name, when he enticed
Israel in Sittim on their march from Nile
to do him wanton rites, which cost them woe.
                              . . . with these in troop
came Astoreth, whom the Phoenicians called Astarte,
queen of Heav'n, with crescent horns,
to whose bright image nightly by the Moon
Sidonian virgins paid their vows and songs . . .
to idols foul. Thammuz came next behind,
whose annual wound in Lebanon allured
the Syrian damsels to lament his fate
in amorous ditties all a summer's day,
while smooth Adonis from his native rock
ran purple to the sea, supposed with blood
of Thammuz yearly wounded: the love-tale
infected Sion's daughters with like heat . . .
                              After these appeared
a crew who under names of old renown –
Osiris, Isis, Orus and their train –
with monstrous shapes and sorceries abused
fanatic Egypt and her priests to seek
their wand'ring gods disguis'd in brutish forms . . .
Belial came last, than whom a spirit more lewd
fell not from Heav'n, or more gross to love
vice for it self . . .
All these and more came flocking, but with looks
downcast and damp, yet such wherein appeared
obscure some glimpse of joy to have found their chief
not in despair, to have found themselves not lost
in loss it self – which on his count'nance cast
like doubtful hue. But he, his wonted pride
soon recollecting, with high words that bore
semblance of worth, not substance, gently raised
their fainted courage and dispelled their fears,

then strait commands that at the warlike sound
of trumpets loud and clarions be upreared
his mighty standard. That proud honour claimed
Azazel as his right, a Cherub tall,
who forthwith from the glittering staff unfurled
th'imperial ensign . . . ,
at which the universal host upsent,
a shout that tore Hell's concave, and beyond
frighted the reign of Chaos and old Night . . .
Advanced in view they stand, a horrid front
of dreadful length and dazling arms, in guise
of warriors old with ordered spear and shield,
awaiting what command their mighty chief
had to impose . . .
               And now his heart
distends with pride, and, hard'ning in his strength,
glories . . .
               He above the rest
in shape and gesture proudly eminent
stood like a tow'r; his form had yet not lost
all her original brightness nor appeared
less than Archangel ruined . . .
               But his face
deep scars of thunder had intrenched, and care
sat on his faded cheek, but under brows
of dauntless courage and considerate pride
waiting revenge. Cruel his eye, but cast
signs of remorse and passion to behold
the fellows of his crime, the followers rather
(far other once beheld in bliss), condemned
for ever now to have their lot in pain,
millions of Spirits for his fault amerced
of Heav'n, and from eternal splendors flung
for his revolt, yet faithful how they stood,
their glory withered . . .
               He now prepared
to speak, whereat their doubled ranks they bend
from wing to wing and half enclose him round

with all his peers. Attention held them mute.
Thrice he assayed, and thrice in spite of scorn,
tears such as angels weep burst forth. At last
words interwove with sighs found out their way:
'O myriads of immortal spirits, O powers
matchless – but with th'Almighty, and that strife
was not inglorious, though th'event was dire –
. . . this infernal pit shall never hold
celestial spirits in bondage, nor th'abyss
long under darkness cover. But these thoughts
full counsel must mature: peace is despaired,
for who can think submission? War then, war
open or understood, must be resolved.'
He spake: and to confirm his words, out flew
millions of flaming swords, drawn from the thighs
of mighty Cherubim. The sudden blaze
far round illumined Hell. Highly they raged
against the Highest, and fierce with graspèd arms
clashed on their sounding shields the din of war,
hurling defiance towards the vault of Heav'n . . .
Meanwhile the wingèd heralds by command
of sovran power, with awful ceremony
and trumpet's sound throughout the host proclaim
a solemn council forthwith to be held
at Pandaemonium, the high capital
of Satan and his peers. Their summons called,
from every band and squarèd regiment
by place or choice the worthiest, they anon
with hundreds and with thousands trooping came
attended . . .
thick swarmed, both on the ground and in the air,
brushed with the hiss of rustling wings, as bees
in springtime, when the Sun with Taurus rides,
pour forth their populous youth about the hive . . .
thus incorporeal spirits to smallest forms
reduced their shapes immense, and were at large,
though without number still, amidst the hall
of that infernal court. But far within,
and in their own dimensions like themselves,

the great Seraphic Lords and Cherubim
in close recess and secret conclave sat –
a thousand demi-gods on golden seats,
frequent and full. After short silence then
and summons read, the great consult began.

10.8

Peccant Humours:
Molière, *The Doctor In Spite of Himself*,
2.4

Pre-modern medicine – like medicine today – relied on the standard science of the time, and magic did the same. Also, in pre-modern texts like Ficino's *Three Books on Life*, where medicine stops and magic starts is often hard to say (8.4–13). And so, when Aristotelian science – or 'natural philosophy', to use the contemporary term – lost credibility after the Middle Ages, the loss did collateral damage to medicine and magic. Molière made comedy out of the wreckage: the absurdity of empty language – medical double-talk especially – is a favourite in his plays. The wood-cutter Sganarelle (S) is a drunk, a glutton and a doctor despite himself, cudgelled (literally) into that role by his wife's trickery. His assignment is to make the speechless Lucinde (L) speak again, though the girl's failure to communicate is tactical (to avoid a marriage) – not physical. Lucinde's father, Geronte (G), is a gullible fool, whom Sganarelle enjoys duping.

*

S *(pointing to Lucinde)* Is this the patient?

G Yes. I have just the one daughter, and if she were to die, I'd be the saddest person in the world.

S Careful then: she can't die except on doctor's orders . . . *(turns to Lucinde)* What seems to be the problem? What's bothering you? Are you feeling bad?

L *(points to her mouth, her head and under her chin)* Anh, ee, onh, anh.

S What's that you say?

L Anh, ee, onh, anh, anh, ee, onh.

S What?

L Anh, ee, onh.

S Anh, ee, onh, anh, anh. I don't get it. What kind of talk is that?

G   That's what's wrong with her, sir: she's turned mute, and so far no one can say why . . . We're asking you to try everything you can to relieve her illness . . .

S   *(turns to Lucinde)* Give me your arm. *(to Geronte)* Your daughter's pulse indicates that she's mute.

G   Why yes, you're right, sir. That's her ailment. You've hit it instantly! . . .

S   We great physicians know what's wrong right away. An uninformed person would have had trouble, telling you 'it's this', then 'it's that'. But me – I go straight to it and let you know that your daughter is mute.

G   Right! But could you please tell me where the problem comes from?

S   Nothing simpler: it comes from her losing speech.

G   Exactly. But please, what's the cause of her losing speech?

S   All the leading authorities will tell you that the action of her tongue is blocked.

G   Then what are your views on tongue blockage?

S   Aristotle makes some quite nice comments about it.

G   Yes, I think he does.

S   A great man – truly!

G   No question.

S   A really great man in every way – much better than me all around. *(gesturing)* But to get back to our consultation, I find that this blockage of the tongue has been caused by certain humours that we experts call 'peccant': *peccant*, meaning that these humours are of the 'peccant' type, especially since vapours formed by exhalations of influences arising in the affected region and, so to speak – do you understand Latin?

G   Not a word.

S   You don't know any Latin at all?

G   None.

S   *(excited) Cabricias arci thuram, catalamus, singulariter nominativo, haec musa* – the muse – *bonus, bona, bonum. Deus sanctus, estne oratio latinas? Etiam*, yes. *Quare*, why? *Quia substantio et adjectivum concordat in generi, numerum et casus.*

G   If only I had studied! . . .

S   Now these vapours that I'm talking about come from the left side, where the liver is, and pass to the right side, where the heart is located and the lungs (called *armyan* in Latin) are found, communicating with the brain (*nasmus* is the Greek name we give it) by way of the hollow vein that we call *cubile* in Hebrew, and on their way they meet those same vapours as they fill the ventricles of the omoplate, and because those vapours – please follow my reasoning – and because those vapours are in some way malignant – pay close attention, now, please –

G   I will.

S   – because they're in some way malignant, which is caused – now listen

G   I'm listening!

S   – which is caused by the acridity of the humours produced in the diaphragm's concavity, the result is that the vapours – *ossabundus, nequeis, nequer, potarinum, quipsa milus*. And that's exactly what makes your daughter mute! . . .

G   No reasoning could be finer, beyond a doubt. Just one thing jolted me – the location of the liver and heart. It seems you've put them where they don't belong, since the heart is on the left side and the liver on the right.

S   Yes: that's how it used to be. But we've changed all that, and now we have a brand new method for practising medicine.

G   I didn't know. Please forgive my ignorance . . . But tell me, sir, what do you think should be done about this illness?

S   What should be done?

G   Right.

S   My advice is to put her to bed and have her take a good bit of bread drenched in wine.

G   Why do that, sir?

S   Because in the bread and wine, when they are mixed together, there is a sympathetic virtue productive of speech. Don't you know that this is just what people give to parakeets who learn to talk by eating it?

G   That's true! What a great man! Quick – bring on the bread and wine!

10.9
A Virtue Dormitive:
Molière, *The Imaginary Invalid*, finale

Although Molière collapsed during a performance of *The Imaginary Invalid* in 1673 and died a few hours later, his play had already given the history of magic (and science) its best joke – about opium's dormitive virtue. Like Sganarelle's 'sympathetic virtue productive of speech', this flagrant display of vacuous verbiage aims to replace real enquiry into the causes of opium's effects (see 10.8). But it fails – thus making a mockery of the 'occult properties' that shored up so many theories of magic (see 7.10; 9.4). The play's polyglot finale is a song-and-dance send-up of the granting of a medical diploma: think of a scene, mainly in mock-Latin, by Gilbert and Sullivan – but with a French accent. Before quizzing a candidate, the faculty gather to wish themselves health, wealth and good appetite, as indicated by Molière's very full stage-direction.

*

THIRD INTERMEZZO

(This is a burlesque – with recitative, singing and dancing – of a ceremony to confer a medical degree. In step with the music, several assistants march on stage, decorate the hall and place the benches. Then the whole group enters and all take their places: eight carry huge enema-syringes; next come six apothecaries and twenty-two professors – accompanying the person to be accepted as a physician – and then eight surgeons dancing with two singing.)

MASTER OF CEREMONIES

Teachers most sage,
doctors on stage,
gathered here to vote and pass –
you experts on drugging

and enema-lugging –
the wishes of the *facult-ass*,
to all: good health;
to each: much wealth;
and don't forget *bon appetit*!

Che bella cosa – medicine!
It's *ben trovata* where we've been!
What a fine *inventio*
our medical *professio*! . . .

Always racing for our cures,
the whole big *tout le monde* adores
us as the gods of healing –
kings and princes fall down kneeling.
In light of that, let's *conservare* –
that's our goal, our *travaillare*:
for us to keep what we have got,
communis sensus says we ought.

So when we think about admitting,
we'd better see whom we'll be getting –
a candidate *capabilis*
to keep us *honorabilis*.

For that task, I've called you here,
and I'm sure you'll find it clear
that our candidate's *perfectum* –
he'll say nothing *incorrectum*.
There's nothing more to make you wait.
So go ahead: interrogate!

THE FIRST TEACHER

If you will, Lord High Headmaster,
and please, my *confrères* medical –
you sages of the sticking plaster –
please find my words acceptable.
I have a question that won't keep:
why does opium makes us sleep?

CANDIDATE

Why opium makes us sleep, you ask me:
that's how you test me, how you task me,
doctor most *doctissimus*!

So to your quiz
my answer is
a VIRTUE DORMITIVE,
whose nature is
to soften up the senses.

CHORUS

Good, good, good! Oh great! Oh good!
That's how to answer, how one should!
He's done so well, he'll now *entrare*
within our club *familiare*!

10.10

A Cunning Man, Hight Sidrophel: Butler, *Hudibras*, 2.3

Samuel Butler turned thirty in 1642, not long after civil war broke out in England; Oliver Cromwell's rule was ending when he started *Hudibras* around 1658. Hudibras, a Presbyterian Quixote, takes his name from a knight in the *Faerie Queene* who 'reason with fool-hardize overran'. He follows the 'peevish, cross . . . sect whose chief devotion lies in odd perverse antipathies' – the Puritan rigorists who had kept Britain bloody for much of the poet's adult life. Ralph, the knight's squire, is appalled by that desiccated religion and opposes his master's rigidity in Church government. For a happier way, he turns to theosophy:

> For mystick learning wondrous able
> in magick, talisman and cabal . . .
> he Anthroposophus and Floud
> and Jacob Behmen understood . . .
> in Rosy-crucian lore as learned
> as he that *vere adeptus* earned.

A 'true adept' in alchemy, Ralpho takes his lead from Fludd, Vaughan and the Rosicrucians (see 11.2, 8, 10). When Hudibras flops – as usual – with the widow whom he tries to court, Ralph wants to consult 'Sidrophel, the Rosy-crucian', who also has a sidekick – Whachum. Sorcerer's apprentice and ghostwriter for Sidrophel's astrological pamphlets, Whachum is second banana in the wizard's con-games, which ignite the brawl that closes this part of the poem.

*

> Quoth Ralph: 'Not far from hence doth dwell
> a cunning man, hight Sidrophel,
> that deals in destinies dark counsels

and sage opinions of the Moon sells,
to whom all people far and near
on deep importances repair.
When brass and pewter hap to stray,
and linnen slinks out of the way . . .
when yeast and outward means do fail
and have no pow'r to work on ale,
when butter does refuse to come
and love proves cross and humoursome:
to him with questions and with urine
they for discov'ry flock – or curing.'

Quoth Hudibras: 'This Sidrophel
I've heard of and should like it well
if thou canst prove the Saints have freedom
To go to sorc'rers when they need 'em.'

Says Ralpho: 'There's no doubt of that.
Those principles I quoted late
prove that the Godly may alledge
for any thing their priviledge
and to the Dev'l himself may go
if they have motives thereunto . . .

Has not this present Parliament
a ledger to the Devil sent,
fully impowr'd to treat about
finding revolted witches out?
And has not he, within a year,
hang'd threescore of 'em in one shire? . . .

Did not the Devil appear to Martin
Luther in Germany for certain,
and wou'd have gull'd him with a trick
but Martin was too politick . . .
appear in divers shapes to Kelly,
and speak i' th' nun of Louduns belly? . . .
Do not our great Reformers use

this Sidrophel to foreboad news,
to write of victories next year,
and castles taken yet i' th' air?' . . .

Quoth Hudibras: 'The case is clear –
the Saints may 'mploy a conjurer,
as thou hast prov'd it by their practice.
No argument like matter of fact is,
and we are best of all led to
mens principles by what they do.
Then let us strait advance in quest
of this profound gymnosophist,
and – as the Fates and he advise –
pursue or wave this enterprise.'

This said, he turn'd about his steed,
And forthwith on th' adventure rid,
where leave we him and Ralph a while
And to the conjurer turn our stile . . .

He had been long t'wards mathematicks,
optics, philosophy and staticks,
magick, horoscopy, astrologie,
and was old dog at physiologie . . .
So in the circle of the arts
did he advance his nat'ral parts
till falling back still, for retreat
he fell to juggle, cant and cheat.
For as those fowls that live in water
are never wet, he did but smatter . . .

H' had read Dee's *Prefaces* before
the Dev'l, and Euclide o're and o're,
and all the intregues 'twixt him and Kelly,
Lescus and th' Emperor wou'd tell ye.
But with the Moon was more familiar
than e'er was almanack well-willer.
Her secrets understood so clear
that some believ'd he had been there,

knew when she was in the fittest mood
for cutting corns or letting blood,
when for anointing scabs or itches
or to the bum applying leeches . . .

He made a planetary gin
which rats would run their own heads in
and come of purpose to be taken
without th' expence of cheese or bacon.
With lute-strings he would counterfeit
maggots that crawl on dish of meat . . .
detect lost maiden-heads by sneezing,
or breaking wind of dames or pissing,
cure warts and corns with application
of med'cines to th' imagination . . .
He knew whats'ever's to be known,
but much more than he knew would own:
what med'cine 'twas that Paracelsus
could make a man with, as he tells us . . .

A paultry wretch he had, half-starv'd,
that him in place of zany serv'd,
hight Whachum, bred to dash and draw
not wine but more unwholesome law,
to make 'twixt words and lines huge gaps,
wide as meridians in maps,
to squander paper and spare ink
and cheat men of their words – some think.
From this by merited degrees
he'd to more high advancement rise,
to be an under-conjurer
or a journeyman astrologer.

His bus'ness was to pump and wheedle,
and men with their own keys unriddle,
and make them to themselves give answers
for which they pay the necromancers,
to fetch and carry intelligence
of whom and what and where and whence,

and all discoveries disperse
among th' whole pack of conjurers . . .
Beside all this, he serv'd his master
in quality of poetaster
and rimes appropriate could make
to ev'ry month i' th almanack . . .

And as in prisons mean rogues beat
hemp for the service of the great,
so Whachum beats his dirty brains
t' advance his master's fame and gains,
and, like the Devil's oracles,
put into dogrel-rimes his spells
which, over ev'ry month's blank page
i' th' almanack strange bilks presage.
He would an elegy compose
on maggots squeez'd out of his nose . . .

Those two together long had liv'd
in mansion prudently contriv'd,
where neither tree nor house could bar
the free detection of a star.
And nigh an ancient obelisk
was rais'd by him, found out by Fisk,
on which was written – not in words,
but hieroglyphic mute of birds –
many rare pithy saws concerning
the worth of astrologick learning.
From top of this there hung a rope
to which he fasten'd telescope,
the spectacles with which the stars
he reads in smallest characters . . .

This feat fell out not long before
the Knight, upon the forenam'd score
in quest of Sidrophel advancing,
was now in prospect of the mansion,
whom he discov'ring, turn'd his glass
and found far off – 'twas Hudibras.

'Whachum,' quoth he, 'look yonder: some
to try or use our art are come.
The one's the learned Knight. Seek out
and pump 'em what they come about.'

Whachum advanc'd, with all submissness
t'accost 'em but much more their bus'ness . . .
He ask'd them whence they came, and whither
their bus'ness lay. Quoth Ralpho, 'hither.'
'Did you not lose . . . ?' Quoth Ralpho, 'nay.'
Quoth Whachum: 'Sir, I meant your way.'

'Yon Knight,' quoth Ralpho, 'is a lover,
and pains intolerable doth suffer:
for lovers' hearts are not their own hearts,
nor lights nor lungs . . . and so forth downwards.'
'What time?' Quoth Ralpho, 'Sir, too long:
three years it off and on has hung.'
Quoth he, 'I meant what time o' the day 'tis.'
Quoth Ralpho: 'Between seven and eight 'tis.'
'Why then,' quoth Whachum, 'my small art
tells me, the dame has a hard heart
or great estate.' Quoth Ralph: 'A joynter,
which makes him have so hot a mind t'her.'

Meanwhile the Knight was making water
before he fell upon the matter.
Which having done, the Wizard steps in
to give him suitable reception,
but kept his bus'ness at a bay
till Whachum put him in the way,
who having now, by Ralpho's light,
expounded th' errand of the Knight
and what he came to know, drew near
to whisper in the conj'rer's ear . . .

Quoth Hudibras: 'If I appear
unseasonable in coming here
at such a time to interrupt
your speculations, which I hop'd
assistance from and come to use,
'tis fit that I ask your excuse.'
'By no means, Sir,' quoth Sidrophel.
'The stars your coming did foretell:
I did expect you here and knew
before you spake your bus'ness too.'
Quoth Hudibras: 'Make that appear,
and I shall credit whatsoe're
you tell me after on your word,
howe're unlikely or absurd.'

'You are in love, Sir, with a widow,'
quoth he, 'that does not greatly heed you,
and for three years has rid your wit
and passion without drawing bit.
And now your bus'ness is to know
if you shall carry her – or no.'

Quoth Hudibras: 'You're in the right!
But how the Devil you came by't
I can't imagine. For the stars,
I'm sure, can tell no more than a horse . . .
But if the Devil's of your counsel,
much may be done, my noble Donzel.
And 'tis on his accompt I come
to know from you my fatal doom.'

Quoth Sidrophel: 'If you suppose,
Sir Knight, that I am one of those,
I might suspect and take the alarm
your bus'ness is but to inform.
But if it be, 'tis ne'er the near:
you have a wrong sow by the ear.
For I assure you, for my part,

I only deal by rules of art
such as are lawful, and judge by
conclusions of astrology.
But for the Dev'l, know nothing by him,
but only this, that I defy him.'

Quoth he: 'Whatever others deem ye,
I understand your metonymie,
your words of second-hand intention
when things by wrongful names you mention,
the mystick sense of all your terms
that are indeed but magick charms
to raise the Devil and mean one thing,
and that is down-right conjuring –
and in itself more warrantable
than cheat or canting to a rabble,
or putting tricks upon the Moon
which by confed'racy are done . . .
The Rosy-crucian way's more sure
to bring the Devil to the lure.
Each of 'em has a sev'ral gin
to catch intelligences in . . .
Bumbastus kept a Devil's bird
shut in the pummel of his sword
that taught him all the cunning pranks
of past and future mountebanks.
Kelly did all his feats upon
the Devil's looking-glass, a stone,
where playing with him at bo-peep,
he solv'd all problems ne'er so deep.
Agrippa kept a Stygian pug
i' th' garb and habit of a dog
that was his tutor, and the cur
read to th' occult philosopher,
and taught him subt'ly to maintain
all other sciences are vain.'

To this, quoth Sidrophello: 'Sir,
Agrippa was no conjurer,
nor Paracelsus, no, nor Behman,
nor was the dog a cacodaemon . . .
As for the Rosie-cross philosophers
whom you will have to be but sorcerers,
what they pretend to is no more
than Trismegistus did before,
Pythagoras, old Zoroaster,
and Apollonius their master,
to whom they do confess they owe
all that they do and all they know.'

Quoth Hudibras: 'Alas! What is't to us
whether 'twere said by Trismegistus
if it be nonsense, false or mystick
or not intelligible or sophistick?
'Tis not antiquity nor author
That makes truth truth, altho' time's daughter.' . . .

Quoth Sidrophel: 'It is no part
of prudence to cry down an art
and what it may perform deny
because you understand not why . . .
Do not the hist'ries of all ages
relate miraculous presages
of strange turns in the world's affairs
foreseen b' astrologers, soothsayers,
Chaldaeans, learn'd genethliacks
and some that have writ almanacks?' . . .

Quoth Hudibras: 'You lie so ope
that I, without a telescope,
can mind your tricks out and descry
where you tell truth and where you lye:
For Anaxagoras, long agon,
saw hills as well as you i' th' Moon,
and held the Sun was but a piece

of red-hot-ir'n as big as Greece . . .
But what, alas, is it to us
whether i' th' Moon men thus or thus
do eat their porridge, cut their corns,
or whether they have tails or horns?
What trade from thence can you advance
but what we nearer have from France? . . .
So when your speculations tend
above their just and useful end,
although they promise strange and great
discoveries of things far set,
they are but idle dreams and fancies.' . . .

At this deep Sidrophel look'd wise,
and staring round with owl-like eyes,
he put his face into a posture
of sapience and began to bluster:
for having three times shook his head
to stir his wit up, thus he said . . .

'Who made the Ballance or whence came
the Bull, the Lion and the Ram?
Did not we here the Argo rigg,
make Berenice's periwig?
Whose liv'ry does the Coachman wear?
Or who made Cassiopaea's chair?
And therefore, as they came from hence,
with us may hold intelligence.
Plato deny'd the world can be
govern'd without geometree . . .
Then much less can it be without
divine astrology made out
that puts the other down in worth,
as far as Heav'n's above the earth.'

'These reasons,' quoth the Knight, 'I grant
are something more significant
than any that the learned use

upon this subject to produce.
And yet th' are far from satisfactory
t' establish and keep up your factory.

Th' Egyptians say, the Sun has twice
shifted his setting and his rise;
twice has he risen in the west,
as many times sett in the east.
But whether that be true or no,
the Dev'l any of you know . . .

Plato believ'd the Sun and Moon
below all other planets run.
Some Mercury, some Venus seat
above the Sun himself in height.
The learned Scaliger complain'd
'gainst what Copernicus maintain'd . . .
swore 'twas a most notorious flam,
and he that had so little shame
to vent such fopperies abroad
deserv'd to have his rump well claw'd –
which Monsieur Bodin hearing swore
that he deserv'd the rod much more . . .
Cardan believ'd great states depend
upon the tip o' th' Bear's tail's end . . .
Some say the Zodiack constellations
Have long since chang'd their antique stations
above a sign, and prove the same
in Taurus now, once in the Ram,
affirm the trigons chop'd and chang'd,
the wat'ry with the fiery rang'd.
Then how can their effects still hold
to be the same they were of old?

This, though the art were true, would make
our modern soothsayers mistake,
and in one cause they tell more lies
in figures and nativities

than th' old Chaldaean conjurers
in so many hundred thousand years –
beside their nonsense in translating,
for want of accidence and Latin . . .

And yet with canting, sleight and cheat,
'twill serve their turn to do the feat,
make fools believe in their fore-seeing
of things before they are in being,
to swallow gudgeons e're th' are catch'd
and count their chickens e're th' are hatch'd.
Make them the constellations prompt
And give 'em back their own accompt,
but still the best to him that gives
The best price for't, or best believes . . .

There's but the twinkling of a star
between a man of peace and war,
a thief and justice, fool and knave,
a huffing officer and a slave,
a crafty lawyer and a pick-pocket,
a great philosopher and a blockhead,
a formal preacher and a player,
a learn'd physician and manslayer,
as if men from the stars did suck
old age, diseases and ill-luck,
wit, folly, honour, virtue, vice,
trade, travel, women, claps, and dice,
and draw, with the first air they breathe,
battle and murder, sudden death.
Are not these fine commodities
to be imported from the skies,
and vended here among the rabble,
for staple goods and warrantable?' . . .

Quoth Sidrophel: 'To let you know
you wrong the art, and artists too
since arguments are lost on those

that do our principles oppose,
I will (although I've don't before)
demonstrate to your sense once more
and draw a figure that shall tell you
what you, perhaps, forget befel you,
by way of horary inspection,
which some account our worst erection.'

With that he circles draws and squares
with cyphers, astral characters,
then looks 'em o're, to understand 'em,
although set down hob-nab, at random.

Quoth he: 'This scheme of th' heavens set
discovers how in fight you met
at Kingston with a Maypole idol
and that y' were bang'd both back and side well.
And though you overcame the bear,
the dogs beat you at Brentford fair,
where sturdy butchers broke your noddle,
and handled you like a fop-doodle.'

Quoth Hudibras: 'I now perceive
you are no conj'rer, by your leave:
that paultry story is untrue,
and forg'd to cheat such gulls as you.'

'Not true?' quoth he. 'Howe'er you vapour,
I can what I affirm make appear.
Whachum shall justify't t' your face
and prove he was upon the place.
He play'd the saltinbanco's part,
transform'd t' a Frenchman by my art.
He stole your cloak and pick'd your pocket,
chews'd and caldes'd ye like a blockhead:
and what you lost I can produce,
if you deny it, here i' th' house.'

Quoth Hudibras: 'I do believe
that argument's demonstrative.
Ralpho, bear witness, and go fetch us
a constable to seize the wretches.
For though th' are both false knaves and cheats,
impostors, jugglers, counterfeits,
I'll make them serve for perpendiculars
as true as e'er were us'd by bricklayers.
They're guilty, by their own confessions,
of felony, and at the sessions,
upon the bench, I will so handle 'em . . . '

Quoth Sidrophel: 'I do not doubt
to find friends that will bear me out.
Nor have I hazarded my art
and neck so long on the state's part
to be expos'd i' th' end to suffer
by such a braggadocio huffer!'

'Huffer!' quoth Hudibras. 'This sword
shall down thy false throat cram that word.
Ralpho, make haste, and call an officer
to apprehend this Stygian sophister.
Meanwhile I'll hold 'em at a bay
lest he and Whachum run away . . . '

To make his way through Hudibras,
Whachum had got a fire-fork
with which he vow'd to do his work.
But Hudibras was well prepar'd
and stoutly stood upon his guard.
He put by Sidrophello's thrust,
and in right manfully he rusht.
The weapon from his gripe he wrung
and laid him on the earth along.
Whachum his sea-coal prong threw by
and basely turn'd his back to fly,

but Hudibras gave him a twitch
as quick as lightning in the breech,
just in the place where honour's lodg'd,
as wise philosophers have judg'd,
because a kick in that place more
hurts honour than deep wounds before.

Quoth Hudibras: 'The stars determine
you are my prisoners, base vermine!'

II

Magic in an Age of Science

Figure 19: Nothing Up My Sleeve: Hocus Pocus Junior

Matthew Hopkins, an undistinguished young man from Manningtree in Essex, began his career as a witch-hunter in March of 1645 by accusing 'seven or eight of that horrible sect of witches living in the towne where he lived'. Hopkins claimed that witches sent 'the Devill like a beare to kill him in his garden'. Dozens of witnesses came forward to testify against the thirty-six women who were tried the next summer, leading to nineteen executions. During the next two years, in a country ravaged by civil war, more charges were filed in other counties and more trials were held, resulting in many judicial murders. Events of such intensity and velocity justify words like 'frenzy', 'craze' and 'panic'.

Hysteria of a different kind – much noise, but no slaughter – was 'enthusiasm' in the England of Robert Boyle and Henry More. More was a Cambridge theologian who corresponded with Descartes. Boyle wrote the *Sceptical Chymist* and discovered a law of gases. Boyle was aware of a common view: that only a 'whimsicall enthusiast' like John Dee, with an inflated sense of religious inspiration, would claim to 'make angels themselves quit their heaven to court his company'. But both Boyle and More thought that evidence of 'converse with spirits' could defend the Christian faith against 'atheism'. Such testimony might come from Rosicrucians, who saw 'angels of God ascending and descending'. When the first Rosicrucian pamphlets advertised such visions, some readers responded enthusiastically.

The reform 'in these latter days' that motivated Rosicrucian propaganda had been expected by Paracelsus. Decades later, on the eve of the Thirty Years War, unity and harmony were Rosicrucian ideals, reflecting affinities between human microcosms and the macrocosm and requiring a 'perfect method' to end the conflicts that Satan incited. To find such a method, Brother *CR* went looking for secrets of the Orient in all the subjects of natural philosophy – alchemy especially – as well as theology and Kabbalah. When he returned to Europe and offered to teach what he had learned, the professors laughed.

Frustrated like Paracelsus by ignorance and arrogance, *CR* still had hope, observing that the world was pregnant with reform and labouring to deliver it. He built a house of study – named for the Holy Spirit and cloistered for a celibate brotherhood – and he chose three disciples (*GV*, *JA* and *JO*) to share his struggle. Their task was to make an exact record of his teachings, axioms to govern the world until the end of time – just around the corner. The brothers wrote in a magical language and prepared a secret book given to *CR* in Damascus. Then they recruited four others, left the Holy Spirit's house and dispersed throughout Europe. The mission of the eight was to cure the sick without charge while staying silent under *CR*'s seal.

But the pamphlet that tells this story breaches the Fraternity's silence to proclaim that 'Europe is with child and will bring forth . . . a general Reformation', making it timely to find more recruits. The brothers challenge the wise to 'behold the present time . . . and to declare their minde', taking care to disclaim two errors. First, there is no heresy in the Rosicrucian rules, which reflect the 'most clear and pure' faith of German Christians. Second, Rosicrucian alchemy is not 'the ungodly and accursed gold-making' that cheats the credulous to turn a profit.

Imminent upheaval of the worldly order had been a Christian hope and promise since the time of the Gospels. And there were always some, like *CR* and his Fraternity, ready to encourage the expectation in flamboyant ways. More serious, rational and systematic – by far – was Francis Bacon's programme in works of the same period on method and natural philosophy. To promote a reform of philosophy, he first declares the current model a failure. The old philosophy is a scandal begun by the Greeks, continued by the scholastics and past due for liquidation. While cataloguing errors of the past, Bacon surveys the literature on natural magic by Ficino, Porta and others – giving special attention to the demotic occultism of Paracelsus. And he has harsh words for them all. Yet his criticism of philosophy as a relic of decadence leaves him tied to its principles and purposes, and nowhere more than with magic.

Hoping to rescue natural philosophy, Bacon sees natural magic as part of its burden, but he would rather reform magic than do without it. He proposes a method to make it intelligible and useful, even to investigate witchcraft and sorcery as troves of useful data. Magic, properly understood, 'applies the knowledge of hidden forms to . . . wonderful operations, and by uniting . . . actives with passives, displays the wonderful works of nature'. Absent this insight, magic will keep decaying, smothered by degenerate traditions.

Published in 1605, Bacon's vernacular manifesto *On the Advancement of*

Learning makes magic part of the progress of philosophy. After his death in 1626, philosophers kept him in the limelight, placing him conspicuously in the canon of their subject – though with little attention to his plans for magic. Before Leibniz died ninety years later, sympathy with such notions vanished in academic philosophy: Leibniz had a hand in its extinction. Like Bacon, he was hungry for books. Like Gabriel Naudé, he was a librarian who shelved them in collections that still made space for learned works on magic by writers like Agrippa and Campanella. Magic books were badges of erudition when Leibniz was young, while Molière and Butler were producing their devastating burlesques. This ambitious and polycephalous genius could see, however, that the occult philosophy was on its way out, as he did his part to clear the path.

When Newton's genius collided with his own in mathematics and physics, an older Leibniz extended the fight to theology – which was of vital interest to all the contestants. A surrogate for Newton in this endless dispute was Samuel Clarke, who translated the master's *Opticks* into Latin in 1706. Nine years later, Clarke debated Leibniz by correspondence. In these letters, where Leibniz denounced Newton's gravitational force as 'a scholastick occult quality', the harshness of the charge was plain to all the parties: they all agreed that occultism was dead and gone for respectable thinkers. The slander smeared Newton with scholastic metaphysics and the occult philosophy sustained by it through the sixteenth and seventeenth centuries – the period of the witch-craze in Europe. Clarke published the letters in 1717, which was also the year of the last trial (though not the last lynching) for witchcraft in England.

Just a little earlier, however, during the decade when Leibniz and Newton were born, English courts had executed more accused witches (mostly women) than ever before or since: it was the time of Hopkins and the Essex trials. Since nothing on that scale happened again in England, Henry More – a university professor who took broad views of religious differences – might have drifted with the tide away from witchcraft. But he and other progressives, like Joseph Glanvill, seeing that crime as well documented and repeatedly confirmed by the courts, seized on it as a proof to defeat 'atheism' – commonly understood as denying the soul's immortality, not God's existence. If the soul survives the body's death, it must live on as the unbodily item – a spirit – that used to inhabit the body. The Devil and his demons are spirits. When they manipulate witches physically, spirits connect with human bodies; the makings of a doctrine of immortality are then secure, and so is the existence of God: QED.

For many modern readers, stories about witches and ghosts are merely childish and not at all threatening. Not so for More, Glanvill and Boyle: they all worried about the drumming demon of Tedworth. The celebrated haunting of John Mompesson's house started in 1661. Investigations traced the disturbances to an earlier incident: in a local village, Mompesson had caused a drum to be confiscated from William Drury, about whom nothing is known beyond his brushes with the law. At a later stage of Drury's troubles, when he was arrested for stealing pigs and jailbreaking, the charges against him cited the witchcraft statute. Just two decades after the Essex horror, the stakes were high for such an accusation.

Was Drury a village wizard or just a street musician and petty thief? No one knows. After his drum ended up at Mompesson's house, reports of strange noises, smells and sights piled up – notably a drumming sound along with 'affrights, vexations and tossings up and down' of the Mompesson children. Glanvill investigated and recorded the story. After he died, More republished his report. Both took the haunting to be factual and to confirm 'the article of our future existence' by proving 'the being of spirits and apparitions'. At the end of his account, Glanvill promises to do the same for 'witches and diabolick contracts'.

Some observers of the Tedworth excitement suspected fraud, and Boyle eventually shied away from Glanvill's more flamboyant claims. But Boyle himself looked for spirits in a strange place – speculating that the Philosopher's Stone might serve as a conduit for talks with angels. Though he never published these suggestions, he took the time to put them in literary form – a dialogue that yields nothing to Dee's diaries for bizarre angel-magic. Interlocutors in the dialogue who expect the Stone to lure angels need a 'medium' to bridge 'the distance between the humane nature and that of an unbodied spirit'. One solution to this 'grand difficulty' is the evil done by witches and magicians – confirmed by scripture and 'the almost universall consent of mankind'.

In the eyes of Gabriel Naudé, such consent was feeble and all too predictable. Of his two occupations, designing libraries shaped his views more than practising medicine, though both were important. His *Apology for All the Great Persons Falsely Suspected of Magic* describes itself accurately. By showing how brilliant eccentrics like Paracelsus were defamed by vulgar prejudice and sloppy thinking, he undercuts the evidentiary basis for loose talk about magic: he aims to make accusations of magic – or witchcraft – less plausible without fully confronting the theoretical arguments for magic as a natural phenomenon or the theological dogmas behind the witchcraft trials. Two years before publishing his *Apology*, Naudé had reacted in the same way to the Rosicrucian scare of 1623 in Paris: the whole thing was a joke, he declared, and Paris fell for it.

Both Naudé and Bacon made procedural recommendations to change people's thinking about magic, but only Bacon addressed the salient problems of natural philosophy with substantive proposals for reform. Other new ideas were to come from leading intellectuals before the occult philosophy became so disreputable that reform was no longer an option. Tommaso Campanella and Athanasius Kircher, a rebel Dominican and an irrepressible Jesuit, were controversialists of great renown and advocates of magic: their critics recognized their talent. But contemporary reviews were harsher for Robert Fludd and Thomas Vaughan, a London physician and a priest from Wales: both introduced the new theosophy to England.

Where Henry More fits in this situation is hard to say. He often impressed his peers, but his theosophical speculations made a bad impression on those who held the view abandoned by his *Kabbalist Conjectures*: that the place to look for science is *not* the Bible. Like Pico, More added Hebrew wisdom to the godly pagan theology that Ficino had traced to Pythagoras and other predecessors of Plato. He also had access to traditions of Kabbalah that evolved after Pico died. His enquiries convinced him that truths of natural philosophy were hidden in the Hebrew text: this much of his story – simply stated – was venerable Kabbalist doctrine. Just what 'the true philosophick Cabbala' might amount to was a trickier question, and he changed his mind about it more than once – in writings whose volume and density are perplexing. If erudition alone could have given More the discipline he needed, his achievement might be clearer.

Though clarity and rigour were not strengths for Fludd or Vaughan, what they accomplished is plain enough: giving theosophy a public face after its underground passage from fugitive remarks by Paracelsus to proclamations by the Rosicrucian Invisibles, whom Fludd and Vaughan both defended. Vaughan published a translation of a Rosicrucian pamphlet in 1652. By then, More had stopped replying to Vaughan's rebuttals of More's attacks on him, which started in 1650. More classifies Vaughan as one of those enthusiasts who 'dictate their own conceits and fancies . . . as if they were indeed authentick messengers from God Almighty'. Descartes had set a new standard for rationality, according to More, and Vaughan was oblivious. He also violated the rule that More himself would break in the *Kabbalist Conjectures*: that no philosophy can be 'safely gathered' out of scripture.

Scripture has epistemic priority in science and provides the crucial evidence: this had been Fludd's position before it was Vaughan's, and it was one of Kepler's reasons for taking Fludd on in 1619, before the completion of Fludd's masterpiece, his *History of Both Worlds*, a book that must be seen in the original to be appreciated. The strange images in this huge volume convey more about theosophy than its text. Fludd's famous diagram of the macrocosm – Nature has Art's monkey on a leash, and she is chained to the Godhead – displays a theosophical cosmology better than Fludd's words could describe it. 'Talkative, loud, thinly learned, inconsistent . . . a fluctuating Fludd': that was one dismissal of his writings. Judged by the standing of his enemies, however, Fludd was a considerable figure: Kepler, Marin Mersenne, Pierre Gassendi and J. B. van Helmont took the time to belittle him.

Fludd died in London in 1637, when Descartes finally went public with his *Discourse on the Method*. At that time, Campanella was the most famous philosopher in France, after spending half his life jailed in Italy. He and Bruno – both renegade Dominicans – got into trouble with the Inquisition around the same time in the 1590s. Though Campanella was the greater threat to public order, he survived and wrote abundantly – on magic, among many other topics. Vitalism (everything is alive) and pansensism (everything is sentient) are the core of his novel philosophy of magic. Vitalism had been common in earlier theories, which usually saw the universe as more like a giant animal than a big machine. Campanella was original in explaining this organic view of nature – and of magic – that others had simply asserted. Like the lawyerly Bacon, he chose the wrong path in natural science, but he was a more skilled philosopher.

Athanasius Kircher, like all Jesuits of his day, was superbly educated in the classics, philosophy and theology; he completed the Order's strenuous requirements for full membership in 1628. He was an omnivore of the intellect, exploring antiquities, archaeology, astronomy, cartography, instrumentation, mathematics, music, philology, physics and many, many languages. Since his talents won him patronage and his books made money, he had the means to take his enquiries wherever he chose, and he chose everything. A continuing focus of his work was magnetism, an ancient enigma that William Gilbert had begun to demystify in 1600. A mechanical account of magnetism was part of Cartesian physics. Well aware of such theories, and anxious to keep Jesuit science current, Kircher identifies magnetism as nature's fundamental force – and as magical energy. Despite his own interest in this puzzling phenomenon, Descartes called Kircher a fake and would not read his books.

Campanella, Fludd, Kircher, More and Vaughan were innovators. Like the fastidious Descartes, they all broke the rules of scholastic natural philosophy in order to replace its doctrines. But the project of a natural *philosophy* – under new management – remained normative for Kircher and Campanella, even while they sought to transform it. For Fludd and Vaughan, however, the new norms were distinctly *theosophical* – when theosophy itself was a novel and indistinct enterprise. When Kircher's critics called him a theosophist, they could point to a section on 'theosophical metaphysics' in his book on Egyptology. But what he discusses there is the 'secret sanctuary of Egyptian theology' concealed in hieroglyphic writing and deciphered by himself, not a private 'mysticall walk', as in Vaughan's *Theomagical Anthroposophy*.

Campanella, Fludd, Kircher, More and Vaughan were innovators, as were Descartes, Galileo, Leibniz, Locke and Newton. Some innovations had a future that we still inhabit, while others did not. Among the first five modernizers, Campanella and Kircher command our respect as masters of their own defunct sciences but not as contributors to ours. No sciences, dead or living, were truly mastered by the other three. All five were convinced that magic would thrive as natural philosophy achieved its reform, but for many others that conviction was merely enthusiastic.

Noble Ends: Bacon,
The Advancement of Learning, 1.4.1–11

Bacon complains that educated people in recent times have examined 'words and not matter'. But their mistake was not as bad as the 'degenerate learning' of the scholastics, which lacked any 'soundness'. Even worse was the 'deceit or untruth' in two kinds of study in Bacon's day – religious and scientific. In response, people were treating miracles reported by clerics as 'as old wives' fables . . . to the great scandal and detriment of religion'. Bad judgement about matters of fact had also damaged 'the credit of natural philosophy with the grave and sober kind of wits'. Imagination had trumped reason in three sciences especially – magic, astrology and alchemy. Since their aims were noble, however, Bacon would rather reform than eliminate them. Published in 1605, his call for reform in natural philosophy – which includes natural magic – is especially keen on alchemy's prospects as a source of 'inventions and experiments, as well for the disclosing of nature as for the use of man's life'.

*

There be therefore chiefly three vanities in studies whereby learning hath been most traduced. For those things we do esteem vain which are either false or frivolous, those which either have no truth or no use. And those persons we esteem vain which are either credulous or curious. And curiosity is either in matter or words, so that in reason as well as in experience there fall out to be these three distempers . . . of learning: the first, fantastical learning; the second, contentious learning; and the last, delicate learning – vain imaginations, vain altercations and vain affectations – and with the last I will begin . . .

These four causes concurring – the admiration of ancient authors, the hate of the schoolmen, the exact study of languages and the efficacy of preaching – did bring in an affectionate study of eloquence and copie of speech, which then began to flourish . . . Then grew the learning of the schoolmen to be utterly despised as barbarous . . . Here therefore is the first distemper of learning, when men study words and not matter . . .

The second, which followeth, is in nature worse than the former. For as substance of matter is better than beauty of words, so contrariwise vain matter is worse than vain words . . . It is the property of good and sound knowledge to putrefy and dissolve into a number of subtile, idle, unwholesome and . . . vermiculate questions, which have indeed a kind of quickness and life of spirit but no soundness of matter or goodnesse of quality. This kind of degenerate learning did chiefly reign amongst the schoolmen, who having . . . Aristotle their dictator . . . and knowing little history, either of nature or time, did – out of no great quantity of matter and infinite agitation of wit – spin out unto us those laborious webs of learning which are extant in their books . . .

This same unprofitable subtility or curiosity is of two sorts: either in the subject itself that they handle, when it is a fruitless speculation or controversy . . . or in the manner or method of handling of a knowledge . . . Their method . . . rests not so much upon evidence of truth proved by arguments, authorities, similitudes, examples, as upon particular confutations and solutions of every scruple, cavillation and objection – breeding for the most part one question as fast it solveth another, even as . . . when you carry the light into one corner, you darken the rest . . . In the inquisition of nature they ever left the oracle of God's works and adored the deceiving and deformed images which the unequal mirror of their own minds or a few received authors or principles did represent unto them . . .

For the third vice or disease of learning, which concerneth deceit or untruth, it is of all the rest the foulest as that which doth destroy the essential form of knowledge, which is nothing but a representation of truth . . . This vice therefore brancheth itself into two sorts: delight in deceiving and aptness to be deceived – imposture and credulity which, although they appear to be of a diverse nature . . . yet certainly they do for the most part concur . . .

This facility of credit, and accepting or admitting things weakly authorized or warranted, is of two kinds, according to the subject: for it is either a belief of history (as the lawyers speak, matter of fact) or else of matter of art and opinion. As to the former, we see . . . this error in ecclesiastical history, which hath too easily received and registered reports and narrations of miracles wrought by martyrs, hermits or monks of the desert and other holy men and their relics, shrines, chapels and images, which – though they had a passage for a time by the ignorance of the people, the superstitious simplicity of some and the politic toleration of others, holding them but divine poesies – yet . . . when the mist began to clear up, they grew to be esteemed but as old wives' fables, impostures of the clergy, illusions of spirits and badges of Antichrist, to the great scandal and detriment of religion.

So in natural history we see there hath not been that choice and judgement used as ought to have been – as may appear in the writings of Plinius, Cardanus, Albertus and divers of the Arabians, being fraught with much fabulous matter, a great part not only untried but notoriously untrue, to the great derogation of the credit of natural philosophy with the grave and sober kind of wits . . .

And as for the facility of credit which is yielded to arts and opinions, it is likewise of two kinds: either when too much belief is attributed to the arts themselves or to certain authors in any art. The sciences themselves which have had better intelligence and confederacy with the imagination of man than with his reason are three in number – astrology, natural magic and alchemy – of which sciences, nevertheless, the ends or pretences are noble.

For astrology pretendeth to discover that correspondence or concatenation which is between the superior globe and the inferior. Natural magic pretendeth to call and reduce natural philosophy from variety of speculations to the magnitude of works. And alchemy pretendeth to make separation of all the unlike parts of bodies which in mixtures of nature are incorporate. But the derivations and prosecutions to these ends, both in the theories and in the practices, are full of error and vanity which the great professors themselves have sought to veil over and conceal by enigmatical writings and referring themselves to auricular traditions and such other devices to save the credit of impostures.

And yet surely to alchemy this right is due, that it may be compared to the husbandman whereof Aesop makes this fable: That when he died told his sons that he had left unto them gold buried under ground in his vineyard. And they digged over all the ground, and gold they found none. But by reason of their stirring and digging the mould about the roots of their vines, they had a great vintage the year following. So assuredly the search and stir to make gold hath brought to light a great number of good and fruitful inventions and experiments, as well for the disclosing of nature as for the use of man's life.

II.2

News of the Invisible Brethren:
A Rosicrucian Manifesto

Johann Valentin Andreae finished his theological studies at Tübingen in 1614, when the Rosicrucian manifestos started to appear, at first in German. When he was younger, had he already invented 'Brother CR ... the chief and original of our Fraternity'? Hard to say: invisibility was the Brotherhood's modus operandi, and Andreae himself wavered on the issue later in life. In 1623, Rosicrucian posters went up in Paris, causing excitement for nearly a year and (for a while) delighting the hoaxers who posted them (see 11.4). Ever since, the adventures of Christian Rosenkreutz – the Candide of theosophical fiction – have proved irresistible. Writing as Eugenius Philalethes, his alchemical *nom de guerre*, Thomas Vaughan brought out an English version in 1652 (see 11.10).

*

Fama Fraternitatis
Or a Discovery of the Fraternity
Of the Most Laudable Order of the Rosy Cross

Seeing the only wise and merciful God in these latter days hath poured out so richly his mercy and goodness to mankind, whereby ... justly we may boast of the happy time wherein there is not only discovered unto us the half part of the world which was heretofore unknown and hidden, but he hath also made manifest unto us many wonderful and never-heretofore seen works and creatures of nature, and moreover hath raised men, indued with great wisdom, which might partly renew and reduce all arts – in this our age, spotted and imperfect – to perfection, so that finally man might thereby understand his own nobleness and worth, and why he is called Microcosmos and how far his knowledg extendeth in nature.

Although the rude world herewith will be but little pleased but rather smile and scoff thereat, also the pride and covetousness of the learned is so great, it will not suffer them to agree together. But were they united, they might . . . collect a perfect method of all arts. But such is their opposition that they still keep and are loth to leave the old course, esteeming Porphyry, Aristotle and Galen – yea, and that which hath but a meer show of learning, more than the clear and manifested light and truth . . . And although in theologie, physic and the mathematic the truth doth oppose itself, nevertheless the Old Enemy by his subtilty and craft doth shew himself in hindering every good purpose by his instruments and contentious wavering people.

To such an intent of a general Reformation, the most godly and highly illuminated Father, our Brother *CR*, a German, the chief and original of our Fraternity, hath much and long time laboured, who, by reason of his poverty – although descended of noble parents – in the fifth year of his age was placed in a cloyster where he had learned indifferently the Greek and Latin tongues, who upon his earnest desire and request, being yet in his growing years, was associated to a Brother *PAL* who had determined to go to the Holy Land.

Although this Brother dyed in Ciprus and so never came to Jerusalem, yet our Brother *CR* did not return but shipped himself over and went to Damasco, minding from thence to go to Jerusalem . . . By his skill in physic he obtained much favour with the Turks . . . became by chance acquainted with the wise men of Damasco in Arabia, beheld what great wonders they wrought, and . . . made a bargain with the Arabians that they should carry him for a certain sum of money to Damasco. He was but of the age of sixteen years when he came thither, yet of a strong Dutch constitution. There the wise men received him (as he himself witnesseth) not as a stranger but as one whom they had long expected . . .

He learned there better the Arabian tongue, so that the year following he translated the book M into good Latin, which he afterwards brought with him. This is the place where he did learn his physick and his mathematics . . . After three years he returned again with good consent, shipped himself over Sinus Arabicus into Egypt, where he remained not long, but only took better notice there of the plants and creatures. He sailed over the whole Mediterranean Sea for to come unto Fez, where the Arabians had directed him . . . It is a great shame unto us that wise men, so far remote th'one from th'other, should not only be of one opinion, hating all contentious writings, but also be so willing and ready – under the seal of secresy – to impart their secrets to others . . .

At Fez he did get acquaintance with those which are commonly called the Elementary Inhabitants, who revealed unto him many of their secrets – as we Germans likewise might gather together many things if there were the like unity and desire of searching out secrets amongst us. Of these of Fez, he often did confess that their Magia was not altogether pure and also that their Cabala was defiled with their religion. But notwithstanding he knew how to make good use of the same and found still more better grounds of his faith, altogether agreeable with the harmony of the whole world, and wonderfully impressed in all periods of times.

And thence proceedeth that fair concord – that as in every several kernel is contained a whole good tree or fruit, so likewise is included in the little body of man the whole great world, whose religion, policy, health, members, nature, language, words and works are agreeing, sympathizing and in equal tune and melody with God, heaven and earth. And that which is disagreeing with them is error, falsehood and of the Devil, who alone is the first, middle and last cause of strife, blindness, and darkness in the world. Also, might one examine all and several persons upon the earth, he should find that which is good and right is always agreeing with itself, but all the rest is spotted with a thousand erroneous conceits.

After two years, Brother *CR* departed the city Fez and sailed with many costly things into Spain, hoping well – he himself had so well and profitably spent his time in his travel – that the learned in Europe would highly rejoyce with him and begin to rule and order all their studies according to those sure and sound foundations. He therefore conferred with the learned in Spain, shewing unto them the errors of our arts and how they might be corrected, and from whence they should gather the true *inditia* of the times to come and wherein they ought to agree with those things that are past . . . and pre-scribed them new axiomata whereby all things might fully be restored.

But it was to them a laughing matter, and being a new thing unto them, they feared that their great name would be lessened if they should now again begin to learn and acknowledge their many years' errors . . . The same song was also sang to him by other nations, the which moved him the more – because it happened to him contrary to his expectation – being then ready bountifully to impart all his arts and secrets to the learned if they would have but undertaken to write the true and infallible axiomata . . . as that which he knew would direct them, like a globe or circle, to the onely middle point and centrum . . .

Verily we must confess that the world in those days was already big with those great commotions, labouring to be delivered of them, and did bring forth painful, worthy men who brake with all force through darkness and barbarism and left us who succeeded to follow them . . . Such a one likewise hath Theophrastus been in vocation and callings. Although he was none of our Fraternity, yet nevertheless hath he diligently read over the Book M, whereby his sharp ingenium was exalted. But this man was also hindered in his course by the multitude of the learned and wise-seeming men, that he was never able peaceably to confer with others of his knowledg and understanding he had of nature . . .

But that we do not forget our loving Father, Brother *CR*, he – after many painful travels and his fruitless true instructions – returned again into Germany . . . There, although he could have bragged with his art, but specially of the transmutations of metals, yet did he esteem more heaven – and the citizens thereof, man – than all vain glory and pomp. Nevertheless, he builded a fitting and neat habitation, in the which he ruminated his voyage and philosophy and reduced them together in a true memorial. In this house he spent a great time in the mathematics and made many fine instruments . . . whereof there is but little remaining to us . . .

After five years came again into his mind the wished for Reformation and . . . he undertook with some few adjoyned with him to attempt the same. Wherefore he desired to that end to have out of his first cloyster . . . three of his brethren – Brother *GV*, Brother *JA* and Brother *JO* – who besides that they had some more knowledg in the arts then at that time many others had, he did bind those three unto himself to be faithful, diligent and secret, as also to commit carefully to writing all that which he should direct and instruct them in, to the end that those which were to come, and through especial revelation should be received into this Fraternity, might not be deceived of the least sillable and word.

After this manner began the Fraternity of the Rosie Cross, first by four persons onely. And by them was made the magical language and writing, with a large dictionary which we yet dayly use to God's praise and glory and do finde great wisdom therein. They made also the first part of the Book *M*. But in respect that that labour was too heavy and the unspeakable concourse of the sick hindred them, and also whilst his new building (called *Sancti Spiritus*) was now finished, they concluded to draw and receive yet others more into their Fraternity. To this end was chosen Brother *RC*; his deceased father's brother's son, Brother *B*; a skilful painter, *G*; and *PD*, their secretary – all Germains except *JA*. So in all they were eight in number, all batchelors and of vowed virginity. By whom was collected a book or volumn of all that which man can desire, wish or hope for.

Although we do now freely confess that the world is much amended within an hundred years, yet we are assured that our axiomata shall unmovably remain unto the world's end, and also the world in her highest and last age shall not attain to see anything else. For our *rota* takes her beginning from that day when God spake *fiat* and shall end when he shall speak *pereat*. Yet God's clock striketh every minute, where ours scarce striketh pefect hours. We also stedfastly beleeve that if our brethren and fathers had lived in this our present and clear light, they would more roughly have handled the Pope, Mahomet, scribes, artists and sophisters, and showed themselves more helpful – not simply with sighs and wishing of their end and consummation.

When now these eight Brethren had disposed and ordered all things in such manner as there was not now need of any great labour, and also that every one was sufficiently instructed and able perfectly to discourse of secret and manifest philosophy, they would not remain any longer together but – as in the beginning they had agreed – they separated themselves into several countries, because that not only their axiomata might in secret be more profoundly examined by the learned, but that they themselves, if in some country or other they observed anything or perceived some error, might inform one another of it.

Their agreement was this: first, that none of them should profess any other thing then to cure the sick, and that gratis; second, none of the posterity should be constrained to wear one certain kind of habit, but therein to follow the custom of the country; third, that every year, upon the day *C*, they should meet together at the house *Sancti Spiritus* or write the cause of his absence; fourth, every brother should look about for a worthy person who, after his discease, might succeed him; fifth, the word *CR* should be their seal, mark and character; sixth, the Fraternity should remain secret one hundred years . . .

But this we will confesse publickly by these presents to the honour of God, that what secret soever we have learned out of the Book *M* – although before our eyes we behold the image and pattern of all the world – yet are there not shewn unto us our misfortunes nor hour of death, the which only is known to God Himself, who thereby would have us keep in a continual readiness. But hereof more in our *Confession*, where we do set down 37 reasons wherefore we now do make known our Fraternity, and proffer such high mysteries freely, and without constraint and reward. Also we do promise more gold then both the Indies bring to the King of Spain. For Europe is with child and will bring forth a strong child who shall stand in need of a great godfather's gift . . .

Howbeit we know after a time there will now be a general Reformation both of divine and humane things, according to our desire and the expectation of others. For it's fitting that before the rising of the Sun there should appear and break forth Aurora or some clearness or divine light in the sky.

And so in the meantime some few, which shall give their names, may joyn together, thereby to increase the number and respect of our Fraternity, and make a happy and wished for beginning of our philosophical canons prescribed to us by our Brother *RC*, and be partakers with us of our treasures (which never can fail or be wasted) in all humility and love to be eased of this world's labour, and not walk so blindly in the knowledge of the wonderful works of God . . .

But that also every Christian may know of what Religion and belief we are, we confess to have the knowledg of Jesus Christ – as the same now in these last days, and chiefly in Germany, most clear and pure is professed, and is nowadays cleansed and voyd of all swerving people, hereticks, and false prophets – in certain and noted countries maintained, defended and propagated . . .

But now concerning (and chiefly in this our age) the ungodly and accursed gold-making which hath gotten so much the upper hand, whereby under colour of it many runagates and roguish people do use great villainies and cozen and abuse the credit which is given them – yea, nowadays men of discretion do hold the transmutation of metals to be the highest point and *fastigium* in philosophy. This is all their intent and desire, and that God would be most esteemed by them and honoured which could make great store of gold, the which with unpremeditate prayers they hope to obtain of the all-knowing God and searcher of all hearts. We therefore do by these presents publickly testifie that the true philosophers are far of another minde, esteeming little the making of gold, which is but a parergon, for besides that they have a thousand better things. We say with our loving Father *RCC* . . . he doth not rejoice that he can make gold, and that, as saith Christ, the devils are obedient unto him, but is glad that he seeth the heavens open, the angels of God ascending and descending, and his name written in the book of life . . .

So, according to the wil and meaning of Frater *CRC*, we his brethren request again all the learned in Europe who shal read (sent forth in five languages) this our *Fama* and *Confessio*, that it would please them with good deliberation to ponder this our offer, and to examine most nearly and sharply their arts, and behold the present time with all diligence, and to declare their minde . . . And although at this time we make no mention either of our names or meetings, yet nevertheless every one's opinion shal assuredly come to our hands – in what language so ever it be – nor anybody shal fail, whoso gives but his name, to speak with some of us, either by word of mouth, or else, if there be some lett, in writing.

And this we say for a truth: that whosoever shal earnestly and from his heart bear affection unto us, it shal be beneficial to him in goods, body, and soul. But he that is false-hearted or onely greedy of riches, the same first of all shal not be able in any manner of wise to hurt us, but bring himself to utter ruine and destruction. Also our building – although one hundred thousand people had very near seen and beheld the same – shal for ever remain untouched, undestroyed and hidden to the wicked world.

In the shade of thy wings, Jehova.

11.3
Heresy No Magic:
Naudé, *Apology*

The ghostly Rosicrucian visitation of 1623 in Paris might have exposed the city to Protestants, atheists, libertines, naturalists, alchemists or even Paracelsians: who knew? There was enough panic to go around. A few were quick to spot the ruse, but only Gabriel Naudé wrote a book to declare it a practical joke, making his reputation with an acid brew of vernacular wit and Latinate erudition (see 11.2, 4). A librarian and a physician, he was well placed to search the huge load of books and pamphlets produced by Paracelsus and his followers (see 9.4). That 'grand heresiarch in philosophy, medicine and religion' was one of the beneficiaries of Naudé's *Apology for All the Great Persons Falsely Suspected of Magic*. He sees Paracelsus as weird and unorthodox: fair enough. His larger point is to distinguish befuddlement, novelty and opacity from the alleged crimes of magic for which people were still being killed.

*

Today the grand heresiarch in philosophy, medicine and religion is Theophrastus Paracelsus, the zenith and rising sun of all the alchemists: I think that those who want to free him from the charge of magic – yet without prejudice to other accusations made against him – have good reason. They can claim that the novelty of his ideas, the difficulty of his style and the obscurity of a great many of the words commonly encountered by those who leaf through the pages of his books . . . leave the reader so puzzled and unclear about what he means to say that one can go forward only by groping through the twists and turns, never knowing how to tell if he is talking about a turd or a pill, a stone or a piece of bread, the Devil or Nature.

There is good reason to suspect that he uses magic (like Trithemius) to make things enigmatic, cover up his teachings and not reveal the emptiness of his art, which he surely believes will be much more admired if it is less understood . . . As for my own opinion, I have not read far enough in the dictionary of this author's phrases prepared by Rulandus that I can evaluate his works. To understand them on this question of his magic, I am glad to follow the opinion of his main interpreters, Severinus the Dane and Croll, who see in it only a cover to conceal his teachings . . .

Jacques Gohory, who has been the main accomplice of Paracelsus in France, believes that the names of the many spirits that he regularly brings into his books – though one might take them to be the Devil's own falcons – should be interpreted as various extracts and essences, as properties and preparations, actually the mineral, vegetable and animal ingredients used to make up his remedies. It's also true that Johann Oporinus – his assistant for a long time and apparently the one who revealed everything now held against him – never mentions magic or invocations.

Wetter, who stayed with him for twenty-seven months, says only that he threatened – when drunk – to make a thousand demons come in order to show his power and control over them, not failing to mention what many claim about the familiar demon contained in the pommel of his sword. I do not want to bring up the view of the alchemists who maintain that this item was the secret of the Philosopher's Stone. If the pommel contained anything, there is better evidence for thinking that it must have been two or three doses of the laudanum that Paracelsus wanted never to be without: he did amazing things with it and used it as a universal medicine for healing all kinds of illness.

Still, someone might say that it does no good to collect these proofs for striking Paracelsus from the list of magicians: not satisfied with making magic one of the four pillars of medicine, he also tried to reveal its precepts and nature to us in all his books . . . In view of his boasting about knowing all the types of magic, however, I find it astonishing that he never chose to use them to do anything – as if it were not better to confirm this novel doctrine by one of his experiments than to follow the usual path of the charlatans who let loose a torrent of common, popular eloquence to extol the marvellous potency of their drugs . . .

But a more acceptable view, which I do not wish to deny, comes from those who say that a major advantage which learned and industrious people have over the ignorant is their ability to shape new systems and principles, changing the order, content and method of the sciences by lengthening or shortening them as they prefer – like the strap of a stirrup. They also say that Paracelsus was one of those people, wanting to change the face of magic as he had also done in philosophy and medicine and as he claimed he could do in religion, threatening to submit the Pope and Luther, both of them, to his maxims, as often and as much as he wished.

For this reason, even though condemning him as a heretic may well be fair since his views about religion were grossly perverse, I still believe he should not be suspected of magic. This is because magic is not a theory or a speculation that anyone can derive and explicate in the way that seems right to him. Magic is practical, using the circle and invocations, things that none of the authorities who oppose the teachings of Paracelsus – as I have just shown – has ever claimed that he liked to do.

II.4
Crazies and Contagion:
Naudé, *Apology*

Before summing up his *Apology*, Naudé has used the standard categories of natural (permitted) and demonic (forbidden) magic, but theoretical distinctions are not his meat (see 8.10, 14). What moves him are rules of evidence and methods of inquiry, applied to expose gullibility and other sins of mental sloth. As a planner of libraries, he knew all about the easy multiplication of authority in the age of the printed book. 'The number of crazies is infinite,' he warns, 'and contagion is very dangerous in the press.' The worst carriers of diseased information, he claims, are the same books that infuriated Reginald Scot – written by 'our demonographers', like the learned Jean Bodin (see 9.14). Full of passionate intensity, these 'persons of great credit and merit' have 'never rejected any story, no matter how fabulous and ridiculous'. Naudé shows how they get away with it, supplying a taxonomy of bad judgement.

*

After having shown in all the preceding chapters, giving reasons general and particular, how it could come about that so many distinguished and famous persons have been suspected of magic, and having reached the conclusions that I thought were needed to defend them in all these cases, I believe one can ask nothing more from my effort now except, as I bring this *Apology* to a close, to note what the real reasons and various motives are that sustain all these slanders, giving them more credence every day, and – unless we put things in order – what wrong and harm they bring with them . . . It seems to me quite reasonable to trace the causes of such suspicion to three facts.

The first is that everyone believes with complete conviction that the strongest proof and greatest assurance of truth we can get depends on general acceptance and universal agreement, which cannot be entirely false and concocted – as Aristotle says in book 7 of his Ethics – combined with the view that following someone's path seems plausible and, by all appearances, friendly and fair. For this reason, it always happens that those who are the latest to get involved in writing and producing books – the demonographers, but other authors too – stand on that maxim and never think to examine what they see as believed and taken for true by all their predecessors, by all those who have written on such a subject before them.

The result is that deceit grows by contagion and cheers go up not for judgement and knowing what the causes are but for following the steps of the person who started the dance. Not once do they consider that anyone who wants to be thought wise and prudent must be suspicious of everything that makes people happy ... and everything that most people approve, taking care not to get snared by the usual popular views, seeing that most of them are usually grandiose in the extreme, that the number of crazies is infinite and that contagion is very dangerous in the press ...

The second fact is that most of those who enjoy writing and putting something of their own in the spotlight are generally arrogant enough to try this only in their spare time. And since they write not so much to benefit an audience by carefully searching for the truth but rather to satisfy their own trivial ambition or to meet a need that forces them into service ... their habit is also to keep the work very light and to take as few pains as possible, having no intention of distracting themselves with long and difficult inquiry into the leading authorities – on a topic about which they have found it necessary to spread all these stories and slanders ... Since – for the reasons I have mentioned – they have failed to win glory by the quality of their writings, they have tried to make themselves notable enough by their quantity ... applying their method of making scrupulous, word-by-word copies of what the authorities have said hundreds and hundreds of times.

For that purpose, something quite useful to them is my third and final explanation for the spreading of all these lies, which is nothing more than the habit, introduced some time ago, of promoting the polymath – the person who speaks about each aspect of every item and about each item in every aspect, having no other aim in writing but to collect and assemble all that can be said ... And so it's no wonder if those who follow such a method exactly find themselves loaded down – like merchants who try to get rid of lots of worthless goods but just end up spoiling their other wares and depriving them of value, though it would help them much more to keep those things in good condition ...

It certainly is strange that Delrio, Le Loyer, Bodin, De Lancre and Godelman, who were or still are persons of great credit and merit, have written with such passion on the subject of demons, sorcerers and magicians yet have never rejected any story, no matter how fabulous and ridiculous, from that whole huge pile of deceits and absurdities that they have mixed helter-skelter with accurate and authentic accounts . . . The writings of the demonographers are so fat and swollen with so many fables that they nearly smother the truth, running the risk . . . of resembling that great Colossus of Rhodes, which was ruined only by its huge and haughty size . . .

Experience provides considerable evidence, to tell the truth, that nothing is more dangerous than mixing in trivialities and stories that are dubious or plainly false with matters of consequence because . . . ordinary people, lacking the capacity to judge things in their own terms, let themselves be swept along by the views of those whom they take to be the wisest . . . Hence, it would best serve the honour of our demonographers – and would clarify and preserve the truth about their subject – if they were scrupulous from now on about pushing no story or authority except after examining all the circumstances carefully, choosing . . . not to fabricate these frivolous, baseless accusations . . . that the Devil insinuates indetectably into the reputations of good people.

II.5

Cold Slain by Heat: Campanella, *On Sense and Magic*, 2.26

'Every being desires its own good': Campanella's maxim was not really new, but what he got from it is impressive – a physical and metaphysical basis for vitalism and pansensism as the core of a theory of magic (see 9.8). The Creator always exists, revealed as a Trinity of Love, Power and Wisdom. Most creatures will cease to exist, but not space and matter: having no opposites, they compete with nothing to maintain their being. The first contest between opposites pits heat against cold, giving form to the matter that fills space and producing the physical differences that mark all other creatures. To all of them, out of his own essence, God gives not only the love of being that makes them want to persist but also the power and wisdom to act on that desire. 'The whole world has a power to sense' because of God's design.

*

Here I shall establish a new principle, that every being desires its own good – even more its greater good and its greatest good most of all. Next, I find that to be preserved in life and existence is the greatest good for all beings, which is why cold opposes heat, heat opposes cold and each seeks to extend its being and destroy the opponent in order to be secure in its own life, and so each moves to its own place where it can best survive – fire on high, air above the soil, water in the sea, people in cities. To be preserved in existence, each seeks to eat: for the sake of its own life, the wolf destroys sheep and every harmless animal, the sheep destroys grass and plants, other animals destroy other things and the human destroys them all for his own good . . . For all things preservation will therefore be the greatest good, and for that purpose nature has provided us with all our actions, powers, shapes, limbs and organs.

The space where beings are located I take to be the first immortal being because space has no opposite: as the basis of every created entity, it accepts everything, living or not, that can subsist only within it. Next I take matter to be immortal because it has no opposite, accepting everything and, when divided or combined, becoming rare or dense, hot or cold, staying always the same in substance but not in appearance, depending on what its forms are. One can say, nonetheless, that matter is less immortal than the space in which it sits.

After these I put the hot and the cold – active principles within each thing that can live only in matter, where they battle one another for supremacy. Because they are mortal, God has given them the power to spread, multiply and generate on their own so that they will not be completely destroyed. This seems miraculous, as heat and cold increase where they can prevail, and as the first enlarges and expands from the Sun to the land, the second from the land to the air. Whatever they do, it all comes from wanting to be preserved and made eternal. Place and matter do not have this power of enlargement because they are not mortal and exist as the basis of created things.

Then I find stones and metals emerging in places where they expand and grow, converting the earth's liquid into themselves and producing mountains of great height, which cannot be done quickly, only over time, in the way that bones grow. And they lack the power to generate another stone or metal because they are made of hard matter that resists heat and cold for a long time and because they do not have as much need to expand and live in other things like them – nor can one see as much intelligence in them. But plants, being more sensitive and apt to die, spread and sprout in order to generate something like them in which to live, and then they rise up from their innate heat . . . Animals, since they are formed from a finer ungenerated substance, move around and away from the place where they are born because the earth is not enough food for them, as it is for plants . . .

But if this is how it goes with these things, the main question to be asked is who their architect is, where such great skill might be housed and whether there is some part of the human being that aims at something other than preserving this life. Surely we must answer that either God – or else some very noble deity – constructs these things directly as well as a divine soul that dwells in them and directs them, since no directions can come from an authority that does not understand the directions. Clearly, such things do not appear to be products of a mindless power nor of an animal or human soul but of something much more rational, and the greatest intelligence of all seems to guide them . . .

There is no doubt that the first Wisdom, the highest Mind of all, is – surpassingly – within all things and that all things are within her, and that this Wisdom, without being moved, is the quickest of all, going from one end of the All to the other and acting to produce everything as the main agent of which every other agent is an instrument. Hence, mistakes made by the instruments are not Wisdom's, and they actually honour her. That God who is the First Power, First Wisdom and First Love, however, has given all things the power to live and has provided as much wisdom and love as are needed to preserve them, providing them for as much time as the First Mind has deemed to be necessary – and this cannot be eliminated.

Therefore, heat has the power to exist, knows how to exist and loves to exist, as does each and every thing, and it desires to be eternal like God. And for God no thing dies, it merely changes, though to one thing another thing seems dead, and that thing really is dead in the way that fire seems bad to cold and, for cold, really is bad, though for God each and every thing lives and is good . . .

When cold is slain by heat, God helps the enlargement of heat but not the destruction of cold, except incidentally inasmuch as the heat is enlarged. But he permits the cold to be affected by not giving it a power of resistance greater than the other's power of action. Had Calvin thought about this, he would not have made God an active cause of sin – which is a defect of perfect action but is not itself an act. God helps the action because it extends existence, but he does not help make the order defective, which would contribute to non-existence, something repugnant to God. The whole world has a power to sense, then, like rays of the Sun from the First Wisdom. And Wisdom, in the wisest way possible, guides those rays into each and every thing: if the thing appears to be mindless, the mindlessness is the thing's, while the Wisdom belongs to the First Mind.

II.6

Consensus: Campanella, *On Sense and Magic*, 3.13–14

Heat itself senses the hostility of cold in order to prevail against it. This heat is sentient not just in animals and plants but also in stones and even artificial things – a magnetic compass, for example. Although this vital energy is more manifest in animals, it works in everything. Each thing is made for an end, either by God or by a lesser designer, and each shares a common sentience or 'consensus' with its end or goal. A ship, well made and well piloted, sails to the port that has this sense in common with it – an energy built into its timbers. When the remora, a magical fish, sticks to a ship and numbs it, the energy weakens and the ship's journey is hindered.

*

Even though they are denser than any other things, stones and metals do not lack sensation . . . Inside them they all contain heat, which is why stones show this on the outside when struck, like metals when they are rubbed hard, producing ash and a smell of sulphur, so that what you can see heating up, bursting into flame and throwing off sparks is those stones and metals – not the result of air being struck. They all have sense, then, because heat is sentient. Moreover, all metals and stones feed and grow, having the Sun's help in transforming the soil where they are first born, no differently than a plant in liquid . . .

There can be no doubt about sensation in plants since they are born, they feed, they grow and they produce seed and offspring like animals . . . Some plants turn as they follow the Sun's longitudinal movement, while others follow the latitudinal motion, meaning that sensation must be shared by heavenly and earthly things. Not only the lion and the cock are solar: plants and metals have sensation in common with the heavens, which is proved by the magnet.

By these examples we recognize the truth of astrology and the power of the occult wisdom that the ancients called 'magic'. And we can see that it is not just natural things that have sensation in common with the goal for which they were made but also artificial things because the same soul of the world guides them both, and hence they are very much alike. In the sea are 'chain fish', 'armoured fish', 'bishop fish' and various other man-made things.

Accordingly, since a ship was made to move through the sea, it shares some sense with this goal. For we see another ship of the same weight and shape being more averse to the journey because it shares less of this sense . . . The ship's wood has the sense of navigation, but the remora takes it away by causing numbness in the ship, and the whole ship is numbed and fights its natural movement as the numbness increases. As the sense of a rabid dog multiplies in us and makes us dog-like . . . so the remora acts on the wood in proportion to its effect on the wood, just as the lion is affected by the cock, the elephant by the mouse, the fisherman by the torpedo and the sheepskin drum by the wolf's pelt.

Science is Magic: Campanella, *On Sense and Magic*, 4.5–6

The sciences of nature underwrite technologies to imitate or assist nature. By finding and directing the natural love and hate in sentient things, all sciences and technologies 'are in the service of magic'. Ordinarily, when people talk about 'magic', they have those efforts in mind but do not understand them. The real magic is everywhere in nature – as Plotinus said long before – but harder to grasp (see 5.5).

*

A 'work of magic' is everything done by scientists who imitate nature or help it along with some unknown technique: not only the common people but the whole human community says so, the result being that not only the sciences as usually described but also all the others are in the service of magic . . . As long as a technique is not understood, they call it 'magic', but afterward it is ordinary science. The invention of gunpowder and of printing was something magical, and so was the use of the magnet, but today everyone understands these techniques, which are commonplace. This is also true of clocks, and when mechanical techniques no longer dazzle, the objects involved become open to public view. But since problems of medicine, astrology and religion are rarely discussed so widely, the ancients bring back the art of magic for these questions.

Animal spirit, being by nature mobile and passive, is disposed to be affected by anything and taken in by it, more or less, in various ways, and the soul that is wrapped up in spirit is affected along with it and goes in too. The main effects are pain and pleasure, which are intense sensations of the good or harm that is done. Love and hate are dispositions towards good or against harm that are not sensed in a unitary way, which turns them into delight and suffering . . . A person can be called a 'magician' if he knows how to use plants, actions and other appropriate things to produce all these results in a human being.

A Little World in Action: Fludd, *Mosaicall Philosophy*

The *Meteorology* that Descartes published in 1637 is very different from Robert Fludd's book – printed posthumously in 1638 – on the same material: 'meteors', meaning phenomena (thought to include comets and shooting stars) above the surface of the earth but below the sphere of the moon. To save those appearances in the sky, Descartes proposed a revolutionary matter-theory. But Fludd used his idiosyncratic account of meteors – illustrated by experiments with a 'weather-glass', a crude barometer – to defend the biblical faith of Solomon against pagan Aristotelians. The evidence for his theosophical defence is 'ocular' or observational but also scriptural. And the Spirit of Solomon's Wisdom breathes in his Christianized Kabbalah: Wisdom is the first emanation from a transcendent Godhead, contracted into Nothing but also dilating to emanate the All. Fludd – a critic of Aristotle and an early defender of the Rosicrucians – goes straight from this Kabbalist theology to physics and meteorology: God's willing (Volunty) and not-willing (Nolunty) become manifest as light and darkness and then as heat and cold (see 11.5–6). Calling those forces divine, Fludd sees God working in nature when water rises and falls in his weather-glass. His vision is theosophical, a new framework for Agrippa's 'occult philosophy': macrocosm and microcosm, harmony and dissonance, sympathy, antipathy and an 'all-working Spirit' as principles of magic.

*

Whereas the minds of worldly men are at this very day erected and soared up even unto the highest pitch of infidelity, insomuch as they require and demand after signes and ocular demonstrations . . . or else they will in no case be drawn to believe . . . since I onely am to enter the lists against the ethnick philosophers who by their inventions have framed out the wisdom of this world . . . I will make choice of ocular demonstration to serve me in this combat . . . to tame and subdue that unreasonable monster – incredulity . . .

I ought to have . . . an experimentall instrument or spirituall weapon which

may carve out a ready way to the truth by a manifest and infallible demonstration objected even unto the eyes of such as are infected with extream infidelity,
that they may thereby turn from their vain and sophisticating philosophy –
with the wisdom of the world on which it is erected – and become unfained
and faithfull schollars and proficients in the true and sacred philosophy
or Wisdom of God. I will make therefore election of such demonstrative
machins for my purpose as is vulgarly knowne amongst us . . . and this instrument is commonly styled . . . the weather-glasse . . .

The ethnick philosophers did surreptitiously assume and ascribe unto
themselves those principles of their philosophy which of right did appertain
unto the wise and divine philosopher Moses and did mask or gild over their
theft with new names or titles . . . In like manner . . . the weather-glasse hath
many counterfeit masters or patrons in this our age who . . . do vainly glory
and give out that it is a masterpiece of their own finding out. As for myself . . .
neither can I rightly arrogate or assume unto myself the primary fabrick of
this instrument . . . for I confess that I found it graphically specified and
geometrically delineated in a manuscript of five hundred years antiquity at
the least . . .

This our experimentall instrument is composed of three parts, whereof two
of them are more essentiall and proper unto the nature of the engin or machin:
namely, the *matras* or *bolt's head* and the *small vessell* of water into the which

Figure 20: Fludd's Weather-Glass

the nose or orifice of the matras . . . ought to enter. And the other is more accidentall, as being onely ordained to sustain the glasse firmly in his perpendicular position . . .

Touching the matras or bolt's head, it is a round or ovall glasse with a long and narrow neck whose orifice (or mouth and nose) ought to bee proportionable unto the rest of the neck. And it must be prepared after a two-fold manner. For first of all, the long neck of it being put perpendicularly into the small vessell, being full of water, so that it do touch the bottom of the vessell, we ought to measure from the . . . top of the water and begin our division into degrees, still ascending upwards till we come unto the very ball, be it round or ovall . . . Dividing of the neck or pipe of the matras in the middle . . . I mark the place of the division with the figure 1 and so count my degrees downward and upward unto 7 – after this manner: 7 6 5 4 3 2 1 2 3 4 5 6 7 . . . As for the small vessell of water, you see it here also described, with the proportion of the pipe of the matras that descendeth into the bottome of it, which is so farre from division as it entreth into the water . . .

Not a few will object and say that no convenient comparison can be made between this our small artificiall machin and that naturall fabrick or organ of the world forasmuch as the spirit in our glasse is everywhere inclosed and strictly included in his vessell . . . But the case is far otherwise in the spirit which is contained in the vast cavity of the world . . . Yea verily, and I averre boldly, that the whole world – or worldly round – is as well and compleatly stuffed or filled with spirit or aire as is this our artificiall vessell or experimentall machin – which if it should not be, it would consequently follow that vacuity would be admitted into the nature of things, the which would be but an absurd thing in a philosopher to credit . . . I would in this regard have each discreet reader to understand that when he beholdeth this instrument's nature, he contemplateth the action (as it were) of a little world . . .

I wish them for their better direction to listen unto Solomon: . . . 'By the Spirit of Wisdom I came to know certainly how the world was made and the power of the elements and the beginning, end and middle of times.' . . . Since Wisdom is the centre, root or cornerstone of all things, how should the centre be known and not the circumference? . . . And for this reason, this divine Spirit is termed rightly of the wise philosopher Hermes the centre of every thing, whose circumference is nowhere but yet it comprehendeth all circumferences that are.

We may therefore collect out of the foresaid speech of Solomon that Wisdom discovered unto him: first, all the abstruse mysteries which do concern the making of the world, as she did unto Moses; secondly, the nature and power of the elements, with the hidden act and miraculous generation of the meteors framed out of an elementary stuffe, and of their wondrous properties; thirdly, the reason and manner how the winds are produced, with the astronomicall division of the year, the scituation of the starrs in heaven and their astrologicall natures; fourthly, the necessaries belonging unto the art of physick . . . fifthly, the secrets of all things occult and therefore of the angels – yea, and of God himself, by consequence – and in this is the mystery of theology comprehended . . .

As for the act of this eternal actor or operator in the ayre, water and earth for the production of meteors, it is most evidently expressed in plain terms by Holy Writ. Saith Job . . . 'God by his Wisdome doth adapt a waight or ponderosity unto the ayre and hangeth up the waters in measure and giveth bounds or maketh a law for the rain and prepareth a way for the lightings of the thunders.' In which words, he sheweth that this one Spirit of Wisdome – in whom is the power as well of contraction or condensation as of dilatation or rarefaction – . . . can make the aire more thick and ponderous by condensation and so reduce it into a cloud, or by rarefying it into a more thin and subtile consistence render it in the form of lightning. And evermore the aire so altered receiveth his shape or figure from the Alterer . . . And thus the clouds, the lightnings, the thunder, the comets, the frost, hayl, snow and ice are created daily by this operating Spirit . . . which I can produce out of the Book of Verity to prove that all meteorology is founded on this Spirit . . .

Concerning the excellent art of physick or medecine, the wise man saith . . . 'from God cometh every kind of healing or curing,' which being so, it is certaine that the only actor in healing and curing is immediatly from this all-working Spirit . . . Salomon's confession . . . sayeth . . . 'by Wisdome I knew the natures of living creatures, the raging conditions of beasts, the differences of plants and the vertues of roots – yea, all the mysteries of creatures, as well occult as manifest, were revealed unto me by Wisdome, which is the worker of all things' . . . that heavenly Spirit which did bestow on herbs, animals and minerals their virtues – as well hidden and secret as apparent and evident . . .

And although ethnick philosophers and physitians have by practicall effects or sensuall observations and demonstrations a *posteriori* found out the occult properties in plants, as for example, of the piony to cure the falling-sickness, of herniaria to respect the rupture, of tussilago to be proper for the lungs . . . yet because they are ignorant of the centrall grounds of sympathy and antipathy, which consisteth in the Voluny or Nolunty of one and the same Spirit, they can give no other reason for such hidden things but only that they

are . . . of a hidden property . . . And so we receive from these learned doc-
tours nothing else but . . . a thing unknown by a more unknown . . . Touching
the harmony of this world, and how every sublunary element and superlunary
sphear are disposed by an essentiall kind of symphoniacall accord, the whole
file of Scripture doth confirm that it is effected by this Wisdom . . .

According unto the Rabbies' or Cabalisticall Doctors' opinion, the eternall
Sapience, which is the radicall beginning or unity of all things – when it
remained, as it were, quiet and at rest, as being retracted in the dark abyss –
was in regard of our weak capacities esteemed as *Ain* – that is to say *Nihil* or
'Nothing.' . . . And yet out of this *Nihil* was revealed unto us Infinity, forasmuch as the emanation which issued from it is All in All, and yet without all,
as it is that fountain out of which the universall waters are drawn, which is
the existence of all things . . . And that catholick and bright-shining-forth –
or fiery and formall vertue – is sent out, which doth impart an essence unto
every thing. And in conclusion, both the *externall* or passive and *internall* or
active of all creatures in the world do issue out of this *eternall*, which is *nihil*
in regard of us but *omnia* in *omnibus et extra omnia* in respect of itself, in
whose eyes darkness and light, invisibility and visibility – and therefore all
potentiall nothing or first matter and actuall something – are one and the
same thing in essence, without any difference . . .

[God] filleth all the world and yet remains in himself without all, in the
very self-same nature of a unity as he was. For as he seemed in the eyes of
man's weak and fragil capacity to be *Ain* or *Nihil* before he would create any
thing, yet was he both unity and infinity unto himself and therefore was
complicite All in All in himself – namely, as he to our blinded fancy
appeareth . . . [the] dark and deformed Aleph. Also, though he shined forth
of darkness and by the revelation of his hidden Wisdom or essence made all
things, as well visible as invisible, to exist formally, and so made dark Aleph
to be changed into light Aleph, yet nevertheless he remaineth all one in himself and passeth not beyond the limits of his uniformity, for . . . 'his darknesse
unto him is as his light.' . . .

In this Spirit's patent, manifest and positive nature – or as he is termed,
'light Aleph' – . . . he moveth or sendeth out his emanation from the centre
towards the circumference, and, revealing himself upon the dark face of the
abysse, maketh the invisible . . . potentiall *Nihil* to appear in act, being first
animated by his bright presence in the form of waters . . . So that as the other
privative or northern property did produce rest and vacancy from operation
(by attraction or contraction from the circumference unto the centre), so in
this his positive or southern and orient property (by dilating himself· or

sending out his active beam, brightness or emanation from the centre towards
the circumference), he doth beget and procreate motion, being accompanied
by the essentiall act of heat or calidity, which operateth continually upon the
effects of cold, in resisting, dissolving and destroying of them . . .

This formall champion of light – namely, heat – warreth perpetually against
the cold gardian of darknesse. For the one can have no dominion in the aire
untill the other by little and little be exiled. And therefore as the light principle, with all his branches, is said to be the father of position, act, information,
plenitude, motion, life, health and heat, so also doth heat operate according
unto the nature of his restless and ever operating father, which is light, to
destroy the effects of darkness and cold . . .

Two opposit vertues, namely cold and heat do spring from one and the
same Spirit in radicall essence, by which it operateth actually and essentially
by a double property, forasmuch as they produce in the catholick element of
the sublunary world opposite effects to effect the will of the Creator in the
aire and upon the earth and seas . . . Passive natures . . . are brought forth
by the mutuall action and opposition of the two foresaid essentiall vertues,
which do spring and have their root or beginning either in the divine nature's
Nolunty and privative existence or Volunty and positive emanation . . .

Seing then that it is water – that is the catholick passive – out of the which,
as being the common subject of all things, the shape of the whole world and
everything therein was and is carved out and fashioned . . . and that the eternall creating and all-inacting Spirit of the Lord is the universall actor which
moveth All in All in the waters . . . in and by an infinity of organs – as angels,
Sun, Moon, starrs, winds, fire and so on, as in many places of scripture we
find it – it must needs follow that he is the agent, as well in the contraction
and dilatation generally without the glasse as particularly within the glasse.

Wherefore as the Sun, the hot winds, and the fire or naturall heat of man's
body have their dilative property from his emanating and inacting vertue and
do alter by it the cold aire, the winds and water from his privative disposition,
so it followeth that as well the dilatation of the aire in the glasse as contraction is the immediate act of this Spirit's positive or privative property. For
when this Spirit bloweth from the north or west, the aire is contracted more
or lesse into a narrower room within the glasse, and that is proved thus:
namely, because the water is drawn up higher into the neck of the glasse, lest
a corporall vacuity should be admitted in nature.

And again, it is most apparent that the aire in the glasse is by so much the
more contracted by how much the northern cold hath dominion in the outward aire, because it is gathered into a more strait place of passage then it was

before the water was elevated up. On the other side, if the hot winds or summer Sun do inflame the externall aire, then the included aire will also dilate itself and in its dilation require a larger space. That the aire is so dilated by heat, it is plainly demonstrated in that the water is struck down by so many degrees lower than it was. Again, if one put his hand on the top of the ball of the glasse, the water will sinke, for the aire will forthwith be dilated . . . Thus you see it evidently confirmed by an ocular demonstration that cold doth contract, inspissate and make gross the included aire, which is argued by the drawing up of the water and straitning the aire. And again, that heat doth dilate and dissipate – by the enlargement of the aire in hot weather or by laying of the hand on the bolt's head, which is made evident by the beating down of the waters.

Note, I beseech you – ye that will not be over-partiall on the Peripateticks' behalfes – the two notable errours of the Aristotelians: whereof the first is manifested in that they hold for a maxim that . . . heat doth congregate and gather together things of one nature. Now you see it here ocularly demonstrated that heat doth operate the contrary, for it dissipateth and disperseth the aire, which is of homogeneall parts, and therefore it doth not congregate it. But it is cold that doth congregate, compact and gather homogeneall things together as well as heterogeneall. For you see in our instrument that it contracts and gathers together the aire – yea, and water – in a straiter and narrower place . . .

The other of their palpable errours is also described by this ocular experiment, for whereas they say that the Sun, starrs, and fire – yea, and all heat whatsoever – doth attract and draw unto it the vapours and humidity of the earth, waters and so on, we find the contrary by this our experimentall glass: for in onely laying the warm hand upon the glass, the aire dilates itself immediately and is so far from being attracted by the heat that contrariwise it flyeth away from the hand. And that this is so, it appeareth by the striking down or precipitation of the water.

II.9
Proof Positive:
Hopkins, *Discovery of Witches*

In the middle of the English Civil War, with government badly strained, Matthew Hopkins worked as a witch-hunter – paid for his services – in the eastern counties of England. About two hundred people, roughly a fifth of the total in England since 1559, were executed because of his actions or influence. During those eighty-six years, when hatred of Catholics was savage in England, the law made martyrs of 260 papists but killed four times as many as witches. In some places the only victims were women. Describing his activities in 1647, Hopkins focuses on the Essex village where he lived. He describes his methods – interrogate the accused constantly, deprive them of sleep, submerge them in water – along with the evidence that most impressed him: testimony from neighbours and other accused persons; parts of the body (extra nipples, for example) deemed unnatural. Polythelia (the clinical term for the famous witch's teats) occurs in roughly one of fifty women, but more than twice as often in men: Hopkins talks about 'Devill's marks'. Before he went to work, accusations of witchcraft in England seldom involved night-flight, sabbats or Satanic sex. But his *Discovery* – so different from Scot's polemic of the same title – relies on the continental conception of witchcraft, well advertised by that time in books and pamphlets (see 8.1–3, 19; 9.14).

*

Figure 21: A Witch Names Her Familiars

In March, 1644, he had some seven or eight of that horrible sect of witches living in the towne where he lived, a towne in Essex called Maningtree, with divers other adjacent witches of other towns, who every six weeks in the night (being alwayes on the Friday night) had their meeting close by his house, and had their severall solemne sacrifices there offered to the Devill, one of which this discoverer heard speaking to her imps one night, and bid them goe to another witch, who was thereupon apprehended and searched by women who had for many yeares knowne the Devill's marks, and found to have three teats about her, which honest women have not. So upon command from the Justice, they were to keep her from sleep two or three nights, expecting in that time to see her *familiars*, which the fourth night she called in by their severall names and told them what shapes, a quarter of an houre before they came in, there being ten of us in the roome.

The first she called was *Holt*, who came in like a white kitling. Second, *Jarmara*, who came in like a fat spaniel without any legs at all; she said she kept him fat, for she clapt her hand on her belly and said he suckt good blood from her body. Third, *Vinegar Tom*, who was like a long-legg'd greyhound with an head like an oxe, with a long taile and broad eyes, who when this Discoverer spoke to and bade him goe to the place provided for him and his angels, immediately transformed himselfe into the shape of a child of foure yeeres old without a head, and gave halfe a dozen turnes about the house and vanished at the doore. Fourth, *Sack and Sugar*, like a black rabbet. Fifth, *Newes*, like a polcat.

All these vanished away in a little time. Immediately after this witch, confessed severall other witches from whom she had her *imps* and named to divers women where their marks were, the number of their marks and *imps* and imps' names, as *Elemauzer, Pyewacket, Peck in the Crown, Grizzel Greedigut* and so on, which no mortall could invent.

And upon their searches the same markes were found, the same number and in the same place, and the like confessions from them of the same imps, though they knew not that we were told before. And so peached one another thereabouts that joyned together in the like damnable practise, that in our Hundred in Essex twenty-nine were condemned at once, four brought twenty-five miles to be hanged where this Discoverer lives, for sending the Devill like a beare to kill him in his garden.

So by seeing diverse of the false papps and trying wayes with hundreds of them, he gained this experience, and for ought he knowes, any man else may find them as well as he and his company, if they had the same skill and experience . . . The parties so judging can justifie their skill to any and shew good reasons why such markes are not meerly naturall . . . For never was any man tryed by search of his body but commonly a dozen of the ablest men in the parish or elsewhere were present, and most commonly as many ancient skilfull matrons and midwives present when the women are tryed, which marks not only he and his company attest to be very suspitious, but all beholders . . .

The reasons in breefe are three, which for the present he judgeth to differ from naturall marks, which are, first, he judgeth by the unusualnes of the place where he findeth the teats in or on their bodies, being farre distant from any usuall place from whence such naturall markes proceed . . . second, they are most commonly insensible and feele neither pin, needle, aule and so on thrust through them; third, the often variations and mutations of these marks into severall formes confirmes the matter . . .

If a witch hear a month or two before that the *witch-finder* (as they call him) is comming, they will and have put out their imps to others to suckle them, even to their owne young and tender children. These upon search are found to have dry skinnes and filmes only and be close to the flesh. Keepe her twenty-four houres with a diligent eye that none of her spirits come in any visible shape to suck her, the women have seen the next day after her teats extended out to their former filling length, full of corruption ready to burst. And leaving her alone then one quarter of an houre and let the women go up againe, and shee will have them drawn by her imps close againe: *probatum est* . . .

[The Devil] seekes not their bloud, as if he could not subsist without that nourishment. But he often repairs to them and gets it, the more to aggravate the witch's damnation and to put her in mind of her covenant. And as he is a spirit and prince of the ayre, he appeares to them in any shape whatsoever, which shape is occasioned by him through joyning of condensed thickned aire together, and many times doth assume shapes of many creatures. But to create any thing he cannot do it: it is only proper to God. But in this case of drawing out of these teats, he doth really enter into the body [of a] reall, corporeall, substantiall creature and forceth that creature (he working in it) to his desired ends, and useth the organs of that body to speake withall to make his compact up with the witches, be the creature cat, rat, mouse and so on . . .

In the infancy of this discovery, it was not only thought fitting [to deprive the accused of sleep] but enjoyned in Essex and Suffolke by the magistrates, with this intention only – because they being kept awake would be more the active to cal their imps in open view the sooner to their helpe, which oftentimes have so happened. And never or seldome did any witch ever complaine in the time of their keeping for want of rest. But after they had beat their heads together in the [jail], and after this use was not allowed of by the judges and other magistrates, it was never since used, which is a yeare and a halfe since.

Neither were any kept from sleep by any order or direction since, but peradventure their own stubborne wills did not let them sleep, though tendered and offered to them . . . And the meaning of walking of them at the highest extent of cruelty was only they to walke about themselves the night they were watched, only to keepe them waking: and the reason was this, when . . . they be suffered so to couch, immediately comes their familiars into the room and scareth the watchers and heartneth on the witch . . .

It is not denyed but many were so served [by tying them up and throwing them into deep water] as had papps and floated, others that had none were tryed with them and sunk – but marke the reasons. For first the Divel's policie is great in perswading many to come of their owne accord to be tryed, perswading them their marks are so close they shall not be found out. So as diverse have come ten or twelve miles to be searched of their own accord and hanged for their labour – as one Meggs, a baker, did, who lived within seven miles of Norwich and was hanged at Norwich Assizes for witchcraft. Then when they find that the Devil tells them false, they reflect on him, and he – as forty have confessed – adviseth them to be swome and tels them they shall sinke and be cleared that way. Then when they be tryed that way and floate, they see the Devill deceives them againe, and have so laid open his treacheries . . .

[Hopkins] utterly denyes that confession of a witch to be of any validity when it is drawn from her by any torture or violence whatsoever: although after watching, walking or swimming, diverse have suffered, yet peradventure magistrates with much care and diligence did solely and fully examine them after sleepe and consideration sufficient. Second, he utterly denyes that confession of a witch which is drawn from her by flattery: for example, '*if you will confesse, you shall go home, you shall not go to the [jails] nor be hanged*', and so on. Third, he utterly denyes that confession of a witch when she confesseth any improbability [or] impossibility, as flying in the ayre, riding on a broom and so on. Fourth, he utterly denyes a confession of a witch, when it is interrogated to her and words put into her mouth, to be of any force or effect . . .

In brief he will declare what confession of a witch is of validity and force in his judgement to hang a witch: when a witch is first found with teats, then sequestred from her house, which is onely to keep her old associates from her, and so by good counsell brought into a sad condition, by understanding of the horribleness of her sin, and the judgements threatned against her; and knowing the Devil's malice and subtile circumventions, is brought to remorse and sorrow for complying with Satan so long, and disobeying God's sacred commands, doth then desire to unfold her mind with much bitterness; and then without any of the before-mentioned hard usages or questions put to her, doth of her owne accord declare what was the occasion of the Devil's appearing to her – whether ignorance, pride, anger, malice and so on was predominant over her – she doth then declare what speech they had, what likeness he was in, what voice he had, what familiars he sent her, what number of spirits, what names they had, what shape they were in, what imployment she set them about to severall persons in severall places (unknowne to the hearers) – all which mischiefes being proved to be done, at the same time she confessed to the same parties for the same cause and all effected, is testimony enough against her, for all her denyall . . .

God suffers the Devill many times to doe much hurt, and the Devill doth play many times the deluder and impostor with these witches, in perswading them that they are the cause of such and such a murder wrought by him with their consents, when and indeed neither he nor they had any hand in it, as thus: we must needs argue he is of a long standing, above six thousand yeers, then he must needs be the best scholar in all knowledges of arts and tongues and so have the best skill in physicke, judgement in physiognomie and knowledge of what disease is reigning or predominant in this or that man's body – and so for cattell too – by reason of his long experience. This subtile tempter knowing such a man lyable to some sudden disease (as by experience I have found) as plurisie, imposthume and so on, he resorts to divers witches: if they know the man and seek to make a difference between the witches and the party, it may be by telling them he hath threatned to have them very shortly searched and so hanged for witches, then they all consult with Satan to save themselves.

And Satan stands ready prepared with a *'what will you have me doe for you, my deare and nearest children, covenanted and compacted with me in my hellish league and sealed with your blood, my delicate firebrand-darlings'*. 'Oh thou,' say they, 'that at the first didst promise to save us, thy servants, from any of our deadly enemies' discovery and didst promise to avenge and slay all those we pleased that did offend us, murther that wretch suddenly who threatens the downfall of your loyall subjects.' He then promiseth to effect it.

Next newes is heard the partie is dead, he [Satan] comes to the witch and gets a world of reverence, credence and respect for his power and activeness – when and indeed the disease kills the party, not the witch nor the Devill, onely the Devill knew that such a disease was predominant. And the witch aggravates her damnation by her familiarity and consent to the Devill and so comes likewise in compass of the lawes. This is Satan's usuall impostring and deluding but not his constant course of proceeding, for he and the witch doe mischiefe too much. But I would that magistrates and jurats would a little examine witnesses when they heare witches confess such and such a murder, whether the party had not long time before, or at the time when the witch grew suspected, some disease or other predominant which might cause that issue or effect of death.

II.10

The Ancient Real Theosophy:
Vaughan, *Anthroposophia theomagica*

In the period before his *Anthroposophia* was published, Thomas Vaughan was educated at Oxford, while Oxford was fighting two wars: one conflict ended when Charles I was beheaded in 1649; dethroning Aristotle was also underway but took longer. Vaughan fought for the King in England's Civil War and against the Aristotelians – or Peripatetics – at the university and afterward. He also feuded endlessly with another innovator, the Cambridge philosopher Henry More (see 11.11). Thomas was ordained, but like his twin brother, the poet Henry, he also practised medicine when many physicians saw alchemy as the key to healing. Writing as Eugenius Philalethes, he continued his alchemical work after the Restoration. One report says that he died from breathing mercury fumes. Dedicated to 'those most noble and truly reborn RC brothers', the *Anthroposophia* is a study of 'man and his state after death' and is 'grounded on his Creator's proto-chimistry' (see 11.2, 8). Echoing Paracelsus and Fludd, Vaughan's alchemy is theosophical: scripture provides data for science, whose aims are religious and 'theomagical'. Vaughan defends these novelties in a preface to the reader on the soul's mystical flights out of the body.

*

I look on this life as the progresse of an essence royall. The soul but quits her court to see the countrey. Heaven hath in it a scaene of earth, and had she bin contented with ideas, she had not travelled beyond the map. But . . . her descent speaks her original: God in love with his own beauty frames a glasse to view it by reflection, but the frailety of the matter excluding eternity, the composure was subject to dissolution.

Ignorance gave this release the name of death, but properly it is the soules birth, and a charter that makes for her liberty. She hath severall wayes to break up house, but her best is without a disease. This is her mysticall walk, an exit only to return. When she takes air at this door, it is without prejudice to her tenement. The magicians tell me 'the soul of one being goes out, and another comes in'.

Some have examin'd this, and state it an expence of influences, as if the soul exercised her royalty at the eye, or had some blinde jurisdiction in the pores. But this is to measure magicall positions by the slight, superficial strictures of the common philosophy. It is an age of intellectuall slaveries: if they meet any thing extraordinary, they prune it commonly with distinctions, or dawb it with false glosses till it looks like the traditions of Aristotle. His followers are so confident of his principles, they seek not to understand what others speak, but to make others speak what they understand. It is in nature as it is in religion; we are still hammering of old elements, but seek not the America that lyes beyond them . . .

The Peripateticks when they define the Soul, or some inferior principle, describe it onely by outward circumstances, which every childe can do, but they state nothing essentially . . . They conceive their principles irregular and prescribe rules for method, though they want matter. Their philosophie is like a church that is all discipline and no doctrine . . . Besides, their Aristotle is a poet in text, his principles are but fancies, and they stand more on our concessions than his bottom. Hence it is that his followers, notwithstanding the assistance of so many ages, can fetch nothing out of him but notions . . .

Their compositions are a meer tympanie of termes. It is better then a fight in Quixot to observe what duels and digladiations they have about him. One will make him speak sense, another nonsense and a third both: Aquinas palps him gently, Scotus makes him winch, and he is taught like an ape to shew severall tricks. If we look on his adversaries, the least amongst them hath foyld him, but Telesius knock'd him in the head and Campanella hath quite discomposed him. But . . . this Aristotle thrives by scuffles, and the world cryes him up when trueth cryes him down.

The Peripatetickes look on God as they do on carpenters, who build with stone and timber, without any infusion of life. But the world, which is Gods building, is full of spirit, quick and living. This spirit is the cause of multiplication, of severall perpetuall productions of minerals, vegetables, and creatures ingendred by putrefaction, all which are manifest, infallible arguments of life. Besides, the texture of the universe clearly discovers its animation . . .

Thou wilt tell me perhaps, this is new philosophy and that of Aristotle is old. It is indeed, but in the same sense as religion is at Rome. It is not the primitive trueth of the creation, not the ancient, reall theosophie of the Hebrews and Egyptians, but a certain preternaturall upstart, a vomit of Aristotle, which his followers, with so much diligence, lick up and swallow. I present thee not here with any clamorous opposition of their patrone but a positive expresse of principles as I finde them in nature. I may say of them as Moses said of the fiat: 'These are the generations of the heavens and of the earth in the day that the Lord God made the heavens and the earth.' They are things *extra intellectum*, sensible practicall trueths, not meer vagaries and rambles of the braine.

The True Philosophick Cabbala: More, *Conjectura cabbalistica*, 2.3

Henry More was an early admirer of Descartes in England. Unlike Fludd and Vaughan, he was taken seriously by other British advocates of the new science – devout Christians who worried that the mechanical philosophy was eroding the foundations of religion. In the interest of piety, More proposes a reading of the Bible that stays faithful to the (Hebrew) text, explains natural science, accords with reason and supports Christian theology. He traces this 'philosophick Cabbala' to Plotinus, Plato and Pythagoras – claiming that Pythagoras learned from the Jews and worked miracles that prove his theories. His ancient metaphysics is a good match for Cartesian physics: it is not fanciful, rash, inconstant or too inquisitive – 'curious' is More's word. Since it fits the biblical text, this Kabbalah is not unrestrained or enthusiastic. And nothing with such good results is too curious, More contends, nor is it rash for Christians to reveal the secrets of religion. On one charge – inconsistency – he seems more vulnerable, having changed his mind about theosophy: he no longer holds that 'scripture does not teach men philosophy'.

*

Let us now take a general view of this whole Cabbala and more summarily consider the strength thereof . . . As for the truths themselves, first, they are such as may well become so holy and worthy a person as Moses if he would philosophize – they being very precious and choice truths and very highly removed above the conceit of the vulgar and so the more likely to have been delivered to him or to Adam first by God for a special mysterie. Secondly, they are such that the more they are examined, the more irrefutable they will be found, no hypothesis that was ever yet propounded to men so exquisitely well agreeing with the phaenomena of nature, the attributes of God, the passages of Providence and the rational faculties of our own minds. Thirdly, there is a continued sutablenesse and applicability to the text of Moses all along, without any force or violence done to grammar or criticisme. Fourthly and lastly, there is a great usefulnesse – if not necessity – at least of some of them, they being such substantial props of religion and so great encouragements to a sedulous purification of our mindes and study of true piety.

Now for the dignity of the persons, such as were Pythagoras, Plato and Plotinus, it will be argued from the constant fame of that high degree of virtue and righteousnesse and devout love of the Deity that is everywhere acknowledged in them, besides whatsoever miraculous has happened to them or been performed by them.

And as for Pythagoras, if you consult his life in Iamblichus, he was held in so great admiration by those in his time that he was thought by some to be the son of Apollo . . . His looks and speeches did so wonderfully carry away the minds of all that conversed with him that they could not withhold from affirming that he was . . . the offspring of God – which is not to be taken in our strict theological sense but according to the mode of the ancient Greeks, who looked upon men heroically and eminently good and virtuous to be divine souls and of a celestial extract . . . This eminency of his acknowledged amongst the heathen will seem more credible if we but consider the advantage of his conversation with the wisest men then upon Earth: to wit, the Jewish priests and prophets, who had their knowledge from God as Pythagoras had from them. From whence I conceive that of Iamblichus to be true which he writes concerning Pythagoras his philosophy, that it is 'a philosophy that at first was delivered by God or his holy angels'.

But that Pythagoras was acquainted with the Mosaical or Jewish philosophy there is ample testimony . . . It was a common fame that Pythagoras was a disciple of the prophet Ezekiel. And though he gives no belief to the report, yet that learned antiquary Mr Selden seems inclinable enough to think it true in his first book *On the Natural Law Among the Hebrews*, where you may peruse more fully the citations of the . . . authors. Besides all these, Iamblichus also affirms that he lived at Sidon, his native countrey, where he fell acquainted with the prophets and successors of one Mochus, the physiologer or natural philosopher . . . which, as Mr Selden judiciously conjectures, is to be read . . . 'with the prophets that succeeded Moses the philosopher'.

Wherefore it is very plain that Pythagoras had his philosophy from Moses. And that philosophy which to this very day is acknowledged to be his, we seeing that it is so fitly applicable to the text all the way, what greater argument can there be desired to prove that it is the true philosophick Cabbala thereof?

But there is yet another argument to prove further the likelihood of his conversing with the prophets, which will also further set out the dignity of his person, and that is the miracles that are recorded of him. For it should seem Pythagoras was not only initiated into the Mosaical theory but had arrived also to the power of working miracles, as Moses and the succeeding prophets did. And very strange facts are recorded both in Porphyrius and Iamblichus, as that . . . he shewed his thigh to Abaris the priest and that he affirmed that it glistered like gold and thence pronounced that he was Apollo . . . I shall only adde his predictions of earthquakes . . . his present slaking of plagues in cities, his silencing of violent winds and tempests, his calming the rage of seas and rivers and the like . . .

And now I have said thus much of Pythagoras . . . there will be lesse need to insist upon Plato and Plotinus, their philosophy being the same that Pythagoras his was, and so alike applicable to Moses his text. Plato's exemplarity of life and virtue – together with his high knowledge in the more sacred mysteries of God and the state of the soul of man in this world and that other – deservedly got to himself the title of 'divine.' . . . But as for miracles, I know none he did . . . For his acquaintance with the Mosaical learning . . . Numenius the Platonist . . . ingenuously confesses 'what is Plato but Moses in Greek?'

As for Plotinus, that which Porphyrius records of him falls little short of a miracle, as being able by the majesty of his own minde – as his enemy Olympius confessed – to retort that magick upon him which he practised against Plotinus, and that, sedately sitting amongst his friends, he would tell them: 'now Olympius his body it gathered like a purse, and his limbs beat one against another'. And though he was not instructed by the Jewish priests and prophets, yet he was a familiar friend of that hearty and devout Christian and learned Father of the Church, Origen, whose authority I would also cast in, together with the whole consent of the learned amongst the Jewes.

For there is nothing strange in the metaphysical part of this Cabbala but what they have constantly affirmed to be true. But the unmannerly superstition of many is such that they will give more to an accustomed opinion – which they have either taken up of themselves or has been conveyed unto them by the confidence of some private theologer – to the authority of either Fathers, churches, workers of miracles or (what is best of all) the most solid reasons that can be propounded, which if they were capable of, they could not take any offence at my admittance of the Cartesian philosophy into this present Cabbala: the principles and the more notorious conclusions thereof offering themselves so freely and unaffectedly and so aptly and fittingly taking their place in the text that I knew not how with judgement and conscience to keep them out . . .

For mine own part (but not without submission to better judgements), I should look upon Des Cartes as a man more truly inspired in the knowledge of nature then any that have professed themselves so this sixteen hundred years. And being even ravished with admiration of his transcendent mechanical inventions for the salving the phaenomena in the world, I should not stick to compare him with Bezaliel and Aholiab, those skilful and cunning workers of the Tabernacle who, as Moses testifies, were filled with the Spirit of God, and they were of an excellent understanding to finde out all manner of curious works . . .

In defence of my philosophick Cabbala, it will not be unseasonable to subjoin something by way of apology for the Cabbalist, for I finde myself liable to no lesse then three several imputations, viz. of trifling curiositie, of rashnesse and of inconstancy of judgement.

And as for the first, I know that men that are more severely philosophical and rational will condemn me of too much curious pains in applying natural and metaphysical truths to an uncertain and lubricous text or letter, when as they are better known and more fitly conveied by their proper proof and arguments then by fancying they are aimed at in such obscure and aenigmatical writings. But I answer: ther is that fit and full congruity of the Cabbala with the text – besides the backing of it with advantages from the history of the first rise of the Pythagorical or Platonical philosophy – that it ought not to be deemed a fancie but a very high probability that there is such a Cabbala as this belonging to the Mosaical letter . . . And then again for mine own part, I account no pains either curious or tedious that tend to a common good. And I conceive no smaller a part of mankinde concerned in my labours then the whole nation of the Jewes and Christendome – to say nothing of the ingenious Persian nor to despair of the Turk, though he be for the present no friend to allegories . . .

But for the imputation of rashnesse in making it my businesse to divulge those secrets or mysteries that Moses had so sedulously covered in his obscure text, I say it is the privilege of Christianity – the times now more then ever requiring it – to pull off the vail from Moses his face. And that though they be grand truths that I have discovered, yet they are as useful as sublime and cannot but highly gratifie every good and holy man that can competently judge of them.

Lastly, for inconstancy of judgement – which men may suspect me of, having heretofore declared the Scripture does not teach men philosophy – I say the change of a man's judgement for the better is no part of inconstancy but a virtue, when as to persist in what we finde false is nothing but perversenesse and pride. And it will prove no small argument for the truth of this present Cabbala, in that the evidence thereof has fetch'd me out of my former opinion wherein I seemed engaged.

But to say the truth, I am not at all inconsistent with myself, for I am still of opinion that the letter of the Scripture teaches not any precept of philosophy concerning which there can be any controversie amongst men. And when you venture beyond the literal sense, you are not taught by the Scripture, but what you have learned some other way you apply thereto. And they ought to be no trash nor trivial notions nor confutable by reason or more solid principles of philosophy that a man should dare to cast upon so sacred a text, but such as one is well assured will bear the strictest examination . . . And he that ventures beyond the letter without that guide will soon be bewilder'd and lose himself in his own fancies. Wherefore if this philosophick Cabbala of mine, amongst those many other advantages I have recited, had not this also added unto it – the aim of advancing the divine life in the world – I should look upon it as both false and unprofitable.

Magnetisms: Athanasius Kircher, *Nature's Magnetic Kingdom*, 1

Working in Galileo's shadow but with enormous energy and flair, Father Athanasius Kircher tried to lead the Jesuits out of the wilderness of scientific disgrace. He began to publish on magnetism in 1643, when he also brought out another huge book on the language of ancient Egypt. *Nature's Magnetic Kingdom, a Physiological Discussion of Nature's Triple Magnet*, is a later and shorter review of the same themes. He studied magnetism for decades, treating it as a universal force – as Newton would do with gravity. But unlike Newton he found direct traces of this energy in plants and animals, describing it in organic and vitalist terms. Magnetism is his channel 'to that real wisdom called "magic"'.

*

Just as the World-Nature, universal and all-changing, spreads through all the world's limbs, governs this universe in a definite order and rules it with changeless constancy, so it is impossible for the universe not to be ruled by a kind of law – divine, architectonic and protective – that by intention and right reason administers all things sagely and protects them with its providence.

The reason of that architectonic mind is really nothing but the changeless law of Nature that Plato calls God's art. Others name it the handmaid, assistant or instrument of the Craftsman by whom all things are managed, sustained and exist. Just as this law, as old as the world, was bound to it by the Craftsman most wise at the ineffable direction of his divine providence – necessity by decree, so to speak – so there is nothing in the whole line of animals, plants and minerals that one can see suffused with any special power unless, so to speak, that thing is subject to the rule of this law . . .

Everything in the world partakes of this law since there is no thing, not even the smallest, into which it does not direct some energy. Thereby it sustains and protects what it has begotten, keeping it strong within, protected against all troubles and actions contrary to its nature. Since this changeless natural energy, implanted in each and every thing, is not always one of those qualities that the philosophers call manifest and elementary, I have thought it not at all unfitting to use 'magnetism' for the same quality, generally occult and defying description, called *colcodea* by the Arabs and by the Hebrews a tool of divine power – a form hidden and active in all things that others describe as a quality of sympathy and antipathy.

My thinking is that every power like this that exists within things generally acts – by analogy with the magnet – through a kind of attraction and repulsion. This attraction is a kind of love whereby, through natural desire, things seek what is good, friendly and similar to them. And repulsion is the anger in a kind of hatred whereby they strive to get rid of the bad, unfriendly and dissimilar.

And this is the reason why I have titled this little book *Nature's Triple Magnet*: besides distinguishing the magnetisms of each thing from magnetism as such, I describe the attractive and repulsive energy concealed in each thing not just in theory but also by experimental demonstration, as well as the matching application of actives to passives that produces astonishing effects – the sole aim of our magnetic technology. Using a special new method, I track down the bindings of the whole universe and hence of all bodily things. In fact, whoever possesses these keys has a gateway to all the information one could want about hidden things: he can boast of finding the gate open to that real wisdom called 'magic' that all real philosophers seek.

II.13

A Demon Witnessed by Multitudes:
Joseph Glanvill to Lord Brereton

Glanvill, a friend of Henry More and a clergyman, was also a friend of the new philosophy (see 11.11). His first book, *On the Vanity of Dogmatizing*, develops the mitigated scepticism of Marin Mersenne more than the rationalism of Descartes. Knowing how fragile faith was in his 'searching and incredulous age', Glanvill also attacked 'modern Sadducism' in the title of his book, meaning by that phrase the 'disbelief of spirits' and the consequent subversion of faith in immortality encouraged by innovations in philosophy. Writing to Lord Brereton, a founder of the Royal Society, he describes his investigation of a cause célèbre that also attracted the King's attention. Starting in the spring of 1661, the owner of a house in Tedworth, his family, his neighbours and a stream of visitors reported a 'thumping and drumming' in the house as well as strange smells and sights that Glanvill and others traced to a demon. Less suspicious than others of fraud or delusion, Glanvill went to the house, talked to the locals, read documents and wrote a report. His motive was to find 'evidence against Sadducism, the disease of our age'. His results were 'to demonstrate that there are spirits that sometimes sensibly intermeddle in our affairs'.

*

Now though you, my Lord, are in no danger of that cold and desperate disease, the disbelief of spirits and apparitions, nor need confirmation in the article of our future existence, yet being ingaged by my promise . . . to send your Lordship the story of the drummer at Mr Mompesson's house at Tedworth . . . I have now at length put the most of those particulars I could obtain into your hands . . .

Master John Mompesson of Tedworth in Wiltshire, being about the middle of March in the year 1661 at a neighbouring town called Ludgarshal, heard a drum beat there . . . He enquired of the bayliffe of the town . . . what it meant. The bayliffe told him that they had for some dayes been troubled by that idle drummer, who demanded money of the Constable by vertue of a pretended pass . . . Mr Mompesson . . . found that his pass and warrant were forgeries . . . The fellow then confest the cheat and begg'd earnestly for his drum. But Mr Mompesson . . . left the drum with the bayliffe and the drummer in the Constable's hands, who it seems after, upon intreaty, let him go.

About the midst of April following, when Mr Mompesson was preparing for a journey to London, the bayliffe sent the drum to his house. And being returned, his wife told him that they had been much affrighted in the night by thieves in his absence and that the house had like to have been broken up. He had not been at home above three nights when the same noise returned . . . a thumping and drumming on the top of his house, which continued a good space and then by degrees went off into the air . . .

After a month's racket without, it came into the room where the drum lay, where it would be four or five nights in seven, making great hollow sounds and sensibly shaking the beds and windows. It would come within half an hour after they were in bed and stay almost two. The sign of its approach was an hurling in the air over the house. And at its recess they should hear a drum beat, like the breaking up of a guard. It continued in this room for the space of two months, the gentleman himself lying there to observe it. And though it was very troublesome in the forepart of the night, yet after two hours' disturbance it would desist and leave all in quietness. At which time perhaps the laws of the Black Society required its presence at the general rendezvous elsewhere.

About this time the gentleman's wife was brought to bed: the noise came a little that night she was in travail but then forbore for three weeks till she had recover'd strength. After this civil cessation, it returned in a ruder manner than before, applying wholly to the younger children, whose bedsteads it would beat with that violence that all present would expect when they would fall in pieces. Those that laid their hands upon them could feel no blows but perceived them to shake exceedingly. It would for an hour together beat what they call 'roundheads' and 'cuckolds', the 'tattoo' and several other points of warre – and that as dexterously as any drummer – after which it would get under the bed and scratch there as if it had iron tallons. It would lift the children up in their beds, follow them from one room to another and for a while applyed to none particularly but them . . .

On the 5th of November, 1662, it kept a mighty noise, and one of the gentleman's servants observing two boards in the childrens' room that seemed to move, he bid it give him one of them, and presently the board came within a yard of him. The fellow added 'nay, let me have it in my hand', upon which it was shuft quite home. The man thrust it back, and the daemon returned it to him, and so from one to another at least twenty times together till the gentleman forbad his servant such familiarities. That morning it left a sulphurous smell behind it, very displeasant and offensive, which possibly, my Lord, some would conjecture to be a smack of the bituminous matter brought from the mediterranious vaults to which we may suppose the vehicles of those impure spirits to be nearly allyed.

At night the Minister of the place, one Mr Cragge, and many of the neighbours came to the house and went to prayer at the children's bedside, where at that time it was very troublesome and loud. During the time of prayer, it withdrew into the cockloft, but the service being ended, it returned. And in the sight and presence of the company, the chairs walked about the room, the childrens shooes were thrown over their heads, and every loose thing moved about the chamber. Also a bed-staffe was thrown at the Minister . . .

Figure 22: The Drumming Demon of Tedworth

It would sometimes lift up the servants with their beds and lay them down again gently without any more prejudice than the fright of being carried to the drummer's quarters. And at other times it would lie like a great weight upon their feet. 'Twas observed that when the noise was loudest and came with the most suddain and surprizing violence, yet no dog would move. The knocking was oft so boysterous and rude that it hath been heard at a considerable distance in the fields and awakened the neighbours in the village, none of which live very near this house.

About the latter end of December, 1662, the drummings were less frequent and the noise the fiend made was a gingling as it had been of money . . . After this it desisted from its ruder noises and imployed itself about little apish tricks and less troublesome caprichios. On Christmas Eve, an hour before day, one of the little boyes arising out of his bed was hit on a sore place in his heel by the latch of the door, which the waggish daemon had pluckt out and thrown at him . . . The night after Christmas Day, it threw all the old gentlewoman's cloaths about the room and hid her Bible in the ashes. In such impertinent ludricous fegaries it was frequent. And such passages are to me considerable intimations that the imps of witches and other troublesome appearing spirits are not alwayes devils – as I have discours't in my 'Considerations about Witchcraft' . . .

About the beginning of January, 1663, they were wont to hear a singing in the chimney before it came down. And one night about this time lights were seen in the house, one of which came into Mr Mompesson's chamber, which seemed blue and glimmering and caused a great stiffness in their eyes that saw it – an intimation that this daemon had its vehicle from the bituminous mines of the lower regions. After the light, something was heard coming up the stairs, as if it had been someone without shooes. The light was also four or five times seen in the children's chamber . . . During the time of the knocking, when many were present, a gentleman of the company said, 'Satan, if the drummer set thee a work, give three knocks and no more,' which it did very distinctly and stopt. Then the Gentleman knockt to see if it would answer him as it was wont, but it remained quiet. He further tryed it the same way, bidding it – for confirmation – if it were the drummer, to give five knocks and no more that night, which it did accordingly and was silent all the night after . . .

After this, the old gentlewoman's Bible was found in the ashes open, the paper side being downwards. Mr Mompesson took it up and observed that it lay open at the third chapter of St Mark, in which there mention is of the unclean spirits falling down before our Saviour, of his giving power to the

Twelve to cast out Devils, and of the scribes' opinion that he cast them out through Beelzebub. The next night they strewed ashes over the chamber to see what impressions it would leave, and in the morning found in one place the resemblance of a great claw, in another of a lesser, some letters in another, which they could make nothing of, besides many circles and scratches in the ashes – all which I suppose were ludicrous devices by which the sportful daemon made pastime with humane ignorance and credulity.

About this time, as I formerly told your Lordship, my curiosity drew me to the house to be a witness of some of those strange passages. It had ceas't from its pranks of drumming and ruder noises before I came. But most of the more remarkable circumstances before related were confirmed to me there by several of the neighbours together who had been present at them. At that time it used to haunt the children. I heard it scratch very loudly and distinctly in their bed, behinde the boulster . . .

The drummer was tryed at the Assize at Salisbury for some petty fellonies he had committed, and there these passages also were produc'd and urg'd. He was condemn'd to the Islands and was accordingly sent away, but – I know not how – made a shift to come back again. And 'tis observable that during all the time of his restraint and absence the house was in quiet. But as soon as ever he came back, the disturbance also returned. He had been a souldier under Cromwel and used to talk much of gallant books he had of an odde fellow's who was counted a wizard . . .

Thus, my Lord, I have given your Honour the summe of the relation which I extracted from Mr Mompesson's own letters – the same particulars also he writ to the Doctor of the Chair in Oxford . . . a Gentleman of whose veracity in this account I know not the least ground of suspicion . . . You know, my Lord, the credit of matters of fact depends much upon the consideration of the relators. And if they cannot be deceived themselves nor supposed any wayes interested to impose upon others, we may and we ought to acquiesce in their reports. For upon these circumstances all humane faith is grounded, and matter of fact is not capable of any proof besides but that of immediate sensible evidence.

Now this gentleman cannot be thought ignorant himself of the truth and certainty of what he relates, it having been done in his family and himself a witness – and that not of a little circumstance or two, but of a hundred, not for once or twice only, but for the space of some years, during which time he was a concerned and inquisitive observer. So that it cannot with any shew of reason be supposed that any of his servants abused him, since in all that time he must needs have detected the deceit. And what interest could any of his family have had . . . to continue so long, so troublesome and so injurious a fallacy? Nor can it with anything of more probability be imagined that his own melancholly deluded him since – besides that he is no crasie or imaginative person – that humour could not have been so lasting and pertinacious. Or if it were so in him, can we think he infected his whole family and those multitudes of his neighbours and others that think themselves as well assured of those actions, of which they were witnesses, as himself? These are wilde supposals and not like to tempt any but those whose wills are their reasons . . .

What interest could he serve in maintaining such a cheat – if it were one and he knew it to be so? He suffered by it in his name, in his estate, in his affairs and in the general peace of his family. Those that believ'd not any thing of spirits or witchcraft in those transactions – which were not a few – took him for an impostor. Those that did, many of them judg'd the permission of such an extraordinary evil to be the judgement of God upon him for some notorious impiety. Thus his name was continually exposed to censure and his estate suffered . . . To which, if I adde the continual hurry that his family was in, the affrights, vexations and tossings up and down of his children, and the watchings and dissturbance of his whole House – in all which himself must needs be the most concerned person – I say the putting together of these circumstances will be evidence enough that he could have no interest in designing to put a cheat upon the world in which he would most of all have injured and abused himself . . .

After things were weighed and examined, several that were prejudicated enough before went away strongly convicted. To which I adde that there are divers particulars in the story in which no abuse or deceit could have been practised: as the motion of boards and chairs of themselves, the beating of a drum in the midst of a room and in the air when nothing was to be seen, the heat that fill'd a whole room without fire in excessive cold weather, the scratching and panting where nothing ordinary could be suspected for the cause and several others such like – all which have numbers of sober and uninterested persons to attest them.

'Tis true, my Lord, that when the gentlemen the King sent were there, the house was quiet and nothing heard or seen that night. And this was confidently and with triumph reported by many as an evidence of the untruth of the story. But certainly 'twas but poor logick to conclude in matters of fact from a single negative – and such a one against numerous affirmatives – and to inferr that a thing was never done because omitted at such a season, and that no body ever saw what this man or that did not. By the same rule of consequence, I may say that there were never any robbers upon Salisbury Plains because I have often travelled over them and never met any of those sorts of violence, and the Frenchman inferred well that said there was no Sun in England because he was six weeks here and never saw it.

This, my Lord, is the common argument of those that deny the being of apparitions: they have travel'd all times of the night and never saw any thing worse than themselves, and it may be so; therefore, spirits and apparitions are bugs and impostures. But why do not such arguers conclude that there was never a cutpurse on Ludgate Hill because they have past that way a hundred times and were never met with by any of those nimble practitioners. Certainly, he that denyes apparitions upon the confidence of this negative – against the vast heap of positive assurances – is credulous if he believe there was never any highwayman in the world if he himself was never rob'd. And the tryals of Assizes and attestations of those that have [been robbed], if he will be just, ought to move his assent no more in this case than in that of witches and apparitions, which have the very same evidence.

Thus, my Lord, I have given your Honour the sum of this affair, and I have taken notice of and recorded the particulars of the relation not to satisfie curiosity or feed the humour that delights in wonders . . . But I consider it as a great evidence against Sadducism, the disease of our age. And though those passages are not so dreadful, tragical and amazing as there are some related in stories of this kinde, yet are they never the less probable or true for being less prodigious and astonishing. And they are strange enough to prove themselves the effects of some invisible extraordinary agent and to demonstrate that there are spirits that sometimes sensibly intermeddle in our affairs.

And I think they do it with as many clear circumstances of evidence as any thing that is extant. For these things were not done long ago, or at far distance in an ignorant age or among a barbarous people. They were not seen only by two or three of the melancholick and superstitious and reported by those that made them serve the advantage and interest of a faction. They were not the passages of a day or night nor the vanishing glances of an apparition. But those circumstances were near and late, publick, frequent and of years continuance, witnessed by multitudes of competent and unbiast attestors and acted in a searching and incredulous age – arguments enough for the conviction of a modest and capable reason. This relation, my Lord, you perceive proves the being of spirits and apparitions but not so directly that of witches and diabolick contracts, and therefore, while I am about it, I shall adde the other narrative which I promised your Honour.

II.14
Angel Midwives:
Leibniz, Letter to Thomasius

Writing in 1669 to his teacher, Jacob Thomasius, who had just published a history of ancient philosophy, the young Leibniz flatters the older man, whose tolerance for scholasticism was stronger than his student's. Leibniz argues that the 'reformed' thought of his century – not antiquated scholastic physics – is in tune with Aristotle, especially on the issue of substantial form. Since that doctrine was the basis of conventional accounts of the soul's immortality, Leibniz walked on thin ice by materializing form as shape (*figura*) and locating the only source of motion in God. He faces the same threat of 'atheism' that disturbed Boyle, Glanvill and More (see 11.11, 13, 15). Reviewing various solutions to the mind/body problem, he sees Campanella's pansensism as more coherent than the scholastic contrivances (see 11.5–7). But he mocks Agrippa for getting the same results in a cruder way by attaching an angel to every physical object (see 9.1, 3).

*

Your 'little taste' of a history of philosophy can't have that title. It's more appetizing than all the others, showing what a difference there is between bare lists of names and those deep accounts that you provide of how the teachings relate to one another . . . Most of the others know more about antiquity than about the subject and have given us lives instead of the teachings . . . You have Patrizi, Telesio, Campanella, Bodin, Nizolio, Fracastoro, Cardano, Galileo, Bacon, Gassendi, Hobbes, Descartes, Basso, Digby, Sennert, Sperling, Derodon, Deusing and many others to name for ripping apart the mantle of philosophy . . .

I don't mind saying that more things please me in Aristotle's books *On Physics* than in the *Meditations* of Descartes – that's how Cartesian I am! And I'll also bet that all eight books can be accepted without damage to the reformed philosophy . . . Who wouldn't welcome his substantial form? There's nothing more real than prime matter. The only question is whether the points about matter, form and change that Aristotle discussed abstractly are to be explained by size, shape and motion. The scholastics say no, the reformers yes. To me the view of the reformers seems not only more accurate but also more in agreement with Aristotle . . .

Once Aristotle has been reconciled with the reformed philosophy, what remains is a demonstration of its own truth, just as the Christian religion can be confirmed both from reason and history and also from sacred scripture. What must be confirmed, then, is that nothing exists in the universe but mind, space, matter and motion . . . But if we show that nothing else is needed to explain the world's phenomena and their possible causes . . . that by itself will establish that the better hypotheses are those of the recent thinkers who use only those things to deal with the phenomena . . .

The better hypotheses are the clearer ones. Now the human mind can really imagine nothing other than mind (when it thinks about itself), space, matter, motion and what results from their relations. Anything you add is just words that can form names and combine in various ways but cannot produce explanations or understanding. Can anyone imagine a being that does not take part in extension or thinking? So why bother to posit souls of animals and plants, bodiless forms of elements and substantial forms of plants that lack extension?

In his book *On the Sense in Things and On Magic*, then . . . Campanella was more correct – though actually wrong, while conforming to his own hypotheses – to attribute sense, knowledge, imagination and will to those substantial forms that lack extension in soulless things. Not out of tune with him is Agrippa's occult philosophy – he assigns an angel to each thing as its midwife . . . This takes us back to as many tiny gods as there are substantial forms –a pagan polytheism, essentially. Accordingly, an attribute of their devices is appetite along with that natural instinct which is also the source of natural cognition and then of an axiom: 'nature does nothing in vain' or 'everything avoids its own destruction' or 'like enjoys like' or 'matter desires a nobler form' and others of that sort. But the fact is that there is no appetite and no wisdom in nature, although a beautiful order emerges from it because it is God's clock.

Clearly, then, the hypotheses of the reformed philosophy – because they are clear and not superfluous – are better than the scholastic hypotheses . . . This makes it plain that we must take our explanation of all qualities and changes from size, shape, motion and so on, and that heat, colour and the rest are nothing but fine motions and shapes. For the rest, I daresay there will never be resistance against atheists, Socinians, naturalists and sceptics unless this philosophy is firmly established.

II.15

Intercourse with Good Spirits: Boyle,
Dialogue on the Converse with Angels

Robert Boyle is best known for the *Sceptical Chymist*, a title that might suggest complete opposition to alchemy or even the whole occult philosophy. On the contrary, an abiding passion for Boyle was alchemical gold-making, and his target in that famous book was just one line of alchemical speculation – a textbook version of the Paracelsian theory of three elements (see 9.4–5). Before releasing a second edition of the *Sceptical Chymist* in 1680, Boyle had sketched – but never finished or published – another work, where seeking the Philosopher's Stone 'has higher aims than . . . to Transmute inferior mettalls into gold'. Four friends debate the Stone's use as bait for Angels: Arnobius (A), Cornelius (C), Eleutherius (E) and Timotheus (T). All but Timotheus have recently visited a fifth friend, Parisinus, and have seen additions to his library. Arnobius and Eleutherius defend alchemical angel-magic as a cure for an atheist sickness – 'that cold and desperate disease, the disbelief of spirits and apparitions,' in Glanvill's words (see 11.13).

*

T   Since I saw you coming all three together out of Parisinus's house, give me leave to ask you whether any of you has taken notice of the new sett of books that he has lately added to his library . . .

A   When I came in, I found him in his study and was somewhat surpris'd to find there a collection of . . . old books about the Phylosophers-stone . . .

T   I presume, then, that you cannot but wonder, as well as I do, that a man versd in rationall and experimentall Phylosophy . . . should with so much application of minde peruse those dull Authors that deserve to be left in as great an obscurity as they affect in their aenigmaticall writings . . .

E   You mistake the scope and drift of Parisinus's studyes, for . . . I am induc'd to guess that in his Hermetick attempts he has higher aims then the acquiring of the skill to Transmute inferior mettalls into gold . . .

A   What Eleutherius does but suspect . . . has bin long my opinion, for I think his ambition reaches higher then gold or anything that gold can purchase . . . The main reason why Parisinus so much vallues and cultivates the study of Hermetick Phylosophy is that he . . . hopes that the acquisiton of the Philosophers-stone may be an inlett into another sort of knowledge and a step to the attainment of some intercourse with good spirits . . .

T   Having allways lookt uppon Parisinus both as a rationall person and as a good christian, I cannot but exceedingly admire that he should think it either possible or lawfull for him, by the help of a red powder – which is but a corporeall and even an inanimate thing – to acquire communion with incorporeall spirits . . . Since an Apostle tells us that even the divell can transforme himself into an Angel of light, tis very dangerous to have, much less to procure, the conversation of Angels . . . But if . . . Parisinus . . . could be sure that the spirits . . . [do not] assend out of the bottomless pitt, yet how will he acquit himself of an idolatricall commerce with spirits? . . . I shall add another dissuasive . . . for I dare appeal to all judicious men whether they do not think it an ambition fitter for some whimsicall Enthusiast then for so learned a man as Parisinus to hope that, if he could turne silver into gold, he might make Angels themselves quit their heaven to court his company . . .

E   I confess . . . that it seems somewhat unaccountable and therefore incredible that a little powder, that is as truly corporeall as pouder of post or of brick, should be able to attract or invite incorporeall and intelligent beings, that have neither need nor use of gold, to converse familiarly with those that – perhapps by chance or fraud – have made themselves possessors of a few drams or ounces of Transmuting pouder. For what affinity or congruity can there be betwixt the stupid and inanimate Elixir and a rationall and immortal spirit that these happy beings should delight to hover about it and . . . discover themselves in a sensible way to the chymist? . . .

A   How ever weighty these arguments may be, I know they are not new to Parisinus . . . I will tell you the substance of . . . what he lately sayd to me upon the subject in the presence of Cornelius . . . Two mediums there are by which this intercourse may be made probable. And first, that there are witches and magicians, I presume Timotheus will not deny. For besides the almost universall consent of mankind, the scripture its selfe in divers places declares no less . . .

C   Lett me add that though the scripture were silent, our own times afford us undeniable instances of the converse of evill men with evill spirits. And I my selfe know severall persons – divers of them Physitians and men of parts and not superstitious but rather the contrary – who have converse with spirits even in visible shapes . . .

A   If then there be an intercourse betwixt men and Demons, the grand difficulty . . . from the great disparity in nature between a man and a spirit falls to the ground. For the difficulty in point of Physick or Phylosophy rises from the distance between the humane nature and that of an unbodyed spirit as such, and so consists in Physicall, not in morall qualifications . . . I shall now proceed to my second Medium, which consists of some instances of Spirits – whom we have more reason to look upon as good than bad – that have conversed with men. There is in the Daemonology of the famous and learned Bodine . . . a memorable story of a good spirit or Genius that for many years familiarly assisted a friend of his, from whose own mouth he had the relation . . .

E   You put me in mind of a gentleman . . . who, having been bred a Physician and being an excellent Mathematician, was much cajold and at last perverted by a famous writer who, by many friends and foes, is thought the subtilest Atheist of our times. This Gentleman, when . . . one day I askt him . . . how he came to be converted from Atheism . . . told me that he had met with an eminent person . . . who was able to performe by skill in naturall phylosophy much more than he himselfe could ever do, and yet despised the world – and the preferments and advantages he was possesd of in it – because of the great impressions that were made on his minde by his converse with spirits, both good and bad, though the company of the latter was very unwellcome . . .

16

The Kingdom of Darkness: Leibniz, Correspondence with Samuel Clarke, 1 and 5

Gravitational force – the core of Newton's physics – drew fire from critics who insisted that only mechanical causes operate in nature. Realizing that force acting over distance would look like a defection from mechanist principles, Newton had framed his *Principia* with praise for 'the moderns, rejecting substantial forms and occult qualities'. Leibniz, Newton's fiercest opponent, turned those words against him. When he called Newton's gravity 'a scholastick occult quality', he accused his rival of contradicting himself with bankrupt notions that they both despised – the hylemorphic metaphysics that their peers had rejected, thereby depriving magic of its philosophical basis (see 7.12; 9.12–13). Writing as a herald of Enlightenment, Leibniz charges that Newton's ideas hinder not just science but also religious reform and 'bring us back again into the Kingdom of Darkness'. England was not yet 'weary of light,' says Leibniz, in the good old days when Boyle lived: the sceptical chemist had died in 1691. The alchemical enquiries shared by him and Newton were unknown to Leibniz, who himself sometimes took alchemy seriously (see 11.15).

*

Natural religion itself seems to decay (in England) very much. Many will have human souls to be material. Others make God himself a corporeal Being. Mr Locke and his followers are uncertain, at least, whether the soul be not material and naturally perishable. Sir Isaac Newton says that space is an organ which God makes use of to perceive things by. But if God stands in need of any organ to perceive things by, it will follow that they do not depend altogether upon him nor were produced by him.

Sir Isaac Newton and his followers have also a very odd opinion concerning the work of God. According to their doctrine, God Almighty wants to wind up his watch from time to time: otherwise it would cease to move. He had not, it seems, sufficient foresight to make it a perpetual motion. Nay, the machine of God's making is so imperfect – according to these gentlemen – that he is obliged to clean it now and then by an extraordinary concourse and even to mend it, as a clockmaker mends his work . . .

According to my opinion, the same force and vigour remains always in the world and only passes from one part of matter to another – agreeably to the laws of nature and the beautiful pre-established order. And I hold that when God works miracles, he does not do it in order to supply the wants of Nature, but those of Grace. Whoever thinks otherwise must needs have a very mean notion of the wisdom and power of God . . .

In good philosophy and sound theology, we ought to distinguish between what is explicable by the natures and powers of creatures and what is explicable only by the powers of the Infinite Substance. We ought to make an infinite difference between the operation of God, which goes beyond the extent of natural powers, and the operations of things that follow the law which God has given them and which he has enabled them to follow by their natural powers, though not without his assistance. This overthrows attractions, properly so called, and other operations inexplicable by the natural powers of creatures. Which kinds of operations the assertors of them must suppose to be effected by miracles or else have recourse to absurdities: that is, to the occult qualities of the schools, which some men begin to revive under the specious name of 'forces'. But they bring us back again into the Kingdom of Darkness . . .

In the time of Mr Boyle and other excellent men who flourished in England under Charles II, nobody would have ventured to publish such chimerical notions. I hope that happy time will return under so good a government as the present. Mr Boyle made it his chief business to inculcate that every thing was done mechanically in natural philosophy. But it is men's misfortune to grow, at last, out of conceit with reason itself and to be weary of light. Chimeras begin to appear again, and they are pleasing because they have something in them that is wonderful. What has happened in poetry happens also in the philosophical world. People are grown weary of rational romances . . . and they are become fond again of the tales of fairies.

As for the motions of the celestial bodies and even the formation of plants and animals, there is nothing in them that looks like a miracle except their beginning. The organism of animals is a mechanism, which supposes a divine preformation. What follows upon it is purely natural and entirely mechanical. Whatever is performed in the body of man and of every animal is no less mechanical than what is performed in a watch. The difference is only such as ought to be between a machine of divine invention and the workmanship of such a limited artist as man is . . .

I objected that an attraction – properly so called or in the scholastic sense – would be an operation at a distance without any means intervening. The author answers here that an attraction without any means intervening would be indeed a contradiction. Very well! But then what does he mean, when he will have the Sun to attract the globe of the Earth through an empty space? Is it God himself that performs it? But this would be a miracle, if ever there was any. This would surely exceed the powers of creatures. Or are perhaps some immaterial substances or some spiritual rays or some accident without a substance or some . . . other I know not what the means by which this is pretended to be performed? . . .

That means of communication (says he) is 'invisible', 'intangible', 'not mechanical'. He might as well have added 'inexplicable', 'unintelligible', 'precarious', 'groundless' and 'unexampled'. But it is *regular* (says the author), it is *constant* and consequently *natural*. I answer: it cannot be regular without being reasonable; nor natural unless it can be explained by the natures of creatures. If the means which causes an attraction, properly so called, be constant and at the same time inexplicable by the powers of creatures and yet be true, it must be a perpetual miracle. And if it is not miraculous, it is false. 'Tis a chimerical thing, a scholastick occult quality . . .

All the natural forces of bodies are subject to mechanical laws, and all the natural powers of spirits are subject to moral laws. The former follow the order of efficient causes, and the latter follow the order of final causes. The former operate without liberty, like a watch. The latter operate with liberty, though they exactly agree with that machine, which another cause, free and superior, has adapted to them before-hand.

Bibliography

INTRODUCTION
and
PART 1: STUDY NO ABOMINATION

Texts in English

The Jewish Study Bible, ed. A. Berlin and M. Z. Brettler. Oxford: Oxford University Press, 1999.

The Revised English Bible with the Apocrypha. Cambridge and Oxford: Oxford University Press and Cambridge University Press, 1989.

Suggestions for Further Reading

Blenkinsopp, Joseph, *A History of Prophecy in Ancient Israel*. Rev. ed.; Louisville: Westminster John Knox Press, 1996.

Bohak, Gideon, *Ancient Jewish Magic: A History*. Cambridge: Cambridge University Press, 2008.

Bloom, Maureen, *Jewish Mysticism and Magic: An Anthropological Perspective*. New York: Routledge, 2007.

Copenhaver, Brian, *Magic in Western Culture from Antiquity to the Enlightenment*. Cambridge: Cambridge University Press, 2015.

Evans-Pritchard, E. E., *Witchcraft, Oracles and Magic Among the Azande*. Oxford: The Clarendon Press, 1937.

—, *Theories of Primitive Religion*. Oxford: The Clarendon Press, 1965.

Rabin, Elliott, *Understanding the Hebrew Bible: A Reader's Guide*. Jersey City, NJ: KTAV, 2006.

Weber, Max, *Ancient Judaism*, trans. H. Gerth and D. Martindale. New York: The Free Press, 1952.

—, *The Sociology of Religion*, ed. T. Parsons and A. Swindler, trans. E. Fischoff. Boston: Beacon Press, 1993.

—, *The Protestant Ethic and the Spirit of Capitalism and Other Writings*, ed. and trans. P. Baehr and G. Wells. London: Penguin, 2002.

PART 2: POWER IN THE NAME OF JESUS

Texts in English

Meeks, Wayne A., ed., *The Writings of St Paul*. 2nd ed.; New York: Norton, 2007.

Miller, Robert J., ed., *The Complete Gospels: Annotated Scholars Version*. Rev. ed.; Sonoma: Polebridge Press, 1994.

Mounce, Robert J., *The New International Commentary on the New Testament: The Book of Revelation*. Rev. ed.; Grand Rapids: Errdmans, 1998.

Suggestions for Further Reading

Arnold, Clinton E., *Ephesians: Power and Magic; The Concept of Power in Ephesians in Light of Its Historical Setting*. Cambridge: Cambridge University Press, 1989.

Bernstein, Alan E., *The Formation of Hell: Death and Retribution in the Ancient and Early Christian Worlds*. Ithaca: Cornell University Press, 1993.

Johnson, Luke, *The New Testament: A Very Short Introduction*. Oxford: Oxford University Press, 2010.

Kee, Howard C., *Miracle in the Early Christian World: A Study in Sociohistorical Method*. New Haven: Yale University Press, 1983.

Pagels, Elaine, *The Origin of Satan*. New York: Random House, 1995.

Smith, Morton, *Jesus the Magician*. New York: Harper and Row, 1978.

Sorenson, Eric, *Possession and Exorcism in the New Testament and Early Christianity*. Tübingen: Mohr, 2002.

PART 3: FIRE PRIESTS, *MAGOI* AND *MAGEIA*

Texts in English

Boyce, Mary, *Textual Sources for the Study of Zoroastrianism*. Chicago: University of Chicago Press, 1984.

Clement of Alexandria, *Exhortation to the Heathen (Protrepticus)*: http://www.earlychristianwritings.com/text/clement-exhortation.html.

Diogenes Laërtius, *Lives of Eminent Philosophers*, from Perseus: www.perseus.tufts.edu.

Jowett, Benjamin, trans, *Dialogues of Plato Translated into English with Analyses and Introductions*. Oxford: The Clarendon Press, 1875.

Pausanias, *Description of Greece*, from Classical E-Text: http://www.theoi.com/Text/Pausanias.

Strabo, *The Geography*, from Lacus Curtius: http://penelope.uchicago.edu/Thayer/E/Roman/Texts/Strabo/home.html.

Suggestions for Further Reading

Boyce, Mary, *Zoroastrianism: Its Antiquity and Constant Vigour*, Costa Mesa: Mazda Publishers, 1992.

Frazer, J. G., *The Golden Bough: A Study in Magic and Religion*. Abridged, New York: Macmillan, 1922.

Hall, Edith, *Inventing the Barbarian: Greek Self-Definition through Tragedy*. Oxford: The Clarendon Press, 1989.

Lévy-Bruhl, Lucien, *How Natives Think* (*Les Fonctions mentales dans les sociétés inférieures*), trans. L. Clare. London: Allen and Unwin, 1926.

Romm, James, *The Edges of the Earth in Ancient Thought: Geography, Exploration and Fiction*. Princeton: Princeton University Press, 1992.

PART 4: DRUGS, CHARMS AND FAIR WORDS

Texts in English

Apuleius, *The Defence*, trans. H. E. Butler, from Internet Classics Archive: http://classics.mit.edu/Apuleius/apol.html.

—, *On the God of Socrates*, trans. H. Gurney, in the *Works of Apuleius*, from archive.org: https://archive.org/details/worksofapuleiusnooapul.

Cicero, *On Divination*, trans. W. A. Falconer, from *Lacus Curtius*: http://penelope.uchicago.edu/Thayer/E/Roman/Texts/Cicero/de_Divinatione/home.html

Hippocrates, *On the Sacred Disease*, from Internet Classics Archive: http://classics.mit.edu/Hippocrates/sacred.html.

Homer, *The Odyssey*, ed. and trans. Albert Cook. 2nd ed.; New York: Norton, 1993.

Plautus, *Mostellaria*, trans. H. T. Riley, from Perseus: http://www.perseus.tufts.edu/hopper/text?doc=Pl.+Mos.+1.

Pliny the Elder, *Natural History*, trans. J. Bostock and H. Riley, from Perseus: http://www.perseus.tufts.edu/hopper/text?doc=Plin.+Nat.+toc

Ptolemy, *Tetrabiblos*, trans. F. Robbins, from *Lacus Curtius*: http://penelope.uchicago.edu/Thayer/E/Roman/Texts/Ptolemy/Tetrabiblos/home.htm

Virgil, *The Aeneid*, trans. R. Fitzgerald. New York: Random House, 1983.

—, *The Eclogues*; *The Georgics*, trans. C. D. Lewis. Oxford: Oxford University Press, 1983.

Suggestions for Further Reading

Barton, Tamsyn, *Ancient Astrology*. London: Routledge, 1994.

Dickie, Matthew W., *Magic and Magicians in the Greco-Roman World*. London: Routledge, 2001

Graf, Fritz, *Magic in the Ancient World*, trans. F. Philip. Harvard: Harvard University Press, 1997.

Lloyd, G. E. R., *Magic, Reason and Experience: Studies in the Origins and Development of Greek Science*. Cambridge: Cambridge University Press, 1979.

—, *Demystifying Mentalities*. Cambridge: Cambridge University Press, 1990.

Nutton, Vivian, *Ancient Medicine*. 2nd ed.; London: Routledge, 2013.

Ogden, Daniel, *Greek and Roman Necromancy*. Princeton: Princeton University Press, 2001.

PART 5: THE PRIMAL MAGE AND SORCERER

Texts in English

Betz, Hans Dieter, ed., *The Greek Magical Papyri in Translation, vol. I: The Texts*. Chicago: University of Chicago Press, 1986.

Copenhaver, Brian P., *Hermetica: The Greek Corpus Hermeticum and the Latin Asclepius in a New English Translation with Notes and Introduction*. Cambridge: Cambridge University Press, 1992.

Firmicus Maternus, Julius, *Matheseos libri viii: Ancient Astrology, Theory and Practice*, trans. J. Bram. Bel Air: Astrology Classics, 2005.

Iamblichus, *De mysteriis*, trans. E. Clarke, J. Dillon, J. Hershbell. Atlanta: Society of Biblical Literature, 2003.

Kyranides: On the Occult Virtues of Plants, Animals and Stones. London: Christopher Warnock, 2006.

Philostratus, Flavius, *The Life of Apollonius*, trans. F. C. Conybeare: http://www.livius.org/ap-ark/apollonius/life/va_00.html.

Plotinus, *The Enneads*, trans. S. MacKenna, ed. J. Dillon. London: Penguin, 1991.

Porphyry, *Life of Plotinus*, trans. S. MacKenna, in Plotinus, *The Enneads*, pp. cii–cxxix.

Proclus, *On the Priestly Art According to the Greeks*, trans. B. Copenhaver in *Hermeticism and the Renaissance: Intellectual History and the Occult in Early Modern Europe*, ed. I. Merkel and A. Debus. Washington, DC: Folger Books, 1988, pp. 102–10.

Synesius, *On Dreams*, trans. A. Fitzgerald: http://www.livius.org/su-sz/synesius/synesius_dreams_01.html.

Zosimos of Panopolis, *On the Letter Omega*, ed. and trans. H. M. Jackson. Missoula: Scholars Press, 1978.

Suggestions for Further Reading

Brown, Peter, *Society and the Holy in Late Antiquity*. Berkeley: University of California Press, 1982.

Dodds, E. R., *The Greeks and the Irrational*. Berkeley: University of California Press, 1968.

Fowden, Garth, *The Egyptian Hermes: A Historical Approach to the Late Pagan Mind*. Cambridge: Cambridge University Press, 1986.

Principe, Lawrence, *The Secrets of Alchemy*. Chicago: University of Chicago Press, 2013.

Shaw, Gregory, *Theurgy and the Soul: The Neoplatonism of Iamblichus*. University Park: The Pennsylvania State University Press, 1995.

Siorvanes, Lucas, *Proclus: Neoplatonic Philosophy and Science*. New Haven: Yale University Press, 1996.

Smith, Andrew, *Porphyry's Place in the Neoplatonic Tradition: A Study in Post-Plotinian Neoplatonism*. The Hague: Nijhoff, 1974.

—, *Philosophy in Late Antiquity*, London: Routledge, 2004.

PART 6: ARMIES OF SORCERY AND FLIGHTS OF ANGELS

Texts in English

Athanasius of Alexandria, *Life of Anthony*: http://www.documentacatholicaomnia. eu/04z/z_0295-0373__Athanasius__Vita_Sancti_Antonii__EN.doc.html.

Augustine, *On Christian Teaching*, trans. J. Shaw: http://www.documentacatholica omnia.eu/04z/z_03540430__Augustinus__De_Doctrina_Christiana_Libri_ Quatuor__EN.doc.html.

—, *The City of God*, trans. H. Bettenson. Harmondsworth: Penguin, 1972.

Eusebius of Caesarea, *Preparation for the Gospel*, ed. and trans. E. Gifford. Oxford: Hart, 1903: http://www.tertullian.org/fathers/eusebius_pe_00_intro.htm.

Eustathius of Antioch, *On the Belly-Myther, Against Origen*, in *The 'Belly-Myther' of Endor: Interpretations of 1 Kingdoms 28 in the Early Church*, ed. and trans. R. Greer and M. Mitchell. Atlanta: Society of Biblical Literature, 2007, pp. 63–157.

Eutychianus, *A Miracle of the Virgin Mary Concerning Theophilus the Penitent*, in Philip Palmer and Robert More, *The Sources of the Faust Tradition: From Simon Magus to Lessing*. New York: Oxford University Press, 1936, pp. 58–77.

Lactantius, *Divine Institutes*, ed. and trans. A. Bowen and P. Garnsey. Liverpool: Liverpool University Press, 2003.

Martin of Braga, *On the Correction of Peasants*, in J. N. Hillgarth, ed., *Christianity and Paganism, 350–750: The Conversion of Western Europe*. Philadelphia, University of Pennsylvania Press, 1985, pp. 57–64.

Origen, *Homilies on Jeremiah; Homily on 1 Kings 28*, trans. J. Smith. Washington, DC: Catholic University of America Press, 1998.

Pseudo-Dionysius, *The Complete Works*, ed. and trans. C. Luibheid and P. Rorem. New York: Paulist Press, 1987.

—, 'The Acts of Peter', in *New Testament Apocrypha, II: Writings Related to the*

Apostles, Apocalypses and Related Subjects, ed. W. Schneemelcher and E. Hennecke, trans. R. Wilson. Cambridge: James Clarke, 1992, pp. 271–321.

—, *The Jewish Life of Christ, Being the Sepher Toldot Jeshu:* ישו תולדות ספר *or the Book of the Generation of Jesus*, ed. and trans. G. Foote and J. Wheeler. London: Progressive Publishing, 1885.

Suggestions for Further Reading

Bartlett, Robert, *Why Can the Dead Do Such Great Things? Saints and Worshippers from the Martyrs to the Reformation*. Princeton: Princeton University Press, 2013.

Brown, Peter, *Augustine of Hippo: A Biography*. 2nd ed.; Berkeley: University of California Press, 2000.

Herrin, Judith, *The Formation of Christendom*. Princeton: Princeton University Press, 1987.

Louth, Andrew, *The Origins of the Christian Mystical Tradition from Plato to Denys*. Oxford: The Clarendon Press, 1981.

MacMullen, Ramsay, *Christianity and Paganism in the Fourth to Eighth Centuries*. New Haven: Yale University Press, 1997.

Nock, Arthur D., *Conversion: The Old and the New in Religion from Alexander the Great to Augustine of Hippo*. London: Oxford University Press, 1961.

Pagels, Elaine, *The Gnostic Gospels*. New York: Random House, 1979.

Scott, Alan, *Origen and the Life of the Stars*. Oxford: The Clarendon Press, 1991.

Stead, Christopher, *Philosophy in Christian Antiquity*. Cambridge: Cambridge University Press, 1994.

PART 7: ARTS OF MAGIC THAT ASTONISH US

Texts in English

Albertus Magnus, *Book of Minerals*, trans. D. Wyckhoff. Oxford: The Clarendon Press, 1967.

Aquinas, Thomas, *Commentary on the Sentences*, trans. R. McInerny: http://dhspriory.org/thomas/Sentences.htm.

—, *Summa contra gentiles*, trans. A. Pegis et al. New York: Hanover House, 1955–7.

—, *Summa theologica*, trans. Fathers of the English Dominican Province. Westminster: Christian Classics, 1948.

Burchard of Worms, *Corrector*, in John R. Shinners, *Medieval Popular Religion, 1000–1500*. Toronto: University of Toronto Press, 2006, pp. 441–56.

Dante Alighieri, *Inferno*, trans. A. Mandelbaum. Berkeley: University of California Press, 1980.

Emerald Tablet. http://www.sacred-texts.com/alc/emerald.html

Lull, Ramon, *Ars brevis*, in *Doctor Illuminatus: A Ramon Lull Reader*, ed. and trans. A. Bonner. Princeton: Princeton University Press, 1995.

Newman, William, *The Summa perfectionis of pseudo-Geber: A Critical Edition, Translation and Study*. Leiden: Brill, 1991.

Oresme, Nicole, *De causis mirabilium*, in Hansen, *Marvels of Nature*, pp. 135–362.

Picatrix: Liber Atratus Edition, trans. J. Greer and C. Warnock. np: Adocentyn Press, 2011.

Ptolemy, *Centiloquium*: http://www.skyscript.co.uk/centiloquium1.html.

Suggestions for Further Reading

Bartlett, Robert, *The Natural and the Supernatural in the Middle Ages*. Cambridge: Cambridge University Press, 2008.

Cohn, Norman, *Europe's Inner Demons: An Enquiry Inspired by the Great Witch-Hunt*. London: Sussex University Press, 1975.

Evans, G. R., *The Thought of Gregory the Great*. Cambridge: Cambridge University Press, 1986.

Flint, Valerie, *The Rise of Magic in Early Medieval Europe*. Princeton: Princeton University Press, 1991.

Hansen, Bert, *Nicole Oresme and the Marvels of Nature*. Toronto: Pontifical Institute of Medieval Studies, 1985.

Idel, Moshe, *Golem: Jewish Magical and Mystical Traditions on the Artificial Anthropoid*. Albany: State University of New York Press, 1990.

Kieckheffer, Richard, *Forbidden Rites: A Necromancer's Manual of the Fifteenth Century*. Stroud: Sutton Publishing, 1997.

—, *Magic in the Middle Ages*. Cambridge: Cambridge University Press, 1990.

Marenbon, John, *Medieval Philosophy: An Historical and Philosophical Introduction*. London: Routledge, 2007.

PART 8: ANCIENT WISDOM AND FOLLY

Texts in English

Champier, Symphorien, *Dialogue Against the Destructive Arts of Magic*, in Brian Copenhaver, *Symphorien Champier and the Reception of the Occultist Tradition in Renaissance France*. The Hague: Mouton, 1978.

Ficino, Marsilio, *Platonic Theology*, ed. and trans. M. Allen and J. Hankins. Cambridge: Harvard University Press, 2001–6.

—, *Three Books on Life*, ed. and trans. C. Kaske and J. Clark. Binghamton: MRTS, 1989.

Institoris, Heinrich and Jakob Sprenger, *The Hammer of Witches: A Complete Translation of the Malleus maleficarum*, ed. and trans. C. MacKay. Cambridge: Cambridge University Press, 2009.

Pico della Mirandola, Giovanni, *900 Conclusions, in S. A. Farmer, Syncretism in the West: Pico's 900 Theses (1486); The Evolution of Traditional Religious and Philosophical Systems*. Tempe: MRTS, 1998.

—, *Oration on the Dignity of Man: A New Translation and Commentary*, ed. and trans. F. Borghesi, M. Papio, M. Riva. Cambridge: Cambridge University Press, 2012.

Suggestions for Further Reading

Allen, Michael, *The Platonism of Marsilio Ficino: a Study of His Phaedrus Commentary, Its Sources and Genesis*. Berkeley: University of California Press, 1984.

—, *Nuptial Arithmetic: Marsilio Ficino's Commentary on the Fatal Number in Book VII of Plato's Republic*. Berkeley: University of California Press, 1994.

Black, Crofton, *Pico's Heptaplus and Biblical Hermeneutics*. Leiden: Brill, 2006.

Copenhaver, Brian, *Magic in Western Culture from Antiquity to the Enlightenment*. Cambridge: Cambridge University Press, 2015.

Copenhaver, Brain and Charles Schmitt, *A History of Western Philosophy, 3: Renaissance Philosophy*. Oxford: Oxford University Press, 1992.

Garin, Eugenio, *Astrology in the Renaissance: The Zodiac of Life*, trans. C. Jackson, J. Allen, C. Robertson. London: Routledge, 1983.

Idel, Moshe, *Kabbalah in Italy, 1280–1510: A Survey*. New Haven: Yale University Press, 2011.

Klaasen, Frank, *The Transformations of Magic: Illicit Learned Magic in the Later Middle Ages and Renaissance*. University Park: Pennsylvania State University Press, 2013.

Trevor-Roper, H. R., *The European Witch-Craze of the Sixteenth and Seventeenth Centuries and Other Essays*. New York: Harper and Row, 1956.

Walker, D. P., *Spiritual and Demonic Magic from Ficino to Campanella*. University Park: Pennsylvania State University Press, 2000.

PART 9: ANCIENT WISDOM MODERNIZED

Texts in English

Agrippa von Nettesheim, Henry Cornelius, *Three Books of Occult Philosophy*, trans. J. Freake, ed. D. Tyson. St Paul: Llewellyn Publications, 1993.

Bruno, Giordano, *Cause, Principle and Unity; Essays on Magic*, ed. and trans. R. Blackwell, R. De Lucca, A. Ingegno. Cambridge: Cambridge University Press, 1998.

Dee, John, *Diaries*, in Meric Casaubon, *A True and Faithful Relation* (London: Maxwell, 1659): Early English Books Online.

—, *The Hieroglyphic Monad*, ed. and trans. C. H. Josten, 'A Translation of John Dee's Monas Hieroglyphica' *Ambix* 12 (1964): 84–221.

McLean, Adam, ed., *The Rosary of the Philosophers*. Edinburgh: Magnum Opus Hermetic Sourceworks, 1981.

Paracelsus, *The Labyrinth of Wandering Physicians*, in *Essential Readings*, ed. and trans. N. Goodrick-Clarke. Berkeley: North Atlantic Books, 1999.

Porta, Giambattista Della, *Natural Magick by John Baptista Porta, a Neapolitane, in Twenty Books*. London: Thomas Young and Samuel Speed, 1658: Early English Books Online.

Scot, Reginald, *The Discoverie of Witchcraft*, London: William Brome, 1584: Early English Books Online.

Suggestions for Further Reading

Anglo, Sydney, ed., *The Damned Art: Essays in the Literature of Witchcraft*. London: Routledge, 1977.

Clulee, Nicholas, *John Dee's Natural Philosophy: Between Science and Religion*. London: Routledge, 1988.

Ginzburg, Carlo, *Ecstasies: Deciphering the Witches' Sabbath*, trans. R. Rosenthal. London: Penguin, 1991.

Hannaway, Owen, *The Chemists and the Word: The Didactic Origins of Chemistry*. Baltimore: Johns Hopkins University Press, 1975.

Harkness, Deborah, *John Dee's Conversations With Angels: Cabala, Alchemy and the End of Nature*. Cambridge: Cambridge University Press, 1999.

Macfarlane, Alan, *Witchcraft in Tudor and Stuart England*. London: Routledge, 1970.

Pine, Martin, *Pietro Pomponazzi, Radical Philosopher of the Renaissance*. Padua: Antenore, 1986.

Rowland, Ingrid, *Giordano Bruno: Philosopher/Heretic*. New York: Farrar, Straus and Giroux, 2008.

Thomas, Keith, *Religion and the Decline of Magic*. New York: Charles Scribner's Sons, 1971.

Webster, Charles, *Paracelsus: Medicine, Magic and Mission at the End of Time*. New Haven: Yale University Press, 2008.

PART 10: MAGIC SEEN, HEARD AND MOCKED

Texts in English

Butler, Samuel, *Hudibras, the First and Second Parts, Written in the Time of the Late Wars, Corrected & Amended, with Several Additions and Annotations*. London: John Martyn and Henry Herringman, 1674: Early English Books Online.

Jonson, Ben, *Volpone and Other Plays*, ed. M. Jamieson. London: Penguin, 1966.

Marlowe, Christopher, *The Complete Plays*, ed. F. Romany and R. Lindsey. London: Penguin, 2003.

Mewe, William, *Pseudomagia: A Neo-Latin Drama*, ed. and trans. J. Coldewey and
    B. Copenhaver. Nieuwkoop: De Graaf, 1979.
Milton, John, *Paradise Lost: A Poem in Twelve Books*. London: S. Simmons, 1674:
    Early English Books Online.
Molière, *The Misanthrope and Other Plays*, ed. and trans. D. Coward and J. Wood.
    London: Penguin, 2000.
—, *The Miser and Other Plays*, ed. and trans. D. Coward and J. Wood. London: Pen-
    guin, 2000.
Shakespeare, William, *A Midsummer Night's Dream*, ed. R. McDonald. London:
    Penguin, 2000.
—, *The Tempest*, ed. P. Holland. London: Penguin, 1999.
Spenser, Edmund, *The Faerie Queene*, ed. J. Hales. London: Dent, 1910.

Suggestions for Further Reading

Findlen, Paula, *Possessing Nature: Museums, Collecting and Scientific Culture in Early
    Modern Italy*. Berkeley: University of California Press, 1994.
Grafton, Anthony and Nancy Siraisi, *Natural Particulars: Nature and the Disciplines
    in Renaissance Europe*. Cambridge: MIT Press, 1999.
Greenblatt, Stephen, *Will in the World: How Shakespeare Became Shakespeare*. New
    York: Norton, 2004.
Howarth, W. D., *Molière: A Playwright and His Audience*. Cambridge: Cambridge
    University Press, 1982.
Hume, Anthea, *Edmund Spenser: Protestant Poet*. Cambridge: Cambridge University
    Press, 2008.
Lewis, C. S., *The Discarded Image: An Introduction to Medieval and Renaissance Litera-
    ture*. Cambridge: Cambridge University Press, 2012.
McEvoy, Sean, *Ben Jonson: Renaissance Dramatist*. Edinburgh: Edinburgh University
    Press, 2008.
Quint, David, *Inside Paradise Lost: Reading the Designs of Milton's Epic*. Princeton:
    Princeton University Press, 2014.
Riggs, David, *The World of Christopher Marlowe*. New York: Henry Holt, 2004.
Wasserman, George, *Samuel 'Hudibras' Butler*. Boston: Twayne, 1989.

PART 11: MAGIC IN AN AGE OF SCIENCE

Texts in English

Bacon, Francis, *The Two Bookes of Francis Bacon of the Proficience and Advancement of
    Learning, Divine and Humane, to the King*. London: Henrie Tomes, 1605: Early
    English Books Online.
Clarke, Samuel, *A Collection of Papers, Which passed between the late Learned*

Mr. Leibnitz and Dr. Clarke in the Years 1715 and 1716. London: Knapton, 1717: http://www.newtonproject.sussex.ac.uk.

Fludd, Robert, *Mosaicall Philosophy Grounded Upon the Essentiall Truth or Eternal Sapience, Written First in Latin and Afterwards Thus Rendred into English by Robert Fludd, Esq*. London: Humphrey Moseley, 1659: Early English Books Online.

Glanvill, Joseph, *A Blow at Modern Sadducism in Some Philosophical Considerations About Witchcraft, and the Relation of the Famed Disturbance at the House of M. Mompesson, with Reflections on Drollery, and Atheisme, by Jos. Glanvill, Fellow of the Royal Society*. London: E. Cotes for James Collins, 1668: Early English Books Online.

Hopkins, Matthew, *The Discovery of Witches, in Answer to Severall Queries Lately Delivered to the Judges of the Assize for the County of Norfolk, and Now Published by Matthew Hopkins, Witch-finder, for the Benefit of the Whole Kingdome*. London: R. Royston, 1647: Early English Books Online.

More, Henry, *Conjectura Cabbalistica or a Conjectural Essay of Interpreting the Minde of Moses According to a Threefold Cabbala: viz., Literal, Philosophical, Mystical or Divinely Moral, by Henry More, Fellow of Christs College in Cambridge*. London: James Flesher, 1653: Early English Books Online.

—, *A Collection of Several Philosophical Writings of Dr Henry More . . . as namely, his Antidote against Atheism, Appendix to the Said antidote, Enthusiasmus triumphatus, Letters to Des-Cartes, &c., Immortality of the soul, Conjectura cabbalistica*. London: James Flesher for William Morden, 1662: Early English Books Online

Naudé, Gabriel, *The History of Magick By Way of Apology for All the Wise Men Who Have Unjustly Been Reputed Magicians, from the Creation to the Present age; Written in French by G. Naudaeus, Late Library-keeper to Cardinal Mazarin, Englished by J. Davies*. London: John Streater, 1657: Early English Books Online.

[Vaughan, Thomas,] *Anthroposophia theomagica, or a Discourse of the Nature of Man and His State After Death, Grounded on His Creator's Proto-chimistry and Verifi'd by a Practicall Examination of Principles in the Great World, By Eugenius Philalethes*. London: Printed by T. W. for H. Blunden at the Castle in Corn-hill, 1650: Early English Books Online.

—, *The Fame and Confession of the Fraternity of R. C., Commonly of the Rosie Cross, with a Praeface Annexed Thereto, and a Short Declaration of Their Physicall Work, by Eugenius Philalethes*. London: J. M. for Giles Calvert, 1652: Early English Books Online.

—, *The Works of Thomas Vaughan*, ed. A. Rudrum and J. Drake-Brickman. Oxford: The Clarendon Press, 1984.

Suggestions for Further Reading

Coudert, Allison, *Leibniz and the Kabbalah*. Dordrecht: Kluwer, 1995.

Dobbs, Betty Jo, *The Foundations of Newton's Alchemy, or 'The Hunting of the Greene Lyon.'* Cambridge: Cambridge University Press, 1975.

Ernst, Germana, *Tommaso Campanella: The Book and the Body of Nature*, trans. D. Marshall. Dordrecht: Springer, 2010.

Gaukroger, Stephen, *Francis Bacon and the Transformation of Early-Modern Philosophy*. Cambridge: Cambridge University Press, 2001.

Hall, A. Rupert, *Henry More: Magic, Religion and Experiment*. Oxford: Blackwell, 1990.

Huffman, William, *Robert Fludd and the End of the Renaissance*. London: Routledge, 1988.

Kahn, Didier, 'The Rosicrucian Hoax in France (1623–24)', in W. Newman and A. Grafton, eds., *Secrets of Nature: Astrology and Alchemy in Early Modern Europe*. Cambridge: MIT Press, 2001.

Lindberg, David and Robert Westman, *Reappraisals of the Scientific Revolution*. Cambridge: Cambridge University Press, 1990.

Newman, William, *Atoms and Alchemy: Chymistry and the Experimental Origins of the Scientific Revolution*. Chicago: University of Chicago Press, 2006.

Principe, Lawrence, *The Aspiring Adept: Robert Boyle and His Alchemical Quest*. Princeton: Princeton University Press, 1998.

Rice, James, *Gabriel Naudé, 1600–1653*. Baltimore: Johns Hopkins University Press, 1939.

Stewart, Matthew, *The Courtier and the Heretic: Leibniz, Spinoza and the Fate of God in the Modern World*. New York: Norton, 2006.

Stolzenberg, Daniel, *Egyptian Oedipus: Athanasius Kircher and the Secrets of Antiquity*. Chicago: University of Chicago Press, 2013.

Yates, Frances, *The Rosicrucian Enlightenment*. London: Routledge, 1972.

Notes

INTRODUCTION

Fig. 1, Anon., Mass of St Gregory, 1475–1500, British Museum.

PART 1: STUDY NO ABOMINATION

Introduction

Fig. 2, from Anon., *La Miroir de la redemption de Romain lignage*, 1483.

prodigious . . . understand Deut. 29:2–3
portents and wonders see 1.1

1.2

divided water from land Gen. 1:6–9

1.6

decision of the Urim Num. 27:21
casting lots 1 Sam. 14:40–42

1.7

God . . . his image Gen. 1:27
spoke . . . out of the fire Exod. 3:1–2

1.11

I am YHWH *. . . before me* Exod. 20:2–3
useth divination . . . necromancer Deut. 18:10
made an Asherah . . . Ahab see 1.13, also Ashtaroth and Astarte in 9.3 and 10.7
whole army of the heavens see 1.7, 11

1.12

In the year . . . died Uzziah, King of Judah, died in 733 BCE

1.13

whole army of heaven see 1.7, 11
On the day . . . to hide meaning unclear

1.18

demon named Asmodeus traditionally, the Destroyer, though the original was probably Spirit of Wrath: see 9.3

PART 2: POWER IN THE NAME OF JESUS

Introduction

Fig. 3, Jacobus de Teramo, *Belial*, 1516.

false . . . prophets see 2.9
unclean spirits see 2.7, 18

2.2

false prophet . . . devil Acts 13:4–12
and you, Bethlehem cf. Micah 5.1

2.3

the Devil . . . his purpose Shakespeare, *The Merchant of Venice*, 1.3.98
not by bread . . . God's mouth Deut. 8:3
he will order . . . stone Ps. 91:11–12
Do not tempt . . . God Deut. 6:16
you shall worship . . . serve Deut. 10:20

2.4

herd . . . iron wand Ps. 2:9
1,260 days see Rev. 11:2, reflecting Dan. 8:9–14, where pagans will persecute the godly for 42 months of 30 days each

2.6

the Lord said . . . footstool Ps. 110:1

2.7

a huge herd of pigs since Jews would not keep pigs, the region is gentile
Ten Cities as just explained, a gentile confederation mainly east of the Jordan

2.9

ruinous horror something or someone (like the Antichrist) who will desecrate the
Temple; see Dan. 9:27, 11:31, 12:11

2.10

Beelzeboul, the demon prince see 2 Kings 1:1–17; also sections 9.3; 10.2, 7; 11.13

2.11

his cure is 'a marvel' John 9:30
Go and wash . . . Siloam 'send,' the root verb, is *shalach* in Hebrew; the pool had ritual
uses, and the sending highlights the divine mission of Jesus

2.15

a few words of power John 5:8; Luke 13:12
called . . . Hermes the messenger god and divinity of language

2.16

python spirit the Pythia at the Delphic Oracle got her name from a snake killed by
Apollo when he took over the shrine

PART 3: FIRE PRIESTS, *MAGOI* AND *MAGEIA*

Introduction

Fig. 4, Johannes of Hidesheim, *Legenda sanctorum trium regum*, 1490

James Frazer see Copenhaver, *Magic in Western Culture*, chapters 1, 2 and 15
Night-roamers . . . initiates see 3.3
behaviour . . . repellent see 4.2, 6–7

Some say . . . in Persia see 3.7
a magus . . . invocation see 3.6
wisdom from . . . the gods see 3.4

3.1

translation adapted from Boyce (1984)

3.2

translation adapted from Boyce (1984)

3.3

Clement of Alexandria reports fragment 14 of Heraclitus in *Protrepticus*, 22.2
Erechtheids a tribal group in ancient Athens

3.4

translation adapted from Jowett (1875)

3.6

hippomanes the plant that causes horse madness

3.7

Zamolxis see 4.3, where Plato mentions Zamolxis as a king of Thrace
Hermodorus a student of Plato who wrote in the middle of the third century BCE
Xanthus a native of Lydia who wrote about his homeland in the fifth century
But they condemn statues see 5.11, 13; 8.13
Sotion wrote a *Succession of the Philosophers* in the second century
Dinon wrote about Persia in the fourth century
Hermippus . . . Hecataeus Eudoxus of Cnidus and Eudemus of Rhodes studied astron-
    omy and geography in the fourth century, when Theopompus of Chios wrote
    history and Hecataeus of Abdera studied the philosophies of various peoples; a
    century earlier Hermippus of Smyrna wrote biographies
Clearchus of Soli wrote on many subjects in the fourth century

PART 4: DRUGS, CHARMS AND FAIR WORDS

Introduction

Fig. 5, Oxford, Bodleian Library, MS Ashmole 304

harmful sorcery see 4.16

Plautus see 4.8

magia is an art . . . young princes see 3.4; 4.16

full of cunning . . . magicking see 4.6

chants . . . and states see 4.6

In our time . . . agreement see Copenhaver, *Magic in Western Culture*

Pythagoras . . . about it see 4.14

obligated . . . nails see 4.13

No one . . . curses see 4.13

when people . . . Virgil see 4.13

dark . . . magic see 4.11

black . . . sickles see 4.11

What ancient . . . false see 4.9

often refuted . . . Magi see 4.14

Still . . . in the dark see 4.14

magi . . . con-men see 4.2

purifications and chants see 4.2

4.2

human effort . . . power of divinity see 4.13; 6.9, 11; 7.9, 14; 10.2; 11.9 on coercing gods or demons

4.3

translation adapted from Jowett (1875)

Zalmoxis see also 3.7; spellings of the name are erratic in the original texts

Abaris . . . Far North a legendary holy man or shaman

4.4

translation adapted from Jowett (1875)

like a well-tuned lyre Heraclitus, fragment 51

4.5

translation adapted from Jowett (1875)

4.6

translation adapted from Jowett (1875)

4.7

translation adapted from Jowett (1875)

4.8

grabbed his guest . . . murdered homicide aggravated by an unspeakable breach of hos-
    pitality and compounded by touching the victim and becoming ritually unclean
Hades . . . to Hell the god Hades is the ruler of Hell

4.9

Chaldaean art . . . tribal name 'Chaldaean' could be either an ethnic name (for people
    who lived in a region of Mesopotamia) or an occupational term (for astrologers)
taking the auspices interpreting the behaviour of birds for divination
Sibylline verses books of verse oracles uttered by women called Sibyls: see 4.12, 6.4
Hall of the Leapers the Salii were priests whose rituals involved dancing
Bacis like a Sibyl, a Bacis may have been a female oracle
Epimenides a prophet of the late seventh or early sixth century BCE
Etruria the territory of the Etruscans
you say . . . lies hidden Quintus addresses Marcus

4.10

Pontus the Black Sea region, far from Rome and therefore exotic

4.11

Massylian from Marseilles, far from Carthage
Western Ones the Hesperides, daughters of Night, in the far West
the dragon a dragon guards the Temple of the Hesperides
clothing he had left . . . a replica of him Aeneas
Erebus god of the underworld
Hecate . . . Diana Hecate/Diana, with three faces, watches at crossroads: see 4.12
Avernus the lake at the entrance to the underworld: see 4.12
love's cure-all flesh from the head of a new-born foal

4.12

death had undone so many T. S. Eliot, 'The Wasteland', l. 63; Dante, *Inferno*, 3.55–7

Sibyl Scarefoe see 4.9 on the Sibyls, this one at Cumae named Deiphobe or Scarefoe

Diana's see 4.11

Grey Eye's girl the Sibyl is the daughter of Glaucus, a grey-eyed sea god

Euboea Cumae, a colony of Greeks from the island of Euboea

Acheron a river in the underworld

Dis the ruler of the underworld

Cocytus a river in the underworld

Tartarus the underworld

who's Juno in the underworld Proserpina, Pluto's wife, reigns like Juno

Birdbane 'birdless' in Greek is *aornos*, *Avernus* in Latin: see 4.11

Hecate an underworld deity: see 4.11

Persephone Proserpina, Pluto's wife and Queen of the underworld

Riverflame Phlegethon, a flaming river in the underworld

Centaurs . . . Geryon all monsters, like the Chimaera, with horribly mismatched parts

4.13

Osthanes a name (with various spellings) attached to magical lore attributed by Greek authors to Persian followers of Zoroaster: see 3.7, 4.14

Democritus the atomist philosopher from Abdera, a contemporary of Socrates, was sometimes confused with Bolos Democritus, an Egyptian of the third century BCE who wrote about magic

Tullus Hostilius traditionally the sixth king of Rome; Numa Pompilius, the second king, was revered for founding the religion described by his books

augurs priests appointed by the Roman state to oversee official rites of divination (see 4.9)

Twelve Tables traditionally Rome's first laws written for public viewing, begun in 451 BCE

Theocritus a Greek lyric poet of the third century BCE whom Virgil imitated in his *Eclogues* (see 4.10)

Marsi a people of central Italy famed as magicians, allied with Rome and then absorbed by Roman expansion around 90 BCE

command a deity on coercing gods and demons, see 4.2; 6.9, 11; 7.9, 14; 10.2; 11.9

Homer see 4.1

Theophrastus a student of Aristotle and his successor; botany was one of his specialities

Cato the elder Cato, who died in 149 BCE, despised Greek medicine but recorded traditional remedies for family use

Nemesis her name means 'righteous anger' or 'retribution'

Nonianus . . . Mucianus both were public figures when Pliny was alive

Psylli, Marsi and Snake-Born the Psylli were African snake-charmers, like the 'snake-born' Ophiogenes from Cyprus, but the Marsi (just mentioned) were from Italy

4.14

three others medicine, religion and astrology, which Pliny calls 'astronomy'

six thousand years for the chronology, see 3.1–2, 7

Eudoxus . . . Hermippus see 4.3

Agonaces Pliny probably means that Agonaces, otherwise unknown, taught Zoroaster, not Hermippus

Apusorus . . . Tarmoendas Pliny knows only the names of these Oriental wizards

Homer's total silence see 4.1

Proteus . . . the Sirens . . . Circe Proteus is a shape-shifting god of the sea in the fourth book of the *Odyssey;* the Sirens try to enchant Odysseus with their singing in book 12, but Circe (see 4.1) has warned him to plug his ears

invoking the underworld book 11 of the *Odyssey* describes the hero's descent to the underworld

Telmessus . . . Chiron's two of the three cities called Telmessus in Asia Minor were famous for diviners; women from Thessaly in north-east Greece were known for sorcery, at least in Latin literature, but the region was also the home of Achilles, who was taught there by Chiron, a centaur; Thrace, further north and east, was the land of Orpheus

Osthanes see 4.13

Pythagoras, Empedocles, Democritus and Plato legends about the Greek philosophers included travels to the Orient to find wisdom

Democritus see 4.13

Apollobex . . . Dardanus these obscure characters have Oriental origins in common

Moses, Jannes, Lotapes Pliny identifies Jews as legendary magicians; Jannes and Jambres (or Mambres) are named in 2 Tim. 3:8 as having 'withstood Moses'; Lotapes may be *iota pê,* a garbled fragment of a Greek transliteration of YHVH, the holiest name of God in the Bible

Twelve Tables see 4.13

Cornelius Lentulus and Licinius Crassus the names serve only to fix a date

water . . . axes various physical instruments of divination

Tiridates a Parthian adventurer made King of Armenia by Nero in 66 CE

4.15

the aether's eternal nature 'aether' was one name for the matter of the heavenly bodies thought to move eternally in perfect circles, unlike lower earthly objects made of the four elements – fire, air, water and earth – whose motions in straight lines are finite

4.16

Plato describes see 3.4

Zoroaster and Oromazes see 'Ohrmazd' in 3.1, 'Ahura Mazda' in 3.2 and 'Oromazdos' in 3.5

Plato – in a different passage see 4.3

Anaxagoras . . . Epicurus: the first three were pre-Socratics who philosophized about the natural world; Epicurus, born in 341 BCE, followed the atomism of Leucippus and Democritus

Epimenides . . . Ostanes Epimenides and Pythagoras were holy men of the seventh and sixth centuries about whom little is known, though much has been said about Pythagoras; Orpheus is a mythical figure; see 4.13 for Ostanes

Empedocles a Sicilian author of philosophical poems, *On Nature* and *Purifications*, who died in 432 BCE

guardian spirit see 4.17

a boy fell down for epilepsy, the 'falling disease', see 4.2 and 4.18

You look for fish see 5.12 for the *naukratês* or 'shipmaster'

bands of wool see 4.10

by moonlight . . . birthing mare see 4.11

Theocritus see 4.13

She of the Triple Crossroads see 4.11 for Hecate

Neptune . . . Phocus all four are Roman gods of the sea, the wrong kind for doing magic, according to Apuleius

then he collapsed see 'a boy fell down' and 4.2, 18

the pay-off . . . divining see 4.9 for divination and Roman civic religion

boys do this miracle Varro and Cato, greatly respected scholars, confirm the use of boys as mediums in divination

Plato's claim see 4.4–5, 16

lodgings for the divine power see 5.4, 11

Epilepsy . . . collapses see 'a boy fell down' (just mentioned) and 4.2, 18

Father Liber a Roman version of Bacchus or Dionysius who presided over one of the rites or 'divine mysteries' in which Apuleius, like many upstanding Romans, was initiated

Carmendas . . . Hostanes see 4.13–14, where Pliny lists these wizards from the East

worshipping wood see 5.11 and 5.13

4.17

Plato says . . . not how it goes see 4.5 for Plato's remark: 'Though gods don't mix with humans, through this spiritual connection come all the communion and all the conversation that gods have with humans.'

the aether above see 4.15

'demons' see 5.4, 5.10 and 6.4

as Plato states see 4.5

middle divinities see 5.4 and 5.10

PART 5: THE PRIMAL MAGE AND SORCERER

Introduction

Fig. 6, PGM 78. 1–14, from the Betz edition

See how . . . parts away see 5.10

Plotinus, the philosopher . . . in the body see 5.4

*body (*sôma*) the soul's tomb (*sêma*)* Plato, *Gorgias*, 493A

Man was formed . . . cosmos itself see 5.8

Saturn will . . . for magic see 5.8

nothing to . . . the Fates see 5.9

the pull . . . system see 5.5

the All . . . under spell see 5.5

the primal mage and sorcerer see 5.5

only the self-intent . . . bewitchment see 5.5

'embodied' and 'disembodied' see 5.7

the sage . . . enchanted love see 5.5

Hecate of the many names see 5.6

let _____ *come . . . need* see 5.6

Peter's . . . Simon Magus see 2.18; 6.1

ventured sorcery . . . star-casting see 5.4

his body shrivelled . . . tight see 5.4

discovered . . . one another see 5.5

victim of magic see 5.5

divine man see Brown, *Society and the Holy*, pp. 131–2

expert on the spirit world see 5.2

demon's work see 5.2

do not yield . . . property see 5.14

undescribable remedies . . . substance see 5.14; also 5.3, 10, 12

mixture . . . of divinity see 5.11

content . . . humans see 5.11

depraved spirits see 5.13

god-making in 5.11 see 'thus does man fashion his gods'

a demon differs . . . soul see 5.10

makes the body . . . chains see 5.10

theurgy see 5.10 and 5.13

plants, stones and spices see 5.11

Even when . . . not thinking see 5.10

from the sympathy . . . powers see 5.16

priestly see 5.16

ancient wise men . . . one another see 5.16

Flax-leaved daphne . . . manifestation see 5.16
spirit's 'manifestation' see 5.4, 10, 16
laurel . . . salt water see 5.16
mixing some . . . divine powers see 5.16

5.1

Pythagoras . . . silence although Pythagoras was far older than Apollonius (see 4.15), many later sages claimed to follow his teachings, including the rule of silence
Empedocles . . . to Egypt see 4.14
guardian spirit see 4.17
Anaxagoras . . . predictions Pliny and others claimed that he predicted the fall of a meteorite in 467 BCE

5.2

Alcestis . . . Hercules the hero rescued Alcestis by defeating Death in a wrestling match after she had sacrificed herself for her husband

5.3

the lion fears only the cock see 5.16
sea-stunner this Mediterranean fish, the electric ray (*narkê*), was often paired with the shipmaster (*naukratês*) as physical proof of magical power: see 5.12

5.4

translation adapted from MacKenna's version in Plotinus, *The Enneads*
malign diphtheria . . . ulcers see 5.9
he followed Ammonius very little is known about this teacher except the names of his students
Persian methods and . . . Indians since Plotinus made it only as far east as the Euphrates, his direct contact – if any – with Persians and Indians will have been limited
tenth year . . . fifty-nine 263 CE
Olympius, an Alexandrian . . . pupil of Ammonius the incident may have occurred not in Rome but in Alexandria, when both Olympius and Plotinus were studying with Ammonius
guiding spirit see 4.17
Our Tutelary Spirit Ennead 3.4
The Sacred Marriage . . . veiled words the marriage of Zeus and Hera, understood as an allegory
searchingly into horoscopy to oppose astrological determinism

Zoroaster . . . Mesus the Gnostics opposed by Plotinus produced writings under names
  like Zoroaster and his ancestor Zostrianus; for this Nicotheus or a different one, see 5.7
Against the Gnostics Ennead see 2.9
You shall hear . . . Good and kindly Porphyry quotes the full text of the oracle, which
  he may have written, and then comments on it
to free himself and rise . . . lifting himself freed from the body to experience mystical
  ecstasy
Plato . . . in the Symposium see 4.4–5

5.5

translation adapted from MacKenna's version in Plotinus, *The Enneads*
his reasoning part cannot be touched intellect and will, the non-bodily higher faculties
  of the soul, have no role in magic, but the soul's lower part, its 'unreasoning element', is in touch with the body's senses and can be enchanted, so that the 'entire
  life of the practical man is a bewitchment' and 'contemplation alone stands
  untouched by magic'

5.6

Hecate see 4.11–12
Dione the mother of Aphrodite by Zeus
Daughter Persephone, daughter of Zeus and Demeter, the wife of Hades who reigns
  in the underworld: she is named directly later in the spell
Adônai . . . Damnameneus Hebrew names of God occur frequently in magic spells,
  with others like 'thoughtful Damnameneus', sometimes identified as one of the
  Dactyls (Fingers) of Mt Ida in Crete who worked in metals

5.7

two-parted the Ω has two branches
seventh . . . Kronos the seventh and last vowel in the Greek alphabet signifies Saturn,
  the seventh and most distant planet
Nikotheos not identified, but mentioned again in a later passage
Ocean 'Ωκεανός begins with *omega*
it says the quotation is not exact, but see Homer, *Iliad*, 14.201, 246, 302
sulphur water 'divine water' also translates the Greek; distillation – perhaps of alco-
  hol, among other substances – was the main use of the apparatus described by
  Zosimos; in later alchemy, the sulphur that replaces one of the usual elements
  (earth, air, fire and water) is not the substance now called 'sulphur'
On Furnaces and Apparatus the collection of notes on alchemical apparatus and technique introduced by Zosimos in his remarks *On the Letter* Ω
suit the Times . . . Fate changes for stars and planets as Lords of Fate, see 4.15; 5.8–9

guardian demon . . . hateful see 4.16–17; 5.1, but this malevolent demon keeps incompetent alchemists tied to the body and Fate

figured stars . . . Times: relations among heavenly bodies, like 'aspects' (see 5.8), are understood geometrically but are also visible as figures in the zodiac

Hermes . . . 'mindless' for a similar remark in a Hermetic treatise, see Copenhaver, *Hermetica*, p. 22, ¶ 3

On Natures no such title survives among the Greek Hermetica, where 'nature' occurs frequently

Zoroaster works on many topics, including alchemy, were attributed to the Persian prophet: see 4.13–16; 5.4

philosophers . . . higher than Fate the mistake made by Plotinus, according to Firmicus in 5.9

Hesiod . . . Epimetheus Zosimos refers several times to Hesiod's story about Pandora, where the repentant Prometheus is the disembodied human person and the reckless Epimetheus is the same person embodied and bound by Fate

'what do humans . . . wealth' the words are not Hesiod's, but see Epictetus, *Discourses*, 4.9.2

Fate's evils . . . magic Zoroaster teaches the opposite of what Plotinus taught, on the authority of Hermes: see 5.4–5

On the Inward none of the Greek Hermetica has this title, but see Copenhaver, *Hermetica*, p. 51, where celestial tormentors 'use the prison of the body to torture the inward person'

the nameless Triad the 'spiritual' person gains mastery by achieving the proper balance among three faculties of 'mind', 'soul' and 'spirit', which reflect an unnamed divine Triad

tablet . . . written Iamblichus mentions a Hermetic revelation by Bitus and describes it as carved in hieroglyphics in a temple: see Iamblichus, *Myst.* 267.11–68.11; Fowden, *Hermes*, pp. 139–53

thrice-great . . . surpassingly great: 'thrice-greatest' (τρισμέγιστος) is usually a title of Hermes: see 5.12

the Serapeion this sanctuary maintained the only library still active in the region around 300 CE, when Zosimos was writing

Ptolemies . . . Greek and Egyptian the Hebrew Bible was translated as the Greek Septuagint under Ptolemy II, who died in 246 BCE; tradition claims no such project for a translation into Egyptian (or Coptic), and Asenas is unknown

the whole sphere the heavens with their four cardinal points, as in 5.8

alpha . . . mu in Hebrew, Adam's name has only three letters (אדם), where the Greek Ἀδάμ uses four

Nikotheos already named but never identified

Light . . . lights in Greek the same letters (φως), accented differently, spell 'light' and 'man'

they persuaded unnamed demonic tempters, serving the Impersonator who will soon be described

clothe in the Adam entombed in the outer carnal Adam, the inner Light dims

Hesiod said Zosimos returns to his allegory on Pandora, previously introduced

Jesus . . . came to Adam saving the inner Adam of light, not the outer Adam of flesh

the demon . . . wants to deceive: a kind of Antichrist, but also 'the Devil . . . who deceives the whole world', as in 2.4

nine letters the Greek word for 'Fate' (Εἱμαρμένη) has nine letters, starting with a diphthong; many names could fit this pattern, perhaps by treating the letters as numbers, as in the gematria used later by Kabbalists

Epimetheus . . . his brother the Pandora allegory, as before

well-timed tinctures returning to the incompetent alchemists attacked in the second paragraph

the poet Homer, *Odyssey*, 8.167–8, inexactly

bone-setting priest this craft that changes, like alchemy, is a perfect fit because the healers, like alchemists, make books to illustrate their procedures and apparatus, like the gear for distillation shown in the notes introduced by the treatise *On the Omega*

those people . . . hunger the incompetent alchemists again

skeletons of the furnaces a sketch of a furnace is like an illustration in a book on bone-setting

the Philosopher Bolos Democritus, as in 4.13

5.8

Craftsman the Demiurge of Plato's *Timaeus* but also the biblical Creator

five planets those that are visible to the naked eye: Mercury, Venus, Mars, Jupiter and Saturn

Petosiris and Nechepso fragments of texts about astrology and divination by these legendary Egyptians can be seen (in Greek) at http://www. hellenisticastrology. com/editions/Riess-Nechepso-Petosiris.pdf

Aesculapius and Hanubius for the first, see 5.11; the second could be the god Anubis or perhaps a poet of the first century CE, Anubio, who wrote about astrology

Myriogenesis such a book by Asclepius would have set forth the influence of each part of the zodiac – by degree, minute and second – ignoring the constellations themselves

Ascendant the part of the zodiac (or a planet in it) rising on the eastern horizon at some moment, also called the 'horoscope'

cardines the four 'hinges' of the zodiacal circle: the Ascendant rising in the east, the Mid Sky directly overhead, the Setting directly opposite the Ascendant and the Low Sky opposite the Mid Sky

nativity a birth-chart or horoscope

5.9

long-haired philosopher see 5.8

Fate see 5.7–8 and the Headnote to Part 5

Socrates . . . Plato's demise both ended badly, according to Firmicus

broken . . . mutilated Porphyry, in calmer language, also describes the illness that killed Plotinus: see 5.4

5.10

it purveys . . . under spell see 5.5

how a demon differs Iamblichus restates questions asked of him by his teacher, Porphyry, writing a *Letter to Anebo*, said to be an Egyptian priest

procession the flow of being from One, Mind and Soul down into the All

manifestations . . . apparitions various forms in which divinity shows itself

5.11

temple gods . . . near to humans gods at the lower end of the hierarchies described by Iamblichus in 5.10; their visits to the temples are something to be 'endured', according to the last paragraph of this selection

cleanest part . . . whole body if the signs are stars and planets, they have no bodies, but what most obviously distinguishes one Egyptian god from another is its head, often of an animal, as in 'the figures of gods that humans form': see 5.13

statues ensouled statues come alive when gods descend into them

your ancestor Asclepius, the disciple of Hermes addressed in the dialogue, is a descendant of the god Asclepius, a Greek version of the Egyptian Imhotep, a divinized mortal

quality of these gods . . . power of divinity: the 'plants, stones and spices' that lure gods into statues have a magical 'quality'; they are the 'tokens' and 'symbols' described by Iamblichus in 5.10; see also 5.12, 16

in tune . . . harmony see 5.5, 5.12 and 5.16 for the magic of harmony and sympathy

5.12

plants and stones and spices see 5.11

sympathies and antipathies see 5.5 and 5.16

Kyranides . . . Harpocration the title of the book is *Kyranides*; one author is a mythical king of Persia, the other a writer called Harpocration from Alexandria, but perhaps not Valerius Harpocration, a lexicographer of the late second century CE

thrice-greatest Hermes Hermes Trismegistus, the Greek Thoth of the Hermetica: see 5.11

men who lack knowledge revealed knowledge (*gnôsis*) is the passport to salvation

pass it on in the way that Hermetic wisdom was transmitted from Hermes to Asclepius: see 5.11

Syriac . . . slab wisdom preserved for the ages from time and defilement by recording it on a durable monument in foreign writing was a common motif in the literature of the period

Old-Time Book another Hermetic text

special properties including magical power, like the 'qualities' of the *Asclepius*: see 5.11

5.13

plants and stones and spices see 5.11

theurges see 5.10 for theurgy

matter . . . selected like the 'plants, stones and spices' of the *Asclepius*: see 5.11

the Craftsman's the divine Demiurge of Plato's *Timaeus*, as in 5.8

processions see 5.10

Marshal . . . Grandmaster heads of different levels of the demonic hierarchy

Chaldaean prophets Neoplatonists after Plotinus, but not Plotinus himself, came to
    revere the enigmatic verses of the *Chaldaean Oracles*, probably composed in the
    third century CE: see 5.15

5.14

calling . . . method rational see 4.2, 18

specific natures idiopathic diseases, to use the modern terminology, that did not fit the
    usual diagnostic categories

disgusting drugs could be either simple – made from a single plant, like peony for
    epilepsy, for example – or compounded, and some ingredients might be bizarre or
    repulsive, like 'the burnt skin of a cave-mouse': see 4.18

5.15

tokens see 5.10–11

signify everything thinking of the universe as a book that can be read

limbs of a single whole the universe as an immense organism with sentient organs and
    limbs, not a huge machine with inert parts

pledges like tokens and symbols: see 5.10–11

we feel a pain magical action at a distance is like referred pain in the body

lyre . . . harmony musical resonance is another physical analogue of magical action at
    a distance

a sage stationed outside the world repeating a point made by Plotinus in 5.5: 'Supposing the
    magus to stand outside the All, his evocations and invocations would no longer avail.'

5.16

priestly knowledge knowledge of magical theurgy is priestly because of its rituals that
    invoke the gods with due reverence

the last . . . earthly manner connecting the bottom of the cosmic hierarchies with the
    hypercosmic summit: see 5.11, 13

brought divine powers . . . to one another likeness is magical

untouched action at a distance, as in magnetism, is a key problem for theories of magic

luminaries the two luminaries are the sun and the moon

lesser . . . size physical size and strength are less potent than placement in the hierarchies of the All: see 5.11, 13

angels . . . stones a hierarchy and a channel of magic

composite statues and fumigations see 5.11, 13

blended separate signs signs are like tokens, symbols and pledges: see 5.10–11, 15

laurel . . . sea water a list like those in 5.12

consecrations theurgic rituals

PART 6: ARMIES OF SORCERY AND FLIGHTS OF ANGELS

Introduction

Fig. 7, Cathedral of Saint Lazaire, Autun

Marlowe . . . *Faustus* see 10.2

the cunning . . . sacrifices to them see 6.15

The great Pan see 6.6

ignorant peasants . . . demons see 6.14

Lucifer was ejected see 2.4 and 10.7

Devil's signs see 6.14

the silliest . . . house see 6.11, also 4.13–14

despicable . . . denial see 6.15

pacts . . . with demons see 6.11

all the marvels . . . of demons see 6.9

this noxious . . . science see 6.9

dark technology . . . sorceries see 4.11 and 6.9

no less detestable . . . account see 6.11 with 1.10, 6.2 and 6.3

black magic see 7.6

We must scrutinize . . . historically see 6.2

a demon-ridden hag . . . together there see 6.3

a woman . . . ghosts see 1.9 and 1.11

the poetry . . . at school see 6.3

astrology, haruspicy . . . magic see 6.4

almighty Jupiter . . . demons see 6.5

What power . . . submit see 6.5

make syllogisms . . . of the Magi see 6.8

since shape-shifting . . . Devil's deceit see 6.7

mentioned in the Acts Acts 17:34

nine orders . . . Iamblichus see 1.4; 5.10
the angel . . . unto Mary the beginning of the prayer called the 'Angelus'
intricate hieratic figures . . . have no figure see 6.13
canonical Acts see 2.18
he astonished . . . magic see 2.18
amazed . . . flying see 6.1
for putting . . . through me see 6.1
Like Moses and Aaron see 1.1
signs . . . emissary see 6.1
as they both . . . amazed see 6.16

6.1

semi-tertian and quartan fevers, often from malaria, classified by their cyclic symptoms
students . . . confirmed committed followers of Peter
Stratonicus not otherwise identified
Gemellus . . . Castor not otherwise identified
Aricia . . . Terracina small towns near Rome

6.2

First Book of Kings 1 Samuel in the Hebrew Bible became 1 Kings in the Greek Sep-
   tuagint used by Origen
Then the woman . . . narrator's voice the woman in the Witch of Endor story is unnamed;
   Origen comments on 1 Sam. 28:11, where the narrator of the story reports what the
   woman said
Raise . . . he said 'he' is Saul, the King who wants to speak to Samuel, the dead prophet
When the woman . . . she said 1 Sam. 28:12–14
no surprises . . . justice Origen's notional opponent cites 2 Cor. 11:14–15
What is written . . . prostrating himself 1 Sam. 28:14
why ask . . . partner 1 Sam. 28:16–17

6.3

the all-holy sentences the words of the Bible in 1 Sam. 28
myth-in-the-belly in Greek *gastêr* is 'belly', and 'myth' is a subsidiary meaning of *muthos*
a myth depicts Eustathius caricatures Greek epic poetry, despised by some Christians
   for its polytheism, while recognizing that its stories are convincing

6.4

the Devil's emissary see 6.1
Piety is . . . knowledge of God the first Hermetic quotation may allude to the Greek

original of *Asclepius* 28; the second is very close to *C. H.* 9.4, for which see Copenhaver, *Hermetica*, pp. 28, 84, 151–2, 246–7

Perfect Discourse the original title in Greek of the *Asclepius*

evil angels quoting *Asclepius* 25; see 'baleful Angels' in Copenhaver, *Hermetica*, pp. 82, 242

Erythraean Sibyl because these pagan texts seemed to support Christian doctrine, Lactantius respected both the Hermetica and the *Sibylline Oracles*, the latter attributed to female prophets from various exotic sites like the Red (Erythraean) Sea: see *Orac. Sib.* 3.228

magicians . . . call those demons up see 5.10–11

divine names see 1.16–18; 2.1, 3–4, 10

6.5

this sign the sign of the cross, as a gesture, a prayer or an image

Christ's name see 2.8, 10, 16

nor can . . . questions Virgil, *Georgics*, 3.491

entrails of the victims see 4.9

God's temple a Christian church

Aesculapius or Apollo gods of healing

Homer . . . the other not the Greek *daimôn* names a spirit that is *theios* or 'divine', whether its actions are good or evil, helpful or harmful; in Homer (see *Od.* 16.364–70) a *daimôn* is generally a god; but in the only place (Matt. 8:31) where *daimôn* appears in the New Testament, demons are 'unclean spirits' according to another version of the same story: see 2.7; 5.10, 13; 6.6

Father of them all Saturn or Kronos is the father of Zeus, father of the gods

from below from hell

two days see 6.2 for the harrowing of hell

sacred mysteries the sacred mysteries are the Bible: for allusions to the Bible in the Hermetica, see Copenhaver, *Hermetica*, pp. lvii–lviii, 99–109, 112–13, 120–21

6.6

not gods . . . like humans here demons rank lower than gods because they are 'earthly' or embodied, but they are not mortal, according to the speaker, who would be refuted if the story about Pan were true: see 4.17; 5.10; 6.5

bad demons divinities can be malevolent

Echinades . . . Paxi in the Ionian Sea

Thamus . . . Egyptian Tammuz was a Mesopotamian god who perished prematurely but may have been resurrected; one reading is that the sailor misunderstood a lament for the god as someone calling his name, and that Pan, which means 'All', is another name for the same god

Palodes the site is probably on the Albanian coast, east of Corfu in the Ionian

Tiberius Caesar . . . that reign Tiberius ruled from 14 to 37 CE; according to Luke 3:1;
    John the Baptist began to preach 'in the fifteenth year of . . . Tiberius'

begging . . . hell see 2.7

6.7

the Enemy see 1.16–17

navel . . . belly euphemism for female genitals

left for the tombs tombs had long been sacred in Egypt, where Christians treated the
    burials of their saints with the same reverence

shape-shifting . . . Devil see 6.2

6.8

give a reason . . . cross the philosophers mistakenly treat Anthony's faith as if it needs
    the support of reason

using an interpreter Anthony's native language was a late form of Egyptian, written in
    modified Greek characters as Coptic

you worship . . . likenesses see 5.11

Osiris . . . Kronos Typhon is a primordial monster who survives when Zeus defeats
    him as well as Kronos, his own father; in Plutarch's account, Isis collects the parts
    of the body of Osiris that Typhon has dismembered

signs and wonders the miracles recorded by the Gospels

illusions of the Magi see 6.1; cf. 2.2

6.9

the most famous poet Virgil: see 4.11

another line of his Virgil: see 4.10

as Cicero noted a few words from such a law in the Twelve Tables survive, but not
    where Cicero noted them – perhaps in a lost part of the treatise *On the Laws*

Apuleius . . . accused see 4.16

we need . . . to the gods see 4.17

6.10

demons come halfway see 4.17

thrown down see 2.4

6.11

amulet as distinct the distination is mine, not universally recognized

characters magical signs used for ritual purposes

dancing gestures can be magical

bringing the body . . . naturally plants can be emetic, purgative and so on because of their natural properties, but the powers of such things used as signs are not natural

silliest practices see 4.13

nativity-makers astrologers who make horoscopes for their clients: see 5.8

if they could . . . its Lord Wisdom 13:9

Samuel . . . Saul see 6.2–3

no charms . . . avoid Augustine is wary about demons even when their presence is not obvious

6.12

makes . . . blazing fire Ps. 104:4–5, or 'he makes the winds his messengers, fiery flames his servants'

God did not . . . judgement 2 Pet. 2:4

Look . . . your path Mark 1:2

Malachi . . . angel the prophet's name means 'my messenger' or 'angel'

we read . . . women they loved Gen. 6:4

Goths . . . Rome the sack of Rome in 410 by Alaric prompted Augustine to write the *City of God* in order to refute those who blamed Christianity for the disaster

Seth the son of Adam, father of Enosh and ancestor of humanity after Cain killed the virtuous Abel and the killer's children died in the Flood: Gen. 4:25–5:32

6.13

ox . . . thrones three of the four 'living creatures' of Rev. 4:7, modelled on Ezek. 1:5 and widely used in Christian art, with the fourth figure of a human, to represent the authors of the four Gospels; Ezekiel also saw wheels (1:16–21) and a throne (1:26) in his vision

Thearchy the Trinity on high

nine revelatory . . . arrays inspired by biblical names for angels of different types, like Seraphim and Cherubim, Dionysius groups angels into three groups of three

first hierarchy . . . principalities the nine groups are Seraphim, Cherubim, Thrones, Authorities, Lordships, Powers, Principalities, Archangels and Angels

6.14

thrown out see 2.4; 10.7

worship creatures see 6.11

one demon . . . another pretended see 6.4–6

day of Mars . . . Saturn as in Spanish: *martes, miércoles, jueves, viernes, sábado*

Lord's day Spanish *domingo*, from *dies dominicus* or 'Lord's day' in Latin

renouncing . . . cross one of the promises made at baptism, performed by making and speaking the sign of the cross, as in Matt. 28:19

Holy Creed the Creed, a profession of belief, is also used at baptism

6.15

kept protesting 'I do not want to be made a bishop' was the conventional response, but Theophilus persisted

cunning . . . Adversary see 1.16–17

sign of the cross see 6.5, 14

blessed baptism . . . defiled see 6.14

6.16

King Jannaeus Alexander Jannaeus, who ruled Judea for the first quarter of the first century BCE, was exceedingly unpopular

Joseph Pandera the name may or may not be fictional

God's secret Name Jews and many others saw the Tetragrammaton, יהוה, the Name that could not be spoken, as a source of magical power; there were many other secret names of God

Helena . . . Jannaeus his wife, who succeeded him in 76 and ruled for nine years, was named Salome Alexandra, not Helena

the Sages unlike her husband, Salome supported the Pharisees and was very popular with them

Sages . . . Judas the story connects the betrayer of Jesus with one of the rabbinical parties – perhaps the Pharisees

Jesus . . . wonders see 1.1; 6.1

they both . . . in the air see 6.1

PART 7: ARTS OF MAGIC THAT ASTONISH US

Introduction

Fig. 8, Olavus Magnus, *Historia de gentibus septentrionalibus*, 1555

lecturing . . . Christ see Evans, *Gregory the Great*, p. 9

breaking rules . . . taught Gregory of Tours, *History of the Franks*, 1

City of God . . . On Christian Teaching see 6.9–12

Apuleius . . . Proclus see 4.15–17, 5.13, 16

all things . . . thinking see 7.1

lower is like . . . single thing see 7.1

separate fire . . . thick see 7.1
Zosimos . . . Letter Ω see 5.7
applies 'medicines' see 7.16
in the silence . . . life again see 7.2
Graeae . . . striges one-eyed Grey Sisters, Fates, vampires, fortune-tellers and screech-owls
Burchard's . . . Decretum see 7.2–3
Cornelius Agrippa see 9.2–3
Asmodeus . . . and witches see 9.3
maleficium see 4.16
Golem see 7.5
answer all questions see 7.17
Oresme . . . Pomponazzi see 7.19 and 9.1
Firmicus Maternus . . . on astrology see 4.15; 5.8–9 and 7.4
images in the skies . . . actions see 7.4
a wise soul . . . nature see 7.4
images and faces see 7.4
get power . . . figure see 7.9
Augustine's worries see 6.11
faces in the heavens . . . on earth see 7.4
faces in this world see 7.4
labelled necromancy see 7.6
necromantic talismans see 7.9
Greek Magical Papyri see 5.6
decans see 7.8
a man rises . . . in his hand from the *Picatrix*, chap. 11
belongs to . . . garment see 7.8
zaare zaare raam see 7.7
The apex . . . necromantic books see 7.9
a third is astronomical . . . in the heavens see 7.9
also mental . . . only from minds see 5.11; 6.10–11
imperceptible . . . permitted see 5.3, 12, 14
gets power . . . stars see 7.12
the demons that help . . . magic see 7.12
prayer . . . humble heart see 7.21
invocations . . . bonded spirit see 7.21
to sanctify . . . secret names see 7.21
Greek Magical Papyri see 5.6
Aquinas . . . modern times see 8.1–3

7.1

What is lower . . . higher see 5.16
turned into earth . . . from the thick perhaps an alchemical process

7.2

all that you do . . . Christ Coloss. 3:17

Parcae for the Fates, see the Introduction to Part 7

three Sisters the *Parcae*

silence of night . . . stretches of land flying at night became a theme of witchcraft accusations: see 7.3

forty days (a carina) a quarantine or period of forty days of penance

7.3

after the first . . . spoiled Tit. 3:10–11

Diana . . . Herodias Diana's associations with the forest link this female deity with remote sites favoured by witches; the Herodias whom Mark (6:14–29) makes responsible for beheading John the Baptist is a likely suspect for wickedness, but the name has probably been altered

angel of light 2 Cor. 11:14–15, as in 6.2

Ezekiel . . . in the spirit Ezek. 37:1

Paul . . . in the body 2 Cor. 12:2

all things . . . by him John 1:3

7.4

Ptolemy . . . Iesure see 4.14

only what is universal . . . through form a genuine science of astrology must know immaterial forms as universals

circles the heavenly bodies move only in perfect circles

nativity horoscope: see 5.8, 6.11

prevent . . . evil astrology is practical

choices astrology can guide one's decisions; one crucial choice is at what moment to make a talisman in order to connect it with a heavenly body: see 7.6, 9

physical temperament . . . stars the influences of the stars and planets blend to match or not match the blending or temperament of matter in earthly bodies

A wise soul . . . nature a good farmer who does not control nature can make adjustments: likewise the astrologer

faces in the heavens constellations or decans or both: see 7.8

7.5

Making a Golem Eleazar's commentary is translated, with help from Fabrizio Lelli, from the Przemysl edition of Zupnik and Knoller, fol. 15ᵛ

the souls . . . in Harran Gen. 12:5: Kabbalah often comments cryptically on small and seemingly meaningless passages of the Bible

two are better than one Eccles. 4:9

it is not good . . . suit him Gen. 2:18: this passage shows that the two previous quotations also bear on the theme of creation, the model for making a Golem

In the beginning Gen. 1:1

221 Gates two-letter combinations of the letters of the Hebrew alphabet, used as a basis for meditation and inducing an ecstatic trance

every limb and organ of the human body and thus the Golem

alef, alef . . . alef mem instructions for combining the vowels with each other and with consonants

7.6

Producing images making talismans: the spirit of a constellation works on the body of a gem while a zodiacal or decanal image is carved on it

talismans . . . forceful the Arabic *telsam* transliterates *telesmos*, meaning 'ritual' in Greek

smoke to attract . . . images see 5.11

elixir . . . different, cleaner bodies the *xêrion* or 'healing powder' of Greek alchemy, a substance with the power to transmute, became the *al-iksir* or elixir of Arabic alchemy, which transmutes metals by healing them, a process of cleansing in this Latin text

the wash . . . fire and water making the elixir by balancing the four elementary qualities goes back to Arabic texts of the eighth or ninth centuries attributed to Jabir-ibn-Hayyan, the namesake of Geber, a Christian, from whom see 7.15

the same elixir . . . the filth see the previous comment on 'elixir'

This word elixir . . . strength see the previous comment on the etymology of 'elixir'

choosing hours . . . are based see 7.4 and 9 on choices

constellations . . . science of images the zodiac

7.7

Dragon's Tail the Tail and Head are two parts of the path marked out where the moon crosses the ecliptic

ascendant see the notes on 5.8

good aspect . . . first house moving through the four quadrants of the zodiacal circle (see 5.8), planets lie at various angular distances, called aspects, from one another and from other heavenly bodies and locations; a trine aspect is an angle of 120 degrees, a sextile aspect is 60 degrees; a house is a sector of the ecliptic or zodiac, usually a twelfth

face a decan, as in 7.8

bezoar stone a mass of hard material found in the stomach or intestines of an animal

Solomon's sign the hexagram shown after the magic words

7.8

each division . . . a face three decans for each of the twelve signs of the zodiac

Fig. 9, Johann Engel, *Astronomium planum in talavlis*, 1488

7.9

cover up . . . profess astronomy Albert proceeds through a series of distinctions, first
between (I) necromancy and (II) astronomy, then – in the paragraphs that
follow – between two kinds of astronomy, (*A*) the first dealing with the structure of
the heavens, (*B*) the second with 'judging the stars', the latter including both a mathematical and a physical or 'natural' component; this is an outline of his analysis:

    I. Necromancy
        A. talismans for invocation
        B. talismans for exorcism
   II. Astronomy
        A. structural
        B. judicial
           a. theoretical
           b. practical
              i. revolutions
              ii. nativities
              iii. interrogations
              iv. choices, including talismans

a certain man . . . philosophy probably Albert himself, a renowned philosopher
structure . . . inside one another the traditional universe of concentric spheres
changes in this world's objects . . . heavenly bodies what we now call 'astrology' is the
    type-B astronomy, as explained in a preceding note, that studies such changes
That science has . . . rings and seals type-B astronomy, using both mathematics and physics,
    includes (*a*) introductory physical theory and (*b*) its subsequent application or practice,
    the latter in four parts: (*i*) revolutions, (*ii*) nativities, (*iii*) interrogations and (*iv*) choices;
    talismans – also described in necromancy (*I*), which is not astronomy (*II*) at all – come
    under type (*iv*) practical astronomy or 'choices', at the finale of the whole system
The principles of judging physical principles are the theoretical introduction to the system
The part about revolutions this application (*i*) of the theory in (*a*) relies on knowledge
    of the simple and complex motions of the five visible planets and two luminaries
    (sun and moon) to predict or explain great physical and historical changes
The part about nativities . . . in aspect this application (*ii*) of the theory in (*a*) produces
    a horoscope or birth-chart; *hyle* and *alchodes* are planets or locations that determine
    the length of life

The part about interrogations this application (iii) of the theory in (*a*) asks about the effect – generally human – of a celestial cause examined horoscopically at the time the question is asked

And then . . . the time that is best this application (*iv*) of the theory in (*a*) uses a person's horoscope to choose whether or not to take an action: see 7.4 and 6

talismans are of three kinds the next paragraphs sort talismans, some of which come under (iv), into three types; the first necromantic kind (I.A) commits the worst sin by invoking demons; the second (I.B), also necromantic, exorcizes demons and is only a little better; the third kind, under (II.iv) is astronomical and not forbidden; it neither invokes nor exorcizes demons, and uses no linguistic signs to communicate with them: see 6.11

Greek Toz and . . . Hermes Toz comes from Thoth, Belenus from Apollonius

This does not . . . as coerced demons invoked by talismans only deceive their users into thinking that the magic coerces them: see 4.2, 13; 10.2

Solomon's Almandal . . . Raziel's titles of magic books suggesting Hebrew or Arabic originals

form must . . . obey images in the heavens permitted talismans are astronomical because figures, not ceremonial words or 'characters' (see 6.11), are put on them just at the moment when a heavenly body of the same (or opposite) figure will influence their making

But choices . . . is rash see the eighth saying in 7.4

Ptolemy's ninth saying see the ninth saying in 7.4

be no writing of characters . . . worship not just figures but also some words are permitted because their use is not ceremonial – not for 'worship' – but compare what Aquinas says in 7.12

7.10

substantial forms . . . a certain species substance is associated not only with species but also with solidity and stability

not come from . . . species and the form hot/cold and wet/dry, the qualities of the elements (fire, air, water, earth), are material, but the form shared in all the individual substances of a species is immaterial

hidden to us though we cannot perceive the qualities called 'occult' or 'hidden', their physical and metaphysical basis is intelligible, according to Albert, for whom such qualities are imperceptible (like the human soul, for example) but not mysterious: see 9.4

7.11

the eastern triplicity a triplicity is a group of three zodiacal signs associated with the same elementary qualities, in this case hot and dry for fire, located in the East where the sun rises

outside the zodiac . . . craft of images this winged horse, ridden by the warrior-hero Bellerophon, is not a zodiacal constellation; Bellerophon's name means 'spear-slayer' or perhaps 'slayer of Belleros'

steady . . . dryness features associated with the most remote and slowest planet

astronomy, magic . . . made of stones this may imply a distinction between amulets and talismans, described by Albert in 7.9

zoron . . . to aphron a magnet's north and south poles, from Arabic, probably from a translation of a commentary on the physics by Alexander of Aphrodisias: see 5.3

7.12

spiritual substances demons or angels

various ingredients from . . . the heavens see 5.11–12, 16; 7.10–11

So it is not true . . . heavenly bodies some magical effects are caused naturally by the heavens, but others are not

a statue moves by itself see 5.11, 13

since in living . . . On the Soul Arist. *De anima*, 415^{b}13

producing . . . destroys the other Arist. *Phys.* 208^{a}9–10

But no substantial form . . . remains when a piece of bronze gets a new figure as a statue, the substance or substantial form of the bronze remains: see 7.10

it is a human . . . produces a human Arist. *Phys.* 194^{b}13

statues . . . necromantic art see 5.11; 7.6–9

This excludes . . . in their mouths Augustine, *City of God*, 8.23–6, citing Asclepius, 23–4 as in section 5.11; also Ps. 135:15–16

It remains to ask . . . magic in the next paragraphs Aquinas argues that magic uses language to send messages to persons, whom he eventually shows to be demons

characters and figures . . . message not just ceremonial characters or magic words are forbidden but also figures, since they address persons with minds, contradicting what Albert says in 7.9, near the end: also 6.11

But if someone says . . . from a heavenly body compare 5.16; 7.9, 11

But because figures . . . only to some mind while still excluding written messages, Aquinas entertains an exception to his previous exclusion of figures: carving an artificial form, the figure of a scorpion, on a ruby puts it in a species of artificial objects, just as its specific form puts it in a natural species of gems

Break up the sky . . . Anebo citing Porphyry from Augustine, *City of God*, 10.11

The next question . . . naturally evil Aquinas concludes his argument by showing that the minds addressed by magic belong to demons, whose deeds are evil but are not themselves evil by nature, since God created them as angels

Porphyry . . . the evil deeds: citing Porphyry from Augustine, *City of God*, 10.11; see also 5.10 and 13

7.13

only . . . the uneducated see 7.2–3

true faith . . . fell from heaven see 2.4

Because the primal . . . tempted the woman since the original sin was sexual and insti-
gated by a woman, some blamed women as the most dangerous tempters

7.14

everything . . . in a prophet's vision as in 1.4 or 1.12

angels . . . Abraham Gen. 18:2; 22:11–18

The assumed body . . . its mover for humans, the soul that enlivens the body is also its
form, but angels are not the forms of the bodies that they use

Augustine says that . . . semen was taken Augustine, *City of God*, 15.23, as in 6.12; *On the
Trinity*, 3.8.13

7.15

stinking spirit . . . living water alchemical sulphur and mercury, not the usual elements: but see the later note on *mercury runs*, and also 5.7

multiplied in mines . . . earth alchemical changes occur naturally in the earth

quicksilver . . . into an earth alchemical mercury and sulphur need artificial
processing

a different principle . . . becoming a metal sulphur and mercury undergo processes of
cooking, dissolving, separating and mixing

calcination slow heating and stirring to produce a calx – an ash or stone

sulphur becomes . . . completes the metal here, as in later alchemy, a tincture transmutes
another substance: see also 5.7

nature's . . . path to completion completion *(perfectio)* is the aim of the alchemical
process

Arsenic . . . than sulphur arsenic and sulphur work the same way

mercury runs . . . from sticking a plausible description of metallic mercury

a complete metal . . . become gold see the previous note on *completion*

copper . . . by artifice making gold is the aim of the alchemical process

7.16

excrement . . . alters them separating and cleaning as in 7.15; excrement as an organic
product comes naturally to the lexicon of alchemy, whose processes are often biological and sexual

brightens . . . lemony colour transmuted gold needs to look like natural gold

natural weight . . . signs of completing transmuted gold needs to be as heavy as natural gold

parts . . . packed close perhaps density as well as weight

first degree . . . the third Geber is thinking quantitatively, though crudely

the stone . . . by elevation the Philosopher's Stone

7.17

A Brief Art translated from Lull, *Ars brevis* (Rome: Silber, 1485)

a path . . . all methods Peter of Spain, *Summaries of Logic*, 1.1

one letter . . . several meanings Lull's key idea

In this figure . . . a conclusion in this syllogism – every *A* is an *M*; every *M* is a *B*; therefore, every *A* is a *B* – *A* and *B* are the 'extremes' and *M* is the 'middle'; if my task is to prove that every *A* is a *B*, to construct the necessary argument I must find the middle that will connect *A* with *B*, the subject and predicate of the conclusion

then the principle . . . up the ladder in a classification by genera and species, the most general genera will be at the top of the ladder (or tree, in the usual version), the least general or most specific species at the bottom, just above the individuals that constitute each species

Fig. 10, Ramon Lull, *Ars brevis*, 1485

their '-tive' correlates . . . '-able' correlates the '-able' correlates are above at the level of the angel, higher than the '-tive' correlates of the imaginative and the growing

7.18

As I dropped Dante, the poet, is the narrator, descending through the narrowing circles of hell

This cruel hostel . . . watch how glancing at Dante, Minos interrupts his instructions to the damned

To which my guide Virgil, another great poet, is Dante's guide, protecting him against Minos

his destined journey .. is willed Dante, still alive, does not belong in hell, but Minos cannot stop his journey there because God has willed it

7.19

the last refuge . . . to God this phrase became proverbial in complaints about far-fetched explanations of phenomena considered magical

assign singular . . . circumstances lacking universal or general explanations, anomalies treated as evidence for magic cannot qualify as science

maniacs . . . from a demon Avicenna, a famous physician and Aristotelian philosopher, would not recommend natural cures for a patient possessed by a demon

power of imagination . . . love Oresme and Avicenna treat imagination and emotion as natural, without being sure about their mechanisms

Sometimes the species . . . my soul in this case, the Latin *species* means 'image' or 'appearance'; one theory of vision explained that very fine species were emitted by external objects and reached the eye; other species affected the other four senses; Oresme extends the model to speculate about how Socrates might influence another person's imagination with the contents of his mind

the species . . . or the organ emitted species, which are physical, explain action at a distance; another explanation is spirit *(spiritus),* a very fine medium for such emissions and transmissions: see 7.6, 15

truly against . . . the Philosopher Oresme sees action at a distance as violating a basic principle – the requirement for contact action – of Aristotelian physics, despite support from distinguished thinkers like Avicenna and al-Ghazali

7.20

Fig. 11, Bayerische Staatsbibliothek Munich, MS Clm 849

The technique for the Latin text and commentary, see Kieckheffer, *Forbidden Rites,* pp. 47–98, 208–11

hoopoe bird like the jynxes of 5.15, which are probably either wrynecks or wagtails, hoopoes were thought to have magical power

Oymelor, Demefin starting with names as strange as those found in the Greek Magical Papyri (see 5.6), the invocation proceeds with phrases from the Creed

7.21

The book . . . begins for the Latin text, see Kieckheffer, *Forbidden Rites,* pp. 256–69

abstain . . . fasts and prayers ritual purification, fasting and prayer in church were normal Christian practice; putting a book on the altar would be difficult for anyone but a priest

a priest's . . . stole vestments worn while saying mass

seven psalms . . . litany Psalms 6, 32, 38, 51, 102, 130 and 143 are the seven penitential Psalms, associated with fasting, abstinence and other penances in Lent; a litany is a prayer, sometimes very long, addressed by names or titles to God, the Virgin and or the saints

the power . . . conjurations unauthorized rituals: see 7.9

On, Jesus Christ . . . Adonay several of these reflect biblical names of God in Hebrew, others are Greek, some are unclear

exorcized and invoked invoking summons a demon and is always forbidden; exorcizing a demon is not permitted unless duly performed by a minister of the Church: see 7.9

7.22

By my invoking for the Latin text, see Kieckheffer, *Forbidden Texts,* pp. 276–85

Iannes and Mambres for Jannes and Jambres, traditionally the wizards of Pharaoh defeated by Moses, see 2 Tim. 3:8, also 1.1 and 4.14

ancient serpent Satan as Mirage

threw . . . from heaven see 2.4

I exorcize . . . lampstands see 7.21 for exorcism and 7.7 for the seal or sign of Solomon, which could be used on a signet ring; in Rev. 1:20, the seven golden lampstands are seven churches

PART 8: ANCIENT WISDOM AND FOLLY

Introduction

Fig. 12, Alciato, *Emblematum liber*, 1531

Nicole Oresme see 7.19

get power . . . conjurations see 7.21

make a spirit come see 7.22

Plotinus . . . about magic see 5.5, 10, 13, 15–16

secrets of Kabbalah see 7.5

maleficium see 4.16

Malleus . . . Exodus see 1.5

Pierre Bayle . . . Bekker thinkers of the early Enlightenment

this heresy . . . sorcerers see 8.3

guilty . . . author of lies see 8.19

almost all . . . demoniacs see 7.19

evil demon . . . World see 8.17

makes a mistake . . . Leviticus see 1.8 and 8.18

image-makers . . . evil demons see 8.8

cosmic harmonies . . . Platonist see 4.4–5; 5.5 and 5.16

Henry More . . . Newton's see 11.11, 13–16

8.1

ascribe natural . . . hidden see 7.13

demons have . . . imagination see 7.13

the only witchcraft . . . to demons see 7.13

they . . . are called witches see 7.13

Bishop's Canon . . . image or likeness see 7.3

divine law . . . kill witches see 1.5

Augustine's comments see 6.12

8.2

succubi and incubi a succubus specializes in sex with human males, an incubus with females

no fewer than forty-eight as lawyers and bureaucrats, the Dominican inquisitors kept records

8.3

What else . . . every day often attributed to John Chrysostom but not found in his sermons on Matthew at 19:10, 'it is good not to marry', but found with that passage in an anonymous Latin text in Migne, *Patrologia Graeca*, 56:803

There are three . . . vagina Prov. 30:15: the Latin is *os vulvae*, as in the Vulgate, which could also be 'womb'; in the Jewish Study Bible the next verse names the four things as 'Sheol, a barren womb, Earth that cannot get enough water, and fire which never says "enough"'.

8.4

soul that is led – not intellect the One and Mind, the two higher hypostases, are shielded by Soul from involvement in lower activities like magic: see 5.4–13.

God's bait . . . lures Ficino interprets what Synesius says, based on his own reading of the *Chaldaean Oracles*, about magical birds (jynxes) that lure gods down to earth: see 5.15

8.5

In the world's body . . . pregnant both kinds of spirit, terrestrial and celestial, are material, but the celestial kind is not metabolized or distilled from elementary matter

somehow not a body . . . somehow a body Ficino labours to describe the crucial intermediate state of spirit

spirit feeds within Virgil, *Aen.* 6.726

Plotinus and Porphyry see 5.4–5

Timaeus the Pythagorean Timaeus of Locri is the main speaker in Plato's dialogue, named after him, on cosmology

8.6

Greater Bear . . . Jupiter the constellation Ursa Major (the Big Dipper) is very visible but not in the zodiac; Corvus the Crow is less visible

Thebit the philosopher Thabit ibn Qurra wrote on astronomy and other subjects – including talismans – in the ninth century, but this recipe seems not to be from his book *On Images;* the title of the anonymous *On Images or Rings of the Seven Planets* makes it a possibility

The ancients . . . gradually warms up the ring warms when worn: see 7.9 and 22

Thomas Aquinas . . . agrees Thomas cites Aristotle, *Magn. mor.* 1207ª26–35 in the *Summa Against the Heathens*, 3.92; see also 7.12

8.7

In the Hundred Sayings . . . like those things see 7.4

Haly . . . commenting Haly Ibn Ridwan worked in the tenth century, but the commentary on the *Centiloquium* was probably by Ahmad ibn Yusuf, who died in 912

bezoar see 7.7

Archytas a Pythagorean philosopher and mathematician of the fourth century was said to have made a wooden dove that flew

Trismegistus . . . harm them as well see 5.11

Hebrews . . . golden calf Exod. 32: see also 1.3

Porphyry . . . the same thing: see 5.4, 10, 13, 15: also Iamblichus, *Myst.* 151.6–10, 160.5–161.1, rejecting Porphyry's view

From each . . . hangs a series see the 'orders' and 'chains' in 5.16

There is no . . . fear the cock see 5.16

8.8

Proclus . . . Moon's series see 5.16

In the glasses . . . at the tip a magnetic compass

in the order . . . Bearish items 'orders' and 'chains' in 5.16

Iamblichus . . . demons and deceived see 5.11 and 13

In Florence . . . vinegar evaporated a limestone fossil, perhaps a crinoid stem, might bubble in strong vinegar

So interconnected . . . those people see 5.16

physician . . . kindling heating, cooking, healing and other natural processes are models for magical action

seems not to get . . . a figure see 7.12

the reason seeded see 8.4

images . . . interpret Plotinus see 5.4–5

8.9

what images . . . talk about Ficino uses information from the *Picatrix* but never mentions it: see 7.8

Albert . . . in his Mirror see 7.9

Thebit Benthorad Thabit ibn Qurra, as in 8.6, and Ptolemy as the supposed author of the *Centiloquium*: see 7.4

as an official theologian . . . on images a fair description of Albert's position in 7.9

Thomas Aquinas . . . concedes less also a fair account of what Thomas says in 7.12

In his book . . . nothing of them see Aquinas, *De fato* 5; *De occ. op. nat.* 17, 20, also 7–11, 14, 16

Indeed, Iamblichus . . . astrological method see 5.10, 13

heating . . . hammering a natural process, like cooking, healing and others that Ficino, like Proclus, treats as models for magic: see 5.16; 8.8

Ptolemy and Haly see 7.4 and 8.7

8.10

Hellebore's . . . toxic and destructive both common species of the plant, black and white, are toxic, but both had medical applications, suggesting an analogy with talismans, according to Ficino

an image directed . . . star-blasted see 5.4

effect on a distant object Ficino doubts the possibility of action at a distance: see 5.15–16; 7.19

Arabs and Egyptians . . . work wonders Ficino is thinking of the god-making passages of the *Asclepius* and of related material originally written by Muslims and Jews in Arabic: see 5.11

astral spirits . . . vapours, lights and sounds natural channels to transmit magical action

8.11

But the very . . . warm air and spirit are purer than the earthy and watery components of medicines

8.12

indwelling spirit . . . degree see 5.4

Lord of your geniture 'geniture' is the same as 'nativity' or 'horoscope', whose Lord (to put it simply) is the planet in the Ascendant, but Ficino adds detail further on: see 5.8; 6.11, 7.4

every person . . . was born since a *daimôn* was not evil for the Greeks, the pagan notion of a 'personal demon' evolved easily into Christian 'guardian angel'; also, since Christians like Ficino thought of the stars and planets as alive, planetary and stellar angels would also seem reasonable: see 6.5

Porphyry looks . . . person is born Iamblichus, *Myst.* 272.12–276.15; Firmicus Maternus, *Math.* 2.25.2, 10

8.13

a kind of tinder . . . body see 5.16

Soul is also . . . technique see 5.16

Everywhere nature . . . Synesius too see 5.5 and 15

stirs the mass . . . huge body Virgil, *Aen.* 6.726–7

Ptolemy has . . . the land see 7.4

Plotinus himself . . . worldly powers Plotinus, *Enn.* 4.3.11; also section 5.11

Synesius see 5.15; 8.4, 7

The very Mercurius . . . adds songs see 5.11

sages of Egypt . . . ministers of religion see 5.11, 13; Iamblichus, *Myst.* 4.10–12, 176.1–8, 249.2–8, 278.5–8

Hebrew astrologer . . . David Bil Samuel ibn Zarza, citing David ben Billya, both Jews of the fourteenth century

my first thought . . . blessed Thomas see 7.12

Porphyry says . . . cleansed see 5.13

Mercurius, however . . . divine power see 5.11, 8.4, 8.8; Plotinus, *Enn.* 4.3.11

8.14

goêteia . . . mageia 3.7; 4.1–2, 11; 5.1–2;

As Porphyry says . . . divine Porphyry, *Abst.* 4.16.1

no, Fathers . . . greatest the Fathers are the Cardinals gathered in consistory, to whom Pico had planned to deliver his speech

One is . . . the other see 4.14

To learn . . . secret doctrines see 4.14

Xalmosis . . . Oromasus see 3.1–2, 4; 4.3, 16

If we ask Plato . . . body healthy see 3.4; 4.3

Carondas . . . Dardanus see 4.15 and 17

Homer . . . his Ulysses see 4.1

Eudoxus and Hermippus see 3.7; 4.3, 14

Alkindi . . . William of Paris Al-Kindi (d. 870) was best known to Latin readers for his book *On Rays* – forces emitted by heavenly bodies; William of Paris and Roger Bacon were prominent philosophers of the thirteenth century who supported the notion of natural magic

Plotinus also . . . lord and prince see 5.4–5

the Greeks . . . how natures are kin see 5.5, 16

jynxes of the Magi see 5.15

marries . . . vine see 5.5, with Virgil, *Georg.* 1.2, 2.221; Horace, *Epod.* 2.9–10

full are the heavens . . . glory Isa. 6:3

dogs . . . strangers Seneca, *Dial.* 7.19.2

8.15

our Esdras . . . Origen Pico takes the story of Kabbalah's origin mainly from the apocryphal 2 Esdras, or 4 Esdras in the Latin Vulgate; see also Hilary, *Treatise on the Psalms,* 2.2; Origen, *Commentary on Matthew,* 10.6–8

Jesus Nave Joshua, who succeeded Moses and was called a prophet, *navi*

to give something . . . about wisdom Matt. 7:6; 1 Cor. 2:6–7

Pythagoras wrote . . . in between Iamblichus tells the story about Pythagoras and his
daughter in his *Life of Pythagoras*, 28.146; the line about Aristotle's *Metaphysics*
comes from Aulus Gellius, *Attic Nights*, 20.5.12; see also Plato, *Letter 2*, 312D–E;
Origen *Commentary on Matthew*, 14.11–12; Pseudo-Dionysius, *Ecclesiastical Hierarchy*, 1.4

But after Cyrus . . . Zorobabel Zerubbabel ruled Judea as a Persian province and began
to rebuild the Temple in the early sixth century, when Cyrus released the Jews
from Babylon.

Once Esdras . . . have I done it 2 Esdras 14:42–8, where 70 newer books are kept secret
when 24 older items of an original 94 are made public; for the number 70, see also
Numb. 11

vein . . . of knowledge 2 Esdras 14:47

Sixtus IV . . . no small cost during the papacies of Sixtus IV (1471–84) and Innocent
VIII (1484–92), a Jewish convert, Guglielmo Raimondo Moncada, worked at the
Vatican as a teacher and translator whom Pico later hired – under the name Flavius
Mithridates – to teach him Hebrew and translate books of Kabbalah

Our Augustine . . . Platonists Aug. *Conf.* 7.13, 26, 8.3

Antonio Cronico . . . on the Trinity the conversation probably happened by 1482; Dattilo, Joab in Hebrew, was a common name; Jews cornered by Christians like Pico
and his host, a powerful Venetian, had little chance of resisting

8.16

Magic . . . Conclusions Pico divided his 900 theses or conclusions into two groups,
identifying the latter as 'following his own opinion'; these 26 theses on magic
come from the second group

natural magic . . . not prohibited in keeping with the teachings of Aquinas, Albertus,
Ficino and many other learned Christians: see 7.9–12; 8.4–7

Magic . . . natural science the basis of natural science was Aristotle's physics, matter
theory, cosmology and psychology, often called 'natural philosophy' – the theory
implemented by the practice of natural magic

ternary and the denary three-fold and ten-fold, alluding to the Christian Trinity and
the ten features of God called *sefirot* ('countings') by Kabbalists: see 8.17

characters . . . act of Kabbalah Kabbalah reads words in Hebrew as numbers because
the letters of the alphabet are also numerals, so that *alef* is 1, *bet* is 2, *gimel* is 3 and
so on; see also 6.11; 7.9, 12

8.17

Kabbalah . . . Conclusions these theses are taken from 47 conclusions 'following the
teaching of the Hebrew Kabbalist sages' that conclude the first half of Pico's collection: see 8.16

Cherubim . . . and Isim Mighty Ones, Flamers, Thrones, Living Ones, Heroes, Watchers, Wheels, Princes and Men: see also 6.13

The letters . . . from the other the Triagrammaton, a three-lettered name of God, could be either *Yehu* or *Yeshu* – both with three letters in Hebrew; one method of assigning numerical values to letters gives 21 for *Yehu*, while *Yeshu*'s value is 19, and the same method gives 21 for *Satan*; Pico saw this as a great secret because he thought that *Yeshu* was a Hebrew form of Jesus

One who knows . . . by day Compassion, the sixth of the *sefirot*, rules by day; absent at night, it makes way for Judgement, the fifth, the source of evil demons

Job said . . . Commanders Job 25:2

By the flying fowl . . . humans Kabbalists interpreted the flying things of the creation story as angels visible to humans, unlike the unseen angels mentioned as birds in the next verse: Gen. 1:20–1

No angel . . . changes Cherubim and Seraphim have six wings; Kabbalists described six-winged angels as unseen and never changing; since they always remain angels, they never turn into demons or humans: Gen. 1:21; Isa. 6:2; Eccles. 10:20

In the whole Law . . . Numerations every part of every letter of the Torah is meaningful in Kabbalah

8.18

Whatever Other . . . Conclusions these theses are taken from the 72 'kabbalistic conclusions following my own opinion' that conclude the second half of Pico's collection: see 8.16 and 17

Whatever the rest . . . into practice in these three theses, Pico's description of Kabbalah as practical and visionary is opaque, perhaps because it was as daring as it was novel; the theory is visionary, focused on God's names *(shemot);* the practice aims to connect with the *sefirot* and produce changes in the Godhead itself, starting with techniques of magical ecstasy; the desired vision is of God – the beatific vision; the three lower levels of visioning suggest natural philosophy, metaphysics and theology; the highest level is ecstatic union with God, when the four combine in a single *merchiava*, a vision of the chariot *(merkavah)* like the one described by the prophet Ezekiel: see Ezek. 1–3:27

Someone with . . . Holy Spirit the quaternary is a magical number (1+2+3+4 = 10), a guide to summing the sums of the four letters in four names of God: *Ehyeh* (21) + *Adonay* (65) + YHVH (26) = YHVH + *Elohim* (26 + 86 = 112), where 86 is also a magical number: see a subsequent thesis for the tetraktys

If humans . . . from now 514 years passed between 1486 and 2000; if the day of Pico's prediction in 1486 was Sunday, 7 December, when the *Conclusions* were published, the end of time should have come on 1 January 2001, one day after the end of the second millennium; 25 days may be just an accident of Pico's schedule before his planned speech in Rome, but finding a meaningful 25 in Kabbalah would take little ingenuity

The way . . . of the Lord in a holy death, the body parts from the soul after and because the soul has already left the body in a prophetic rapture that unites the human mind with God's divine Intellect

One who is . . . Judgement for a Neoplatonist like Proclus, being 'rationally intellectual' was an elevated state of the soul; *Binsica* is a Latinization of 'kiss' (*nesiqah*) preceded by the preposition 'in' (*be*). The death of the kiss is the holy death just described

One who has . . . Saturday God rested on the seventh day, and the standard order of the week for Christians was Sunday through Saturday; assigning planets to days was more fluid, however; before Christ came, the day of rest on Saturday was ruled by the moon, understood as the Sabbath and the lowest of the ten *sefirot*; after Christ came, a change to Sunday moves the holiest day from the bottom to the top of the lower seven *sefirot*

Whatever the rest . . . the first Pico correlates the five planets, two luminaries and three higher spheres with the ten *sefirot*; the Building is the seven lower *sefirot*: see 11.8 for a later version of Kabbalist cosmology

Whoever knows . . . to tenth given the correlations of the previous conclusion, Pico draws on standard astrological associations – Mars with the anger that violates the sixth commandment, for example – to extend his Kabbalist astrology to Christian morality

When Kabbalists . . . which forbids the seventh and eighth are *sefirot*, which are also Saturn and Venus, and the lower seven are the lower *Merchiava* or Chariot; the seventh gives sons and the eighth does not forbid them, correlating with the commandments of Saturn to keep the Sabbath and of Venus not to steal

If he is . . . ineffable name the quaternary, discussed in a previous thesis, is also an amulet, the tetraktys – an equilateral triangle of four points on each side and one in the centre; counting from any apex through four rows of points, all the points add up to ten: $1+2+3+4 = 10$; if each row is replaced by as many of the letters (which are also numbers) of YHVH, God's holiest name, as can fit, starting with *yod* at the apex and then with *yod* again at the right of each row, the sum becomes 72: 10 *(yod)* + 15 *(yod + he)* + 21 *(yod +he + vav)* + 26 *(yod + he + vav + he)*; as a divine name, 72 is hidden in three verses of Exodus 14, each of which contains exactly 72 letters; aligned and read vertically, they produce 72 angelic names of three letters each; thus, the mystical 72 comes from YHVH in the same way that the denary comes from the quaternary: see Exod. 14:19–21

From the . . . rational nature The *shem ha-maforash* or 'pre-eminent name' was made explicit or interpreted when God gave Moses the priestly blessing for Aaron to use; the blessing includes YHVH three times; for each occurrence of the name there are 24 different arrangements of its four letters, summing to 72: Num. 6:22–7

Just as Aristotle . . . philosophically Pico knew Maimonides not only as the most eminent Jewish Aristotelian but also as an authority studied by Kabbalists; his *Guide for the Perplexed* could be read by Christians in a medieval Latin version

Just as . . . the Law astrology reads the stars and planets as God's heavenly scripture just as Kabbalah reads the *sefirot* as God's supernal scripture recorded in the Bible

8.19

claim to go . . . things described above see 7.2–3; 8.2
the power of imagination see 7.19; 9.1
the author of lies John 8:44

PART 9: ANCIENT WISDOM MODERNIZED

Introduction

Fig. 13, Anono, *Rosarium philosophorum*, 1550

as when a juggler . . . familiar see 9.14
Champier's Dialogue . . . in 1486 see 8.1–3, 19
maleficium see 4.16
will be as cunning . . . monuments Marlowe, *Doctor Faustus*, 1.19–20, 119; see also 10.2
an impenitent . . . art of divination Rowland, *Bruno*, pp. 228, 258–60, 274
the inadequacy . . . teach see 9.1
Fludd's theosophy see 11.8
Thomas Vaughan see 11.10
The ancient writer . . . secret inspiration Pseudo-Dionysius, *Celestial Hierarchy*, 2.5; see also 6.13
the magical . . . other arts see 9.4
very much . . . cannot pronounce see 4.13–14
it was a matter . . . perfect see 8.15
Matter is . . . all things see 9.12

9.1

the intelligences . . . spheres on Aristotelian grounds, Aquinas accepted the existence of spiritual movers for the heavenly bodies, though he doubted that they are life-giving souls
Theophrastus . . . evident wisdom students and interpreters of Aristotle: see 3.7
St Thomas Aquinas see 7.12
the Peripatetics Aristotelians like Pomponazzi
by God . . . second causes although an omnipotent God can act directly and miraculously on the world, the action is normally indirect, through 'second causes' in nature

9.2

the archetypal . . . Craftsman see 5.8, 13
This magic . . . noblest see 8.14

Apuleius . . . rule of religion see 4.16
Magic includes these . . . subjects see 4.14

9.3

the 'ineffable' . . . in Exodus see 8.18

if you fall . . . the earth see 2:3

I shall rise . . . of old Isa. 14:13–15; see also 2.10

lying spirit . . . Ahab's prophets see 1.11, 13

that woman . . . belly in 1 Sam. 28:7, the woman called a 'belly-talker' by the Greek Septuagint is described in the Latin Vulgate as 'having a python' *(habens pythonem)*, which reflects Acts 16:16, where a girl 'has a python spirit' that makes her a diviner and alludes to the snake of the Delphic oracle: see 1:10; 6.2–3

Theut in Plato Thoth (or Hermes Trismegistus), said by Plato to have invented gambling: *Phaedrus*, 274C–D

vessels of iniquity . . . with Belial the Hebrew name probably means 'worthless'; Gen. 49:5–6; 2 Cor. 6:15

The avengers . . . Asmodeus see 1.18

Their prince is Satan . . . to make Rev. 13:13–14, where the false prophet is a subordinate of the Antichrist, not Satan himself; see also 2.4

holding the four . . . bad faith Rev. 7:1–2, where one angel restrains four others who can 'hurt the earth' with winds; Mereri is the 'bitter destruction' of Deut. 32:24, perhaps personified in Job 3:5 and connected by Agrippa with the demon prince of Ephes. 2:2

The furies . . . devastator Rev. 9:11 – reflecting Job 28:22 – interprets the Hebrew Abaddon (Destroyer), 'the angel of the bottomless pit', as equivalent to Apollyon (Destroyer) in Greek

slanderers . . . our God in Hebrew *Ashtaroth* seems to be a plural of *Ashtarteh*, probably an analogue of Aphrodite, a goddess widely worshipped in the ancient Middle East and named nine times in the Hebrew Bible (see 1.11), generally using the plural to name a *type* of heathen divinity; for the 'accuser' of Rev. 12:10, see also 2.4

the tempters . . . avarice the New Testament uses *mamônas* , as in Luke 16:9–13, for the wealth or property that divides people from God; see Ps. 78:49 for evil angels

the Devil . . . vale of tears see 2.4

for fear . . . road Matt. 8:28

Isaiah . . . dragons Isa. 13:21–2, 34:11–15; Ps. 91:13

scorpion . . . Perversity Luke 10:19, 16:9; John 12:31, 14:30, 16:11; and section 2.10 for the 'demon prince'

Origen's view . . . felt Origen discusses these issues in his work *On Principles*, 1.5.3, 1.8.4, but not as Agrippa says; see also Matt. 8:31, Luke 8:32–3 and section 2.7

Theologians share . . . equally compare what Aquinas says in 7.13

Book of Tobias . . . Asmodeus see 1.18

special guardian . . . the flesh see 4.16–17; 5.1, 7; 8.12

Raziel . . . fornicator Agrippa's interpretations are correct for Gabriel and Raphael, but only Gabriel and Michael are biblical; for Raphael see 1.18; Raziel's name is attached to the medieval *Book of Raziel the Angel*, which mentions Anial or Haniel, and Aniel is one of the 72 names that make up God's ineffable name, for which see 8.18

Zapkiel . . . Amixiel see 8.18 for Kabbalist astrology, combined here with angel lore

Urieus . . . Mahazael names on the pattern of Urieus (Oriens), Amaymon, Paymon and Egyn appear frequently in later medieval magic books; for Azazel see 1.8; Samael, Azael and Mahazael are Kabbalist

Book of Temples . . . Lights the *Zohar* or parts of it, falsely attributed to Shimon bar Yochai, a rabbi of the second century CE

Book of Formation the *Sefer Yetzirah*, in circulation by the tenth century, was a wellspring of later Kabbalist speculation

There is a . . . table see 8.18 for the *shem ha-maforash*

Fig. 14, Agrippa von Nettesheim, *Opera omnia*, 1600

9.4

the art of the Signed . . . into it Paracelsus, *Astronomia magna, oder die gantze Philosophia sagax der grossen und kleinen Welt* (Frankfurt: Martin Lechler for Hieronymus Feyerabend, 1571), fol. 29ᵛ

hidden . . . occult things Paracelsus understands 'occult' to mean 'hidden' in the sense of 'covered' but able to be uncovered: see 7.10

human body . . . distinct organs the basic principle of the physiognomy of analogies among features of human, animal and plant bodies

any body has . . . are spiritual the hidden analogies are powerful because they are spiritual as well as physical

not Galen . . . established anew one book about medical magic by Paracelsus would make good the loss of everything written by the leading physicians of antiquity and the Middle Ages

Magic, as I said . . . its gifts magical anatomy is not physical dissection but a spiritual analysis of signatures

Though the parts . . . with what visible effects of celestial causes reveal the invisible arcana

the Magi . . . luminous body the quest of the Magi is a model for astronomical discovery of the arcana: see 2.2

9.5

Sulphur and Mercury . . . names see 5.7, 7.15

Our Mercury . . . is Mercury see Figure 13

there is nothing . . . not Mercury an invitation to transmute everything

the whole elixir see 7.6

the dragon . . . tinctures see 5.7 and 7.15 for tinctures

Lucas . . . Morienus in the twelfth century, when Robert of Chester produced a book *On Composition in Alchemy,* he brought the word *alchimia* into Latin, to title an Arabic text of instructions by a monk called Morienus; other attributions in this passage are apocryphal (Plato), fictional or unknown

Almisadir listed with mercury, sulphur and arsenic by Constantine of Pisa in his *Book of the Secrets of Alchemy* in the thirteenth century: perhaps ammonium chloride, distilled from urine

9.6

Seeing magick . . . shewed before the translation is from the 1658 edition of Porta's *Magick,* p. 3

witty clever

physician . . . physick natural scientist; natural science

common simples ordinary botanical remedies

cunning skill

glasses mirrors

sleights techniques

9.7

We are now come . . . alchymy matters the translation is from the 1658 edition of Porta's *Magick,* pp. 160–4

golden liquor . . . immortal one understanding of the elixir, but see 7.6, 9.5

brickle brittle

knapt broken

voided cleared

mastery a feat or procedure

powned crushed

rigoles furrows

wrested or writhen strained or twisted

reflexed reflected

blower a technician using a bellows

flighted put to flight

9.8

We pass . . . whereof the translation is from the 1658 edition of Porta's *Magick,* pp. 190–92

experiment . . . experiments sometimes an observation or 'experience' rather than a test, and never, in the modern senses, a designed, controlled and reproducible test of an explicit hypothesis; nonetheless, Porta's approach to magic is markedly empirical

mariner's compasses . . . writ about them magnetic needles on two compasses would
    somehow pick out the same letters
Anaxagoras . . . living stone Aristotle, *De anima*, 405ᵃ13–22
Epicurus . . . inveighs against this Galen, *Natural Faculties*, 1.14; Lucretius, *On Nature*,
    6.906–1089
complicated tangled
pits of loadstone . . . Galen Galen, *Natural Faculties*, 1.14, as previously
smeered greased
calx see 7.15

9.9

Someone who knows . . . distance Agrippa, *Occult Philosophy*, 2.1
Now I am come to the translation is from the 1658 edition of Porta's *Magick*, pp.
    190–92
catoptrick glasses mirrors
burning glasses mirrors arranged to focus light for burning
how letters may be cast out a primitive image projector
plain glass plane mirror
in the beginning the first words of John's Gospel
sight pupil

9.10

Fig. 15, John Dee, *Monas hieroglyphica*, 1564

the style called Pythagorean proverbially silent, secretive and obscure
not one dot . . . of circles see 8.17, especially thesis 33
quadrate mystery . . . symmetrical squaring the circle
Hebrew . . . sacred language gematria, notarikon and *tzyruph* are ways of combining,
    calculating and permutating the numerical letters of the Hebrew alphabet: see 8.16
This real Kabbalah . . . creation Rom. 1:20

9.11

Instructions from Angels the translation is by Meric Casaubon, in Dee, *Diaries*, pp. 13,
    239 and 34–5 in separate pagination
the Stone the crystal ball used by Kelley and Dee, or perhaps St Dunstan's book about
    the Philosopher's Stone
Oriens, Egym, Paynim and *Mayrary* for the first three, see 9.4; for Mereri see 9.3
God will not . . . secret wisdom see 8.15 on pearls and swine
the angel of God . . . in his journey see 1.18

9.12

call him 'the great demon' see 4.5

hypostasis see 8.4

all the seeds are hidden see 8.8

David of Dinant . . . Avicebron Solomon ibn Gabirol, a Jew who wrote in the eleventh century, and David of Dinant, a Christian of the early thirteenth century, both had controversial views about matter and its relation to God

9.13

three-headed . . . metaphysical Cerberus, the dog who guards hell, has three heads

in the Physics . . . well disposed Arist. *Phys.* 188ª31–88ᵇ15; *De anima*, 414ª11–12

numbness . . . nets see 5.3

purely material principle . . . act together compare 7.19, 8.19 and 9.1

Hippocrates . . . believe most source unknown

9.14

Abominable and Devilish the selection is from Scot, *The Discoverie of Witchcraft*, London: William Brome, 1584, pp. 14–18

ingraffed implanted

powrd poured

coosened cozened, defrauded

coosenuges cozenages, deceptions

juggler conjurer

knacks tricks

familiar a witch's spirit helper, often in animal form

trumperie fraud

Cardanus Girolamo Cardano

spoile confiscated property

sithens since

haereticae depravitatis Bernard Gui, *Procedure for Inquisition into the Wickedness of Heresy*, an inquisitor's manual of the early fourteenth century

the fift . . . the Eight regnal years: 1563 and 1542

some canon some point of Church law

a foolish pamphlet . . . 1582 one of four anonymous pamphlets about witchcraft in Essex printed between 1566 and 1589, *A True and Just Recorde*, written in part by Brian Darcy, whose relative, the second Baron Darcy of Chiche, died in the previous year, thought to have been bewitched

Ri. Ga., a Windsor man in 1579 Richard Galis published a witchcraft pamphlet, *A Brief Treatise Containing the Most Strange and Horrible Cruelty of Elizabeth Stile*

usuallie regularly

PART 10: MAGIC SEEN HEARD AND MOCKED

Introduction

Fig. 16, Christopher Marlowe, *The Tragicall History of the Life and Death of Doctor Faustus*, 1620

Fig. 17, Stockholm, National Library, Codex Gigas, 13th century

Fig. 18, Ulisse Aldrovandi, *Mostrorum historia*, 1642

Medieval books . . . from the sky see 1.1; 2.1, 18

Porta's books . . . Paracelsus see 9.4, 8–9

I can call . . . for them 1 Hen. 4, 3.1.52–4

the mind is . . . of Heav'n see 10.7

to justify . . . to men Milton, *PL*, 1.26

Plautus . . . look foolish see 4.8 and Chaucer, *The Canon's Yeoman's Tale*

Rose Garden . . . empty language see 9.5

of power . . . omnipotence Marlowe, *Doctor Faustus*, 1.56

10.1

Merlin's Enchanted Sword for the text, see Spenser, *The Faerie Queene*, as in the Bibliography

heben ebony

coverd curved

kend knew

amenaunce behaviour

bylive quickly

prowest bravest

paynim non-Christian

Sar'zins fowly Saracens grievously

eftsoones forthwith

greedily avidly

and Archimage . . . vaine Pyrocles asks Archimago for the sword that he had brought for Braggadocchio

faine happily

beteeme grant

smart pain

dint a blow in battle

fone foes

forst allow

wroth angry

weenest supposes

troth truth

brond sword
dight properly

10.2

Within This Circle for the text, see Marlowe, *The Complete Plays,* as in the Bibliography
welkin sky
hest bidding
characters see 6.11; 7.9, 12; 8.16
Acheron see 4.12
Beelzebub see 2.10, 9.3
Demogorgon possibly a garbled form of 'Demiurge'; see also Damigeron in 4.16
Franciscan . . . devil best dressing Satan's servant as a friar was funny to Marlowe's
    anti-Catholic audience, especially since Franciscans were proverbially greedy,
    lecherous and hypocritical
Did not . . . per accidens the spell cast by Faustus is only an indirect or accidental cause
    of the presence of Mephistopheles; the direct cause is Satan's wish to put souls in
    hell for denying God: see 7.9
confounds hell in Elysium sees hell as heaven
the old philosophers the old pagan philosophers, because they are unbaptized, cannot
    be in Heaven
God threw . . . damned with Lucifer see 2.4, 10.7

10.3

Fairies and Hobgoblins for the text, see Shakespeare, *A Midsummer Night's Dream,* in
    the Bibliography
lob a clumsy lout
passing exceedingly
changeling a human child stolen by fairies
spangled starlight sheen starry night sky
square prepare to fight
that all so that all
Robin Goodfellow Puck's name
skim . . . barm barm is the head on beer; Puck interferes with everyday domestic tasks
beguile enchant
gossip's old woman's
crab crab apple
dewlap loose skin around the throat
rash wanton irresponsible
Corin . . . Phillida poetic names for a shepherd and shepherdess
bouncing . . . buskined big with leather leggings

Hippolyta . . . Theseus the Queen of the Amazons is to be married to the King of Athens
ringlets circle dances
rheumatic respiratory
distemperature disorder
Hiems Winter
childing bountiful
mazèd bewildered
henchman page or squire
vot'ress a woman bound by vows of religion to serve someone, like a nun
shun . . . spare avoid
chide fight
bolt arrow
love-in-idleness pansy
leviathan whale

10.4

A Spirit Too Delicate for the text, see Shakespeare, *The Tempest*, as in the Bibliography
quality retinue
to point exactly
on the beak . . . bowsprit in every part of the ship
distinctly in separate places
coil commotion
Not a soul . . . asleep after the storm, the ship's crew is safe, still under Ariel's spell
Midseason . . . glasses two hour-glasses past noon: 2 p.m.
give me pains . . . performed me since you're giving me orders, let me remind you of
    your unkept promise to me
moody haughty
Before . . . be out before the time of Ariel's service is up
bate shorten
grown into a hoop bent double with age
Argier Algiers
This blue-eyed hag . . . child Sycorax was pregnant with Caliban
hests orders
mine art . . . thee out Prospero's magic released Ariel
peg stuff
correspondent obedient

10.5

The Simple Idiot for the text, see Jonson, *Volpone and Other Plays,* as in the
    Bibliography
heretic . . . to convert him the heresy is not believing in alchemy

costive of belief reluctant to believe

gulled tricked

the work is done the alchemical work

aludels pear-shaped glass vessels

bolt's-head long-necked flask

on D pieces of apparatus with their contents are labelled A, B, C and so on

tinct tincture: see 5.7; 7.15; 9.5

imbibition soaking

St Mary's bath a double boiler or *bain marie*, an invention attributed to an early alchemist named Mary

lac virginis virgin's milk, a white fluid – water with lead oxide and alum

calcined . . . calx see 7.15

reverberating in Athanor being heated with flame in a furnace

crow's head . . . were the crow removing the crow's head is one step in an initial stage of blackening (*nigredo*) or decomposition, but a cockscomb is a fool's hat

ferret a smelly animal but also a metal ring for a bottle

inceration making waxy

projection throwing into a crucible

balneo vaporoso steam bath

As if at first . . . natural mine alchemy multiplies gold by imitating natural processes: see 7.11

Get you . . . and hooks items of base metal to be turned into gold, ostensibly, though when Subtle promises to 'change all metals', he intends to sell these household goods

materia liquida liquid matter

For where it is . . . doth in earth summarizing the alchemical process

He'll bray . . . be brayed to bray is to pound in a vessel like a mortar, but also to skin an animal, and so to cheat

Of your elixir . . . to name Jonson had read many books like the *Rose Garden* (see 9.5) in order to collect these terms, which are obscure and convincing at the same time

intending . . . obscure their art alchemists obfuscated their procedures in order to conceal them

perplexed allegories . . . ours common Sir Epicure has 'cleared' or explained the myth of Sisyphus to back Subtle's claim that alchemical enigmas are sacred; but Surly knows that the alchemist's work, like the labour of Sisyphus, always fails to move its stone to the goal; 'common' is 'public', like the next character who enters, Dol Common, a prostitute, and to make alchemy public is a desecration

10.6

Fake Magic the translation is adapted from Mewe, *Pseudomagia*, as in the Bibliography

magical rings see 7.20 and 10.2

Let Janus take care with two faces, Janus looks forward and backward

10.7

A Summons for the text, see Milton, *Paradise Lost*, as in the Bibliography

The mind . . . of Heav'n see 10.2, at the end

He . . . Almighty God, who controls the thunder, like Jupiter

Satan . . . Beelzebub see 1.13, 16–17; 2.3–4, 10; 9.3; 10.2

Princes, potentates, warriors see 6.13

cope vault

princely dignities . . . thrones see 6.13

known . . . by various names see 9.3

Moloch in Lev. 20:2–5 and elsewhere, Molech's heinous evil may be the cultic sacrifice
   of children

Chemos the Moabites are the people of Chemosh in Num. 21:29 and Jer. 48:46

Peor the Lord (Baal) of Peor was also a Moabite god, as in Num. 23:28 and Num. 25

Astoreth . . . Astarte see 9.3

Thammuz . . . Adonis see 6.6

Orus Horus

Belial see 9.3

Azazel see 1.8

amerced deprived as punishment

when the Sun . . . rides the sun is in Taurus in April and May

10.8

peccant diseased and infectious

Cabricias . . . et casus gibberish, though most of the words are Latin

armyan . . . nasmus . . . cubile gibberish again

omoplate shoulder blade

ossabundus . . . milus gibberish

10.10

A Cunning Man for the text, see Butler, *Hudibras,* as in the Bibliography

reason . . . overran Spenser, *Faerie Queene,* 2.2.17

peevish . . . antipathies Butler, *Hudibras,* 1.1.205–6

For mystick . . . earned Butler, *Hudibras,* 1.1.523–40

Sidrophel, the Rosy-crucian Butler, *Hudibras,* 2.3 argument; see also 11.2

hight named

When brass . . . or curing the cunning man, Sidrophel, responds to complaints of missing household goods, failed recipes and minor ailments

The Saints . . . the Godly Ralph (who has no standing) assures Hudibras that a good
   Presbyterian can consult a cunning man

Has not this . . . in one shire Parliament supports witch-hunting; a 'ledger' is an agent

Kelly Edward Kelley, John Dee's 'skryer': see 9.11

speak . . . belly nuns of Loudun in France had claimed to be possessed by demons, leading to a trial and the burning of a priest in 1634

to write . . . th'air predicting the outcome of battles during England's Civil War

gymnosophist an exotic holy man

stile pen

juggle, cant and cheat Sidrophel is a con-man

Dee's Prefaces . . . Emperor John Dee wrote a preface for the first English Euclid; an associate was Albert Alasco, a Polish nobleman; for the Emperor and Kelley, see 9.11

well-willer an eager student

fittest mood astrological states of the moon

planetary gin . . . heads in an astrological mouse-trap

what med'cine . . . make a man with a later work *On Nature*, incorrectly ascribed to Paracelsus, says that a 'little human' *(homunculus)* can be produced by incubating semen in a closed vessel, but Paracelsus himself had moral reservations: see 7.5; 9.4

zany a comic sidekick

squander puper . . . words prepare legal documents in the most wasteful and costliest way

His bus'ness . . . could make the zany's main job is to extract information from his master's clients that will then be fed back to them; he also serves as the ghost-writer for Sidrophel's almanacs

bilks deceptions

found out by Fisk Nicholas Fisk, a physician and astrologer

This feat . . . come about when Sidrophel sees Hudibras and Ralph approaching with his telescope, he sends Whachum to quiz them

Yon Knight . . . doth suffer Ralph explains his master's bad luck with his beloved, a widow

joynter a woman who has the sole rights to an estate

The stars . . . foretell Sidrophel claims to know the whole story from his astrology

Donzel squire

But for . . . nothing by him Sidrophel insists that his magic is entirely natural

The Rosy-crucian . . . lure the Rosicrucians are better than Sidrophel at the diabolical magic that Sidrophel falsely disclaims

Bumbastus Paracelsus: see 9.4

Kelly John Dee's skryer with his crystal ball: see 9.11

Agrippa see 9.2–3

Trismegistus . . . time's daughter Francis Bacon's slogan, 'truth is the daughter of time,' values progress over antiquity, including the ancient authority of Hermes Trismegistus

genethliacks makers of horoscopes

But what . . . dreams and fancies even equipped with telescopes, stargazing has no useful product

Who made the Balance . . . above the earth Sidrophel's arrogance evades the import of

God's questions in Job 38:31–3: 'Cans't thou bind the sweet influence of Pleiades or loose the bands of Orion? . . . Knowest thou the ordinances of heaven?'

Th'Egyptians . . . tails end in astronomy the ancients disagreed about the basics, just like the moderns: Copernicus, Girolamo Cardano, Julius Caesar Scaliger and Jean Bodin

Some say . . . of old the sun no longer rises in the zodiacal signs at the times established for them by ancient astrologers

accidence the grammar of inflected words, specially in the classical languages

gudgeons small fish easily caught; also people easily fooled

huffing blustering

a formal . . . player a rigorous preacher and a lazy person

fop-doodle a fool

saltinbanco's fraud's

draw a figure . . . by my art Sidrophel performs an 'interrogation', as in 7.9, here called a 'horary inspection' and his 'worst erection' because casting a horoscope on the spot is hard to bear; he gets the knight's sad story right because Whachum, disguised as a Frenchman, has extracted the information from him and Ralph

chews'd and caldes'd tricked and cheated; for the second word, pronounced *kal-deezed*, see 4.9 on the Chaldaean art

perpendiculars the sorcerer and his apprentice are crooked, but Hudibras threatens that they will hang straight, like a bricklayer's plumb line

sessions a local court run by a justice of the peace – like Hudibras

huffer blustering fool

Stygian sophister diabolical liar

gripe grip

fire-fork . . . prong a forked tool for use with coal

twitch . . . breech Hudibras kicks Whachum in the rear

PART 11: MAGIC IN AN AGE OF SCIENCE

Introduction

Fig. 19, Anon., *Hocus Pocus Junior, the Anatomie of Legerdemain: The Art of Jugling Set Forth in His Proper Colours, Fully, Plainly and Exactly, So That an Ignorant Person May Thereby Learn the Full Perfection of the Same, After a Little Practise*, 1635

seven or eight . . . garden see 11.9

whimsicall . . . atheism see 11.15

angels of God . . . descending see 11.2

in these latter . . . method see 11.2

like Paracelsus see 9.4

axioms 'axiomata' in 11.2; the word was a term of art in the huge literature inspired by Peter Ramus

Europe is . . . gold-making see 11.2

applies . . . works of nature Bacon, *De augmentis*, 3.5

a scholastick occult quality see 11.16

affrights . . . diabolick contracts see 11.13

medium . . . of mankind see 11.15

the true philosophick Cabbala see 11.11

dictate their . . . safely gathered More, *Enthusiasmus triumphatus*, 43 (p. 29) in *A Collection*

mysticall walk see 11.10

II.1

Noble Ends the text is from Bacon, *Advancement*, pp. 17–22

the hate of the scholmen see 11.16

affectionate eager

copie abundant variety

vermiculate sinuous

little history . . . or time 'history' is any knowledge based on critical and empirical inquiry

facility of credit credulity

narrations . . . and images see 6.7–8

Plinius . . . Arabians see 4.13–14; 7.9, 16

pretences . . . pretendeth aims . . . aims

auricular traditions hearsay

II.2

News of the Invisible Brethren the text is from Vaughan, *Fame and Confession*, pp. 1–32

happy time . . . creatures of nature new discoveries in exploration, science and technology

Microcosmos a lesser world mirroring the greater

The Old Enemy Satan

our Brother CR Christian Rosenkreutz

indifferently equally well

brother PAL initials in capital letters, as in *CR*

Dutch German

physick see 9.6

Sinus Arabicus Arabian Gulf

inditia signs

Theophrastus Paracelsus

Sancti Spiritus Holy Spirit

rota cycle

fiat . . . pereat let it be . . . let it perish

the word CR Christian Rosenkreutz?
Aurora dawn
runagates apostates
cozen impose upon
fastigium peak
parergon accessory
Fama and *Confessio* Rosicrucian manifestos, the *News* and *Confession*

11.3

Trithemius the learned abbot Johan Heidenberg of Trittenheim wrote about nearly
    everything, including magic
Rulandus . . . Oporinus Martin Ruland, a Paracelsian, wrote a dictionary of alchemi-
    cal terminology; Peder Sorensen (Severinus), Oswald Croll and Jacques Gohory
    were prominent in the same field; the printer Johann Herbst (Oporinus) started as
    an assistant to Paracelsus, and biographies mention Wetter as a servant

11.4

Aristotle . . . in book 7 NE 1145b5–7
Delrio . . . haughty size Johann Godelman, a Protestant lawyer, Martin Delrio, a Jes-
    uit, Pierre le Loyer and Jean Bodin added their voices to the testimony on witches,
    demons and ghosts

11.5

a new principle . . . its own good new only in the naturalist version that Campanella
    inherited from Telesio and Bruno: see Aristotle, *NE* 1094^{a}1–2
Then I find stones . . . intelligence in them see 7.15

11.6

the remora . . . numbs it see 5.3, 12
the lion . . . the cock see 5.16
the remora . . . causing numbness as just noted
torpedo the electric ray

11.8

A Little World the text is from Fludd, *Mosaicall Philosophy*, pp. 1–9, 17–21, 48, 53–7
ethnick pagan
objected put before
machins devices

engin or machin apparatus or device

matras or bolt's head a long-necked vessel made of glass, as in 10.5, but Dee's device is a glass tube open at one end with a bulb at the closed end

Touching regarding

pipe tube

fabrick structure

spirit or aire see 7.6, 15, 19; 8.5, 10–11

vacuity . . . to credit Fludd excludes any vacuum

a little world an artificial microcosm: see 5.6, 8.0, 11.2

By the Spirit . . . Wisd. 7:17–22

Hermes the centre . . . that are the second aphorism of the *Book of Twenty-Four Philosophers*

The foresaid . . . comprehended according to Wisd. 7, through God's wisdom we have knowledge of the world and the elements, their creation and continuation, the seasons, the heavens, winds, animals, plants and the human mind

Saith Job . . . thunders Job 28:20–26

Book of Verity the Bible

from God . . . curing Ecclesiasticus 38:1–2

by Wisdome . . . of all things Wisd. 7:20–22

piony . . . falling-sickness see 4.2, 18; 5.14

occult . . . hidden property see 7.10, 9.4

from these learned . . . more unknown see 11.16

According unto . . . his light Fludd conflates the Christian doctrine of creation from nothing *(ex nihilo)* with the Kabbalist *tzimtzum* (contraction), whereby God creates the world by withdrawing from a point at the centre of his boundless light; since *'ain* in Hebrew is 'nothing' and *sof* is 'end', *'ain sof* is 'infinity' or, in a religious sense, the Infinite; after *'Ain Sof,* the first of the ten *sefirot* is the Crown, *Keter*, and Wisdom is the second, *Hokmah*: see 8.16–18

revealing himself . . . abysse Gen. 1:1–2

privative . . . orient property see the headnote to 8.17

This formal champion . . . positive emanation see 11.5

Wherefore as . . . in nature local physical expansion and contraction demonstrate God's actions in the universe; the Spirit, itself both theological (the Holy Spirit) and physical (spirit, air, wind), links the two levels

strait confined

inspissate condense

precipitation being forced down

11.9

Fig. 21, Mathew Hopkins, *The Discovery of Witches*, 1647

Proof Positive the text is from Hopkins, *Discovery*, as in the Bibliography *kitling* kitten

Sack white wine or sherry

Peck peak?

peached accused

all beholders anyone who looked

aule awl

filmes tongues?

close to the flesh skin tight around the flesh?

seekes not . . . covenant see 4.2, 13; 6.9, 11 and 7.14 on pacts, coercion and worship

couch go to sleep

heartneth on emboldens

policie artfulness

Assizes session of a county court

reflect on look to

adviseth . . . floate advises them to be tried by being thrown into water, when floating and not sinking will be a proof of guilt

sad worn out

God suffers . . . any hand in it compare 7.2–3; 8.1, 19; 9.14

six thousand yeers after the creation

plurisie imposthume chest pain, cyst

jurats officials

11.10

The Ancient Real Theosophy the text is from Vaughn, *Anthroposophia*, sig. B1ʳ-B5ʳ

those most . . . proto-chimistry Vaughn, *Anthroposophia*, tp, sig. A3r,

progresse journeying forward

scaene view

glasse mirror

expence . . . pores release through openings in the eyes or pores

common philosophy . . . Aristotle see 11.16

irregular . . . fancies Aristotelian principles are not governed by rules

notions fantasies

tympanie of termes empty, inflated terminology

Quixot the novel *Don Quixote* by Miguel Cervantes was first translated into English in 1620 and was enormously popular: see 10.10

digladiations fencing

palps handles

Telesius . . . Campanella see 11.5–7

spirit see 7.6, 15, 19; 8.5, 10; 11.8

discovers reveals

these are the generations . . . earth Gen. 2:4

extra intellectum beyond understanding

11.11

The True Philosophick Cabbala More, *Conjectura*, 1653, pp. 183–93
conceit understanding
the text of Moses the first five books of the Bible
sedulous diligent
for Pythagoras . . . life in Iamblichus see 8.15
a philosophy . . . angels Iamblichus, *Life of Pythagoras*, 13.62.4
that learned antiquary . . . citations John Selden, *De jure naturali et gentium juxta disci-
plinam Ebraeorum* (1640)
at Sidon . . . Moses the philosopher Iamblichus, *Life of Pythagoras*, 3.14.2
thigh . . . like gold Iamblichus, *Life of Pythagoras*, 28.135.2; Porphyry, *Life of Pythagoras*,
28.1–3
Numenius . . . in Greek Numenius of Apamea, a Platonic philosopher of the second
century CE, cited by Eusebius, *Preparation for the Gospel*, 9.8.1–2 (411^d–12^a); 'ingenuously' means 'candidly'
As for Plotinus . . . against another see 5.4; 'retort' is 'throw back'
familiar friend . . . Origen Plotinus and Origen had the same teacher, Ammonius Sac-
cas: see 5.4
nothing strange . . . Cabbala see 8.15, 11.8
Bezaliel and Aholiab artisans chosen by God and assigned by Moses to assist with the
building of the Tabernacle: Exod. 35:30–36–7
lubricous slippery, elusive
sedulously carefully

11.12

Magnetisms from the Amsterdam, 1667, edition of the Latin text
Nature . . . God's art Plato, *Soph.* 265D3
Craftsman see 5.8, 13; 9.2
magnetism . . . occult see 8.8, 9.8
colcodea the level of the divine that emanates forms – Avicenna's 'giver of forms' or
qulqude'ah, Latinized as *colcodea* since the Middle Ages

11.13

Fig. 22, Joseph Glanvill, *A Blow at Modern Sadducism*, 1668

A Demon Witnessed by Multitudes the text is from Glanvill, *Sadducism*, pp. 95–125
the article . . . existence the eleventh clause of the Creed asserts that the dead will rise
hurling roaring wind
its recess when the wind stopped
the Black Society Satan and his demons: see 10.7

roundheads . . . tattoo types of drum-beat

mediterranious subterranean

cockloft attic room

prejudice harm

apish foolish

caprichios pranks

waggish mischievous

fegaries pranks

the Twelve . . . Beelzebub the apostles: see Mark 16:17; Luke 4:33–6; and sections 2.8,
      10, 16

gallant salacious

bugs scarecrows

Now this gentleman . . . capable reason a full summary of points supporting the evi-
      dence and testimony gathered for the drumming

11.14

Angel Midwives translating the text edited by C. J. Gerhardt (Berlin: Wiedemann,
      1875), pp. 15–26

Patrizi . . . Deusing thinkers of the last two centuries who were critics of Aristotle

eight books the eight parts of Aristotle's *Physics*

the reformed . . . matter and motion the new science and philosophy after Galileo and
      Descartes, basing its physics not on the traditional qualities (hot/cold, wet/dry)
      but on quantifiable structural properties of matter in motion

God's clock once the Creator sets the universe in motion, it operates independently
      according to laws of nature already established: see 11.16

Socinians having denied that Christ is the second Person of the Trinity, followers of
      Fausto Sozzini were seen by many Christians as heretics

11.15

Intercourse with Good Spirits the text is from Principe, *The Aspiring Adept*, App. 3, pp.
      310–17

Hermetick alchemical

the divell . . . Angel of light 2 Cor. 11:14–15, as in 6.2, 7.3

conversation of Angels see 9.11

Enthusiast in Boyle's day, 'enthusiasm' was religious belief and behaviour – especially
      the latter, often associated with excessive emotion – taken to be inappropriate

pouder of post ground sandstone

Transmuting pouder the Philosopher's Stone as the main agent of transmutation

Elixir see 7.6; 9.5, 7; 10.5

the scripture . . . no less see 1.1, 5, 10; 2.2, 18

our own times . . . visible shapes see 11.9–11, 13

the grand difficulty . . . qualifications see 9.1

Bodine Jean Bodin

Atheist . . . Atheism in Boyle's day, usually not outright rejection of theism but denying a doctrine – like immaterial spirits or the immortality of the soul – regarded as essential for belief in God

11.16

The Kingdom of Darkness Clarke, *A Collection of Papers*, London: Knapton, 1717, pp. 3–5, 265–76

the moderns . . . occult qualities Newton, *Principia* (1686), preface

God . . . mends his work see 11.14

occult . . . schools see 7.10; 8.8; 9.4; 11.8, 12

some men . . . forces Newton and his followers on gravity

Charles II the King was restored in 1660 and died in 1685

plants and animals . . . in a watch a thoroughly mechanical account of nature, but not of its 'divine preformation'

operation at a distance on action at a distance, see 5.15–16, 7.19, 8.10

a scholastick occult quality as just previously